Sex, Career and Family

Other P.E.P. Studies
published by Allen & Unwin

Sex, Career and Family

Including an International Review of Women's Roles

MICHAEL P. FOGARTY
RHONA RAPOPORT
ROBERT N. RAPOPORT

P.E.P.
12 Upper Belgrave Street

LONDON · GEORGE ALLEN & UNWIN LTD

FIRST PUBLISHED IN 1971

© George Allen & Unwin Ltd., 1971

ISBN 0 04 301029 6

PRINTED IN GREAT BRITAIN
in 10 point Times Roman
BY T. AND A. CONSTABLE
EDINBURGH

Acknowledgements

This report results from a study sponsored by the Leverhulme Trust. P.E.P. and all concerned with the study wish to express their appreciation for the Trust's encouragement and financial help.

The report is very much a team effort both between individuals and organisations. Political and Economic Planning and the Human Resources Centre of the Tavistock Institute of Human Relations have collaborated in it. Michael Fogarty was, during most of the study, a member of the staff of P.E.P.; Robert Rapoport was a member of the staff of the Tavistock's Human Resources Centre; and Rhona Rapoport held appointments in both institutions.

The organisational studies were made by Isobel Allen, Patricia Walters, John Allen, and Helena Smith and Fred Martin, under Michael Fogarty's general supervision. The intensive family interviews were conducted not only by the Rapoports, but under their supervision by David Armstrong, Stephanie White, Elizabeth and William Collins. Research assistance on the analysis of different kinds of data was given by Helen Morton, Rosemary Fison, Gerhardt Christiansen, Dorothy Rapoport, Janet Philps, and Susan Voorhees.

The surveys and their analysis involved a complex of interlinked activities. Two of the surveys (1967 graduates and 1960 graduates) were conducted with the help of Research Services Ltd, the third (1968 sixth formers) with the help of Donald Hutchings and the Oxford Institute of Education, but at the date of closing this report was not completed. Help with statistical analysis, computer programming and the machine aspects of the processing of survey materials was given by Andrew Bebbington and Elliott Mittler. Different parts of the processing were accomplished with the help of Survey Analysis Ltd, Professor Elliot Jaques of the School of Social Sciences, Brunel University, and Brunel University Computation Department, The Atlas Computer at Chilton, and English Electric (Lector Form method used in the sixth form Survey). A good many people helped with various aspects of this work, and must be thanked though with the proviso that they are not to be held responsible for its shortcomings: notably J. Hailstone and D. House at Chilton, L. Hawkins at S.A.L., Derek Jolly of English Electric, and Andrew Bebbington of the London School of Economics. Professor R. K. Kelsall and Mrs Anne Poole of Sheffield University were very helpful in relation to establishing a sampling frame for the 1960 Graduate Study based on their own graduates' survey.

A very special kind and degree of gratitude is expressed to two highly committed American research workers – Alice Rossi and Lotte Bailyn. Alice Rossi helped with ideas and encouragement from her own very rich experience in a related type of study. Without her generous sharing of ideas, preliminary findings and research instruments even before she had published them herself the authors could never have attempted so much in so short a time. Lotte Bailyn helped at a crucial stage in the data analysis by taking on a sub-study of couples that served as a pilot analysis for the larger groups surveyed. She contributed immensely with her clarity in thinking through problems of data analysis. Neither, of course, is responsible for the conclusions.

Colleagues in a number of countries of Eastern and Western Europe, in North America, and in Israel helped through correspondence and by arranging study tours. Special comparative reports on East and West Germany were written by Christine Kulke and Ingrid Sommerkorn.

The help and encouragement of colleagues at P.E.P. and at Tavistock and Dublin have been indispensable. The project as a whole, as a creative venture in collaborative research among specialists in different disciplines has benefited by the broad vision of all concerned in developing collaboration where it promised to be fruitful, regardless of organisation boundaries. Mrs P. Pinder conducted at P.E.P. simultaneously with the present study a review of *Women at Work* generally – not only of highly qualified women – which was published as a P.E.P. Broadsheet in 1969.

The project has benefited from time to time from the guidance and advice of its panel of advisers who, in accordance with P.E.P. practice, remain anonymous.

Steadfast secretarial support from Ann Eccles (P.E.P.) and Elizabeth Burrett (Tavistock) have helped to keep order amid the projects' rising mountains of paper and to bring this report to see the light of day. Gill Riordan's editorial assistance is gratefully acknowledged.

Contents

PART FIVE: CONCLUSIONS

Part One

Introduction

Foreword

Are Women a Special Problem?

The terms of reference underlying this report are concerned with women, and in particular women and top jobs: how to get more of the former into the latter. As the study developed it extended not only to women in top jobs but to women's opportunities in professional and managerial work at graduate level generally. It also focused increasingly – and this is the point the research team wish to emphasize in this Foreword – on the general pattern of relationships between men and women. Limitations of time and material have prevented the team from following out this approach as fully as they would have wished or as the title of the report implies. At a number of points this report will still give the impression of dealing with a 'women's question'. But the need to lay equal stress on rethinking the roles of men and women, not those of women alone, is a key part of the message which the team would like to convey. The case for careers for highly qualified women at a level commensurate with their abilities, and on an equal footing with men, can be argued on several grounds: personal interest and family need, civil rights, or, more cold-bloodedly, the need of the economy to use its biggest reserve of untapped ability. Whatever the ground of the argument chosen, if there is to be movement in this direction, it is necessary not only to develop woman's own occupational competence and to break the barriers of discrimination, but also to work out new attitudes and relationships between men and women in the family as well as in working life.

The research team's assumptions and conclusions on how to go about this are set out in the chapters that follow, especially in Chapters I, V and XIII. It will be noticed that the team has paid particular attention to 'dual-career' families as defined in Chapter IX. It is not the team's intention to set up these families as a unique or universal model to which all should conform. The team's own view is pluralistic. Many different patterns of family and working life are likely always to be needed to fit different talents and inclinations, and

17

many options should be open. But 'dual-career' families are particularly interesting for the way in which they are pioneering – often, as will be shown, very successfully – a style of living which combines full participation for the wife as well as the husband in high-level employment together with the maintenance of the traditional values of family life. They do so in the face not only of the inherent problems and strains of the pattern of living which they have chosen, but also of misunderstandings, resistance and lack of material facilities which could be done away with if the value of their way of living were more widely appreciated.

But the point to stress here is not the value of any particular solution to the problem of rethinking sex roles in the light of the case for women's careers. It is that as the study has proceeded its accent has come to be more and more on sex roles rather than on women. If the problems arising from women's careers are to be successfully solved, men as well as women will need to join in working out a further series of changes – over and above the many which have already taken place – in men's as well as women's patterns of living; and men as well as women, as will be argued, have a strong interest in doing so.

Men and women, moreover, will not cease to be men and women in the process. One of the most significant findings of the family studies reported here is that dual-career and similar patterns do not imply masculine women or feminine men, any more than they need imply any disadvantage to children. Past views on this have been biased by the fact not only that those women who fought their way through the barriers of discrimination to reach top positions had often to be exceptionally tough – especially in the generation which made the first breakthrough – but also that so many of the women who reached these positions hitherto have been single. Women and men who remain single after usual marriage age tend, as will be shown, to diverge from the attitudes of their own sex towards those of the other. The present studies have paid special attention to married men and women, and in their case no necessary or even probable correlation appears between a wife having a career and the feminization of men or the masculinization of women.

Chapter I

The Special Problem of Women's Promotion to Top Jobs

WHY DO WOMEN HOLD SO FEW OF THE HIGHEST POSTS?

In its initial concern with women's employment at high levels this enquiry has had a double focus. It began by studying the discrepancy between women's obvious contribution to the lower and middle ranks of many highly qualified professions and the much smaller number of women in higher posts. Women outnumber men by three to one among assistant teachers in the basic grade, but are outnumbered by men among the heads even of primary schools; by as much as six to one among the heads of comprehensive schools. Among hospital doctors in England and Wales women provide 25 per cent of house officers but only 7 per cent of consultants. In the Administrative Civil Service women provide 17 per cent of Assistant Principals but only 3 per cent of Under-Secretaries. At the moment there is no woman Permanent Secretary at all. Why do discrepancies like these exist, and what might be done about them? From this point of view the focus of the enquiry has been on top jobs in a relatively narrow sense. The research team's preliminary broadsheet on *Women and Top Jobs*[1] illustrated the dividing line between 'top' and lower jobs in this sense by examples such as:

Posts above and below the 'top' job line

Industry	Head of a major division or function, company employing 2,000-5,000	Senior manager in a similar company, responsible to the head of the major division or function
Civil Service	Under-Secretary (Assistant Secretary marginal)	Principal
Hospital Board	Consultant	Medical Assistant, Senior Registrar

[1] P.E.P., 1977

19

IS WOMEN'S PROGRESS TOWARDS AN EQUAL SHARE IN
HIGHER PROFESSIONAL AND MANAGERIAL WORK
GENERALLY LEVELLING OFF?

But as the enquiry has proceeded it has developed a second and
stronger focus on the constraints which seem still to be holding
down women's share in higher professional and managerial work
generally, not only in posts at the very top. Women's entry into a
number of higher professions in Britain has followed a sequence
from breakthrough to acceptance onto a plateau suggesting stagna-
tion. In architecture, for example, the doors of the profession were
opened by the 1920s, and by the 1950s a number of those who first
came through them had established themselves as accepted senior
practitioners. The number who reached the very top and were accepted as leaders of the profession was small, but, in proportion to
the number of women practising, may if anything have been higher
than among men. But the total number of women architects remained
small, only around 4 per cent of all the architects practising, and
showed no sign of rapid increase. Women architects had become an
accepted but apparently permanent minority. In the Administrative
Civil Service, the universities, and the higher ranks of the B.B.C. the
story has been similar. Women doctors moved through the same
stages a generation earlier, reaching by the 1920s and 1930s the
standing which women architects reached by the 1950s. In politics
the pattern has been similar though the timing has been different.
The first woman M.P., Constance Markievicz, was elected in 1918,
though as a Sinn Feiner and from 1919 a Minister in Dail Eireann
she did not take her Westminster seat. The first woman actually to
take a Westminster seat was elected at the end of 1919. By the 1930s
women were well established in the House and there had been a
woman Cabinet Minister. By the 1960s, if not by the 1950s, a noticeable proportion of women Members were of the standing which
would let them reach for the top places in politics. But the total
number of women M.P.s has remained small.

There are, of course, other fields in which women have still to
achieve even the earlier stages of breakthrough and acceptance, in
particular in the higher levels of business bureaucracy. Women
owner-managers of small and medium firms are an accepted though
once again a minority part of the business scene, but women at
the top of the management ladder in big business hierarchies remain
very rare indeed. The Oxford University Appointments Board noted
in its report for 1968 that over 90 per cent of the public service jobs
notified to it that year were open to women as well as men. In private

industry and commerce, however, two-fifths[1] of the jobs notified were closed to women; and whereas in the private sector women with specialist qualifications had relatively good opportunities – only 28 per cent of the technical jobs notified were closed to them – women were barred from 57 per cent of first jobs requiring a non-technical Arts qualification of the kind which women more commonly have. Half of all openings for articles with solicitors and accountants in private practice were also closed to women. Nationalized industries took an intermediate place with 72 per cent of jobs open and 28 per cent closed.

But the central question is: when women have come so far in so many higher professions, and not merely have doors been opened but many women have found that they can actually walk through them and on upwards to the top, why has further growth in the numbers who do so apparently been blocked? Between the Census years 1921 and 1931, in the decade immediately following the first opening of the doors to women in many professions, the number of women in higher professional work in Britain rose nearly twice as fast as the number of men, by 3 per cent a year against ·8 per cent. This was the classic decade of breakthrough. From 1931 to 1951 the two rates of growth were much closer together, though women still had a slight edge over men with an annual growth rate of 3·6 per cent against 3 per cent. But from 1951 to 1961 the number of men went on growing at 4·5 per cent a year while the number of women actually fell by nearly 1 per cent a year. The fall was accounted for mainly by a drop in the number of women professionally employed in religion. But the number practising medicine also fell, the number of women in science and the writing professions rose much more slowly than the number of men, and at a time when engineers were multiplying faster than any other major profession, and surveyors and accountants were also increasing fast, the report from which these figures are taken continued to record women in these fields as 'too few to show separately'. In higher administrative, professional and managerial work as a whole the number of women rose in these years in England and Wales from 40,000 to 50,000, at 1·7 per cent a year, but the number of men rose from 450,000 to 660,000 at 3·8 per cent.[2]

This actual fall in women's share in higher professions did not continue through the first half of the 1960s, but neither did women resume their advance. The percentage of 'managers, large establishments' in England and Wales who were women was almost exactly

[1] The corresponding figure for 1967 had however been 52 per cent.
[2] Knight, R., 'Changes in the Occupational Structure of the Working Population', *JRSS*, Series A, 1967, Part 3. 1951-61 figures are for England and Wales, earlier figures are for Great Britain.

the same at the Census for 1966 as at that of 1961 (Table I.1). So was the percentage of women in a range of higher professions (Table I.2); excluding the biggest, school teaching, in which the percentage of women fell. In some individual professions women made dramatic proportional gains, but for the group of higher professions as a whole this was offset by the fact that some of the biggest increases in the absolute number of professional people employed were in professions where women are only weakly represented. So, for instance, the number of women engineers and technologists classified as such[1] grew faster than the number of men, but in absolute figures the increase was 700 for women and 70,000 for men. Spread over the grand total of all men or women in the higher professions, the former figure influences the average rate of increase very little, whereas the latter influences it a great deal.

Table I.1

Men and Women 'Managers, Large Establishments', England and Wales Censuses of 1961 and 1966

Number (000s)	1961	1966
Men	517·3	548·2
Women	76·4	81·9
Total	593·7	630·1
Women as per cent of Total	12·9	13·0

Nor do the 1961-66 figures suggest that the pattern of recruitment has been such as to lead automatically to a big advance in women's share in the higher professions over the next few years. This would be the case if, for example, the increase in the number of women working in the professions had been concentrated at entry ages. In that case it could be expected that the overall percentage of women in each profession would rise as the big new contingents came in behind them. Different professions have of course different recruitment problems and patterns, but on the average of the whole group of higher professions it seems (Table I.3) that the increase in the number of women was evenly spread over entry and older age groups, though with a relatively small increase in the main child-bearing age group, 25-34. Inland Revenue figures for the middle 1960s shows that whereas women represented nearly one-third of all employees, they were outnumbered by men

[1] In Table I.2 'engineers and technologists' and 'scientists' excludes qualified scientists and technologists who are classified under other headings, for example as school or university teachers.

22

Table I.2

Men and Women Active in Certain Professions, England and Wales, Censuses of
1961 and 1966

	Number of men and women in each profession or group, 1966 (000s)		Women as percentage of total in each pro-fession or group, 1966 (%)	Increase in number in each profession or group, 1961-1966 (%)	
	Men	Women		Women	Men
Medical practitioners	43·0	9·4	18	13	−3
Dentists	11·05	1·3	11	48	−5
Engineers and technologists	267·9	1·8	1	60	35
Scientists	52·2	4·1	7	23	16
University teachers	15·7	2·4	13	69	57
Accountants, company secretaries, etc.	100·0	17·7	15	33	20
Surveyors, architects	78·5	1·5	2	−6	16
Barristers, solicitors	30·4	1·5	5	49	8
Authors, journalists, etc	29·8	9·1	23	20	no change
Theatre, art	43·2	23·4	35	9	44
Clergy, members of religious orders	33·8	10·2	23	−25	−17
Social welfare workers	22·3	25·1	53	39	11
Professional workers not classified elsewhere	30·0	14·9	33	9	27
All the Above (1961)	757·9	122·4	14 (14)	16	18
School etc. teachers (1961)	210·1	285·2	57½ (59)	9	15
Senior Civil Servants, M.P.s, etc.	29·2	3·7	11	3	10
Senior local government officers	32·2	5·85	15	56	15
Personnel managers	10·3	4·1	28	40	32

by twenty to one in the range of P.A.Y.E. incomes from £2,000 to £2,999 and by fifty to one above £5,000.[1] Neither the Census nor any other figures show any automatic reason to expect this sort of relationship to change greatly in the next few years.

It is common to find that the graph representing the development of some social custom or practice or the advancement of a group is S-shaped. There is a slow start, a rapid acceleration as the new development takes hold, then a tendency for the curve to flatten as a state of equilibrium is reached. The curve of women's movement

Table I.3

Increase per cent in the number of women in certain age groups in certain professions, Great Britain, Census of 1961 and 1966.

	Age-group				
	20-24	25-34	35-44	45-54	55-59
Higher professions summarized as 'all above' in Table II	21	9	27	20	20
School, etc., teachers	−6	9	33	−6	9
Senior Civil Servants, MPs, etc.	no change	56	−35	31	17
Senior local government officers	155	23	68	50	45
Personnel managers	77	43	43	22	61

into a number of higher professions has clearly followed this pattern, and a state of at least temporary equilibrium has been reached. The question is: is this equilibrium a permanent resting place, or is it (what is also commonly found) a pause before moving into a new S-curve of further advance? If and when the gates of sectors such as large-scale business management, of certain technical professions, where women's opportunities are still formally or informally more restricted, are opened wider, can one expect that there too the number of women who actually pass through the gates will stabilize itself at a low level?

THE BLOCKED ROAD TO THE TOP – A BY-PRODUCT OF THE GENERAL CONDITIONS OF WOMEN'S EMPLOYMENT?

In one way the answer might seem to follow simply from a consideration of women's position in employment generally.[Study after

[1] Report of the Commissioner of Inland Revenue for the year to March 31, 1966, Cmnd. 3200, Table 53.

study in recent years has pointed out that women generally, quite apart from any question of promotion to top jobs, tend not to be offered the same chances of training for skilled work or promotion as men nor to be motivated by their education or work environment to take them; that they tend to be segregated into 'women's work', devalued by unequal pay, treated as lacking in commitment to their work and as unsuitable to be in authority over men, and trained and encouraged not merely to accept these conditions but to think them right; and that husbands, the community (for example as regards nursery schools and shopping hours) and employers have only half-heartedly adapted to the change in the women's labour market due to the increasing share taken in it by married women. If factors like these account for women's poor representation in skilled and super-visory work generally, surely they account still more powerfully for women's under-representation in work in the highest ranges. If and when these general shortcomings in women's employment oppor-tunities are cured, will this not automatically entail that more women will be qualified for the top jobs and will aim for and reach them?

There is substantial truth in this suggestion, and these general background factors which affect all women in employment play a major part in this report. But even as regards the general run of women's employment, other work by P.E.P. has shown that it is unprofitable to think in terms of wide sweeping measures of change without considering in detail the specific problems of women in particular occupations, industries and districts.[1] The question of equal pay, for example, presents itself in very different forms accord-ing to the exact nature of the inequality – unequal rates, unequal earnings, job segregation – and the probable consequences of chang-ing it and the views and traditions of the parties concerned. The problems of family life when both the husband and wife work occur in one form in a traditional textile community geared for generations not only to married women's work but to shift work, and in another form in suburban district with a new population where these patterns have hitherto been rare.

JOBS AT THE TOP: THE CASE FOR A SPECIAL STUDY

In investigating the question of women in higher professional and managerial work, one quickly becomes aware that this, even more than most other sectors of women's work, is a world of its own. This has been the case historically. In the Civil Service, for example, though demands for equal pay have always had the backing of women of all grades, there was for many years a division over the

[1] Pinder, P., *Women at Work*, P.E.P., 1969.

marriage bar between clerks and typists on the one hand and women in the higher professional and administrative grades on the other. The rule at that time was that women were normally to be dismissed on marriage, with a gratuity. The associations representing clerks and typists were inclined to uphold it on the grounds that the dismissal of married women, who might be assumed to have relatively low commitment to their work, cleared the road to promotion for the single women who were committed to and dependent upon it; that the married women themselves might be worse off if they kept an employment opportunity of which not many would make use – or not for long – but lost their gratuity; and that in any case rapid turnover of staff on routine jobs was desirable. On the other hand women in the higher grades, having a deep commitment to their work, fought this rule consistently.

High personal commitment to work is one of the factors marking off the holders of qualified jobs in all countries. A Polish study[1] found that the proportion of married women who return to work after maternity leave ranges upwards from 35-40 per cent in low skilled work in the clothing industry or as waitresses and barmaids to 75-85 per cent in most professional and managerial occupations and 95 per cent in the case of doctors and teachers. In France 70 per cent of women graduates were working at age 50 in 1962 compared to 40-45 per cent of women with only a basic education.[2] Of American women aged 45-54 in 1964, the proportion working was 43 per cent for those with elementary education but 85·5 per cent for those with five or more years of college.[3] In England and Wales 40 per cent of all married women aged 25-44 were working at the time of the Census of 1961, but 57 per cent of those who completed their education at 20 or over. The reasons for this high commitment are mixed. Higher pay and better pension prospects or other fringe benefits, as compared to those found in the general run of jobs, certainly play their part. But the Polish finding is that cash differences count for less in holding married women to their jobs in more interesting professional and managerial work than in routine office or factory jobs, and an English study finds that among English married women directly financial reasons for working count for much less among middle-class women than among women from the working class.[4]

[1] Kurzynowski, A., *Occupation and Continuity of Employment of Young Mothers* (trans. from Polish), in M. Sokolowska (ed.), *Kobieta Wspolczesna*, Warsaw, 1966.
[2] 'L'Emploi Feminin', in *Etudes et Conjoncture*, December 1964, p. 62.
[3] U.S. Department of Labor, *Handbook on Women Workers*, 1965, p. 195
[4] Klein, V., *Working Wives*, Institute of Personnel Management, 1958, p. 25.

Not only can the holder of a qualified job be expected to have a relatively strong personal interest in it; in addition, high-level jobs tend by their nature to demand an exceptionally high degree of commitment. In terms of time this is not always true. It is often practicable for a medical consultant, for example, to work less than full time, and in very many high-level jobs there is more freedom than in ordinary factory or office work to adapt working hours to family needs or to take time off for emergencies; perhaps counting it off against a more generous number of days' vacation than is usually allowed in more junior posts. But top posts, especially if they have a large management content, are more likely than junior posts to have to be filled full time, at least in present conditions; how far this is necessarily or permanently true is discussed in Chapter XII. They often entail bursts of unavoidable overtime, and sometimes in effect continuous overtime. Above all, reaching as apart from holding them commonly calls for greater persistence in a career and more competitive drive to get to the top than is needed at more modest levels of aspiration. The point of persistence is often not so much to acquire experience and operating skills – this is obviously important, but the time needed for it can be relatively short – as to build and maintain the network of personal relations needed both for operating purposes and to make a candidate visible to those who decide promotions.

High personal commitment to work and heavy demands from the job raise problems for family life, especially in the case of married women with children. These problems press all the harder because, as the present study has confirmed, women qualified at this high level tend to be particularly conscientious mothers and particularly aware of findings by research workers such as Bowlby about the danger to children from lack of maternal care in their first years. On the other hand, women working at high levels have exceptional resources for dealing with their family problems. They are by definition people of high intelligence, usually highly educated, and likely, seeing the sort of work that they do, to be capable organizers. So, often, though by no means invariably, are their husbands. Women in this position are likely to be earning substantial salaries or profits themselves, and their husbands may well be doing likewise. A family in which the wife as well as the husband is working full time and earning at the level usual for honours graduates will be doing poorly if its income when the parents are in their middle thirties is under £4,000 to £5,000 a year. If the husband is doing well in his profession, an income at this level can be reached even if the wife works part time. Earnings at age forty to fifty may be much higher. Two averagely successful general practitioners can expect to earn between them £8,500 a year, and two medical consultants can expect to end up, even without any distinction award, with a family income (including normal supplementary earnings) of around £11,000. A Civil Service Assistant Secretary married to an Under-Secretary will also have an income approaching £12,000, and where one or other partner is in a senior business post the level may be higher still. Money, if not exactly the answer to all family problems, does certainly oil the wheels in matters such as housing, home help and maintenance, shopping, transport and holidays.

To have a husband qualified and working at a high level is always significant for a wife's career, but may affect it in either direction. A high total income, whether earned primarily by the husband or by both partners equally, can release the wife for outside work by facilitating domestic management; but the husband's high income may also remove the incentive for his wife to work (unless the job is particularly tempting) or at least to work sufficiently to qualify for a top job. It is again a general international finding that, other things being equal, the proportion of wives working falls off the higher the husband comes on his country's income scale.[1] Income taxation plays a part here, for under current British rules a husband and wife are taxed slightly less heavily than two single persons until their combined income (assuming it is all earned) approaches £5,000, but more heavily above that level. Two single people each earning, say, £3,500 a year would in 1968-69 have paid a further £687 in tax if they had increased their earnings by £1,000 each, but a husband and wife earning a total of £7,000 between them would have paid an additional £1,138 if they had done the same.

Again, while the husband's job and his social status and contacts may open up for his wife job opportunities which she might not otherwise have had, they may also reveal other avenues of interest which she prefers to follow rather than work herself. She may gear her entertaining and other social (including social service) activities to backing up his career, or use his status and contacts as the starting point for a network of friendships and voluntary social or political activities of her own, or simply join in on his own network out of interest. As an American study notes,

'Business and professional men are more apt to take their wives with them in leisure-time activities of various sorts, with the result that their wives know most of their friends quite well. This acquaint-

[1] On British graduate wives, see Aregger, C. E. (ed.), *Graduate Women at Work*, Oriel (for British Federation of University Women), 1966, p. 33.

ance is gained partly while entertaining in the home and partly through joint activities elsewhere. In general, co-educational leisure-time patterns characterize high-status marriages. . . .[1]

The same study notes on the one hand that wives' satisfaction with their marriages tends to be greater the higher the husband's social status and education – especially if the wife's education runs level with his – but on the other that the husband's power of decision within the family tends also to rise in line with his education, social status, and occupational success. This need not in itself diminish the wife's chance of a successful career. The question whether highly qualified husbands support their wives in seeking careers more or less than those less highly qualified is a separate one. At the least, however, it means that the wife's career decisions need more than in other social groups to be co-ordinated with the husband's. One area where this may be particularly important is in the geographical location of jobs. High-level jobs tend to be both individual and scarce, and this makes it harder to match the interests of both husband and wife within commuting distance of their home than if they were in work of a kind more commonly available. Soviet man-power planners have run into this difficulty as much as their opposite numbers in the West.[2]

Even if these differences between higher-level and other work did not exist, women's work at top levels in both the senses defined earlier – at the topmost level of all and in higher qualified work generally – would deserve separate study because of its significance for work at other levels. This significance can be general and symbolic; a flag on the top of the building encouraging by its presence – or discouraging by its absence – women whose own careers are unlikely to be affected in any more specific way. It can be much more direct in lower-level professional (or even craft) and managerial work. Promotion into many middle management and professional jobs depends not only on the immediate needs of the job itself but on whether the candidate will eventually be eligible for more senior posts on the same career line. Even if lower-skilled jobs are not them-selves on a line leading to the top, the appointment of women to top jobs may unlock the door to jobs lower down simply by making it harder to deny that women are capable of undertaking them. The greater the number and the wider and higher the range of work of woman engineers or architects, the harder it is likely to be to main-

---

[1] Blood, R. O., and Wolf, D. M., *Husbands and Wives*, Free Press, Glencoe, 1960, p. 169.

[2] Dodge, N. T., *Women in the Soviet Economy*, John Hopkins, 1966, pp. 234-236.

tain the present effective, though informal restrictions on recruiting women as, for example, draughtsmen.[1]

THE P.E.P. ENQUIRY

It is from these lines of thought that P.E.P. started when in 1966 it was invited by the Leverhulme Trust to organize a study of women's work and opportunity in occupations at graduate level. The general conclusions of the study are presented in this report. A number of more specialized reports are also being published. With help from the Tavistock Institute of Human Relations a research team was recruited, including an economist (Michael Fogarty) specialized in management and labour market studies, a sociologist and psychoanalyst (Rhona Rapoport) specialised in family studies and a social anthropologist (Robert Rapoport) specialised in community studies. Fourteen other British, Irish and American research workers have been involved in the project either part-time or for short periods of full-time work, and a wide range of contacts has been built up with people working in related fields in eastern and western Europe, Israel, and the United States.[2]

THE RESEARCH TEAM'S ORIENTATIONS: VALUES AND ASSUMPTIONS UNDERLYING THE PROJECT

a *The development of social theory*

Social science excludes value judgments as far as possible in obtaining the facts to answer a question and in working out the most economical theory to link them, but inevitably involves a substantial

[1] In 1968 only 1·5 per cent of draughtsmen in British industry were women. See Chapter III, Table 6 of this book.

[2] A second volume on *Women and Top Jobs – Four Studies in Achievement*, published simultaneously with this report, includes studies by Patricia Walters of women in the Administrative Civil Service: by Isobel Allen on women in the B.B.C. and in managerial and professional work in two large companies (referred to below, for anonymity, simply as Company A and Company B): and by John Allen of women company directors (a study made in collaboration with the Institute of Directors). A study by Helena Smith and F. Martin of women architects will be published separately. A third volume by Rhona and Robert Rapoport, to appear in 1971, will analyse more fully the material on life cycles and careers in relation to family life. P.E.P. is also publishing separately studies by Christine Kulke and Ingrid Sommerkorn comparing the experience over women's careers and family life of East and West Germany, and has published Mrs P. Pinder's study *Women at Work*, on equal pay and equal opportunity for women. Mrs Pinder's study was undertaken under a separate project but parallel to the Leverhulme project. A broadsheet on *Women and Top Jobs* was published by P.E.P. in 1967 as part of the first stage of the Leverhulme project.

degree of value judgments in selecting which questions to ask and assigning more or less weight to different aspects of the answers. One such value judgment is about the value of social science itself. Social like other science proceeds to some extent by chasing its own tail. A value judgment normal for professionals in this field as in others is that it is a good thing to advance the state of their own art. One question or clue leads to another, and is followed up for its contribution to building or reforming a system of social theory, irrespective of any specific relevance it might have to present practical problems. Eventually, the resulting improvement in social science techniques or in general understanding of social structures and attitudes may be expected to have a practical use, but that is not the immediate consideration.

An approach of this kind has played its part in the present study. The market for women workers presents some of the most intriguing problems of labour market theory in general, and one of the further reports just mentioned will go in more detail into the contribution of this project both to the methodology of the social sciences and to the general theory of the family in industrialized societies.

b *Commitment to a cause*

Another type of value judgment concerns the extent to which a study is to be seen as serving not merely some practical purpose but a cause. It has been conventional in social science to avoid ethical judgments and to study the data of human life as does a physical scientist observing matter in test-tubes. This is, of course, itself an ethical position, which carries disadvantages as well as the advantages of objectivity and detachment. It leads to a tendency to concentrate on sterile problems and to abdicate to others, often less competent for the purpose, the role of consultant on matters of importance to society as a whole. The tendency to eschew an ethical position also often masks further implicit ethical judgments; for example, that what is and has been, or what is feasible for the future, is good. Alice Rossi carries this argument forward in a passage directly relevant to the present field of work:

'What I am suggesting is that sociology should be involved in the hard task of establishing goals for a future in terms of which we effect changes in the present. This normative dimension of planning is what Hasan Ozbekhan claims is most needed at this time, to correct the tendency in modern society for the futurists to focus only on technological feasibility, so that the sole criterion of decisions and actions is what man 'can' do, which then becomes what he 'ought' to do. In other words, modern industrial societies have failed to develop an ethic commensurate with our technology. (On a small scale as much can be said about sociology as a field.) The old ethics of traditional religion and family life have lost much of their meaning and guiding power, but neither the social sciences nor politics have made any serious attempt to develop a new ethic (Ozbekhan, 1967). This means there exists an opportunity for all of us in the behavioural sciences, and perhaps particularly for the younger generation, since the older one seems merely to bemoan the 'end of ideology', and to resist attempts at a new one, to learn the skills of our professions and to apply these as a counterforce against the feasibility-focussed technologists. This means bringing out of the corridors and into the classrooms serious dialogue about what a 'good' society could be, what a university could be, what a family could be, what the life of men and women could be. It means too, that armed with a tentative and flexible ideology, we focus our research and our action on testing approximations toward that goal and changing both as our knowledge increases.'[1]

The view taken in this book runs in the same direction. Women's position in contemporary society is in many respects unsatisfactory. An explicit aim of the study is to facilitate the attempts being made by many people – educational, governmental, industrial and individual – to evolve better ways of managing the situation out of which this unsatisfactory state has arisen; with, of course, particular reference to the question of women and higher qualified work.

Immediately, attempts to change the position over women and work, highly qualified or other, take place within the social and economic framework existing here and now. In the longer run they are one of the forces changing this framework; in the direction, ultimately, of what some authors[2] have called the post-industrial society. This concept suggests that, as productivity rises, the urgency to work to provide minimum or even affluent standards of material wellbeing will diminish. With it will diminish the need to persuade or compel people, and especially men, of high ability to concentrate as strongly and exclusively on building the material foundations of society as has been traditional in the past. It does not follow that the need for able people to commit themselves strongly to work of other kinds will disappear. The highly creative artist or scientist will not necessarily cease to be dedicated in even the most affluent society, nor will the problems of politics or higher management necessarily

[1] A. Rossi, *The Road to Sex Equality*, paper to a seminar on Social Inequality, University of Chicago, February, 1969.
[2] E.g. Kahn, H. and Wiener, A. J., *The Year 2000*, Macmillan, 1967.

32

become any simpler. But there could at least come a time when there is less material urgency about work than now.

In a variety of ways people could then move more easily towards the concept of (to turn Marcuse's title on its head) 'multi-dimensional man' and develop the idea of shaping their lives not as a succession of inescapable compulsions but as a multi-faceted work of art. On the one hand they could feel free to weigh the claims of work against other interests, such as those of family life. On the other they could feel free to adopt towards work of all kinds the 'game-like' attitude which already applies substantially to work like that of the artist, the basic scientist or the politician. Work organization, hours and methods could be determined more from the standpoint of the worker's and his (or her) family's satisfaction and less exclusively from that of productivity. As Woodward and others have pointed out, the social and technical organization of work in advanced societies is already moving that way as a result of existing technical and market needs, even apart from any direct consideration of workers' welfare or wishes.

In present conditions in even advanced societies work remains for many people a necessary evil, something to be endured, to which at best one becomes habituated. On the other hand, for many of the highly qualified the world of work already has an entirely different character. It is for them an area within which major satisfactions may be derived, sometimes superior to those of other spheres of life, including elements of family life, of leisure and of responsibility for and participation in the development of the community as a whole. Work at other levels may even now incorporate elements of this kind. In the view of analysts like Bell, Trist and Gross, work in the post-industrial society is likely to become more and more this type of activity and to offer growing scope for personal development and fulfilment or, in Maslow's term, 'self-actualization'. It is envisaged that a balance will be struck between competition and co-operation, between team work and individual effort, between bureaucracy and 'network' patterns of management, and between autonomous work groups and central direction.[1]

One assumption of this book is that access to this major area of self-development and actualization ought to be open equally to men and to women, and that pathways within it should depend on personal capacities and wishes rather than on ascribed characteristics such as traditional sex roles. The standards of productivity already achieved in the advanced industrial countries indicate that the prospect of a post-industrial society need not be utopian. It is a prediction of a possible future, given the appropriate conditions and influences,

[1] References on pp. 183-184.

and it is this prediction and prospect that gives the present study its long-term perspective.

The method of the study, however, takes account of the orientation of social science towards answering questions factually, whatever value judgments may have entered into the original selection of the questions. The aim of the enquiry has been not directly to determine policy – this would be to go beyond a factual answer to the questions set – but to light up in a factual way the issues which must be faced in any policy aimed at the general end which the team has taken as given. It is to facilitate the development of strategies, whether at the political level, by employers, or by individual families, for adapting working and family life to the personal needs and interests of both men and women, by clarifying the problems and choices which strategies of this kind will involve.

c *Multiple answers, not a new stereotype*

A further assumption of the research team has been not so much a value judgment as a generalization – which has been confirmed by the evidence of the enquiry itself – from previously available facts. It is that in the long run the needs both of individual men and women and of the community, counting gains in terms of economic efficiency as well as of personality and inter-personal relations, are likely to be best met if women and men base their career and family choices principally on their abilities and needs as individuals and not on sex-typed or other group stereotypes or norms. Women (like men) should have the training opportunity and encouragement to work more, or less, as they individually decide, in the light of each one's own personality and responsibilities towards others. This view does not exclude a role for group norms. Public opinion, the expression of group norms, will still need to be won over to encourage women to act in this way and not simply to follow traditional rules. But the role of group opinion should be to encourage personal choice, not to force it into standard moulds.

(*i*) *The general principle of relying on individual, not group, differences.* The general rule that roles should be assigned primarily in terms of individual, not of sex or other group, differences is unlikely to be challenged at the level of pure principle. In a quite general way few will deny that it pays, in terms of both money and personal welfare, to design jobs and use selection procedures so that people and jobs are accurately matched; or that a richer form of marriage can be achieved when each partner is free to develop his or her own personality and neither personality is suppressed. Nor is there any evidence of differences in the potential abilities of men and women, given the right type of socialization and training, which would justify either the maintenance of segregated spheres for the two sexes or any regular superiority of one over the other.

It is a fact that the observed characteristics of men and women form, not two distinct patterns, but 'large overlapping curves in which many boys would be in their temperament more like most girls than like most boys'.[1] So for example a study of ambition among boys and girls in English schools shows that in schools of every type the average boy is more ambitious than the average girl, but the average girl has an ambition score in the same bracket as around 20 per cent of boys (depending on the type of school), and in a higher bracket than 12 per cent to 15 per cent.[2] So, again, other studies show that women tend to be more field-oriented than men – more inclined, that is, to make judgments in the context of their immediate environment rather than of some remote, more abstract, possibly more universal framework[3] – but also that many men are more field-oriented than many women and many women less field-oriented than many men.

Those sex differences that do exist, other than the most directly physical ones, appear to an uncertain but substantial extent to be time- and culture-bound, and from the point of view of social usefulness – in work or otherwise – there is no *prima facie* reason to prefer one pattern to the other. Field-orientation is again an example. Many of both sexes are likely to have acquired their particular orientation, not because of some basic genetic condition, but through their specific experiences in our society at the present time. In so far as sex differences in field-orientation exist, it seems likely that the orientation characteristic of each sex has advantages. The low field-orientation which tends to be found among men, the ability to rise above an immediate context and judge in a wide framework, is certainly a socially valuable attribute. But there is also reason to

[1] Riesman, D., *Some Dilemmas of Women's Education*, The Educational Record, 1965; see also, among the references on pp. 183-184, Maccoby, 1967; Erikson, 1964; Stoller, 1969.

[2] Veness, T., *School Leavers*, Methuen, 1962, p. 161.

[3] Witkin in Riesman, 1965. In Witkin's research, it was found that men could set a tilting chair into alignment in a tilting room better than women because, he argued, women paid too much attention to the 'field' outside the apparatus and were therefore not as effective in concentrating on the task at hand. Aside from the issue of how 'intrinsic' this tendency is, Riesman notes that to imply that this 'field-dependent' tendency is less desirable than the more focused task-orientation is a masculine definition of the situation. One might equally have said that males were less aware of their immediate environmental situation and valued order above responsiveness (Riesman, 1965). One might have said that the men tended to be 'blinkered' in their approach.

think that high field-orientation, whether in a man or a woman – the ability to respond strongly and sympathetically to an immediate environment – is an undervalued attribute, whose development could enrich many work situations.

It is certainly likely to remain the case that the most common or typical pattern for a woman's career in work and marriage differs from the most common or typical pattern for a man. But the team's assumption is that it is reasonable for these average or typical differences to be over-ridden far more often than at present by differences among individuals of either sex. A greater variety of family and career patterns will be needed to cater for the men and women who diverge from the average for their own sex. The typical marriage may still be one in which the husband has higher career ambitions than his wife. But it will also be possible to find cases where both have strong career ambitions, or neither has, or the wife has but the husband has not. All of these patterns will be equally legitimate, and it will be equally desirable in each case to adjust the roles of the two partners at work and at home to the actual needs and potential of their personalities.

The case for this view can be summed up in terms of three rationales:

The manpower rationale is that it is in the interest of society to discover and make the most effective use of its talent. This requires optimum matching of job and person. To use in the housewife role a highly qualified woman who dislikes housework, simply because there are inadequate arrangements to relieve her of this role, is inefficient. It is similarly inefficient to use in a factory job a man with a special interest in child care, simply because child care is stereotyped as feminine.

The human rights rationale[1] is that a central problem for society is to find patterns which will maximize the realization and protection of the right of women as of men to equal opportunity to participate in social activities for which they personally are suited.

The social change rationale notes that social forces are pushing *de facto* towards a more egalitarian and libertarian culture which will make it more possible for women to participate equally with men in all the valued spheres of life and in moulding these spheres of life for the future, and that this is a trend of which policy-makers concerned not only with what is desirable but with what is practicable must take note.

(ii) Historical constraints; an evolutionary approach. The research team is not arguing that the rule of assigning roles primarily in terms

[1] Goode, see p. 184.

of individual rather than sex-typed differences is one to be followed rigidly in societies at all stages of technical and social development and without regard to the need for learning time and continuity. A number of constraints have stood in the way of applying this rule in particular societies in the past, and to some extent still do.

A major constraint has been that social and economic conditions at a given time and place may not and often have not permitted the creation of a wide enough variety of roles, especially work roles, to cater for the whole range of human personalities. There is no particular reason to suppose that the patterns of work roles consistent with consumer needs and current technologies will always correspond to the range of abilities and interests available, or capable of being made available by training. There is somewhat more reason to suppose that this correspondence could be achieved today than in the past. But certainly in the past there have never been enough challenging and interesting work roles on offer to match all the human abilities available, even if the most dynamic possible use had been made of the possibilities of adapting jobs and re-qualifying people within the limits set by technology in each time and place. Probably there are not enough roles of that kind available here and now – whatever might be achieved by future reforms – especially at the highest levels of skill and responsibility.[1] Who is then to fill such roles of this kind as there are; especially when, as in the case of women's advance towards top jobs, there is a conflict between new claimants and a class of existing incumbents? How is the necessary rationing to be done?

Rationing can be on the basis of ability; all can be given the chance to qualify, and the most able will get the available jobs. But it is also necessary at least to consider the thesis that it may be the lesser evil to disqualify some possible competitors from the start, for example women or married women, either arbitrarily or because a particular group has alternative roles open to it; in the case of married women, for instance, the role of a mother and full-time housewife. Given that some will in any case be disappointed and their talents underused, which policy is less damaging to individuals and society: to have numbers of able and qualified people for whom no jobs matching their abilities are available and who are conscious of having been defeated in a meritocratic race, or to tell certain people that they will not be allowed even to qualify for reasons which in no way reflect on them personally, reasons which, in Lord Melbourne's famous words, have no damned merit about them? Supposing that for good reasons the practice of reserving certain posts for certain groups has become established, but that the force of these reasons

[1] Fogarty, M. P., *The Rules of Work*, Geoffrey Chapman, 1963, Chapter V.

is now diminishing, at what point does it become worthwhile to incur the trouble and, for some, disruption of upsetting the *status quo*? The ways in which questions like these are answered have differed from one period and society to another. The differences depend both on values and attitudes in each society and on the actual balance of demand and supply in the market for high ability.

In the present enquiry questions such as these raised themselves in the form that, whereas staff shortages are found in Britain in many areas of middle and junior professional and managerial work, it is only in rare and temporary cases that qualified candidates cannot be found for top jobs. If women are to have more access to these jobs, some men now holding them or candidates for them will be displaced. Many employers see the introduction of women into top jobs as offering in these circumstances at best a marginal gain, likely to be outweighed by the trouble which the operation would cause. This issue will be considered in its place below.

Another constraint arises from the fact that it is difficult to assess personal needs and abilities precisely enough to make accurate adjustment between personality and work or other roles possible. Even so apparently straightforward a procedure as assessing a candidate's suitability for a job can have a wide margin of error. Similarly, a husband and wife will not necessarily find it easy to understand and adjust to each other's personality. Alike in work and in family life, people may not even be aware of their own potentialities unless this awareness is forced on them, and even a careful investigation of their potential may discover only what they have been trained into in the past, not what they might arrive at in the future. It was observed of a certain Roman emperor that 'no one would have doubted that he was capable of ruling, if only he had never ruled'. For women in top jobs the present study shows that this saying could often be reversed; no one, including very often themselves, would have believed that they could rule if they had not done it. Judgments of individual cases on an individual, case-by-case basis, as both sociologists and economists have pointed out, can have a systematic and self-reinforcing bias. Thus, for example, repeated judgments that individual women are unfitted for promotion may and do lead to a conviction on the part of employers that women in general are unfitted or unlikely to be considered, so that they cease even to try effectively for it. Or, again, an assessor who sees only part of a problem, for example an employer who sees women's or men's work potential but not their family or other circumstances, may through ignorance bring about a damaging clash of roles or an overload of commitments.

If in the face of risks like these the administration of work and society is to remain manageable, and individuals are to be given some certainty of where they stand and of at least a minimum of respect for their potential and needs, the best available answer – even if only a rough and ready one – may be to stereotype roles to some extent and to assign people to them by categories rather than as individuals. To be treated as a member of a category such as 'husband', 'wife', or 'woman worker' is in principle less likely to provide for one's personal abilities and needs than if one were dealt with as an individual, but in practice may come nearer to the mark if judgments on individual cases are likely to be inaccurate, arbitrary or biased.

So for example there may well be a case, which will be considered below, for positive discrimination in training and promotion in favour of women as a class, to correct the effects of systematic biases against them in the past.

So again, though past conventional definitions of a housewife's role did not give scope for the full range of women's abilities and interests, they may nevertheless in their time and place have offered to a high proportion of married women more security and a better approximation to personal needs and interests than could have been achieved in any other way. The risk of creating overload and a clash of roles through inadequately considered role assignment, as will be underlined in later chapters, is in present conditions a very real one.

Finally, any process of major social change involves a time constraint. Time is needed to assemble and deploy human and material resources. To relieve housewives' overload and the clash of work and family roles calls for a number of material measures which cannot be developed at short notice. If more women work, fewer will be as available as in the past not only for the care of children but for other home-making activities such as the care of the aged and disabled, or for voluntary and community activities of the kind women have traditionally supported. To the extent that it is wished to replace working wives in these roles – the qualification is important – it will be necessary to add to professional services: those of the nurse, the professional social worker, the professional group worker who organizes neighbourhood and community activities. This may involve reconsidering occupational roles in terms both of sex-typing and of status. To attract more and better staff into child-minding activities, for example, the status attached to these activities is likely to have to be raised to become commensurate with the value placed on child mental health. There are similar implications for schools, home help arrangements, and a variety of other services. Changes like these have wide implications for public and private expenditure and manpower planning. They cannot be disposed of at short notice or without considering possible prior claims for other social purposes.

Learning time is needed to work out new policies and win support for them in the face of ignorance and misunderstanding. If progress towards the ideal of treating each person in accordance with his or her personal interests and capacities is blocked by old stereotypes and attitudes, it is unreasonable to expect these to disappear overnight. Attitudes on sex roles and family life tend to be deep-rooted. Even where they are obsolete or unfounded, to attack them suddenly, sweepingly and in a revolutionary way risks promoting a backlash which can cause more conflict and delay than a more differentiated and evolutionary approach would have needed in the first place.

In a case like that of family and work there is a 'building site' problem. Family life, careers, and the relation between them cannot simply be demolished or suspended to leave a clear field for reconstruction. They have to go on, and reconstruction must proceed around them while they retain much of their present form. There is also a problem in a case like this of ensuring that the whole of a complex of issues and the great variation of individual circumstances have been taken into account. Dramatic, sweeping measures of change are certainly possible and can be useful, but risk riding rough-shod over legitimate differences between the circumstances of individuals and families, and creating a façade behind which problems remain unsolved and may even be aggravated. The sweeping changes brought in by the Marxist governments of Eastern Europe are impressive, as will be shown, and some suggestions for Britain based on them will be put forward later. But it is also the case that many housewives in Eastern Europe have found themselves propelled from under-employment as full-time housekeepers to over-employment, often severe, in a combination of house and outside work, before any adequate relief for this overload was available. A simple, narrowly focused ideology made a sharp, decisive, change in their status possible, but precisely because it was so simple and narrow made it harder to anticipate the problems which would arise from then on or even to recognize them quickly and openly when they did arise.

The research team thus accepts that in bringing about change in an area like that of family, careers, and sex roles the main weight should be placed on an evolutionary rather than a revolutionary approach. The changes considered here, especially the most basic changes in sex roles, are of the kind whose full realization may need to be spread over decades – if not generations – rather than years. They need to be driven forward continuously and with force but through a strategy staged over time; and they need to come about primarily by education, example, and inducement, operating through many channels and leaving many options open.

d *A problem of men and women, not of women alone*

Another orientation of the team – again a generalization from previously available facts, confirmed by the enquiry's own evidence – has been towards the idea that any worthwhile policy about women and top jobs must be thought of in terms of changing the working and family habits of men as well as women; not simply or primarily of giving women their chance within a traditionally male pattern of behaviour in top jobs and careers leading to them. There is a negative and a positive way of looking at this, each valid in its own fashion.

On the negative side, better access for women to top jobs could mean fewer opportunities for men in their work and less freedom from domestic responsibilities. How far and under what conditions will this be acceptable?

On the positive side, the interests and abilities of men as well as women are distributed over a wide curve, and one of the points emerging from the discussion of men's and women's roles in recent years is that men too have lost through being forced into stereotyped patterns of behaviour. There has for example been a tendency to under-rate the role of the father in the family and to permit work pressures to grow in a way which makes it hard for him to exercise it in full. The stress laid in boys' education on independence and forceful behaviour has helped among other things to bring it about that in 1967 thirty-six men went to prison in England and Wales for every one woman, and that men have a substantially greater prospect, compared to women, of accident and death.[1] The loss from tendencies like these does not fall equally on all men. For some, traditional training in forcefulness and independence provides just the stimulus they need; but others, who find themselves at a less central point in the distribution of men's interests and abilities, are pushed into breakdown and delinquency. If the role of father and of host in the family circle tends to be under-estimated by comparison with men's roles in work, it is those men whose interests and abilities specially fit them for this role who are likely to lose most. Men as well as women are likely to gain from a more explicit recognition of the variety of interests and abilities in each sex and of the need to adapt work and family roles to it.

The original question of the enquiry was whether more women can or should take up top occupational roles traditionally reserved to men, It develops into the question whether men – or more men – might not gain by behaving in ways traditionally more usual in the

---

[1] Comparative international statistics on men's and women's accident and death rates are conveniently summarized in Council of Europe, European Population Conference, 1966, Vol. I, papers 15-18 and 29.

life cycles of women, for example by concentrating for a time on home and community responsibilities at periods when a growing family particularly needs this, and cutting work commitments accordingly, or by accepting a permanently more limited occupational role so as to leave room for a wider range of family or other interests outside.

e *Varied but not permissive*

The research team's argument is not that the choice of roles by men and women in work and the family should be left completely open. Certainly it should be varied to suit individual circumstances; new stereotypes should not be substituted for old. To take, for instance, the world-wide movement in recent years towards participation by husbands and wives in activities traditionally characteristic of the other sex and towards joint decisions, and to derive from it a new stereotype for roles within marriage, would break the rule of treating individuals as individuals just as much as to continue the older stereotype of segregated roles. But neither is the selection of roles in work and marriage simply a matter of each individual's arbitrary choice.

One objective limit is set by individuals' own abilities and temperaments. The distribution of roles in a society needs to take account of the actual curve of distribution of temperaments and abilities, not to depart arbitrarily from it. A second limit is set by the constraints already mentioned; for practical reasons, some degree of institutionalization of men's and women's roles and of compromise between individual and social needs is likely to remain necessary. People can accommodate to institutional limits to some extent, thanks to the plasticity of human personality. Individuals' interests and abilities are usually flexible and can be re-directed within wide limits without significant loss to the individual. But this flexibility has its limits, and some unresolved conflicts between personal needs and what is socially practicable are likely to remain.

'The right view', as the research team wrote in its earlier broadsheet on *Women and Top Jobs*,[1] is:

'Neither that individuals must always adjust to institutional requirements nor the reverse. It is that there is a continuous interplay between the two processes. In contemporary society there is both a range of behaviours which best fit current conditions of living . . . *and* a need for individuals and groups, such as the family, to select from within this range the behaviours which fit their own time, place, and individual circumstances, and to de-

[1] P.E.P., 1967, p. 63.

velop from these their own set of rules. All options must be open according to the needs and abilities of . . . not only those directly involved but members of the wider community and those whose interest may be affected by precedents set now. At any one time and place any particular institution may take a variety of shapes, and from society's point of view any of a number of these may be equally acceptable.'

OUTLINE OF THE REPORT

The results of the enquiry are reported below in four divisions.

Part II puts the problem of women and top jobs in Britain in perspective by reviewing recent developments in Eastern Europe on the one hand and in Western countries – the United States, certain countries of Western Europe, Israel and Britain – on the other. Starting from very different ideological points of view, attitudes and policies in the East and West have tended to converge. This convergence and the questions which it either has answered or leaves still unanswered is the theme of Part II.

Part III considers, on the basis especially of the enquiry's own national surveys, the career and family patterns envisaged by young, highly qualified women in Britain today. It goes on to consider the practicability of reconciling a career for both husband and wife at high levels with successful family life. It does this on the basis both of generally available material about mothers' and fathers' employment and child care and, especially, of a series of intensive case studies of married couples made during the enquiry. A number of the couples studied have to all appearances succeeded in reconciling a full career for the wife with successful family life. Others have tried, but have found this pattern less viable for them than a more traditional one. All the couples are unbroken (though there may have been a previous marriage) and have children. In most of them the wife has worked continuously, with only the minimum break needed for the actual birth of her children. In the light of their and others' experience, what strategies are available to husbands and wives who want to combine successful family life with a dual-career pattern? To what conditions is each strategy likely to be appropriate, and under what conditions are families likely to discover appropriate strategies and adopt them?

Part IV picks up the results of studies of women's experience in the five occupations already mentioned, in the management of two large firms, as directors in business generally, in the B.B.C., in the Administrative Civil Service, and as architects – together with more general material on other occupations, especially the more established fields of women's professional work such as medicine, teaching, and social service. How, if at all, has women's performance in these occupations tended to differ from that of men, particularly as regards differences which might affect promotion to the top? What has been and seems likely to be the experience in these occupations of highly qualified women's availability for work, as apart from their ability once they are at work? The life cycles and career patterns of married women have tended and seem likely still to tend to differ from those traditional among men – whatever may happen to some men's life cycles in future – because of having children. This seems likely to remain true even if a woman has a strong commitment to her career and hopes to minimize any interruption to it. Her motivation at different stages of her career, the effort she is ready to put in at a given age, and the time at which she is ready and fitted for promotion are all likely to differ from a man's. These features of married women's careers seems likely not only to remain, at least for the majority of today's younger married women, but to continue to affect the careers even of single women, especially by influencing the attitudes which girls acquire in their education and the image and expectation of employed women in the minds of employers. In any case married women are the vast majority in older age groups, and it is from them that any great increase in the number of women in top jobs would in practice have to come. How far, then, is it possible without loss of economic efficiency to adjust employers' policies for recruitment, training, job design and placement, and promotion in order to give married women as good a chance as men of similar ability and qualifications of reaching the top? What have employers and the economy to gain from this? Have employers given it serious consideration? Is there any industry, firm, or profession in Britain where it has been done successfully; and, if so, what action would be needed to reproduce this success elsewhere?

Finally, Part V considers possible long-range implications of the enquiry, and of parallel work by P.E.P. on the agencies promoting equal pay and opportunity for women, not only for work but for marriage, men's and women's roles, and the role of love and affection in society. From the whole body of findings and discussions it then draws out possible implications for policy and action.

Part Two

An International Review of Experience

Chapter II

The Experience of Eastern Europe[1]

In none of the other countries examined in the P.E.P. study has so sustained and forceful an effort been made to bring women into business and social leadership as in the Marxist countries of Eastern Europe. Some features of this effort are specific to these countries, but many are of universal relevance and separable from the application of a generally Marxist system. The experience of Eastern Europe thus provides a useful perspective in which to foresee the future problems of Western countries, especially as regards the problems which remain when the formal and traditional barriers to women's progress still common in the West have been abolished. The Soviet Union now has more than half a century of experience in this field, and the other East European countries most of a generation, and it is with their experience that it is useful to begin.

Behind the drive which the socialist countries have made to bring women first of all into work outside their homes and secondly into positions of leadership in work lie two chief factors. The first and most important is ideological. The family holds a key place in Marxist thinking as the basic cell of society, with essential functions in a number of fields. Over and above its most obvious function in the birth and early rearing of children, the family has a part to play in education, in shaping and satisfying emotional relationships between the family members, and in consumption and production. But it cannot perform these functions to the best advantage so long as mothers (or married women in general) are restricted to the role simply of a housewife.

'Mere' housewives are seen by Marxist thinkers as subject in capitalist society to a double alienation. They are not independent but in a sense the property of their husbands. Where a dowry is paid or some similar arrangement is made, this relationship is of course underlined; but it exists, in the form of a relation of dependence and

[1] The material for this chapter is drawn primarily from the Soviet Union, Poland, Czechoslovakia and the German Democratic Republic.

subordination, even where there is no question of property in this material sense. 'Mere' housewives are also alienated in that they are shut off from the main stream of work and social interchange, the means used by human beings to make themselves fully human. Through work and social interchange man takes hold of nature and society and transforms them so as to fit them to his needs, and at the same time shapes his own personality to take account of natural and social imperatives. In this way he creates in one and the same operation himself, nature and society, and by adapting each of these three to the others he brings conflict and alienation between them to an end. From this process of creation and mutual adaptation, the central human adventure, the mere housewife is shut out. At most she can take part in it indirectly through her husband and children. The loss is not only hers. Society and the family also lose the contribution which she might have made. Her role even within the family will suffer, for she cannot be as effective as she might have been as a partner to her husband or as mother to her children. A women's organization underlines what women themselves have to gain by wider work opportunity:

'Why is so much emphasis placed on women's work, on their economic equality? Because it is precisely the economic liberation of women, their raised status and their independence, which are the indispensable conditions for their equality with men in society.' [1]

Lenin stated more broadly that:

'A victory for socialism is impossible until a whole half of toiling mankind, the working woman, enjoys equal rights with men; and until she no longer is kept a slave by her household and family.' [2]

This ideology can be given different accents according to the circumstances of each time and place. In the Soviet Union official attitudes to family relationships and to questions such as divorce or abortion swung through a wide arc in the first twenty years after the October Revolution, from extreme permissiveness to a Victorian emphasis on stability, duty and discipline. Analysis of a Polish women's magazine shows that between the early and the later 1950s the 'propaganda model' of the family presented by the journal changed sharply:

'Propaganda model (1) was characterized above all by the strict subordination of the family to a wider group. It did not represent

---

[1] Brejchova, Jirina, and others, *Women in Czechoslovakia*, Czechoslovak Women's Committee, Prague, 1963, p. 24.

[2] Quoted in Webb, S. and B., *Soviet Communism – A New Civilization?*, University Labour Federation edition, 1936, p. 815. See generally *Wladimir Iljitsch Lenin–Zur gesellschaftlichen Stellung der Frau*, Deutsche Akademie der Wissenschaften, Berlin (East), 1970.

the traditional and institutionalized concept of the family, as Burgess used to perceive it. What chiefly distinguished it from that concept was its reduction in the family's role. This reduction occurred at the macro as well as the micro level. The family's role was limited chiefly to procreation. The model was marked out by the equality of relationships within the family, associated with the rule that differences in men's and women's roles ought not to be accentuated. This rule followed in its turn from the accent laid on activities outside the family and work activities on the part of both husband and wife, of parents and children. The chief innovation in this model was to harmonize family and work roles, especially in the case of the wife.

'Propaganda model (2) was sharply distinct from model (1). It approximated to the basic concept of the family as seen by Parsons. In this model the main accent was on expressive and integrative functions, and therefore on the role of the wife as person and mother, and on the role of the family in the socialization and self-expression of individuals. It rested on the principle of the individualization of interpersonal relationships. The sentiments of the spouses and of parents and children were assigned a high value in it'.[1]

All over Eastern Europe in the last few years there have been changes in attitudes towards the form of care to be preferred for pre-school children; more will be said on this below.

But variations like these in Marxist thinking about women's employment, substantial as they sometimes can be, centre round a norm which does not change. Full work opportunity for women, including mothers, remains an aim of social policy throughout Eastern Europe. This aim is at least on occasion treated as important enough to outweigh considerations of economic efficiency:

'In drawing women into social labour the Soviet State was wittingly taking a measure that was unprofitable from the economic viewpoint. This was done with a view to ensure the speediest liberation of women. For instance, in Central Asia and in the Transcaucasian Republics where women were taking no part in social labour, such branches of industry were being set up as allowed of employing Moslem women. There were even factories staffed exclusively by women, although the cost of production at such factories was much higher.' [2]

[1] Kloskowska, A., (University of Lodz) in Lauwe, P-H. Chombart de (ed.) *Images de la Femme dans la Société*, Editions Ouvrières, Paris, 1964, pp. 115-6.
[2] Statement by the Soviet Women's Committee on *The Role Played by Women Engineers and Scientists in the U.S.S.R.* to the Second International Conference of Women Engineers and Scientists at Cambridge, 1967: cyclostyled.

49

An American investigator has developed an ingenious economic model to express how, in practice, Soviet manpower planners decide on the optimum proportion of women to recruit for particular branches of work or education. He found however that Soviet economic literature could give him no guidance on this, for: 'With few exceptions, Soviet authors tend to view the employment of more women as desirable under all circumstances.' [1]

Clashes between economics and women's advancement are not always resolved in favour of women; this will be discussed below. But often there has been no clash anyway. Economic considerations (including the economic consequences of demography) have often favoured greater participation by women in the work force and their increased employment in top posts, and this has been a second major factor behind the drive for women's employment in Eastern Europe, above all in the Soviet Union and East Germany. The Soviet Union had over 25,000,000 war deaths in the Second World War, and this was imposed on top of massive losses in the First World War, the revolutionary civil war, and the agrarian revolution, famine and purges of the 1930s. Some of the dead were women. But most were men, and the upshot was that whereas before the First World War the number of men and women in the population of working age was nearly the same, in 1946 women outnumbered men by three to two, or in absolute numbers by twenty million. Further, the deficit was not only among younger men. It was actually largest in the middle and older age groups whose members might be expected to fill top jobs.[2] There has also been what might be called an artificial deficit of younger qualified men for civilian work as a result of the high degree of mobilization of the Soviet armed forces. In 1959 it is estimated that 18·5 per cent of Soviet male graduates were in the forces.[3]

East Germany likewise had heavy war losses among men, and in addition, until the building of the Berlin Wall, a substantial loss of both men and women through emigration to the West. This has left East Germany with an exceptionally high proportion of the elderly and of boys and girls of school age. At the Census of 1964 the proportion of the population under 18 or over 60 was 49 per cent in East Germany compared to 34 per cent in West Germany, whereas the proportion aged 30 to 50 was only 21 per cent against 24½ per cent. In the age group from 35 to 59 women outnumbered men by

---

[1] Dodge, N. T., *Women in the Soviet Economy*, John Hopkins, 1966, p. 46.

[2] Dodge, *op. cit.*, pp. 6 and 15 and Appendix 1. See also United Nations Economic Commission for Europe, *The European Economy in 1968*, Ch. III, Table IV.

[3] Dodge, *op. cit.*, p. 198.

about three to two.[1] It goes without saying that a shortage on this scale of working population generally and of men of mature working age in particular is highly favourable to the advancement of women.

It has also been characteristic of the method of planning used in the East European countries to experience from time to time special surges of economic advance, with over-full employment and a need to call all hands to the pump.[2] These too have been periods specially favourable to women's advancement. So, for example, a severe shortage of industrial labour developed in the Soviet Union around 1930, during the first Five-Year Plan. Its effect in stimulating women's employment was superimposed on earlier discussions of how to improve women's status by bringing more of them into employment. When in due course the general shortage of labour was relieved the pressure to recruit women dropped.[3] In Poland there was severe pressure on the labour market in the years of reconstruction and industrialization after the Second World War. What might almost be called the rediscovery of the family in Poland in the early 1960s dates from the time when this pressure eased and the need to employ wives and mothers became less urgent. The drive which developed in East Germany in the early 1960s to bring more women into senior positions can be traced not least to a shortage of middle and senior managers and specialists during and after the Seven-Year Plan of 1959-65.

TYPES OF ASSISTANCE EXTENDED TO WOMEN IN EMPLOYMENT

The methods used in Eastern Europe to ensure that women are recruited and given the chance of training and of selection for higher posts have included the removal of discrimination against them, the creation of positive discrimination in their favour, the promotion of a favourable public opinion, and action to adapt working and social life to the ways in which a woman's life cycle necessarily differs

[1] *Die Lage der Familien in Mitteldeutschland*, pp. 238-239; in Bericht über die Lage der Familien in der Bundesrepublik Deutschland, January 1968, Deutscher Bundestag, Drucksache V/2532: and *Die Frau in der Gesellschaft*, Zentralinstitut für Information und Dokumentation, East Berlin 1966, p. 5 and UN Economic Commission for Europe, *loc. cit.*

[2] A planned economy can proceed either from one short-term equilibrium position to another, achieving structural change by a succession of marginal adjustments, or directly from one economic pattern to another which is structurally different, creating short-term disequilibria and bottlenecks in the process. Both methods have been used in Eastern Europe.

[3] Schwarz, S. M., *Labour in the Soviet Union*, Cresset, 1953, Chapter II; Dodge, *op. cit.*, pp. 63-64.

from a man's: especially to ensure that a woman's job shall not be prejudiced by maternity.

Discrimination is barred in the first place by constitutional guarantees. So for instance the Soviet constitution of 1936 lays down that:

'Women in the U.S.S.R. are accorded equal rights with men in all fields of economic, state, cultural, and social life. The possibility of realizing these rights of women is ensured by affording women equally with men the right to work, payment for work, rest, social insurance, and education, state protection of the interests of mother and child, granting pregnancy leave with pay, and the provision of a wide network of maternity homes, nurseries, and kindergartens' (Article 122).

From the earliest days of the Soviet Union general guarantees of this kind have been translated into specific legal and administrative measures to ensure that women do in fact have the benefit of these rights. Among these are provisions for equal pay and an equal right to employment – if employment is unlawfully refused to any person, including any woman, the public prosecutor's service is required to intervene[1] – for equal access to education, and for co-education (except for a brief and limited experiment in separate education in the Soviet Union in the late 1940s and early 1950s) with a common and unspecialized curriculum.

'The high enrolment for girls is of great significance in view of the uniform academic curriculum, heavily weighted with science, which is required throughout the entire primary and general secondary school system. This uniform curriculum for both sexes unquestionably has a strong favourable influence upon the attitude of girls towards mathematics and science. Also, the polytechnical orientation which characterized Soviet education in the 1920s and which has been re-emphasized since the reform of 1958 serves to familiarize girls as well as boys with the practical applications of science.'[2]

In planned and centrally controlled economies national policy on women's recruitment reaches local personnel administrators with the force not merely of persuasion but of a political and industrial directive. For senior posts in particular, under the system known in the Soviet Union as *nomenklatura*, appointments require party approval. Central control of publicity media makes it possible to

---

[1] Tatarinova, N. and Korshunova, E., *Living and Working Conditions of Women in the U.S.S.R.*, International Labour Review, October, 1960, p. 346.

[2] Dodge, *op. cit.*, p. 108; see also L. S. Souter, and Winslade, R., *Women Engineers in the U.S.S.R.*, Caroline Haslett Memorial Trust, 1960.

bring all propaganda channels to bear to create a public opinion favourable to women's work in the sense both of motivating women themselves and of obtaining the necessary co-operation from husbands, managers, and the operators of shops and other service facilities.

Representatives of the East European regimes tend to insist more strongly than their opposite numbers from the West on the importance of the law and of general, standardized, administrative measures for re-defining the status of women inside as well as outside the family.[1] East Germany's 1965 Code of Family Law is a particularly clear-cut illustration. The Code rewrites family law with the aim of guaranteeing to married women, especially mothers, their husbands' co-operation in freeing them to take the job that suits them.

'Both spouses must take their share in the education and care of the children and in housekeeping. The mutual relations of the spouses are to be given a form which permits the wife to combine her occupational and social activities with motherhood. If a spouse not hitherto occupied decides to take up an occupation, or a spouse decides to undertake further education or to work in a social activity, the other spouse must support this project of (the first) partner with comradely consideration and help.'[2]

The official commentary notes that this does not mean that the spouses must play an identical part – 'that would be schematism' – but that both must feel fully responsible for the house and family, and the husband 'must not be satisfied only to give a hand'. It also makes it clear that this is a directive not only to husbands and wives but to managements and trade unions.

'That the working wife and mother should stay at home when her child is ill, or should excuse herself early from a social activity at the plant so as to fetch her child from the day-nursery, is seen as a nuisance but inevitable. There is still too little understanding and consideration for the fact that the male worker too is a husband and father. The idea that the education and care of the children and the housework are chiefly the wife's business is not yet wholly overcome. So much could be changed by a different organization of plant and social work and a different style of working.'[3]

If the spouses live separately, either can under East German law claim maintenance from the other if this is necessary because of age,

[1] Comment based notably on contributions to the United Nations Seminar on the Status of Women, Iasi, Romania, August 1969.
[2] Article 10 of the *Familiengesetzbuch*: from *Das Familienrecht der D.D.R. – Lehrkommentar*, Staatsverlag der D.D.R., Berlin, 1967
[3] *Ibid.*, p. 50.

illness or the care of children. But the wife like the husband has no right to maintenance if these grounds do not apply; she must get herself a job. She has however the right to maintenance while training for a profession, if she has not previously done so; she cannot be required to take any job that comes. The husband can claim maintenance from the wife if the same circumstances should apply to him.[1]

To remove discrimination against women, or motivate them equally with men, may sometimes require at least temporary discrimination in their favour, as in certain instances already mentioned. One was the Soviet Women's Committee's case of plants which recruited Central Asian women as a contribution to social change, even though these women's work was less economic than that of men. Another was the Soviet government's action in the period of labour shortage during the first Five-Year Plan. In order to expand the industrial work force as a whole, the Soviet government temporarily set for plant managers higher quotas for the employment of women and for the admission of women to factory training schools than the managers would have chosen for themselves.[2]

A further case in East Germany in the early 1960s concerned specifically women in middle and top jobs. The Politbureau of the Central Committee of the Socialist Unity Party issued in 1961 what came to be known as the Frauenkommuniqué,[3] pointing out that women were too rarely promoted to supervisory and managerial positions and calling both for a national debate and for action by all government and social organizations to increase the proportion of women in these positions. A Scientific Advisory Council and a research centre were set up to work on problems of women's advancement. Plans for the advancement of women, worked out in collaboration with the Advisory Council, have to be incorporated into the research and action plans of the various economic and political agencies of the State. Managers and administrators are required to report regularly on action taken for women's advancement. If they fail to co-operate, the Advisory Council is in a position to take up the matter at top ministerial level.[4]

East European governments have seen no necessary contradiction between encouraging women's work at all levels and maintaining

---

[1] *Familiengesetzbuch*, Article 18 and p. 82. The 1968 *Fundamentals of legislation of the U.S.S.R. and the Union Republics on Marriage and the Family* express the same principles as the East German Code, though in less detail.

[2] Dodge, *op. cit.*, pp. 63-64; Schwarz, *loc. cit.*

[3] *Die Frau – der Frieden und der Socialismus*, Zentralkommittee der S.E.D., December 23, 1961.

[4] Law of 20. X. 1966, superseding a Ministerial Order of 12. V. 1964; and information from the Deutsche Akademie der Wissenschaften, where the research centre is situated.

a classical type of legislation protecting women from work likely to be damaging to them but not to men, in view of the differences between men's and women's physical constitution and especially of women's role as mothers. The Soviet Union specifically rejects the view of 'certain representatives of the international women's movements (who) look on women's privileges as discrimination against female labour'.[1] In war and periods of economic strain protective legislation tends to be suspended or ignored, as also happens in Western countries. But in normal times, though details differ from country to country, the aims and range of protection are similar to those usual in the West. In the Soviet Union, for example, national and provincial legislation and the safety rules of individual industries are used to ban women from heavy and regular underground work, from many types of work on seagoing fishing vessels, from the use of dangerous materials and tools (for example pneumatic hammers, under the safety rules of the oil and chemical industries), and from work on high smoke stacks. A pregnant woman is normally excluded from night work and overtime, and has to be transferred to light work if this is medically required. After the fourth month she has the right to refuse work assignments involving travel.[2] Provisions for medical care, maternity benefit, family allowances, tax allowances, and housing, though again differing in detail from country to country, are also conventional in terms of practice in the West.

What is more distinctive about East European practice is the protection given to a mother's job, and the practical help offered to employed mothers in the way of day nurseries and nursery schools. A Soviet manager cannot legally refuse to hire a woman because she is pregnant, nor can he reduce her pay or dismiss her on the ground of pregnancy. After a birth a mother in the Soviet Union is entitled to protection of four kinds: eight weeks' paid maternity leave, to which annual leave is usually added; up to three months' unpaid maternity leave, after which she can still return to her own or an equivalent job; a further period, up to one year from the birth, for which she can stay away from work without diminution of her rights to benefits such as sick pay, maternity benefit, or pension, which depend on continuity of employment; and, if she returns to work while still nursing her baby, paid time off for nursing it. Provisions in the rest of Eastern Europe are on similar lines. The time allowed under the first three of these provisions has tended to lengthen in recent years. A Czech degree of 1964, for example, extended paid

[1] Tatarinova, M., *Women in the U.S.S.R.*, Novosti, Moscow, p. 79.
[2] Dodge, *op. cit.*, pp. 57-75, summarizes Soviet protective legislation and related industrial provisions since 1918; including the protection referred to in the next paragraph.

maternity leave from 18 to 22 weeks, and there has since been a further extension to 26 weeks. Under Czech legislation a mother's right to return to her old job runs up to one year from the date of her child's birth, and she can remain out of employment without diminution of her pension for up to three years.[1] A Hungarian law of 1967 provides that a mother may stay out of work for up to three years after a birth and will during this time, after the expiry of her paid maternity leave, be paid an allowance equivalent to about 40 per cent of the wage of an average woman earner. At the end of the three years she is entitled to return to her former employer in the same or a similar job.[2]

The East European countries have also made massive efforts to put at mothers' disposal day nurseries and nursery schools, both for educational reasons and to make it easier for mothers to work. In the Soviet Union the number of places in permanent nurseries (including nursery places in kindergartens) increased from 62,000 in 1928 to 736,000 in 1950 and 2,253,000 in 1964. The number of children enrolled in kindergartens was 130,000 in 1928, 1,169,000 in 1950 and 4,737,000 in 1964.[3] Total provision of both kinds together rose, on a slightly different basis of calculation, from 1,788,000 places in 1950 to 4,428,000 in 1960 and 8,534,000 in 1967.[4] The pace of development and the emphasis as between nurseries and kindergartens differs from one country to another, but the general trend of development in East Germany, Poland, and Czechoslovakia has been similar.

Considerable efforts have been made in Eastern Europe to improve shopping, catering and other public service facilities so as to lighten the double load on married women of employment and housework, of which the East European régimes are very much aware. Time budgets for the Soviet Union, Czechoslovakia, and East Germany between 1959 and 1966 show employed housewives with small families to be spending typically four to six hours a day on household chores; husbands, as Russian, East German, and Romanian studies bring out, spend only a fraction of the same time on them.[5]

[1] Brejchova, op. cit., p. 31-2, and Czechoslovak State Population Committee, Czechoslovak Population Problems, 1965, first section.

[2] Women in Hungary, Hungarian Women's Council, Budapest 1968, p. 37.

[3] Dodge, op. cit., pp. 78 and 84.

[4] Zhenschchiny i Deti v. S.S.S.R., Statistika, Moscow, 1969, p. 126, The Z.D. figures do not reassign nursery places in kindergartens (758,000 in 1964) to the 'nursery' category, whereas Dodge's do: there are also some more detailed differences.

[5] See e.g. Dodge, op. cit., pp. 93-96, for the Soviet Union; The Daily Régime of Employed Women in Prague, Czechoslovak Population Committee, loc. cit., W. Köppert in Frau und Wissenschaft, Berlin, Akademieverlag, 1968, pp. 64-5, D.D.R.: for Romania, H. Cazacu, 'Facteurs Sociaux, Economiques, Biologiques et Budget de Temps', Revue Romaine des Sciences Sociales, 1968, pp. 35-44.

East Germany and Czechoslovakia have developed organized 'grand-mothers' movements' to provide help for working wives.

East Germany has also established, over and above the normal right of access of all women to any field of education or specialist training, special classes for housewives who wish to train as engineers or economists. 'Admission to these classes is open to women who have an exceptional load of domestic work as mothers and house-wives, and for that reason cannot follow courses in an ordinary class.'[1] The level of work required is the same as in an ordinary class, but, subject to this, principals of schools are required to adjust the timetable to the housewives' convenience. They have also to arrange for any necessary periods of practical work in enterprises or elsewhere, and, in so far as participants are already employed, to negotiate with the employing enterprise an appropriate period of released time (up to twenty hours a week) with pay at up to 80 per cent of each woman's previous earnings. More generally, P.E.P.'s East German report notes, women in East Germany have benefited from the division of professional training courses into relatively short, self-contained, units which are easier than longer continuous courses to fit into the typical pattern of a married woman's life.

HOW SUCCESSFUL HAVE THESE MEASURES BEEN?

As regards women's actual success in reaching the top, Eastern Europe has what might be called a 'yes-but' situation. The propor-tions of women qualified for higher posts, active in the work force, and actually holding posts of senior responsibility, has risen sharply in Eastern Europe since the Marxist régimes took over. But the pro-portion of women at or near the top, though in many fields higher than in the West, is still far short of equality with men. In the Soviet Union in particular, where two generations have passed since the revolution as compared to one in the rest of Eastern Europe, women's progress towards the top has shown signs of levelling off.

Taking first the test of qualifications, there has been a dramatic advance in women's opportunity in higher education. In Prague in the early 1960s the proportion of men of all ages with university education was four times higher than the proportion of women, but in the age group 24-29 the ratio fell to two to one, and in the group aged 20 to 24 the proportions were almost equal.[2] In East

---

[1] *Decree on the Further Education of Women in Special Classes in the Specialized Schools of the D.D.R.*, 25. vii. 67, s. 4. The experimentation leading up to this decree began after the Frauenkommuniqué: *Gesundheitliche und Soziologische Probleme der berufstätigen Mütter*, conference report, Deutsche Gesellschaft für die gesamte Hygiene, Rostock, 1966, p. 85.

[2] Srnska, *loc. cit.*, p. 402.

Germany, which has a relatively low proportion of women in higher education – 26 per cent of all students in 1964 – the ratio of women students to the total female population nevertheless rose from 12 per 10,000 in 1953 to 32 per 10,000 in 1963.[1] In Russia before the revolution women already made up 20-25 per cent of students.[2] This general average did not increase much during the first years of the revolution, though there was a particularly sharp breakthrough in medicine. But there was a big general increase during the late 1920s and 1930s – the time of the first two Five-Year Plans – and by the early 1950s women made up over half of all Soviet students (Table II.1). In 1959, whereas in age-groups over 45 the proportion of men with higher education was still three times as high as the proportion of women, in the age-group 30-34 the proportions were about equal.[3]

Table II.1, however, also brings out the other side of the story. In the Soviet Union, where the Marxist experience has been longest, the advance of women in higher education has been checked and at one time even reversed. Whether the figures are taken overall or faculty by faculty, it appears that a peak was reached in women's participation in higher education in the early 1950s; as early as the 1930s in the case of medicine. Since then the proportion of women

Table II.1

Women in Higher Education in the Soviet Union

(i) *Women as percentage of all day and evening students in higher educational institutions*

	Industry construction transport communications	Agricultural	Economics and law	Medicine	Education, culture	All
1928	13	17	21	52	49	28
1933	22	32	36	75	50	37
1937	28	30	41	68	48	43
1950	30	39	57	65	72	53
1955	35	39	67	69	72	52
1960	30	27	49	56	63	43
1962	28	25	NA	54	62	42
1968-69	35	27	59	55	65	47

Zhenschchiny i Deti v S.S.S.R., Statistika, Moscow, 1969 (1928, 1960, 1968-69) p. 56, and Dodge, *op. cit.*, p. 112.

[1] *Die Frau in der Gesellschaft*, op. cit., pp. 58-63.
[2] Dodge, *op. cit.*, pp. 102-3.
[3] Dodge, *op. cit.*, p. 283.

(ii) *Women as percentage of all receiving 'candidate' (Ph.D.) degrees*

	1936-37	1956-68	1959-61	1962-64
Biology	37	67	52	53
Chemistry	26	53	51	38
Geology	23	27	27	27
Physics, mathematics	6	23	15	17
Applied science				
Medicine	29	54	53	47
Agriculture, veterinary	20	36	33	29
Technology	4	19	16	12
Non-scientific fields	21	32	27	25
All fields	21	33	30	28

Dodge, *op. cit.*, p. 137.

(iii) *Women as percentage of all receiving 'doctoral' (higher doctorate) degrees*

	1936-37	1956-58	1959-61	1962-64
Biology	24	29	36	31
Chemistry	8	18	18	40
Geology	9	11	10	23
Physics, mathematics	8	0	4	8
Applied science:				
Medicine	11	51	41	42
Agriculture, veterinary	0	13	11	13
Technology	0	4	4	3
Non-scientific fields	8	20	16	11
All fields	10	15	18	21

Dodge, *op. cit.*, p. 138.

students has fallen. It has recovered from its lowest level, but, even allowing for demographic changes, women were somewhat worse placed in 1968 than in 1955 in all faculties except that of industrial construction, transport and communications. In 1955 the proportion of women in higher education corresponded almost exactly to the proportion of women in the whole population then aged 20-29. By the early 1960s it was running up to 7 per cent behind; women made up 50 per cent of the population aged 20-29 in 1965 compared to 43 per cent in higher education in 1964. By 1969 the gap had narrowed again to 2·5 per cent. Women were 47 per cent of all in higher education in 1969 and 49·5 per cent (estimated) of the total population aged 20-29 in 1970. But in 1969-70 a boy still had around 10 per cent more chance than a girl of being enrolled for higher education.[1] Soviet figures show that in recent years the proportion of women has been consistently higher, branch by branch, among second-level specialists with a 'special secondary' education than among specialists with higher education.[2]

Women's share in degrees at the Ph.D. level ('candidate' degrees) in the Soviet Union has always fallen well short of that of men and, like their share in higher education in general, has fallen since the 1950s. Women's share in advanced doctorates was still climbing in the early 1960s, though with differences from faculty to faculty, but lagged still further behind men than their share in Ph.Ds. In Poland similarly it seems that the level at which women's opportunity lags furthest behind men's is not, as in some Western countries, the Ph.D., but the higher degree level corresponding to the German 'Habilitation'.

Considering next the fields of work which women enter, the education figures show that women in Eastern Europe are now taking a substantial part in less traditionally feminine professions such as engineering, the law, medicine and economics. This impression is underlined by the figures in Tables II.2 and II.4 for women actively employed in some of these professions. But once again there are reservations. Some professions and branches of professions remain more feminine than others. A woman in the Soviet Union who enters engineering can compete in practically any area of the profession. So for example the Soviet Women's Committee notes how

Table II.2

Women in Non-traditional Professions in Eastern Europe

(i) *Percentage of women among specialists with certain qualifications in the Soviet Union*

	1913	1928	1941	1954	1960	1964	1966
Engineers, geologists	—	—	15	29	29	31	30
Physicians	10	45	61	76	75	74	72
Legal personnel	—	—	15	32	32	32	—
						(1963)	
Economists, economic statisticians, commodity specialists	—	—	31	59	57	63	63
Agronomists, veterinarians etc.	—	—	25	41	39	41	40

Dodge, *op. cit.*, p. 194. *Zhenschchiny i Deti v S.S.S.R.*, *op. cit.*, p. 98.

[1] Population figures from Economic Commission for Europe, *The European Economy in 1968*, Chapter III, Appendix I.
[2] Tatarinova, *op. cit.*, p. 50, *Zhenschchiny i Deti v S.S.S.R.*, *op. cit.*, pp. 98 and 100.

(ii) *Percentage of women among certain specialists in Poland, 1964*

Engineers	11
Physicians	44
Dentists	80
Lawyers	24

Sokolowska and Wrochno, *op. cit.*, Table 10.

(iii) *Percentage of women among personnel in legal work in East Germany*

	1950	1958	1963
Judges	19	30	32
Advocates:			
in the civil service and in local			
government service	NA	NA	23
other	NA	NA	7
Notaries	1	20	23
Notaries' clerks	$3\frac{1}{2}$	29	51
Lay justices in local courts	NA	NA	41

Die Frau in der Gesellschaft, op. cit., p. 234.

Nina Samusenko, 'an outstanding turbine constructor', has earned the nickname of 'Turbine Regulation Goddess'.[1] But whereas in engineering-industrial institutes in the U.S.S.R. in the 1950s the proportion of women among students of food technology and of technology of the consumer goods industry ran around 75 per cent, in power and transport engineering and machine building the proportion of women dropped to 20-25 per cent.[2] In medicine, in spite of the high proportion of women in the profession generally, men have tended to dominate in certain fields, notably surgery.[3] Women continue to show a preference for professions such as teaching or medicine rather than for technology, and for mental work rather than physical work or (as in construction site work) the direct management or supervision of heavy physical work. In general (Table II.1 (i) and II.2 (i)) the Soviet figures show a tendency for women's penetration of non-traditional fields to level off since the 1950s.

[1] 'Because she spares no effort in teaching the foremen and workers.' Soviet Women's Committee, *loc. cit.*, p. 9.

[2] Dodge, *op. cit.*, p. 126. For similar figures for Czechoslovakia in 1965-66 see *Statistical Abstract* for Czechoslovakia (Orbis, Prague 1968), Table 99. Economics and law appear as an overwhelmingly feminine faculty: 87 per cent of the students in vocational and secondary vocational schools in 1965-66 were women. For East Germany, see G. Schnelle in *Frau und Wissenschaft, op. cit.*, p. 93.

[3] Dodge, *op. cit.*, p. 129.

In the Soviet Union as elsewhere, whether in the West or in the East, women continue to fill many of the lowest-skilled and lowest-paid physical jobs.[1] As they move away from these they may move into traditional areas of male physical skill. The percentage of women among machine and hand setters in printing, for example, rose in the Soviet Union from 12 per cent in 1926 to 78 per cent in 1959.[2] But they often also bypass these areas and look for an outlet rather in office work or a profession. In 1959 the proportion of women among Soviet engineers was 32 per cent, but among craftsmen in the metal industries the proportion fell to 15 per cent for turners and 6 per

Table II.3

Women's Participation in the Work Force, Eastern Europe

(i) *Soviet Union: Percentage of women who are in the work force at certain ages*

(a) *Urban women*

Age	1926	1939	1959
10-15	13	NA	4
16-59	40	45	67
60+	28	9	13

(b) *All women*

Age	1926	1959
15-19	80	63
20-24	93	81
25-29	75	80
30-34	75	78
35-39	77	77
40-44	77	76
45-49	77	75
50-54	72	69
55-59	68	55
60-64	55	48
65-69	47	35
All ages	52	49

Dodge, *op. cit.*, pp. 33, 35, 36.

[1] Kulke quotes recent East German figures showing that women constitute 75-90 per cent of the workers in pay groups I-III (lowest) on industry, but only 4-6 per cent in groups VI-VIII (highest). In the East German economy as a whole in 1963 the proportion of wage and salary earners on rates of over 600 marks a month was 43 per cent for men but 7 per cent for women. 11 per cent of men but 50 per cent of women were on rates below 400 marks. For earnings figures for Poland see Sokolowska and Wrochno, *op. cit.*

[2] *Die Frau in der Gesellschaft*, p. 182.

(ii) *East Germany:* (*a*) *Percentage of wives who are in the work force:* employees only (e.g. excluding co-operative or private farmers), 1964

Wife's age	No. of children	Wife working				Wife not working
		Full-time	Part-time		Total	
			25 hours a week or more	24 hours or less		
18-24	0	88	3	1	92	8
	1	64	8	6	78	22
	2	49	4	10	63	37
	3 or more	35	5	2	42	58
	All sizes of family	68	6	5	79	21
25-39	0	77	8	5	90	10
	1	52	12	12	76	24
	2	47	10	13	70	31
	3 or more	38	9	11	58	42
	All sizes of family	52	10	11	73	27
40-49	All sizes of family	48	11	14	73	27
50-59	All sizes of family	38	7	10	55	45
60 and over	All sizes of family	15	3	4	22	77
All ages	All sizes of family	48	9	10	67	33

Die Frau in der Gesellschaft, op. cit., p. 162-3.

(*b*) *Families with husband present: per cent of wives who work in families where the husband's income is at a given level, 1967*

Per cent of wives working where the number of children is	Net income of husband (East German marks)				
	under 400	400-599	600-799	800-999	1,000 or over
0	78	73	69	65	57
1	88	84	78	73	$64\frac{1}{2}$
2	91	81	75	$64\frac{1}{2}$	52
3 or more	92	75	67	58	40

P.E.P. report on East Germany (C. Kulke): based on *Statistisches Jahrbuch der D.D.R.* 1968, p. 446.

SEX, CAREER AND FAMILY

(iii) *Czechoslovakia, 1961*

(a) *Women in the non-agricultural work force (excluding apprentices)*

	Total employed 1948 000s	Total employed 1966	Increase in employment 1948-66 000s
Men	2,300	2,908	608
Women	914	2,340	1,426
Total	3,214	5,248	2,034
Women as per cent of Total	28	45	70

Statistical Abstract for Czechoslovakia (Orbis, Prague 1968) Tables 25 and 26.

(b) *Married women in the work force (percentage)*

Age	Czech regions Of total	Of married women with 3+children	Slovak regions Of total	Of married women with 3+children
20-24	63	30	47	15
25-29	58	41	41	23
30-34	63	55	47	34
35-39	70	63	47	40
40-44	72	66	49	42

Czechoslovak State Population Committee, *Czechoslovak Population Problems*, Prague 1967, p. 28.

[*Table* II.3 *continued opposite*

cent each for fitters and for installation and maintenance mechanics.[1] There are plenty of women agricultural technicians (Table II.4 (iii)), but the woman tractor driver, whose well-padded shape has caused such joy to Western cartoonists over the years, turns out to be a myth, except of course (as in the West) in war-time. By the middle and late 1950s women were only 0·75 per cent of all Soviet tractor drivers.[2] A number of mental work professions in the Soviet Union and Poland show the combination familiar in the West of feminization and low pay, with the same difficulty as in the West in saying which of these developments is the hen and which is the egg.[3]

Though co-education and a common curriculum have done much to increase girls' readiness to enter non-traditional occupations,

[1] *Die Frau in der Gesellschaft*, and see p. 169 for farm mechanics (women were 1·4 per cent of those employed in this craft in 1959).
[2] Dodge, *op. cit.*, pp. 169-70.
[3] *Ibid.*, pp. 129 (medicine), 133 (science and technology), 137; Sokolowska and Wrochno. *op. cit.*

64

Table II.3 (continued)

(iv) *Seven East European countries: percentage of all women of certain ages who were in the work force at certain dates*

Age	Bulgaria 1956	Bulgaria 1965	Czechoslovakia 1950	Czechoslovakia 1961	East Germany 1950	East Germany 1964	Hungary 1949	Hungary 1960	Poland 1950	Poland 1960	Romania 1956	Romania 1966	U.S.S.R. 1959
15-19	52	39	71	54	73[1]	55[1]	56	52½	59	43	75[3]	43[3]	62
20-29	69	78	56	63			39	52	64½	65½	76	77	80
30-39	75	86	48	62	46[2]	69[2]	30	50	62	65	73½	79	78
40-49	76	86	52	67			27	51	64	69	75	77	75
50-54	65	68	48	59	34	58½	25	46	60	65	73	71	67
55-59	54	35	41½	42			27	31	55	60	68	59	49
60+	29	10	18	15	11	13½	22	22½	36	37	46	28	39
All 15+	62	61	47	50	41	48	32	43	59	59	70[4]	62¼[4]	67

[1] 15-24   [2] 25-49   [3] 14-19   [4] All 14+

United Nations Economic Commission for Europe, *The European Economy in 1968*, Ch. 3, Table II.

c

East German and Polish studies show that substantial differences in boys' and girls' interests remain and are likely to bias their occupational choice.

'From the boys' interest profile, comprising geographical interests with a tendency towards the exotics of travel; technological orientation towards the exploitation of natural forces; historic-political interests with the accent on war events; and sports with the stress on personal achievement, it would appear that boys' interest in nature is utilitarian. Boys are interested in man as an individual active in every way and battling against the odds. Similarly, the statement that the girls' interest profile is characterized by geographical-biological and socio-historical interests (philosophy, psychology, languages, art, gymnastics), allows us to suppose that girls are preoccupied with nature from the receptive point of view, and with man mainly as a sensitive participant in the human community.'[1]

Table II.4

Women in Senior Posts, Eastern Europe

(i) *In industrial management*

(a) *Soviet Union* (*December 1963*) *and Poland* (*1958*)

	Women as percentage of all in each category in each country	
	U.S.S.R.	Poland
Plant directors	6	2
Chief engineers	13	2
Heads and deputy heads of:		
Workshops	12	
Shifts, sections, groups, etc.	20-22	
Production departments		6
Economic departments		15
Chief and senior accountants	36	20
Economists, statisticians, planners	79	39
Engineers	38	—
Technicians	65	—
Foremen	20	—
All industrial employees	45	—

M. Sokolowska and K. Wrochno, *Some Reflections on the Different Attitudes of Men and Women towards Work*, International Labour Review, July 1965, p. 41: *Zhenschchiny i Deti v S.S.S.R.*, *op. cit.* p. 102: Dodge, *op. cit.*, p. 179.

[1] R. Radwilowicz in Sokolowska (ed.), *Kobieta Wspolczesna, op. cit.*

(b) *East Germany, 1963: centrally controlled nationalized industry* (%)

Plant directors	3
Technical directors	4
Chief accountants	14
Office managers and supervisors	46
Planning group leaders	17
Engineers and technicians	7
Other leadership posts	9

Die Frau in der Gesellschaft, op. cit., p. 61.

(ii) *In banking: Polish National Bank, 1963* (%)

Directors	4
Assistant directors	5
Department heads	16
Head bookkeepers	32
Senior planning inspectors	44
Senior supervisors	77
Bookkeepers	93
Tellers	93

M. Sokolowska and W. Wrochno, *op. cit.*

(iii) *In agricultural management: collective and state farms and other state agricultural enterprises, Soviet Union, 1956* (%)

Collective farm chairmen and directors of state farms	2
Agronomists	40
Livestock technicians	44
Veterinary surgeons and auxiliaries	18
Other technicians	14
All workers and employees	31

Dodge, *op. cit.,* p. 202.

(iv) *In scientific work* (%)

	U.S.S.R. 1950	U.S.S.R. 1961	Poland 1962
Professors	6	8	3
Associate/assistant professors	15	18	13
Senior assistants	31	29	—
Other assistants	48	51	—
Assistants and scientific workers, unspecified	—	—	31

Die Frau in der Gesellschaft, op. cit., p. 76: and M. Sokolowska and K. Wrochno in M. Sokolowska (ed.), *Kobieta Wspolczesna,* Warsaw 1966.

(v) *In higher educational work*

(a) *Soviet Union, 1950 and 1960*

	Women scientific workers in higher educational institutions (%)	
	1950	1960
Directors and deputies	5	5
Deans	7	9
Department heads	11	12
Professors	9	11
Associate/assistant professors	21	24
Others	33	34

Dodge, *op. cit.*, p. 207.

(b) *Yugoslavia, 1958-59 (%)*

	Professors and lecturers	Assistants
Universities, including:	*6*	*28*
Medicine	12	34
Economics	7	38
Philosophy, mathematics, science	7	35
Law	7	25
Technology	2	15
Veterinary science	1	26
Agriculture and forestry	—	29
Academies of art, including:	*18*	*39*
Art	6	13
Applied art	7	8
Music	22	64
Theatre, etc.	25	31

Die Frau in der Gesellschaft, *op. cit.*, p. 67.

(vi) *In school teaching: Soviet Union (%)*

	1950-51	1964-65	1968-69
Directors:			
secondary schools	21	20	23
primary schools	61	72	78
Teachers (not directors):			
grades 8-11 (oldest)	67	68	—
5-7	74	76	75
1-4 (youngest)	67	87	87

Dodge, *op. cit.*, p. 205, and *Zhenschchiny i Deti v. S.S.S.R.*

(vii) *In medicine: Soviet Union, 1956 (%)*

Heads of medical establishments, chief physicians, deputies	57
Heads of divisions, laboratories, etc.	73
Other physicians	82
Dentists	83
Medical auxiliaries, nurses	93
Laboratory technicians	94
Heads of pharmacies	80
Pharmacists and pharmaceutical chemists	92

In absolute numbers:

	Men	Women
		000s
Heads of medical establishments, chief physicians, deputies	19	25
Heads of divisions, laboratories, etc.	12	32
Other physicians	34⎫ 38	156⎫ 174
Dentists	4⎭	18⎭

Dodge, *op. cit.*, p. 210. *Zhenschchiny i Deti, v S.S.S.R. op. cit.*, p. 76, gives the following figures from the Census of 1959:

	No. of Women (000s)	Women as per cent of all
Chief physicians and other leaders of public health institutions	23	52
Physicians	265	79
Dentists	26	83
Medical auxiliaries and nurses	306	84
Pharmacists etc.	56	95
Nurses	689	99½

(viii) *In various occupations: Czechoslovakia, 1961 (%)*

Universities: all academic staff	10
Managers of administrative services: heads of administrative units and economic administrations	15
Executive posts in management and the economy	18
Controllers, inspectors, auditors	27
'Responsible posts' in:	
transport and communication	28
municipal services, housing	30

M. Srnská, *Employment of Women in the Czechoslovak Socialist Republic*, International Labor Review, November 1965, p. 400.

(ix) *In trade unions* (%)

    (a) *East Germany, 1965*

        Shop stewards ('confidence men')   38

        Plant committees:
            members   44
            chairmen   27

        National executive committees (individual unions and congress):
            members   42
            chairmen   12

    (b) *Soviet Union, 1959-62*

        Plant and local committees:
            organizers   67
            members   49

        Republic and province committee members and candidates   41
        Central committee members and candidates   43

    Die Frau in der Gesellschaft, op. cit., pp. 241 and 250.

(x) *In politics* (%)

    (a) *Central committees of the Communist Party*:

Soviet Union	1941	$1\frac{1}{2}$
	1961	3

        East Germany, 1967:

Secretaries of the central committee	—
Politbüro members and candidates	5
Central committee (members and condidates)	12

    (b) *National Parliaments:*

Soviet Union	1961	27
East Germany	1964	$27\frac{1}{2}$
Poland	*c.* 1960	13

    (c) *Local government*:

        Soviet Union, 1961

Regional and county councils	40
City councils	41
Rural district councils	40
Settlement (commune) councils	41

THE EXPERIENCE OF EASTERN EUROPE

East Germany

	Councillors		Holders of local government posts			
			Senior		Middle level	
	1960	1964	1961	1964	1961	1964
Regional councils	25	31	5	9	23	27
County councils	18	22	8	12	27	35
County boroughs	21	25	7	9	—	58
Towns and communes	16	19				

Dodge, *op. cit.*, p. 214; *Die Frau in der Gesellschaft, op. cit.*, pp. 227, 230-1, 233, 249; Sokolowska and Wrochno, *op. cit,* Kulke, *op. cit.*

An East German study notes that girls in older school classes significantly surpass boys in conduct, orderliness and application, and generally in avoiding disciplinary offences, and provide a higher proportion of youth group leaders. It adds however that a reason for the greater proportion of girls among group leaders may simply be that teachers find girls more manageable, and that:

> 'Boys' disciplinary difficulties should not be given a wholly negative evaluation nor girls' better disciplined behaviour a wholly positive one. On the contrary, the profile of boys' negative disciplinary behaviour includes such elements of a positive kind as determination, boldness, initiative, self-possession and surplus strength, whereas the profile of girls' positive disciplinary behaviour also includes less valuable factors such as credulity towards authority, fear of punishment, shyness, a tendency to hang back and emotionality'.[1]

Similar differences come to light in the training of Soviet men and women engineers and affect their suitability for posts of different types. Girls' conscientiousness makes them valued in research work, but 'men remain superior in giving firm decisions'.[2]

As regards actual participation in the work force – as apart from the level and field of qualifications – a strong opinion has been built up in all the East European countries in favour of women's right to work[3]: and, especially in the Soviet Union, of their duty to do so.

> 'The Soviet Union has succeeded in creating an atmosphere in which a woman feels apologetic if she does not work. The author

[1] K. Otto, 'Psychische Geschlechtsunterschiede', in *Frau und Wissenschaft*, Akademieverlag, (East) Berlin, 1968, pp. 116-17.
[2] Souter and Winslade, *op. cit.*
[3] On Poland see Kloskowska, *op. cit.*, and Kloskowska and Markowska in *Polish Perspectives* for January 1968.

71

recalls a dinner party at which he questioned each woman in turn about her work. Around the table with their husbands were a physician, a teacher, a retail executive and a woman who confessed with embarrassment that she did not do any work at all, but stayed at home to take care of her children. This reaction was characteristic. . . . As a young girl from a high-income family put it, "When all your friends are working, it is no fun not to work".'[1]

Two Czechoslovak psychiatrists note that whereas in certain societies 'the most suitable solution' may be for mothers of small children to stay at home, women brought up to adopt the attitudes towards a career promoted today in Eastern Europe will find this frustrating. 'Their mental balance may be endangered', and it may be best for their children as well as themselves if they go to work.[2]

The proportion of women and especially of married women with children who do in fact remain in the work force in Eastern Europe is by Western standards extraordinarily high (Table II.3). The high percentage for the Soviet Union as early as 1926 (Table II.3 (i) (b)) is less surprising than it might seem, for at that time the Soviet Union was primarily an agricultural country and the high figure was due to members of farm families helping on the farm. As industrialization developed, and employment came increasingly to mean working away from home, the proportion of women in the work force might have been expected to decrease. Instead (Table II.3 (i) (a)) the proportion of urban women aged 16-59 who are in the work force rose by 1959 from 40 per cent to 67 per cent[3] and in the country as a whole three-quarters to four-fifths of the women of the age when they are most likely to have small children continued to be recorded as at work. In one sample of Soviet women about a quarter of those who had themselves reached child-bearing age before the revolution reported that their mothers had at one time or another worked outside their homes, but of those who had been children in the first two decades of the revolution from half to two-thirds reported that their mothers had done so. In the same sample 68 per cent of married women aged 31-40 in 1940 were working even though they had children, as against 84 per cent of those without children.[4] The Czech and East German figures in Table II.3 underline that in Eastern

---

[1] Dodge, *op. cit.*, p. 53.

[2] Knoblochova, J. and Knobloch, F. *Family Psychotherapy, in Aspects of Mental Health in Europe*, World Health Organization 1965, p. 85.

[3] See the similar figures for Romania in United Nations Economic Commission for Europe, the *European Economy in 1968*, Ch. III, p. 205. In the age group 20-54, the participation rate for all women in Romania rose only slightly from 1956-66 but that in urban districts rose from 45 per cent to 60 per cent.

[4] Inkeles, A. and Bauer, R. A., *The Soviet Citizen*, Harvard 1959, pp. 205-206.

Europe today a substantial number even of mothers with three or more children continue to work. From the revolution of 1948 until 1966 women provided over two-thirds of the increase in the non-agricultural work force in Czechoslovakia, and rose from 28·5 per cent of it to 44·5 per cent. The expectation in Eastern Europe is that the rates of women's participation in work will increase further during the 1970s.[1]

The tendency to remain in the work force or to come back quickly to it after the birth of a child is particularly marked among people who have higher qualifications or who come from a professional or other white-collar background. In the first years after the Soviet Revolution it was above all women from the white-collar classes who moved into work away from their homes.[2] East German figures show that the proportion of women who are in the work force rises from 57 per cent of those without a craft skill or professional qualification to 84 per cent of university graduates. A local study in Rostock showed that the proportion of mothers with small children who are in employment rises from 42 per cent where the mother has only primary education to 83 per cent where her education is at university level.[3] Some 67 per cent of the mothers of small children in this study whose husbands were in a professional job were themselves working, compared with 45-50 per cent of those whose husbands were clerks or shop-floor workers.[4] Polish findings on the more rapid return to work after a birth by women in higher and professionally qualified jobs were quoted earlier.[5] Another analysis shows that in the age-group 18-29 in Poland 55 per cent of women with elementary education are employed, but 80 per cent of those with secondary and 90 per cent of those with higher education.[6] In Hungarian experience most primary educated women use their right to three years' leave after a birth, but only a fraction of university graduates do so.[7]

Career commitment tends to differ between highly qualified and unqualified women in a qualitative as well as quantitative sense. Lower qualified women contacted in East European studies tend to explain that they work out of economic necessity, or because of the

---

[1] United Nations Economic Commission for Europe, *op. cit.*, Table 9.

[2] Inkeles and Bauer, *op. cit.*, p. 205.

[3] *Die Frau in der Gesellschaft*, *op. cit.*, p. 161: *Gesundheitliche und soziologische Problems der berufstätigen Mütter, op. cit.* p. 17.

[4] *Ibid*, p. 18.

[5] Chapter I, p. 26.

[6] Sokolowska and Wrochno, *op. cit.*

[7] Szabady, F., *Study of the Impact of a Family Protection Measure—the Allowance for Child Care in Hungary*. Paper to the Seventh World Congress of Sociology, Varna, 1970.

73

insecurity of depending wholly on a husband in times of war, revolution, migration, and the break-up of established relationships, and
that they might well wish to concentrate on their home if these
pressures were taken off.[1] They tend often to feel only an external
relationship to their work, to judge it in terms not of the job itself
but of surrounding factors such as supervisors' attitudes, social contacts on the job, or workplace amenities,[2] and to 'take their home to
work' – have their minds running on domestic issues while at work –
rather than take their work home.[3] They tend easily to be absent or
to stay at home beyond the statutorily recognized time after a birth.[4]

Higher qualified women, on the other hand, tend to internalize
their work, to be satisfied with it, to 'take it home'; often, as Czech
and East German informants comment, to the extent of creating
greater tensions and difficulties in their family life than are experienced by lower-qualified women.[5] Where a lower-qualified woman
might judge a manager or supervisor in terms of his personal relationship to her as a subordinate, higher qualified women are more likely
to judge him in terms of his ability to plan and direct the job as such.[6]
Though higher- like lower-qualified women feel the pressures of
economic need and insecurity, they would probably still be following
their careers if these pressures were removed.[7] They see themselves[8]
as capable of handling senior jobs – one study obtained their managers' confirmation that they are in fact successfully doing so – though
also as often being discriminated against when there is a choice
between promoting a woman or a man. A Polish study[9] found a
substantial proportion to be interested in promotion even though
they were mothers with dependent children. Excluding about 20
per cent of respondents who were uninterested in promotion because
they liked their present job, 60 per cent of the women in the sample
who had dependent children wanted promotion, as well as 70 per
cent of those who had none.

[1] Piotrowski, J. in Chombart de Lauwe, op. cit., (Poland): Inkeles and Bauer,
op. cit. pp. 203-207 (esp. p. 207) (U.S.S.R.).
[2] Mielke, M. in Frau und Wissenschaft, op. cit., p. 89 (East Germany): see also
the study reported by Steiner, ibid., pp. 50-1.
[3] Sokolowska, International Labour Review, op. cit., p. 45 (Poland).
[4] Kurzynowski, loc. cit., (Poland),
[5] Below pp. 91, 95-6, 97-8. See Dodge, op. cit., pp. 56-7 and 233; Sokolowska,
op. cit.; K. Wrochno, 'Women in Directing Positions Talk about Themselves', in
Kobieta Wspolczesna, op. cit., and 'Aspekte qualifizierter und leitender Tätigkeit
von Frauen in Polen' in Frau und Wissenschaft, op. cit.; and Souter and Winslade,
op. cit.
[6] Mielke, op. cit.
[7] Inkeles, E. G. and Bauer, loc. sit.; Steiner, loc. cit.
[8] Wrochno, articles cited.
[9] Wrochno, Women in Directing Positions, op. cit.

The fact remains, however, that even in Eastern Europe most women – especially of course most mothers – spend a smaller proportion of their life in the work force than most men. Statistics published hitherto also show a tendency for them to retire younger. This may be partly a function of the low qualifications and earning capacity of today's older women, who had less opportunity than girls in recent years to get a good qualification. There might therefore be a change as better qualified younger women come up towards pension age. But Dodge's analysis for the Soviet Union suggests that early retirement, before reaching 60, is common even among highly qualified women specialists.[1] Popular attitudes continue to support the idea that, whereas a husband's first commitment should be to his work, a wife's should be to her household.[2] This need not and does not prevent a high commitment to work on the part of women intellectuals, but even in their case may lead to their refusing the overtime and other special commitments needed to get and hold a top job.[3] In the Soviet Union in the 1940s, young white-collar women showed much more career commitment than other young women or than blue-collar men, but markedly less than white-collar men.[4] Women with high formal qualifications, which guarantee their opportunity to return to work when they wish to do so, may become more inclined to pick and choose between jobs than others less sure of themselves. In particular, they may tend to stay out of work after the birth of a child until exactly the right job turns up.[5] For all family sizes, East German figures show the proportion of wives working to fall sharply as their husbands' income rises to a comfortable level (Table II.3 (ii) (b)).

As has been said, official and scientific opinion has moved in recent years towards recognizing that the periods for which a mother is free to stay out of work after a birth without losing her job or social security rights have been too short to be satisfactory from the point of view either of mothers themselves or of young children.[6] Longer career breaks for maternity have not been merely tolerated but encouraged. It has also been increasingly recognized, given that

[1] Dodge, *op. cit.*, p. 188.
[2] E.g. the analysis by Kloskowska in Chombart de Lauwe, *op. cit.*, and the discussion of the East German Family Code quoted above, p. 53.
[3] E.g. Dodge, *op. cit.*, p. 233. On women doctors, see M. G. Field, *Doctor and Patient in Soviet Russia*, Harvard 1957, p. 193. For a similar finding for women architects in Romania, see below, p. 84.
[4] Rossi, A., *Generational Differences in the Soviet Union*, Ph.D. Thesis, Columbia University, 1954, p. 202.
[5] Kurzynowski, A., 'Occupation and Continuity of Employment of Young Mothers', in *Kobieta Wspolczesna*, *op. cit.*
[6] Above, pp. 55-56.

maintenance of the population requires that a proportion of families should have three or more children, that in these families there may be a particularly strong case for the mother to work full-time as a housewife:

> 'This discovery gives the women acting as housewives a different social position: due to their merit in upholding the level of reproduction, they become much more useful for society than believed until now.'[1]

Adding together the probable loss of time through childbearing, child care, general absence or withdrawal from work and early retirement, it looks as if a professional woman in the Soviet Union might possibly be available for work outside her home for perhaps 13-14 per cent less time than a man with a similar qualification.[2] The cutback in women's share in higher education in the Soviet Union around 1960 can be explained partly by military or para-military needs: for example, the need to provide enough men doctors for the armed forces or to give priority in admission to higher education to veterans. It was also influenced at least for a time by a rule that most of those admitted to higher education must have two or more years of employment experience. Women may have been more liable than men to get lost to education during this interval. Dodge's study suggested that a modification of this rule in 1965 to permit more admissions direct from secondary school might lead to a higher proportion of girls being admitted. The figures of admissions for 1968-69 show that this forecast was probably right. But after allowance is made for these factors, it still looks, as Dodge argues, as if Soviet policy reflects a hard-headed calculation that women's lifetime productivity outside the home is likely, ability for ability, to fall short of men's and that the qualifications required from women to justify their admission to universities and other institutions of higher education should be correspondingly higher than those called for from men.[3]

In the early 1960s, on the figures quoted above, men's chance of getting a place in higher education in the Soviet Union exceeded women's by upwards of 30 per cent. This clearly was exaggerated

[1] Kucera, *op. cit.*, in *Czechoslovak Population Problems*, 1967, p. 29.
[2] Dodge, *op. cit.*, pp. 233-234; see also pp. 113-118 on his model for the economics of education. Dodge estimates the time lost through having a typical number of children (two), through staying out of work after each baby and generally through extra sickness and absence compared to men, as about 6 per cent of a professional woman's working life. Other factors leading to a lower participation rate by women in work, especially early retirement, add to another 8 per cent.
[3] Dodge, *op. cit.*, p. 116.

in relation to a potential loss of career time of 13-14 per cent. On Dodge's model the sharp improvement since then in women's chances of a higher education might be interpreted, not as a stage on the road towards complete equality, but simply as a recognition that the gap had become too wide.

Women's success in actually reaching the top in Eastern Europe presents the same mixed picture (Table II.4). It is not surprising to find (Table II.4 (i) (a)) that the proportion of women plant directors and chief engineers was lower in Poland at the end of the 1950s, little more than a decade after the Marxist revolution, than in the Soviet Union nearly half a century after October 1917. It is the modest proportion of women in directing jobs in the Soviet Union or in a country of such strongly orthodox Marxism as East Germany that is striking. Women's achievements in Eastern Europe do not fall short – far from it – of their achievements in the West. But they do fall far short of what Marxist theory might lead one to expect. At managing director level in industry women are outnumbered by men in ratios from fifteen to thirty to one, according to country. At the corresponding level in Soviet agriculture they are outnumbered by fifty to one, and in East German agriculture by a hundred to one; in fact by two hundred to one in the case of state farms as apart from co-operatives.[1] Even when the proportion of women in a profession as a whole is high, as in medicine or teaching, the proportion of women at the top is much less impressive. It is striking at first sight that in medicine in the Soviet Union in the middle 1950s women held over half the posts as heads of medical establishments, chief physicians or their deputies (Table II.4 (vii)). If, however, the number of these jobs held by men and women is compared with the number of men and women who are in the relevant professions and qualified to hold them, it appears that there was one male doctor or dentist at the top for every two below head of division level, but only one woman at the top for every seven in the lower ranks.[2] In Poland, 49 per cent of male primary school teachers hold supervisory posts, but only 10 per cent of women.[3]

Dodge has a particularly interesting discussion of women's productivity and distinction in scientific research in the Soviet Union. In proportion to the number of specialists in each field, women's output of scientific papers runs far behind that of men – from a half

[1] Kulke, *op. cit.*
[2] Field, *loc. cit.*, found that among high-ranking physicians named in the Soviet journal *Medical Worker* men outnumbered women by four to one at a time when in the medical profession, as a whole, women outnumbered men in almost the same proportion.
[3] Sokolowska and Wrochno, *op. cit.*

to a fifth in a number of fields – and women win relatively few awards. In 1957-64 women received $2\frac{1}{2}$ per cent of the Lenin Prizes awarded in technology, 3 per cent in science and 6 per cent in the arts. Even the most outstanding woman scientists tend to be collaborators rather than leaders:

> 'Although these women are doing important research, all are working in collaboration with or under the direction of men who have greater professional distinction. The real guidance of the research appears to be firmly in the hands of men.'[1]

In every occupation and East European country for which figures have been collected, women's share diminishes the nearer jobs approach to top executive management, to national as apart from local leadership, to steering a business in a market as apart from carrying on administration inside the framework of a plan, to original research and initiatory work,[2] and to the direct control of traditionally male types of physical work. This is not to say that in these areas women's share disappears. Women provided, for example, in the Soviet Union in the middle 1950s, 10 per cent of the heads and leading specialists of construction enterprises.[3] But it diminishes and has sometimes to be artificially made good. Eastern Europe has plenty of examples of the 'statutory woman', familiar on Western committees, who is appointed not simply on her personal merits but because a woman member of this or that body is deemed necessary. It is curious, a Polish comment notes, how easily one can always name the top women in an East European country. A few in each country at any one time turn up again and again in different posts.

Women in Eastern Europe have a well-established position as specialists (including top jobs in such non-traditional fields as engineering), in areas such as research and technology and in functional (including office) as apart from operating management. Twenty-five per cent of personnel managers in East Germany, for example, are said to be women. Women also do relatively well (Table II.4 (ix) and (x)) in elected posts – especially, as one comment from East Germany points out, those posts that are unpaid – where selection is likely to be influenced by the need to make a public demonstration of Marxist principle. But even where women are strongly represented in the middle ranks they tend to miss the more specifically managerial top

---

[1] Dodge, *op. cit.*, p. 204, and generally Ch. 12. The reference is to women working at the Institute of High Molecular Compounds at Leningrad, but Dodge quotes their case not in isolation but as 'a clear illustration' of a common pattern.

[2] See besides Dodge, *loc. cit.*, G. Schnelle in *Frau und Wissenschaft, op. cit.*, pp. 94-95.

[3] Dodge, *op. cit.*, p. 204.

jobs, including top management in professional and (Table II.4) academic life, and top executive jobs even on the political and trade union side.

WHAT IS THE EXPLANATION ?

What is the reason for this apparently only limited success in bringing women to the top? It is *not*, in the first place, that women have shown themselves lacking in ability to use the educational opportunities opened up to them in Eastern Europe, or any necessary reluctance (as apart from reluctance in accidental present circumstances) to develop career interests outside traditional fields. Though the proportion of women entering non-traditional fields such as industrial technology still falls short of that of men, an East German study notes that this may be due more to the failure of technical educators and enterprises to present their case to girls effectively than to any underlying resistance on girls' part. In the particular career guidance experiment reviewed in that study, three out of five of a group of older schoolgirls who had shown no previous interest in a career in technology switched their interest in that direction after a new form of presentation was tried.[1] Dodge summarizes a number of observations of Soviet schools and colleges to show that 'schoolgirls appear to have no inhibitions about tackling technical work, and the technical streams of secondary schools have between 40 and 45 per cent girls',[2] and that in technical and scientific as well as in other subjects girls tend to do as well as boys, if not marginally better.[3] It seems clear that the fall in the proportion of women in Soviet medical schools has not been due to shortcomings in the school qualifications of women applicants. It is on the contrary a case of women being turned down even though academically better qualified.[4] Very generally:

'The question which we are raising would scarcely be intelligible to a Soviet student or educator. They are so accustomed to women's participating effectively in all fields of study and at all levels of learning that the possibility of sex differences usually has not occurred to them. This confidence in the intellectual capacity of women appears to be borne out by the academic record of students.'[5]

[1] Schneider, G. 'Entwicklung Technischer Interessen bei Mädchen', in *Frau und Wissenschaft, op. cit.*, pp. 74-75.
[2] Quoted by Dodge from Souter and Winslade, *op. cit.*, p. 15.
[3] Dodge, *op. cit.*, pp. 229-231.
[4] *Ibid.*, p. 113.
[5] *Ibid.*, pp. 229-230.

It is also, as has been seen, *not* the case that women in Eastern Europe who have the qualifications for professional and managerial jobs show a lack of job commitment or a tendency to drop easily in and out of the work force. Nor, again, is the problem the survival of patriarchal ideas of the family. Certainly many traditional attitudes persist. Czechoslovak women persistently seek a husband more highly qualified than themselves[1] (what will happen, an informant asks, as the improvement of women's qualifications sharply reduces the chance that they can find one?) and Polish working-class men are reluctant to find their wives earning more than they earn themselves.[2] In all the East European countries custom and practice determine that the wife still does most of the housework and stays at home in a family emergency. In Czechoslovakia the law still allots the right to leave work for this purpose to the wife and not the husband, and speaks of the husband as the breadwinner.[3] Women in Poland and East Germany still find themselves discriminated against over promotion; above all, Polish studies suggest, in industry.[4] In Central Asia, the Soviet government has fought a prolonged and still unfinished battle against Moslem concepts which restrict women's role.[5] In at least one East European country an informant prominently identified with women's advancement has found herself regarded as, in Marxian terminology, a dogmatist – the Marxian equivalent of a religious fundamentalist – because she insists on reminding her party colleagues of the statements on this subject of such founding fathers as Engels and Lenin. The actual record of the Soviet Union over women's advancement, as apart from the principles underlying it, prompts Dodge to wonder whether this area of Soviet policy has had as high a priority in reality as Soviet leaders would claim.[6]

But these remaining traditional attitudes, in so far as they are simply traditional, are likely to fade away; and in so far as what appear to be traditional attitudes, for example over the division of labour in the home, have a future, the basis for their survival is no longer the traditional one. Patriarchal concepts of the family are dead

[1] Prokopec in *Czechoslovak Population Problems, op. cit.,* 1965.

[2] Kloskowska in Chombart de Lauwe, *op. cit.,* p. 105. See also the comment on some East German wives' reluctance to accept a promotion which would give them a greater responsibility or status than their husbands, by Kallabis in *Frau und Wissenschaft, op. cit.,* p. 39.

[3] See e.g. the use of 'breadwinner' in *Czechoslovak Population Problems,* 1967, p. 4.

[4] Wrochno, *op. cit.*: Mielke, *loc. cit*: Kallabis, *loc. cit.*: and the *Frauenkommunique.*

[5] Dodge, *op. cit.,* especially pp. 53-4, deals with this in detail.

[6] Dodge, *op. cit.,* p. 246.

in Eastern Europe and have been replaced with concepts of a more egalitarian kind. Kloskowska and Markowska document this change for Poland.[1] Inkeles and Bauer document for the first generation after the Soviet revolution not only the shift towards wives working but also the decline of emphasis in Russian child-rearing on traditional values and relationships and the increase of emphasis on personal and intellectual development and on 'getting along'[2]. Western visitors and investigators in the Soviet Union repeatedly stress the equality of intellectual as well as marital relations between men and women, and the readiness of men to accept women as intellectual equals and to work with them on that basis.[3]

The real question in Eastern Europe today – though this is often not clearly acknowledged in Eastern Europe itself – is not whether to follow traditional or newer patterns but, given that the traditional basis of relationships within the family has ceased to be accepted, what form to give the new basis which is now taking shape. As Kloskowska points out, the pattern of roles, and especially of work roles, that tends to emerge in practice in the Marxist countries among urban families which have changed from a patriarchal to an egalitarian type of marriage is by no means necessarily the one proposed to them in Marxist propaganda models. Will the new pattern be one which assigns to men and women similar roles in work and the family, subject only to the minimum of differences required by biology? Or will it provide, within an egalitarian framework, for a continuing fairly sharp division of labour, with wives giving their primary attention to the household and husbands to outside work, such as Kloskowska finds to be emerging in Poland? Will it provide for a pattern of roles varying from one married couple to another or from one social class to another, for example as between working class and professionally qualified couples?

a *Overload*

One very important factor in the new patterns of marriage and women's work emerging in Eastern Europe is the continuing overload – typically, as was said earlier, four to six hours a day of household activities on top of a job – on wives who are also working

---

[1] In Chombart de Lauwe, *loc. cit.*, and *Polish Perspectives* for January 1968.

[2] Inkeles and Bauer, *op. cit.*, p. 221.

[3] E.g. D. and V. Mace, *The Soviet Family*, Hutchinson, 1964, p. 108. (quotes also L. Daiches, *Russians at Law*, Michael Joseph, 1960): G. Z. Bereday, *The Politics of Soviet Education*, Stevens, 1960, p. 66: and Souter and Winslade, *op. cit.*

outside the home. Soviet, Czech, East German, and Romanian references illustrating this have already been cited.[1] In Poland:

'The chief problem of women in directing positions – according to their own evaluation – does not flow from the traditional attitude to woman's advancement nor from their own feminine traits. It primarily results from the lack of time to fulfil all obligations, from the difficulties in the way of full engagement in professional matters. All a woman's time off the job – it is hard to speak of "leisure" time – is taken up fully and completely by matters connected with her role as wife and mother.'[2]

Overload could in principle be relieved by moving more swiftly towards a more equal distribution of tasks within the family, by shifting more of the care of children to nurseries and other collective agencies, or by improving housing, household equipment and services available to the housewife so as to lighten the domestic load. All three lines of approach are being used in Eastern Europe. But all three run into difficulties.

One reason for difficulty over the first two of these approaches has certainly been the survival among both men and women of traditional attitudes. But there are also others of a more permanent and fundamental kind. Nursery as apart from kindergarten care has proved too expensive to be expanded at the rate which East European governments might have wished. New thinking about child care, in Eastern Europe as in the West, has tended to stress the dangers of institutionalization and the need to set limits to collective provision as apart from family care. New thinking about the overall role of the family, in relation to all its members and not only to the children, has tended in a similar direction. These issues over the role of the family and collective care are considered again below.

Delay to the improvement of housing and of household equipment and services has arisen to some extent out of ideological debates about the sort of provision to be made. Opinions vary from one East European country to another, and from time to time about the emphasis to be placed on public catering as against the private kitchen, or on encouraging families to instal their own washing machines as apart from using public ones. Soviet policy recognizes that work in the home 'is productive labour which contributes towards the national income,' but insists that it is less efficient

[1] Above, p. 56. For a comment from direct observation by Western investigators, see D. and V. Mace, *op. cit.*
[2] Wrochno, *loc. cit.*

because scattered and under-mechanized and that it should be accepted only so long as:

'The present level of development of the production forces makes work around the house and in subsidiary economies an objective necessity for part of the population. . . . Measures being adopted eventually will result in the family's everyday needs being met by public services. There will be no need then for personal subsidiary economies.'[1]

So extreme a view would not necessarily be accepted in other socialist countries. But in any case the chief immediate difficulty has been a practical one which applies to the Soviet Union as much as anywhere else. The biggest obstacle in this area has been reluctance to divert from other political and social objectives the capital and productive resources which a major drive to relieve the housewife's load would require. Until recently no East European country gave high priority to the housewife or, generally, to the consumer. The ratio of housing space to population and general development of household and retail services was allowed to lag far behind what is acceptable in the consumer-oriented economies of the West. Dodge, for example, notes from as recently as the beginning of the 1960s that in the Soviet Union:

'Hot water is practically unavailable, even in the cities, where it is estimated that less than 3 per cent of the urban population is supplied with hot water; even in Moscow only 10 per cent of all apartments have hot water. This means that almost every drop of hot water in the Soviet Union must be heated in a pot on the stove, and the family laundry alone can take the equivalent of two strenuous days a week.'[2]

Lack of resources for helping the housewife has been compounded by muddle in the use of such resources as there are. Retail management and the planning of retail and service networks are not among the brightest jewels in the Communist crown.

What might happen to married women's motives to work as a result of future housing reform in Eastern Europe is a matter for speculation. Reform might well do as much to discourage a fuller commitment to work as encourage it, with little net change on balance. Cramped and ill-equipped housing and lack of privacy

---

[1] Tatarinova, loc. cit., p. 25. See also United Nations Economic Survey of Europe in 1968, p. 185.
[2] Dodge, op. cit., p. 97.

encourage activities outside rather than in the home and facilitate social control. The pressure of public opinion, which in Eastern Europe favours work and other activities outside the home, is less easy to avoid than in the conditions of a Western suburb.

But no speculation is needed about the effects here and now of present conditions in housing, retailing and other areas affecting the housewife's overload such as husband's help or child care. Their upshot, so far as the Polish working class families studied by Klos-kowska are concerned, is that these families tend to find that there is still a solid basis in East European reality for a division of labour between man and wife in which the wife treats the running of her home as a full-time job, which it in fact often is. For many of the professional women studied by Dodge in the Soviet Union, equipped with high qualifications and ability but 'unable to escape the endless distraction and worries of caring for a husband and children', 'the price of excelling in their profession is simply too high . . . to pay'. They settle for a middle-level job with fixed hours and commitments and leave the top to the men.[1] A group of Romanian woman archi-tects, when asked why they tended (as was the case) to be even more reluctant than was usual among their male colleagues to seek pro-motion to administrative jobs, gave as one reason their strong pre-ference for staying near the drawing board and the site. But others were the difficulty of reconciling child care, shopping and other family responsibilities with the overtime and other extra commitments at the top, and simply that 'we've enough administrative problems at home'.[2]

b *Changing norms for child rearing and general relationships in the family*

The Marxist approach to the family can, as has been said, be inter-preted in various ways. There is little sign in Eastern Europe of a general challenge to it, and Western observers have shown that there are good reasons for this. The Maces, in particular,[3] go so far as to claim that Soviet social (as apart from political) conditions in the early 1960s represented an optimum for family life, and that this was reflected in the actual level of family relationships. Even the Stalinist repression had a favourable by-product in that families tended to grow closer together. This was especially marked in families

[1] Dodge, *op. cit.*, pp. 232-33.
[2] In the provincial architect's office at Iasi; personal report by one of the authors.
[3] D. and V. Mace, *op. cit.*

at the professional and managerial level; farmers' and manual workers' families tended to be physically more dispersed and disrupted.[1] But within the accepted overall framework of Marxist concepts of the family, there has been a growing volume of debate relevant, among other things, to the question of women's work and especially of continuous and high-level work.

One factor has been a tendency to shift from the first to the second of Kloskowska's two 'propaganda models' quoted at the beginning of this chapter; from a concept which minimizes the role of the family and stresses its members' outside obligations to one which emphasizes its role as an intimate and united group, concerned with its members' formation and emotional support.[2] Geissler documents a shift of opinion of this kind for East Germany, though he also points out that the institutional pattern corresponding to this shift has not yet taken shape. What is important for children, he suggests, is not only contact with the mother but membership in a stable and harmonious family where roles are distributed more than in the past in terms of individual personality and character, and whose members have time for one another and for a range of common activities. They must have 'time for free time' together. The care and warmth of such a family is also important for the old and the sick. Though 'time for free time' is a basic condition for a family of that kind, this does not mean that the wife should stop working outside the home. Outside work remains a basic condition not only of her equality within her marriage but of her accumulating a range of experiences and points of view common to herself, her husband and the children, and of a free and easy exchange of ideas between them. But it may well become necessary for a wife to limit her outside commitments, especially when the children are very young and the role of the mother is specially important compared to that of the father. She may, for example, need to work for periods part-time.[3]

Another factor has been recent experience and studies in the areas of demography and child rearing. The experience of the East European countries is that there is a strong negative correlation between married women's employment and fertility. To have one or perhaps two children and to continue in work while the children are small appears practicable. To continue with three or more young children is much more rarely practicable (Table II.3 (ii) and (iii)). This reflects itself in a tendency for those working mothers with the strongest work commitment – especially those with higher qualifications who

[1] Inkeles and Bauer, op. cit., p. 211.
[2] See above, pp. 48-49.
[3] Geissler, A., 'Probleme der Familie" in Probleme und Ergebnisse der Psychologie, 1965; No, 13, pp. 16-29 and No. 14, p. 38.

are likely to work most continuously – to stop at one or two.[1] Granted that the slowing down or reversal of population growth to which this leads is undesirable from the point of view of the State, what is to be done? There appears to be a division of opinion here. Specialists from Poland and Czechoslovakia seem to tend towards:

> 'Favouring the increase of economic activities of women caring for older children, that is of women roughly speaking over thirty years of age, while aiming to reduce the employment of women in the years of their highest fertility.'[2]

Those from East Germany and the Soviet Union prefer to stress the case for facilitating the employment of the mothers even of larger families by better provision of nurseries, nursery schools and household and public facilities. But within this difference of emphasis, certain common findings emerge.

First, institutional care, other than day care, for very young (and even for not so very young) children is being discredited:

> 'As many works have shown, the morbidity and the physical and psychological development of children become progressively less favourable, the greater the share taken by social child-rearing institutions in the total process of child rearing. . . . All reach broad agreement that the conditions for children's development deteriorate along the sequence family upbringing – day nursery – weekly boarding nursery – permanent institutional home.'[3]

In East Germany there has been a tendency to make less use of weekly nurseries because of their damaging effect on children.[4] In the Soviet Union, the government's efforts at certain times to promote boarding schools have met with considerable popular resistance, except for the children of families with special problems.[5] In Czecho-

---

[1] Kucera, *loc. cit.*, for Czechoslovakia; Dodge, Ch. II, esp. p. 27, for the Soviet Union: and see Table III and United Nations Economic Commission for Europe, *op. cit.*, pp. 185 and 214 ('concern has been expressed in several countries that the incidence of female employment is already excessive and has had some adverse influence on such aspects of family life as child bearing and child rearing'). Tatarinova, *op. cit.*, p. 15, claims that Soviet figures show that 'the working woman has a better chance of marriage and motherhood'. But the figures which she quotes show for middle-aged urban women a strong correlation between having three or more children and having a relatively small number of years in employment, or none at all.

[2] Kucera, *op. cit.*, p. 30.

[3] Geissler, *op. cit.*, p. 23.

[4] E.g. E. Schmidt-Kolmer, *Pädagogische Aufgaben und Arbeitsweise der Krippen*, (East) Berlin 1968, p. 16.

[5] Dodge, *op. cit.*, p. 39, cf. Mace, *op. cit.*, pp. 276-277.

slovakia, a series of follow-up studies on children in institutions, beginning in the middle 1950s and becoming available for publication in the early 1960s, confirm the findings of Western investigators such as Bowlby about the damage that institutional care may do to children's development.[1] Many children, the Czech studies show, cannot stand the 'monotonous stimulation' of life in even a weekly nursery – let alone longer-term care – with its continuous noise and movement and lack of periods of peace at home. The Czech studies have encouraged not only a turn towards family and day rather than longer-term institutional care but a loosening in the uniform, somewhat rigidly disciplined methods of upbringing which the Alts[2] observed in Soviet nurseries and which were at one time standard over most of Eastern Europe. In child rearing as in other aspects of family life, there has been a marked swing towards emphasis on individual and personal development and on the family as a central agent for it.

The tendency to discredit institutions does not extend to day nurseries, still less to kindergartens. The Czech studies suggest that a small percentage of children, perhaps 5 per cent, cannot stand a full day in a nursery, and perhaps 30 per cent to 40 per cent of those using nurseries do not in fact stay for the afternoon. An East German writer, Neubert,[3] touched off a lively discussion by suggesting that under socialism nurseries and other institutions for young children are a transitional phenomenon, likely in the end to be superseded by a system under which young mothers would be released from work for several years and then helped to return in their thirties. But he seems to have had only limited support, not only from the political side but from medical and social scientists. The verdict of East European scientific studies seems in general to be that, subject to reservations such as those just mentioned from the Czech studies, good day care plus employment for the mother is favourable rather than otherwise to the personal and intellectual development even of pre-nursery school children, and strongly favourable to that of children at nursery school age and over. East German and Czech studies, for example, point out that 'mother employed' correlates positively with children's school performance,[4] though the evidence does not all

---

[1] Bibliography (with English translation of titles) in J. Langmeier and Z. Matajcek, *Psychicha Depriacia v Detstve* (Psychological Deprivation in Childhood), Bratislava 1967 (bibliography, not text).
[2] Alt, *op. cit.*, pp. 11-117: see also pp. 165-6 (primary education) and 265-6.
[3] Quoted in Geissler, *op. cit.* p. 17.
[4] A. Grandke, H. Kuhrig and W. Weise, *Zur Situation und Entwicklung der Familien in der D.D.R.*, Neue Justiz 8/1965, pp. 234-235: J. Prokopec, 'Progress of Children of Employed Women at School', summary in *Czechoslovak Population Problems*, 1965, *op. cit.*, p. 25.

run in the same direction.[1] Studies on this point note that the positive relationship is explained in part by the greater tendency for mothers with better education to be in employment, and that a whole complex of other factors may be involved:

'The influence of the mother's employment on children's school performance depends on many important factors, in particular on her attitude to her occupation and family, her conditions of work, the attitude of her family to her work, and . . . the general family situation.'[2]

But at this point considerations of practicability take over. The quality of nursery care, even more than that of kindergartens, varies from one place and country to another. Informants comment that it is probably higher on the whole in East Germany than in Czechoslovakia, and in Czechoslovakia than in Poland. But everywhere it can be patchy and, if provided to a good standard, with a staffing ratio appropriate to very small children and with good accommodation and medical facilities, it becomes expensive to parents, the State or both. In Czechoslovakia, in recent years, operating costs (including food) per place seem to have been about $2\frac{1}{2}$ times as high in nurseries as in kindergartens, and the cost per place per year in nurseries was equivalent to about 30 per cent of the average salary of employees of all grades.[3] How this affects parents will of course depend on how the charge is spread. In all East European countries, the State carries a high proportion of the cost. But whereas in Czechoslovakia charges to parents at a given income level are higher for nurseries than for nursery schools, the Soviet Union follows the opposite policy. Not surprisingly, in the Soviet Union demand for the limited number of nursery places 'substantially outruns the supply'.[4] Whoever has to bear it, the charge is substantial. Taking into account also the tendency of mothers of very young children to

---

[1] E.g. a Czech diploma thesis by E. Ronova on *An Enquiry into the Results of Pre-School Training in Kindergartens and at Home*, 1967, finds that in their first year of primary school, kindergarten trained children have a less good record, especially in behaviour, than those brought up wholly at home. An important factor in this study appears to have been the greater resemblance of the standards of behaviour expected in school to those expected at home than to those usual in the kindergarten. Kindergarten children tend to be more restless, disobedient, talkative and lacking in concentration.

[2] Grandke, *loc. cit.*

[3] Estimate from figures supplied by the Czechoslovak Ministry of Health, from *Czechoslovak Population Problems, op. cit.*, 1967, pp. 8-9, and *Statistical Abstract* for Czechoslovakia, *op. cit.*, Table 27. Capital costs do not appear to be included. East German figures show an even less favourable ratio of costs in nurseries to costs in kindergartens.

[4] Dodge, *op. cit.*, p. 81.

be absent from work relatively often because of the child's illness or other problems, and the loss of production to which this leads, the East European governments appear to have concluded that nurseries should be given a much lower priority than nursery schools. In the Soviet Union in 1962 about 37 per cent of urban children of the relevant ages were in kindergartens but only 12 per cent in permanent nurseries; though perhaps another 10 per cent could find a temporary place in seasonal (summer) nurseries.[1] East Germany, at a time when it had nearly 60 per cent of its children of relevant age in kindergartens, had 20 per cent in nurseries and envisaged only 25 per cent by 1970. Czechoslovakia at the end of 1967 had 11 per cent of its children under three in nurseries, and envisaged only a 'not so marked' increase in nursery places in the next years, chiefly in the larger cities; whereas in 1965 the proportion of children aged three to six who were in kindergartens had already reached 48 per cent.[2]

To these economic difficulties in the way of nursery provision has to be added the difficulty which mothers – once again, especially mothers of small children – often find in organizing care at home. This of course is also part of the problem of overload. Grandmothers are a great resource, but a Polish study points out that very active involvement of the grandmother in a three-generation family can lead to serious conflicts or to the breakdown of a marriage.[3] In 74 three-generation families studied, 48 had disturbed family relationships, and in 42 of these cases the disturbance was attributed to 'the destructive interference' of grandmothers. Grandmothers may also in the long run be a diminishing resource, especially in families with higher education; but this is subject to what was said about above the age of retirement. It remains to be seen whether, as the proportion of older women who have had secondary or higher education and corresponding careers increases, the proportion who wish to continue their own careers will increase as well. *Prima facie* it might, but the continuing tendency for women to retire earlier than men seems likely at least to apply a brake.

An approach which could solve simultaneously the problems of convenient care at home and of nursery provision, together with

[1] Dodge, *op. cit.*, pp. 78 and 84. 'Nurseries' includes nursery places in kindergartens.

[2] Information from the Czechoslovak Ministry of Health and the Deutsche Akademie der Wissenschaften. The demand for more nursery places in East Germany is illustrated in *Gesundheitliche und Soziologische Probleme, op. cit.*, pp. 19 and 26-7: but see also p. 57, where 'shortage of nursery places' appears to count for much less in the decision of mothers not to work than a general wish to be with and care for their children.

[3] Ziemska, M. *Inter-personal Relations in Two- and Three-Generation Families*, in *Kobieta Wspolczesna, op. cit.*

many of the problems of overload, is the idea of a 'service house', as developed notably in Sweden: an arrangement in which nursery facilities with full staffing and equipment are built into a block of flats along with restaurants and other service and recreation facilities. This approach has been examined in East Germany, but judged too expensive in terms of both capital and operating costs for the country's present stage of development. The nearest approach actually used is that of the planned neighbourhood in which facilities are provided for a group of blocks or housing areas. This, though it ensures that facilities shall be near at hand, relieves the housewife of the difficulty of combining adequate child care with employment, or even housekeeping, to a much smaller extent than the 'service house', in which facilities are under one roof and inside one enclosure and the children can be left to run free. It seems from recent press references that Soviet planners may be coming to the same conclusion on grounds of public preference as well as of cost.[1]

The upshot of all these considerations on child care is that a new balance of views is beginning to show itself in Eastern Europe. There would probably be general agreement in Eastern Europe, in spite of an occasional challenge like Neubert's, with Geissler's view that 'We cannot accept, either for the mother herself or for society, that there should be a break in work of several years after birth'.[2] But many would also accept his view that:

'During the first six years and especially during the first three years of life we can only accept social institutions for child rearing as a supplement to upbringing in the family, though one which becomes increasingly necessary as the child grows older.'[3]

Sokolowska[4] notes that here again certain Soviet investigators tend to put this point the other way round, and to talk of family care for very young children as a practical substitute for collective care in nurseries pending the creation of a better nursery network. Since, however, this network is still only in course of being built, they come for practical purposes to the same conclusion as Geissler. Whether on grounds of principle or of practice, there has developed in all the Eastern European countries the tendency already mentioned to extend the periods of paid leave, unpaid leave, and leave without the guarantee of the same job but with preservation of pension rights, on

[1] Cf. the discussion of attitudes to a pair of new service houses in Moscow, *The Times*, 27.11.68.
[2] Geissler, *op. cit.*, p. 23.
[3] Geissler, *loc. cit.*
[4] M. Sokolowska, *The Household—Unknown Working Environment:* English translation of her article in *Studia Socjologizsh*, 1963/3.

which mothers can rely after the birth of a child. There is also increasing readiness to accept that mothers of young children may work part-time. The accent differs from one country to another. East German comments insist much more strongly on continuity of employment – though it can be part-time employment – than, for example, those from Czechoslovakia. But the general trend is common to Eastern Europe as a whole.

These tendencies, however, will not necessarily be as helpful to highly qualified women, with their high degree of career commitment, as to women working at lower levels. There is certainly evidence that professionally qualified women may be readier than others to stay out of work to look after their younger children; that they are more likely to be critical of defective nursery provision and to have resources (their own or their husbands') which let them stay out of work longer to choose a good job on which to return. But the tendency for them to work through or to stop only briefly is strong enough for a number of informants to note that professionally qualified mothers are liable to be a case requiring special help. On the one hand they are a category for which further and better nursery provision is likely to be needed; bearing in mind also that these tend to be the mothers both who can best afford nursery fees, and also whose outside work is valuable enough to the state to be worth subsidizing. On the other hand they may be in special need of psychological help, for they are more likely than others to feel a conflict between their own career needs and the views on child rearing which they like others increasingly accept. This tension has been found to come to the surface in marriage and child guidance, and can reflect real underlying difficulties for the children.

c *Reconciling family and work roles*

Overload and new thinking about the family and child-bearing are two strong reasons why married women in Eastern Europe may find it hard to reconcile their work and family roles. A third is that, in spite of the prolonged efforts of the East European governments, it is still common to find that employing agencies have not developed recruitment, training and promotion practices adapted to the typical life cycle of married women. Some clashes are inevitable and have to be resolved as they go, for example the problem of finding suitable work for both members of a married couple when both are highly qualified and there is a question of transferring one to a new area. Souter and Winslade[1] and Dodge[2] give rather different impressions

---

[1] *Op. cit.*   [2] *Op. cit.*, pp. 235-6.

of what may happen in the Soviet Union in a case of this kind. The former say that the husband may well follow the wife if she has the more senior post. The latter suggests that in practice it is usually the wife's career that is disrupted. The two findings are compatible in that wives' promotion probably tends in practice to lag behind that of husbands. Dodge however also suggests that women may be more inclined than men to resist assignments to remote or unpopular areas, which may form part of the build-up of career experience and of a promotion ladder.

But even where there is no unavoidable clash of this sort, informants indicate that East European employers often go only part of the way towards allowing for women's different life pattern. The legal provisions for the protection of mothers are not always strictly observed.[1] It would be interesting to know whether differences exist in this respect between lower and higher qualified women, bearing in mind that it may be more difficult for an enterprise to keep a senior or specialized job open than to re-employ a returning mother in one of a number of standard jobs. An enterprise which is a good employer may go out of its way to help a professional woman who has temporarily dropped out of her job to keep in touch with it,[2] or may create part-time jobs for mothers of young children. East German law lays on employers a duty to create part-time jobs for mothers. But it seems that it can be somewhat a matter of chance whether these things are done in the ways that best help a professional woman to build up her training and experience and win promotion, or even are done at all. Women do in practice lose ground in the promotion race in their child-bearing years, and may not get much help from management in accelerating back to the point which they might otherwise have reached. The unhelpful attitude of some Polish managers towards women seeking promotion is brought out not only in the study by Wrochno already cited but in another on the special employment problems of women who are sole family breadwinners.[3] East German studies point out that top jobs themselves are liable, without any compelling reason, to be organized in a way which makes it hard for women to combine holding them with family responsibilities.

'The organization and style of work in leading posts is still often irrational and burdensome, so that women would be able to occupy posts of this kind only under extreme strain.'[4]

[1] Cf. Dodge, op. cit., p. 73 (dismissals do occur).
[2] Souter and Winslade, op. cit.
[3] Wrochno, op. cit., and K. Wrochno, Working Conditions of Women as Sole Family Breadwinners, in Kobieta Wspolczesna, op. cit.
[4] Kallabis, H., in Frau und Wissenschaft, p. 30.

'Through a false conception, men's work and the in many ways less than optimal organization of leadership functions, with the working conditions associated with them, are at present treated as the generally valid standards by which women's work is judged. . . . A central task . . . will therefore be, among other things, to organize leadership processes more rationally.'[1]

Overall, the impression from informants is that the East European régimes have put much less thought than their principles would seem to require into the concrete problems of gearing promotion and training practices to the life cycles and attitudes of women as well as men, and in particular to developing for women career patterns which could lead to the top. It does not seem that there has been enough pressure from the side of the labour market to induce them to do so. All the East European countries have experienced shortages of qualified staff, in periods and places severe, and these shortages have been a powerful reason for training and promoting women. At times, for example during the first twenty years of industrialization in the Soviet Union,[2] it was hard to find qualified staff for even the most senior posts: though at that time there were relatively few women in the Soviet Union with qualifications in non-traditional fields available to take advantage of this shortage. But today it is not at the top that shortages make themselves felt. In the Soviet Union, East Germany, or Czechoslovakia qualified men will normally be available to fill a plant director's job or a professorial chair. It may still of course happen that a woman is the best qualified candidate for a top job. But in the East as in the West, promotion pyramids grow narrower towards the top and the supply of qualified competitors tends to exceed the demand. The labour market factors which have favoured women's advance into lower and middle profession and managerial levels do not operate so strongly as a rule from then on towards the top.

d *Feminine identity*

A further factor in women's uncertain record of career achievement in Eastern Europe is uncertainty not so much over feminine identity as over its implications for working life. Though Communist parties in the East as in the West have had their share of 'steel-hardened

[1] Mielke, *op. cit.*
[2] See the accounts of Soviet management in this period by G. Bienstock, S. M. Schwarz and A. Yugow, *Management in Russian Industry and Agriculture*, Oxford 1944, Ch. 9; and D. Granick, *Management of the Industrial Firm in the USSR*, Columbia 1954, Ch. 3.

cadres' whose feminine characteristics have been trained into invisibility – the Communist like the French revolution has had its *tricoteuses* – they have never been feminist in the sense that they 'disregard the natural characteristics which mark women out for a special place in the collective'.[1] Observers like the Maces note the absence in the Soviet Union of any wish to blur sex identification for either men or women or any tendency to do so in fact. The expression of feminine identity which they observe in practice in the Soviet Union differs in some ways from that common today in countries such as America or Britain; but a number of the differences go in the direction of older and more traditional British or American models, not of anything radically new. Sex as such is played down, but qualities such as 'self-effacing modesty, tenderness, and maternal warmth',[2] are accented.

In the Soviet Union as in other countries, the particular form in which femininity is expressed is linked to the country's past history and present state of development, and may well change in future. It may also vary from one social group to another. Inkeles and his colleagues[3] note as a general, not sex-linked, finding that personality traits such as emotional expressiveness, a strong drive for relatedness with people, and impulsiveness which characterize the general population of the Soviet Union are much less characteristic of university-trained people in professions and higher administration. But there is no visible reason as yet to expect a movement towards blurring sex differences in the Soviet Union, and information from other East European countries points the same way. For Poland, for example, Sokolowska and Wrochno comment that the case for more women at the top is not simply to have more of the same qualities which men already supply but to use more fully the complementary qualities of the two sexes.[4] An East German directive on management training for women goes out of its way to accent women's potential contribution to communications, training, and broadly the field of human relations, in a way not found in parallel discussions of training for men.[5]

The question is rather, granted that sex differences are to be accepted and turned to account, which actual or possible differentials are to be given a positive valuation, and which are to be rejected?

[1] Alexandra Kollontai (People's Commissar for Public Welfare from November, 1917), quoted in Mace, *op. cit.*, p. 96.

[2] Mace, *op. cit.*, pp. 110-112.

[3] A. Inkeles, E. Hanfmann, H. Beier, *Modal Personality and Adjustment to the Soviet Socio-Political System*, Human Relations, 1958/1.

[4] Sokolowska and Wrochno, *op. cit.*

[5] Directive of July 7, 1968, quoted in Kulke, *op. cit.*

Among the differences between the sexes noted or alleged by both internal and outside observers as currently existing in Eastern Europe – most of these have already been mentioned – are that girls and women tend to be more conscientious and disciplined than boys and men, but less path-breaking; than girls' interests tend to run to the humanities, to 'maternal' fields such as teaching or medicine and to mental work, rather than to outdoor work, technology, or mastering nature as such, that women tend to be more emotional, personal, and concerned with detail than men, and less able to deal logically and objectively with broad issues; that they tend towards ancillary rather than leadership roles; that married women tend to defer publicly to their husbands, and to be reluctant to earn more or reach higher than them; and that both women and men tend to accept that a mother, unlike a father, will treat her domestic role as primary.[1] Some of these differences are resisted by the Marxist parties and governments, and efforts are made to remove them: for example by co-education on a common curriculum, giving girls the same chance as boys of developing technical interests and entering non-traditional fields of work; by encouraging work co-operation and directness of speech between boys and girls; or by insisting that though a mother's domestic role is important it is not exclusive. New agreed rules are emerging; notably that feminine roles have in any case to include both a career and motherhood, and that in the choice of careers there should in principle be equal opportunity and free choice for women and men alike. Practical necessity disposes of many remaining doubts. Many mothers, for example, have to work simply to make financial ends meet.

But there remains a margin of uncertainty, due not only to the difficulty of escaping from old conceptions but to incomplete definition of new ones. If it is asked where the elimination of sex differences is to stop – short of eliminating them altogether, which is ruled out – no clear answer emerges in Eastern Europe in either theory or practice. If it is asked further how far sex-role differences are seen as capable of being eliminated, whether or not it is desirable to do so, once more no clear answer emerges.[2]

This margin of uncertainty is particularly marked in the case of highly qualified married women whose husbands are also in highly qualified and high-earning careers. If having more than one or two children is incompatible with a career highly valued both by society and by a woman herself, what should be her priority? How is she to

[1] See in particular the articles by Wrochno, Sokolowska, Kloskowska, and Radwilowicz on Poland: Dodge (230ff.), Souter and Winslade, and the Maces on the Soviet Union: and Otto, Schneider, Mielke, and Kallabis on East Germany.
[2] See especially Sokolowska and Wrochno, *op. cit.*, and Sokolowska, *op. cit.*

balance her priorities between free time for her children – especially now that it is increasingly accepted in Eastern Europe that a mother may need in her children's interest to take up to two or three years off work after each child is born – and a career which involves getting quickly back to work or 'taking work home'? Especially, once again, if she can afford financially not to work? In making such a choice, what degree of shortcoming is it right for her to tolerate in the quality of nurseries and nursery schools? Suppose that her husband's and her own career pull in different geographical directions, on what principles are he and she to decide how the choice is to be made? Should she accept a promotion to a level higher than his if it is in an entirely different field, or in the same field, or if it puts him under her command? East German law[1] requires that the husband's own role be modified to the extent needed to make his wife's career practicable. How far in practice is his wife justified in pressing him to go in this? Would it be reasonable, for example, if the case seemed to indicate this, for the couple to reverse their roles altogether and for the husband to take a primarily domestic role permanently or for a long period? Would to go so far be consistent with the general Marxist approach to the differentiation of sex roles: and, if not, where is the line to be drawn?

On questions like these no fixed or agreed view seems to exist in East European practice, nor even in theory or as a matter of political intention. A Czech study notes that role relationships within marriage top the list of subjects on which women would like advice from a marriage advisory centre, and links this specifically to women's changing educational and career patterns.[2] Another notes that at least during a transition period, 'psychotherapists have to be prepared for varying concepts of both the masculine and feminine roles'.[3] Other informants comment that a significant factor behind the rising divorce rate in some East European countries is the growing insistence of women on a revision of roles within marriage, but note a lack of clarity and agreement about the lines of this revision and how far it is to go.

CONCLUSION

The experience of the East European countries shows that it is possible by public policy to accelerate sharply women's movement into new areas of work and the solution of the problems of family

---

[1] Above, p. 53.
[2] Wynnyczuk, V. in *Czechoslovak Population Problems, op. cit.*, 1967, pp. 22-23.
[3] Knoblochova and Knobloch, *op. cit.*, p. 87.

life and child care associated with this. Particularly as regards action in the public sectors, it provides a number of valuable suggestions about how this is to be done. The point to be underlined here, however, is that the flattening of the curve of women's advancement which is apparent in the West is apparent also in the East. The East European experience helps to define, but does not answer, a number of the questions about this which have also proved central to P.E.P.'s enquiry.

The fact that the Marxist régimes of Eastern Europe have not achieved for women an equal share in top jobs does not simply reflect a failure of political decision or a hangover of outdated views from the past; though both of these have played their part. At least three other conclusions relevant to P.E.P.'s enquiry need to be drawn.

First, when the formal and customary barriers to women's advancement are removed, as has to a great extent been done in Eastern Europe, there remain not only technical problems which may take time to appreciate and resolve – for example those of re-casting employers' recruitment and promotion practices to allow for women's different life cycle – but genuine clashes of priority between socially desirable objectives, for example those which arise over the expenditure needed to improve housing, neighbourhood services, or the provision of nursery schools. It also necessarily takes time to work out the patterns of behaviour on the part of husbands, wives and children which are appropriate in dual-career families in the interests of all their members, or rather to define the range of patterns from which it is useful to choose and the criteria for choosing between them. It takes time, again, to work out in the light of these changes and win general acceptance for a new pattern of masculine and feminine roles, with a much wider range of variation and choice than in the past. The experience of Eastern Europe is a useful checklist of problems which will need to be solved in the West and reminder of the difficulties of solving them, rather than a source of already completed answers.

Secondly, the experience of Eastern Europe underlines that in many ways it is for people of high qualifications that problems in these areas are likely to be hardest to solve. In a material and financial sense the hardest problems are obviously those of the poor; of the mother of four children who has to work to make ends meet, or of the family in defective or overcrowded housing. But in a psychological sense the strain on families at the professionally qualified level may be greater. These are the families where the wife is most likely to be deeply committed to her career and to a wide network of interests, and most inclined to 'take her work home'. Her husband may well be in the same position. But these are also the families which are liable to demand the highest standards of child care and to be most critical of substitute care for children; those which will not simply take the standards of nurseries, kindergartens or grandmothers as they find them. East European informants note that these factors do as a matter of fact often result in a higher level of tension for both parents and children in intellectual families than in working-class families, and in actual or threatened breakdowns in marital and parent-child relations.[1] These special problems of highly qualified dual-career families, as apart from the general run of families qualified at lower levels, have been a main area for the P.E.P. enquiry to explore.

Thirdly, a study of the research material on Eastern Europe and of the dates at which it became available suggests strongly that the Marxist régimes until recently lost heavily, in terms of their own objectives, by taking too strong an ideological line on women's advancement. The point is not that they were wrong to have well defined objectives, but that they too easily assumed that the answers to their questions were straightforward and could be quickly discovered by administrators. It is not possible, as was said in Chapter I, to carry on research in a field like this without some ideological preconceptions, including some estimate of the kind of question likely to prove relevant and of the answers likely to emerge. But a rigid advance commitment to a particular approach can inhibit necessary research by blocking off important questions. The Soviet Union might well have moved faster along the lines desired by its government if the assumption had not grown up, as Dodge points out, that it was irrelevant to raise questions about women's economic performance or academic capacity – what *type* of capacity or performance, as well as what level – at all. Since the early 1960s it seems that this lesson is being learnt in Eastern Europe, though, as yet, not wholeheartedly in every country. An advantage of the type of assumptions underlying the present enquiry, as set out in Chapter I, is that they leave open the question of what the actual range and shape of patterns of behaviour over marriage and careers is to be; open enough to ensure that no avenues of enquiry need be blocked.

[1] Informants especially from East Germany and Czechoslovakia.

Chapter III

The Experience of Western Countries – Ideologies and Trends

It is often said that women's position in employment, and especially in highly qualified employment, is fundamentally different in Eastern Europe from what is found in Western countries such as Britain, West Germany, France, Sweden, or the United States. But when the situations in the West and the East are reviewed together, the similarities stand out even more than the differences.

In the West as in Eastern Europe the proportion of women, especially married women, who are in the work force has risen steeply through the last generation. There has been the same tendency for women's share in higher education to increase rapidly – whether measured by the absolute number of women studying or by the proportion which women students make up of their age group or of the whole student body – and for women with higher education to show a high level of career commitment. There has been the same tendency for the family and community to develop in ways which make it easier for married women to work outside the home if they so wish: for shopping, housing, and other services to improve, for the number of large families and of births after age 30 to fall, and for husbands to take a larger and less patriarchal part in the running of their homes.

There are the same tendencies in the West as in the East for the proportion of girls who reach college to remain at least marginally lower than the proportion of men; for women to take a much smaller share in postgraduate study than in study at undergraduate level; for even highly qualified women to spend substantially less of their potential working time in employment than correspondingly qualified men; and for women's career paths to stop well short of the top. When the reasons for these negative tendencies are listed they turn out again to be very much the same in the West as in the East; overload; problems of the care of young children; slowness on the part

99

of employers to adapt their recruitment and promotion practices to the differences between the life cycles of women and men; and uncertainty over how in modern conditions masculine and feminine roles should be defined.

The chief difference between Eastern Europe and the West, and it is a major one, is that in the West the pressure for women to move into work has been less clearly directed and usually weaker.

One reason is that there has tended to be less pressure on Western labour markets. This point must not be overstated; in the advanced Western countries employment prospects for well qualified people in recent years have been good, and several have had at least an approximation to full employment overall. But there is still much truth in it. In Britain the growth of the work force, and especially the employment of traditionally 'secondary' workers such as married women, has been checked or even reversed from time to time by balance-of-payments difficulties. In West Germany and Israel immigration was heavy after the Second World War, and postponed the achievement of full employment for many years. Ireland, a country of particularly heavy emigration, has developed what might be called a widow's cruse situation. An improvement in employment opportunities inside the country has been likely to reflect itself in a fall in emigration which partly or wholly refills the reservoir of unemployed. Sometimes it has more than refilled it, when the improved opportunities have led a particularly large number of potential emigrants to take a chance at home. In that case unemployment has paradoxically become heavier after an increase in employment than it was before. In general, Western governments have been less ready than those in Eastern Europe to force the pace of structural change in their economies in peacetime to the point of creating major and lasting scarcities of qualified staff, such as have proved so helpful to women's advance in the East. They have not been able to avoid scarcities of that kind entirely, for example the scarcity of teachers in Britain, but have been less willing than Eastern Governments to court them deliberately.

A second main reason why the pressure for women to work has been less strong and consistent in the West than in the East is that ideologies about family life and women's work, and especially the ideologies which are publicly expressed and most directly influence policy, are less uniform in the West than in Marxist countries. The governments, employers and social movements of Eastern Europe follow in principle a single aim, however much it may be varied or neglected in practice. In Western countries a much wider range of ideologies challenge and compete with one another, from near-traditional at one end of the scale to radical 'new feminist' at the other.

This greater openness in the West to the competition of ideas has proved to have both advantages and disadvantages. The Western approach has been more successful than the Eastern in ensuring that awkward issues shall be brought into the open, that there shall be no inhibitions about research, and that the risk of imposing one-sided and ill-considered solutions shall be minimized. Though, for example, there has been a higher proportion of working mothers in Eastern Europe than in the West, the most basic research on child care in families where the mother works – including research showing the advantages of mothers working – has been done in countries such as Britain and the United States. Some of the best East European studies had for years to be carried on underground to avoid political difficulties. Ideological freedom has been reinforced in the West with the freedoms of a market-oriented economy and, in most Western countries, of competition between political parties for votes. In the relatively open and competitive conditions which result it has been easier for families in the West than in Eastern Europe to make their wishes about housing, houschold equipment and retail services effective. Though Western provision in these respects has often been defective, it has generally been well ahead of what is available to families in the East.

On the other hand the Western approach, and particularly the competition of ideologies, has made it harder to draw the threads of debate together and weave them into clear-cut policies. The movement of older married women into work has been much more *ad hoc* and piecemeal in the West than in Eastern Europe. It has been related more to labour market pressures, which themselves have tended to be weaker than in the East, and less to any overall view of the needs of the family and the economy. It has been less rapid than in the East. Even after the swift advance of the last few years, participation rates for older women in the work forces of most Western countries remain by the standards of Eastern Europe relatively low. In most countries and sectors of the labour market they still stop short of the threshold at which the weight of social custom and practice supports rather than holds back the married woman who works. Legal, administrative, and educational provisions have only slowly been adapted to the new situation. The rights of working mothers, for example, have been much more effectively institutionalized in the East than in the West. Few Western countries – Israel and Austria are among the exceptions – provide a working mother with as good a guarantee of her right to return to a job or of her seniority and social security rights as is usual in Eastern Europe. Few, again, have

101

had as clearcut a policy as the Eastern European countries for the provision of kindergartens and nurseries. The movement of women into work in the West has also tended more than in the East to follow customary channels. There has been less tendency in the West for women to break into fields such as engineering which are not traditional for them.

THE IDEOLOGICAL DEBATE

Western like Eastern European countries have turned sharply away from patriarchal conceptions of marriage, based on inequality between husband and wife and on the idea of the father as the master. Remnants of it survive, but few accept it as the ideal for the future. The ideologies which replace it form a continuous series with no sharp boundaries between them, but for present purposes, and with the accent on attitudes to women's work, can be taken as falling into five competing groups.[1]

a *Role segregation, with a strong preference for the housewife at home*

Kelly,[2] for example, argues that a pattern in which the wife works is likely to overload her through the need to do both her domestic and her outside job. Families which accept this pattern may well be underestimating the time and effort needed for creative home-making, and overestimating the cash gain from outside work after allowing not only for the expense of doing it but also for the more expensive way of housekeeping which it entails, and for the loss of some of the production and services which are undertaken by full-time housewives without pay. When wives work there may be a tendency for the size of families to drop below the optimum for either family life or national population policy, since working wives tend to have fewer children. There may be psychological damage to children through too early and prolonged separation from their mothers, on the lines indicated notably by Bowlby.[3] There is likely to be confusion between masculine and feminine roles, as the husband moves into the housework area and the wife into outside work. This will have repercussions on husband, children and wife alike. The children will be left confused, with no clear model for sex identification. The husband, who is the

---

[1] See also the summary by Dahlström in E. Dahlström (ed.), *The Changing Roles of Men and Women*, Duckworth 1967, Ch. 6.

[2] Kelly, G. A., *The Catholic Family Handbook*, Robert Hale, 1961, Ch. 11.

[3] The reference is to Bowlby's 1952 study of *Maternal Care and Mental Health*, World Health Organization 1952, not to his somewhat revised position taken in his later work.

natural head of the house and provider, will find his role devalued and is likely consciously or unconsciously to resent this. The wife may lose her primacy in intuition and love and the leading role in the family which it gives her, and may achieve no compensating gain.[1] As a result of all these factors she is likely to suffer from guilt, tension and physical strain.

An ideology of this kind, underlining the idea of the man as head of the house, could obviously be understood in an old-style patriarchal sense, but it is clear from the context that this is not what is intended. Junker,[2] in a German study, shows that there is no necessary or, in modern conditions, even probable connection between the two concepts. He found widespread support among German husbands and wives for statements such as 'The husband is master in the house', or 'The wife's realm is her household; everything else is the husband's business'. There was, however, no correlation between these views and either objective or subjective indicators of inequality or lack of partnership in marriage. Junker concludes that the point of phrases like these is not acceptance of inequality but a preference for a husband whose role, though equal, will be distinctively masculine. Junker's (and Kelly's) view comes close to Kloskowska's finding in Poland that in current conditions many married couples accept that there is a case, not for inequality in marriage, but for maintaining a clearcut division of labour along traditional lines.

b *Housekeeping as primary for wives, a job as complementary*

Junker goes on to develop a line of thought related to Kelly's, but distinct enough to rate as a separate ideology. On the one hand he argues that:

> 'The woman who decides for marriage and children has to take a fundamental decision for or against the family. She has to decide whether to locate the central point of the further development of her personality in the family or in a profession. There is no valid compromise.'[3]

For the married woman with children a job can be complementary to her main role, but not a full commitment.

But on the other hand Junker recognizes that a job, so long as it remains complementary, can have a valuable part to play in a married

---

[1] De Lestapis, S., *Amour et Institution Familiale*, Spes, 1948, Ch. 7.

[2] Junker, R., *Die Lage der Mütter in der Bundesrepublik Deutschland*, Deutscher Verein für öffentliche und private Fürsorge, 1966, Part I, Vol. 2, pp. 233 ff., esp. p. 257.

[3] Junker, *op. cit.*, p. 276.

103

woman's life cycle. Professional training is valuable to her for developing her personality and for her integration into society, and also as an insurance in case of widowhood or separation. But conditions should be such that she is free to select her own optimum balance between domestic and outside work. She should not be forced by financial and social needs into a permanent, full-time, commitment to the world of work, where, over and above any other difficulties, her family commitments will always leave her at a disadvantage. There should be better financial guarantees for a case such as widowhood. A range of institutions should be created to help housewives to widen their outside interests and develop skill in making game-like use of their free time. Advanced societies are moving towards a world of games rather than work, and in this world housewives could in effect become the professionals. A housewife may well wish to move into and out of work, appearing on the work scene as a helper rather than a competitor, and treating work as a game and not merely as a means of earning an income. Work can be valuable to her if it is game-like and supplementary to her main role, but not as a central commitment in her life.[1]

c *Alternating home and work roles: the three-phase model*

This model is especially associated with the names of Alva Myrdal and Viola Klein.[2] Myrdal and Klein accept that many families will, and probably should, follow a pattern like that proposed by Kelly while their children are young; certainly they should do so while the children are very young. But even if 'young' is extended to age 15, this will leave an average married woman in Western countries such as Britain with twenty years of free working life after her young-child period is over and before reaching retiring age. Unless she works in these years she is likely to be isolated, functionless, and dissatisfied, for Myrdal and Klein do not accept that voluntary, amateur activities can today provide her with a full and satisfying role.

'Sharing in the life activities of the community generates a sense of purpose which is essential to human fulfilment. This is particularly the case in a society like ours, where the obligation to make a constructive contribution to the social effort has become a generally accepted ethos and where this contribution is measured by professional standards and on the basis of tangible results.'[3]

[1] Junker, *op. cit.*, esp. pp. 32-33, 187-190, 262, 271-276.
[2] Myrdal, A., and Klein, V., *Women's Two Roles*, 2nd ed., Routledge & Kegan Paul, 1968, esp. Chs. 9 and 10.
[3] *Ibid.*, p. 189.

The older woman with free time in any case owes a contribution to society 'in terms of the accepted definition of work'.

'It is therefore suggested that women should visualize their life-span as a succession of three phases, each dominated mainly by one function; a period of training and education, followed, if possible, by years devoted to raising a family; these, in turn, being succeeded by a period during which past training and experience are put to wider social use.'[1]

In this three-phase model 'education, family and work can be blended to a harmonious whole', and women can achieve a clear direction for their lives. But this is possible only if women choose and train for a career seriously and recognize that employers and society will expect them to yield a return for the training they receive. The careers which most of them choose will need to be of a kind easy to combine with marriage, to keep up with during the time when a mother has young children – perhaps by working part-time or at home – and to return to afterwards in spite of broken experience. They will often be traditionally feminine careers, such as teaching, but traditionally masculine jobs like that of an estate agent may also qualify. On the other hand, 'professions such as that of a surgeon or diplomat would be very difficult to reconcile with family responsi-bilities', for they involve continuous commitment or problems such as travelling or frequent transfers to posts in new places. They should be chosen only by women who 'are willing to work on the same con-ditions as men'.[2]

The three-phase model avoids any difficulty over the separation of mothers and young children, and leaves a clear distinction between masculine and feminine roles. It could on the other hand still leave housewives overloaded with a combination of outside and home responsibilities, especially at the time when they have continuing responsibility for children but are beginning to move back into out-side work. Myrdal and Klein suggest a number of angles from which the overload problem could be attacked, including better nursery and other public service facilities, service houses, and more equal sharing by husbands in the work of the home. The addition to the national income through increasing the proportion of married women in work might be used to make possible a reduction in work-ing hours for both men and women to, say, six a day, so releasing more of men's as well as women's time for activities at home, and incidentally getting rid of the present discrepancy between the work-ing hours of a child in school and of most mothers in full-time work.

---

[1] *Ibid.*, p. 153.   [2] *Ibid.*, p. 157.

The three-phase model also requires improvements by employers and the State in the rules for maintaining mothers' job rights up to, say, two years after a birth; and in facilities for keeping a wife in touch with work during the time when she is working at home, for re-training and re-employing older women, and for part-time work as a means both of keeping in touch and of re-entering.

d *The continuous career pattern, with minimum interruption for maternity*

This ideology has been developed in the West both by Marxists, on lines similar to the official ideologies of the East European countries, and by 'new feminists' with a civil rights rather than a Marxist approach.[1] The Marxist approach tends to put the heaviest stress on the value of work, both for personal development and for society. The civil rights approach has more to say on the reform of relationships within the family. But these are differences of emphasis within a common frame of reference. On both approaches, the three-phase model is rejected on the grounds that it separates women for too long from participation outside the home, that it limits the fields in which they can expect to work and the level of promotion they can hope to achieve, and that it achieves no compensating gain in family life and child care.

Attacking a position similar to Kelly's, the Marxist writers Michel and Texier say:

'Put in this way, the Church's position reveals its misunderstanding of a basic value of the modern world, that of work in a regular occupation. It is accepted today that work is not only the fullest form of integration into society but the outstanding means of personal formation and development.'[2]

Many occupations do not yet measure up to this standard, but this will be cured by participation, not by standing aside.

'We cannot accept the limited view which would deprive women of the three results of work: development of the feminine person-

---

[1] A good example of the Marxist approach is A. Michel and G. Texier, *La Condition de la Française d'Aujourd'hui*, Gonthier, 1964. Examples of the civil rights approach are *The Status of Women in Sweden*, Report of the Swedish Government to the United Nations, 1968 – see also Dahlström, *op. cit.*, including his reference to E. Moberg's *The Conditional Emancipation of Women*, 1961; A. Rossi, *Equality Between the Sexes – An Immodest Proposal*, Daedalus, 1964; B. Friedan, *The Feminine Mystique*, Penguin, 1965; C. Bird, *Born Female*, McKay, 1968; and E. Sullerot, *Demain Les Femmes*, Laffont-Gonthier, 1965.
[2] Michel and Texier, *op. cit.*, II, 172.

ality, better understanding of adolescent children, and closer intimacy of the married couple.'[1]

Myrdal and Klein would of course also accept that work outside the home is important for women. But the practical conclusion which they draw is very different. Their three-phase model admits a relatively long break in mother's working life while their children are young. The Marxist and civil rights approaches agree that some break is needed and that mothers should have discretion about its length, but stress the case for keeping it short and maximizing the continuity of careers. Whereas Myrdal and Klein ask that girls should be trained predominantly for careers, many of them traditionally feminine, which are easy to combine with a three-phase life cycle, the more radical supporters of the dual-career pattern have no such inhibitions. Girls should have the same opportunity as boys of qualifying for non-traditional careers and acquiring an interest in them. Tendencies in education to convey a segregated picture of careers and lives should be combated. Girls should follow technical classes equally with boys, and boys housework classes equally with girls. Textbooks and career guidance material should be checked for any tendency to present women and men predominantly in traditionally sex-typed roles.[2]

The civil rights approach has come close to being the official and generally accepted ideology of at least one Western country, Sweden,[3] and the Swedish Government's report on *The Status of Women* is a classic statement of it.

'A decisive and ultimately durable improvement in the status of women cannot be attained by special measures aimed at women alone; it is equally necessary to abolish the conditions which tend to assign certain privileges, obligations, or rights to men. No decisive change in the distribution of functions and status as between the sexes can be achieved if the duties of the male in society are assumed *a priori* to be unaltered. . . . The division of functions as between the sexes must be changed in such a way that both the man and the woman in the family are afforded the same practical opportunities of participating in both active parenthood and gainful employment. If women are to attain a position in society outside the home which corresponds to their proportional membership of the citizen body, it follows that men must assume a greater

[1] *Ibid.*, p. 173.
[2] See especially the Swedish report on *The Status of Women, op. cit.*
[3] Though, as in Eastern Europe, it is as well to add for the record that ideology is one thing and day-by-day practice is another.

share of responsibility for the upbringing of the children and the care of the home. A policy which attempts to give women an equal place with men in economic life while at the same time confirming woman's traditional responsibility for the care of home and children has no prospect of fulfilling the first of these aims. This aim can be realized only if the man is also educated and encouraged to take an active part in parenthood and is given the same rights and duties in his parental capacity. This will probably imply that the demands for performance at work on the man's part must be reduced: a continued shortening of working hours will therefore be of great importance. In this context it would be advisable to study how reductions in working hours could best be distributed over the working week with a view to making it easier for husbands to do their share of work in the home.'[1]

The common assumption of Western society that a wife has a right to be supported by her husband must be combated, for it discourages her from making the serious commitment to a career which is needed for her own and her family's welfare. Certainly the right of a parent to stay at home when the family needs this must be safeguarded, for example by appropriate social security provisions. But the best parent to stay at home will not on every occasion or at every stage of the family cycle be the mother. Fathers too must have the right to take time out for their family duties.[2] Between this and the shortening of men's as well as women's working hours, the contribution by men to the national income will be reduced. But the reduction is likely to be more than offset by the extra working capacity made available on the part of women; extra in terms not only of quantity but of quality in the sense of stronger career commitment and better qualifications than have been usual for women in the past. A Swedish informant illustrates the possible quantitative gain in working capacity with a simple piece of arithmetic about the number of careers in a family:

$$1 + 0 = 1$$
$$\tfrac{3}{4} + \tfrac{3}{4} = 1\tfrac{1}{2}$$

The questions about overload, child care and the possible blurring of masculine and feminine roles raised by other ideologies take a particularly strong form in the case of the continuous-career ideology, which departs furthest from the norm of the housewife at home. On the overload issue supporters of the continuous-career pattern see the more equal sharing of duties in the home as the first safeguard, and better provision of nurseries, kindergartens, service houses, and

---

[1] *The Status of Women in Sweden, op. cit.,* p. 4.   [2] *Ibid.*

other social facilities as the second. The argument that child care need suffer through this substitute care or through the absence of mothers from their homes is rejected. Granted that it is likely to be psychologically damaging to young children to be boarded for long periods in institutions, it is denied on the basis of recent studies that any such results need follow from day care in good nurseries or, even more so, in kindergartens. For older children it is argued that there is likely to be a double psychological – not only material – gain when their mother has an outside job. First, the mother is likely to have, by comparison with a full-time housewife, a greater range of experience, more personal maturity, more ability to take a detached view, and less time and temptation to be over-protective and dominant. Secondly, there is the gain from the greater and more active presence of the father in the home.

Masculine and feminine roles, it is finally argued, are not being blurred. They are being re-written in the light of the new conditions of family and working life, and the new definitions are as clear as the old and more satisfying. Industrial society has exaggerated the segregation of masculine and feminine roles. The new definitions are in many ways a return to the older tradition of the farmer and craftsman. The mother in those days and at that social level – the upper-class tradition was often different – presented to her daughter a model not of full-time child care but of mixed productive and child-care activity. The father, playing his part around the home, presented a masculine model to his children in a way made unnecessarily difficult today by the segregation of husbands' activities outside the home from wives' activities within it. Children were usually cared for by a wide circle of relatives or fellow-villagers, and much less exclusively than today by their parents alone.[1]

e *Multiple patterns on a base of equal opportunity*

This is the ideology which the research team itself accepts, and which has already been presented in Chapter I. The point, as was said there, is not that married couples should feel that they have a completely free choice as to the way in which they will define their respective roles. There is present for each couple a range of objective conditions, including on the one hand the abilities and temperaments of wife and husband and on the other the conditions of the society in which they live. These conditions define the roles which it is reasonable for the wife and the husband in each case to adopt. The argument is that the patterns of work and family activity by husbands

---

[1] Cf. Rossi, *op. cit.*, p. 615.

and wives which emerge in this way, assuming that they are chosen reasonably and that unnecessary barriers to choice are removed, are likely to spread over a very wide range. Some families at least – the question 'how many' is a matter for research – are likely to find themselves best suited by each of the patterns recommended by the four previous ideologies, from segregated roles to continuous careers. One might for example expect relatively many families where the wife has low qualifications, and so probably low earning capacity, a relatively uninteresting job, and a low degree of career commitment, to decide for the segregated-role or complementary-job pattern; especially as low qualification may also go with low ability to cope with the difficulties of a continuous-career pattern. On the other hand a relatively large proportion of families where the wife's qualifications are high might be expected to decide for continuous careers. Three-phase patterns might be found at either end of the scale.

This multiple choice ideology does not simply take existing abilities, qualifications and social conditions as given. It is dynamic in that the personal and social conditions of which it takes account are not only those that exist but also those that will come into existence or that might be brought into existence by a policy decision. Its point is simply that in any conditions which are foreseeable or which it is practicable to create, married couples are likely to find themselves in a wide variety of situations relevant to the choice between the home and work roles theoretically open to a husband and wife. Society will need to accept that the patterns of activity actually developed by husbands and wives should be varied enough to match this variety of situations. The problem is not to enforce a standard pattern but to facilitate an appropriate choice.

THE ACTUAL COURSE OF DEVELOPMENT IN THE WEST

a *Participation rates and the 'network effect'*

The ideologies of family life and women's work set out above have, of course, very different practical implications. Under the ideology of segregated roles few if any married women (unless they were widowed or separated) would be in paid employment. Under the ideology of continuous careers nearly all would be working, except during the months immediately before and after a birth.

The segregated-role pattern was common in the West until a generation ago. It remained usual in the 1960s in countries such as the Netherlands, Norway and Ireland where (Table III.1) the proportion of middle-aged women working has been as low as 5 per cent or 10 per cent for married women with husbands present, and in the range from 15 per cent to 25 per cent for all women together.[1]

Britain, however, is one of several advanced[2] Western countries which have been changing fast through the last generation in the direction of a three-phase, continuous-career, or at least complementary job pattern. As recently as 1946 the Royal Commission on Equal Pay noted it as normal – that is, as the expected practice in peacetime – for only around 10 per cent of married women of all ages to be in paid work.[3] Proportions around this level had been returned at the Censuses of 1911, 1921, and 1931. But the Commission covered itself[4] by noting that the withdrawal of women from war work 'had been somewhat slower than was expected', and that, in the new conditions of the post-war labour market, full employment and a general shortage of manpower were giving rise to appeals to women to stay on. At about the same time, in 1944, a government Social Survey report[5] noted that 44 per cent of the married women workers questioned and 63 per cent of the single and widowed disapproved in principle of work after marriage, and that over half the married women felt that if a job were open to a man or a woman it should go to a man. Nevertheless it forecast, on the basis of the expressed intentions of women war workers, that the work force was likely to contain more older and married women after the war than it had before.

As it turned out, the proportion of married women and especially of older married women who work has in fact risen sharply during the postwar generation, and not only in Britain (Table III.1). By the early 1960s the proportion of all women in their forties who were working in countries such as Britain, West Germany, France and

[1] Comparisons based on general figures like these, including women working in agriculture, must be treated with care because of the wide differences from one country to another in the Census classification of unpaid family helpers on farms. However, the figures quoted point in the right direction. E.g. B. E. Harrell-Bond, 'Conjugal Role Behaviour', *Human Relations*, February 1969, p. 86, brings out the much higher degree of role segregation in married couples with an Irish husband as compared to couples in the same (English) environment with an English husband. The Irish pattern, which is now tending to change, rests largely on demographic factors, linked in turn to the socio-technical pattern of Irish farming in the nineteenth and twentieth centuries. The demographic factors are summarized in B. Walsh, *Some Irish Population Problems Reconsidered*, The Economic and Social Research Institute, Dublin, 1968.

[2] 'Whereas in the East women's activity rates outside agriculture have been generally rising, the limited evidence suggests that this is so only in some of the advanced Western countries.' United Nations, Economic Commission for Europe, *The European Economy in 1968*, Ch. 3, p. 249.

[3] *Report of the Royal Commission on Equal Pay*, Cmd. 6937, 1946, para. 340.

[4] *Ibid.*, para. 141.

[5] Government Social Survey, *Women at Work*, Central Office of Information, 1944.

111

the United States was in the range from 40 to 50 per cent, and the proportion of married women of this age with husband present who were working ranged from 35 per cent to 45 per cent. Britain moreover is one of the countries, like Sweden and the United States, where these proportions have gone on rising. By the middle 1960s over half of all women in Britain around age 50 were working. The proportion of married women aged 45-49 who worked reached $52\frac{1}{2}$ per cent in 1967 and is expected to be $56\frac{1}{2}$ per cent in 1972 and $61\frac{1}{2}$ per cent in 1981. The proportion of married women of all ages who are working in 1970 is expected to be 39 per cent.

In particular regions and professions the proportion of women and especially of married women who work is well above even the rising general average just quoted. In Britain in 1961 the proportion of married women of all ages who were working averaged 30 per cent, but whereas in Wales, the rural South-West, the North (including Tyneside), and Scotland it ranged between 19 per cent and 23 per cent, it reached 34 per cent in London and the Midlands and 36 per cent in Lancashire and the North-West. Of all women in Britain who were aged 45-59 in 1968, the proportion working was 35-40 per cent in Wales and the Northern region, but 54-56 per cent in the South-East, the West Midlands, and the North-West (Table III.2).

The relationship between the supply and demand factors underlying the rise of married women's participation in work out of their homes, in Britain or in other Western countries, is highly complex and still not fully explored. In a complex analysis of the reasons for the rise in women's participation in the American work force from 1940 to 1960, Bowen and Finnegan conclude that among the factors which played a significant part are:

On the supply side; Positive factors: women's rising educational and income aspirations, and the tendency for goods and services which would formerly have been produced in the household to become cheaper and easier to acquire in the market. Negative factors: the rise in incomes, making it easier for housewives to afford not to work; and, in this particular period, a rise in the proportion of women of working age who had young children currently depending on them.

On the demand side; Positive factors: the rise in women's rates of pay, shorter and more convenient hours of work (including more opportunities for part-time work), and an increase in the proportion of jobs in industry available to women. A negative factor: during the last part of the period, a rise in unemployment.

Other factors mentioned as relevant to particular categories of workers are re-entry requirements – for some groups, such as managers, difficulties over re-entry turned out quite possibly to increase participation through making women who at present hold jobs more reluctant to leave them – and the more or less attractive nature of the work on offer. There proved to be an intriguing relation with the husband's occupation. Wives of labourers, craftsmen, managers, and professional and technical workers showed relatively low rates of participation, whereas participation rates for the wives of operatives, service workers, clerks, or sales workers tended to be relatively high.

The balance of evidence from investigations in Britain as well as other countries is however that the main reason for the rise in married women's employment is to be found on the demand side. More jobs have become available for women than can be filled by the single, separated or divorced women in the labour market. There is a reserve labour force of women who are willing to work – though they are not necessarily pressing to do so, and may have to be persuaded – but who do not formally enter the market unless jobs for them are available. When jobs are hard to get many of them drop out of the work force altogether instead of remaining in it and registering as unemployed. When, on the other hand, jobs become available, this invisible reserve force comes into the open. The ratio of women to men in the work force rises, and this further reinforces demand as women become more familiar and acceptable as workers. At this point, as Bowen and Finnegan show, a further effect develops on the supply side. Women themselves become more used to working. It becomes less necessary than it had been in the first place to lure them into work with high pay or other exceptional inducements. Their participation comes to correlate less with specific factors such as those listed above and more with a general attitude favouring work.[1]

[1] For Britain see especially the review of recent material in R. Thomas and R. Peacock, *Men's and Women's Journeys to Work*, P.E.P. Broadsheet, 1970: notably of J. Bowers; *The Anatomy of Regional Activity Rates*, National Institute of Economic and Social Research (in press); J. S. Swabe, 'Labour Force Participation Rates in the London Metropolitan Region', *Journal of the Royal Statistical Society*, Series AA (General), Vol. L. 32, Part II, 1969; see also E. Eversley and K. Gales, 'Married Women: Britain's Biggest Reservoir of Labour', *Progress*, No. 3, 1969; H. A. Turner, 'Employment Fluctuation, Labour Supply, and Bargaining Power', *The Manchester School*, May 1959.

For America see W. G. Bowen and C. A. Finnegan, *The Economics of Labour Participation*, Princeton, 1969, Ch. 5-7; C. G. Oppenheimer, *The Interaction of Demand and Supply and its Effect on Female Labour Force in the United States*, cyclosyled, based on Oppenheimer's *The Female Labour Force in the United States: its Growth and Changing Composition*, Ph.D. thesis, University of California (Berkeley), 1966; and G. P. Cain, *Married Women in the Labour Force*, Chicago, 1966.

As was said in **Chapter I**, women with high professional qualifications, in Western countries as well as Eastern Europe, show a much stronger commitment to their careers than others, and more readiness to remain in paid work. In Britain the Social Survey noted this in the replies of women war workers to the question of whether they wished to go on working after the Second World War. Seventy-two per cent of professional and administrative workers wished to do so, compared to a general average of 55 per cent and a low figure of 46 per cent for women labourers and packers.[1] A quarter of a century later the Social Survey re-documented the same point.[2] In Britain women with higher qualifications are consistently more likely to work than those with lower qualifications (Table III.3 (i)). They tend in choosing a job to show more interest in the opportunity to use their skills and qualifications – that is, more interest in the job itself – and to give less priority to circumstances incidental to the job such as pay, working conditions, or pleasant working companions (Table III.3 (ii)). They are also less likely than women with lower qualifications to be absent from work. Qualification for qualification, women tend to have a higher level of absence than men, but qualified workers of either sex tend to be absent less often than the unqualified. The working rule which emerges from experience in a number of countries is that women of a given level of qualification tend to have absence similar to that of men with the next lower qualification, but less absence than less qualified workers of either sex. Absence among women administrators, managers, or teachers, for example, tends to match that among craftsmen or clerks among men.[3]

[1] Social Survey, *op. cit.*, p. 17.
[2] Government Social Survey, A Survey of Women's Employment, 2 vols., SS379, 1968. See also the contrast between the work interests of 19-20 year old girls who left school respectively at 15 and at 17-18 in Government Social Survey, *Young School Leavers*, 1969.
[3] For Britain the Ministry of Pensions and National Insurance enquiry into *Incidence of Incapacity for Work*, (H.M.S.O. 1965, Table A.9, A.12, B.9, B.12), found the percentage of men and women who had at least one spell of sickness absence in 1961-2 to be:

	Men	Women 'Other'	Women Married
	%	%	%
Administrators, managers	14	32	28
Teachers	17	28	23
Clerks	25	31	34·5
All skilled manual and routine clerical	28	32	37
Semi-skilled	31	37	44
Unskilled	35	40·5	43
All occupations	*28*	*33*	*39*

See also for the United States the *Report of the Committee on Federal Employment*, 1963, p. 31.

Women in certain professions, such as medicine, stand out in other British studies as having a level of career commitment exceptional even by the standards general among professional women (Table III.3 (iii) (e)). Seventy-two per cent even of married women doctors with children were working in 1962, along with 83 per cent of those without children and 95 per cent of single women. The proportion working among women engineers is similar (Table III.3 (iii) (d)). The figures for both these professions contrast sharply with the low career persistence of social administration students brought out by Table III.3 (iii) (c).

Comparable figures are found in other Western countries. At the age of 50, 70 per cent of French graduates were working in 1962 compared to 40-45 per cent of women with only a basic education.[1] Among American women (Table III.4) the proportion working in 1964 at the ages 45-54 rose from 43 per cent of those with only elementary education to 85 per cent of those with postgraduate education, or from 29 per cent to 63 per cent if the comparison is confined to married women (not widowed, separated or divorced). Bowen and Finnegan analyse the extent to which greater participation by more educated women is due on the one hand to their higher earnings and on the other to job interest and other non-wage factors. Up to first degree level they find a rough balance between the two types of influence, but to women with post-graduate education non-wage factors are much more important. In Germany, women with a higher school leaving certificate (*Abitur*) make up a significantly greater proportion of women in the work force than of housewives at home.[2] Seventy per cent of all women graduates in Germany (the total against which the percentage is calculated includes the retired and disabled) were in the work force in 1961; for graduates in medical fields (doctors, dentists, pharmacists and veterinarians) the proportion reached 77 per cent. The corresponding figures for men were 89 per cent and 93 per cent.[3] In Israel 30 per cent of native-born Jewish women with five to eight years of schooling were in the civilian work force in 1963, but 62 per cent of those with thirteen years or more.[4] In Norway, where the proportion of women and especially married women in employment is generally low, the differences related to education

[1] *L'Emploi Féminin*, in *Etudes et Conjoncture*, December 1964, p. 62. See also the figures in F. Guelaud-Leridon, *Le Travail des Femmes en France*, Presses Universitaires de France, 1964, p. 62.

[2] Microcensus of April 1964. The actual figures are: women with *Abitur* 2·8 per cent of women of the same age in the work force, 2·2 per cent of women not in the work force.

[3] From a 10 per cent preparatory sample for the Census of 1961.

[4] *Women in the Labour Force*, State of Israel Ministry of Labour, (cyclostyled), 1965, p. 59.

are particularly striking. Whereas only 9·5 per cent of all Norwegian married women worked outside their homes in 1960, 55 per cent of women graduates did so.[1]

The rise in the proportion of married women who work in a country like Britain is self-reinforcing, and may become much more so in the future than in the past. Women's work outside the home is one of those social practices, like shift-work, which become more acceptable and tend to have more good and fewer damaging effects the more general the practice is.[2] In the Lancashire textile districts, for example, the dual-career tradition in working-class families is old and well-established, and employers and the community as well as families have become adjusted to it. But there is some way to go before this degree of adjustment to and social support for dual career patterns becomes general, even in those circles where women's tendency to become lifetime workers has been strongest. In Britain today a large proportion even of full-time housewives – still more of women who are themselves working – are likely to answer 'yes' to the question 'Do most of the married women you know go out to work or not?' But contacts with families for the present project have shown that it is still common for families where the wife as well as the husband follows a professional or managerial career to find that neighbours and relatives do not understand how such a family needs to organize its life, or can cope with what people who lack experience with continuous careers see as insoluble problems of overload or of child-care.[3] Outsiders still too easily assume that a wife with a career is free to use her non-working time to fit into patterns of social interaction appropriate to full-time housewives, or that a continuous-career couple must be neglecting their children when in fact they have been able to develop a satisfactory pattern of child care.

By contrast, in the Russian situation referred to in the last chapter, the balance, not merely of political or administrative support but of public opinion, has swung over decisively to the side of women's careers. Where, as in the Soviet Union, most married women and in particular the vast majority of professionally qualified women are working, the mother who is in employment can find full understanding of her problems among her friends and neighbours. The full-time housewife, on the other hand, is forced into concealment and apology even if she has good reasons for staying at home. It seems that the point at which the balance tips lies somewhere

---

[1] Holter, H., Women's Occupational Situation in Scandinavia, *International Labour Review*, 1961, p. 389. See also the Swedish figures charted by Dahlström, *op. cit.*, p. 113.

[2] E.g. F. Zweig, *The Worker in an Affluent Society*, Heinemann, 1961, pp. 56-7.

[3] Below, Ch. IX.

between the higher women's work participation rates shown in the last chapter for parts of Eastern Europe – upwards of 70 per cent of married women in their forties in East Germany and the Czech region of Czechoslovakia, and 75 per cent of all women in this age group in the U.S.S.R. – and the much lower average rates, subject to exceptions for particular occupations and regions, still usual in the West.[1]

Whether the balance of support and opposition in a particular society favours or disfavours work for married women, families cannot ignore it:

'The family itself is always a part of some wider community. . . . This is still true where the family deliberately rejects, or is rejected by, the community, and where the relationship is thus one of withdrawal; the family may choose to spurn the community, but it cannot choose to deny its existence. . . . The individual family's place in these (cultural) systems whether objectively or subjectively assessed, can be ignored neither by the members of that family nor by anyone who tries to understand its internal relationships.'[2]

Over and above their friends and other outside contacts a married couple have to reckon with the attitudes and claims of their extended family, for the extended family remains important, thanks to cars and telephones, even in a world where people are no longer so tied to a particular district or social group.[3] If there is to be a change in the balance of support, someone must break away from existing patterns of activity and pioneer new ones. But pioneering is for pioneers, and not everyone is in a position to face the strains and breaking of relationships which it involves. A Czech study, strongly favourable to women's work, notes nevertheless that if, in a given society, the balance of support is in fact tipped against outside work by married women, it may often be best for child, mother, and the community to recommend a mother of young children to stay at home. This could be true, the study suggests, even if the family's circumstances are such that in Eastern Europe, where the balance of support is different, it would be thought right for the mother to work.[4]

When, then, can it be expected that the break-even point, at which the weight of custom and practice finally turns over on to the side

---

[1] Though the rates attained in one or two Western countries do overlap with those found in parts of Eastern Europe where participation has not gone so far (Table III.1 (iv)).

[2] J. and E. Newson, *Four Years Old in an Urban Community*, Allen and Unwin, 1968, p. 17.

[3] Cf. C. Rosser and C. Harris, *The Family and Social Change*, Routledge and Kegan Paul, 1965.

[4] Knoblochova and Knobloch, *op. cit.*, p. 85.

of the married woman who works, will be reached in the West? This point cannot be precisely defined. But with the rise in participation rates in a number of Western countries, including Britain, it looks as if the zone in which it lies is being approached. If this is true of any of these countries overall, it is likely to be still more true of professions and districts where the proportion of women working is already above each country's general standard.

The present somewhat mixed pattern of social support for married women workers in a country like Britain might be expected to, and does encourage the growth of specific, probably temporary, patterns of social relationships. A woman working in a professional or managerial job is unlikely in present conditions to meet either the diffused, relatively even level of support from her environment which she could expect in a country like East Germany or the degree of doubt and misunderstanding to be expected in countries where the participation rate of mature married women drops, as in Ireland or the Netherlands, to 5 per cent or 10 per cent. Support is likely to be available to her on a selective basis. A continuous-career couple might be expected to shape their network of contacts accordingly, whether consciously or unconsciously; for example, to concentrate their friendships among people not only from the same professional and social background – this would be expected in any case[1] – but with the same attitude to married women's work as themselves. This, as will be shown, is precisely what the British family case studies in the present enquiry have found.

But that is for the short run. For the longer run, the significant point is that in Western countries such as Britain participation rates for women, including older married women, seem to be approaching the level at which, as in Eastern Europe, to have a job becomes the norm. Support for the ideology of role segregation and of the housewife permanently at home is still widespread but has been falling, and there seems little prospect of this trend being reversed. The question is rather, how far will it go, and which of the other ideologies about family relationships and wives working will gain most ground? Will the strongest swing be towards the three-phase pattern, the job as complementary, continuous careers, or some multiple-pattern mixture of the three?

On the face of it, the swing for most of the able and highly quali-

---

[1] Cf. the findings by Inkeles and Bauer, *op. cit.*, p. 201, on friendship patterns in the Soviet Union. On present ambivalent attitudes to working or not working among housewives generally, see, e.g. E. Pfeil, 'Mutterabeit gestern und heute', pp. 137-138, in *Deutscher Verein für öffentliche und Private Fürsorge, Die Mutter in der Heutigen Gesellschaft*, 1964.

fied women with whom this study is concerned, given their strong career commitment, would seem likely to be towards a continuous-career or at least a three-phase pattern. The tendency for British graduates to adopt a three-phase pattern stands out clearly in Table III.3 (iii) (b). But it remains to be proved that the main swing is in either of these directions, for the figures just quoted to show high career commitment by highly qualified women could be consistent not only with continuous-career and three-phase patterns but with Junker's idea of the complementary job. High commitment to having a career does not necessarily imply full-time commitment, flat-out effort to reach the top, or priority for career over other interests even in the child-free phase of a three-phase cycle. Nor at present does it in fact do so in Western countries, any more than in Eastern Europe. The same higher qualified women who stressed to the Social Survey their demand for an opportunity to use their skills and qualifications turned out to show no strong interest in promotion or in further training. In fact they showed less interest in training opportunities than women with lower qualifications.[1] A substantial part of the work done by higher- as well as lower-qualified women is less than full-time. Married women doctors, for example, though the very great majority of them are working at any time, tend over their careers to put in only half the working time of a man or a single woman (Table III.3 (iii) (e) (iii)). This proportion may be dropping, though not necessarily by women doctors' own choice.[2] Though the proportion of women doctors who do *some* work appears to have risen over the last generation, the proportion who work part-time appears to have risen faster and the proportion who work full-time to have fallen (Table III.3 (iii) (e) (i) and (ii)).

A recent British study of part-time work by professional women notes that:

'One of the most important and surprising pieces of information to have come out of this survey is that the majority of women in it have no intention of returning to full-time work.'[3]

The women surveyed had developed a culture very like that which Junker had in mind. The accent laid respectively on work and family affairs varied from case to case, but neither activity was to be

---

[1] Table III.3 (ii).

[2] *Ibid*, and Robb-Smith, *op. cit.*, who notes that in the case of younger married women doctors the anticipated proportion of potential working time actually worked during their careers falls short both of what they would wish and of what women doctors in the same position achieved in the past.

[3] P. Williams, *Working Wonders*, Hodder & Stoughton, 1969, p. 104.

sacrificed to the other, and in particular there was no question of a full-time, overriding commitment to work.

'The women in this survey . . . want a multi-faceted life, and make the point over and over again that each different activity feeds them with stimulus and interest. They are doing what they find is possible, discovering how best to manage. And from the comments of their husbands it turns out that what is possible is a working activity, both domestic and professional, of such wide and energetic proportions that few men would dream of undertaking the equivalent. . . . The picture built up in the questionnaires is of extremely busy, often humorous, adaptable women, fast on their feet, somehow dovetailing the many different demands on them, and happy with their way of life.'[1]

There is no suggestion that these women lack commitment to their careers. Nor does it necessarily follow that they will be barred from top career achievement. The view quoted earlier from East Germany about the irrationality of the present organization of many top jobs applies equally to the West; it may well be more practicable than has been commonly thought hitherto to open a road towards the top for women with less than a full-time career commitment. That is one of the questions to be examined below. But for these women career commitment takes its place in a network of other interests and obligations, in and out of the family – for example a heavy commitment to social or political work – which have at least equal priority. Whatever level of achievement may be open to them now or in future, their careers will quite clearly remain in Junker's sense 'complementary'.

In the same way as these women show no sign of changing their present pattern of work, so also even the segregated-role pattern, though losing support, shows no sign of disappearing; particularly if it is taken to include not only cases where the wife is predominantly home-centred but those where, though not in employment, she carries a heavy load of voluntary social or political work.[2]

It seems, for example, to remain more strongly established in families where the husband works in a business bureaucracy than in those where he is in free professional or academic work.[3] Evidence

[1] R. Williams, *Working Wonders*, Hodder & Stoughton, 1969, p. 18.

[2] On voluntary work see e.g. Aregger, *op. cit.*, p. 47, and B. M. Rodgers, *A Follow-up Study of Social Administration Students of Manchester University*, Manchester, 1963, p. 16.

[3] See M. L. Helfrich, *The Social Role of the Executive's Wife*, Ohio State University, 1965, or the self-examination by wives of business leaders in the papers of the World Congress of the Christian Employers' Association

from a number of countries shows a tendency for wives to drop out of the work force when their husbands' income reaches high professional or managerial levels;[1] or, more precisely, for fewer wives with a given level of professional qualification to work than would do so if their husbands were earning less. The real significance behind findings like these has, however, to be checked, for the wife who gives up a formally separate career may still be working as a family helper in her husband's career. Cases where this happens shade over from the purely social support given by a wife who has an increasing role as hostess for her husband as he rises in his profession to the direct and close involvement in their husbands' careers of the wives of many parsons or of some independent businessmen. As hostess the wife may still be following a segregated-role pattern. Where she also becomes more directly involved it may be more correct to speak of a complementary-job or even a dual-career pattern.[2]

The question of how much support each pattern of attitudes to women's work can expect to gain thus remains an open one, and is one of the central issues with which later chapters are concerned.

b *Education, qualifications, and occupations*

Given a particular level of commitment to the work force, the career options open to a woman as to a man depend not only on ability but on qualifications. In Britain as in other Western countries the number of girls completing a full secondary education and proceeding to higher education has increased sharply over the last generation both absolutely and in relation to the size of the age group. By the later 1960s the proportion of girls staying at school to 17 or over had doubled compared to the mid-1950s. By 1965 the absolute number of girls staying to 17 exceeded the combined total of boys and girls who stayed ten years earlier. The number of girls staying to 17 is expected to double again by the 1980s (Table III.5 (a) (i)).

Though girls still lag behind boys, the growth in the proportion of the age group staying to 17 and obtaining two or more A levels – the minimum normal qualification for a university – has been greater

---

(U.N.I.A.P.A.C.), Brussels, 1968. Some of the conflicts arising are brought out in the paper in that series by C. Duboy, and by J. M. Pahl, 'Managers and their Wives', in *Marriage Guidance*, November 1968.

[1] E.g. for Britain, Aregger, *op. cit.*, p. 23; for U.S.A., *Handbook on Women Workers*, *op. cit.*, p. 29.

[2] Cf. the analysis of the roles open to an executive's wife in Helfrich, *op. cit.*, Ch. 6 (family-centred, community-centred, 'creative', consultant, career, student); and Aregger, *op. cit.*, p. 87.

for them than for boys. 'Bit by bit the sex gap is closing.'[1] The experience is that the great majority of girls as well as boys who stay and who obtain the minimum qualifications for university entrance, do in fact go on to one or other kind of full-time education (Table III.5 (a) (v)). By 1967 some 12·5 per cent of all girls in the relevant age group in Great Britain were entering full-time higher education, and this proportion is expected to rise substantially (Tables III.5 (a) (iv) (a) and (b)). For men and women together 609,000 places are likely to be needed in higher education in England and Wales in 1980-81 against 382,000 needed for 1971-72.[2]

Similar rises in the proportion of girls completing a full secondary education have taken place in other Western countries (Tables III.5 (b) (i) and (ii), III.5 (c) (i) (c), III.5 (d) (i) and (ii)). The figures for France and the U.S.A. are particularly striking. In France the proportion of girls qualifying in the very tough *baccalauréat* has risen steadily decade by decade until in the 1960s it caught up with that of boys. In the United States the number of girls graduating from high school has consistently exceeded the number of boys, and by 1964 the proportion of the relevant age group (both sexes together) who graduated reached 76 per cent. Data from the U.S.A., Germany, France and Sweden also show a rapid increase in the number of girls who proceed to higher education, absolutely and as a proportion of the age-group (Tables III.5 (b) (i), (iii) and (iv), (c) (ii) (a), (d) (i) and (ii), and (e)).[3]

So far, the educational picture in Western countries is encouraging for women's prospects of career success. But it has a number of shadows. In the first place the British figures show a tendency for girls, age for age, to achieve at least marginally less good results than boys in G.C.E. A level, and for a smaller proportion of women than of men to achieve first class honours at the universities (Table III.5 (a) (iii) and (vii)). The difference in G.C.E. performance among leavers at age 17 is, however, as has been said, expected to diminish, and in the universities women balance their low proportion of first class honours with a high proportion of second class degrees. In university faculties with a highly selected body of women students, for example medicine, women may regularly do better than men.[4]

---

[1] Layard, R., King, J., and Moser, C., *The Impact of Robbins*, Penguin, 1969.

[2] Layard *et. al., op. cit.*, p. 93.

[3] A number of Swedish data are summarized in *The Status of Women in Sweden. The Statistical Abstract of Israel*, 1968, Tables T/22 and T/31, shows that in 1966-67, 5,640 girls (Hebrew education) passed the matriculation examination against 4,948 boys, and in 1967-68, 10,072 women were studying for bachelor degrees in academic institutions against 11,260 men.

[4] E.g. the comment of the *Report of the Royal Commission on Medical Education*, Cmnd. 3569, 1968, para. 302: 'The work of women medical students is

Secondly, there is a tendency everywhere for boys' and men's persistence in education to exceed girls' in higher age groups, in more advanced education (these two of course commonly go together), and in part-time higher education, where persistence depends most heavily on the student's own drive. In France, Germany and the United States the tables show that the percentage of women students compares less well – though in France only marginally so – with that of men at college than at high school level. This also appears to be true in Sweden, though the gap is closing fast.[1] In Britain the Labour Mobility Survey of 1963 (Table III.5 (a) (xi)) showed that women's school and college qualifications tend more than men's to fall into the lower part of each range; O level rather than A level for school qualification, diploma or 'minor professional' rather than a degree at college level. In recent years the number of women entering higher studies (universities, further education and teacher training) has increased faster than the number of men – by 114 per cent against 91 per cent for entrants into full-time education in England and Wales, comparing 1967 with 1961.[2] But only a few years back, in the late 1950s and early 1960s, men entrants were increasing faster than women.[3] At the beginning of the 1960s, when the proportion of girls staying at school till 17 was about four-fifths of that of boys, the proportion proceeding to some kind of higher education was only one-third of that of boys (Table III.5 (a) (i) and (iv)). By far the greatest part of the difference arose because men were readier to seek higher education part time, on either a day or an evening basis. This point about part-time study applies also to postgraduate qualifications in a field like medicine. Though younger women doctors in Britain have, if anything, less difficulty than men with the examinations for their initial qualification, fewer of them go on to take postgraduate qualifications, and the women – especially the married women – tend to do less professional reading than the men.[4]

---

widely acknowledged to be better, on average, than that of the men students'. But A. G. W. Whitfield, 'Women Medical Graduates of the University of Birmingham 1959-63', British Medical Journal, 5th July 1969, notes that at Birmingham women medical students gain markedly fewer prizes, scholarships and distinctions than men, though about the same proportion obtain honours degrees.

[1] The Status of Women in Sweden, pp. 34-35.

[2] Layard and others, op. cit., p. 116

[3] Report of the Committee on Higher Education, Cmnd. 2154, 1963, p. 263. In full time day education men increased by 89 per cent in 1954-62 against 53 per cent for women; in part time day education by 96 per cent against 79 per cent. Women had a higher rate of increase than men only in universities (full time).

[4] Stanley, G. R., and Last, J. M., Careers of Young Medical Women, cyclostyled, 1968: Department of Social Medicine, University of Edinburgh; and Whitfield, op. cit.

At higher degree level women drop still further behind men, both in Britain and elsewhere. In 1965-66 women contributed a quarter of the first degree graduates in Britain, but only 9 per cent of those receiving higher degrees. Even among these, women took a larger share of master's degrees and a smaller share of doctorates (Table III.5 (a) (viii) and (ix)). Similar situations are found in America (Table III.5 (d) (iv), Sweden (Table III.5 (e)), and Israel.[1]

From the fact that women's interest in education and training tends to fade sharply once the period of training runs beyond under-graduate age and cuts into what are usually the first years of married life, it does not follow that it is impracticable to revive it later. There are obvious difficulties in providing renewed education and training for relatively immobile married women. But these difficulties have not prevented important developments in professional education and re-education for older women in a number of countries, perhaps most notably the United States, but also including Britain; especially, so far as Britain is concerned, in teaching. Drucker among others has pressed the case for a general reform of education, affecting men as well as women, whereby full-time school or college education would cease much sooner than is now usual for professionally quali-fied people, but education linked to and building on experience would continue up to or beyond retirement.[2] Men who spend their lives in a single professional field, he suggests, are likely to go stale well before retiring age; there is a case for opening the road to a new career for everyone in their forties or even fifties. Women, clearly, have an even greater interest in a reform on these lines than men.

The third shadow on the record of women's educational progress in Western countries in recent years is that Western women still tend much more than men, or than women in Eastern Europe, to concen-trate their interest in a few subject areas and to aim for a limited range of occupations. In English[3] schools, girls' sixth-form courses are concentrated heavily on Arts subjects, while boys divide them-selves more evenly between Arts and Science (Table III.5 (a) (ii)). In the universities (Table III.5 (a) (vi)) girls are practically absent from technology and less well represented than men in pure science. They are also somewhat under-represented in medicine, although here the

[1] *Statistical Abstract of Israel*, 1968, Table T/31: in 1967-68 women made up 47 per cent of bachelor degree students in academic institutions, but only 22 per cent of students for masters and doctoral degrees.

[2] Drucker, P. F., *The Age of Discontinuity*, Heinemann, 1969, Pt. IV.

[3] This comment would be much less true of Scottish schools, where in 1967 girls in sixth forms were divided almost equally between combined Science/Arts courses and pure Arts courses. *Report on The Flow of Candidates in Science and Technology into Higher Education*, Cmnd. 3541, 1968, p. 53.

number of women has been restricted by the policy of certain medical schools and not necessarily by women's own choice.[1] In the late 1950s and the first half of the 1960s the proportion of women students who took pure science increased, but this was offset by a fall in the proportion studying medicine. The proportion taking Arts or Social Studies actually increased.

Girls' interest in the humanities and in social studies rather than in science can be shown to have a strongly positive side, which is brought out in the Government Social Survey's 1968 report on *Young School Leavers*. Girls who left school at 17 or 18 appear in this report as sharing with men who left at the same age a strong, realistic interest in studies and activities likely to help in choosing and doing well in a career, but also as having wider general interests than the men. They tend to want broader courses and to be less preoccupied with examination success. They show more concern than the men with personal and moral development, with art and spare-time interests, and with general knowledge, travel, and a wide range of contacts away from home; as well as with home management.[2] Another study presents evidence that, if girls have reacted against science – and especially the physical sciences – this may be because science has too often been presented to them in too technical and material a light, leaving them with the impression that the choice between Arts and Science is 'people versus test-tubes'.[3]

But whatever its positive aspects, the tendency of women to acquire only a limited range of qualifications at school and university adds strength to the further tendency for them to concentrate their career choices in a limited range of occupations. A much higher proportion of girls than of men decide at the point where they leave school to train for teaching, and go direct into a teachers' college (Table III.5 (a) (iv)). Of those who go to university, a far higher proportion than among men, whether measured overall or faculty by faculty, also choose teaching for their career (Table III.5 (a) (viii)). A higher proportion of women than of men take jobs in other public services; the civil service, local government service, and the hospital service. The proportions practising medicine or entering publishing, entertainment, and other communication industries are at least

[1] See *Report of the Royal Commission on Medical Education*, Cmnd. 3569, 1968, paras 301-303.
[2] *Young School Leavers*, report of an inquiry carried out for the Schools Council by the Government Social Survey, *op. cit.* On travel, see Table III 5 (a) (viii). In every faculty, a higher proportion of British women graduates than of men take jobs overseas.
[3] Pheasant, J. H., *The Influence of the School Organisation and Curriculum on the Choice of Exam Subjects made by GCE Candidates*, London Ph.D. thesis, 1960.

125

within range of those found among men. On the other hand far smaller proportions of women than of men go into industry and commerce or into fields such as law, accountancy, and banking. Women scientists who do enter industry are more likely than men to do so because the job is a technical one for which their degree qualifies them, and less likely to enter as prospective administrators or managers: but this does not hold for entrants from Arts or Social Studies.[1] Overall, a survey in the mid-1960s showed more than two-thirds of the women graduates then working in Britain to be concentrated in teaching (mainly school teaching) and research, and a further 16 per cent in medicine and dentistry; only 15 per cent were in all other occupations together (Table III.5 (a) (x)). The similar contrast in Germany[2] between the concentration of women's occupations and the relatively wide spread of men's is brought out in Table III.5 (ii) (c) and (d).

It is a hen and egg question whether girls in Britain refrain from entering a wider range of non-traditional occupations because they do not have the qualifications for them, or do not seek the qualifications because they have no intention of entering these occupations. What is clear is that women cannot expect to enter these occupations, or at least to go far in them, until more of them do acquire the relevant qualifications. A recent survey of the directors of eighty-two British companies showed that 61 per cent had professional or academic qualifications of some kind, and three-quarters of the qualifications identified were of a kind, in engineering, accountancy and law, which few women gain.[3] Industrial surveys show both that the percentage of graduates among industrial managers has risen sharply and that two-thirds to four-fifths (according to the sample) of all

[1] The Psychological Research Centre, *Undergraduates and their Choice of Jobs*, 1968, Table E. This is the prospect as seen from women's own point of view. For the employer's angle see the comment of the Oxford University Appointments Board (Report for 1968) noted in Chapter I, pp. 20-21; a smaller proportion of the technical jobs in industry and commerce reported to the board in 1968 were closed to women than of the jobs open to general Arts graduates.

[2] See also for the U.S.A. Table III.5 (d) (v) and (vi); for France, III.5 (b) (iv) and for Sweden, III.5 (f). Table III.5 (g) gives comparative figures of women in non-traditional occupations in several countries. Figures for Israel are given in the *Statistical Abstract of Israel*, 1968, Tables T/25-T/30 (number of students or recipients of degrees in certain fields). Individual fields show divergences from one country to another. For example in Israel, where a law degree is normally a preparation for a professional practice and not (as in most of Western Europe) for fields such as general administration, women were 18 per cent of all students receiving bachelors degrees in law at the Hebrew University in 1967-68: contrast the figures in Table III.5 (g).

[3] Betts, R., 'Characteristics of British Company Directors', *Journal of Management Studies*, February, 1967.

graduates in management, including around 60 per cent of the graduates who reach top management and the board, are scientists or technologists.[1] Women are under-represented in the first of these fields and almost wholly absent in the second.

Some changes in the direction of women's qualifications and careers do certainly take place. Cambridge women graduates of 1952-53 spread their career choices over a markedly wider field than those of 1937-38.[2] Though the census of 1961[3] showed women to constitute only 7 per cent of the number of scientists and technologists in active work, it recorded at any rate a handful of women metallurgists and civil, mechanical, electrical and chemical engineers, and several thousand practising women scientists – mathematicians, biologists, chemists and physicists in that order – mainly in teaching, but with 4,700 in other fields. Women do find their way into industry, finance, and the law. A London Chamber of Commerce survey found a significant number of women executives 'in four occupations sometimes imagined to be male preserves – directors, accountants, company secretaries . . . and legal advisers'.[4] In work like that of computer programmers, systems analysts or market research women have made their way in significant numbers into new professional occupations which have not had time to become sex-typed and where there is a shortage of qualified staff. Changes over time in France and Sweden are brought out in Tables III.5 (b) (iv) and III.5 (f).

These changes, however, are small, and it does not seem that there is an automatic tendency in any Western country for increases in women's willingness to qualify for and enter non-traditional occupations to come fast enough to produce a major shift in the pattern of women's qualifications and employment even over a considerable number of years. In markets of all kinds buyers and suppliers tend to follow established channels unless a force exceeding some threshold of significance arises to compel a change. The level of the threshold varies from one market to another, but seems to be particularly high in labour markets, where social conventions reinforce the factors of trouble, cost and risk which hold back the exploration of new sources and outlets in markets of all kinds. This applies with particular force to the demarcation of men's and women's work and

[1] A number of studies are summarized in D. G. Clark, *The Industrial Manager*, Business Publications, 1961.

[2] Craig, *op. cit.*, p. 71.

[3] See also Chapter I, Table I.2 (Census of 1966), where however the figures quoted are for technologists and scientists classified as such, as apart, e.g. from those classified as school or university teachers.

[4] London Junior Chamber of Commerce, *Women Executives*, 1966.

to differentials related to sex and skill.[1] It seems that in many non-traditional occupations in Western countries no force to increase the recruitment of women has yet made itself felt strongly enough to pass the threshold of significance. Though, for example, there have been women engineers in the leading Western countries for most of two generations, the proportion of women among engineering students in countries such as Britain, the U.S.A., Canada, Sweden and Belgium towards the end of the 1960s remained of the order of 1 per cent, and was not significantly different from the proportion of women among engineers already practising.[2]

The forces underlying the sex-typing of occupations run deep. They originate in early childhood,[3] and are reflected in the schools. A German study notes how even in newer school textbooks women are rarely presented as having careers at all, let alone careers outside traditional fields.[4] In Sweden it has been official policy in the last few years to modify school-teaching so as to promote individual rather than sex-typed subject and career choices by both boys and girls:

'Schools should aim at making it clear to pupils that the differences between individuals of the same sex are greater than any average difference between the sexes as a whole. Their lessons in domestic science and civics should leave pupils in no doubt as to the equal responsibilities of husband and wife in the home. Textbooks and other teaching aids ought not to further entrench traditional ideas concerning the separate role of the sexes but on the contrary . . . actively combat them.'[5]

When, however, in the school year 1966-67 Swedish pupils were asked to choose occupations for a spell of practical vocational experience, boys still put engineering, building, the metal trades, and the electrical trades and similar technical fields at the top of their lists, while girls chose health and medical services, teaching, and commercial and office work.[6]

An American study suggests that no very powerful pressure towards non-traditional occupations can be expected from women graduates

---

[1] Fogarty, M. P., *The Just Wage*, Geoffrey Chapman, 1961, Ch. 5; and *Personality and Group Relations in Industry*, Longmans, 1956, Ch. 8, (esp. p. 199). See also P. W. S. Andrews, *Manufacturing Business*, Macmillan 1949, Chs. 5 and 6.

[2] *Proceedings of the Second International Conference of Women Engineers and Scientists*, Cambridge, 1967.

[3] See the references on p. 149, footnote 1.

[4] Sollwedel, I., 'Das Mädchen und Frauenbild in den Lesebüchern der Volksschulen', in *Informationen für die Frau*, March 1968.

[5] *The Status of Women in Sweden*. p. 29.

[6] *Ibid*, pp. 30-32.

themselves. Alice Rossi found only 7 per cent of recent American women graduates to qualify as 'pioneers', defined as women whose long-range career goals are in predominantly masculine fields.[1] Most of the remainder were 'traditionals'. They had long-range career goals, but preferred to confine them to fields where women predominate. A minority were 'homemakers', aiming to be full-time housewives, and even less likely than the 'traditionals' to pioneer.

How far, in the face of conditions like these, it is likely to be practicable or desirable to turn the interests of well-qualified women towards non-traditional fields will be taken up again in later chapters. Where, in particular, is the drive and entrepreneurship needed for this purpose to come from in the absence of automatic forces likely to be effective for change? Can we, for example – this will be a question for Chapter VI – detect signs in Britain today, in spite of Rossi's findings, of a new and more 'pioneering' attitude among younger women graduates themselves?

c *Achievement: jobs at the top*

Given that men still tend to have an edge over women in qualifications relevant to top jobs, and that even highly qualified women tend to participate in the work force somewhat less fully than similarly qualified men, either of two consequences might follow for women's prospects of reaching top jobs. Women might be under-represented at the top by some fraction corresponding to their lower average participation rate and qualifications: that is, to the proportion which women contribute to the total time worked by men and women together in highly qualified occupations, or to the proportion which they constitute of the holders of degrees or other qualifications for entering these occupations. Or they might be under-represented by some greater fraction; on the basis that only those who participate full-time and at full pressure, and are prepared to seek qualifications beyond the entry level, are in the race for the top at all. On this second model there would be plenty of women in the basic grades of professional and administrative work, but the proportion of women would taper very sharply towards the top; quite apart from any further restrictions that might be imposed by prejudice and discrimination.

The second model, on the evidence quoted in the last chapter, applies substantially in Eastern Europe. It is also the common model in the West. In Britain the Inland Revenue's statistics of incomes charged under Pay-As-You-Earn – wages, salaries, Forces pay, and

[1] Rossi, A. S., 'Who wants women scientists?', in *Women and the Scientific Professions*, M.I.T. Symposium, M.I.T., 1965, pp. 79-80.

certain pensions and fees – show that women are overwhelmingly outnumbered in the higher income ranges.

Women as per cent of All P.A.Y.E. income earners in each range, 1964-65[1]

Income Range £	Men	Women	Women as per cent
	000s		of all in each range
5,000 and over	47	0·9	2
3,000-4,999	131	5	4
2,000-2,999	313	16	5
800-1,999	8,317	524	6
500-799	4,652	1,599	25
275-499	1,909	3,359	64
Total	15,369	5,504	26

The Inland Revenue figures are subject to a number of qualifications. More women than men work part-time, and this must tend to increase the proportion of women in the lower income brackets. Women are liable to receive lower pay than men for the same job, and in occupations where women predominate the general level of pay tends to be low. For these reasons, lower pay for a woman does not necessarily mean less responsibility. In certain professions women's relatively poor showing at the top may reflect neither unequal pay for the same job nor a true shortfall in achievement, but rather a tendency to see certain types of work in which women happen to specialize as less valuable to the consumer than they actually are. In universities, for example, there is evidence that women tend to be marginally more interested than men in teaching and less in administration and (less markedly) research;[2] but it is research and administration which tend, whether for men or for women, to be the roads to high rank and pay.

The general impression given by the Inland Revenue figures is, however, correct, and is confirmed by the more specific figures for Britain, France, Germany, and the U.S.A. summarized in Table III.6. The particular figures chosen are by way of illustration; figures for

[1] Report of the Commissioners of Inland Revenue for 1965-66, Cmnd. 3200, 1967, p. 76.

[2] For Britain see I. Sommerkorn, *The Position of Women in the University Teaching Profession in England*, London University Ph.D., 1966, pp. 119-121 and 132-146. For the U.S.A. see J. Bernard, *Academic Women*, Meridian Books, 1966, Chs. 9-12; but also the strong reservations by R. J. Simon, S. M. Clark and K. Galway, 'The Woman Ph.D. – A Recent Profile', in *Social Problems*, Autumn 1967.

other occupations and countries tell the same story.[1] Everywhere, whether in industry and commerce, in national or local government administration, in universities, or in hospitals women's share of posts tapers sharply towards the top. This is true, though somewhat less so, even in an occupation such as teaching where there is a high proportion of older women (Table III. 6 (v) (a)). At the very top, women's proportion of posts tends everywhere to be minimal.

There are of course certain predominantly feminine occupations which women have in effect to themselves, along with the controlling positions within them, for example that of a general (not necessarily a mental) hospital matron (Table III.5 (a) (xii)[2]). Not surprisingly, women hold a relatively high proportion of managerial posts in occupations where a high proportion of women are employed. Two-thirds of all women 'managers, large establishments', in England and Wales in 1961 (Table III.6 (i) (a)) were in a small group of occupations where they constituted 20 per cent to 50 per cent of all managers as the Census defines them; in education, medical services, retailing, hotels and catering, laundries and dry-cleaning, and 'miscellaneous services'. Another fifth were in industries such as textiles, clothing, food, and paper and printing, and in wholesaling and in national and local government. All other fields together accounted for only one-seventh of women managers, and in these other fields only one manager in twenty-five to thirty was a woman.

But the professions which women have to themselves tend to be in a functional or supporting position, like that of a nurse, rather than a position of overall control; and, generally, women tend to be in support roles rather than line or general management. If they reach senior positions, it is likely to be as specialists rather than as general directors. British women university teachers meet little discrimination up to the level of Senior Lecturer or Reader; the line tends to be drawn between these senior but not usually managerial posts and the authoritative role of a professor.[3] In industry and commerce a woman is more likely to become a staff manageress or buyer than the manager of a large store. She is more likely to reach a senior position in scientific or market research or as a systems analyst than to become the manager of a works. Women doctors' interests may take them into any area of medicine, but those of them who obtain postgraduate qualifications are less likely than men to do so in the

[1] E.g. Holter, *loc. cit.*, p. 393, for Norway.
[2] See also on this the proposals of the Committee on Senior Nursing Staff Structure, H.M.S.O., 1966.
[3] This point is accurately perceived by women university teachers themselves. See I. Sommerkorn, *The Position of Women in the University Teaching Profession in England*, London University Ph.D., 1966, p. 155.

toughly competitive and prestige-giving fields from which the leaders of the profession tend to be drawn and more likely to qualify in 'minor specialities'.[1]

Women who do reach the top in present conditions in a country such as Britain tend to be untypical of women in general in ways related not necessarily to their ability but to their motivation and to the social pressures to which they are subject. Women graduates today usually expect to take a career break, or at any rate to drop from full to part time, during the period when they have small children. The road to the top is not absolutely barred for women who follow this pattern. The British Federation of University Women found in the middle 1960s that 5 per cent of women graduates with interrupted careers nevertheless reached salaries of £2,000 or more, and a very few passed £3,000. But of women in the same sample with uninterrupted careers 15 per cent reached £2,000 and 4 per cent reached £3,000.[2] Married women with interrupted careers accounted for less than a fifth of the women executives in the London Chamber of Commerce's enquiry,[3] even at the modest level of salaries included, down to less than £1,000 a year. More than three-fifths of the women covered in that enquiry were unmarried. The only sub-group which came near to matching the normal time-table of women's lives was the company directors, of whom two-thirds were married and over half had interrupted their careers. It is significant that this is the group in which marriage and inheritance rather than straightforward promotion is likely to have played the greatest part in getting to the top.

It does not appear that there is at this time any clear or strong tendency in Britain, or in most other Western countries, for the proportion of those women who enter highly qualified professions and who then go on to achieve top posts to increase. The position remains as set out in Chapter I. Following the removal of barriers to women's entry into a number of professions such as architecture, engineering or the Administrative Civil Service around the time of the First World War – earlier in a few professions, such as medicine – a limited number of women entered these professions. Among these few, not surprisingly, there was a relatively high proportion of 'pioneers' in Alice Rossi's sense, who not merely entered but persisted very much as a man might have done, many of them remaining unmarried. Informants in the present enquiry remember these women as the 'battleaxe generation'. In due course, the women who persisted in this way began to appear at the top; in small numbers before

[1] Stanley and Last, *op. cit.*, Whitfield, *op. cit.*
[2] Aregger, *op. cit.*, Table XII.
[3] London Junior Chamber of Commerce, *op. cit.*, App. 3.

1940,[1] and in increasing numbers thereafter as more of them acquired the necessary seniority in professions where the gates were opened around 1920.

But at the present time, leaving aside the accidents of marriage or other relationships which might bring a woman to the top of a family business otherwise than on the normal line of promotion, it seems on the face of it that the proportion of professionally qualified women likely to climb a career ladder in the style which leads to the top on traditional masculine lines is unlikely to be as great as it was in that older generation. The age of marriage has fallen and the likelihood of marrying has increased among professional people as in other social groups.[2] This carries with it the prospect of a greater incidence of career breaks than in the older generation, though with the difference that the break today tends to be at the birth of the first child and not at marriage.[3]

It does not follow that the prospects of increasing the proportion

---

[1] See for example the data on doctors' careers in the 1930s in Kettle, *loc. cit.*

[2] In 1931, 41 per cent of women aged 25-29 in England and Wales were single; in 1966 this figure dropped to 13 per cent. At age 35-39 the proportion still single fell from 21 per cent to 8·5 per cent. In the next few years the trend towards earlier marriage will be encouraged by demography. Women marry men on the average two or three years older than themselves, so that when the number of births falls, as it did from 1947 to 1955, a relatively small number of women born in year X+3 find themselves matched twenty years later with a larger number of men born in year X. After 1955 the number of births rose from year to year so that by the later 1970s the situation will be reversed and women of marriageable age will find themselves outnumbering men. Highly educated women tend to marry later than women in general, but are tending like them to marry earlier than in the past. At the Census of 1961, 11 per cent of all women in England and Wales aged 30-34 were unmarried, but 27 per cent of women doctors. But whereas only 18 per cent of the women doctors who qualified from 1920 to 1929 were married within two years of qualifying, 48 per cent of those who qualified in 1955-59 were married by that stage. As many as 37 per cent of those who qualified in the 1920s were still unmarried in 1962. 55 per cent of teachers with a postgraduate diploma who started teaching in 1936 were unmarried at age 30, but only 37 per cent of those who started in 1949. Data from Censuses; J. A. Rowntree, *On the Falling Age of Marriage and Decrease of Celibacy*, European Population Conference (Council of Europe), 1966, Paper C8; Ministry of Education, *Statistics of Education 1964*, Pt. II, Table I; *Women in Medicine*, Office of Health Economics, 1966, p. 27; R. K. Kelsall; *Women in Teaching*, H.M.S.O., 1963, Table 12b; see also Aregger, *op. cit.*, pp. 9-10; B. Rodgers, *A Follow-up Study of Social Administration Students of Manchester University*, Manchester, 1963, pp. 19, 31-32, P.E.P., Graduate Wives, (*Planning 361*) (summarizing a study by Judith Hubback).

[3] Aregger, *op. cit.*, pp. 19-24. Among women graduates in Britain covered by Aregger's study who had interrupted their careers, 60 per cent of those aged 65 or more gave marriage as the reason for the break and only 17 per cent children, whereas of those aged 25-34 only 32 per cent mentioned marriage but 55 per cent children.

of women in top jobs must be written off. Face impressions may be misleading. As will be argued especially in Part III, continuous-career patterns of marriage could become more widespread spontaneously or could be encouraged to do so. Action could be taken to develop a pioneering spirit among more women; this will be raised particularly in Chapter XI. Career patterns and job specifications could be modified – this will be considered particularly in Chapter XII – so as to give more chance of reaching the top to women who have career breaks and spells of part-time work, or who cannot accept unlimited overtime as a condition of promotion. That would be equivalent to switching from model (2) of the pair with which this section began to model (1). If that change were made without otherwise changing women's educational and career patterns, women would continue to hold a smaller proportion of top than of all jobs, for their average qualifications and average availability for work would fall short of those of men and their careers would still be over-concentrated in particular occupational fields. The tendency for women's share in jobs to taper off almost to nothing at the top would, however, be far less strong than now. The chance of reaching the top for the woman who did obtain relevant qualifications and enter an appropriate field, but did not wish to sacrifice her family life to her career, would be greatly increased. How far it is practicable and economic to bring this about will be the central issue of Part IV.

Chapter IV

The Experience of Western Countries – Emergence of a New Accent

DISCRIMINATION NOT THE CENTRAL ISSUE FOR
THE LONG RUN

In reviewing the experience of Western countries it becomes increasingly evident that there is a gap, or rather a change of character, between the short-term and long-term problems which have to be faced. The issues which arise in the short run are largely those of discrimination and of overcoming outdated beliefs. In Western countries, as in Eastern Europe, informal beliefs and practices inherited from the past often still stand in the way of women who wish to combine a career with family life. In addition, as a result of the piecemeal and *ad hoc* development of the movement of women into work and the absence of clear lines of policy, open and formal discriminations against women continue in the West in a way which would not be tolerated in Eastern Europe. It is still common in Britain to find women refused equal pay, the chance to compete for traditionally male jobs, or the right to access to executive clubs or dining rooms.[1] Here and now, discriminations like these constitute an important problem, and are rightly a first target for reformers.

These, however, are historical survivals; support for them is crumbling, and in the not so very distant future they seem likely to lose much of their importance. Equal pay has become the accepted policy of the European Economic Community and of the public services of Britain and the United States, and now also, under The Equal Pay Act of 1970, of the private sector in Britain.[2] The idea that most women are transients who do or should disappear

[1] See Ch. I, p. 21, for examples of restraint on competing for certain jobs. The occupational studies reported below in Part IV threw up a number of cases where women are more or less formally refused consideration for jobs in certain areas (especially general and production management), or refused access to executives' normal social facilities.

[2] See also the statement on *Equal Pay for Women* issued by the Institute of Personnel Management in March 1969; and P. Pinder, *Women at Work*, P.E.P., 1969.

from the work force on marriage – implying that they are not worth considering for lengthy training or long-range careers – has been undermined by both research and experience. Older married women, especially those with high qualifications, are flocking back into the work force. Research, which will be summarized below, has demolished the idea that for a mother to work is necessarily damaging to her children or her marital relations. In particular circumstances it may be; but, equally, in other circumstances the effects of a mother's employment has been shown to be altogether favourable.

As women's participation in the work force rises and the range of professions or levels of work from which they are barred becomes smaller, it has become harder to defend such restrictions as remain or even to find public defenders of them at all. Whatever may be said in offices or round lunch tables, fewer and fewer men are prepared to go on public record with dismissals of women's suitability for professional and managerial posts like those collected from certain British managers by Brock,[1] or like the resounding declaration of a German professor, about 1960, that a woman giving a professorial lecture is out of place; lecturing is a secondary sexual characteristic[2].

Restrictions on entry into particular professions have become hard to uphold in the light not only of women's demonstrated performance in nearly all professions in an individual country such as Britain but of the differences which exist both within Western countries and between them, as well as between the West and the East. If Denmark can have 70 per cent of women dentists, and a dental service which is recognized in many respects to be of outstanding efficiency,[3] it becomes hard to see any technical or professional reason for limiting Britain to 7 per cent (Table III.5 (g)). Brock's study of industrial firms in Britain found a range of responsible jobs in fields such as personnel management, production management, buying, work study and sales and commercial work for which managers in some firms thought women unsuitable, while in other firms women were in fact doing these jobs to their firms' satisfaction.[4]

In contacts with large employers during the present enquiry little hesitation was found in admitting that women may have the potential for top jobs at least as individual performers, leaders of small

[1] N. Seear, V. Roberts, and J. Brock, *A Career for Women in Industry*, Oliver & Boyd, 1964, esp. p. 80.

[2] H. Anger, *Probleme der Deutschen Universität*, Mohr, Tübingen, 1960, p. 481. Anger's study of German universities is the most formidable quarry of anti-feminist quotations – by Anger's informants, not by him as author – turned up by the P.E.P. enquiry.

[3] Cf. evidence quoted by P. Kaim-Caudle, *Dental Services in Ireland*, Economic and Social Research Institute, 1969.

[4] Seear, Roberts, and Brock, *op. cit.*

groups, or in staff roles. Doubts still tend to be expressed over women in senior managerial as apart from professional and specialist work. But these doubts too are being eroded in a number of ways.

It is now possible to point, in the West as well as in Eastern Europe, to many women who have in fact proved themselves effective as directors and top managers, in a wide range of occupations. Those who have done so by climbing up normal ladders of promotion tend, as has been said, to have been even more exceptional than men who have achieved similar positions, because of the greater difficulties which women seeking promotion have hitherto had to face. There is also, however, the evidence of what might be called the 'catapulted' women, those who reach the top by some accident of family succession and without special strain. It does not seem that these women, with their more normal family life and less ruthlessly selected personal characteristics, perform in a significantly different way from what might be expected of, say, a younger son who took over a family business in the same circumstances. The conclusion of a German study of women heads of businesses is that though some differences can be noted between the performance and attitudes in top jobs of women and men, and between those of women who reached the top by different routes, the resemblances are in each case overwhelmingly more important than the differences.[1] It will be shown below that the conclusion from British evidence is similar.[2]

New thinking about the nature of management, and the qualities which it requires in the technically advanced and swiftly changing conditions of a modern economy, have underlined the value for top management not only of those qualities in which women tend to overlap with men but of those traditionally distinctive of women. Evidence on this also will be considered below. In situations requiring complex change and group consensus on it, distinctively 'feminine' qualities seem at least as likely to be effective as those traditionally developed in men. For present-day top management, situations of just these kinds are increasingly important.

At still another level it can today be argued that, over the years, the evidence to disprove women's ability to fill senior posts has so often been shown to be confused and contradictory, and *a priori* arguments against women's capacity have so often collapsed when put to a practical test, that today the burden of proof rests with anyone who argues that women cannot be found with the ability to fill some position hitherto filled by men. The occupational studies in the present enquiry – the Administrative Civil Service is a particularly good example – show how time after time resistance was put

---

[1] H. Hartmann, *Die Unternehmerin*, Westdeutscher Verlag, 1968.
[2] Chapter XI.

up to the appointment of women to a certain managerial or professional post, but proved to have no substance when some accident of personal pioneering, political pressure or labour market shortage brought it about that a woman was in fact appointed.

In so far as the remaining restrictions on women's entry into particular fields or levels of work are formal and open, experience has shown that it is relatively easy to compel their removal once the will to do so is there. The British Civil Service has achieved complete formal equality of opportunity for women at all levels. The American Federal Civil Service swept away at one blow a large number of job specifications requiring that only men be appointed, simply by asking the appointing agency in every case to state the reasons why this requirement was made.[1] Equal Employment Opportunity legislation in America has also been effective in getting rid of many formal and open discriminations in job advertisements, collective contracts, and conditions of promotion or appointment.

Informal discrimination is of course a more difficult matter. When it is considered along with those formal restrictions which remain, it is clear that to remove the restrictive legacies of the past will still take a massive effort. The size of this effort should not be underestimated, particularly as it is required now and not in some distant future for which long preparation could be made. But the further one looks ahead, the clearer it becomes that the leading edge of the debate on women's careers in Western countries needs now to be elsewhere.

THE CENTRAL ISSUE: NOT ABOUT ADMITTING WOMEN TO EXISTING STRUCTURES, BUT ABOUT ADAPTING STRUCTURES TO WOMEN'S PRESENCE IN THEM

As the perspective lengthens and more consideration is given to long-term issues, the accent shifts from the negative task of removing obstacles to women's entry into a world of work designed for and by men, to the more positive aim of adapting both work and family life to the presence in the world of work of women as well as men. The debate in the past about removing restraints on women's admission to one or another occupational or political role tended to proceed on an assumption – unchallenged, or challenged only by far-out thinkers or at the level of rhetoric – that these roles themselves would not be much changed in the process. To a substantial extent the same was true even of roles within the family. Though traditional patterns of family life and of girls' upbringing were expected to, and did, change in many ways, it tended still to be assumed that men's career paths would continue as before and that the division of

---

[1] Report of the Committee on Federal Employment, *op. cit.*, p. 17.

household roles would normally follow the segregated-role pattern.

Today it is precisely on this point that the question of women and top jobs is beginning to centre. To remove restrictions while leaving occupational and family roles basically as they were opened the path to the top for a few unusual women. But this was a limited achievement. 'Average' or 'typical' women, with husbands and children and with life cycles, interests and abilities different from those of average or typical men, can find employment of some sort in a society where the division of roles in the household and the recruitment practices of employers remain fairly close to traditional segregated-role lines. They are likely to be barred, however, even in the absence of formal discrimination, from many of the senior and responsible jobs to which women of the same ability but with a more exceptional life cycle can have access. The figures in Chapter III show that this is in fact the usual pattern. The question now is: how far will it be of advantage to society, including both men and women, to revise household roles and employment practices so as to give these 'average' women their chance of a full career to the top? Should career patterns be altered so as to give women who follow a three-phase or complementary job pattern more chance of reaching the top, or can family patterns be altered to make a continuous-career pattern more practicable for highly qualified women with family responsibilities? If so, how is it to be done?

In trying to answer this question the long-term issues which remain to be clarified in Western countries – as apart from the immediate problem of discrimination – seem remarkably like those found in Eastern Europe. The long-term obstacle to women's advancement into high-level careers in Western countries is *not*, as has been shown, that highly qualified women are lacking in career commitment. Their career commitment is serious, and at a level far above that of less qualified women, though still tending to fall somewhat short of men's. It is *not* that women are excluded from education up to undergraduate or basic professional level. The percentage of women who take advantage of such education remains smaller in a country like Britain than the percentage of men, but has been rising steadily. It is *not*, as has just been argued, that women with the potential for top jobs cannot be found. The point is rather that the same attention has not yet been given to weaving women's careers into the customs and practice of occupations and of the family – including the activities of men as well as women – as has been given to the careers of men. The problems important for the long run are, as in Eastern Europe, those of reconciling high-pressure careers for women with child care and other family responsibilities; of overload through carrying both a home and an outside job; of re-thinking what it means to be a man or a woman in the new conditions created by women's careers; and of the clash between women's life cycles and career patterns designed to fit the life cycles of men. All these problems will remain even when discrimination has gone.

The facts are complicated, situations are varied, and Western countries have a confusion of competing ideologies about women's high-level careers. The problem is not one of choosing between straightforward alternatives such as discrimination and non-discrimination. It is to define a variety of realistic options, backed by practical understanding of what each implies and by the measures needed to make each effective, as models which men and women can use in their differing individual circumstances, and round which a range of public policies can be built.

a *What are to be the norms of child care and marital relationships, and what conditions do they impose on men's as well as women's careers?*

In a study by the British Federation of University Women of the attitudes of married women graduates who consider returning to employment,[1] child care proved to be the most urgent consideration.

'The major preoccupation of these married women graduates was the welfare of their children; this outweighed all other considerations. There were widespread misgivings about the effect on the children of the mother's return to work, but there was also a good deal of disagreement among the women about the likelihood of its having bad effects. By no means all would agree with those whose attitude was that only the mother can properly look after her children and that any substitute, however competent, can be only a poor second best and involves a risk of causing emotional disturbances in the children. . . . Other women would be prepared to engage someone to look after the children, especially when they feel that it is desirable that the children should have more contacts both with adults and with other children. These mothers do, however, need to be sure that whoever looks after the children is suitable and competent and would be good for them, and this uncertainty acts as an impediment to a return to work.'

Other studies, notably in America,[2] have underlined a further set of questions about the influence of women's careers not so much on parent-child relations as on relations between husbands and wives themselves.

In this whole area research in the last few years has shifted the

[1] Aregger, *op. cit.*, pp. 85-86.
[2] E.g. R. O. Blood and D. M. Wolfe, *Husbands and Wives*, Free Press, 1960.

140

accent of discussion significantly.[1] Fifteen or twenty years ago it was common to meet statements stressing on Kelly's lines that for a wife to work is likely to harm her relationship with her husband, or flat statements such as Bowlby's 'the mother of young children is not free, or at least should not be free, to earn'.[2] Today a much more variegated picture has emerged. The category 'mother working' no longer appears very useful in forecasting relationships in a family. It is the circumstances of her work that are all-important.

The effects of a mother's employment on her children of school age and above, and on her relations with her husband, may be more or less favourable according among other things to whether it is usual in a particular district or social group for married women to work; to whether the wife herself has been working long enough to have the problems of reconciling her job and her family in control; to her attitude to her job; to her educational level and her social class, which correlates with levels of education, income and capacity to take responsibility and solve problems; to her job level relative to her husband's;[3] to her husband's own competence in and attitude

[1] See e.g. *Deprivation of Maternal Care*, World Health Organization 1962, which follows up J. Bowlby, *Maternal Care and Mental Health*, World Health Organization 1952; reviews of largely American research material in M. L. and L. W. Hoffman (eds), *Review of Child Development Research*, Russell Sage Foundation, 1964; F. I. Nye and L. W. Hoffman, *The Employed Mother in America*, Rand McNally, 1963; I. Stolz, 'Effects of Maternal Employment on Children', *Child Development*, 1960; and A. F. Siegel and N. B. Haas, The Working Mother— A Review of Research, *Child Development*, 1963; British studies such as C. Heinicke, 'Some Effects of Separating Two-Year-Old Children from the Parents', *Human Relations*, 1956; J. W. B. Douglas and J. M. Blomfield, *Children under Five*, George Allen & Unwin, 1968, and *The Home and the School*, MacGibbon & Kee, 1964; S. Yudkin and A. Holme, *Working Mothers and their Children*, Michael Joseph 1963; T. W. Moore, Children of Full-time and Part-time Mothers, *International Journal of Social Psychiatry*, 1964, and *The Outcome of Full-time and Daily Substitute Care of Pre-Schoolchildren*, British Association for the Advancement of Science, Section J, 1967; and J. Jones, 'Social Class and the Under-Fives', *New Society*, Dec. 22, 1966; kibbutz studies by E. M. Spiro, *Children of the Kibbutz*, Harvard, 1958; A. I. Rabin, *Growing up in the Kibbutz*, Springer, 1965; P. B. Neubauer (ed.), *Children in Collectives*, Thomas, 1965; Y. Amir, *The Effectiveness of the Kibbutz-Born Soldier* (typescript), 1968; Y. Amir in *Human Relations*, Vol. 21, 1969; B. Bettelheim, *The Children of the Dream*, Thames & Hudson, 1969; and references to German studies in Junker, *op. cit.*, and *Die Mutter in der Heutigen Gesellschaft*, Deutscher Verein für öffentliche und private Füsorge, 1964 (esp. the article by E. Pfeil), and R. König, Die Stellung der Frau in der Modernen Gesellschaft, *Gynäkologie und Geburtshilfe*, 1968, I: and the Scandinavian studies in Dahlström, *op. cit.*, especially Ch. 3 by P.O. Tiller.

[2] Bowlby, *op. cit.*, p. 91.

[3] This does not necessarily refer to difficulties arising from the wife having a superior job. At least one study indicates that a wide discrepancy the other way – the wife's level far below the husband's – can also be damaging.

to his work and family roles – this will be explored further in Part III – and to whether she is working full- or part-time. On this last point, there is research support for the view of *Working Wonders* that for many women part-time work permits a combination of roles with more positive value both for the women themselves and for their families than any other. There is also, however, evidence that highly-qualified middle-class women are more likely than women with fewer personal and monetary resources to have the capacity to achieve an equally positive combination of work and family roles while carrying a full-time job.[1]

If women who wish to work, whether because it is socially customary or because of their own career commitment, are held back from it, the evidence is that the results are likely to be damaging to their families as well as themselves. The reverse also holds; damage is likely to result if mothers who see (and may objectively have) good reasons for not working are nevertheless forced into work. This tells in favour of employment for highly qualified women, whose career commitment and capacity to cope with the problems of combining a family and a career are likely to be high. From another point of view, however, whereas mothers who are forced into employment can at least adopt a matter-of-fact, guilt-free, attitude to it – precisely because of its inevitability – the middle-class wife who works from choice may feel much greater tension and guilt over possible neglect of her family, and this may adversely affect her family as well as herself.

Mothers' employment tend to have positive value for the girls in their families; girls tend to become more self-reliant, to be less dependent, and to grow up with a wider range of adult models in mind. The evidence suggests on the other hand that boys may become over-dependent. But for boys the influence of the mother working is much more likely to be marginal. Recent research lays increasing stress on the importance of the role of the father for both boys and girls, but for boys in particular. Where a mother's work appears to be damaging to the boys in her family the right diagnosis may be that the root of the damage is not the mother's work but the absence of the father or his inadequacy in his role either in the family or in his job. A father's absence or inadequacy may lead, among other things, to over-dependence on the mother, and this in turn to 'compensatory masculinity'. Lacking a reliable masculine model, a boy may in that case grow up without a clear understanding of what masculinity means; feel that his masculinity has to be proved and tend to express it aggressively; and himself run into marriage difficulties later on.[2]

[1] See especially Douvan in Nye and Hoffman, *op. cit.*

[2] See, besides the other references quoted, an Irish study by I. Hart on 'The Social and Psychological Characteristics of Institutionalized Young Offenders in

Because the father is absent or inadequate, the mother in such a case may have to work. But this, in so far as it has negative effects, may be no more than an extra complication in a situation of which it is not the cause; and its effect can be positive and at least make a bad situation better. If the fact that the mother works encourages the father to reduce his work and other outside commitments and participate more in his family, its effects may be particularly positive.

'It is surprising how society has accepted with strange equanimity the fact that fathers may hardly appear at all as members of their families except in a state of physical exhaustion.'[1]

As regards children under school age, increasingly fine distinctions are now made as to the circumstances in which separation of a child from its mother is liable to be damaging. Where there is stable care, whether by an individual or through a group such as an Israeli kibbutz, it does not seem that any lasting damage, or indeed any damage at all, need follow from the mother's absence from even a small child for part of the day. Unstable care by a succession of individuals, or prolonged absence of the mother, as where a child is in a hospital or other institution, or, of course, care of poor quality is a different matter, and here the risk of damage is high. Even where stable care is concerned there are conditions to be made. Many for example would argue that, though the larger family or community group can help in care, there must be one or at most a pair of main mother-figures, one of them preferably being (as in a kibbutz) the mother herself. Margaret Mead has, however, argued from cross-cultural studies that over the childhood period as a whole, given the right conditions, care shared among a large group may well yield better results – depending on the particular society and its needs – than care focused heavily on the mother.[2] The highly practical assessments of kibbutz and non-kibbutz recruits by the Israeli Army appear to bear this out.[3]

Ireland', *Administration*, Summer 1968; and his article in *Economic and Social Review*, Autumn 1969.

[1] Yudkin and Holme, *op. cit.*, p. 165.
[2] In *Deprivation of Maternal Care, op. cit.*
[3] Amir, *op. cit.* One so far unpublished study suggests that the point may be that a kibbutz upbringing tends to make little difference either way to children's basic personality structure, but does, like a good English boarding school, tend to convey skills and understandings useful when initiative is required in a group situation. The kibbutz recruit seems also to have a feeling of relative freedom and autonomy over against an institution such as the Army; this helps him to avoid over-identification and the tendency to deal with problems 'rightly' rather than realistically. Information from I. A. Antonovsky, Israel Institute of Applied Social Research.

Kibbutz specialists note that one factor in these good results may be that, under a well-planned system of group care, parents may have more free time in which to interact with their children, and more chance to influence school and nursery teaching, than in a system of care by individual families in which home and school are sharply separated and homes themselves are loaded with domestic chores. Something similar has been found in the present study in dual-career families in which the parents have been forced by the pressure of their commitments to think deliberately ahead and reserve time for their children; possibly more time, and better used, than would have been available in practice in a family with segregated roles.[1]

Child care has been the main focus of debate in Britain, but other aspects of family relationships are now also coming into the picture. A number of recent studies of the aged, for example, raise for Western countries the issue brought up by Geissler in East Germany. Given that the three-generation and generally the extended family remains a reality in a country such as Britain, what patterns of family, work and community life are most consistent with the family's function in providing care, contacts and a constructive task in life for the elderly?[2] A similar question can of course be asked about family care for the disabled. In Britain in 1965 some 13·5 per cent of all employed women over 45, 16·5 per cent of all women earning over £1,040 a year, and 17 per cent to 18 per cent of non-employed women over 45 had responsibility for one elderly person or invalid or more. Women with heavy responsibilities of this kind were particularly likely to be not working and unlikely to go back; and women with any responsibility of this kind made up 15 per cent of part-time workers but only 7 per cent of full-time.[3]

The problem is to extract from the bewildering mass of research material and practical experience now available a series of models of child care and other family relationships for the case where the mother is or might be working – especially, for present purposes, where she is highly qualified and working in a corresponding job – which can be offered to families to fit their individual circumstances. Such models must of course take account of the same very practical

[1] A professional man working in an Israel kibbutz told the authors of his experience during a period of work in England, where he was living with his family in normal English individual family style. Although his job involved a good deal of work at home, his children complained how little they saw of him compared to the situation in the kibbutz.

[2] Especially the British studies by the Institute of Community Studies (by Young, Willmott, Townsend and Marris), or Rosser and Harris, *op. cit.*

[3] A. Hunt, *A Survey of Women's Employment*, Government Social Survey, SS 379, H.M.S.O. 1968, pp. 110-111.

issues of cost and availability of services as have arisen in Eastern Europe. It is not only in East Germany that the Swedish concept of the 'service house', with its own nursery facilities and school as well as its restaurant and other communal facilities, has been judged too expensive for general use. Very similar criticisms of service houses were made to the authors in Sweden,[1] where informants pointed out in addition that this particular pattern of living is not to everyone's taste. Attitudes to nurseries and nursery schools are strongly influenced by the relation between costs and resources in the sense not only that, in Britain as in Eastern Europe, financial considerations delay nursery provision by public authorities,[2] but also that families which can afford more costly alternatives may prefer these. The British Federation of University Women found, somewhat to their surprise, that nursery schools came low on the list of British women

---

[1] *Welt am Sonntag*, August 17, 1969, reported as an original and hitherto untried experiment a proposal to build a first service house in Germany, aimed at middle income groups 'from the teacher to the administrative civil servant'. For this group the costs seemed to be taken as tolerable. A first move towards this project, though strongly backed by women deputies and social scientists, failed not on financial grounds but through ideological objections: but the move was being renewed.

[2] Average recent costs for Britain are:

	Cost per place	
	Capital	Recurrent (per annum)
		£
Day nurseries (1967-68)	800	334
Nursery schools (1969)		
classes of 20	320	150
classes of 30	270	100

Figures from the Department of Health and Social Security and the Ministry of Education and Science. Capital costs are for building costs only; site and equipment costs have to be added, and, in the case of nursery schools, architects' fees. About one-sixth of the cost of local authority day nurseries is recovered from parents. The age range of nurseries is from 0 to 5; nursery schools take children of 2, 3 and 4. Day nurseries are continuous through the day and year, nursery schools operate only in school hours and terms. An industrial firm quotes the recurrent cost plus depreciation and replacements for its nursery for children aged 2½-5 in 1967 as about £160 per place or £185 per child actually accommodated; 1969 figures would be about £210 or £235 (R. and M. Kingsley, *An Industrial Day Nursery*, Institute of Personnel Management, 1969). On the extent of nursery school provision see T. Blackstone, *Where Nursery Schools Are*, *New Society*, October 9, 1969. In 1965 10 per cent of all children in England and Wales aged 3-5 were in nursery schools, 6 per cent in maintained and 4 per cent in independent schools. From then till 1969 the number of maintained places increased very slightly and that of independent places rose to a substantial but uncertain extent. French costs for nurseries were quoted in 1969 as 25 francs per child per day – 42s. 6d. before the devaluation of August 1969 and 37s.-37s. 6d. after it – of which families would pay 3 to 12 francs.

145

graduates' priorities, whereas domestic help heads the list.[1] Similarly, a French study notes that women with higher education, which is likely to coincide with good housing, high salaries, and the ability to recruit domestic help, tend to give nurseries relatively low priority.[2]

The studies reported below in Part III are a first contribution, which it is intended to develop further in Volume III, towards working out a set of models for matching women's and men's career patterns with the various functions of their families. But much more work than has been possible in the present enquiry will be needed before a definitive set of models can be set down.

b *How is the sheer load of work involved in running a large family to be reconciled with the wife's career?*

The problem of overload ranked second only to that of child care for the participants in the special local studies of British women graduates in the British Federation of University Women's enquiry.

'Most women consider that shedding most of the load of housework is necessary if they are to return to work. . . . There is the difficulty of obtaining help. . . . There is the difficulty of unreliability; many of the domestic workers are married women and they too have domestic chores of their own. There is the fact that some women do not like employing people. . . . Finally, there is resentment at what must be paid to domestic workers.'[3]

This quotation puts the overload problem in a somewhat narrow light. Overload is related to the pressures of child care and general family management as well as to domestic work in the more mechanical sense. Its solution depends, certainly, in part on mechanization, delegation, and good organization within the home, and on better shopping and service facilities outside it. Professional women in a country such as Britain start at an advantage over women in similar positions in Eastern Europe in that they have much higher standards of housing and domestic equipment. They have also the advantage of far more efficient and accessible shopping and service facilities. In all countries, West or East, employed women gain as compared to full-time housewives from what might be called the reverse application of Parkinson's Law. Domestic work, as household time budgets from both Eastern and Western countries show, expands to fill the time available for it. Working wives in general, and highly

[1] Aregger, *op. cit.*, pp. 39-40.
[2] A. Michel, *Needs and Aspirations of Married Women Workers in France*, International Labour Review, July 1966, pp. 46-49.
[3] Aregger, *op. cit.*, p. 86.

qualified wives in particular, tend to respond to the shortage of time for their domestic work by showing greater skill than non-working wives in organizing such time as they have and by achieving eqnal results with less time and effort.[1]

But over and above questions about shops, washing machines, and domestic help, the overload problem raises issues of a more basic kind about relationships within the family and between the family and society, overlapping with those just raised about the care of children or the elderly. A family can certainly relieve its overload by using collective care for its young children or by identifying itself with a community capable, as in a service house or a kibbutz, of giving close and continuing support. But how far is it wise for it to do so, and how far is it economic for the community at large to help it by subsidizing service houses or other collective facilities? Though grandparents can be helpful, they themselves are often the first to see dangers in becoming too closely and continuously involved in the management of their children's household. How far can they or other relatives reasonably go in helping to relieve parents' overload at the stage when there are dependent children? How many grandparents in any case are likely to remain available to help, at an age when they have energy to spare, as the work participation rate of married women in their fifties rises?

A major resource for reducing wives' overload is, of course, husbands' co-operation in the home. A high degree of co-operation is today normal. 'Most Woodford men are emphatically not absentee husbands';[2] they share the housework and the care of children with their wives and carry a largely independent responsibility for household repairs. Similar comments are repeated in other surveys.[3] But in the great majority of cases there is still a limit. The husband continues to carry the primary responsibility for work and the wife for the home, and in family emergencies or times of family overload it is the wife's career, not the husband's, which is expected to give way. Swedish official policy today insists, like East German family law, that the duty to cope with domestic emergencies should be equally shared. Can it be assumed that this policy of fully equal shares will be accepted elsewhere in the West?

---

[1] E.g. time budgets for working and non-working housewives quoted in Dahlström, *op. cit.*, p. 31 (Sweden), Junker *op. cit.*, Vol. I, p. 442 (Germany), *Le Travail des Femmes en France*, Notes et Etudes Documentaires, 12th November, 1966 (France).

[2] P. Willmott and M. Young, *Family and Class in a London Suburb*, Routledge and Kegan Paul, 1960, p. 21.

[3] E.g. Harrell-Bond, *loc. cit.*, and H. Gavron, *The Captive Wife*, Routledge and Kegan Paul, 1966.

When all other practicable means of relieving overload have been used, in what proportion of cases will the solution still turn out to be the traditional one; that is for one partner in a marriage to concentrate on housework full-time? The division of labour in families tends to become more, not less, clear-cut as the load of domestic work increases; in the West as in the East, mothers of three or more children are likely to become (or remain) full-time housewives. For how many couples, in what circumstances, is a full and clear-cut division likely to remain desirable?

Overload, in short, cannot be treated only as a mechanical or managerial problem, though these are elements in the problem. If solutions for it are to be acceptable they must follow from more basic judgments about the desirability of different patterns of living in both the conjugal and the extended family. Once again, it will be the purpose of Parts III and V to contribute towards developing, out of the mass of research and experience now available, practical working models suited to families in varying circumstances.

c *What are to be the norms of masculine and feminine behaviour?*

The question of how a married couple divides its housework is relatively superficial. With all respect to Kelly's school of thought, it is hard to believe that the family will be in danger if men develop an interest in cooking and shopping[1] or women in plastering the domestic walls. Nor need the family be threatened, as current Swedish policies seem to suggest, if married couples conclude that everyone cannot be a jack-of-all-trades and wives and husbands tend still to specialize in skills of different kinds; dress-making or cooking special meals on the one hand, mechanical and electrical maintenance on the other. But behind superficial points like these, as well as behind the more far-reaching issue of how far to carry specialization on the one hand in earning and on the other in domestic management, there lies the very basic question of what being a man or a woman in the social conditions of the next decade should mean. Is the aim, as Alice Rossi puts it, in terms parallel to those commonly used in discussing race relations, to be 'cultural pluralism', 'total assimilation' of the minority (women) into the masculine culture, or a 'melting-pot model' which 'assumes a gradual transformation of both the immigrant and the host culture'?[2]

---

[1] In certain Middle Eastern cultures the fact that the husband monopolizes shopping is in any case an element, not of equality or participation, but of inequality and a patriarchal system of family relationships.

[2] A. Rossi, *The Road to Sex Equality*, cyclostyled paper to a seminar on Social Inequality, University of Chicago, February 1969.

Though the interests and aptitudes of individual men and women overlap, well-established differences are found in Western as in other cultures between typical or modal men and women; whatever their origin, and disregarding for the moment the question whether they can or should be modified. Men tend, in Parsons's term, to have an instrumental-adaptive role and the personal characteristics appropriate to it. They tend to exceed women in forcefulness, in the capacity to analyse a situation and break through to new patterns, and in mathematical and mechanical ability; and generally, in objective, abstract, impersonal thinking and the definition of formal structures and rules.[1] Women on the other hand tend to take what Parsons calls an expressive-integrative role. They tend to exceed men in the ability to make the best of relationships within a given framework; in responding sympathetically to a given situation, as apart from abstracting from it and creating a new and original one; in dealing with interiors rather than structures; in meticulous application rather than the fixing of broad outlines. They tend also to have the advantage in qualitative, not necessarily precise, but expressive methods of thinking and communication; in language and feeling

---

[1] A number of relevant studies are summarized by Kagan and Gallagher in M. L. and L. W. Hoffman, *op. cit.*, and E. Maccoby, 'Women's Intellect' in S. M. Farber and R. H. L. Wilson (eds), *The Potential of Woman*, McGraw-Hill, 1963. See also T. Parsons and R. F. Bales, *Family, Socialization, and Interaction Process*, Routledge & Kegan Paul, 1956; the contributions by R. J. Lifton and Eric Erikson to *The Woman in America*, American Academy of the Arts and Sciences, 1964, and by Erikson, B. Bettelheim and A. Rossi, to *Women and the Scientific Professions*, M.I.T., 1965; U. Bronfenbrenner, 'The Changing American Child', *Merrill-Palmer Quarterly*, April 1961; W. E. Vinacke, 'Sex Roles in a Three-Person Game', *Sociometry*, 1959; L. M. Terman and C. C. Miles, *Sex and Personality*, McGraw-Hill, 1936, and L. M. Terman and M. J. Oden, *The Gifted Group at Mid-Life*, Stanford, 1957; J. W. Getzels and P. W. Jackson, *Creativity and Intelligence*, J. Wiley, 1962; E. P. Torrance, *Education and the Creative Potential*, Minnesota, 1963; M. A. Coler, *Essays on Creativity in the Sciences*, New York University Press, 1963; A. Steinmann and D. J. Fox, *Self and Ideal Sex-Role Perceptions of Men and Women*, paper to American Psychological Association convention, New York, September 1966; D. W. MacKinnon, 'The Characteristics of Creative Architects' in M. Whiffen and H. Bush-Brown (eds), *The Teaching of Architecture*, Cranbrook, 1964 (for American Institute of Architects); P. Stringer, 'Masculinity-Femininity as a Possible Factor Underlying the Personality Responses of Male and Female Art Students', *British Medical Journal of Social and Clinical Psychology*, 1967; M. Wallach and H. Kagan, *Modes of Thinking in Young Children*, Holt Rinehart & Winston, 1966. The reference to Barnard is to his *The Functions of the Executive*, Harvard, 1938; that to Schumpeter is to his *Capitalism, Socialism and Democracy*, Allen & Unwin, 1943. On current thinking on the relation between genetic and cultural factors see D. C. Glass (ed.), *Genetics*, Russell Sage Foundation, New York, 1968, notably the contributions by Bressler, Halsey and Haller on pp. 178 and following.

rather than mathematics; in what Chester Barnard labelled the 'non-logical' (not to be confused with illogical) and informal as apart from the formal and mathematical approach to problems. Women tend to be more conciliatory, concerned with service rather than power, and with acceptability and consensus rather than with competition and Schumpeter's 'storm of creative destruction', which breaks a situation to pieces and creates a new one. Their training tends to be specially concerned with personal relationships and small groups, and to leave them with an interest in people rather than problems. For qualified women with high earning capacity money is important in many ways: as a symbol of professional and personal recognition – 'if a woman in operational research does not receive equal pay and training, she will definitely change her job'[1] – and in terms of the personal and family standard of living which it makes possible. But it tends to matter less to women than to men in terms of power and wealth as such. Women are more likely than men to be, not necessarily unambitious, but ambitious in an unspecialized way, concerned less with achieving top success in a particular field than with balanced achievement – often meaning in practice satisfactory as apart from top achievement in a broad range of life interests.

These differences are perceived by employers, and are often given as a reason for limiting women's promotion opportunities or restricting women to certain fields. As the authors wrote in the initial broadsheet of the present enquiry:

'Many employers accept that women can perform well in posts where they work on their own or with a small group, but consider them a bad risk as managers of larger groups. Women are said to be too emotional to make good managers, too inclined to judge by personalities and to intrigue, too little aware of the rules of discipline, loyalty to a wider group, and objectivity needed to run a large organization with success. Women in management are said to be short-term in their outlook, to crack under pressure and take shelter behind men, and to lack creativity, adaptability and force. These considerations will not necessarily exclude women from management altogether. One large retail organization, for example, makes a specific place for the 'womanly woman', who becomes the staff manageress or the assistant store manager, the manager's right-hand man – his 'day-time wife', as one study puts it – but never carries overall or top responsibility. It is where top-level line responsibility is concerned that many men and also, it appears from surveys, many women feel that women are a poor risk.'[2]

[1] M. C. Elton and A. Mercer, 'Growth and Mobility in Research', *Operational Research Quarterly*, 1966.
[2] Women and Top Jobs, P.E.P., 1967, p. 51.

In any case, since the interests even of women with a strong career commitment tend to be more diffuse than those of men, employers note that there is often more readiness on the part of a woman of top ability than of a man to settle for something less than a top job.

It is clear from the evidence of the P.E.P. study, as well as of previous enquiries, that employers both in Britain and elsewhere often perceive the differences between men and women inaccurately.

(1) There is a tendency to attribute to all woman an undifferentiated set of characteristics, whereas in fact there are substantial differences in respect of these characteristics both between individuals and between groups of women of different social background, education and training. The feminine characteristics thought by employers to disqualify women for higher posts, for example high absence or turnover, or low job and career commitment, tend often to be those common among working-class housewives rather than among highly-qualified professional women. Again, employers often appear to underestimate the extent to which, given the wide differences between individuals of either sex, the personal characteristics of women overlap those of men, so that many members of either sex are likely to be fitted for roles more typical of the other. There is a tendency for their expectations of woman's behaviour in a work role to be cast in terms of the behaviour they note in wives, sisters, or mothers in a domestic role, and for too little allowance to be made for the fact that a woman can and often does adopt entirely different styles of behaviour at home and at work.

(2) Women show and are expected by society to show less aggression in seeking promotion than men. It seems that many employers overlook the fact that in spite of this a woman may be as capable as a man of doing a senior job if others take the initiative in helping her to reach it.

(3) Employers today accept that certain traditionally feminine characteristics, such as meticulous application, can have a special value for routine manual and clerical work. They have been slower to appreciate that other traditionally feminine characteristics, such as quick responsiveness to a total situation, skills in using a 'non-logical' approach, and a service or educational rather than a power- or wealth-seeking outlook, may be acquiring a special value for higher management as participative systems of management, based on groups rather than individuals and on networks of diffused initiative rather than hierarchies, replace older more formal and authoritarian systems.

(4) Employers may tend to overestimate the extent – admittedly

substantial – to which women's and men's characteristics are rooted in genetics, and underestimate the degree to which they can be changed by late as well as early training.

Nevertheless, there is obviously substance in employers' insistence that the difference between women and men may affect women's (and men's) suitability for certain types of employment. What account, then, are individuals or policy-makers to take in future of masculine-feminine differences, having regard to the needs and problems of families as well as jobs?

The range of roles, or potential roles, to be taken into account is clearly far wider than in the past, since in Western as in Eastern Europe the door has been opened in recent decades for a comprehensive reassessment of the roles of both sexes. The once conventional stereotype of segregated roles – on the one hand the housewife without outside employment, on the other the bread-winner free to contract out of all but a few domestic commitments – has lost the near-monopoly which in many social groups it used to have. Particular married couples or societies may, as has been said, still prefer segregated roles to overlapping roles in the family or to three-phase, continuous-career, or complementary-job patterns of employment. But now their choice has to be justified. The justification for the once conventional patterns can no longer be taken as self-evident. The replacement of concepts of general masculine superiority with ideologies of equality and partnership, besides being a major change in itself, has opened the way for the consideration of many others. It creates a more open atmosphere in which the actual advantages or disadvantages of conventional masculine and feminine characteristics, and the case for encouraging or combating them, can be more reasonably assessed.

One of the options open is to continue to accept differences in masculine and feminine roles along traditional lines. They are not always irrelevant or wrong. The problem often is not to escape from them but to use them to better advantage. As Junker's research or the evidence of *Working Wonders* shows, equality and partnership do not necessarily imply identity or interchange-ability of roles. Men and women may still specialize in different activities and follow very different life cycles. The movement of women into careers, and particularly into high-level careers, may sometimes involve choosing between traditional femininity and what would once have been regarded as a conventional masculine style of behaviour. But research and experience have shown that this need not be so. 'Masculine' behaviour at work can be consistent with 'feminine' behaviour at home, since home and work roles are commonly segregated and can be entirely different. Conventionally 'feminine' as well as 'masculine' characteristics can in any case, as has been said, be valuable at top as well as other levels of professional and managerial work precisely because of the different contribution which they offer. There is no need to prefer one to the other or to standardize the two on some common model. The problem, Erik Erikson suggests, is not that women's distinctive vision is a myth but that so little use has been made of it.

In at least one major area, that of creativity, success depends on combining masculine and feminine characteristics in the same person. Creativity requires 'feminine' sensitivity and intuition – non-logical qualitative thinking, and free association not limited by abstract schemes – and ability to create order within a framework, as well as 'masculine' capacity for analysis, forcefulness and breaking through previously established frameworks. Research on creativity has shown that it cannot be identified with the characteristics of either sex alone.

In other areas it is possible to benefit from the distinctive characteristics both of men and of women not by combining them in one person but by collaboration between the two sexes in which the members of each sex are assigned to appropriate roles. The American Y.M.C.A. and Y.W.C.A. report an unusual case where it was possible to compare directly men's and women's performance in managing parallel and overlapping tasks.[1] The men's method of working tended to be formal and, in Weber's sense, bureaucratic. They were inclined 'to move more through administrative fiat'. They showed force and drive, but were 'production-centred', concerned more with getting limited tasks speedily and effectively carried out than with developing sensitivity to all the factors in their environment and setting new or wider objectives. If a new job had to be done, they tended not to work it out in committee but to hire a specialist and tell him to get on with the job. Women on the other hand started from the fact that:

> 'The woman's role is of necessity more related to involvement with the less mature in growth producing experiences. Not being the "head of the house" she must depend upon group decisions rather than authoritarian unilateral ones.'[2]

The women tended to work much more than the men through groups and discussion, bringing in a wider social and occupational range

[1] L. W. Dodson, *The Role of the YWCA in a Changing Era*, Y.W.C.A. of New York, 1960; and information from the National Council of Churches, New York.

[2] *Loc. cit.*, p. 84.

of people than the men, with less tendency to confine participation to established high-status specialists, and with less formality. They irritated the men by using these methods in cases where authoritative and bureaucratic methods would despatch business more effectively within clear boundaries, but on the other hand succeeded better than the men in developing sensitivity to a wide range of new social issues and to the action which they would require. They were more aware than the men of community needs, as apart from needs arising in their own institutions. They were also readier to accept a duty to serve the community as opposed to concentrating solely on the needs of their own group. The conventionally masculine approach proved successful in some parts of the work to be done and the conventionally feminine approach in others. The problem, evidently, was not to choose between the two but to combine them.[1]

But the options open also of course include new role patterns. Experience has shown not merely that differences between the typical interests and abilities of men and women can be complementary and of value to society, in top jobs as in other spheres, but also that there is no particular reason to suppose that those differences which happen to be typical today are necessary or ideal either now or for the future. They are, to an important extent, not inherited but shaped by history, culturally handed down and liable to be geared to the conditions of the past rather than the present. They can be and may need to be modified today and in the future. Further, though the average or typical characteristics of the two sexes differ, those of individual men and women overlap, and cannot and should not all be fitted into standard sex patterns, notably in a case like that of the creative artist where personality needs to draw from both sets of characteristics. Education, training, employment practices and, generally, social customs and attitudes need to be designed, as in the campaign now being developed in Sweden, to leave options open to individual men and women and to permit the evolution of typical or average patterns in the directions that new circumstances require.

The point, however, is not merely that new masculine and feminine roles may be appropriate. It is also to recognise that the task of defining which are the roles appropriate to each type of personality and work of family situation has still be be completed.

[1] The findings from the Y.M.C.A./Y.W.C.A. case are directly in line with more general findings about the respective usefulness of formal and informal 'authoritarian' and 'democratic' management, not specially linked to sex roles; see Fogarty, M.P., *The Rules of Work*, Geoffrey Chapman, 1963, Chapters 12 and 13.

There is widespread uncertainty even about what masculine and feminine behaviour is currently to be expected, let alone what might or should be expected in future. The end of the Y.M.C.A./Y.W.C.A. story was less happy than its beginning. In principle, the best results could have been obtained by treating the men's and women's approaches as complementary and using both. What actually happened was that, in the absence of good understanding by each sex of how and with what effect the other worked, the men and women, using their respective approaches, irritated each other to the point where they could no longer work together at all.

In a study covering ten countries, including Britain, of samples mainly of highly educated groups, Anne Steinmann finds general agreement between men and women on the characteristics of the 'ideal' man or woman. A woman should have an even balance between self- or career-oriented and family interests. A man should be more strongly oriented to his own career and development, but should have a family interest as well.[1] When however men or women are asked what they think is the ideal picture of members of their own sex in the minds of members of the other, a very different impression emerges. Women think that men want them to be far more traditionally 'feminine' than men actually do. Men think, equally incorrectly, that women want a 'feminine type' of man. Women, further, are found to think that men have a much more traditionally 'masculine' ideal of the masculine role than men in fact have. In this atmosphere of mutual misunderstanding it is only too easy to see how clashes like that in the Y.M.C.A./Y.W.C.A. case can arise.

But even if factual misconceptions like these were removed, many unsettled questions and grounds for dispute would remain. In his study of German women employers[2] Hartmann notes that a woman employer may have in effect to write her own role description and impose it on society, since for her, unlike her masculine equivalent, there is no ready-made role waiting. A woman climbing the promotion ladder in a large British firm may well find herself condemned as unfeminine and aggressive if she seeks promotion vigorously, but overlooked if she does not. If she has a child, she is likely, unlike her opposite number in America, Israel or Eastern Europe, to find that there is no socially sanctioned set of rules on how she should act to continue her career. How long a break should she take after a birth? Should she return at all? Can she reasonably ask for a period of part-time work? Will she be badly regarded if she takes time off for family emergencies? She is on her own in these matters and, like the German woman employer, has to write her own role.

[1] Steinmann, *op. cit.*   [2] Hartmann, *op. cit.*, Ch. 5.

A man may run into similar difficulties over the clash between his work and his family responsibilities. Is it acceptable for him, as a man, to turn down a possible promotion, transfer, or simply a spell of overtime, on the ground that this clashes with his duties at home? Is it reputable for him to adopt the broad, multi-dimensional pattern of ambitions characteristic of many women, to settle for an interesting middle-level job, and to give a large part of his attention to non-work interests? Will he, if he does so, be written off as a dilettante? Margaret Mead quotes with disapproval the case of American husbands who do in fact choose to give priority to non-work interests, even in a situation where the claims of work are being pressed beyond all reasonable limits:

'A very large manufacturing concern in this country, when they were getting ready to prepare men for the next step up in the echelon, called them in and said, "Now this next step you're going to be groomed for is a tough one, and it's going to take sometimes as much as eighteen hours a day. Go home and ask your wives and children if they will let you." True to our picture of American life, they went home, and half of the wives and children vetoed it immediately, so the men didn't make any effort to go on. The family said "No! We like picnics." The company took the group that did go on, and they harried them. They would just let them get home, sit down to dinner, and they'd call them back. Sunday morning the family would just have the picnic all packed, and the telephone would say, "Come back to the plant." That got rid of another 50 per cent. Then they took the few that were left and promoted them.

'This is serious. This is a situation in which life in the suburbs – the plumbing, the babies, the azaleas, and the cub scouts – is given precedence over the job of production and distribution which is necessary to this country.'[1]

What, in circumstances like these, is it reasonable for a man to do?

More generally, as was underlined in Chapter III, the ground rules by which men and women choose between continuous-career, complementary-job, three-phase or segregated-role patterns for their working and family life have still to be worked out. What factors of ability, opportunity, family size, social and managerial skill, personal interests and attitudes should determine the choice of one or the other? And, granted that men's and women's interests and abilities overlap, how far and in what circumstances is it reasonable to carry the reversal of sex roles? There is unlikely to be much con-

[1] M. Mead, quoted by L. R. Sayles, *Individualism and Big Business*, McGraw-Hill, 1963, pp. 85-86.

troversy today if a wife whose children have grown up takes a job, or a husband helps with the housework and perhaps takes over completely in an emergency. But there is still likely to be social disapproval if the husband concentrates wholly and permanently on the housework, or if the wife insists on her career in circumstances which could interfere with her husband's career or throw on him the primary responsibility for seeing that the children are not neglected. Where, if anywhere, is the line to be drawn?

A whole new expanse of country has been opened up in the matter of sex roles. The problem now is to draw the map which will help people to choose from among the vast variety of directions offered by the new geography the course which accurately fits their needs. Here as before, what is needed is to devise a set of models corresponding to the variety of individuals' circumstances; a range of norms rather than a single standard solution, taking account not only of individuals' abilities and interests but of what is practicable in foreseeable social conditions. The studies reported in Part III are designed first of all to throw more light on how men and women in Britain do in fact currently understand their roles, and secondly to provide suggestions as to what are likely to prove practicable and acceptable role patterns in future.

d *How far can and should work as well as family patterns be adapted to fit women's distinctive life cycle?*

Though it may not be easy for a qualified woman to find a job in a small town or country district, 'the lack of suitable work or difficulty in finding it' turned out not to be a prominent issue in the British Federation of University Women's special studies.

> 'The main difficulty here is that the available jobs are not adapted to the women's circumstances, and that it is difficult for them to meet employers' requirements about hours of work.'[1]

This appeared as the third major difficulty, after child care and overload, in the way of graduates returning to work. Recruitment and promotion procedures for senior posts have been geared traditionally to the life cycle of men, who normally remain in continuous employment, can work a full day, can concentrate on their job to the relative exclusion of domestic affairs, and do not need a career break or reduction in their commitments during the time they have young children; though men may, of course, have unforeseen career breaks for other reasons, as happened most strikingly during the Second World War.

[1] Aregger, *op. cit.*, p. 87.

High fliers in any occupation tend to take off around age 30, at the time when women are most likely to be tied with young children. A woman, like a man, who misses her chance then may get no second one, and the Census shows how likely this is to happen. In 1966 men 'managers, large establishments' in Great Britain outnumbered women by five or six to one at the entry age to high-level careers, 21–24, and also at ages 45 and over; but by no less than ten to one at age 25–34. The woman with top potential who has to hold back at age 25–34 may still get promotion later, but is unlikely to have the chance of rising as high as a man of equal merit who avoids delay at this point. If a woman in her small-child period wishes to keep contact with her career or to work her way back into it, she is likely to find in many occupations that part-time work and other arrangements for maintaining continuity are a hit-and-miss affair, depending on personal and local factors rather than a general rule, and that there are few or no regular arrangements for re-recruitment or retraining. If a woman does reach near to the top she may well find that the relative quality of her work counts for little, at a level where there are anyway plenty of qualified competitors for top jobs, compared to the fact that her competitors are not only more aggressive in seeking promotion, but under less pressure to set limits to their commitment of time.

It is in principle possible to adapt the career pattern of a firm or profession to allow for women's different life cycle, and yet to leave women with the same opportunities of advancement as men. Steps towards doing this could include not only a change in recruitment, training and promotion policies for women themselves – organized career breaks for maternity, opportunities for keeping in touch and part-time work during a family's small-child period, better arrangements for re-recruitment and retraining – but greater encouragement to fathers as well as mothers to weight their interests towards the family during the small-child period or to take time out for school holidays or family emergencies; or measures such as a general reduction in daily or weekly working hours applicable to both sexes.

However, a number of these measures are controversial from the point of view both of the efficiency of production and of their repercussions in other directions, including women's own interests. There has been controversy on whether part-time work is desirable for women with a serious career commitment. The economic case for recruiting women is much more obvious in the basic grades of qualified occupations, in many of which demand for staff has tended to outrun supply, than in the top jobs in which no obvious shortage of qualified candidates exists and the admission of women as candidates may seem to upset established prospects of promotion, reduce morale, and create unrest. In the quotation above, Margaret Mead suggests that in some Western countries encouragement to fathers to reweight their interests towards the family has already gone far enough to damage work efficiency in top jobs.

The occupational studies reported in Part IV are intended to throw light on controversies like these, and on the question of which policies for adapting working life to women's life cycle are likely to prove economic and acceptable from the point of view of employers and the economy in general as well as of women themselves.

e What are to be the personal and social strategies for the next stage?

The new approach to the issues raised by women's careers which began to take shape during the 1960s all over the Western world is directed, as has been said, not simply to removing formal obstacles while leaving family and work systems basically unchanged but to modifying all the systems involved – men's roles, women's roles, work and family organization – in relation to each other. So far, however, the overall strategies for doing this have not acquired a clearcut shape. In Part V an effort will be made to move on beyond the conflict of ideologies still prevalent in the West to at least an outline of a possible strategy. This has to be worked out in relation not only to the objectives considered in Parts III and IV – in particular to the models suited to different family circumstances and to what is practicable in the general circumstances of each country – but to the action which it is reasonable to expect from the various agents themselves. Eli Ginzberg has noted[1] how graduate women themselves tend to fall into four groups in terms of their approach to planning their own future. The Planners, as he calls them, pursue a single goal or set of goals throughout their lives. The Re-casters may shift direction once or twice in their lives as required by changes in their values or circumstances. The Adapters swing with events, re-shaping their aims as their family and other circumstances change. The unsettled fail to achieve clear aims at all. Without necessarily accepting Ginzberg's classification, allowance has to be made for these and a variety of other distinctions between the ways in which individuals and different groups and institutions are likely to contribute to shaping the future. For the reasons set out in Chapter I, the strategies finally evolved are likely to be different in the case of highly qualified women, with their stronger career commitment and other distinctive problems, from those appropriate to women's careers in general. All this will be the subject of Part V.

[1] E. Ginzberg and A. M. Yohalem, *Educated American Women: Self Portraits*, Columbia 1966.

Part Three

Studies of Family and Work Careers

Chapter V

The Conceptual Framework of the Research

A number of the assumptions underlying the P.E.P. studies as a whole – not only the family and sample studies – were set out in Chapter I. The research itself has focused on the idea of a life cycle; on the typical patterns of development found in the life histories of men and women in particular directions at key turning points.

The conceptual framework used views the processes of formulating ambitions, career development, family life and so on through time. The reason for this emphasis is that it has become increasingly apparent that many of the generalizations made in the literature about the pressures on, or the wishes or involvements of women, their husbands, and employers are *phase specific*. Generalizations holding for one time of life may not hold for others, and therefore a framework is necessary that makes it possible to analyse factors at play by specific phase of the life cycle.

Furthermore, the research is *process orientated*, and focuses on how movement or change occurs from one phase to another. As women move from the roles involved in one phase into those of the next phase, a process of reorganization is at work. To accomplish the reorganization, there is a necessary *un*-organization, a certain amount of turbulence, and then a new organization forms around the role expectations and obligations in the new situation. Individuals vary in the degree of disorganization and turbulence subjectively experienced. If one seeks to alter a structural situation during the steady state between critical transition points, one may expect to encounter resistance. This is an important perspective in relation to the policy implications of the research findings and will be returned to in that context.

The overall development cycle is difficult to delineate on the basis of social status transitions because these become differentiated at a very early age into different role systems – school, work, family and other roles. In a very general sense the life cycle can be seen as a whole career, which is made up of the stages of infancy, youth, adulthood and old age. Running through these stages of the life career are various sub-careers (e.g., the work career, the school career) which last for different lengths of time within the life career and have different characteristics. All of the careers are made up of concatenations of phases, which have the following properties:

Phases in the Life Career

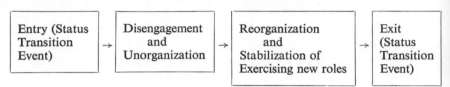

For example, the entry-event in the family role career is birth (in relation to one's parental family) or marriage (in relation to one's family of procreation). Marriage involves, in part, disengagement from child roles in the family as well as engagement with the new role of husband or wife.

The nature of these transitional and reorganizational processes is sometimes explicitly recognized in the language. For example, when a person leaves school or university there is a double set of terms used, one denoting the entry aspect of the event and the other denoting the exit aspect. (It is sometimes called 'graduation', sometimes 'commencement'.) The cliché jokes around marriage ('I'm not losing a daughter, I'm gaining a son') also indicate this duality.

The type of conceptual framework required in fact is multidimensional. As already indicated, the life career is seen as being made up of several sub-careers and the life cycle is characterized by an increasing differentiation of roles making up the various streams; the interplay between the different life-cycle sub-careers is one part of the multidimensional framework. Some elements of the interplay may be visualized when considering the stages in three of the role systems— family, education and work.

Forces in the different sub-career lines interplay. The demands of the marital role must be balanced against the demands of educational or occupational roles. There are also other influences which can operate to determine the way the reorganization process is resolved, or even whether or not the entry to the new status is attempted. Looking at this conception graphically in relation to the specific

164

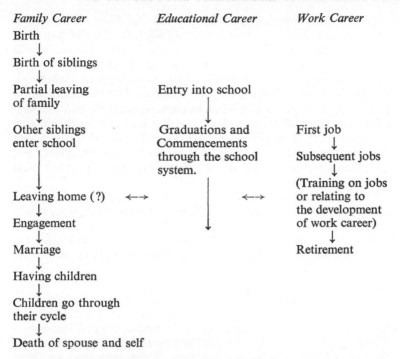

career line of *work*, the following may be posited as a way of systematizing the multidimensionality of influences:

Multidimensional Framework for Analysing the Processes of Work-Career Status Transitions

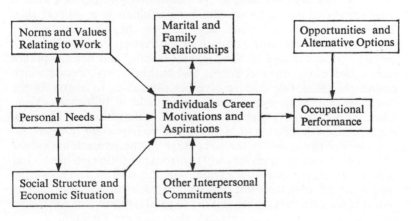

At each critical transition point the field of forces shifts and a person's motivations and aspirations may alter. A young person who, because of the array of forces at home and in school, may have a high level of aspiration in the sixth form may lower it in response to forces encountered later, e.g. in the interpersonal area or in the work opportunity area, or in the actual job situation. It is the examination of these forces as they are at work in contemporary Britain that will be focal in the analysis to follow. Getting into and performing in responsible high level jobs requires a special array of forces which have been appreciated in a general way by some observers, but which have also been subject to considerable distortion and to biased or stereotyped thinking.

The critical task at present is to detail and analyse the range of factors which are functioning in different circumstances, since single formulations have so far proved generally unproductive. Consider the status transition of graduation from university in the case of a talented female student. She will probably be in the throes of making several decisions at this point: one alternative may be to go on to postgraduate work and extend the career cycle into another phase; another alternative may involve initiating the family-of-procreation life cycle by getting married to a bright young architect boyfriend who is on the point of emigrating to Australia; a third alternative may be to initiate the occupational life cycle by taking a job as an editorial assistant in a publishing firm. There may also be other alternatives, for instance a moratorium, a period of travel or adventure, etc. She herself may be most interested in pursuing postgraduate study but her parents may prefer to remove her from the educational cycle lest she worsen her chances for a suitable marriage, and they may urge her to take the publishing job, perhaps after a brief secretarial course to increase her usefulness in a support role. They may discourage the marriage because they are reluctant for her to emigrate. Her own strength of motivation, her resolution of certain conflicts related to her personal identity and her acceptance or rejection of her parental norms and authority, will decide which course she takes. She may resolve her difficulties by marrying the boy, thus hoping to escape the parental field of influence. Then, when she arrives in Australia, factors such as the attitudes of her new husband and the location of his work will be important in determining whether she re-enters the next stage in the educational sphere of her life. A new set of choices will confront her following her critical decision to marry and to emigrate, and the field of forces will be somewhat different, since not only will the husband probably become more salient than the parents, but the societal influences of Australian culture may become more operative than those in England.

The simple formulations based on stereotyped conceptions of the appropriateness of certain activities for women which might have held sway in the past are becoming less acceptable as general formulae. The personal, societal and interpersonal influences vary at different periods in the life cycle – the pre-school infancy period, the school period through secondary schooling, the specialized training period (which ordinarily begins after school in university or other colleges but which may take place or continue into the work setting) and the career implementation phase which follows. Each of these periods has sub-phases and various ways in which the work-family-education life cycles are articulated. The events in the different stages (particularly at critical decision points) are highly interdependent. They may be 'used' against one another. A talented woman who fears to enter the competitive world of work may 'use' her wish to be a 'good' mother as a rationale for avoiding entry or re-entry into the work-career cycle. What happens in an individual life cycle level also operates on a larger scale among the institutional sectors of society. In the exploratory interviews during which the research framework was being formulated:

A civil servant in the Department of Education and Science indicated that the prevailing attitude in the department was to see the womanpower issue as not being the concern of the department; the problems lay with industry, not the educational system. A personnel officer in industry indicated that industry wanted more women in top positions but that women (other than the odd 'blue-stocking') did not seem to want high level careers. This was sometimes attributed to women's low career motivation presumably derived from their earlier educational and familial experience.
A secondary school head teacher said that they had advertised headships (schools and departments) that had formerly been women's strongholds but that these jobs were now going to men. A demographic reason was given. Women marry more now, and therefore the career women who would accept demanding jobs with lots of responsibility ('the old war-horses') were a disappearing breed.

The secondary school head did discuss the idea of redefining the headship roles to make them less demanding. Neither she nor anyone else interviewed seriously considered changing men's roles to make it more possible for their wives to take jobs of the kind mentioned above.

Psychobiological differences aside, the typical developmental patterns of girls differ from those of boys in contemporary society. This can be illustrated through the various stages in relation to work careers. The material used is from the literature and from interviews.

167

PRE-SCHOOL INFANCY PERIOD

In this first period, the child's decision points are few but the environmental influences acting upon him are many. There is a voluminous literature on the effects of early childhood experience on the formation of adult character. The early, pre-school years are held by many authorities on human development to be the most critical for the establishment of enduring tendencies and attitudes that affect subsequent experience. Much of the early work along these lines, for example that by the classical psychoanalytic theorists, is now regarded by most social scientists as suggestive rather than definitive. Contemporary researchers tend to concentrate not on specific acts in relation to early experiences with weaning, toilet training and so on, but on the patterns of inter-personal behaviour which surround the handling of these issues. The aim is to discover in these patterns the influences on the child's conception of itself and others that affect subsequent definitions of its world. Some of the mechanisms involved in the early experiences that form the basis for little girls' conceptions of what is right and proper for females and little boys' conceptions of what is right and proper for males have been delineated by Hartley. She indicates how sex-typed 'moulding' of children occurs in families, e.g. by dressing up little girls to look 'pretty' and 'feminine', by channelling their interests towards dolls and toy houses, and by 'gentling' girls (in Maccoby's terms) in contrast to the 'roughhousing' of boys, and in the use of all sorts of sex-typed symbols (dress types, cosmetics *v.* tools) and exposure to activity patterns (dolls *v.* guns). Girls are very early led to *prefer* certain modes of conduct and activity that contrast to those preferred by boys. How much of this is biological and how much cultural is still imprecisely defined. However, there is much to support (in modified form) the early caricatured assertion of the cultural relativity of sex-roles by Margaret Mead (1935).[1]

Within the larger pattern of cultural values, it is the family that provides a major part of the mediating influences affecting early development. Family structures vary in any society and particularly in a complex society but the variation is not random. There are, in general, two groups of determining factors: those that are related to sub-cultural groupings sharing a common style of life, in for instance social class or ethnic groups; and those that are related to familial situations which cut across sub-cultural lines, such as whether or not there is a high degree of tension between child and father and/or mother. There is some suggestive evidence that both kinds of factors are related to career performance in later years, although

[1] For references throughout Part Three see lists at end of each chapter.

there is a great need for more definitive research in this field. Alice Rossi has shown in her American study that there are several characteristic family constellations underlying high career aspirations in women; those women, for example, who had 'tense' relationships with their mothers and close relations with their fathers, or whose mothers provided successful career models, or whose parents experienced considerable domestic tension and discord are more likely to have high personal career aspirations, whatever their social class background, than their peers from more tranquil or normatively 'adjusted' early household environments (Rossi, 1965). These patterns must be regarded as specific for this time in history, but not necessarily valid for other periods, or for other societies.

In relation to performance potentials, relating development of intellectual ability to the differences in the sex-role moulding experiences of early childhood is complicated by the fact that many of the most widely used intelligence tests were standardized to eliminate items that differentiated between the sexes so that boys and girls could be measured against the same norms. For this reason much of the information about the development of intelligence is reported in terms that are not very sensitive to sex differentials, and the most important lines of differentiation have been by sub-culture, e.g. social class. In recent years, psychologists have begun to develop tests that measure different dimensions of intellectual and creative ability, and findings like the following begin to emerge (Maccoby, 1963).

Girls seem to excel in the development of verbal skills while boys excel in mathematical skills; boys develop a more analytic approach to thinking and reasoning while girls are more global and influenced by their socio-environmental field. The tendency for the more analytic approach and greater display of interest and talent in scientific and mathematical fields by the boys seems to relate to childhood experiences associated with allowing or training for independence. Girls are more protected and 'mothered' than boys, and this may account to some extent for this differentiation. The finding by Roe and others that scientists tend in their early childhood to be 'loners' gives support to this line of observation. This would be an example of a situational pattern, i.e., one that may occur in various subcultural settings. Another sort of variable that cuts across sub-cultural groupings is demographic – notably position in the birth order. There is some evidence that first children have higher aspirations than subsequent children and girls with elder brothers seem to have higher aspirations than girls who do not have these male exemplar/rivals (Price, 1969).

An example of sub-group patterning along class lines stems from the tendency in middle-class culture for the father to go out to work while the mother remains constantly available at home. This reinforces the tendency to form from the earliest days different images of activities appropriate for each sex These early differences seem to provide a foundation for the emergence later of preferences, values and choices from among curriculum and occupational alternatives that make women choose 'people-oriented' activities and men favour the more independent and enterprising forms of activity. In discussing the action implications of such research findings for recruiting more women scientists, Alice Rossi states:

> 'If girls are to develop the analytic and mathematical abilities science requires, parents and teachers must encourage them in independence and self-reliance instead of pleasing feminine submission. . . . A childhood model of the quiet, good sweet girl will not produce many women scientists or scholars, doctors or engineers. It will produce the competent loyal laboratory assistant' (Rossi, 1965).

This is the stage at which the child has little or no choice as its mother or other adults make most decisions for it. It is here, however, that some fundamental predispositions are laid down affecting how the child will exercise its later options. Conventionally, the mother has played a major role in setting the conditions of a child's environment in this phase as the father tended to be away so much. More recently there is evidence to indicate that the participation of the father has been increasing in child rearing in this early pre-school stage (Yudkin and Holme, 1965).

THE SCHOOL PERIOD (FROM NURSERY SCHOOL TO SECONDARY SCHOOL)

When the child goes through the critical status transition of school entry, he experiences a major change in his life circumstances that sets in motion new moulding influences which continue to develop in strength and diversity through secondary school. *En route* there are a series of transitions – from primary to secondary school and from one level to the next – that may have special significance depending on the degree to which each transition involves change of teachers, fellow-students, school environment and so on. While the choice of major pathways is still in parental hands, particularly in the early stages of school, there are others involved and the child begins to play a more active role in selecting areas of interest and involvement. Teachers become important and make many of the day-to-day decisions governing the child's activities that formerly had been parental prerogatives. The children match themselves and are matched by others against the behaviour of other children; they begin to compare their own family environments with those acting on other children.

This is a time of considerable extension of horizons and increase in the field of interpersonal and societal forces acting on the developing child. These forces may be congruent with one another and achieve an effect which is harmonious, or they may be incongruent and create various kinds of conflict. During this extended period, the issue of wastage becomes salient. As soon as it is legal to do so, students start to 'drop out' of school, usually never to re-enter. Even before this, some drop out psychologically, choosing to take little interest in the curriculum since increasingly high qualifications mean high education or training; this leads almost irrevocably away from the pathways that make it possible for men and women to reach the strata of the 'highly qualified' occupations. A crucial question then becomes that of defining the issues that affect the decision to opt out of the educational career course and, more specifically, the issues that affect women in these decision processes.

It is generally agreed that many more pupils from all strata of society than currently achieve this have the potential to pass at least two subjects at 'A' level if they remained in school and were appropriately motivated; however, a high proportion of young people from the lower socio-economic levels drop out before they reach this point. Indeed, there is some indication that the *more* rather than the *less* able pupils from the lower class groups tend to leave early (Floud and Halsey, 1956; Himmelweit and Swift, 1969). A number of reasons are given for this, such as the influence of parents (whose values are incongruent with those of the school), the individual's dislike of the school and feeling of being discriminated against, the failure of the school to integrate such students into the school society, the influence of peer groups outside the school which may be rebelling against social norms, and the ineptitude of careers guidance services. Enterprising, highly independent youngsters who feel themselves to be cultural misfits in school understandably make choices that provide them with a more gratifying environment. For girls, this shift of involvement may not take them outside of the school altogether but simply involve changes of course within the school.

Pheasant has given attention to the special issue of girls' school careers and found that teachers in a majority of schools tend to influence girls along the lines of conservative societal sex role images. They encourage the selection of 'feminine' course options, particularly where the number of places say in a physics course is limited. Biology is frequently the only science option open to women. Aside

171

from sheer access, it was found that even when girls did have the opportunity to take science courses if they were so inclined, they found its presentation distasteful or meaningless in that it was not really related to the interests of girls and women. The girls are made to feel that the choice is between 'people *v.* test-tubes', and that 'science is harsh and impersonal', or 'physics is a boy's subject' (Pheasant, 1960). Once having missed the chance to take certain 'O' levels many girls are thereby diverted forever from careers in the relevant fields. This is particularly true in science and technology.

In schools where boys and girls are trained separately (as in many high-level British schools producing highly qualified personnel) the tendency is for even the most 'future-minded' schools to pay little attention to the sociological aspects of the future. One headmistress in a top girls' school, for example, indicated that the girls think about career *and* marriage but are not prepared for the difficulties they may encounter in attempting to combine these activities. It is to be expected that the career ideal will give way in any potential clash between the two. The boys, on the other hand, are given a vocationally oriented training, with little or no attention to the relationship between work and family life. If they think of the matter at all they expect that their wives will be the traditional 'helpmate' described earlier.

In the school period, then, there is a progressive increase both in the number and complexity of transition points at which the individual can exercise choices, and in the number and complexity of environmental influences. The choices that a girl makes – to take an interest or not, to stay or drop out, to take a course or not, to take an 'O' level or not, to take an 'A' level or not – all have consequences, often irreversible, for her subsequent availability in the highly qualified human resource pool.

As these stages and aspects of the issue are spelled out, two factors become increasingly apparent: both how complex are the societal forces which must be altered if the course of events is to be affected, and also what might be the most strategic points for the application of effort. Teachers, head teachers, curricula committees, career counsellors and peer groups become involved as well as the individual and his or her family.

THE SPECIALIZED TRAINING PERIOD

The individual who enters this period has already gone through secondary school and opted to continue with training experiences of one kind or another that will lead to high occupational qualifications. A girl's feeling of choice will depend on what she has already done in secondary school, and may already be considerably restricted. By the time they reach this point, most women have been socialized away from 'masculine' interests and from infancy onward guided away from fields leading to 'O' and 'A' level qualifications essential to entering ranges of specialized training. Universities in England tend to require a rather high degree of commitment to a specialized course from the outset, and women who have been guided systematically toward the humanities may never have a chance to 'discover' a scientific interest in themselves, because the courses within which such an awakening may occur are closed to them if prior experiences did not establish the requisite entry qualifications. One of the women scientists interviewed traced the preferences of girls for the humanities and social sciences to their earliest experiences with the sex-segregation of toys, and described the struggle that she personally had to engage in with the university authorities when she wished to change fields. In the face of obstacles placed in the paths of potential girl scientists prior to entering university, she felt that the shortage of applicants for university places in science is understandable. It is a failure of the pre-university levels of education to facilitate women's interests and choices leading in other than the conventional directions.

At any rate, the woman who succeeds at the earlier educational levels and is motivated to continue will, depending on what her choices are at the point of leaving secondary school, undertake one or another type of advanced specialized training. She may go to university or college, enter a firm or other large organization with its own training programme, or she may take an apprenticeship or job in which she sees a possibility for developing in such a way as to reach an ultimately high level of qualifications.

If a girl enters university she will embark on a phase which is usually presented as the most comfortable and easy in her career. Universities are often seen as the most 'universalistic' of all organizations in their high valuation of intellectual performance independently of the ascribed attributes of the student. In fact there are a number of factors in the university or other specialized training institution's situations which modify this picture. Leaving aside the situations which result in sex-segregation in higher education, it is clear that the first thing a girl must do if she is going to achieve high qualifications is to stay the course. There is a rather high drop-out or 'wastage' rate in some fields, and there is a rather widely held preconception that women are more likely to drop out than men. This has been used as a reason for preferential selection of men in some courses for which there is high competition. The higher wastage rate would seem to be caused by a number of sex-specific obstacles. If the girl marries while at university, the expectations of her in the marital

173

role may more often require termination of education than would hold for a boy in similar circumstances, or she may become pregnant (in or out of marriage) and therefore leave the training situation. A girl may have to work with more highly conflicted feelings within herself than a boy from a comparable social class background. This may take a variety of forms. Some middle-class students rebel against having gone to university simply to please their parents; others, perhaps more from working-class backgrounds, may be pursuing a course that seems burdensome, wasteful or incomprehensible to their parents; or, the young woman may face a situation in the university where she is made to feel that being in a competitive situation with young men decreases her chances of dating and marrying.

Once the woman has her first degree, she may either enter employment or, if she is in one of the professions requiring higher qualifications, she may undertake an additional phase of training. By this time the issue of marriage may have become salient, although increasingly it occurs at any stage from secondary school onwards. When the woman marries, she then has to decide whether or not she really wants to go on working. There are many preconceptions current that women do not really want to work and that their employment is frequently a gap-filler between school and marriage, with later re-entry to work seen mainly as a source of supplementary income. Viola Klein's data indicate that this attitude is more often associated with women in less highly qualified occupations while the more highly trained wish to continue work through their lives (Klein, 1966). However, the most frequent current pattern is for married women to work until close to the birth of the first child and then to withdraw from work. The woman who works continuously through marriage, childbirth and the early stages of child rearing is still the exception.

If a well qualified woman does not marry or, if married, does not have children, the immediate post-university period is occupationally a relatively easy one for her. There are many places for university graduates and obtaining a suitable position is not a major problem. Some employers even prefer women at this stage because many of them at this point in their careers are supporting husbands who are continuing with their studies or are in early establishment phases of their own careers. This assures a high level of commitment to the job and a good 'mix' of relatively uncompetitive personnel with those who are more ambitious and competitive. As one informant put it:

'Many men are glad to see a good group of women entering a job situation with them, as this cuts down on the competition that they anticipate in getting promoted into higher level jobs.'

This perception of women begins in the early career period, becomes a clearly defined stereotyped expectation, and is accepted by many women themselves. Some employers feel that when they try to open up new career lines for women, the women themselves limit their aspirations and behave (as they have been conditioned to do) as if they did not really want to work in high level positions.

THE PERIOD OF MARRIAGE AND LATER CAREER DEVELOPMENT

For married women in all occupations, but particularly for those in careers involving high commitment and responsibility to organizations, the birth of the first child is the critical family transition signalling withdrawal from work. The usual pattern for which women have been prepared, and which most accept as 'normal' if not desirable, is that they withdraw fully from work for the period of childbearing and early child rearing at least until the children enter school. When the last child has entered school, the woman may (if she has sufficient energy left and has not changed her interests too radically) re-enter part-time employment. This pattern may be functional in relation to the maintenance of the existing structure of the male role both in the family and in the occupational setting but it is neither congruent with the norm of equal opportunity to choose and enjoy society's resources, nor is it conducive to making the best use of female talent acting as it does against women's chances for reaching really senior positions.

The literature provides abundant documentation for these points. Myrdal and Klein elaborate the 'women's dilemma': women are socialized in terms of broad cultural values to expect that men and women should have equality of opportunity and that they will naturally have a marriage and a career as do men; however, women find in fact that at the child rearing stage they must make a choice (Myrdal and Klein, 1956). They must decide whether to continue to give major energies to their work involvement (as do men), or to their family involvement (as is the most generally accepted course) or to attempt both. Some factors that influence their choice at this point are their self-conceptions, their physical and psychological strength, the attitudes of their friends, the kinds of husbands they have and the nature of their relationships, the work opportunities open to them, and their attitudes towards children and the maternal role. The research evidence on these issues can be considered separately under three headings: the effects on children, the role relationships with the spouses, and the relevance of different types of employment patterns.

The issue of effects on children is a very complex one that has been given a good deal of professional attention as well as being the focus of widespread popular concern. The issue is usually stated in terms of the potential psychological damage imposed on children if their mother works, Bowlby's work on maternal deprivation has had a tremendous effect, not only on its intended target audience of hospital and other institutional administrators, but on parents and others personally concerned with the well-being of children. The mother who is highly educated is likely to be even more interested than most in this issue, whether or not she is particularly maternal. Recent work by Terence Moore and Yudkin and Holme in Britain, and Nye and Hoffman in the United States, as well as experience in Sweden and Israel, have led to a re-consideration of this issue (Moore, 1966; Yudkin and Holme, 1965; Nye and Hoffman, 1963). The general conclusions are, on the whole, negative, i.e. there is no indication that children of working mothers are more deprived than those of non-working mothers. To some extent, however, there are positive indications, i.e. that children may benefit from having a mother happily employed outside the home (presumably in contrast to unhappily 'captured' within) and that girls in particular may benefit from having an active role-model in their mothers. There is some suggestion that in the type of family that fosters a more egalitarian view, so that the mother can work as well as the father if she wants to, the children may also have the benefit of more contact with father.

Bowlby, since the publication of the W.H.O. report on Mental Health, 1951 (which used the maternal deprivation thesis as an argument against women going to work), has himself done further work that suggests that the effect of separation depends on the circumstances, particularly the quality of substitute care (Bowlby, 1965). Ironically, Bowlby's subsequent theoretical work seems to provide an under-pinning for a radical reconceptualization of the whole issue of parental role-relationships in regard to work, and the effects on children. He now speaks of 'attachment theory', emphasizing that satisfactory emotional attachment of some kind is an important need for the growing child but that this need not be tied to such events as feeding. Therefore a framework is provided for delegating many tasks formerly considered inextricably 'maternal' without undermining the basic sense of attachment necessary for healthy development (Bowlby, 1969). The implications of attachment theory for the working through of new solutions to the child care issue have yet to be considered in detail but they are now on the theoretical horizon and if Bowlby's influence is as great in revising popular preconceptions as it was in first establishing them, major changes may be brought about. In terms of the framework used in this study, it is important to note that there is far too little definitive research on the effects on children of various patterns of mother and father working or at home, with associated supplementary or substitute 'mothering' arrangements.

The issue of the husband-wife role relationship is one that is always mentioned tangentially in discussions of women working but has not yet received focal attention. Riesman talks of the need for allaying men's anxieties about their own roles so that they will be secure enough to let their wives work; Erikson writes about men and women having overlapping curves of talent; political pamphlets (citing recent research) indicate that as a result of changes now taking place, men are participating more in all sorts of domestic tasks. The prevailing attitude about the man in relation to the domestic world seems to parallel that which has been prevalent about the women in relation to the world of work, namely, that he is invited to help out if he has surplus time and energy; in many families, men tend to be expected to help out at home to the extent that such help does not interfere with their normal work regimens. Conversely, women may go out to work so long as doing so does not interfere with looking after home, children and husband. This formula has provided a sort of role-complementarity which is only now beginning to be critically re-examined. From the manpower point of view, the argument is that women are being under-utilized if they remain entirely in domestic roles, and that the traditional formula of a period of withdrawal has acted as a barrier to women's reaching top positions of the occupational structure. Humanistically, it has been argued that women who want it ought to have the opportunity for continuous self-fulfilment in work as do men; and, conversely, that men who wish to concentrate on domestic roles ought to have the chance to work out with their wives ways of achieving new and creative balances in the division of labour in the home. Implied in this is the possibility of a new balance of time and energy spent on family activities and work activities, which may benefit men as well as women. Alice Rossi argues that in contemporary society the husband enhances his self-fulfilment as a man if he is able to help his wife to be a fuller woman – and for a highly qualified woman this means to pursue her career (Rossi, 1969).

In relation to the work situation, two issues seem to occupy major attention of contemporary specialists. First, the nature of work seems to be changing in such a way that the more physical, manual types of jobs are becoming less arduous, and the more professional ones more so. If the trends noted by Donald Michael continue, automation will lighten the load on the less qualified thus creating problems of surplus leisure, while the more highly trained technological professions become increasingly overloaded (Michael, 1968). Be this as it may, the general point that seems relevant is that the nature of work is changing. Galbraith and others have argued that less work is actually necessary for the economy of an affluent society, and as the psychological attitude of 'over-valuation' of work becomes less functional either for the society or the individual, various new patterns may emerge which give less salience to work in the overall life-space of the individual (Galbraith, 1960). By so doing, it may become possible to arrange less rigid and confining schedules of work for any given member of the family. This prospect (which is far from being realized) makes it possible to consider many types of arrangement, for example where the husband is released from some of the demands made on him by his work and thereby is able to co-operate with his wife so that she can go out more to work.

The second issue is concerned with barriers to career development. To some extent the issues of women developing so as to rise to the top are similar to those of men. As the pyramid narrows, the competition becomes fiercer, the in-fighting fiercer and the primitive sex-loyalties more operative. Compared to these barriers, the earlier career obstacles are child's play. Prejudices against women entering work in various sectors of the society are relatively mild at lower levels. They are manpower resources much in demand for support level jobs. The problems arise in relation to their progression into the highest positions. Reasons given by employers for the paucity of women in high positions are various:

'Men don't like women bosses';
'Men don't like to have a woman boss at work *and* a boss at home';
'Women don't like women bosses';
'Once a woman withdraws to have children, she can't re-enter except at a low level'. (Reasons for this include 'technological obsolescence', 'competitive disadvantage', 'change of interests and motivation', and so on);
'Women don't want it';
'There are prejudices against putting women on the board';
'Women can't keep up the pace' (travel, night work, total commitment);
'Women don't carry their fair load . . . they want equal pay for unequal work. . . .'

Whatever the reasons may be in any given situation it is quite clear from the studies of Seear and her associates, Arreger, and others that women are not successful in entering senior positions in the same proportions as are men with similar qualifications (Seear and Brock, 1964; Arreger, 1966). One lady scientist interviewed denied that obsolescence was a 'real' problem even in highly technical fields because of the fact that people tend to specialize in narrow areas with which it is possible to keep up. In some ways men, who face similar problems of obsolescence, are at a disadvantage as some are tied to specific jobs which occupy their energies and prevent them from keeping up with overall new developments. She attributes the difficulty entirely to the prejudices of people who control access at critical points – the nominators for positions, programmes, candidacies and so on. To paraphrase her, 'it's not being a top scientist that is a problem for women scientists, it's *getting* to be one'.

In general, the conceptual framework and review of salient issues bearing on the framework highlight the course of influences acting on individuals at different stages in their life careers, and how events in earlier stages can affect subsequent events. At the points of status change from one social role to another in the various spheres of life career (family, education, work) critical decisions are made that may affect the entire subsequent career, not only the course of the next stage. At these critical transition points, the personal, inter-personal and societal influences that operate to affect the individual's choice are particularly trenchant. A woman's decision to work thus becomes an issue not only of her own motivation but of the whole pattern of support in her relationships and of the societal pattern of supports and/or impediments in defining sex roles. In considering the formulation of research that will exploit the potentialities of this conceptual framework, a dilemma becomes apparent. If the research worker begins with the later stages of the career, e.g. the peak of the work career, there is more certainty that the subjects studied represent those in focus – namely, women actually *at* the top. Knowledge gained about people who are in this type of position and are functioning under favourable circumstances could be immediately useful to others of comparable talent, functioning in circumstances less favourable but which may be amenable to change. On the other hand, the women *now* at the top were motivated, recruited and developed in social circumstances significantly different from those currently prevailing; thus what would be learned from the reconstruction of their career processes might not be closely applicable to women *en route* to the top today. Conversely, the earlier the researcher goes back in the life cycle for the selection of research foci, the more 'long-term' and contingent the perspective becomes.

METHODS OF INVESTIGATION

This study is an exploration in depth. It seeks, by various methods – qualitative, quantitative, documentary, direct observation, cross-cultural, and so on – to analyse the issues confronting contemporary highly qualified women in relation to their careers. This research, like all research, is based on assumptions, implicit or explicit, and the choice and interpretation of what is done must be assessed in this light. In making the assumptions more explicit, a sounder basis for choice of problems and methods can be made, and a research strategy can be developed which bears on the underlying thinking about the topic. In this way discontinuity between research findings and the discussion of their meaning can be minimized. However, a research strategy depends not only on the explicitness of assumptions and rationales, but also on resources and opportunities available. The choice of methods and strategies in any complex investigation is something that emerges from an interplay between the specific interests, competencies and inclinations of the individual researchers, the financial and personnel resources available, the time span allowed for study and the opportunities in the environment. The strategy of this investigation reflects these considerations.

Ideally, it would have been valuable to undertake a longitudinal study showing how different arrays of influences affect the aspirations of girls and boys as they develop, and how they come to change under the impact of later influences. The way in which the developing individual resolves dilemmas confronting him at the various critical points affects not only himself, but also the society in which he lives. An increased knowledge of the fields of forces bringing about the different kinds of resolutions – in the individual, his interpersonal relationships, his family, community and occupational environments – would be of value both theoretically and practically. However, such a study was ruled out both because of the time and financial limitations for the research and because the rate of social change is so great that the generalizations arrived at after a long-term longitudinal study might be of limited value for subsequent generations. Early in the research period it became clear that there were great differences in outlook and experience of women now at the top and women rising into top positions.

It was decided therefore that the groups of women who were to constitute the main study sample should be relatively young still and part of the generation that made its career development following the Second World War. The awareness that early marriage and child rearing periods would be most critical was also a factor. Nearly all women marry nowadays, and most have children and seek to reconcile their family roles with their occupational aspirations and roles. A suitable population from which such a sample could be drawn was found in a study of 1960 British University graduates conducted for the University Appointments Boards by Professor

Kelsall of Sheffield University. Professor Kelsall generously consented to allow individuals in his larger sample to be asked whether they would be willing to receive another, longer questionnaire in connection with the present study, and a sub-sample was derived from these responses which seems representative of the larger sample of graduates eight years out of university. The analysis of responses to a lengthy questionnaire covering the entire life-cycle of this sample of 30-year-olds (approximately) provides the core of the data reported in the next three chapters.

The survey instrument used in studying the life careers of the 1960 graduates was based on one designed by Alice Rossi and her colleagues (particularly James Davis and Frank Spaeth) of the National Opinion Research Center in the U.S.A. Borrowing heavily from their experience with a similar survey of graduates had two advantages. It allowed the present study to build upon existing experience of the most up-to-date kind and to evolve a research instrument in a fraction of the time that would otherwise have been required. In addition, it provided the possibility for some comparative analysis to determine similarities and differences between American and British graduates. This instrument attempted, within the limitations of such approaches, to gather information about earlier periods of the individual's life cycle as well as contemporary attitudes and behaviour patterns. However, in order to check on the reliability of information about patterns at earlier periods, and also to gain some insight into possible changes that are going on, two additional surveys were conducted: one of a sample of 1,000 graduates in their final year at University; this period of time was seen as crucial in making choices which would affect subsequent career patterns. In addition, another sample of about 2,000 sixth formers drawn from different types of schools in different parts of the country was conducted, with the collaboration of Donald Hutchings of the Oxford Institute of Education. In the present report the 1960 graduates are in focus with some information about the others provided, mainly in footnote form. Fuller reports on the other studies will concentrate on the special issues of their particular phases and will be published separately, together with a more systematic attempt to view them together as a simulated longitudinal study.

Because the method used for these surveys was a postal questionnaire (or a questionnaire which was 'invigilated' for the sixth form and university samples), their utility was limited to the kinds of analyses that could be validly accomplished with this kind of instrument. Two additional sub-studies were therefore developed to supplement the cross-sectional survey. One of these was the intensive family study, which consisted of an attempt to get to know much more intimately a small number of families in which the wife was pursuing an active and successful career as well as having an intact family with at least one child. A dozen such family studies were made, and, to gain perspective, three additional studies were made of families like the others – which are termed 'dual-career families' – except for the fact that the women concerned had dropped out of the active pursuit of their work careers, preferring to maximize familial patterns or being unable to reconcile the two kinds of pressures. These fifteen intensive case studies attempted to trace the development of the patterns observed through the personal and marital histories of the individuals concerned, and to reconstruct as far as possible the dilemmas that they faced, the stresses and strains that were involved, and how they were resolved and with what consequences for the individuals personally and for their families.

Another sub-study concentrated on the occupational environment. The cross-sectional studies based on the questionnaire approaches described, tapped only the responses of those who filled out the questionnaires, not their relevant environments, say at work. In order to gain an increased awareness of how the different fields of forces interact to affect individual decisions at critical status transition points, it was decided to study both family and organizational or occupational environment intensively in a smaller range of cases, to understand how forces within these environments impinge on individuals and affect their individual careers. Accordingly, after considerable discussion and exploration the five work environments mentioned in Chapter I – architects, the Administrative Civil Service, the B.B.C., women business directors, and women managers in two large companies – were chosen for intensive study by the team concentrating on the occupational studies, and from these environments the family cases were also selected.

There are then three major types of sub-study, each with its specific methods and its advantages and limitations but which form together a fairly comprehensive picture of representative elements of the problem at hand:

(1) Three cross-sectional surveys of highly qualified young men and women in Britain: one survey of sixth formers, one of university graduates in 1967 and one of 1960 graduates eight years out. The last is particularly in focus in the present report as it concentrates on the most problematic life-cycle phase for women – namely when they have young families – and also because it includes retrospective data on the whole life cycle.

(2) A study of the structure and functioning of dual-career families

to show how family life may be reconciled with high level careers (Intensive family studies of fifteen families in a range of occupations related to study type 3.)

(3) A study of occupational environments and career structure. (Five types of occupational and organizational work environments and career structures – relating to the same environments from which the family studies are drawn, and orientated to elucidation of the special career problems faced by women in contrast to men.)

All the sub-studies are exploratory in nature, though some use quantitative and some qualitative data. They are neither hypothesis-testing nor hypothesis-generating in the classical experimental paradigm, but are developed through systematic observation, inductive analysis, testing for patterning in the data in such a way as to build up a picture of the sector of 'reality' in focus and an understanding of how things seem to work in relation to it. Rather than testing a hypothetical relationship between one variable and another under specified and controlled conditions, the interplay of many antecedent and consequent variables under different conditions is examined as they seem to occur in different circumstances of contemporary society. This is to facilitate the search for generalizations and to develop an informed conception of the implications of the findings.

Some of the antecedent factors are conditions of individual, familial, and organizational experience; some of the consequent variables are work behaviour, satisfaction at work, satisfaction at home and personally, and patterns of participation in various spheres of life. These tend to be interactive but the ways in which they interact in relation to specific issues, like changing women's careers, is incompletely understood. The aim is to contribute to the systematic understanding of the interplay of these elements in producing observable career patterns for highly qualified women. This involves men as well as women, and familial as well as occupational institutions.

REFERENCES

Aregger, C. E., *Graduate Women at Work*, B.F.U.W., 1966.
Bell, D., 'Notes on the Post-Industrial Society (I and II)', *The Public Interest*, Nos. 6 and 7, 1967.
Bowlby, John, *Child Care and the Growth of Love*, London: Penguin, 1965.

Bowlby, John, 'Disruption of Affectional Bonds and its Effects on Behaviour', *Canada's Mental Health*, Supplement No. 59, January, 1969.

Davis, James A., *Undergraduate Career Decisions*, Chicago: Aldine, 1965.

Erikson, Erik, 'Inner and Outer Space: Reflections on Womanhood', *Daedalus*, Vol. 92, 2, 582-606, 1964.

Floud, J., Halsey, A. H., and Martin, F. M., *Social Class and Educational Opportunity*, London: Heinemann, 1956.

Galbraith, John Kenneth, *The Affluent Society*, Boston: Houghton-Mifflin, 1960.

Goode, W. J., 'Family Patterns and Human Rights', *International Journal of Social Science*, Vol. XVIII, 41-7, 1966.

Hartley, Ruth, 'A Development View of Female Sex Role Identification' in Biddle B. J. and Thomas E. J. (eds) *Role Theory, Concepts and Research*, New York: John Wiley and Son, 1966.

Himmelweit, Hilde, and Swift, Betty, 'A Model for the Understanding of School as a Socializing Agent', *Trends and Issues in Developmental Psychology*, New York: Holt, Rinehart Winston, 1969.

Klein, Viola, 'The Demand for Professional Womanpower', *British Journal of Sociology*, Vol. XVII, 2, 183-97, 1966.

Laing, R. D., *The Politics of Experience*, London: Penguin, 1967.

Maccoby, Eleanor E., *The Development of Sex Differences*, London: Tavistock Publications, 1967.

Maslow, A. H., *Motivation and Personality*, New York: Harper, 1958.

Mead, Margaret, *Sex and Temperament in Three Primitive Societies*, London: Routledge & Kegan Paul, 1935.

Michael, Donald, *Unprepared Society*, New York: Basic Books, 1968.

Moore, Terence, 'Difficulties of the Ordinary Child in Adjusting to Primary School', *Journal of Child Psychology*, 7.1.17-38, 1966.

Myrdal, A., and Klein, V., *Women's Two Roles, Home and Work*, London: Routledge & Kegan Paul, 1956.

Nye, N. I., and Hoffman, L. W., *The Employed Mother in America*, Chicago: Rand McNally, 1963.

Pheasant, J. H., *The Influence of the School Organization and Curriculum on the Choice of Exam Subjects and Careers made by GCE Candidates*, Ph.D. Thesis, Institute of Education, University of London, 1960.

Price, J., 'Personality Differences Within Families: Comparison of Adult Brothers and Sisters', *J. Biosoc. Sc.* Vol. 1, 177-205, 1969.

Riesman, David, 'Some Dilemmas in Women's Education', *The Educational Record*, 1965.

Rossi, Alice, *see* Davis, James, A.

Rossi, Alice, 'The Road to Social Equality', Paper given to a Sociology seminar at the University of Chicago, 1969.

Seear, N, Roberts, V. and Brock, J., *A Career for Women in Industry*, Oliver & Boyd for The London School of Economics, 1964.

Stoller, Robert J., *Sex and Gender: On the Development of Masculinity and Femininity*, London: Hogarth Press, 1969.

Trist, Eric, *The Relation of Welfare and Development in the Transition to Post-Industrialism*, Los Angeles: University of California, Socio-Technical Division, Western Management Science Institute, 1970.

Yudkin, S., and Holme, A., *Working Mothers and Their Children*, London: Michael Joseph, 1963.

Chapter VI

Work Careers

'My profession is . . . my only fit wife.'

(I. K. Brunel, in Rolt, 1961.)

'A woman has three security valves, a man, a child, a job; in my code it stands in that order, yet in my real life the order is reversed. Also, I believe that only a man with whom I would like to make a couple should be able to calm my anguishes, my distresses; but in real life it's my work that does that. I hate to admit all these contradictions in myself. . . .'

(C. Deneuve, *Life*, Feb. 2, 1969, p. 52.)

INTRODUCTION

The two quotations above show crucial differences in sex roles in relation to career and family life. Men, nowadays nearly as much as in Brunel's day, may admit that their career brings them their primary satisfactions without necessarily jeopardizing their family life. Brunel, the pioneering railway engineer, was passionately dedicated to his work, admitted it publicly and was praised for it while at the same time maintaining family life. For women, as illustrated by Miss Deneuve's statement, family relationships are supposed to be paramount, with career integrated with the rest of their lives in a secondary way or not at all. Where the woman in fact derives primary satisfactions from her career, she may experience conflict and have difficulty in integrating her family relationships into this pattern. Miss Deneuve, even with the enormous financial and other helping resources available to a successful film star, has experienced these strains and has in fact divorced her husband and restricted her contacts with her child so as to pursue her career – despite her wish to 'manage all – have a great career, a happy family life with a man, children and all'.

Alice Rossi notes that the 'helpmeet' conception of the woman's familial role is not compatible with a committed career as a responsible professional, such as a scientist, engineer or doctor, 'except for those rare Amazons among us who live two lifetimes in one' (Rossi, 1965, p. 53); Jessie Barnard in her study of women in academic careers says that 'unless your husband – if you have one – is with you all the way, the going will be rough. In fact, you might do well not to encumber yourself with any other kind of husband but your work' (Barnard, 1963). The male helpmeet to back up the dedicated professional woman (as Brunel's wife backed him up) is an even rarer bird than Rossi's Amazon.

186

In fact, the way in which the contemporary married woman with a family integrates a work career into her life is usually by accommodating to the 'social facts' of life and choosing the least stressful options open to her. Though, as Lotte Bailyn notes, highly qualified women may be assumed to have a range of ability and creative potential comparable to men and, like men, seek to develop a life style in which they can function in their various roles efficiently and productively with some degree of integration between them and satisfactions deriving from them, the social supports for women are lacking. For highly qualified men the probability of developing such a life style is high – not only developing and exercising both work and family roles, but being able to integrate the two and derive satisfactions from both. For women, once the decision is made to have children, a massive dilemma arises. On the one hand, women are seen as fortunate to have the choice as to whether or not they work, as the family livelihood does not usually depend on the wife but on the husband in his role of provider. On the other hand, her range of options is in fact severely curtailed by virtue of the fact that she is expected to carry responsibility for familial roles and to subordinate her own career aspirations to those of her husband, e.g. in relation to location of residence (Bailyn, 1964).

This narrowing of options, coupled with the tendency for environmental institutions to aggravate the difficulties faced by highly qualified women, creates a situation where the onus is thrown very much on to them as individuals to create solutions to their dilemmas. The easiest path is to fall into the conventional role of 'housewife', at least for a time. Another alternative is to make 'irrational' choices, do unsuitable work, be exploited in jobs of lower status or interest than they would command if they were men. Though this may be irritating it has the merit of reducing pressures from the work sphere. A third alternative is for the woman to interrupt her career, dropping out and re-entering as family situation and stage allow.

This chapter will focus on work careers and the comparisons between men and women in relation to how family and other influences affect the development of career aspirations. In the next chapter the focus will be on patterns of family life, and how they are affected by work and other influences. The data on which these analyses are based are from a cross-sectional survey of men and women who graduated from British Universities in 1960.[1] To provide some

---

[1] This survey of 865 men and women 'eight years out' of University is based (as described in the previous chapter) on a larger sampling of 1960 graduates achieved by Prof. R. K. Kelsall who very generously allowed his larger sample to be used as a sampling frame. Technical details are provided in the technical appendix on the sampling methods.

indication of trends underway and also to verify inferences about the developmental process as it relates to different career stages, information on career aspirations is also introduced, usually in footnote form, from another survey that was made of final year University students in 1967.[1]

Aside from selected references to the work of others in this field, a more specific set of references is made to the work of Alice Rossi, from whose American survey of women graduates our own survey instrument was adapted.[2]

In this chapter, after reviewing some of the major research positions in relation to the study of women and careers, the data from the British sample is analysed in terms of the place of career in the lives of women as compared with men, the different kinds of career aspirations that seem prevalent, the sort of occupational choices that are associated with these orientations to career, the intentions about continuous or non-continuous work careers that differentiate some women from others and most women from most men, and finally the kinds of factors that appear to determine the different patterns of career orientation and intention.

As this chapter concentrates on the career side of the analysis being made of the interaction between career and family (the next chapter concentrating on the family side) the position developed is that to understand the career patterns of women it is necessary to recognize that the factors involved are complex and multidimensional. Traditionally the picture was supposedly simpler: men worked as providers while women stayed at home as housewives and helpmeets with a relatively small range of exceptions, e.g. in family businesses or where the women were forced into the provider role. This picture has become increasingly complicated with the increase in egalitarian norms and educational experiences. The issues as they currently stand are that highly qualified women experience the same complexities as men (e.g. of fitting together personal, interpersonal and social influences in the choice and development of an occupational career) plus the additional set of complexities associated with how to manage the issues posed by child rearing. Here women show a range of orientations that affect their career performance and intentions. The purpose of this chapter is to indicate some of the complexities of

---

[1] A third national survey was conducted of a sample of 2,000 upper sixth form students in 1968. This study, undertaken in collaboration with Donald Hutchings of Oxford University, will be reported in a separate publication.

[2] Our survey instruments were adapted from questionnaires used by James Davis, Alice Rossi and Frank Spaeth at the National Opinion Research Centre (NORC) in Chicago. Selected comparisons will be made here where data are available.

this picture as it is seen in highly qualified British women (compared with men at the same stage) eight years after they leave university. A population studied at this time shows a range of attitudinal and behavioural patterns characteristic of the developing person with high qualifications.

Career aspirations – long and generally recognized as different for men and women in our society – are shown to be not simple and fixed (and therefore 'natural') but complex and variable, subject to personal, interpersonal and societal influences of various kinds.

The key issue is how different types and levels of commitment to career arise and are modified. As family commitments, particularly for women, significantly affect and are affected by career commitments, the key issue becomes how more effective integration between the two areas of life can be achieved for women as well as men.

THE NATURE OF CAREER ASPIRATIONS

Among behavioural scientists a number of perspectives have emerged in the study of careers.

Different types of personality are attracted to and adapt differently to the requirements of different kinds of occupations and careers (Roe, 1956). Values as well as needs affect these choices (Rosenberg, 1957; Ginzberg, 1951; Butler, 1968). Careers in different fields have properties that are determined by the nature of the occupation and its history and social context and these influence the behaviour of individuals taking on roles in the specific career fields (Hughes, 1958). Aside from the global characteristics of any given career – such as medicine, law, architecture or business – careers have stages which provide sequences of roles for individuals from the novitiate through retirement and these roles differ according to the nature of the social system in which the career is embedded (Super, 1957; Cogswell, 1969).

The literature on the analysis of careers is extensive (cf. Osipow 1968). In general, the orientation adopted here is that in the study of highly qualified individuals it is important to distinguish between careers and other kinds of job sequences. Careers have the distinguishing characteristic of a developmental quality, even though this may only emerge retrospectively. The job sequences in a career tend to form a meaningful whole and there is a sense of high involvement and motivation (commitment) and progression towards valued goals or achievements (McClelland, 1953). The different approaches to the study of careers have different theoretical orientations, as would be expected, and differ as to whether they are focusing on personal motivations or on roles and their articulation with the social environment. As the current study expressly tries to approach the issue from both perspectives, it is useful to note that each of the perspectives, aside from having certain advantages, tends to have certain disadvantages. The sociological approach has the advantage of seeking regularities and patterns that make it possible to distinguish the more pervasive and effective patterns from the more local and inconsequential. The psychological approach has the advantage of providing information on motivation and personal orientation to the behavioural patterns which may allow for an understanding of dynamic processes as experienced by individuals. The two are most usefully joined in studies of social process and social change, as is the present report.

For such a goal, two elements of perspective are important and the aim is to emphasize them in the current work. First, it is important to take a position that is relatively free of the biases of a particular culture. As will be indicated below, where there is a cultural bias as to what is 'feminine' and what is 'masculine', particularly in the world of work, constraints may be introduced which are irrational from the point of view of the present study. Second, it is important to take a position that allows for a consideration of differentiation and variation in populations as well as the modal or dominant patterns. Where there are changes underway it is often the 'creative minority' which will exercise increasing influence as time goes on rather than the numerically dominant majority at any given time.

In relation to sex differences in career choice and development, different conceptual frameworks seem to be used for the analysis of male careers and for female careers. As males are seen to have the function of status-placement for the family (cf. Parsons, 1959 and discussion below, p. 195), the choice of career for boys is seen in terms of social mobility for the family as a whole. As women make their occupational choices much more against a background of the traditional housewife-mother and as they do not have the function of status-placement for their families, their choices tend to be analysed in terms of their personal identities and familial relationships (Cf. Lidz, 1968 and discussion below). This is not simply a matter of disciplinary differences, but reflects the state of conceptual development of the field. Both perspectives are important. Two leading research clinicians are quoted to indicate how the viewpoint of such observers is biased not only by the clinical source of their data but by the cultural framework within which they live and work. The Czech psychiatrists present their analysis in the cultural frame of the Socialist countries and the American psychiatrist represents middle-class American perspectives and values. These viewpoints, expressed by reputable authorities, are cited to show the nature of the prevailing climate of authoritative opinion within which women entering demanding occupations must function. This also affects the opinions of men which are operative in the marital and occupational situations.

The American middle-class view, buttressed by the clinicians' formulations,[1] is best expressed by Lidz, a respected and leading research psychiatrist (Lidz, 1968). His general observation may be true enough, that:

> 'Although most women will prepare for and enter into an occupation, it is usually a secondary matter, a means of filling time or supporting her husband during his training years and augmenting the family income when she is not caring for children. The selection of an occupation will not be concerned with gaining prestige, wealth, or power, but will more commonly be directed toward finding a job in which she can fill a nurturant role, as in nursing, teaching, social work and medicine.[2]

This reflects a prevailing statistical pattern. The view, however, becomes myopic as Lidz goes on to label traditionally sex-typed roles in terms that imply some biological fitness or natural inevitability:

> 'There are, of course, a number of women who will pursue more masculine careers for a variety of reasons, sometimes because they cannot come to terms with their feminine identity and wish to compete with and surpass men, but also often from fears of marriage and childbirth, or of the dangers of dependency.'[3]

Lidz presents the view from the clinic as though it were generally valid. He does not indicate that there are other motivations for a woman wishing to pursue a career, or having similar career values to men, or that competitiveness or fear of dependency might be as operative for men as for women in their choice of careers. He has no idea of the degree to which competitiveness or fear of dependency

---

[1] It is important to note two things here. First, some Eastern psychiatrists believe that the view expressed above reflects bourgeois capitalism. We believe that it reflects a position prevalent in a society that happens to be bourgeois and capitalist; rather, the psychiatrist is dealing with psychological casualties from his society and is orientated to the norms of this society and tends to lack cross-cultural perspectives. Second, the view expressed here is not held by all psychiatrists. Psychiatrists like Erikson, Bettelheim and Leighton discuss these topics in less ethnocentric terms. At the other extreme are psychiatrists who do not give much thought to the dynamics underlying the behaviour they observe and treat clinically. Lidz's viewpoint is a prevailing one among informed and thoughtful but culture-bound psychiatrists and is presented for this reason – not as a straw-man viewpoint held by a particularly hidebound or narrow-minded minority. It should also be said that Lidz, in discussing topics on sex-differences, shows a keen awareness of sub-cultural differences and their implications.

[2] Lidz, p. 253. [3] *Ibid.*, p. 352.

or masculine elements of identification are prevalent in the population
of women who do not choose 'masculine' occupations. His viewpoint
culminates in a section on occupational choice in which he states:

'Women do not usually need to prove themselves through accomplishment and achievement, and gain more satisfaction from being
admired and loved because of who they are, or because of what
they can give. . . . Although some women enter adulthood with a
fairly firm decision to pursue a career come what may, eventually
marriage usually takes precedence and a career becomes secondary.
Most women recognize, even if the colleges they attend do not,
that being a good wife, and even more being a good mother,
requires many refined abilities and skills and forms a career in
itself. Dissatisfactions with this limiting career will often arise;
this will be discussed in the chapter on marital adjustment. . . .'[1]

This viewpoint contrasts sharply with that of Knoblochova and
Knobloch of Czechoslovakia. While obviously in both countries
there are various types and sources of marital tension, the Knoblochs
tend to see the situation in which marital tensions arise through the
wife's dropping her career, more in terms of the possibility that the
husband is unable to drop a traditional sex-typed conception about
masculine and feminine roles. The Knoblochs state (Knoblochova
and Knobloch, 1965):

'When psychotherapists of different countries meet they are unable
to reach full agreement on a general formula for the healthy and
well-adjusted family, for standards for the masculine and feminine
role, etc. The reason is mainly that standards in different societies
are different and are due to varying conditions; a factor that constitutes adjustment in one society may not do the same in another.
For example, it is impossible to formulate a general conclusion
on whether and how long the mother must stay with her small
children at home and not go to work; it can only be said that in
a certain society in known conditions such-and-such is the most
suitable solution for child and mother.[2] In a society where girls
are principally prepared for the role of housewife and mother,
where vocational possibilities for women outside the family are
limited to auxiliary jobs demanding lesser qualifications, and
where economic conditions lead to strong competition with men,

[1] Lidz, p. 383.
[2] Of course there are some biological invariables due to the needs of baby
and mother, but psychotherapists should not be too certain that they know
what these invariables are. Research has not progressed so far as to afford
reliable conclusions, and the claims made in psychiatric literature are generally
strongly influenced by cultural factors.

the most suitable solution is probably that mothers with small children stay at home. For such a mother it may be bad if, for purely financial reasons, she has to seek a job and leave care of the child to another person or to an institution. On the other hand, in a country with a socio-economic system like that of Czechoslovakia, where the professional career and basic economic independence of women are broadly regarded as essential conditions of their emancipation, where their right to work is embodied in the Constitution, where, from childhood, they are educated with a view to their choosing a profession, and where they will soon be able to achieve the same status as men,[1] it may be frustrating for them to stay at home for a long time with their child. Their mental balance may be endangered, and neurotic symptoms and depressive moods may appear even in reasonably balanced women. Under these conditions, it is best, not only for the mother but also for the child that the mother should go to work and that the care of her children – not forgetting the father's part – should be shared with the nursery school and kindergarten. Clinical experience seems to show that the quality and not only the quantity of maternal care is important for the child. It seems to be better for the child if the employed mother, the satisfactions she enjoys in the family balanced by those she enjoys in her profession, is at home for part of a day than if unbalanced and depressed, she is there all day long. It has been the author's experience over many years that housewives who came to the Psychiatric Clinic as neurotic patients often decided during therapy to go to work. If psychotherapy continued, strikingly more favourable situations for personality change were established: the patients lost a sort of mental lethargy, became more lively, optimistic and resourceful, renewed their lost interests and seemed younger in body and in mind although their lives became more complicated. The nursery schools and kindergartens in Czechoslovakia admittedly leave much to be desired, but they already possess many features which give them an important part in known cases where children staying at home the whole day with frustrated mothers have a more disturbed emotional contact with the mother than a child who spends several hours a day in a nursery.

Quite a few authors in English and American psychiatric

---

[1] In fact, as is described in Chapter II, they have not yet achieved it fully in all parts of public life, but the trend is in this direction. It is a long-term process determined by economic development, the establishment of good nursery schools and kindergartens in sufficient numbers, the mechanization of household work, etc. There are also the negative factors, such as prejudices on the men's side, to be overcome.

literature seem to have an *a priori* concept of the role of housewife as the most ideal for feminine adjustment; if there is marital discord in a family where the wife is a professional woman, it is readily explained by the 'wife's not being well-adjusted to her feminine role'. One instance is of an energetic woman, successful in her profession, coming with her husband who is dependent, clinging and not very successful in anything he undertakes, to the marriage counsellor. The husband suffers from manifest neurotic symptoms, especially in the sexual sphere. The therapist seems from the outset to suppose that the wife is maladjusted to her feminine role, accounting thus both for her striving for success in her profession and also for her husband's inhibitions. The therapist directs her attention to the masculine traits in her character indicated by her interest and success in her job. As a result of therapy, the wife decides to leave her job and stay at home. The husband's self-confidence is increased by the fact that he no longer feels inferior to his successful wife, and in the process of mutual adjustment he loses his symptoms.

If such a case occurred in Czechoslovakia, we would doubt whether permanent marital stability could be achieved in this way. We wonder also how much the preconceptions of the therapist contributed to the outcome of therapy.

In Czechoslovakia, the feminine role is a more complicated concept and covers more functions than, say, before the Second World War. Also, in Czech society the concept is not strictly defined; in a transition period, psychotherapists have to be prepared for varying concepts of both masculine and feminine roles. We do not attempt to convert our patients to our opinions; we approach both the marriage partners' different standpoints in a way that will harmonize them and lead to mutual adjustment. It is useful for the psychotherapist to know the trends of development in his society.

Therapists in Czechoslovakia do, of course, meet the type of woman who is maladjusted to the feminine role as they understand it in the broad framework, where it is not, however, usually felt to manifest itself either in the choice of job or in its execution. To them such a type manifests itself in a lack of interest in marriage or in children, and, if the woman married, in her failure to adapt herself, in a tendency to be ambivalent, aggressive, promiscuous, frigid, to reject childbirth, etc.

We also encounter men who need to feel superior to women especially to their girl friends and wives, and husbands who decline to let their wives go to work – as a result of conditions in their childhood when they formed their conception of roles, the fear of losing their superiority, old-fashioned views (according to prevalent opinion), jealousy and suspicion, etc. But they tend to be considered in our society as cases of insufficient adjustment to the masculine role; their view would not be regarded as socially sound, and they have to seek compromise solutions for their marital relations. In the therapeutic community of the Neurosis Centre, such men would be encouraged to enact model conflicts with women patients. Employment is part of the feminine role concept; neither the therapist nor the patients in a group advise the woman patient to adapt herself solely to the demands of her husband.'

The tendency here is to assume employment generally as a part of the feminine role concept rather than being something 'masculine' if it is formulated in too ambitious terms or in relation to the non-traditional range of 'feminine' jobs.

In sociological analyses a man's identity is very much linked to his occupation and his family is placed in the social structure largely according to his occupation and his success in it. To the extent that women have had occupations outside the home, there has been a tendency for the wife to choose an occupation of appreciably lower status than her husband's or for a husband to choose a wife with an occupation appreciably lower than his own (Parsons, 1959). This serves to maintain the man's function of family status-placement through his work. However, the situation has inevitably become more complex as women increasingly receive similar education to men and have similar interests aroused which in turn lead into increasingly similar ranges of occupational possibilities. Nevertheless, whether for psycho-biological reasons or through cultural lag, the indications of most contemporary research are that women differ from men both in the career-relevant capacities they demonstrate and in the kinds of motivational syndromes they characteristically display in the world of work. However any particular woman may behave, the statistical tendencies are for women to opt still for a more restricted range of occupations and for them to participate in the occupational world with less drive for success in the status-climbing sense.

Perhaps the most useful conceptualization of this situation in sociological terms is that made by Turner. He distinguished two types of ambition, and two types of associated gratification. One type is material ambition, which is associated with jobs or careers where the gratification is assumed to be *extrinsic* to the actual work done; the other is the eminence type of ambition where the desire is for accomplishment and excellence in a line of work where the

195

gratification is primarily *intrinsic* to the work itself (Turner, 1964). Obviously the two may be linked, as McClelland and his colleagues have demonstrated in their studies of the 'achievement motive' (McClelland, 1953). However, they may, under some circumstances, be segregated, and one of the circumstances brought out by Turner and relevant here has to do with women's ambitions, to the extent that they are satisfactorily distinguishable as a group from men's.

Turner argues that married women, when they choose to work, leave the material ambitions to their husbands. They either have a purely supplementing attitude (as in ordinary non-career jobs) or an eminence orientation in which predominantly intrinsic gratifications are sought where there are career-orientations. The women who work merely to supplement their familial material ambitions tend to continue to exercise whatever intrinsic gratifications they seek within the homemaker's role. It is only women who de-emphasize the homemaker role as the sole arena within which they expect to get their major gratifications that seek intrinsic rewards in their careers. They still tend not to equal the men in the degree to which they seek both extrinsic and intrinsic rewards in their careers. Turner does not go into any further speculation as to why this phenomenon exists, but taken together with Parsons's observations about the tendency for career-wives to pursue careers less materially rewarding and/or less eminent than those of their husbands, it appears that this arrangement is in some ways functional for the contemporary family with its historical set of role definitions.

Alice Rossi indicates how these norms are perpetuated in American middle-class families through socialization influences. She writes:

'In her primary group environment, she (the girl) sees women largely in roles defined in terms that relate to her as a child – as mother, aunt, grandmother, babysitter – or in roles relating to the house – the cleaning, cooking, mending activities of mother and domestic helpers. Many mothers work outside the home, but the daughter often knows as little of that work as she does of her father's. Even if her own mother works, the reasons for such working that are given to the child are most often couched in terms of the mother or housewife role. Thus, a girl is seldom told that her mother works because she enjoys it or finds it very important to her own satisfaction in life, but because the money she earns will help pay for the house, the daughter's clothes, dancing lessons or school tuition. In other words, working is something mothers do as adult women. This is as misleading and distorted an image of the meaning of work as the father who tells his child he works "to take care of mummy and you" and neglects to mention that he also works because he finds personal satisfaction in doing so, or that he is contributing to knowledge, peace or the comfort of others in the society.'[1]

As Rossi implies, there should be an increased appreciation of the way in which the hierarchies of values, ordering of ambitions, definitions of roles and areas of gratification, may be changed if socialization influences could be altered. Women's ambitions are not fixed – either biologically or culturally. They are subject to change in response to circumstance. One circumstance that is very familiar involves premature bereavement. If a youngish woman is left a widow, she may be 'catapulted' into a career (e.g. in her husband's business) and once in it she may find that it awakens somewhat dormant capacities in her, from which she derives hitherto unexpected satisfaction. The celebrated 'champagne widows' of France illustrate this. There are other kinds of crises, or critical transitional experiences which stimulate a reorganization of values and patterns of aspiration and gratification. These include marriage and having children (Rapoport, 1961).

THE PLACE OF CAREER IN THE LIVES OF MEN AND WOMEN

Miss Deneuve, in placing family before work as the area of life from which she hoped for the greatest satisfactions expressed the cultural normative view for women in our society. But once involved in career activities which were intrinsically gratifying (as well as extrinsically gratifying, in her case) she found that the sources from which she was obtaining data were not those which she would ideally have liked.

In the cross-sectional survey instruments used, a question was included which sought to gauge the *relative* salience of the different life areas – family, work and so on. The assessment of salience is essential to the topic of central concern to this study, as it is assumed that outstanding achievements tend not to be found where the activity has low salience for the people concerned. By hypothesis, women are unlikely to aspire to the more demanding types of career

---

[1] In a footnote to the above discussion (p. 641), Rossi refers to a study by Ruth Hartley of upper-middle-class mothers of girls in a progressive school in New York City. The working mothers of this sample told their children that they were working out of the home because of financial need. They express their guilt about their working and appear to hold quite traditional concepts of appropriate 'feminine' behaviour which they feel they are violating. An example is given by a well-to-do working mother who loves her work but told her daughter that she works for financial reasons. When asked why she does not tell her daughter that she enjoys her work, she said, 'Well then what excuse would I have for working?' (Hartley and Klein, 1959).

197

jobs if work and career are of low salience to them. A major element in salience is the satisfaction expected or experienced from each area of life; this is used here as an indication of salience.

The sample of 1960 graduates were asked the question: 'Which of the following gives you (*a*) the greatest satisfaction and (*b*) the next greatest satisfaction?'[1]

Your career or occupation
Family relationships
Leisure time recreational activities
Religious beliefs or activities
Participation as a citizen in the affairs of your community
Participation in activities directed towards national or inter-
    national betterment
Running a home
Other

Table VI.1 shows the distribution of responses to the first part of the question, i.e. 'which gives the greatest satisfaction', for the 1960 graduates, broken down by sex and marital stage.

This table shows clearly that the area from which satisfactions are received is a function of sex and marital stage. Both single men and single women experience greatest satisfactions from their careers, whereas the emphasis shifts to family life following marriage and

Table VI.1

Greatest Life Satisfactions by Sex and Marital Stage

1960 Graduates: (Percentages)

	Single men	Married men no children	Married men with children	Single women	Married women no children	Married women with children
Career	53	42	29	42	19	4
Family	11	42	59	14	58	82
All Other & NA	36	15	13	43	24	13
Total percentage	100	99	101	99	101	99
N =	(58)	(79)	(245)	(112)	(73)	(298)

[1] 1967 graduates and 1968 sixth formers were asked the same question, except that the form 'expect to give you' rather than 'gives you' was used to elicit their expectations about these areas, many of which had not yet been experienced.

still more after having children. The sex differences and similarities are also interesting. Though more men than women obtain their greatest satisfactions from their career or occupation at every stage, 59 per cent of the men choose the family as the main area after having children; for the women, approximately the same proportion find the family area most satisfying once they are married, but the proportion rises to 82 per cent after having children. While only 4 per cent of the women retain career as their primary area of satisfactions after having children, 29 per cent of the men retain this orientation at this stage. For both men and women there is about an equal falling off of satisfaction from other areas following marriage and childbirth. (The full table is given in Appendix I.)[1]

In considering both the first and second chosen areas of satisfaction, a picture emerges of a large number of women in this sample who look to their career or occupation as a secondary area of satisfaction. Table VI.2 shows the combined proportions of individuals in the different sex and marital stages who chose career as first or second in importance to them:

Table VI.2

Career as Greatest or Next Greatest Areas of Satisfaction by Sex and Marital Stage

1960 Graduates: (Percentages)

	Single men	Married men no children	Married men with children	Single women	Married women no children	Married women with children
Career as Greatest or Second Greatest Areas of Satisfaction	84	74	80	75	50	30
N =	(58)	(79)	(245)	(112)	(73)	(298)

[1] The 1967 graduates showed a pattern of response that confirmed this picture. Being 90 per cent single, their distributions resembled those of the single respondents, with 30 per cent of the men and 12 per cent of the women indicating that they expected greatest satisfaction from their careers and 53 per cent of the men and 73 per cent of the women from family life. Combining 'greatest' and 'next greatest' satisfactions, family outstrips career for both groups with 80 per cent of the men and 85 per cent of the women falling into one or the other category (as compared with 76 per cent of the men and 69 per cent of the women expecting this much satisfaction from career), making the younger group slightly more 'familistic' in orientation than the older unmarried group. Rossi's findings for women graduates three years out of university are roughly similar to those for the 1967 British graduates.

Thus, 74-80 per cent of all men and single women seem to obtain their greatest or next greatest satisfactions from work, whereas the proportion drops to half for married women without children and to less than a third for married women with children. Even so, it is interesting to note that nearly one third even of married women with young children look to their careers as a *major*, if not the primary source, of their personal satisfactions. This issue will be dealt with at greater length in the next two chapters when interplay of work and family commitments are considered in greater detail. This chapter shows how the *salience* of career (as compared with other areas of potential life satisfactions) relates to types and levels of career aspiration.

COMPONENTS OF CAREER ASPIRATIONS

As indicated above careers have been studied from a variety of perspectives. It would seem that a certain *level* of motivation is necessary to achieve a career that involves high qualifications and persistence of effort; in addition, a certain *type* of motivation is needed for a person to be drawn to and function successfully within a given occupation – and this is *a fortiori* true for women who leave the conventional women's roles. Turner's distinction between two types of ambition in young people has been mentioned (Turner, 1964). However, to accept the extrinsic motivations as quintessentially 'masculine' and the 'intrinsic' ones as 'feminine', simply because a correlation exists between these orientations and sex in a specific cultural contest would, it is argued here, be erroneous. The findings of this report confirm Turner's formulation to a large extent; but there are important qualifications that show how the two types of aspiration may be linked not to sex *per se* but rather to *general* career orientations that happen in this population (as in Turner's) to be statistically correlated with sex. In addition, the emphasis here is on a more dynamic conception of how these types of aspiration change with life stage, reinforcing our fundamental postulate that they are determined to a major extent by the social environment and situation. It follows from this that the orientations and correlation with sex could change as the culture changes.

In actual behaviour, 'extrinsic' and 'intrinsic' motivations (which are theoretical abstractions) are usually combined in various ways. One of the problems in the usage is that the terms 'extrinsic' and 'intrinsic' are sometimes seen in evaluative terms – with 'intrinsic' motivation being seen as more desirable than 'extrinsic'. For this reason, the terms 'horizontal' and 'vertical' ambition are used instead. The latter conceptions also have the advantage of relating the

individual's motivations to a structure in the social environment –
an organization, profession or other occupational structure.

In this section an attempt will be made to assess the differences in
career aspiration between men and women, and in the next chapter
we shall examine the family area before coming to the crux of the
matter for women and their careers – namely, how family and career
may be integrated more effectively for women as well as for men.

a *Levels of aspiration*

The eight-year-out respondents were asked about their present level
of ambition, and also about its level when they were at university
and when they were in secondary school.[1] The data in response to
these questions can be plotted as a 'quasi-time series', showing the
general course of development of the 'vertical' aspirations of men
and women.

Figure VI.1

Recalled Aspirations of Men and Women at Different Points in their
Careers (1960 Graduates) (Percent wanting to 'get to the top' or 'hold
high position')

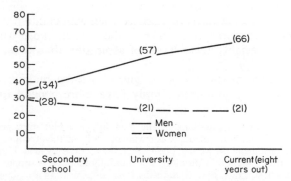

From this it may be seen that among graduates, both young men
and young women recall having had similar levels of aspiration when

[1] The question asked was: 'How would you characterize your level of
ambition?'

    To get to the top
    To hold a high position
    To get along, make a living
    Other
    Didn't think about this aspect

Respondents were asked to reply in terms of what they thought 'now', 'when
they were at University', and 'when they were in Secondary School'.

at secondary school. Roughly comparable proportions of each (about one third) wanted to get to the top or hold a high position. For the men, the picture is one of sharp increase, with more of them aspiring to hold top or high positions as they go through university and leave to enter work and marriage. For the women, in contrast, there is a decline during their university years, and they stabilize at this lower level of aspiration thereafter.[1] Is this pattern true for all men and women, or are there other elements in the situation that differentiate sub-groups within the male and female populations? The critical role transitions of getting married and of having children have been conceptualized as important in the reorganization of values and behaviour (Rapoport, 1961); in the preceding section these factors were shown to affect the relative salience of different life areas. How do they affect occupational ambitions?

Table VI.3 shows the pattern of response by the eight-year-out group to the question on level of aspiration.

Taking together those who wish to 'get to the top' and those who wish to 'hold a high position', it is clear that the most ambitious group among the 1960 graduates is the married men. The single men are appreciably lower. For the women the reverse is true. The proportion of single women who aspire to high level positions is greater than that of married women. For the men, there is little overall difference between the married men with children and those without children. However, amongst the women those with children show appreciably lower levels of aspiration than those without children.

Various interpretations can be given to these findings. Do the more ambitious young men simply have more general drive and

[1] Two alternative explanations of the data are possible: retrospective bias may operate differently for men and for women, with the men recollecting lower levels of aspiration and the women higher than those currently held. However, the assumption that these recollections are substantially accurate is supported by the data from the 1967 graduates. Though the levels of aspiration are higher for this younger group overall, they show a similar patterning. For the 1967 graduates, 59 per cent of the men and 46 per cent of the women recalled having a high level of aspiration in secondary school; then the men rose to 71 per cent at the time of the study (final year university) and the women dropped to 35 per cent of their numbers aspiring to the high level. As in the 1960 graduates sample, the male rise in proportions of high aspirers is sharper than the female drop. The second alternative, an exploration of which is beyond the scope of the current work, is that these figures do not represent rises and drops and stable patterns of aspiration for the same people, but that different individuals make up the picture with a much more complex process of shifts in aspiration underlying the pattern than is apparent. This possibility will have to be explored separately. On balance it is assumed that the overall picture presented will hold up, even if the underlying process producing it is more complex than that suggested.

marry earlier, leaving their more listless colleagues as a group high in unmarried and unambitious types? Or, do the men start off relatively evenly distributed in level of aspiration and then change under the impact of family responsibilities, so that the single ones are able to remain relatively unperturbed by the exigencies of family-life and therefore need not shift their energies so much into the 'vertical' orientations to career ambition? Among the women, why is it that those who are single are more ambitious? Are they people who were always ambitious and refused to allow men and children to interfere with their participation in the occupational world or have they only

Table VI.3

Current Level of Aspiration by Sex and Marital Stage

1960 Graduates: (Percentages)

	Single men	Married men no children	Married men with children	Single women	Married women no children	Married women with children
Get to top	21	18	22	6	6	2
Hold high position	24	56	47	31	18	12
All other responses	55	26	32	62	77	86
Total percentage	100	100	101	99	101	100
N =	(58)	(79)	(245)	(112)	(73)	(298)

recently substituted 'vertical aspirations' for family life? The construction of the developmental pattern of aspirations by recollected levels at the different life-cycle stages is revealing when related to current family stage. Figure VI.2 shows this for men, and VI.3 for women.

It would seem that the single men always were somewhat less ambitious as a group than those who are married 8 years after graduating, but the differences increase following university. The two groups of married men are virtually identical in their level and patterning; the single men start lower, rise only relatively slightly during university days, and then remain stable thereafter with less than half of them showing high levels of aspiration. The women's pattern is shown in Figure VI.3.

203

Figure VI.2

Men's Recalled Level of Aspiration by Life Cycle Stage

1960 Graduates: Men (Per cent wanting to 'get to the top' or to 'hold a high position')

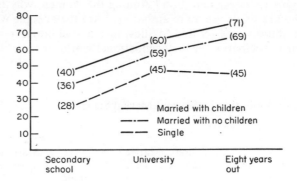

Figure VI.3

Women's Level of Aspiration by Life Cycle Stage

1960 Graduates[1]: Women (Percentages wanting to 'get to the top' or to 'hold a high position')

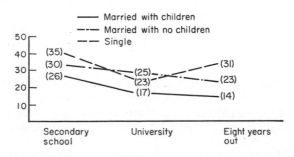

[1] An analysis of individual patterns shows that the overall levels of high aspirers are maintained by about one third of the numbers remaining consistently high, and about two thirds rising from lower levels of aspiration in earlier stages. The individuals who drop out of the high aspiring group are made up of about one third who simply lower their aspirations to the 'get along' category, and about one third who go off the vertical aspiration scale to 'other' or 'don't think about it'.

It can be seen that the women's pattern differs markedly from that for the men. The women who marry are from the outset somewhat less ambitious occupationally than those who do not, though the differences (as with the men) are minimal at secondary school and university and become more manifest at the eight-year-out point. All categories of women depress their levels of ambition, as they recall them, during their university experience, and those who are married continue to depress them, with aspirations being lowest among married women with children. The single women, in contrast, elevate their levels of aspiration following university.

On the basis of questionnaire information it is hazardous to speculate about the precise mechanisms involved here, though there are almost certainly several patterns within the overall development of aspirations shown. The two variant groups – the single men and single women – are interesting and have some traits in common.

Some information on these two groups is available from adjective check lists that were provided for all respondents. They were asked to indicate for a list of 48 adjectives the extent to which they felt each one applies to them. Examination of the responses shows that for several of the adjectives the single men and the single women differ markedly from their married colleagues. The single men describe themselves as somewhat *less* hard driving, ambitious or competitive than the married men. Only 7 per cent, for example, of the single men indicate that they are 'very hard driving', as compared with 18 per cent of the married men. And 16 per cent of the single men indicate that they are 'not at all' hard driving, as compared with 8 per cent of the married men. Single women, by contrast, show the obverse differentiation, being *more* hard driving than other women. Fifteen per cent of the single women indicate that they are 'very hard driving' as compared with the general level of 6 per cent for the married women. Following the same pattern of the single women being like most men in the competitive area, and the single men being more like the women, the single women consider themselves to be more 'rational', more 'intellectual', more 'physically strong' and more 'loyal to an organization', than other women; while the single men consider themselves to be less 'physically strong', less 'methodical', and more 'talkative' than other men. There are fewer 'strong silent' types here.

Aside from the 'vertical aspiration' syndrome of traits, which checks with the responses to the question on aspirations (with the single men aiming lower and the single women higher than the married members of their respective sexes) there are some traits which they share as variant groups. Relatively high proportions of both the single men and the single women indicate that they are 'very reserved' (25 per cent of the single women as compared with about 10 per cent of the married women; 14 per cent of the single men as compared with about 10 per cent of the married men). 16 per cent of the single men consider themselves to be 'very shy' as compared with only 4 per cent of the married men. The single men and single women also consider themselves to be more than ordinarily intuitive. Nineteen per cent of the single men indicate that they are 'very intuitive' as compared with 6 per cent of the married men, and 23 per cent of the single women as compared with 12 per cent of the married women. Both the single men and the single women consider themselves to be 'very cultured' more often than do others of their respective sexes (19 per cent of the single men as compared with 7 per cent of the married men; 16 per cent of the single women as compared with 7 per cent of the married women).

Special to the single women is the greater proportion who consider themselves unattractive to the opposite sex. This is perhaps the counterpart of feeling less physically strong for the single men. A remarkably uniform proportion of about 60 per cent of all the married categories of men and women consider themselves 'somewhat' or 'very' good looking. However, only 46 per cent of the single men and 46 per cent of the single women choose these categories of response. Furthermore, 11 per cent of the single women (as compared with only 3 per cent of the married women) indicate that they are 'not at all attractive to the opposite sex'.[1]

The level of ambition held is of course only partly a question of individual motivation. The activation of motives, or their effective channelling, depends on the environmental circumstances – the economic opportunity structure and, more focally here, the family structure of roles. A special problem is created by the fact that

---

[1] The relationship between physical attractiveness and career development for women has not been given sufficient attention. Ben-David has pointed this out in personal communication. Social mobility studies have indicated how physical attractiveness has operated in women's favour through mate-selection processes. In career development, where competence and achievement are paramount, attractiveness may also be relevant but in different ways. Indeed, there may be a bi-modal pattern operating. Alice Rossi's data indicate on one extreme that short fat girls are more likely to consider themselves unattractive, less likely to marry and therefore more likely to pursue a career, than their peers. Ben-David suggests as a hypothesis, that at the other pole of physical attractiveness there may be another favourable factor for those girls who have career aspirations. Attractive girls may be secure enough in their heterosexual relationships to be able to devote major attention to work tasks – particularly during the courting phase of development – where less attractive girls may be concerned with peripheral preoccupations such as where their next date will come from. There may be other factors operating in favour of attractive women at later phases of their career development. The bi-modal hypothesis deserves further attention.

women who wish to pursue careers have to reconcile this with a heavy burden of residual domestic responsibilities from the traditional housewife role. This is demonstrated in relation to the issue of energy.

A high degree of energy is needed for anyone to pursue a career. This is particularly true for careers that have a high component of vertical aspiration. There was a general consensus among the survey respondents – of the different life-stage groups between the two sexes – about how much time and energy is necessary to make a successful career. About 80 per cent overall feel that it takes maximum time and energy to 'get to the top', with another 10-15 per cent feeling the required energy expenditure as 'medium'. About 70 per cent overall feel that to achieve 'substantial success' takes medium time and energy, with about 25 per cent of the remainder feeling that it takes maximum time and energy even to achieve 'substantial' success.

The overall percentage of women (excluding those who want to be housewives exclusively) who feel that it will take 'maximum' energy for them to get where they want to occupationally reflects the proportions of women to men who are high aspirers. About 20 per cent of women as compared with over 60 per cent of men aspire to reach high positions, and about the same relative proportions indicated that it would take maximum energy to reach the positions they wanted to be in (about 11 per cent of the women as compared with about 27 per cent of the men).

It is, therefore, a matter of general consensus that it takes a lot of energy to reach a high position, and the amount of energy one needs to have available is a function of how high one aspires.

The picture on *levels* of aspiration can be summarized as follows:

Women have a lower level of aspiration than men but men's and women's levels of aspiration are much more nearly alike when they are younger than subsequently. There is a discernible relationship between social role and level of aspiration. As women proceed from school to university to subsequent life following graduation, their level of occupational aspirations drops. The level of aspiration of married women, particularly those with children, falls more sharply than that of the single women. Indeed, the single women's pattern undergoes a transformation following university with more women in this category showing an upswing of ambition. There may be a number of explanations for this. Some women may not want to marry and may develop high career aspirations instead; some may have decided that their chances of marrying are low and so increase their career involvement. Still others may be postponing marriage while they consolidate their career position.

Men, on the other hand, show the obverse picture. Their level of ambition, as a group, rises continuously and sharply as they leave university and marry. For most men this is the pattern and the married men with and without children do not differ from one another as appreciably as do the married women with and without children. The single men, like the single women, are anomalous. Unlike the married men, the proportion of single men with a high level of aspiration does not rise following university. This may be because they do not experience the stimulus of marital responsibilities or it may be because their personality traits are different from those of their marrying graduate classmates.

The preceding section attempted to bring out the overall patterning of levels of aspiration for the population under study, and to indicate some variations particularly as related to sex and marital status. In the sections to follow, some of the more 'intrinsic' or 'horizontal' *types* of aspiration will be brought out.

b *Types of aspiration*

Respondents were asked: 'People's ambitions go in different directions. For each of the ambitions below please indicate the extent that you would like to achieve it'. (Not at all, somewhat, or very much.)

The list, given in the table below, has both 'vertical' and 'horizontal' elements of aspiration. The response pattern for the overall 1960 graduate population was as follows:

Table VI.4

Direction of Ambition Wanted 'Very Much'

1960 Graduates: (Percentages)

Have a reputation for extreme competence in one's field	76
Be creative (e.g. in the arts)	30
Make an important discovery (e.g. in the scientific field)	17
Be rich (to have lots of money)	17
Be powerful (run a big organization or government body)	12
Be famous (be a known name)	7

It is notable that the graduates generally, both men and women, favour the intrinsic types of rewards. They overwhelmingly choose 'a reputation for extreme competence' as the achievement they want 'very much', with creativity falling second by a good margin. There

208

are, however, interesting sex differences, which are shown in the following table:

Table VI.5

Men's and Women's Direction of Ambition by Family Stage
(Per cent indicating they want it 'Very Much')

	Single men	Married men no children	Married men with children	Single women	Married women no children	Married women with children
Be famous	16	13	9	8	4	2
Be rich	26	24	25	6	7	8
Be powerful	21	19	23	3	3	2
Be creative	29	20	29	29	30	31
Make an important discovery	21	24	23	9	10	8
Have reputation for extreme competence in one's field	71	90	85	70	71	64
N =	(58)	(79)	(245)	(112)	(73)	(298)

It would seem from this table that the men wish in much greater proportion than the women to achieve the 'vertical' rewards – wealth, fame, power. These are the elements encompassed in the notion of getting 'to the top'. To 'make an important discovery' also seems to be desired more by men. This ranks overall with the 'vertical' items, and probably implies career success in this sense. The women and the men resemble one another much more closely on the more 'intrinsic' or 'horizontal' value of doing 'something creative' and in wishing to 'have a reputation for extreme competence in one's field'. The men wish the latter somewhat more than the women.[1]

In summary, the men and women resemble one another in their general ranking of directions of worthwhile ambition – placing 'competence' on top while fame and power are at the bottom for each category. Men and women also resemble one another in their high valuation of the 'horizontal' characteristics of their work, particularly 'creativity'.

A second notable finding is that in contrast to *level* of ambition (which is heavily affected by stage of family life cycle) *direction* of

[1] This may be due to deficiencies in the wording of the question 'having a reputation for extreme competence'. The men may give greater emphasis to the 'reputation' part and the women to the 'competence' part.

ambition is not so affected. There are differences between the men and women, particularly in relation to the 'vertical' career values of fame, wealth and power; but these are seen across the range of family life cycle stages and do not vary appreciably with getting married and having children for either sex.

Looking at the direction of aspirations more closely, information was obtained about individuals' specific goals and which of these he/she expected eventually to achieve. Twenty specific goals were suggested and respondents were asked to indicate which ones he/she wanted to accomplish. Ordering the specific goals into seven groupings they can be described as 'general contribution', 'contribution to special field', 'contribution to science or technology', 'contribution to the creative arts', 'personal status', 'successful business' and 'money'. The women – in both the 1967 and the 1960 samples – showed a higher proportion of choices than the men for two of the categories: 'general contribution' (which mostly consisted of items such as writing a book) and 'creative arts'. As a further indication of how the 'moulding' (cf. p. 216 below) process occurs, many of the men expect that they will be successful in ways other than their preferred types of accomplishment. They consider that they will probably eventually attain money and personal status to a greater extent than they say they now want it; and, on the other hand, a smaller proportion than would really like to, feel that they will achieve outstanding scientific or professional contributions of a more innovative or creative kind.

Fully one third of the women indicate that they do not want any of the accomplishments listed; this is true for only 5 per cent of the men. The responses are concerned with *current* wishes and the married women with children contribute the greatest weighting to this percentage among the eight years out people.[1]

Another appreciation of the differences between the 'intrinsic' values seen in their work by men and women is obtained by examining their responses to a question asking for an indication of the relative importance to them of nine career values:

An opportunity to work with people rather than exclusively with things or ideas.
A chance to work at an interesting job with a minimum of disturbance.
A chance to use intellectual problem-solving abilities.
An opportunity to show what I can accomplish.

[1] On the other hand, over 40 per cent of the women as compared with 13 per cent of the men in the 1967 survey also indicated that they did not want any of the options given.

An opportunity to be helpful to other people.
A reasonably stable and secure future.
Relative freedom from supervision by others.
An opportunity to be creative.
An opportunity to maximize income.

The following table summarizes the response pattern, dividing the career-values into three groups: a group in which the men tend to rank the value higher than the women (i.e. a greater proportion of the men choose that value as first or second in importance); a group

Table VI.6

Top Career Values by Sex:

1960 Graduates: (Percentages: men's first, women's second)

GROUP I	GROUP II	GROUP III
Men value these higher than women	Equally high emphasis	Women value these higher than men
Intellectual problem-solving (29 per cent, 23 per cent)	Interesting job (25 per cent, 27 per cent)	Working with people (32 per cent, 52 per cent)
Stable/secure future (20 per cent, 13 per cent)	Freedom from supervision (19 per cent, 17 per cent)	Helpful to others (21 per cent, 37 per cent)
Show what I can accomplish (19 per cent, 10 per cent)	Creative opportunity (15 per cent, 16 per cent)	
Maximize income (16 per cent, 3 per cent)		

in which they are about equal (i.e. proportions within 5 per cent of one another choose the value as first or second in importance); and a group in which women place higher emphasis than men on the value in question.

The values used in this question were adapted from earlier studies by Rosenberg, Moment and others (Rosenberg, 1967; Moment, Simpson and Simpson, 1960). In their studies, a tripartite grouping seems to have emerged with distinctions made between 'intrinsic' values (i.e. things related to actual performance of work tasks of the occupations), extrinsic values (i.e. financial rewards, security), and 'peripheral' values (e.g. opportunity to work with people rather than things). The findings in this present study support the tripartite division; however, *both* men and women choose 'working with people' first. The 'intrinsic' or 'horizontal' values are about equally emphasized by men and women, whereas more men emphasize 'vertical' values and more women the 'peripheral' values.

Other responses on values in the survey reinforce the findings on this question; men consistently show a higher interest in financial rewards, the wish for power, influence, authority, etc., while women show consistently a greater interest in 'stimulating human contacts', helping others, etc. The emphasis on intellectual problem-solving, work with ideas, inventions and discoveries seems to be an area of intrinsic ambition which men hold more highly than women, though this is less marked than findings for the other value contrasts mentioned.

The 1967 graduates also show some association between sex and values in work. The women tend to pay more attention to aesthetic and human relations types of values in their work with the men tending to emphasize 'vertical' ambition accomplishments. To the extent that women hold vertical aspirations, many drop the level under the impact of child-care responsibilities. They do not, however, change their values. They simply, to use Alice Rossi's expression, 'put a lid on' their aspirations. Taking all the women together, only 5 per cent indicate that their career is of no interest to them. This is about the same proportion as for the women on the other extreme who indicate that their career is of great importance to them and that they intend to continue working throughout their lives *and* having children. It is the 90 per cent in between that are of greatest interest, because they are the ones who shift their levels up or down, modify their aspirations and participate in or withdraw from work at different stages of their lives according to their situations.

The situational factors that make for a highly qualified woman working effectively are partly in the external world of occupations and partly in the more personal and intimate areas of their own motivations and familial circumstances. Family circumstances will constitute the main topic of the next chapter. Before that a few remarks on the part played by motivation: it has already been indicated that a high level of aspiration is associated with such character traits as 'hard-driving', 'ambitious', 'competitive', and so on, and with such career values as the wish to 'show what I can accomplish'. Taking level of aspiration as a variable, with some men and some women high on it and some low, what is the effect of this particular dimension on some aspects of work performance – namely occupation chosen, amount of time worked and earned income? The following section shows the relationship between level of aspiration and these elements of career performance for the different groups of respondents in the sample.

OCCUPATIONAL CHOICE AND CAREER PERFORMANCE

The ways in which the level and type of aspiration are formulated by individuals are complex. They also affect occupational choice and performance. Some occupations have a more hierarchical career structure than do others, and by choosing such an occupation one may become automatically involved in 'climbing' however much the initial attraction to the occupation was on 'intrinsic' rather than extrinsic grounds. Some professions reward meticulous cultivation of qualitative achievement with hierarchical rewards more than do others. The very act of choosing most occupations places one in a hierarchical system of ranking so that in deciding to become a mechanical engineer rather than a mechanic, one automatically chooses a higher level of aspiration. Furthermore, some occupations articulate with others in a chain of advancement while others are in relatively closed compartments in the occupational system; if, for example, one chooses to become a musician one can, given drive and opportunities, pass from being an instrumentalist to being a conductor or composer or a professor of music. If, on the other hand, one chooses to be a musical instrument repairman this sequence of career positions is not ordinarily open to one. If one becomes a nurse one cannot become a doctor without leaving the nursing sub-system and entering the medical training sub-system. Furthermore, it is sometimes difficult to assess how much any individual is motivated by extrinsic and how much by intrinsic motives; and these may change in their value for the individual. The cinema idol who after financial success wants to play on the stage even at a much lower level of remuneration exemplifies this; often the components are merged. How much of the Beatles' early career motivation can be attributed to intrinsic delight in expressiveness and artistic accomplishment and how much to crude drives for success? These issues defy appraisal with the survey instrument used here.

Thus aspirations may vary, both in kind and level, with stage in the life cycle and they ought to be seen as encompassing the domestic work role as well as occupational roles in the labour force outside the home. The houseproud woman, who wants to keep up with the Joneses in the size of house, garden and car owned, illustrates the potential pervasiveness of the extrinsic aspiration syndrome on the domestic scene. And the modest housewife – manifesting very little extrinsic aspiration for herself – may drive for her husband's or children's success through the familiar mechanisms of displacement

213

and manipulation. Some individuals compartmentalize their aspirations, as is seen with the driving businessman who reaches for financial success and power during the working day only to retire to the cultivation of a non-instrumental hobby in the evening such as mounting butterflies. An irony arises when the hobby becomes the source of worldly success, as in the case of someone like Ian Fleming, author, 'with his left hand', of the James Bond novels.

The choice of an occupation has, then, a range of extrinsic, intrinsic, and peripheral components. In choosing an occupation, an individual chooses implicitly or explicitly a position in a socially ranked hierarchy of occupations, with associated financial and prestige rewards. Any given choice, however, may be made on intrinsic grounds with little attention to the ranking component of the choice. And, once made, an occupational choice may be pursued with either extrinsic or intrinsic values uppermost in the individual's motivations. Peripheral elements which were minor as original criteria may become crucial. Most individuals function with a blend of the three, difficult except in extreme cases to disentangle. The decision, for example, to be an architect may be initially motivated either by the conception of the architect's position in society as highly prestigious and well-paid, or by the notion of designing beautiful buildings, or of working with interesting people. Once an individual has embarked on the career of an architect, he may use his professional skills primarily to accumulate as much money as possible without reference to the type of work done, or he may attempt to maximize the aesthetic component in his work or the socially significant component without more than minimal reference to the financial aspect, or the 'social' aspects without reference to either of the other two.

Another aspect of occupations and one that is particularly important for this study is that they are frequently socially stereotyped – not only as 'high' or 'low' but as 'masculine' or 'feminine'. Some occupations are 'women's occupations' in terms of prevalent norms, while others are 'men's occupations', and it has been the more pioneering type of women, highly motivated to work, who have crossed over the sex-typed career lines from the nurse-teacher-social worker complex into the 'masculine' territory of science, engineering and business management (Fogarty, Rapoport and Rapoport, 1967; Rossi, 1965; Hughes, 1958).

The choice of occupation is subject to different constraints for women than for men. Both men and women experience their own vicissitudes of indecision, trial and error, testing out and shifting of occupational commitments, but they start with somewhat different conceptions of their suitability for various occupations. There are many theories about why women, even in the current period of

214

W

enlightenment, opt for certain occupations and avoid others. A number of the points made in general discussion of these issues were put into a question, and the respondents were asked for four occupational groups – pure science, applied science and engineering, industrial management, and the 'free professions' – why they thought so few women entered these fields, and why they thought that women, once in these fields, so rarely rose into high positions. The reasons offered as alternative choices for the respondents were:

Such jobs require skills and characteristics which women do not have.
Restricts woman's chance to marry.
Too demanding for a woman to combine with family responsibilities.
Men in this field resent women colleagues.
Most parents discourage their daughters from training for such a field.
Women today want to work only occasionally and on a part-time basis, which they can seldom do in this situation.
Women are afraid they will be considered unfeminine.
Length of training.

The answers to these questions were remarkably uniform across the different groups of respondents. Because the model categories are often not majority choices – the dispersion being considerable – the two categories most frequently chosen for each of the career issues are reported in Table VI.7.

Table VI.7

Perceived Reasons for Women Not Entering and Not Rising to High Positions in Selected Professions

1960 All Men and Women Graduates: (Percentage of Most Frequently Chosen and Second Most Frequently Chosen Reasons)

	Science	Engineering	Management	Professions
Reasons for not entering	Parents (23 per cent)	Parents (21 per cent)	Men resent (21 per cent)	Training (34 per cent)
	Don't know (18 per cent)	Unfeminine (23 per cent)	Parents (20 per cent)	Don't know (20 per cent)
Reasons for not rising	Family (35 per cent)	Men resent (27 per cent)	Men resent (32 per cent)	Family (36 per cent)
	Require full-time (21 per cent)	Family (26 per cent)	Family (28 per cent)	Require full-time (18 per cent)

215

In fact, a relatively small number of all the possible reasons presented were seen as important. Parental influences, men's attitudes and family responsibilities were frequently chosen reasons for difficulties in *all* of the occupational groups. 'Length of training' was seen as a specific barrier to women's entering the professions but would probably be answered similarly had the question been put in relation to men's reasons for not entering the professions.

There are two categories that were indicated as relevant by less than 10 per cent of the sample. The notion that women do not have the requisite skills, and that it would damage their chances for marriage, are very seldom chosen (under 5 per cent overall). For all but pure and applied science, the idea of the field not being feminine was also rejected, though this was thought to be a factor for women not entering engineering (23 per cent) and science (12 per cent). For science and the professions, the full-time demands of the occupation were perceived as a deterrent to women rising to high positions; this was given as the third most frequent reason under industry and engineering.

Occupational choice is seen as a process, or rather two processes: *crystallization* and *moulding*. The two interact, and individuals vary in the degree to which they succeed in accomplishing occupational choices satisfactorily. Some individuals never do crystallize an occupational choice but drift from one to another. This pattern is less frequent among the occupations requiring a high degree of qualifications. The moulding process occurs when an individual responds to social pressures, either positive or negative, to formulate an occupational choice and to develop an effective role within an occupation. An example of negative moulding would be where an individual really wants to do something which is difficult in the circumstances and, succumbing to social pressures, participates in an alternative occupation more or less unhappily. The youthful poet-revolutionary who finds after graduation that there is no ready market for his type of occupational interest may compromise by becoming a teacher of Spanish literature. Depending on his personality, he may be relatively happy with this choice or he may feel deep-seated discontent and express his dissatisfactions in various ways. Research on careers has indicated an early stage of occupational choice in which the choices are either unformulated or based on fantasy – such as the little boy's fantasy of being a cowboy or a jet pilot. While some of the fantasy choices may materialize in subsequent reality, they will in a much larger proportion of the cases be subjected to the kind of moulding process that turns the little cowboy into a grown-up policeman, or the little jet pilot into the grown-up travelling salesman. Crystallization brings clarity and choice into a situation where there was vagueness and indecision. Moulding brings a more 'realistic' or socially acceptable choice into a situation where there may have been unrealistic or unfeasible fantasy previously.

The population studied illustrate these processes very well. Crystallization can be seen to occur from one age group to the next and the retrospective material reinforces the information available from the samples at the different age levels. The overall picture is that about one third of this graduate population had 'no particular occupation' in mind by the time they reached secondary school. This number was reduced to about 5 per cent during the time they were in secondary school, and the proportions are further reduced to 2 per cent by the end of their university career. The less than 1 per cent who are neither housewives nor gainfully employed are almost entirely women. Only one single man indicated that he was unemployed at present. The question of commitment to occupation, however, is another matter. Many graduates try out occupations within a given range and enter occupations temporarily. This is not only true of the occupation 'housewife' but for many of the men as well, including teachers, salesmen, etc. Indeed, the modal category for both men and women graduates is to have had two changes of employer in the eight years since graduation and to have had two changes of kind of work done. (These are not necessarily the same people but the overall proportions are similar.) About a third of the graduates have had two changes in the eight years. The two groups which have modes different from the mode of the graduate population as a whole are single men (the greatest proportion of whom have had three changes of kinds of work done) and the married men with children (the greatest proportion of whom have also had three changes). The reasons for these variant patterns are probably different for the two groups, with the single men being more undecided or uncommitted as a group and the married men with children possibly being upwardly mobile.

This is supported by an examination of reasons given for changing jobs. The graduates were asked their main reason for leaving their last job. The most important single reason for the population as a whole was 'to have a baby' and for the married women with children the figure is 75 per cent. 15 per cent of the overall population have never left a job and the proportion for men only is 25 per cent. Single men and married men with children differ from the other groups in the number of job changes they have had; both have experienced more but for different reasons. A high proportion of single men appear to have left their jobs because of a lack of commitment, whereas the greatest proportion of changes for married men with children came with advancement in a line of work. This is

217

indicated in different ways. Thirty per cent of the married men with children indicate that they left their last job to take 'a better job', as compared with 24 per cent of the single men giving this as the main reason. Furthermore, an analysis of the stability of occupational choice supports this impression. Respondents were classified according to whether they indicated an early choice of occupation which corresponds with their present occupation or not. The proportion of people of all categories who say that their idea of what they wanted to be in secondary school corresponds to what they are in fact currently doing is about one third – the only really variant types being found among the single men, of whom only about 20 per cent indicate this consistency of occupational role. The actual distributions by sex and marital status are:

Table VI.8

Consistency of Occupational Choice

1960 Graduates: (Percentages showing consistent occupational choice)[1]

Single men	Married men no children	Married men with children	Single women	Married women no children	Married women with children
21	42	37	42	38	33

Once again there is a tendency for the single women to resemble the married men in their consistency of career commitment more than they do other women or the single men (who in turn are even less consistent in their career orientations than are married women with children).

What sort of occupations do men and women graduates actually enter, and what are their experiences in them? The issue of women's careers is really a special case of the general problem of occupational choice, because most graduates are trained for a range of possibilities, but most make specific choices only after receiving their general qualifications. Examining the occupations of the eight-year-out graduates in our sample, it can be seen that the pattern reflects the culturally normative sex stereotyping of occupations (Table VI.9).

Thus men outnumber women 15 to 1 in the professions and industry, 3 to 1 in the public service and academic occupations, and

---

[1] Choices were rated as consistent if the individual indicated a serious interest in the *same* occupation at three periods, 'secondary school', 'university', and 'now'.

Table VI.9

Present Occupations of 1960 Graduates (Percentages)

	Men	Women
Architect, accountant, lawyer, engineer	26	2
Industrial manager, business enterprise	15	1
Government (Civil Servant)	6	2
Scientist	11	3
University teacher	16	6
Secondary school teacher	16	21
Primary school teacher	1	4
Publisher, journalist, mass media	2	2
Social worker	2	4
Housewife	0	44
Other	6	10
Totals Percentages	101	99
N =	(382)	(483)

Table VI.10

Median Income in Different Occupations and Percentage of those Groups who are Women

1960 All Men and Women Graduates

	Median Income category (£s per annum)	Per cent of the group who are women
GROUP I Industrial manager, sales personnel, doctor, lawyer, Civil Servant	2,000-2,500	9
GROUP II Engineer, college teacher, others	1,500-2,000	26
GROUP III School teacher, scientist,[1] social worker	1,000-1,500	48
GROUP IV Housewives	None	100

[1] Scientists are in the lowest income group because their median income is in this range. It is unclear from our data whether this is because so many of them are still involved in postgraduate studies and early establishment roles as laboratory assistants, etc., or whether fully employed scientists in this age range are in fact so lowly remunerated.

women outnumber men in teaching and social work. Being a house-wife is an exclusively feminine occupation.

The choice of occupation has consequences for level of income. Table VI.10 shows the different levels of median income by groups of occupations whose median incomes cluster in the same ranges. It also shows how the occupational groups with a greater proportion of men have higher median incomes.

That level of aspiration, independent of type of occupation, has an effect on income is shown in Table VI.11.

Table VI.11

Level of Income and Level of Aspiration by Sex and Family Phase

1960 Graduates: (Percentage of Each Category who are High Aspirers.)

	Per cent earning under £1,500		Per cent earning over £2,000	
	(N)		(N)	
Single men	22	(18)	53	(17)
Married men without children	64	(11)	84	(32)
Married men with children	50	(36)	76	(104)
Single women	31	(71)	75	(4)
Married women without children	18	(51)	25	(4)
Married women with children	13	(290)	33	(3)

It has already been shown that the men as a group earn more than the women. Smaller proportions of all categories of women are in the 'over £2,000' than of the men. However, examining the effect of 'level of aspiration' it is clear that this operates for all categories of earners, men or women. For each category, the proportion of high aspirers in the £2,000+ earning bracket is higher than in the under £1,500 bracket.

Income is, of course, only one indicator of performance at work. The hours per week of paid employment according to sex and marital stage are shown in the following table.

If a 'full-time' job is considered to be over thirty hours per week, over 90 per cent of all categories of men are employed full-time, and for married men the figure is 96 per cent. The women in all categories work fewer hours, though using the 31 hours+ criterion for 'full-time', the single women work as many hours as at least the single men. Of married women without children, nearly 65 per cent approximate a full-time job. The sharp drop comes of course with children, but even here over a third of the married women with children continue to work at least a bit.

What, then, are the determinants of working? One may ask this for men and women, as Pym did in his paper 'Why work at all?' (Pym, 1969). However, in this context the focus is on the question of what differentiates the women who *continue* to work – even while marrying and having babies – from the women who do not. The men, to all intents and purposes, all work; they do not have the same option that the women have, whether this option can be perceived as a special blessing associated with the women's role in society or

Table VI.12

Hours of Paid Employment per Week

1960 Graduates: by Sex and Marital Stage (Percentages)

	Single men	Married men no children	Married men with children	Single women	Married women no children	Married women with children
None	2	0	1	2	13	62
Under 10	2	0	0	2	7	22
11-30	5	4	4	7	16	11
31-40	46	44	44	54	51	4
41+	45	53	52	35	13	0
Totals:						
Percentages	100	101	101	100	100	99
N-NA	(56)	(78)	(242)	(111)	(71)	(291)
NA	(2)	(1)	(3)	(1)	(2)	(7)
N	(58)	(79)	(245)	(112)	(73)	(298)

as a special burden. The problem for the research is to distinguish between the working and non-working women, particularly among those who marry and have children. Because of the special problems raised for women by virtue of childbirth and infant care, 'working' means not only working at any given moment but intention to work more or less continuously through the life cycle. The question, then, becomes what are the patterns of *continuity* in work for married women, and what seems to influence them?

DETERMINANTS OF MARRIED WOMEN'S EXPECTED WORK PATTERNS

A consideration of the factors that determine whether or not a woman continues to work even while having young children involves a number of complexities. For women at the family stages covered in the sample under study, many are now working who may not do so in future. So current work status is not a sure indicator of overall career continuity. To understand career continuities, a study of intentions is necessary in research of this type where samples cannot be followed up.

Women who marry and have children think of the child-rearing period, according to our response patterns, in three major phases: when the children are under 3, which is the youngest age at which the child can be entered into a nursery school and when the infant is

Table VI.13

Married Women's Expected Work Patterns at Different Phases

1960 Graduates: (Percentages intending to work)

	When youngest child is under 3		Children 6-12		All children working/married	
	Married women no children	Married women with children	Married women no children	Married women with children	Married women no children	Married women with children
Full-time[1]	8	5	8	20	41	55
Part-time	20	33	51	61	36	26
Not at all	54	61	25	4	3	1
Don't know	18	2	16	16	20	18
Total Percentages	100	101	100	101	100	100
N =	(73)	(298)	(73)	(298)	(73)	(298)

seen as most in need of 'mothering'; the period of primary school (age 5-12); and when the children are self-sufficient, culminating in the point at which the last child is working or married. These may, of course, be broken into sub-phases, but the crucial phases seem to be marked by the point when the youngest child reaches age 3 at one end, and when the last child is working or married at the other. The distribution of responses for the married women in the 1960 graduates sample – about their behaviour and work intentions during these phases – is shown in Table VI.13. Over 90 per cent of all categories of graduate women expected to work before having children.

[1] These categories are self-defined by the respondent. The choices were given in the questionnaire as listed here.

Looking in greater detail at the figures for the married women, and examining the part played by level of aspiration in producing an expectation about work, the following pattern is discernible:

Table VI.14

Expected Work Pattern[1] by Family Phase and Level of Aspiration

1960 Graduates: All Married Women (Percentages)

	Married women no children		Married women with children	
	High aspiration	Not High aspiration	High aspiration	Not High aspiration
Not work oriented	19	25	14	20
Non-continuous work oriented	44	61	29	54
Continuous work oriented	38	14	57	27
Totals percentages	101	100	100	101
N-NA	(16)	(44)	(42)	(248)

(Total N = 371 . N-NA = 350)
(NA = 21)

This table shows that level of aspiration makes a difference in that a higher proportion of the high aspirers intend to work 'continuously', (however little, in terms of hours per week) than of the non-high aspirers. About 30 per cent of all the women indicate the intention to work at least 'a bit' continuously. The 'non-continuous' work pattern is the modal expectation, while only about 20 per cent are not work oriented. There are some indications in the present sample, though this cannot be tested conclusively, that the married women without children idealize the motherhood state and 'over-express' the intention to drop out when their youngest child is under three. Once the event occurs, some of these women may revise their

---

[1] Expected Work Patterns are defined as follows: continuous Work Oriented includes all those women who plan to work during the period when their youngest child is under 3 (note that this means that some women included in this category may drop out for a time when their older children are under 3). All these women plan to work in later phases of the family cycle as well. Non-Continuous Work Oriented are all those who plan to work at one of the later family phases, but not when their youngest child is under 3. Non-Work Oriented are those who do not plan to work after the children are grown, or who plan to work less in the last phase than in the period when their children were 6-12.

223

intentions to approximate the higher levels of continuous work intention expressed by their classmates who have already had children.[1]

Another factor influencing women's work intentions is their commitment to the idea of women having careers.

Table VI.15 shows, in part, the relationship between commitment to the idea of women's careers and intention to work in different stages of the family life cycle for married women with children.

Table VI.15

Commitment to the Idea of Women's Careers[2] and Expected Work Patterns

1960 Graduates: All Married Women with Children (Percentages)

	Not committed	committed
Not work oriented	33	14
Non-continuous work oriented	45	36
Continuous work-oriented	20	49
NA	1	—
Totals Percentages	99	99
N =	(73)	(91)

This table indicates the very strong relationship between the idea of women's rights in having an opportunity to develop a career and the intention to work. The more commitment exists, the greater is the intention to work. Indeed, the highly committed women show a smaller proportion of intention to have a part-time continuous career than do the non-committed women. In general, however, the committed women are less likely to interrupt, as well as less likely to settle for part-time work than the uncommitted, and their proportions who do not intend to work at all or who wish to lessen their own work involvements over time is very much smaller.

Continuing with the focus on overall life plan in relation to work, which seems crucial for married women with children, the analysis of 1960 graduates' data provides interesting findings. Beginning with the 'intention to work while the youngest child is under 3' as the

---

[1] This interpretation is confirmed by an examination of the 1967 graduates responses, which are very similar to those of the 1960 women without children.

[2] *Commitment* is defined as being in favour of women having a career and *Not* strongly agreeing with the view that a woman cannot make long range plans for her own career because they depend on her husband's plans for his. Cf. Appendix Table VI.A1 and pp. 261-2 for details of this index. In this table only the extreme forms of commitment are excerpted to show the contrast, hence the smaller N. Full and medium commitment are here combined as 'committed'.

crucial dependent variable indicating high individual commitment to career and therefore high potential from the point of view of career development, it is possible to show how a number of career performance variables relate to work intentions.

First, consider how the variable 'intention to work when youngest child is under 3' operates in relation to type of occupation in which the respondent is at the time of survey; then in relation to hours worked; and then in relation to income.

Table VI.16

Occupational Status and Intention to Work When Youngest Child Under 3

1960 Graduates: All Married Women Currently Employed (Percentage Intending to Work when Youngest Child is Under 3)

Occupations	Percentage	Total N =
Sales, personnel, industrial managers	100	(4)
College teacher	79	(19)
Doctor, lawyer, architect, finance, engineer	75	(4)
Primary school teacher	73	(15)
Secondary school teacher	61	(59)
'Other'	61	(28)
Social worker	54	(13)
Housewife[1]	46	(24)
Scientist	43	(7)
		(173)

The occupations fall into two fairly distinct groups – the top professional group (managers, professionals and college teachers) and the second group, which is somewhat less likely to continue, though still intending in relatively high proportions to keep some kind of work going. The schoolteachers split on this outlook, with primary schoolteachers in the first group and secondary schoolteachers in the second. The numbers are small, particularly for primary schoolteachers. However, we do know that of the 14 primary schoolteachers presently working, half are 'high' aspirers while the comparable proportion for secondary schoolteachers is one fifth. This suggests further investigation.

The overriding distinction is, of course, between those who give

---

[1] These women indicate they do some paid work but think of themselves primarily as housewives. It is interesting that nearly half of these women intend to continue working when their infants are under 3, supporting the general picture that the most conclusive thing for a married woman continuing a career developmental pattern is to keep working.

H

'housewife' as their present occupation and those who give one of the listed occupations. For all of the listed occupations, minority though they be, there is a fairly high intention to continue working throughout. What does this mean in terms of numbers of hours currently employed? Are the more fully-occupied more or less likely to intend to continue than the part-timers?

Table VI.17

Current Employment and Intention to Work when Youngest Child Under 3

(Percentage Intending to Work when Youngest Child Under 3)

Current Employment (Hours per week)	Married women without children		Married women with children		All married women	
		(N-NA)		(N-NA)		(N-NA)
None	20	(10)	12	(182)	13	(192)
Under 10	0	(3)	77	(61)	73	(64)
11-30	22	(9)	91	(33)	76	(46)
31 or more	33	(39)	92	(13)	48	(52)
Totals: N-NA		(61)		(289)		(354)
NA (Intention)		(12)		(9)		(21)
N		(73)		(298)		(371)

This table indicates that for married women overall, those who work under 30 hours per week are more likely to intend to continue working through the critical period of young infancy than are those who currently work full-time.

However, this finding has different explanations for different women. As the table shows, the sheer presence of children has a major effect on the pattern. The women with children cluster more heavily in the lower number of working hours per week. The under-ten-hours-per-week (and of course the non-workers) are almost entirely married women with children. The full-time (31+ hours) are mainly women without children, though there is a minority of married women with children who work this number of hours.

The generalization that holds for both groups – married women with and without children – is that the more the woman is working, the more she is likely to intend to continue working (or resume working) when her youngest child is still under 3. But this is much less true for married women without children than those with children.

The married women without children show much less intention

to work when the youngest child is under 3 than do the married women with children. The women who have had the experience of having children show the wish to be working much more strongly than those who do not, the latter showing the 'traditional dream' phenomenon of idealizing maternity (Bailyn, 1970).

For the married women with children, there is a sharp difference between those who have dropped out of work completely and those who continue to work, even if only a very little. The women who drop out of work completely – whether they have children or not – are much less likely than those who continue working to want to work when their youngest child is under 3. For the married women with children, the effect of continued work on future intentions is very marked. If the woman has continued to work at all, she is much more likely to intend to continue than if she has dropped out, and if she has a major job commitment (i.e. 11 hours per week or more) she is almost certain to intend to work continuously.

Table VI.18 shows the effect of current family size on this pattern.

Table VI.18

Number of Children and Intention to Work when Youngest Child is Under 3, by whether or not Currently Employed

1960 Graduates: All Married Women (Percentages Intending to Work when Child Under 3)

Respondent is currently	None or expecting first	(Total) (N-NA)	One or two	(Total) (N-NA)	Three or more	(Total) (N-NA)
Employed	29	(51)	81	(91)	94	(16)
Housewife	14	(7)	11	(135)	15	(40)
		(58)		(226)		(56)

Totals N-NA (340)

NA Intention = (20)[1]
NA Employed = (9)
NA Children = (2)
N = (371)

[1] Twenty married women did not indicate their intentions about working with a child under 3. Of these 14 have no children. Those married women who do not expect to have any children were asked not to answer the question about intentions, hence a higher NA for the employed group, who are disproportionately married women without children (15 as compared with 5 for the married women with children).

This table shows that if a married woman drops out of work, the number of children she has does not affect her work intentions. However, for the women who are in employment eight years after graduation the intention to work continuously (i.e. to be at work when the youngest is under 3) increases with the number of children. The greater number of children the higher is this intention. Some of these women may have stopped working temporarily when their first or second children were very small but by the time the third or subsequent child was born they may have developed a way of handling the situation so that if they were job or career oriented, they could continue to work even while the infant was under 3.

The data on income bear out the 'hours of work' picture.

Table VI.19

Annual Income and Intention to Work when Youngest Child is Under 3

1960 Graduates: All Married Women Currently Employed (Percentage Intending to Work when Infant Under 3)

Current annual earned income	Married women no children		Married women with children	
		(N-NA)		(N-NA)
Under £500	14	(7)	79	(74)
£501-£1,000	25	(4)	93	(15)
Over £1,000	33	(40)	95	(18)
Totals: N-NA		(51)		(107)
NA (Intention)		(11)		(4)
N		(62)		(111)

As already indicated, a greater proportion of the married women without children than of those with children falls within the higher income bracket, as the latter work fewer hours. There is a major difference between the two-sub-groups of married women in that those *with children* have a much higher intention to work when their youngest children are under 3, and the higher their current earnings, the greater their intention. The relation between level of earning and intention is also present for the married women without children.

The attitude variables of 'level of aspiration' and 'career commitment' also seem to affect intention to work, but they are particularly powerful in separating the housewives who intend to work when their youngest child is under 3 from those housewives who do not. Look first at level of aspiration:

228

Table VI.20

Level of Aspiration, Current Employment and Intention to Work when Youngest Child Under 3

1960 Graduates: All Married Women (Percentage Expecting to Work when Youngest Under 3)

Level of Aspiration	Housewives		Employed Married Women	
		Total N-NA		Total N-NA
Not high	6	(175)	64	(120)
High	33	(18)	71	(38)
Totals: N-NA		(193)		(158)
NA (Intention)		(5)		(15)
N		(198)		(173)

This table indicates that, though the number of women among the housewives who intend to work when their youngest child is under 3 is small relative to the proportions for the women who are currently employed, their level of aspiration differentiates these women quite markedly. A third of those with a high level of aspiration intend to work at that point whereas only 6 per cent of the non-high-aspirers have this intention. For the currently employed women, the proportions who intend to work through are much higher, and the difference between the high-aspirers and the non-high-aspirers is much less marked.

Taking 'commitment' as another attitudinal variable – in this instance one of the questions forming the commitment index reported above (p. 224), the pattern emerges as shown in Table VI.21 overleaf.

This table, like the previous one, shows a small but consistent subgroup within the housewife category where there is a relatively high commitment to career and a relatively high intention to work even while the youngest infant is under 3. Indeed, one-fifth of the high commitment housewives intend to work when their youngest infants are under 3.

As for intention to return to work when the children are grown, most married women graduates now have this intention. Only a very small proportion (6 per cent) of the graduate married women indicated a consistent intention to be housewives as an exclusive occupation all their married lives. When asked about intentions to return at specific stages, however, a somewhat larger proportion (about 23 per cent) do not say that they intend to return – perhaps indicating their uncertainties about how this can be accomplished. Alternatively, after experiencing married life, they may prefer not to work. Looking at the statements of intention from the other point of view, however, it is striking how many of the married women graduates do intend to return to work when their children are grown. Seventy-seven per cent of the women in the sample studied indicate this intention specifically; an analysis was made of the factors related to this – differentiating those who do intend ultimately to return from those who do not.

Ultimate intention to return to work is affected by the individuals' perceived salience of work in their lives. Overall, 77 per cent of the married women in the sample intend to work when their children are

Table VI.21

Commitment to Women's Career and Current Employment in Relation to Expected Work Pattern

1960 Graduates: All Married Women

Commitment to women's career[1]	Currently Housewives Percentage expecting to work when youngest child under 3		Currently employed Percentage expecting to work when youngest child under 3	
		N-NA		N-NA
Low	8	(175)	58	(99)
High	23	(18)	80	(59)
Totals: N-NA		(193)		(158)
NA (Intention)		(5)		(15)
N		(198)		(173)

grown. Eighty one per cent of those who indicate that career either gives them 'the most satisfaction in your life' or the 'next most satisfaction' intend to work compared with 72 per cent from among those who do not rate career as salient to them in this way.

The two groups of 'career salient' and 'non-career salient' wives differ in other values and attitudes and in their current situations. Women in the career salient group are more likely to intend to return if their marital relationship is less happy. While 85 per cent of these women intend to return even with a 'very happy' marital relationship, the proportions rise to 95 per cent and 100 per cent for women who indicate that their marital relationships are 'unhappy', or only 'pretty happy'.

[1] Commitment is indicated as in the footnote to Table VI.15. 'Low commitment' is taken as the three lowest categories ('none', 'mixed' and 'secondary'), and 'high commitment' as the top two ('full' and 'medium').

Husband's income is also a factor in the intention to return. The career salient women who are most likely to return are those whose husbands are in the middle range of the current income continua, between £1,500-£2,500 per annum.[1] Ninety-three per cent of those women intend to return, as compared with 73 per cent of those whose husbands earn over £2,500, and 60 per cent of those whose husbands earn under £1,500.

SUMMARY AND DISCUSSION

In this chapter the career aspirations and performance of a sample of women graduates have been described and analysed to some extent in terms of the special constraints operating on married women with children.

For men (with the exception of those who do not marry within eight years of graduating from university), the level of career aspiration tends to rise with time and with the transition into marriage and fatherhood. For women (once again with the exception of those who are unmarried) the trend is the reverse. The patterns which emerge for unmarried men resemble the women's patterns more than those for the other men, and those for the unmarried women resemble the men's, rising in level during the years following university.

The level of career aspirations, however, is only one component of this topic. There are 'intrinsic' or horizontal as well as 'extrinsic' or vertical dimensions of career aspiration, and the women – though dropping their *level* of aspiration when they encounter the difficulties arising from the integration of a career with traditional domestic roles – do not alter their 'intrinsic' aspirations – i.e. the specific kinds of interests and values which they seek in work *per se*. They wish as much as the men and as persistently as the men to have the kind of career in which they can do an interesting job and work relatively autonomously in relation to supervision. Like the men, they value above all the idea of cultivating a reputation for extreme competence in whatever line of work they pursue, and feel that the experience of creativity in work is important. They differ from the men not only in their lesser and diminishing attachment to the more 'extrinsic' or 'vertical' aspects of career accomplishment – high income, high status and authority etc. – but in their greater interest in 'social' (or what has sometimes been referred to as 'peripheral') values – human contact and being of help to people.

[1] The 'husband's income' item had an unusually high non-response rate. In this group of 112 career-salient women, 24 did not give husband's income. However, these 24 married women resembled the middle-income category of women, with 92 per cent intending ultimately to return.

Level and type of aspiration combine to affect occupational choice and orientation to work. For men this affects the field of work chosen and performance within the field. More men graduates than women choose the more remunerative fields and perform competitively within them; they seek a reputation for competence and an opportunity to show accomplishment. For women, the fundamental choice is between the occupational identity of 'housewife' and that of one of the occupational groups for which they were trained or in which they may have worked prior to marriage or having children. For married women, there is a very sharp differentiation between continuing work at some level, thus maintaining continuous identity as a member of an occupational group, and choosing the identity of housewife, however temporarily.

The employed married women work more hours, earn more, have higher commitment to the idea of women's careers and higher levels of aspiration for themselves in their careers than do the housewives. Among working women the career values indicated resemble those of the men in most respects. In relation to the intention to work relatively continuously – as indicated by the intention to work even while there is an infant under 3 still at home – several distinct patterns emerge:

(*a*) the type of married woman who is highly committed to women in general having careers and who works herself. Eighty per cent of these women intend to work 'continuously'.

(*b*) the type of married woman who does not believe very strongly in women's careers generally, but who works herself. Fifty-five per cent of these intend to continue to work.

(*c*) the type of married woman who believes in women's careers generally though she herself is currently a housewife. Twenty-three per cent of these women intend to return to work even before their youngest child reaches the age of 3.

(*d*) the type of married woman who does not believe very strongly in women's careers and who herself is a housewife. Only 8 per cent of these intend to return to work before their youngest child is 3 years old.

The intention to work when there is a young child at home is, then, very complex. It is partly a function of what the woman graduate is actually doing eight years after university. Women who leave occupational life to become housewives are much less likely to intend to return than those who stay in some kind of a job; but a small minority nevertheless do intend to return when their youngest child is under 3.

Among those who do continue working, the intention to work

continuously is also very complex. The highest current earners are not those who are most likely to continue, nor are they the ones who have the fewest children. Higher earnings are associated with longer working hours, and longer working hours are put in by women who have not yet had children. Many of the women who have not yet had children intend to drop out when they have their first child. Those with the greatest intention to work continuously are in the modest earning bracket (£500-£1,000 per annum) and are predominantly part-time workers.

The intention ultimately to return to work is now far more widespread than in the past among married women such as those represented in this sample of graduates. Nearly 80 per cent expect to be working when their children are grown. Examining the variables in their current situation which might distinguish between those who do and those who do not ultimately intend to be working, it is clear that the former group (which includes the early as well as the late returners) are women who expect to get major satisfactions from work. The early returners, as a sub-group, are the ones whose commitment to work is a matter of principle. The later returners may not be committed so much to the general idea of women's careers, but they may recognize that they will want to do something to keep themselves interested, to be useful, etc. Their husbands are likely to be middle-income earners rather than from the higher or lower income groups. The nature of the marital relationship serves as an encouragement to return to work in a distinct sub-group where marital satisfactions are less and the accumulated unhappiness of the 'out' stage presses these women towards re-entry. How this will affect their marital relationship subsequently is not known, though some indications may be seen from the nature of the marital relationships of those wives who are currently working; this will be discussed in the next chapter.

The above findings all show that data on the current behaviour of married women at the early stages of their family life cycle cannot be taken as a simple indicator of their potential work pattern. Future behaviour, as indicated by intentions to work, relates partly to current behaviour (those working *at all* are more likely to continue to work than those who drop out completely to the housewife role), and partly to commitment to the idea of women having careers (in the purposeful developmental egalitarian sense). Three conclusions from this which are relevant on a policy level seem to be indicated:

(*a*) measures which help women who are career oriented to keep working to some degree rather than 'dropping out' into the housewife role altogether are likely to increase their occupational activity.

(b) measures which foster the value of commitment to a career in women, and
(c) measures which reduce the conflict between family roles and work roles should lead to more women graduates staying in work.

Family domestic role obligations are clearly the main elements adversely affecting women's career development and performance. What are they? How do they function now for women graduates, and how do the imperatives of the domestic roles interact with the aspirations in the occupational roles? These are the questions for the next chapter.

REFERENCES

Bailyn, Lotte, 'Notes on the Role of Choice in the Psychology of Professional Women', *Daedalus*, 700-10, 1964.

Bailyn, L., 'Marital Satisfaction in Relation to Career and Family Orientations of Husbands and Wives', *Human Relations*, Vol. 23, No. 2, 1970.

Barnard, Jessie, *see* Mattfield, etc.

Brunel, I. K., *see* Rolt, Lionell T. C.

Butler, *Occupational Choice*, Science Policy Studies, No. 2, London: H.M.S.O., 1968.

Cogswell, Bettey E., 'Some Structural Properties Influencing Socialization', *Administrative Scientific Quarterly*, April 13, 1969.

Deneuve, Catherine, *Life*, February 2, 1969.

Fogarty, Michael, Rapoport, Rhona, and Robert, *Women and Top Jobs*, P.E.P., 1967.

Ginzberg, Eli, *et. al.*, *Occupational Choice*, New York: Columbia University Press, 1951.

Hartley, Ruth, and Klein, A., 'Sex-Role Concepts Among Elementary School-Age Girls', *Marriage and Family Living*, February 21, 1959.

Hughes, Everett C., *Men and Their Work*, Illinois: Glencoe Free Press, 1958.

Knoblochova and Knobloch, 'Family Psychotherapy in World Health Organization', *Aspects of Family Mental Health*, Geneva Public Health Papers 28, 1965.

Lidz, Theodore, *The Person, His Development throughout the Life Cycle*, New York: Basic Books, 1968.

McClelland, David C., *et al.*, *The Achievement Motive*, New York: Appleton-Century-Crofts, 1953.

Mattfield, J. A. and van Aken, C. G. (eds), *Women and the Scientific Professions*, Cambridge, Mass.: MIT, 1965.

Moment, David, 'Pathways of Career Development Revisited', *Harvard Business School Bulletin*, Nov.-Dec. 1960, pp. 27-9.

Osipov, S. H., *Theories of Career Development*, New York: Appleton, 1968.

Parsons, Talcott, 'Age and Sex in the Social Structure of the United States', *American Sociological Review*, Vol. 7, No. 5, 604-16, 1942.

Pym, Dennis, *New Society*, 1968.

Rapoport, Rhona, 'Normal Crises, Family Structure and Mental Health', *Family Process*, 2, 68-80, 1961.

Roe, Anne, *The Psychology of Occupations*, New York: J. Wiley, 1956.

Rolt, Lionell T. C., *Isambard Kingdom Brunel*, London: Grey Arrow, 1961.

Rosenberg, M., *Occupations and Values*, Illinois: Glencoe Free Press, 1957.

Rossi, Alice, 'Women in Science: Why so Few?', *Science*, Vol. 148, 3764, 1196-302, 1965.

Rossi, Alice, 'Equality between the Sexes: An Immodest Proposal', *Daedalus*, 93, 2, 607-52, 1964.

Simpson, R. L., and Simpson, I. H., 'Values, Personal Influence and Occupational Choice', *Social Forces*, 39, 116-25, 1960.

Super, Donald E., *The Psychology of Careers: An Introduction to Vocational Development*, New York: Harper & Row, 1957.

Turner, Ralph H., 'Some Aspects of Women's Ambition', *American Journal of Sociology*, 70, 271-85, 1964.

Chapter VII

Family Patterns and Work

The change in demography and in cultural norms and values, as indicated above, have brought about a situation where many highly qualified women seek to combine work and family life, rather than give up one for the other. Just as highly qualified women show a range of levels and types of aspiration in relation to their careers, so they show a range of attitudes and behavioural patterns in relation to family life – from remaining single without the intention of marrying, marrying and not having children, to the other extreme of marrying and following a traditional homemaker role with no intention of ever working. The idea that women are 'naturally' maternal and domestically minded while men are 'naturally' ambitious and competitive in the world of work is too simple a view to be tenable in today's society. Graduate women, like graduate men, have various attitudes towards careers – in general, and specifically in relation to themselves; and they have different orientations to family life. The aim of this chapter is to describe in some detail the family patterns found among highly qualified women, and to seek out current relationships between family patterns and career orientations.

It has been argued that some highly qualified women want, need and feel that they ought to pursue their careers, and that tying them down to the chores of family life makes for unhappiness for themselves, their children and their marital relationship. It has also been argued that the strains of combining work and family for a woman in the early phases of family development are more than most individuals and marriages can bear, and that it may in some cases be deleterious for the mental health of the developing children. Is the family a blessed haven of personal fulfilment of a psycho-social trap beset with stresses and strains?

Any answer which is formulated to this question is liable to be labelled as obvious, a hazard encountered in reporting the finding of much social investigation. One reason that this hazard exists, of course, is that informed readers entertain a number of hypothetical

236

positions, which are often incompatible with one another and which may be mobilized, according to circumstances, to produce an 'I knew it' sort of response. It is known that families are both helpful and harmful; that marital relationships facilitate the development of each partner, and that they limit this development; that children are a joy and that they are a burden.

In a sense the answer to the question posed above is a new set of questions. As there is no single and simple answer, the question is better put: 'Under what circumstances and for what kinds of people do various kinds of family relationships function in the interests of married women pursuing careers?'

In order to investigate this new set of questions, a number of concepts are employed.[1]

FUNDAMENTAL CONCEPTS: SALIENCE, COMMITMENT AND INTEGRATION

First is the concept of *salience*. People vary in the importance they attach to different areas of their lives and the degree to which they obtain or expect to obtain personal satisfaction from family life, from work or career, and from other areas of life such as leisure activities, participation in community organizations, and so on. On the whole, the population of highly qualified men and women studied are very 'familistic', and place a great emphasis on the extent to which they derive satisfaction from family life. However, individuals and families vary in this, and in the particular part of family life in which they are most involved, e.g. housekeeping, child rearing, or external relationships and activities, and they have different ideas about who should do what in the home.

Apart from domestic involvements and division of labour made necessary by women working, individuals vary in the degree to *commitment* they have to the idea of women working outside the home at all. (For a fuller discussion see pp. 258ff.) A prevalent view in our society today is that highly qualified women should do some kind of work, but that this should not interfere with their domestic duties, as traditionally defined. To this, some add that it should not interfere with the husband and his career requirements. Husbands as well as their wives vary in the degree to which they are committed to women's careers, and the husband's attitude is important to the women – though not absolutely decisive. Some women do not pursue

[1] Particular thanks are due to Lotte Bailyn in relation to the concepts used in this chapter, as well as to Alice Rossi, on whose work the whole survey was based. Bailyn, 1970, applies some of the concepts in the analysis of couples in the sample.

237

a career despite a permissive or even supportive attitude from their husbands, while others do pursue careers despite opposition at home. One recent national survey showed that one-sixth of Britain's wives work despite disapproval on the part of their husbands (Hunt, 1968).

Not only the husband's attitude but also his behaviour is important. Husbands vary, as do their wives, in the ways in which they combine work and family involvements; the concept of *integration* is used to define the range of ways in which men as well as women combine the two major spheres of life (see pp. 267ff.). The 'integrated' husband is one who derives major satisfactions from both work and family – not one to the exclusion of the other. 'Integrated' husbands vary according to whether they are 'family integrated' (i.e. place family first, career second) or 'career integrated' (i.e. place career first, family second). 'Non-integrated' husbands indicate that career or family (but not both) is one of the two principal areas of life satisfaction.

It is in situations in which the husbands give prominence to family satisfactions, and particularly in which there is an integrated orientation to work and family, that the highest degree of marital happiness is found. This does not mean that the highest degree of career orientation will be found among their wives. Career orientations and high expected work intentions on the part of the wives are found in these conditions when the woman is committed and motivated to having a career, but this is only in a relatively small proportion of instances. A higher proportion of women with high work intentions come from a less happy type of marital situation, where the commitment to the ideal of women having careers is perhaps a less important motive for working than the lack of personal fulfilment in the marital relationship – where the husband, for example, may manifest a non-integrated approach, giving overwhelming emphasis to his career. Such women workers may be highly motivated to work outside the home, but may not have as clear a career-orientation. They care less what their work is or what it is adding up to than that they are out of the home and occupying themselves.

There is, it will be shown, no single issue around which the problems encountered by highly qualified women in combining family and career can be resolved. Nor is there one single type of 'career woman' among those who work or intend to return to work. There are different types of orientation to family, and to the relative place of family and work, and different situations in the marital relationship as well as in the labour market which determine the patterns to be observed. There is a range of overall patterns from the old-fashioned 'conventional' housewife who does not work and does not expect to return to work, through the 'career-orientated' wife who

238

does not intend to interrupt her career development more than minimally even to have and rear children. There are some house-wives who are 'reluctant' and wish to return to work as soon as pos-sible, and some workers who are 'unwilling', and would like to stop; there are some who work and intend to continue working, not for the sake of a career but only to avoid boredom. The relationships among these patterns are sought in this chapter.

To study these relationships, the same core sample of 1960 gradu-ates is used as in the previous chapter. These respondents have had more experience with marriage and family life than those in the younger samples. Earlier attitudes will have been tested against actual experience, and to some extent orientations will have had a chance to crystallize. Where it is available and appropriate, informa-tion from the other samples, including the American sample studied by Alice Rossi and her colleagues, will be mentioned in footnotes.

THE FAMILISTIC EMPHASIS

Most of the sample of the 1960 graduates were married by the time they had been eight years out of university and most of them had already at least one child (64 per cent of the men, 62 per cent of the women). Only 15 per cent of the men and 24 per cent of the women were still single at the time of the survey. As shown in the last chapter, the married graduates are decidedly 'familistic' in their values. Most of them, both men and women, indicate that 'family' is the area of life from which they obtain their greatest satisfactions. Family re-lationships are the most salient to graduates as a group.

This does not mean that the graduates want large families. Only 10 per cent indicated that having a large family was an important goal in their lives. Having a large family was a low priority com-parable with the 8 per cent who indicated that what they wanted very much was to lead a life of activity in community organizations. Nor does a 'family' mean involvement in extended or parental family activities and relationships. 'Family' is concentrated in the nuclear family, and it is highly child-centred.[1]

The most frequently chosen item from a list of possible life attain-ments which were provided as things many people want very much in their lives was to 'be a good parent'. Fifty-six per cent of the respondents chose this and 50 per cent indicated that they wanted

[1] It should be noted, however, that the survey research instrument used was not designed to pick up details of the extended family relationships of these graduates. From the more detailed study of a small sample of 'dual-career' families (reported in Chapter IX) it can be seen that while there may not be much active seeking out of grandmothers and other relatives, these couples are ready to give their relatives attention and to accept obligations in relation to them.

very much to 'help my children to develop as I think they should'. These percentages in the 'want very much' category outstrip the wish to 'have enough money to live well' (chosen by 32 per cent of the respondents) or to 'do something important' (only 18 per cent want this very much).

Most of the highly qualified people in the sample want to have good homes and a good standard of living to provide a place to cultivate the *internal* aspects of family life. The home and the children are most important and the neighbourhood much less so; only 20 per cent of the respondents indicate that they want very much to 'live in a good neighbourhood for my children to grow up in'. Again, the internal life of the family matters more than the home, which is a prerequisite but not an end in itself. Table VII.1 shows the progression towards having a separate house with advance in marital phase.

Table VII.1

Type of Residence by Sex and Family Phase

1960 Graduates: Men and Women (Percentages)

	Single men	Married men no children	Married men with children	Single women	Married women no children	Married women with children
Flat or flatlet	40	24	3	58	17	5
House	41	73	96	33	77	94
Other	19	2	1	9	7	1
Totals Percentages	100	99	100	100	101	100
N-NA	(58)	(79)	(242)	(111)	(73)	(297)
NA			(3)	(1)		(1)

Ownership follows the same pattern, with 91 per cent of the married men with children owning their homes and 88 per cent of the married women with children also being in this position. The single people show differences, with 33 per cent of the single men owning their accommodation as compared with only 12 per cent of the single women. About 80 per cent of the families with children (84 per cent of the men's families and 74 per cent of the women's families) live in the conventional pattern, i.e. with the husband going out to work and the wife staying at home as housewife. For about a quarter of the married women graduates with children, both husband and wife work, compared with only 15 per cent of the families of the married men graduates with children.

240

The life inside this highly valued family sphere is examined in some detail as it is by such an analysis that some of the complexities of familial influences can be understood and dealt with. The order of examination does not reflect the order of importance to the individuals. Indeed, the first area is lowest in salience to the respondents.

HOUSEHOLD DIVISION OF LABOUR

In this section the household division of labour is examined as one of the major areas making up family life. Every society has developed a division of labour which is based in part on sexual differences. Men's work and women's work have been distinctly defined in most traditional societies, and to adhere to the culturally evolved patterns was no more than being 'natural' or 'human'. In today's society where sex-differences in tastes, interests and talents are less clearly differentiated, and educational and other formative experiences emphasize individual differences, one would expect new patterns to emerge. Recent research has indicated a trend towards a division of labour in houscholds which is less 'segregated' along traditional stereotyped lines and more 'interchangeable' or 'joint' – i.e. shared by husband and wife together (Bott, 1957). Ideally one might expect that for a population of highly qualified men and women each household would work out, within the confines of its own internal organization, a division of labour uniquely suited to the tastes, inclinations and available energies of the members.

Against this there is the counter-observation that contemporary society is becoming increasingly standardized and homogenized, and in fact resembles the 'battery society' of a chicken farm – with every mum and every dad behaving like all the others, and everyone's values and attitudes moulded by the mass media so as to produce conformity, however much there is an illusion of individuality (Golding, 1969).

The domestic life patterns of the sample of 1960 British graduates are examined in order to determine first how much homogeneity there is in the patterning, and second how conventional is the division of labour in the home. In fact, most British graduates who are housewives think of their domestic activities in several categories. These women show greater enjoyment in some than in others. Shopping, food preparation and the arrangement of social activities are the items most enjoyed; washing, cleaning and child care constitute another grouping of activities, which are seen to belong together and are not liked as much as a group, except for child care, which has its redeeming features. Gardening constitutes a third category

241

and has the characteristic of being the household activity which is most likely to be shared between husbands and wives. The crystallization of these attitudes and activities into the fairly conventional pattern of women being responsible for most of the internal activities and men the external ones is something that occurs over time as the graduates emerge from university into 'real life'; as time goes on, the actual patterns of behaviour deviate from the earlier expressed preferences and are recast into a more socially prevalent mould. The data presented in this section document these patterns and trends. Ten activities associated with the domestic scene were listed and respondents were asked:

'Assuming you were financially able to employ household help, circle the category which best describes how you would *like* each of the following activities to be handled in your household.'

For each of the categories, the respondent (including single men and women who answered in terms of 'how you would like to have these things done if you were married') was given the option of indicating whether he would like to have:

'Husband do it himself most of the time'
'Wife do it herself most of the time'
'Husband and wife to do it together'
'Husband to employ help to do it'
'Wife to employ help to do it'

In the Table VII.2, the modally chosen category is indicated for each of the ten household activities.

Clearly, the population, even the most educated part of it, still regards domestic activities as overwhelmingly a female sphere. The only parts of the domestic round that both men and women would delegate, even given sufficient resources to hire help, are the house-cleaning activities; and even here the modal categories are relatively low indicating a fairly wide range of opinion. The only less frequently chosen category is decorating, which comes out as one of the two preferred 'joint' activities (from the women's point of view – the men just barely prefer to delegate this). Most graduates see only gardening as an area of shared activity.

The *actual* pattern of activities, as distinct from the preferences indicated in the imaginary situation of available outside help, is not greatly different, although subtle variations emerge. Respondents were given a similar list of household activities, with the addition of three shopping items (for food, clothing and household), budgeting and arranging social activities. Taking the overall distributions of activity, this population of eight-year-out graduates shows the following pattern (see Table VII.3 overleaf).

Table VII.2

Preferred Division of Labour in Household Activities

Most Frequent Choices for 1960 Men and Women Graduates[1]

	Men's responses			Women's responses		
		Percentages	Total N-NA		Percentages	Total N-NA
Everyday cooking	Wife	69	(376)	Wife	77	(478)
Special cooking	Wife	55	(379)	Wife	65	(480)
Child care	Wife	67	(375)	Wife	67	(479)
Regular cleaning	Other	37	(378)	Other	41	(479)
Spring cleaning	Other	31	(375)	Other	33	(478)
Washing/ironing	Wife	39	(375)	Wife	53	(481)
Mending	Wife	59	(374)	Wife	63	(479)
Decorating	Other	26	(380)	Husband and Wife	38	(478)
Minor repairs	Husband	67	(377)	Husband	67	(480)
Gardening	Husband and Wife	42	(382)	Husband and Wife	55	(480)
Total N =			(382)			(483)

It would seem from this list that the wife, as expected, does most of the household activities most of the time. This is a higher proportion than is ideally desired by either men or women. There were no categories in which 'other help' figured as the modal category though for household cleaning it reached its peak with 13 per cent indicating that this is how it is handled. Husbands do the minor repairs, also a bit more than ideally desired; and both do gardening though a bit less than the wife would like. Shopping for household items and clothing are 'joint' activities. There are a number of strong secondary patterns, e.g. husband gardening (37 per cent), both shopping for food (27 per cent), both participating in child-care activities (38 per cent) and wife shopping for clothing (40 per cent).

The families of the men graduates differ somewhat in structure from those of the women graduates. This is due to the fact that the wives of the graduate men are drawn from a broader range of educational backgrounds than the husbands of the graduate women. To the men

[1] The most frequently chosen categories are identical where comparable information exists, for the 1967 graduates and the 1960 graduates. Full tables are provided in Appendix Table VI.A1.

243

graduates, the educational attainments of their wives seem often to be less important than their other qualities. The graduate women, on the other hand, tend to marry men with higher educational attainments (and therefore social status) than their own. None of the men graduates' wives have doctorates, whereas 20 per cent of the husbands of the women graduates have reached this level. Two per cent of the male graduates' wives have M.A. degrees as compared with 12 per cent of the women graduates' husbands; and nearly half of the graduate women's husbands are graduates with the B.A. degree, compared with under one-third of the graduate men's wives. One direct structural consequence of this patterning is that the

Table VII.3

Actual Division of Labour in Household Activities

1960 Married Men and Women Graduates: (Percentages of choice in most frequently chosen categories)

Wife does it		Husband does it		Both do it		Help does it
Cooking	92	Minor repairs	80	Budgeting	44	
Special cooking	83			Gardening	46	
Child care	44			Clothes shopping	59	
Household cleaning	74			Household shopping	90	
Washing	91			Arranging social activities	70	
Food shopping	69					

women graduates tend to show a higher proportion of families in which both husband and wife are working. This feature is accompanied on the one hand by a greater tendency towards joint or interchangeable patterns of division of labour in the household, and on the other hand by a greater use of outside domestic help.

The use of hired help relates both to employment of the wife and to the family phase. About 10 per cent of married women with children report having outside help whether or not the wife works outside the home. For the married women without children only 3 per cent of the non-employed wives have domestic help compared with 18 per cent of the employed wives in this category. Thus, the married women with children do more of the household work by themselves

244

than do those without children – more cleaning, more shopping, more food preparation, etc.

Household repairs is an interesting category because in families without children this is an almost exclusively 'husband alone' category, so that there is a shift in the nature of the division of labour when the family has children as well as the sheer quantity that devolves on the married woman. It becomes one of their shared areas of activity. On the other hand, it is likely here that unlike gardening this is the kind of sharing that allows either party to accomplish the repair task, not necessarily together, and all in all it represents primarily another increase in the load of responsibilities carried by married women with children.

How do married women (working or not) evaluate the various tasks for which they have to carry the main responsibility? For each of the categories of household activity described in terms of 'who does it', respondents were also asked how they felt about the pattern that existed, and whether they 'enjoyed it', 'do not mind doing it' or 'dislike doing it'.

On the basis of responses to the 'enjoyment' question on household activities (which includes child care), a correlation matrix was formed. Three clusters were discerned by using a hierarchical linkage analysis[1] (McQuitty, 1960).

(1) *a.* Furniture shopping, clothes shopping, food shopping
    b. Cooking, daily and special; arranging family social activities
(2) Budgeting, washing, (cleaning), child care
(3) Gardening

This means that the women who say they enjoy any one of the shopping activities also tend to enjoy the other shopping activities, and they may be different from those women who enjoy the washing-cleaning-budgeting-child-care activities. Enjoyment of cooking is closely associated with the enjoyment obtained from arranging family social activities; and is more closely related (i.e. more of the same women like both than otherwise) to shopping than to the cleaning-budgeting-child-care area. The location of budgeting with the washing-cleaning cluster rather than the shopping cluster may reflect a general factor of 'economizing' which is an 'end' rather than a 'means'. Had budgeting clustered with the shopping activities it may have reflected the housewife's greater participation with her husband in the overall strategy of budget allocations. For the English

---

[1] Cf. Appendix, Table VII.A2 for correlational matrix used as the basis for the McQuitty clusters. The hierarchical linkage analysis is a form of cluster analysis grouping together the most highly inter-correlated variables in any array.

housewife child care is associated with the least enjoyed household activities.[1]

The clustering of responses to the 'preference' question ('assuming that you were financially able to employ household help . . . how would you *like* each of the following activities to be handled in your household?') is somewhat different. The *preference* clusters for the British study were as follows:

(1) *a.* Weekly cleaning, seasonal cleaning, clothes care
    b. Mending
(2) Gardening, decorating, household repairs
(3) Daily cooking; special cooking
(4) Child care

The most striking element to emerge from these clusterings is the detachment of the child care item from the cleaning cluster. This would suggest that while the cleaning and mending items are chores that most of the wives would prefer to delegate (some minor differences existing between those who prefer to do mending themselves and those who do not) the child-care area is separate. The cooking items remain together as activities either to be done by the wife or delegated, and the same is true for the second cluster which contains the main items in which the men participate.[2]

[1] A comparison with information for the U.S.A. of the household activities enjoyment measures of a sample of women graduates three years after university provided the following clusters:

(1) Furniture shopping, clothes shopping, food shopping
(2) *a.* Child care; daily cooking; food shopping
    b. Special cooking
(3) Cleaning, mending, washing clothes
(4) Gardening.

The American graduate women apparently associate child care with the more enjoyed activities such as food shopping and preparation. Child care for the English housewife apparently calls up images of cleaning while for the Americans the image is of feeding (Rossi, unpublished draft, 1968).

[2] While an 'enjoyment index' could not be obtained for the 1967 graduates as they were for the most part unmarried, they did answer comparable questions on their *preferences*. The main difference between the 1967 and the 1960 graduates' responses is the lowering of the inter-correlational coefficients. This seems to indicate that the older women, after experiencing domestic activities, are more able to distinguish among them; this reduces the high overall correlational patterning which signifies thinking about them as a single set. The full table on the distribution of 'enjoyment' is in appendix Table VII.A4.

The American study shows similar patterning, retaining the closer association between food preparation and child care:

(1) Weekly cleaning, seasonal cleaning, clothes care
(2) Mending

[*footnote continued on next page*

THE CHILDREN AND CHILD-CARE ACTIVITIES

As has been indicated, the sample is very 'familistic' in the sense that the respondents tend to place a high value on family life, particularly the areas concerned with the socialization of their children. Most of them expect to derive major satisfactions from the family area and want this to be the area of life in which they accomplish something worthwhile.

Countering this is the fact that having and rearing young children presents demands as well as gratifications, and that these fall most directly, according to the conventional pattern, on the women. Most women in the sample, and in our society generally, seem to cope with the situation by temporarily putting their career aspirations into abeyance, automatically lowering their ultimate ambitions and restricting themselves to trying to keep their general direction of interest alive. For the most part, they attempt to maximize the gratifications of child care and to minimize its drawbacks. In fact, most of the housewives distinguish in their minds between the chore aspect of child care and the gratification aspect. As was noted in the previous section, the chore aspect is associated with house-cleaning activities, and would be delegated were sufficient resources available for obtaining help. In examining the way most of the graduates – men and women – feel about children and their impact on their careers, the following findings are relevant.

First, this population for the most part want two children and on the whole they keep the family size to the desired level. Furthermore, the women in this sample obtain their desired family size comparatively early in marriage. Table VII.4 shows the distribution of the number of children actually had.

It would seem from this table that there are very few people who have unwanted children, or at least who can say that they have unwanted children.[1] Altogether, the proportion of families that want

---

(3) Gardening
(4) Child care; daily cooking, special cooking

There is a slight preference for the Americans to be more willing to delegate cooking and gardening. In both sets of data there is a high correlation among the items, suggesting a general factor of household activity which may be thought of as a block and accepted or rejected by different subgroups of women, i.e. these women tend to accept or reflect all aspects of household activities.

[1] The tendency not to have more children than desired may also be reflected in the high proportion of women who have four or more children and do not indicate that they have no idea how many they hope for; quite a different situation from the large 'no answer' percentage for those with no children at all.

more than three children is very small and does not differ significantly for the men and women graduates.

Most of the respondents describe their attitudes towards having children as wanting them 'very much'. Over half the married men and women reply in this way, with the only discernible variant pattern among the married graduates being married women without children, 8 per cent of whom indicate that they are not keen to have children at all. Five per cent of the men indicate this.[1]

Table VII.4

Number of Children Hoped For by Number Now Had

1960 Graduates: Married Men and Women

Number of Children Now – Percentage

		0	1	2	3	4+	0	1	2	3	4+
Number of children hoped for	None	5	—	—	—	—	8	1	—	—	—
	One	2	10	—	—	—	1	5	—	—	—
	Two	40	49	59	—	—	54	47	61	—	—
	Three	28	29	20	77	—	17	24	22	59	—
	Four+	12	10	15	19	100	11	15	13	39	86
	No idea+NA	12	3	5	3	—	10	7	4	2	14
Totals percentage		99	101	99	99	—	101	99	100	100	100
N =		(57)	(73)	(132)	(31)	(5)	(71)	(74)	(167)	(51)	(7)

The graduates were asked their opinion about the effects of children on their careers. As might be predicted, particularly in the light of the effects of children on career ambitions reported in the previous chapter, the differences between men and women are very marked. Whereas about 80 per cent of the married men feel that having children makes 'no difference', 70 per cent of the married women indicate that it means that they must 'stop' their career development, and another 20 per cent feel that it hinders their careers. Only about 2 per cent of the women, as compared with about 10 per cent of the men, feel that having children 'helps' them with their careers.

About two-thirds of both the male and female married respondents with children indicate that they felt, before having children, that having children would contribute to their personal development; the other third felt that it would not affect them personally. The per-

---

[1] Aside from personal inclinations, social pressures in our society tend to press in the direction of a woman getting married, and once married to have children. To indicate a wish not to have any children expresses a variant attitude – and this may be understated.

centage goes up to over 90 per cent after having children. The contribution of children to marital harmony as distinct from personal development is, however, another issue which will be discussed later in the chapter.

There are some interesting relationships between number of children desired and had on the one hand, and actual employment pattern of married women on the other. First, it is clear that the number of children already had affects whether a married woman is presently working or not. Table VII.5 shows the percentage of women not working for the different levels of child-bearing.

Table VII.5

Number of Children and Employment

1960 Married Women Graduates: (Percentage Not Working by Number of Children)

	No children	Expecting first	One	Two	Three or more
Not working	10	24	61	60	72
N =	(51)	(21)	(74)	(167)	(58)

The number of children a woman has affects her employment. There are three major breaks in the pattern: the first when 'expecting', the second when the first child arrives, and the third when there are three or more children. The ideal number of children desired may also be determined by one's work status. Considering all the married women who have had at least one child so as to avoid the effect from idealizing the state of parenthood (which is a factor amongst the women without children) the following picture emerges:

Table VII.6

Employment and Number of Children Desired

1960 Married Women Graduates with Children: (Percentage Desiring Two or Less Children)

	Not working	Part-time	Full-time working
	43	58	67
Totals: N-NA	(186)	(109)	(59)
NA (Desire)	(10)	(5)	(2)
N	(196)	(114)	(61)

Sixty-seven per cent of the full-time working women want two or less children (the remaining 33 per cent wanting more) as compared with 58 per cent of the part-timers and 43 per cent of the non-workers who want less than two. This table indicates the relationship between the employment of a woman and her attitude towards how many children she hopes to have. Whether or not a woman works is affected by and affects her attitudes towards domesticity and *a fortiori* towards child bearing and rearing.

The attitudes of married men and women respondents towards child-care practices are fairly uniform, even among those who do not yet have children. The preferred way for a woman to have a young infant (under a year old) looked after if she does go out to work is by a relative in the infant's own home. Married women with children indicate this preference 62 per cent of the time. Married men and women without children still have this as their modal choice though it is no longer a majority choice. Married men without children choose it least (41 per cent). The second most popular choice is not a relative in the relative's home but a hired helper in the infant's home. About 25 per cent overall prefer this arrangement. All other arrangements, including nursery and child-care facilities, are much less frequently chosen. The important point here is that the preference is overwhelmingly for the young infant to be looked after in its own home surroundings.

The pattern remains similar until the child is 3, after which the modal category becomes 'nursery school'. Nearly 70 per cent of the respondents favour this way of caring for the infant between the age of 3 and 6 if the mother goes out to work. After 6 the range of preferred arrangements increases, with domestic helpers being the most favoured.

The modal response categories to the question of what age the infant should be before a married woman should accept an 'exciting job she would like to take, assuming she could arrange for good child care during her absence from home', is 4 or 5 for a part-time job (about 33 per cent indicate this), and 6-10 for a full-time job (27 per cent indicate this choice).

To attempt to get at what constitutes 'good child care' in the minds of the respondents, the following hypothetical proposition was put to all married persons:

> 'Suppose you (or your wife, if you are a man) were offered an excellent full-time job when you had a four-year-old child. Assuming you (your wife) did not need to work, but were (was) interested in the nature of the job itself, indicate whether you (your wife) would accept such a job under each of the conditions listed below.'

The responses are summarized in the following table:

250

Table VII.7

Acceptability of Child-Care Conditions for Mothers Working at Non-Essential Jobs

1960 Married Graduates: (Percentage Indicating that they would accept or 'probably' would accept)

	Married men no children	Married men with children	Married women no children	Married women with children
A very close relative lives nearby and would love to take care of the child	59	47	64	62
There is an excellent house keeper you are sure would take good care of your child	54	44	57	44
There is an excellent all-day child-care centre	63	57	71	53
You could make adequate but not excellent child-care arrangements	18	6	14	8
N =	(79)	(245)	(73)	(298)

From this it would seem that men and women have generally similar attitudes, with women accepting a close relative as a surrogate a little more easily than men, and the married men and women with children being somewhat more cautious about delegating child care generally than are those without children. The most generally acceptable solution for the men is a child-care centre; for the women, a close relative living nearby. These are the most favoured solutions. The most remarkable difference, however, is between 'excellent' and 'adequate' facilities. This population is prepared to accept excellent but not merely adequate day-care facilities for its young children.

The marital relationship has complexities of its own. Unlike domestic chores, this area cannot be delegated. Unlike child bearing, marriage does not provide a major impediment to a woman continuing her career; rather it may impede or enhance her career development depending on the relationship she has with her husband. As has been indicated, there are more complexities in the matter than simply whether or not the husband says he approves of his wife's working. What, then, are the kinds of elements in the marital relationship that affect a woman's orientation to her career and her actual career plans and accomplishments?

THE MARITAL RELATIONSHIP

In our society the marital relationship is generally recognized as central for adults. For graduates the tendency is to marry very shortly after finishing university. Only about 10 per cent in the present sample married before that point and about 50 per cent married within two years following graduation. By eight years out, 85 per cent of the men and 75 per cent of the women are married and most of those who are still single intend eventually to marry. Only 4 per cent of the single men and 6 per cent of the single women indicate that they intend never to marry.[1] Marriage is a highly idealized state, and 70 per cent of the married graduates indicate that they were 'very keen to marry', with a further 25 per cent indicating that they were 'moderately keen'.[2]

About one-third of the married women are married to men the same age as themselves, though under 20 per cent of the men are married to women the same age as themselves. This reflects the greater tendency for women to marry men with whom they are at university. Fifty per cent of the married women with children and 30 per cent of the married women without children state that their spouses were at university with them, as compared with only 18 per cent of the married men with children and 16 per cent of the married men without children. The modal category for the men is, in keeping with general cultural expectations, that they marry a woman 1-2 years younger than themselves, and for the women that they marry a man 1-2 years older. About 25 per cent of each of these groups conform to this culturally normative pattern. For the men there is a greater spread, with about 5 per cent of the men at one extreme marrying women 5 or more years older than themselves, and about 15 per cent marrying women 5 or more years younger than themselves, (12 per cent of the married men with children; 22 per cent of the married men without children). The women rarely marry men that are much younger than themselves (under 2 per cent), though at the other extreme 10 per cent of the married women with children and

[1] An additional small proportion of the single men and women (9 per cent and 4 per cent) indicate that they expect at age 40 some 'other' kind of life situation than being single and working or being married, whether or not working.

[2] Married women without children report considerably less enthusiasm about marrying than those who have children. A higher proportion of them (44 per cent as compared with 33 per cent of those without children) report that their mothers were very keen for them to marry, and a lower proportion (16 per cent as compared with 21 per cent) report that their fathers were very keen. These responses suggest one social pressure among many on people to marry whether or not they want to.

17 per cent of those without children are married to men five or more years older than themselves.

Marriage is followed for most by rapid entry into parenthood; in the 1960 graduates study, 81 per cent of the men and 86 per cent of the women had or were 'expecting' a child. Fifty-eight per cent of the women graduates and 54 per cent of the men had had two or more children by this time (see Table VII.4).

Most of the married graduates – both men and women – report that having children has a consolidating effect on the marital relationship. Just over 60 per cent across the categories of respondents indicate this, while another 30 per cent feel that it makes no difference to the marital relationship.

In general the sample is made up of people who consider themselves to be happy and well adjusted. Respondents were asked about how happy 'you really feel about your marriage'[1]. About 60 per cent of the respondents, across all the categories of married people, indicate that they are 'very happy', with approximately a further 30 per cent of the men and 25 per cent of the women indicating that they are 'pretty happy'.[2] The highest proportion of 'mixed' feelings is reported by the married women with children (16 per cent), and among the married men with children (10 per cent). The married women without children choose 'not happy' and 'unhappy' more than the others at 9 per cent. Married men without children did not show a corresponding level (only 10 per cent 'unhappy'). So the balance is very heavily on the positive side.

As one possible source of marital difficulty, the perception of a mismatch was examined. Respondents were asked whether they ever feel that they married the 'wrong sort of person'. Table VII.8 reports the distribution of responses to this question:

[1] Five response categories were provided: 'very happy'; 'pretty happy'; 'sometimes happy, sometimes unhappy'; 'not very happy'; and 'unhappy'.

[2] Overall, 'global' happiness correlates with marital happiness for the married people, though the levels reported are somewhat lower. For example, the categories given were 'as happy as I'd like', 'pretty happy', 'not too happy' and 'unhappy': Married men without children chose 'as happy as I'd like' 42 per cent of the time (with an additional 52 per cent 'pretty happy'); married men with children 30 per cent and 63 per cent; married women without children 30 per cent and 60 per cent; and married women with children 43 per cent and 50 per cent. Having children is associated with a drop in happiness for men and a rise in happiness for the women. The global happiness ratings give additional information about the single people. They are, in both sexes, less happy than the married people; this is consistent with what has been reported in other studies (e.g. Bradburn and Orden, 1969). The single men choose 'happy as I'd like' only 14 per cent of the time, with an additional 65 per cent as 'pretty happy' while the single women show an even lower percentage of 'happy as I'd like' (9 per cent), though their 'pretty happy' proportions come up to 72 per cent.

Table VII.8

Feelings of Marital Mismatch by Sex and Marital Phase

1960 Graduates: Married Men and Women (Percentages)

	Men		Women	
	No child	Children	No child	Children
Often	0	1	7	1
Occasionally	21	29	17	26
No	80	70	76	73
Total Percentages	101	100	100	100
N-NA =	(78)	(245)	(72)	(298)
NA =	1	—	1	—

Married people who have children tend to have doubts about whether they made the right choice of partner more often than do those with no children. This may be related to the feeling of being tied into the marriage more irrevocably after having had children, and the increase in reported disagreements that stem from the presence of children probably contributes to this feeling as well. (See below.)

It is interesting on the other hand to examine the question of how much the individuals attribute the difficulties they perceive in the marital relationship to themselves and their failure in the role of husband or wife as distinct from the 'other person' and the possibility of having made a wrong choice. Table VII.9 shows the pattern of response to the question, 'Do you feel you are not doing as well as you would like as a husband/wife?'

Table VII.9

Dissatisfaction with Self as Husband/Wife

1960 Graduates: Married Men and Women (Percentages)

	Men without children	Men with children	Women without children	Women with children
Yes often	0	7	10	10
Sometimes	46	51	58	55
No	54	42	32	35
Totals Percentages	100	100	100	100
N-NA =	(78)	(245)	(72)	(298)
NA =	1	1	1	—

Two differences seem to be prominent in this table. First, the women express somewhat more dissatisfaction with themselves as wives than do the men as husbands, and this does not seem to be related to whether or not they have children (indeed, some women without children may express dissatisfaction because they have not yet produced children). Second, the men's frequency of dissatisfaction with themselves as husbands rises with having children. This may be related to the reported increase in incidence of disagreements about division of labour (see below). If so, one possible explanation is that the women put more pressure on the men to help after they have children, and although the men do not fulfil these demands at the same time they feel dissatisfied with themselves for this reason.

To determine something of the dynamics of young family life, questions were asked about the frequency with which respondents and their spouses had disagreements over different issues arising in family life.

'All families disagree about things, regardless of their overall happiness. For each of the following, please indicate how often you and your spouse have disagreements: weekly, monthly, less frequently, rarely or never.'

The categories provided were:

'Religion/politics; use of money; handling of children; in-laws; personal habits; lesiure activities; husband's job; friends; division of labour in the household.'

In general, women report a lower level of disagreement than the men; frequency of disagreement increases for men and women with having children. By and large relatively frequent disagreements are reported as arising from the nine areas by men and women though the order and emphasis varies by sex and family stage. Only three categories are fairly 'heavily' indicated as areas of disagreement, using as a criterion that 20 per cent or more of the respondents indicate that this is an area in which there is weekly or monthly disagreement. At the top of the list is 'personal habits', (36 per cent of the married men without children, 33 per cent of those with children, and 14 per cent and 25 per cent for the two categories of married women respectively); second is 'division of labour' (23 per cent, 24 per cent, 15 per cent and 23 per cent for the four categories of respondent); use of money is third (with 17 per cent, 24 per cent, 20 per cent and 19 per cent for the respective categories of respondents indicating that this is a weekly or monthly area of disagreement). The men indicate more disagreement on 'leisure' than do the women; for them the percentage is about 20 per cent as compared with 12 per cent for the women. 'Children' becomes an area of disagreement among those who have them, with about 20 per cent of both men and women indicating this as an area of weekly or monthly disagreement. The lowest areas of disagreement are 'friends', 'wife's job' and 'husband's job' – all under 5 per cent overall. More of the married men with children indicate disagreements over husband's job' than others (15 per cent as compared with under 5 per cent for all other categories). It is also interesting that the disagreement over 'in-laws' is greater for men with children than for men without children, possibly because the women's parents become more involved in the family life when there are children. On the other hand, for those without children, the women's sensitivity to the 'in-law' problems seems higher than the men's, possibly because at this stage the women resent more than the men the persisting ties with parental families.

For the purposes of this study, two of the areas indicated as causing regular disagreement repay further study. The frequent occurrence of disagreements in relation to 'domestic division of labour' is second in order (after personal habits), and occurs for about 20 per cent of the women. Taking all married women according to how much they are working, there is a sharp difference among the married women with children by whether they work full-, part-time or not at all. This difference, however, does not occur for the married women without children, as is shown in Table VII.10.

Table VII.10

Employment and Disagreements over Division of Labour

1960 Married Women Graduates: (Percentage Indicating Frequent Disagreements[1] over Household Division of Labour)

	Without children	(N-NA)	With children	(N-NA)
Not working	0	(10)	20	(182)
Working up to 30 hours weekly	12	(17)	26	(97)
Working 31+ hours	18	(45)	37	(13)
Totals: N-NA		(72)		(292)
NA (Disagreement)		(1)		(6)
N		(73)		(298)

Frequency of disagreements over division of labour in the household rises sharply with having children and is more frequent among the

[1] 'Frequent' is taken to be monthly or more often.

women with children who work than among those who do not, increasing with the amount of time worked.

The third most frequently indicated area of regular disagreement – 'use of money' – is also interesting in relation to women's employment. Women were asked their reasons for having left work, and two major groupings are discernible: the majority who left for 'domestic' reasons, and the minority who left for other reasons. Among the 'domestic' leavers 16 per cent report frequent quarrels over the 'use of money', while 27 per cent of those who left their jobs for 'other' reasons report disagreements over money. It would seem that the wife's loss of personal income can be more easily absorbed in the marital relationship if she has the compensation of a child than if she has not.

The married graduates in this sample resolve disagreements in three major ways, the women showing slightly different patterns from the men.[1] The most frequently reported way of resolving disagreements is 'by rational discussion' (particularly reported by the women – approximately 36 per cent of the women as compared with approximately 30 per cent of the men). For the men the second most used mode of resolution is 'one gives in one time, the other the next' (about 25 per cent of the men report this as the main way disagreements are resolved as compared with only 13 per cent of the women). For men the third is followed closely by 'a row to clear the air', while for women, this is the second most frequently reported way of resolving the disagreements. The women do not favour the men's second most used method, namely, taking turns to give in. They indicate in greater proportions, as their third most frequently indicated pattern, non-resolution of the disagreements. It is interesting to note (though the numbers are very small) that the men feel in greater proportions than the women that they 'get their own way' while the women feel slightly more frequently than the men that they just 'keep things to themselves' and give in. In general the correspondence between the men and women is fairly good and it is interesting that only about one-fifth of the population indicate non-resolution of disagreements. For the women, this pattern of non-resolution is more frequently reported than for men and it might well be that married women are particularly vulnerable in this way.

THE INTERACTION BETWEEN FAMILY AND CAREER

In Chapter VI some aspects of the interaction between career and family were examined with the focus on career. It was shown that level of aspiration, commitment to the general value of women's

[1] See Appendix II, Table VII.A3 for full table.

rights to have careers, and actual enjoyment patterns all contribute to women's intentions to work. Being in work at present, even if only for a few hours a week, is perhaps the most important indication of the intention to work continuously (as measured by the intention to work when the youngest child is under 3). As far as the more remote work expectations are concerned, i.e. when the children are grown, it was shown that this has become the most prevalent pattern, with about three-quarters of the graduates in the sample having this intention. The most powerful determinant of this general intention is the feeling that work or career is an area of life from which great personal satisfactions are derived. In general (as is shown in the full table in Appendix III) the more commitment that is present, the more continuous is the expected pattern of work.

In this chapter, the dimensions of home and family life are somewhat more carefully dissected, and the specific tasks for which men and women carry responsibility and their feelings towards them are analysed. The centrality of children in family life is highlighted, and though children are of paramount importance to members of both sexes it is seen that child care remains very much the responsibility of women. Highly qualified women experience child care as a source of gratification which operates at least in the short run to compensate for the frustrations that many feel at having to withdraw from their careers, and they have very stringent requirements about the delegation of the care. Nevertheless, 38 per cent of the married women with children in this sample indicate that they expect to be working when their youngest child is still under 3.

a *The complexities surrounding women's career commitment*

The operative pathways and critical decision points for married women returning to work when their youngest child is under 3 are suggested in Figure VII.1.[1] Starting at the left-hand side of the chart it is seen that of all the married women in the sample who provided the requisite information for this analysis (total of 335), 38 per cent (127) intend to work when their youngest child is still under 3.

The factor that most distinguishes the women who expect to work at that point in their family cycle from those who do not is whether

---

[1] This diagram is derived from the A.I.D. scanning process and is reported in the Technical Appendix. A.I.D. stands for Automatic Interaction Detection, a stepwise regression programme described in Sonquist and Morgan, 1964. The figures in the A.I.D. analysis are slightly different from figures reported in other tables because slightly different definitions were used in the two analyses. As far as can be determined, the patterns produced by the A.I.D. analysis and the more conventional procedures match very well.

or not they ideally want to be a housewife now. Just over 50 per cent of the women ideally want to be housewives. Of these only 7 per cent (12 out of 171) intend to work while their youngest child is under 3. The other half of the sample, who ideally prefer to be working, are nearly evenly divided into those who are *not* favourable to married women in general having 'careers' as distinct from 'jobs' (48 out of the 77 who favour careers, or 62 per cent expect to be

Figure VII.1

Work Orientation of 1960 Married Women Graduates[1]

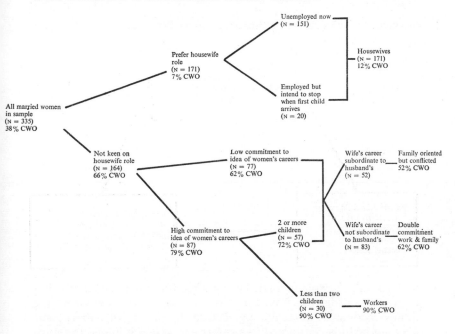

working while their infants are of that age) as compared with 67 out of the 87 (79 per cent) who *favour* women having careers. The chart shows, in this way, the patterning of variables that differentiate the women who expect to work more continuously from those who do not.

The intention to work when the youngest child is still under 3 years old was again used as an indicator of a larger conception of a

---

[1] Here, as elsewhere in this work, 'continuous' work orientation is indicated by the intention to work when one's youngest child is under 3. This is abbreviated here as CWO.

woman's expected work pattern. As mentioned in the last chapter, this is a good indicator of a relatively continuous involvement in work through the family life cycle. Other indicators which might serve as predictors of an individual's career potential are more variable in predicting woman's performance. The reason for this is the impact in society today of situational factors such as the care of children and the orientation of the husband. Thus, high aspiration, full commitment, current performance, and so on, must be viewed in the context of a specific situation before their meaning can be

Figure VII.2

Selected Variables Affecting Women's Career Potentials

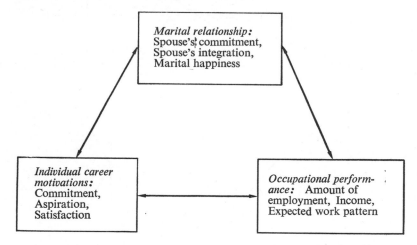

understood. A woman may be working full time reluctantly but doing so in order to support a student husband, or to augment the family income temporarily, e.g. before the arrival of a baby; she may not be fully committed to a career and may not intend to return as soon as possible after having children.[1] Conversely, there are some women who are committed to the idea of women's careers but who withdraw from active working for a period of child rearing; they may work fewer hours and make less money over a given period, such as the one during which the graduates' sample was studied, than some women who are not career-committed but are working to relieve boredom or to supplement family income.

---

[1] Of course, these differences in motivation to work apply to men too. However, in society today men do not have the option not to work. For women, this option may create a psychological burden (Cf. Bailyn, L. 1964).

This complexity presents special problems for analysing the potential of women in the world of work. There is no one given variable or even a single cluster of variables that is clearly useful as the main predictor of career potential. Rather, there is an interrelated set of variables – values, personal inclinations, plans, current performance and type of marital relationship.

Therefore, in this report, a complex set of indicators is used, with a piecemeal analysis of relationships among them. The indicators suggest relevant dimensions of behaviour, attitudes and experience which not only affect ultimate career potentials, but also affect one another. They may thus be seen as an interacting network of variables as shown graphically in Figure VII.2.

In this framework three interacting areas are shown: Marital Relationships, Individual Career Aspirations and Occupational Performance, and the examination will focus on the nine variables shown above (three from each area).

A central variable in the analysis of individual motivation is commitment. Only one aspect of commitment is examined here – namely, commitment to the idea of women having careers. It is defined as an index based on two questions:

(1) What are your attitudes to a married woman engaging in:

a. a 'career' (in which there is a long-term occupational commitment)

b. a 'job' (just to add interest and/or to supplement family income)

c. voluntary activities (not for money, but time consuming)?

Respondents were asked to indicate whether they were 'in favour', 'mixed or neutral', or 'against' each.

(2) 'A married woman cannot make long-range plans for her career because they depend on her husband's plans for his'

Do you:

'strongly agree', 'mildly agree', 'mildly disagree' or 'strongly disagree'.

The construction of the index was described in the last chapter (Appendix, Table VI.A1) and the resulting typology is described in Figure VII.3. The index describes the individual's commitment to the idea of women's careers and it is used for both male and female respondents. For the individual woman, commitment to the idea is used as a variable of personal career-motivation, and her husband's commitment to the idea (or her perception of it, which was also

261

measured in the survey instrument) is used as a variable in the marital relationship which may affect her occupational performance.

Figure VII.3 describes the commitment typology as derived from the answers to these two questions.

Figure VII.3

Types of Commitment to Women's Careers

		Married Women *cannot* Make Long Range Career Plans		
		Strongly Agree	Mildly Agree	Disagree (Mildly or strongly)
Women should have a *career* type of occupational commitment	Favour	Secondary committed (IIIa)	Medium committed (IIIb)	Full committed (IIIc)
	Neutral mixed or against	Non-committed (I)	Mixed committed (II)	Mixed committed (II)

i. *The Non-committed:* Not in favour of women having careers, and agree that married women cannot plan their own careers because of the priority of the husbands' careers.

ii. *Ambivalent or mixed committed:* Mixed, neutral or against women having careers, and mild agreement or disagreement with the proposition that women are not able to plan their careers because of their husbands' careers.

iii. *The committed* (which has 3 subtypes):

   a. Secondary Commitment: where the respondent is in favour of women pursuing careers but at the same time strongly agrees with the proposition that married women cannot make career plans, because of the priority of the husband's career plans.
   b. Medium Commitment: where the respondent is in favour of women's careers, but agrees (though only mildly) that a married woman cannot make career plans.
   c. Full Commitment: where the respondent is in favour of women having careers, and disagree with the idea that married women cannot make career plans because of the priority of their husbands' careers.

These types make sense when viewed in historical perspective, and correspond to some of the distinctions emerging from similar research (Ginsberg, *et al.*, 1966; Mulvey, 1963; Rossi, 1965). The non-committed married woman is the traditional housewife and until recently this was the dominant pattern for women to adopt. For such women, university education is seen primarily as a way of developing oneself personally so that one becomes a better mother, wife and community participant. More recently, as egalitarian values and universal education have gained ground, other patterns have emerged. The mixed commitment or 'ambivalent' type represents, it would seem, the transitional phenomenon which is being experienced by many women who have to some extent taken on new attitudes and have achieved high qualifications but who have also been educated in a traditional context and live in an environment which only partly supports change. As these women are characterized by their lack of a strong position on either of the two commitment indicators of women's careers, they may be expected to perform or not to perform and to be satisfied or not satisfied according to the conditions in their immediate environments (Rossi, 1968).

On the side of more positive commitment, three sub-patterns are apparent. That of 'secondary commitment' is probably the most generally accepted among married women who are in favour of work at all, and it is only among a minority of highly qualified married women with children that the other two patterns of commitment are evident.

The personal and value preoccupations of the married women with ambivalent 'mixed' commitment attitudes revolves around the issue of whether it is possible or not for married women to have careers. The secondary commitment women are clear on this; they think it is a good idea in general but that married women must keep their own career aspirations secondary to those of their husbands. The medium commitment types are less preoccupied with the general value issue of whether women should have careers or not but more with how much of a career or how fully equal to the husband's it should be. The fully committed married women are clear on both these issues. The only problems that arise for them are concerned with feasibility, not values. As has been indicated in the last chapter, only 19 or 7 per cent of the married women with children are fully committed, but nearly three-fifths of these (the largest proportion for any group) intend to work continuously. Adding the medium committed people to the fully committed, there are 91 married women with children (about a third of this category) of whom half intend to work continuously. (See Appendix, Table VI.A1.)

When the effect of commitment on the variables of occupational performance, e.g. current employment and 'expected work pattern', is examined, the utility of the commitment index becomes clearer. Only a very tiny proportion of the non-workers (housewives) with low commitment intend to work when their children are under 3 and a very high proportion (85 per cent) of the high-commitment workers expect to work when their youngest child is under 3. At the same time, similar proportions (over half) of the non-working high-commitment types on the one hand, and the working low-commitment types on the other intend to resume work at this critical period of their child's early infancy.

The ways in which personal factors and marital relationship factors each contribute to a woman's performance in the occupational sphere are complex and their influence is reciprocal. Only illustrative documentation of these influences is possible here. It has already been shown in the last chapter, for example, that level of aspiration (a personal factor) influences work intentions (an occupational performance variable). It was also indicated that personal factors affect whether or not an individual is likely to be married by eight years out of university, and this in turn affects occupational performance – for men as well as for women. Table VII.11 gives another illustration of how a personal factor – commitment to the idea of women having careers – affects present occupational performance.

This table shows that among the married women graduates without children, everyone with any degree of commitment (100 per cent in all three of the positive commitment categories) works. For married women with children, the proportions working fall generally; but a greater number who have a high degree of commitment to the idea of women having careers are working than among those who are not so committed in their personal beliefs and values.

The preceding analysis has focused on the attitudes, values and intentions of married women graduates and has indicated that these variables are all inter-related and affect women's actual patterns of work. In the next two parts of this section, special attention will be given to the issues surrounding the relationship between these work orientations and behaviours and the marital relationship. How much do husbands' characteristics and attitudes affect wives' career performance? How much and in what way does this affect their marital happiness?

b *Career and husband's attitude*

Public discussion of the bearing of the marital relationship on women's work performance indicates both the diversity of opinion

FAMILY PATTERNS AND WORK

and the complexity of issues in this area. At one extreme, not represented in the current sample of highly educated women, is the radical feminine liberation position, which in some instances advocates the abolition of the conventional marriage institution which is seen as the enslavement of women. At the other extreme is the old conventional position, expressed in modified and modernized terms but stemming essentially from the Victorian position and earlier that familial well-being depends on the wife accepting her role as homemaker, dependent economically on the husband but providing for

Table VII.11

Commitment to the Idea of Women's Careers and Current Employment

1960 Graduates: All Married Women (Percentages Working)[1]

Married women without children

	No commitment	Mixed commitment	Secondary commitment	Medium commitment	Full commitment
	73	69	100	100	100
N =	(26)	(16)	(11)	(14)	(6)

Married women with children

	No commitment	Mixed commitment	Secondary commitment	Medium commitment	Full commitment
	19	20	33	33	42
N =	(73)	(99)	(36)	(71)	(19)

him the domestic situation and supports that allow for complementary satisfaction. In Tennyson's terms, all else would be 'chaos' (Tennyson, 'The Princess'). In terms of the Victorian derivative in

[1] The proportions employed and unemployed among the married women are slightly different in this table from those in the tables presented in the last chapter. This is because a different measure of employment was used. In the last chapter the criterion was the answer to the question asking how many hours per week the individual was employed. In this table and in others in the current chapter, the criterion was the answer given to the question: 'Here are six descriptions of the relationship between work and family. Indicate which is closest to yours now.' The choice of 'married (or living as married), husband works and wife runs home' was taken to indicate that the woman was at home not working at present. All other responses – describing a range of women's work situations combined with family life – were taken to indicate some form of employment of the wife. While the figures achieved in this way differ from those derived from answers to numbers of hours employed, the patterning of responses is the same.

contemporary society, what else would a normal woman want than to be at home at the centre of a happy family? (*The Sunday Times*, September 21, 1969). As has already been indicated, the most prevalent pattern nowadays is the interruption of career involvement for a period of domestic concentration followed by resumption of career later on, usually in a low key with little hope of more than marginal participation. However, there are variant patterns in the present-day situation that it is important to analyse and understand – on the one hand, the more conventional domestic pattern and on the other, the more committed career pattern. While the latter is more in focus in the current study, it is the entire range and its characteristics that is important in any ultimate sense and the comprehension of any single pattern is enhanced by an understanding of how it contrasts with the others.

In preceding discussions, the part played by husbands has come into the picture only peripherally. The married women in this sample mostly work as a matter of choice because it is only an insignificant minority who are separated, who have incapacitated husbands, or husbands who are not earning because they are involved in postgraduate studies. Of the five married women who indicate that their husbands earn under £500 per year, three work full-time. Roughly 40 per cent of the women whose husbands earn under £2,000 per year work full-time, and about a quarter of those whose husbands earn over £2,000 work full-time (less for the married women with children, more for those without). These, then, are women who do not have to work, indeed who often work with a family environment of a relatively high income for people of their ages. Their own commitment to the idea of women's careers has been shown to be a factor affecting whether they work or not. What are the factors in their marriages that hamper or facilitate the pursuit of a career and influence their career performance?

Two elements in the relationship will be examined, and then the issue of marital happiness – itself an influence determining occupational performances – will be discussed. The two elements are first, the husband's own orientation to family and career for themselves and secondly, his commitment to the idea of women pursuing careers.

There is a tendency to think that as conventionally men work and women are at home, the problem is a simple one for men as they *must* work, while for women it is complex because they must work against a culturally normative pattern, and work therefore becomes a matter of choice. Men are seen to differ in their degree of ambition, 'thrust', competence and so on, but it is assumed that they must work and that work must occupy their capacities as fully as possible.

266

In general, it is further assumed that the kind of men who are in the sample under examination are likely to derive major satisfactions from their careers – in contrast to less skilled and professionalized workers who may in varying degrees be alienated from their work. The information from this study indicates a range of variation in the way these highly qualified men regard their work and their family life as well as other areas of their lives. Classifying them in terms of the relative salience to them of work, family life and other areas of life gives potentially important insights into the structure of their families. The structural conditions created by a man who is totally immersed in his career, giving his family only peripheral attention, are clearly different and have different implications for the highly qualified wife, from the structure created by the man who places his family first and sets limits on how much he allows his career to make inroads into his time and energies.

Some understanding of men's orientations to their work and family life is one of the important contributions that this study is attempting to make. Much of the research on women and their careers has regarded the problems only in terms of women's talents and motivations. This is important, but not sufficient by itself. The structural elements of the masculine environment mentioned above play an important part, as do the attitudinal elements concerned with the husband's own values about women and their careers. To demonstrate that these actually operate in practice, not only theoretically, the men in the sample were classified in terms of the relative salience (derived satisfaction) for them personally of work, family and other areas of life. This classification is referred to as the men's patterns of *integration*. That is to say, different men integrate their work and family life in different ways. Some place work and family as the two areas of life from which they derive their main satisfactions, while others indicate one or the other as one of their two main areas of satisfaction but not both.

The basis for the classification was the question mentioned in Chapter VI, p. 198:

'Which of the following gives you the most satisfaction in your life?'

Your career or occupation
Family relationships
Leisure-time recreational activities
Religious beliefs or activities
Participation as a citizen in affairs of your community
Participation in activities directed towards national or international betterment
Running a home

The classification derived from the replies to this question is as follows:[1]

i. *The integrated orientation:* here 'career' and 'family' are mentioned as the two areas of life from which the individual gets most satisfactions.

   a. The Career-Integrated – in which career is first, family second

   b. The Family-Integrated – in which family is first, career second

ii. *The Non-integrated orientation:* in which the top two categories may include work or family, but not both.

   a. The Career-Non-integrated – career is first or second, but family is not mentioned as the other principal source of satisfaction

   b. The Family-Non-integrated – family is first or second, but career is not mentioned as the other principal source of satisfaction

As can be seen, this yields a four-fold typology. The married men in the 1960 graduates sample are distributed in the following way along these two dimensions.

Table VII.12

Married Men's Family-Career Orientation

1960 Graduates: (Percent of all Married Men)

		Integration	
		Integrated	Non-integrated
Emphasis	Career	26	11
	Family	43	20
Totals	N =	(213)	(95)
Total Married men	N-NA	(308)	
	NA (Integration)	(16)	
Married men	N	(324)	

Clearly this is a 'family-orientated' sample as has been indicated in various ways already. The most prevalent orientation of husbands is the 'Integrated-Family' orientation, i.e. where both career and family are the major sources of satisfaction, but family is the more important of the two. There are many fewer, proportionately, of the 'Career-Non-integrated' men, who would seem to be striving for

[1] A residual category of 'other' exists (3 per cent for married men). As this is of such small importance both numerically and conceptually in the present study, percentages are based on the four major patterns only.

career success without looking to the family for their satisfactions in a major way.[1]

The husband's orientation to career and family – i.e. the way he *integrates* the two in his own life – provides a structural element in the marital relationship which may influence the wife's employment performance. Similarly, the husband's *commitment* to the idea of a woman having a career may provide another influential element in the marital relationship. The two elements are shown in the following table to be only slightly related to one another:

Table VII.13

Married Men's Orientations to Career and Family and their Commitment to the Value of Women's Careers

1960 Graduates: Married Men Only (Percentages)

	Integration			
	Integrated		Non-Integrated	
Commitment	Career	Family	Career	Family
Non-committed	32	38	26	41
Mixed-committed	31	34	38	41
Committed { Sec. committed	9	9	12	3
Med. committed	20	11	12	7
Full committed	9	8	12	8
Totals: Percentages	101	100	100	100
N-NA	(81)	(132)	(34)	(61)

NA (Integration) = (16)
n = (308+16)   = (324)

There is a tendency for men who place their own greatest emphasis on career as a source of satisfaction to feel also that women should have careers. The smallest proportions of 'non-committed' men are in the career-orientated groups, particularly the Career-Non-integrated, where family life is not seen as a main source of satisfactions. The relatively low proportion of Family-Non-Integrated men who are highly committed to women's careers (15 per cent in the medium

---

[1] It must be kept in mind that this is a university graduate sample, where family values may be higher than in a random cross-section of similarly higher status people in industry and elsewhere who are not graduates. In addition, there is a possible source of bias in that the non-integrated career-oriented males may be less likely to complete a questionnaire of this type, making their sub-group under-represented in the sample. Postal questionnaires provide the further hazard of uncertainty about how privately the form was filled up. Some men may have rated family higher than they might otherwise have done if their wives saw the forms.

and full categories, as compared with 24 per cent and 29 per cent for the two career-orientated categories of men) might indicate a feeling that as career is not that important for men or for women, there is no point in women pursuing a career at all. Such men might prefer wives who were familistic so that both would obtain their main satisfactions from the family and associated activities. The small percentage who are committed to women working may be so either for *laissez-faire* reasons, or because they wish to have their wives make up occupationally for their own attitude. Furthermore, the non-integrated familistic husband may not wish his wife to be too committed to a career because her accomplishments might eclipse his own.

It should be kept in mind that the proportions of married men who are committed in any clear way to the idea of women's careers are small. Just over a third of the married men who emphasize career (i.e. the 'Career-Integrated' and 'Career-Non-Integrated' groups) and a quarter of those who emphasize family are committed to the value position in favour of women's careers. This has implications for their wives. Ideally one would like to know the relationship between these characteristics of married men and their wives' actual patterns of commitment and work. There is only partial data on this for the married men's wives in the sample – namely, whether they are currently working or not. Information on the way in which married men's commitment and their wives' patterns of commitment match is available only in the 'couples' series, where data was obtained for both women and their husbands.[1]

Taking first the data on whether the wives of graduate men are currently working, the total sample of married men may be subdivided into the integrated and non-integrated in their own orientation to career, family and other spheres of life. Then this orientation is combined with the degree of commitment to women's careers. The effect of these two orientations on the percentage of wives working is seen in Table VII.14.

The greatest likelihood that a 1960 graduate's wife will be working is if she is married to a 'Career-Non-Integrated' man, the sort of man who derives great satisfaction from his career and does not derive major satisfactions from family life. Fifty-six per cent[2] of the

[1] All married women in the sample were sent an additional questionnaire with a note addressed to their husbands asking if they too would fill up a questionnaire. Of the 371 married women who returned questionnaires, 224 (about 60 per cent) also returned usable questionnaires for their husbands. The sample of 224 is the basis of the 'couples analysis' which is mentioned from time to time in what follows. Lotte Bailyn has focused on selected topics for detailed study.

[2] The numbers here are very small indeed and so should be viewed with special caution.

wives of this group of men are working, with the men's commitment to women's career making a difference – 75 per cent of the highly committed men's wives, as compared with 50 per cent of the non-committed men's wives, working at the time of the study. Overall, the family non-integrated husbands show the next highest proportion of working wives, though there is only a small difference between this category and the career-integrated group.

Table VII.14

Married Men's Integration, Commitment and their Wives' Employment

1960 Married Men Graduates: (Percentages whose wives are working)

	Integrated		Non-Integrated	
	Career Total N	Family Total N	Career Total N	Family Total N
Low commitment (including non-committed and mixed commitment)	26 (58)	18 (107)	50 (26)	35 (52)
High commitment (including secondary medium and full commitment)	39 (23)	40 (25)	75 (8)	22 (9)
Total percentage working:	30	22	56	33
Total N-NA	(81)	(132)	(34)	(61)

NA (Integration) = (16)
N = (324)

The husband's commitment variable makes a difference for the career-orientated respondents in the direction of increasing the likelihood that their wives will be working. High commitment also makes a big difference amongst the family-integrated. It seems that the wives of these men are influenced by their husbands' values and possibly that it is these husbands who help to make it possible for their wives to work. For the wives of the non-integrated 'familistic' husbands (i.e. those who emphasize family values to the exclusion of work) the reverse is true: for them commitment of the husband to women's careers seems to be inversely related to their actual work. This may be because the husbands in this category have a rather apathetic or *laissez-faire* attitude towards work generally, making the wife's own inclination a more determining element in the situation. The couples analysis (cf. below) supports this idea.

It must be remembered that these figures reflect current work patterns. These, as has been shown in the last chapter, are only part of a network of variables relevant to women's career performance. To consider the issues more thoroughly, one would need to relate these family environmental situations not only to current work status, but

Figure VII.4

Married Men's Integration, Their Commitment to Women's Careers and their Wives' Work Status

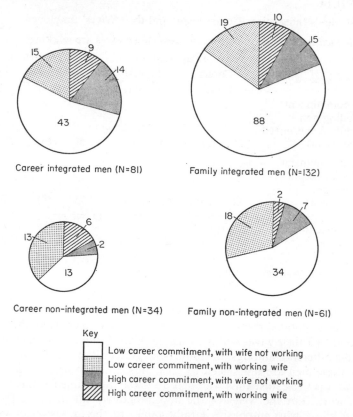

Career integrated men (N=81)   Family integrated men (N=132)

Career non-integrated men (N=34)   Family non-integrated men (N=61)

Key

☐ Low career commitment, with wife not working
▦ Low career commitment, with working wife
▨ High career commitment, with wife not working
▨ High career commitment, with working wife

to intentions, commitment, and the other factors which are likely to determine ultimate performance.[1] The foregoing merely demon-

[1] It must also be remembered that the work performance indicated here is that of the wives of the graduate men, about 80 per cent of whom are themselves graduates or hold some kind of further-study qualifications. A comparison with the couples' information suggests that while their general level of commitment and performance may be lower than that of a purely graduate group, the mechanisms seem to be essentially the same.

strates that the husbands' orientations, both to their own career and family integration and to the idea of women having careers, makes a difference to whether or not wives work.

The following figure shows this in another way:

Figure VII.5

Married Men's Commitment to Women's Careers and their Wives' Work Status

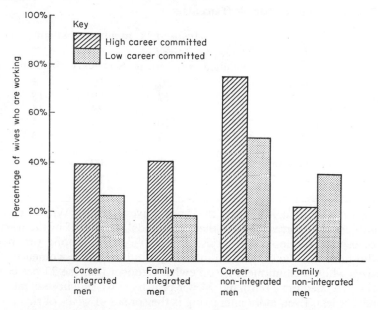

The analysis of the couples' data provides some further insights into the differences indicated within the types of families described. These data show some interesting patterns about the way in which husbands' attitudes and orientations to work and family articulate with their wives' attitudes and orientations. There are some discernible points of disjunction between husbands' attitudes and those of their wives. Just because a husband is committed, verbally, to the idea of women's careers, it does not follow that his wife will automatically subscribe to this idea. Nor does it follow that a wife of a non-committed husband will automatically remain dutifully at home. There seem to be at least two interesting points of disjunction revealed in the couples' analysis that give some clues to the dynamics underlying the pattern of work displayed by the wives of the married men in the sample as reported above. The first relates to the men's

commitments to the value of women's careers, and the second relates
to their integration of satisfaction from work and family. Table
VIII.15 shows the first.[1]

Table VII.15

Value Commitment to Women's Careers

Husbands' Patterns by their Wives' Patterns

1960 Graduates: Couples' Sample (Percentages)

		Husbands' commitment patterns				
		Non-committed	Mixed or ambivalent	Secondary	Medium	Full
Wives' commitment patterns	Non-committed	59	20	15	8	14
	Mixed	17	52	9	18	29
	Secondary	7	3	49	18	5
	Medium	13	20	24	55	24
	Full	4	5	3	3	29
	Totals Percentages	100	100	100	102	101
	N =	(54)	(75)	(33)	(40)	(21)

From this table it appears that most wives have the type of commitment that corresponds to their husbands'. Over half of the wives
correspond for most categories. A sizeable group among the men
who have a 'secondary' commitment attitude towards women have
wives whose commitment is somewhat stronger (i.e. the 27 per cent
who are 'medium'/'full') and 24 per cent have wives whose commitment is less. Even more interesting is the spread of wives of the 'full'
commitment husbands. They show a distinct bimodality, with the
number of wives of 'mixed' or ambivalent commitment as large as
the number of those 'fully' committed. In these cases sanction from
the husbands, or even pressure from them, is clearly not enough, and
it seems that wives have to be ready to show commitment themselves.
The next table contributes further information about this.

Table VII.16 shows that the lowest proportion of medium/fully
committed wives (and correspondingly the highest proportion of
non-committed wives) are among the non-integrated 'careerist' husbands; and even those who are on the committed side are all 'medium'
in their commitment. It was seen in Table VII.14 that 24 per cent
of these non-integrated career husbands endorse high career com-

[1] The data reported here are in L. Bailyn's unpublished memoranda on the
couples' analysis.

274

mitment in their wives. A plausible interpretation of these findings is that some of these careerist husbands give only 'lip service' to the idea of women's careers. This endorsement may be partly a matter of alleviating feelings of guilt arising from their own involvement in their careers to the exclusion of family considerations. The endorsement may not go with actual supportive behaviour which is necessary to facilitate their wives' careers. Though a high proportion of the wives of the non-integrated 'career men' are working (see Table VII.14), they do so without a value commitment to the idea of woman's careers. Their behaviour, then, could be described as a compensatory work involvement which aims to fill the gap left by their husbands' low involvement in them and their family life.

Table VII.16

Husbands' Integration and Wives' Commitment

1960 Graduates: Couples' Sample (Percentages)

		Husbands' Integration			
		Integrated		Non-Integrated	
		Career	Family	Career	Family
	Non-committed	32	26	50	16
Wives'	Mixed commitment	26	29	20	35
commit-	Sec. commitment	12	13	15	12
ment	Med. commitment	22	25	15	33
	Full commitment	8	7	0	4
	Totals Percentages	100	100	100	100
	N =	(50)	(89)	(20)	(51)

Table VII.16 also shows that the highest degree of commitment (taking 'medium' and 'full' together) is found among the wives of the 'family-non-integrated' men, with the other two categories close behind. That is to say, the men that derive satisfaction from their family life – whether this is integrated with satisfaction from career life or not – have wives who express higher commitment to the idea of having careers. It may be that their wives were committed in this way before they married, and/or that they provide an environment for their wives to express such commitment.

c *Career and marital satisfaction*

Some enthusiasts for women's careers may argue that personal fulfilment, particularly of highly qualified women, is dependent on their participating in the world of work. Domestic life alone may be seen as stultifying for these women, and from an extreme viewpoint as a form of enslavement. The working wife and mother is seen as having a well-rounded life, integrating both spheres as her husband does. She is felt to be a more interesting wife, growing with her career as her husband does. She is, so the argument goes, a better mother, more vital and interested in the world around her.

Countering this view is the negative conception of women with careers; such women may be seen as driven by neurotic conflicts, lacking in maternal and feminine characteristics, and neglecting their husbands and children to satisfy personal ambitions or needs. Psychiatrists and paediatricians, basing their views mainly on clinical experience interpreted in a conventional cultural framework, add authoritative voices to the fears and anxieties that place many of the casualties of contemporary family life at the door of the working mother.

What are the facts? This is an extraordinarily difficult area to assess. Just as it is nearly impossible, on the basis of existing research, to reach any satisfactory conclusion about the effects of mothers' work on their children's psychological functioning in later life because of the difficulties in following through and controlling the myriad intervening events, so it is difficult to assess the bearing of wives' employment orientation on current satisfactions; the latter are determined by lifetimes of antecedent factors predisposing one way or another independently of the proximate event of employment. In addition, assessment of something as complex as marital satisfaction for people who tend not to think in simplistic and stereotyped terms by a direct approach questionnaire, must be viewed with great caution. Nevertheless, some research using questionnaire methods has produced interesting and plausible findings on marital satisfaction. Orden and Blackburn, for example, find that marital happiness is higher among working wives who work out of choice than among those who work out of necessity (Orden and Blackburn, 1969). Bailyn points out, on the other hand, that for highly qualified women this element of choice can be a double-edged sword. Because such women usually do not *have* to work for economic reasons, being married to high-earning husbands, they may accept less rewarding jobs or lower status jobs than those to which their qualifications entitle them, for the sake of avoiding conflict (Bailyn, 1964).

It would not be expected that the sort of people who entertain complex conceptions of themselves, their families and careers are as likely as those who more easily accept conventional ways of thinking and acting to indicate in a questionnaire that they are 'very happy'. John Stuart Mill's observation has some relevance here:

'It is indisputable that the being whose capacities of enjoyment are low, has the greatest chance of having them fully satisfied; and the highly endowed being will always feel that any happiness which he can look for, as the world is constituted, is imperfect. But he can learn to bear its imperfections, if they are at all bearable; and they will not make him envy the being who is indeed unconscious of the imperfections, but only because he feels not at all the good which those imperfections qualify. It is better to be a human being dissatisfied than a pig satisfied; better to be Socrates dissatisfied than a fool satisfied. And if the fool, or the pig, are of a different opinion, it is because they only know their own side of the question. The other parties of the comparison know both sides.'

It must be recognized, however, that there is no intention in the present analysis of women and their careers to disparage those who choose the conventional pattern. It is just to emphasize that 'happiness' is not the sole criterion for evaluating a chosen pattern of life. Nevertheless, overall this is a very 'happy' sample of young people. As indicated above, 60 per cent of all the married respondents – in similar proportions across the different sex and marital stage groups – indicate that they are 'very happy' in their marriages and an additional 30 per cent indicate that they are 'pretty happy'. The issue at hand is whether there is any discernible difference in this regard between those who are presently working and those who are not, and whether a commitment to the idea of women having careers has any relevance for marital happiness. This can be examined bearing in mind that it is degree of happiness that is being examined rather than degree of unhappiness.

In examining all married women in the 1960 graduates' sample, it is possible to analyse the proportions of 'very happy' marriages in the different sub-groups – working or not working, and committed or not committed in varying degrees. Table VII.17 shows the patterning of response in this regard.

This table shows that among the 'non-committed' wives, working or not working does not affect their level of marital happiness. When such a wife works, she is probably not very deeply engaged in the work, and does not allow its pulls and pressures to affect her main area of involvement, namely her family. Indeed, it may be that the 'non-committed' wife whose husband is 'careerist' or for other reasons wanting her to work may actually increase marital happiness by going out to work. The same lack of difference between working and non-working is seen less sharply among the secondary-commitment wives. For the ambivalent wives – with 'mixed' or 'medium'

277

commitment – there is a higher degree of marital happiness if they do not go out to work at this time of their family life cycle. Indeed, their high statement of happiness may be seen as a defensive reaction, justifying the sacrifice made of career aspirations at this point in favour of the maintenance of marital harmony.[1] When these 'mixed' or 'medium' commitment women work, they sacrifice a degree of marital happiness. The 'fully committed' wife who stays at home during this period maintains a fairly high level of 'very happy' marriages, namely 50 per cent, though this is lower than for any other commitment category. The question now is why the level of 'very happy' marriages drops so sharply for the 'fully committed'

Table VII.17

Commitment to Women's Careers, Employment and Marital Happiness

1960 Graduates: All Married Women[2] (Percentages who say that they are 'very happy' in their marital relationship)

	Not Working		Working	
Not committed	68	(54)	71	(41)
Mixed commitment	73	(67)	46	(43)
Secondary commitment	59	(17)	52	(27)
Medium commitment	74	(38)	37	(46)
Full commitment	50	(10)	27	(15)
Total Percentages very happy	68	(188)	49	(173)

Totals: N-NA = (361)
          NA =   (10)
          NA = (371)

wives who are employed, bearing in mind that over a quarter still indicate that their marriages are 'very happy', and a further 36 per cent indicate that they are 'pretty happy' in their marriages.

From all that has been reported above, it is clear that the husband's orientation to his own career and family as well as his attitude to

[1] The A.I.D. analysis suggests that the gain in marital satisfaction made by the mixed or ambivalent wives who stay at home is accompanied by a drop in their *personal* satisfaction, and that a corresponding rise in personal satisfaction is found among the committed women who do work at the sacrifice of a very high level of marital happiness.
[2] The analysis of this data by sub-groups of married women – with and without children – shows that the pattern holds up for the sub-groups as well. Non-working married women without children cluster on the low commitment end, as expected, but show similar proportions of marital satisfaction as the women with children in the same commitment group.

women's careers is an important though by no means exclusive determinant of this pattern of response. Table VII.18 shows the relationship between husband's integration of career and family and their marital happiness under conditions of their wives working or not working.[1]

Table VII.18

Husbands' Career-Family Integration, their Wives' Employment and their Marital Happiness

1960 Graduates: All Married Men (Percentages 'very happy')

	Husbands' Integration					
	Integrated			Non-Integrated		
	Career		Family		Career		Family
Wives at home	39	(57)	65	(103)	60	(9)	51	(41)
Wives at work	50	(24)	62	(29)	26	(19)	50	(20)

N-NA 308
NA = 16
N = 326

This table shows that whether their wives are currently working or not makes little difference to their marital happiness for the husbands who emphasize 'family', whether integrated with career or not. An interpretation is that they take into account the needs of their families, including their wives, and arrive at a solution that is appropriate for that family, to maintain the given level of marital happiness. The career-non-integrated men, though endorsing the general idea of women also having careers, do not seem to follow this through in their own families. Where the wives do work, possibly as a compensatory measure, this is not accompanied by high levels of marital happiness. Among the career-integrated husbands, the proportion 'very happy' rises when their wives are working.

---

[1] It is to be remembered that these data are based on the men in the sample, and relate to their wives and families, many of whom are not graduates. The data from the couples' analysis, where both members' information is available and the wives are graduates, shows a similar picture, however, with smaller numbers. Bailyn finds that of 94 working wives in the couples' sample, 45 per cent overall are 'non-committed' and 55 per cent 'committed' in their career orientations. The working wives of 'career non-integrated' husbands show the highest proportion of 'non-commitment', namely 58 per cent. The highest proportion of 'committed' wives (32 per cent) is found among the 'family non-integrated' husbands. The analysis of the graduates' married women data further lends piecemeal support to this picture. Cf. Chapter VIII.

Further information on the importance of the husbands' orientation is contributed by an analysis of the responses of the married women, indicating how their own commitment to the idea of women's careers fits with their husband's and produces different degrees of marital happiness under different conditions of concordance and of wives working.

Table VII.19

Husbands' and Wives' Commitment to Women's Careers, Wife's Employment and their Marital Happiness[1]

1960 Graduates: All Married Women (Percentage 'very happy' in marriage)

		Wife has low commitment		Wife has high commitment	
		Wife is at home	Wife is employed	Wife is at home	Wife is employed
Husband's perceived commitment is:	Low	55	50	15	6
	High	8	5	44	29
	N =	(150)	(64)	(80)	(77)

This table shows that for employed wives, the highest degree of marital happiness is preserved if there is concordance between husbands' and wives' commitment to the idea of women's careers. Where both have a low commitment to the idea, the proportion of 'very happy' marriages is highest; indeed, nearly as high if the wife works as if the wife stays at home. Where both husband and wife agree that women ought to have careers, the degree of marital happiness in the family of the working woman is at its next highest level – nearly 30 per cent 'very happy'. Where there is discord – either because the husband's attitude is favourable and the wife's not, or vice versa – the wife working is accompanied by a much lower level proportion of 'very happy' marriages. However, it should be noted that where there is discord of this kind, the level of marital happiness is not improved substantially by the wife staying at home and not working.

It is also clear that the fact of working is a particularly difficult variable to assess in terms of marital happiness. Whether or not a

[1] Husband's commitment is as perceived by the respondent, who is a married woman (index derived in the same way as own commitment, but in response to parallel questions on spouse's opinions). Marital happiness is as measured by both the respondent's feelings and her perceived spouse's feeling. 'Very happy' is only where *both* partners are seen as 'very happy'.

woman is working currently is conditioned so much by the presence or expected presence of children in the early marital stages and the fact that acceptable alternative ways of handling child rearing are not readily available in our society, that it is mainly the very determined or otherwise unusually motivated married women who work when they have small children. Some of the contemporary experience of stress and strain when a married woman pursues a 'continuous' career is due to the fact that the social structure is not geared to this pattern. Married women's career development is therefore comprehensible only if one takes a whole-career perspective rather than looking at the situation of current employment in a young family. Nowadays, the most frequently encountered orientation, as has been brought out earlier, is to interrupt employment at the period of early childbearing and rearing with the intention of resumption at some point later. Many highly committed women are able to maintain a high degree of marital happiness even though they are not working at a specific period early in marriage because they intend to return later. An interrupted pattern brings gratifications, avoids conflicts, and is generally supported. In the next chapter an index of career-orientations will be presented which shows a more longitudinal picture of the individuals' orientation to work and career in relation to family life, using both the commitment to the general idea of women's careers and the intention of the individual herself as part of the picture. The range of career patterns based on both general ideas and personal intentions will then be related to some of the other factors under examination: among them, marital happiness, which will be seen as an important current factor affecting a woman's overall career pattern.

ORIENTATIONS TO WORK AND FAMILY IN A CHANGING WORLD

The type of data obtained from the populations surveyed (given their age and way in which the samples were obtained) shows strongly that issues and problems in the early family stages have a powerful effect, but the data do not reveal the way in which these issues are dealt with and worked out in the longer run. How many families in which there is dissatisfaction, stress and incongruity between ideals and behavioural patterns stay together over a period of time? Even if they do not dissolve, what are the consequences for them in terms of discord, conflict, unhappiness and stress symptoms if they are not able to make personal resolutions in the absence of socially structured ways of resolving the dilemmas of the highly qualified wife and mother? These are topics for further research, although, of course, they are nonetheless real and pressing for not being covered in the present report. Many topics of importance in this ramifying web of points, issues, dilemmas and implications of various resolutions can only be touched upon. Learning to live with conflict and irresolution is a way of life for a great many people of the kind studied. When a decision point arises where one person's career or personal development in work may have to be sacrificed for the other, it is not easy to work out a solution optimal for both persons, however desirable this might be. The respondents to the survey were presented with four dilemmas of the kind highlighted in this and the previous chapter, and their patterns of resolution – at least on paper – are interesting to record, for they provide some indication of the 'winds of change' in relation to the educated public's conceptions of women's roles. One dilemma was posed as follows:

> John and Mary are married and both are graduating from a university in the south of England. She is a classical philologist and he an engineer. She is offered a post in a first rate northern university, and knows that there is little likelihood that another post in classical philology will come up for her elsewhere in the near future. He could get a job in the north, as good as the one he now has, but he doesn't particularly like living in that part of the country, preferring to live in the south. What decision do you think they should make?

Three options were suggested:

a. Move up to the north and try to work out a way for him to be happy there
b. Stay in the south and try to get her interested in another field, or
c. Move to another country

The acceptance of the need to accommodate a woman's career to the extent indicated in this situation has – life acceptance of women's work after marriage – become very general. Seventy per cent of the respondents overall accept that this couple should move north. The married women top the range with 76 per cent of them endorsing the move north (as compared with 68 per cent of the married men). The single people are the most *un*accommodating, 60 per cent of single women and 67 per cent of single men opting to move north. This dilemma, being rather abstract, probably tapped the respondents' *ideal* conceptions.

The second dilemma perhaps comes a little closer to home:

> Sally is a 27-year-old woman who graduated from university several years ago and is now living in a pleasant home with her

professional husband and two young children. She finds that despite all the good things she has in her life, she is still frequently bored and dissatisfied with her lot. How helpful do you think each of the following suggestions would be for increasing Sally's general satisfaction?

Have another baby
Undertake a programme of serious reading or course of study to prepare for later professional employment
Take periodic vacations alone with her husband
Seek psychiatric advice
Seek religious counsel
Plan interesting excursions and projects with her children
Take a job in a field she is interested in
Develop some absorbing hobby
Become active in a club or community organization

The replies – only those that indicated 'very helpful' – are in the table below. When responses were below 10 per cent, the category is omitted.

Table VII.20

Bored Housewife Dilemma

(Percentages Answering 'Very Helpful')

	Single men	Married men no children	Married men with children	Single women	Married women no children	Married women with children
Serious study	21	25	21	29	44	43
More vacations with husband	14	18	18	15	12	16
Family projects	40	32	36	43	33	38
Take a job	36	54	45	44	56	60
Develop hobby	32	35	37	46	44	46
Community work	28	24	24	41	36	33
N =	(58)	(79)	(245)	(112)	(73)	(298)

This table shows that the most popular solution for the bored *married* women graduates is to 'take a job'. 'Developing a hobby' and 'serious study' share second position in frequency of choice. Married men with children contrast most sharply with married women who have children in the proportions favouring 'serious study for later professional employment' and 'taking a job'. In both

283

cases the men choose these solutions less frequently, being more 'conservative' in their responses.[1]

The third dilemma highlights the residual responsibility that is accepted as 'feminine', and which limits the degree of career commitment that many women can assume under current conditions. Even where there is an egalitarian ethos, it is the exceptional rather than the 'normal' family who adopt it totally. This is indicated by the responses of graduates to the following situation:

Bill and Sue are solicitors, equally dedicated to their work which is for separate firms. They both work very hard, long hours and are often late getting home. They have two small children who are well looked after by competent domestic helpers. However, Bill has been feeling increasingly that he is not being looked after in the way he has wanted and expected in marriage and has been putting considerable pressure on Sue to give up her professional work and be a better homemaker.

Do you think:

That she should quit her work entirely as he suggests?
That she should try to get her firm to put her on to a part-time basis?
That he should reconsider the position and change his expectations at home so that she can continue her career?
That they should consider splitting up so that they could find more compatible marriage partners?

The modal responses to this question were in favour of Sue dropping to part-time work rather than quitting her job altogether. Eighty per cent, overall, favoured this solution. In second and third positions, though both only small minorities about equally chosen overall, were the 'reorganization' and 'quit' solutions. Only 3 per cent of the married women with children (1 per cent of the married women without children) suggested that Sue quit her job – as compared with 10 per cent of married men with children, 14 per cent of married men without children and 12 per cent single men. Divorce was chosen by a negligible proportion. Reorganization was 11 per

---

[1] The response of the 1967 graduates to the bored housewife dilemma was: 'Take an interesting job' was the top solution by both men and women and 'take up a hobby' second for both. Unlike the 1960 graduates, the split between men's and women's views become a qualitative rather than merely a quantitative one at this point, with women favouring the 'serious study' as third solution, but men placing this sixth with family projects, etc., in between. Both men and women, in both the 1960 and 1967 groups, place at the bottom of their listings, psychiatric advice, religious advice and having another baby; none of these is considered very helpful by the majority.

cent overall – the more committed egalitarians – with the men not outstandingly more conservative than the women on this point.

This dilemma was also put more extremely: 'In another situation, the husband is quite satisfied with the situation but one of the children (age 6) is beginning to show severe disturbances (e.g. stammering, bedwetting, school retardation).' Do you think:

The mother should quit her job altogether and immediately?
She should work less time and spend more time with her child?
The parents should both reduce the time they work and both spend more time at home?
None of the above; leave it entirely to professional help.

The pattern of answers to these questions – which is more of a 'crunch' type of question – is as follows. About a quarter of the respondents feel that the wife should quit – and there are no remarkable sex or family stage differences here, other than that the married women without children favoured this somewhat less than the others (16 per cent). Here the most favoured choices are nearly evenly split between dropping to part-time (36 per cent overall) and reorganizing both members' work-family commitments (34 per cent overall). The women favour the part-time solution more than the men (43 per cent of the married women as compared with 36 per cent of the married men); while the men favour the 'reorganization' solution slightly more than the women (36 per cent of married men as compared with 31 per cent of married women).

The patterns of response to these dilemmas (which correspond very closely to the patterns indicated by 1967 graduates as well)[1] are very interesting. They may, of course, be interpreted in various ways, and one may find them either encouraging or disappointing according to one's value position and expectations. It seems clear, however, that the most prevalent attitude is one that can be termed 'new conventional' woman's orientation (cf. p. 304). The prevailing attitude, as in the Bill and Sue story, is in favour of the wife working full-time but only to the point where it does not seriously interfere with either the husband's comfort or the child's health. Then she should reduce her involvement in work to part-time. Where no one really suffers, as in the Sally story, a more egalitarian orientation can prevail, at least in theory.

[1] Both the fully egalitarian position and the completely traditional one are now minority positions. The position favouring a reorganization of family life so as to allow the husband to help more seems to be more widely held, in relation to an ill child. Perhaps men are now more openly acknowledging their role and interest in relation to child rearing than has been true in the past, where discipline rather than nurturance from the male was the emphasis.

ILLUSTRATIVE CASE VIGNETTES – DIFFERENT PATTERNS
OF COMMITMENT TO CAREER

A few vignettes drawn from the questionnaire responses of women graduates, representing the different types of commitment, put a little 'flesh and blood' on to the bare bones of analysis.

Mrs A – _Full Commitment:_ married with three children, 30 years old, English, currently a housewife. Mrs A went to a single-sex grammar school and a civic university both in the north of England, and did her degree in Humanities. She indicates a high ambition in the sense of wishing to hold a high and well-paid position within the teaching profession.

In school, as at university, Mrs A emphasized academic achievement and while she had no specific ideas of what she wanted to achieve she had as her career values: first, the wish to work at an interesting job; second, to have relative freedom from supervision; and third, to work at a job that gives her a chance to use her capacity for intellectual problem-solving. At the bottom of her list are security and high income.

Mrs A is a good example of what we have termed the 'new-conventional' housewife. Though she has high aspirations within her chosen field of schoolteaching, and though she has a full commitment to the idea of women having careers, she does not wish to be working while her children are young, but only later. Her husband is a local government official and they live in a suburban setting where the prevailing atmosphere is one which supports the idea of women working a little but not enough to interfere with home and family obligations. She herself obtains her main satisfactions from family relationships, with second in importance 'running a home'. For this period of her life she is a 'family-non-integrated' woman with high general commitment, but high satisfaction in the traditional role. Both she and her husband are very happy with their marital relationship, and she feels that having children brings husband and wife closer together and has helped her to grow as an individual as well, though she now feels that three is enough, whereas she had wanted four originally.

In her general ideals, Mrs A is more committed to women's careers than her husband, who only mildly agrees or mildly subscribes to the various questions and hypothetical situations with which Mrs A herself gives rather more egalitarian responses. She describes herself as happy, idealistic, rational, rebellious, talkative, and there is a strong tinge of religious orientation in her family background, community activities and self-conception. It is against this, perhaps, that some of her ideas, but not her conduct, are 'rebellious'. But she considers herself not at all 'cautious, dependent, fragile, lazy, loyal to an organization, methodical, middlebrow, moody or reserved'. Her comments about her career are:

✻'Perhaps the area of discontent of a graduate housewife has not been clearly indicated by answers to these questions. The half dozen or so close friends in a similar position also feel, I know, as I do. Five years or so devoted to small children or housework have been enjoyable and enormously rewarding. Probably the next five years will pass in a similar way and be great fun, but ten years out of a job, followed by perhaps part-time service is not a likely route to the top. The years spent as a housewife may have contributed much to general self-fulfilment and enjoyment of life, but there will be a lingering regret that in one's chosen profession, entered with confidence and enthusiasm in one's early 20s, one will in the end be only second rate.'

Another married woman with two children, who is committed to women's careers and has high career aspirations for herself, comments that:

✻'To be a success, a wife has got to be unchallengeable in the various spheres of house, garden, appearance, children, cooking, entertaining, as well as a chosen career. If you fall down on any one of these, you are open to attack. My answers show I am pretty content with my present domestic phase – I have young children and a new house and do not regret the five years I feel I must take off, though I do regret losing my place in the promotion sphere. My view of domesticity, however, would be very different if no retreat from it was ever promised. The successful man is judged by the position he reaches; a successful woman by her ability to keep a number of eggs in the air without smashes and yet to climb as high as she can.'

Mrs B – *Medium Commitment:* married, three children, working part-time (21-25 hours p/week). Mrs B is 29 years old, an English graduate and attended a single-sex direct grant school. She works 21 to 25 hours per week, and earns in the £500 to £1,000 per annum bracket. She hopes to return for a postgraduate degree when she can.

Mrs B married while she was still a student – to an engineer several years older than herself. At that time she wanted a large family as well as a career, and indicates that her original notion was to have four children. Now she has three, but wishes it were only two, as the problems of pursuing her career along with the family have been very great. She is a woman who derives her main satisfaction from career – with family second. She has had to modify her ambitions somewhat. Early on she favoured the law as a career, but is now thinking more of journalism as a long-term career. Her interests throughout school and university have been academic, and her aspirations were in the direction of extreme competence in her field. Her ranking of career values resembles the stereotypically 'male' rather than 'female' ordering of values – she places 'opportunity to work with people', 'creativity', and an 'opportunity to be helpful to others' on the bottom, giving much greater emphasis to the others. Her top three were: 'a chance to work at an interesting job' (a shared 'masculine' and 'feminine' value in this sample), 'freedom from supervision' and 'an opportunity to maximize income'.

When she had her first baby she left her job. Another reason given was that the particular job lacked opportunities for advancement; thus having a baby clinched the decision for her, though she did value the idea of motherhood. She has since gone back to work in a job which is very flexible and stimulating and in which she has a lot of support and co-operation. However, she is not paid as much as she thinks she ought to be, and though she is not actually looking around for another job, she would be receptive should one with that ingredient, along with the others, come along.

She answers the hypothetical questions with a strong egalitarian emphasis – despite her only medium commitment (because of 'mildly' agreeing that a woman cannot plan her career). She feels that John and Mary should move north, that Sally should undertake a programme of serious study, and that Sue should reduce her work to help the disturbed child, but that her husband should also. She feels that there are a complex of reasons for women pursuing careers: to avoid boredom, get stimulation and to have an area of life in which she is recognized in her own right and to fulfil personal needs and ambitions.

She and her husband strongly agree that a woman can establish just as warm and secure a relationship with her children if she works, as a mother who does not work, and strongly agree with the view that parents should encourage just as much independence in their girl children as their sons. In other respects, her attitudes indicate a slight tendency towards having to take a secondary role to her husband's career. This is not entirely an easy accommodation, though she characterizes their marital relationship as sometimes happy and sometimes unhappy (and her husband's view as pretty happy). They have frequent disagreements about personal habits, and about the handling of the children (weekly) and about the use of money and her job (monthly). Nevertheless, she feels that having children, though it has hampered her career, has brought her and her husband closer together, and the marital relationship is the one to which she gives highest priority in her domestic hierarchy of values. Altogether, her own personal development has not been served by having had the children, she feels, as well as it might have, had she been able to work more continuously.

Her self-image reflects the mixture of stereotypically career-oriented and 'feminine' domestic traits that are so often found in the less than full committed types: she considers herself to be 'ambitious', 'intellectual', 'loyal to an organization', 'tense' and 'unconventional' – but not at all 'efficient', 'fragile', 'idealistic', 'pedestrian', 'rebellious' or 'witty'. She has the following general comments about her career experiences:

'It is still practically impossible for anyone without unlimited money and living space to combine family and career, due to the lack of proper child-care facilities, etc. Insufficient advice was given at school in my day on suitable careers for other than full-time career girls, and I don't doubt that this is still the case. Finally, in the better girls' schools there is far too much academic emphasis and nothing or little is given to subjects like cooking, dressmaking, household maintenance, etc., which are as important in their way as Latin and Greek are in theirs.'

Mrs C – *Secondary Commitment:* age 30, went to single-sex direct grant school. She has two children, works ten hours a week as a secondary schoolteacher and earns under £500 per year.

This is an Oxbridge girl who studied humanities and graduated with a second class honours degree. Her ambitions are to be creative, discover something important and to have a reputation for extreme competence in her field. She wants to get to the top and always has done. She has had various ideas for the channels through which this might be accomplished, regarding secondary schoolteaching as a stop-gap. She thinks ahead about various possibilities such as being a writer or starting her own business of some kind that would involve creativity. Creativity is her top career value, with 'a chance to show what she can accomplish' as second, and 'interesting job' as third. At the bottom of her list are 'working with people', 'being helpful' and 'security'. Family is the area of life from which she gets most satisfaction and 'other' the next most satisfying area (apparently, from her other answers, creative activity such as art, whether or not it is geared to a paid occupation).

While both Mrs C and her husband are strongly in favour of women's careers, and feel that a working mother does not necessarily cause emotional damage to her children if she works, they both feel that a woman's career should take second place to her husband's, and that a woman cannot plan her career because this depends on

K

her husband's career. Her husband, who is several years older than she, is a university don earning in the £2,500 to £3,000 range. They both feel that having children brings husband and wife together and she feels that the experience has contributed to her development as a person. Mrs C is in favour of part-time work for a woman while the youngest child is under 3 and full-time when the child is older. She would prefer to have a relative at home looking after her child during the time the child is under 1 year, a close friend between 1 and 3 and nursery school between 3 and 6. Her ideas on child care are fairly traditional in the sense that it is the wife and not the husband who carried almost all of the responsibility in this area. She characterizes herself as: very 'ambitious', 'creative', 'efficient', 'emotional' and 'idealistic', but not at all 'dependent', 'fragile', 'gossipy', 'loyal', 'pedestrian', 'methodical' or 'lazy'. Her social circle is 'conventional suburban', and she reckons that she is unlike most of them in the degree to which she is competitive occupationally. Her comments are:

'It is difficult to know whether marriage and having children, which has been a pretty clear priority for ten years or so, has enabled me to do more of what I want to or less. Had I been obliged to earn full-time to support a family during this time, I might have channelled my career problems into a fully satisfactory occupation. On the other hand, I might have had no time or opportunity at all to do what I wanted. During this time I had no job that was anything but socially satisfying from the point of view of integrating with the community in a fairly helpful way, but have had various chances such as a year of no job after marriage and time at home during the infancy of my first child to do what I wanted – that is to buy materials, hold exhibitions, develop an idea of producing a plastic toy for commercial purposes, study plastics and so on. I always felt that it was essential in order to be creative to resolve personal problems first, but this could either have been because of my instinctive nature as a female person or because I am not essentially creative enough to sustain a full-time career.'

Mrs D – *Mixed Commitment:* is another Oxbridge humanities graduate with a good degree. She has two children and was not working at the time of the survey. She would like eventually to hold a high position and indicates that her most cherished wish to is have a reputation for extreme competence in her field – not to be creative or to make an important discovery. She earlier had the idea of being a university teacher and still has that idea now, though at university she entertained ideas of being a social worker, librarian, secondary schoolteacher, personnel manager or public administrator.

This wife, in contrast to some described earlier, has a strong public-service element in her aspirations. She has as alternatives the career aspirations described above *or* holding high positions in community organizations. Her personal career values reflect this, in that her top three are 'opportunity to be helpful', 'opportunity to work with people', 'freedom from supervision'; the bottom of her list are 'creativity', 'income' and 'interesting job'.

While Mrs D left her last job when her child arrived, and wanted it that way, she feels now that she wishes she could work a little less at home and by implication a little more on a job. The shortage of help makes this difficult. She misses being with people and having the stimulation of the interaction that is available in a highly qualified job.

Mrs D represents the 'new-conventional' pattern, in that she is at home and likes it – with mild discontents – but expects by the time she is forty to return to work. She is in favour of voluntary activities for women, or a job, but against the idea of a career that involves long-term commitment and planning. She mildly agrees with the statement that women cannot plan their careers because their husbands' careers come first. They both feel that it is more important for a woman to help her husband than to have a career herself, though she feels it is important for a woman to work if she needs to fulfil her personal needs and ambitions. She herself derives her primary satisfaction from family life, and secondarily from religious beliefs and activities.

The social circle of the D's is academic, with a strong emphasis on moral conscience. She and her husband are 'very happy' in their marital relationship and they rarely row about anything. Her husband is an architect and they originally wanted four children, though their current ideal size is two. She is conservative in her attitudes towards timing the return of an ambitious woman such as herself, feeling that part-time work can commence when the child is between 6 and 10, but not earlier, and that full-time work should be reserved for when the children are grown. All areas of child-rearing responsibility are seen as the wife's. She regards herself as 'calm, loyal, methodical, quiet', and not at all, 'fragile', 'gossipy', 'hard-driving', 'volatile', 'highly strung', 'lazy', 'outgoing', 'nervous', 'pedestrian', 'poised', 'sophisticated' or 'witty'. Compared with others she knows, she is practical and not competitive or nervous. She has no general comments to make.

Mrs E – *Uncommitted:* This wife has one child, and works part-time. She represents the anomalous situation of having high aspirations – wanting eventually to hold a high position – and yet being non-committed from the point of view of endorsing the idea of women's careers. She went to a co-educational grammar school and university in the Midlands, and read humanities, graduating with a good honours degree. She also had a postgraduate diploma in education. She formed her idea of becoming a secondary schoolteacher when she left university, and this is her current career ideal. Her career values are: first; 'an opportunity to show what she can accomplish', second: 'a chance to work at an interesting job' and third 'an opportunity to be helpful to others'. At the bottom of her list are 'chances to use intellectual problem-solving ability', 'creativity' and 'stable and secure future'.

Mrs E left her job to have her baby and was pleased to leave at that time. The kinds of things she values in a job are more the human characteristics of interaction with her mates, and the short journey to work, though she also wants stimulation. She is somewhat dissatisfied with being a full-time housewife and wishes that she had more help. However, things are as she expected, and she is in general against the idea of women having long-term careers. She favours voluntary activities or a job, if she wishes to work at all. Her husband agrees with this position, though he has more mixed feelings about voluntary activities. They both feel quite strongly that the woman's activities, whether voluntary or a job, should be entirely secondary to the career requirements of her husband. The primary source of satisfaction for her is family life and second is leisure activities.

The social circle of the Es is suburban and most feel that a woman ought to be able to work a little so long as it does not interfere with family life. She and her husband are very happy in their marriage and she never feels that she married the wrong sort of person. Her husband is an accountant and earns in the middle range for our sample, just under £2,000. She originally wanted four children and now wants two, though she feels that having children contributes to her personal development. She favours part-time work until the children are grown, and considers the best arrangement for child care would be a relative in the home. She considers herself to be 'emotional', 'highly strung', 'idealistic', 'loyal', 'moody' and 'tense', not at all 'calm', 'efficient', 'fragile', 'shy', or 'witty'. She says:

'I have been interested to find that although a graduate trained to teach children in the age group of 11-18 years, I have found younger children easy and stimulating to teach. My present part-time post in an infants' school is frustrating solely because of the large numbers in the class. Fifty children in one's care defeats many excellent ideas and methods. The need for more child-care facilities for the babies of women teachers should be urged most persistently at a national level. I am sure that if our children were adequately looked after in their pre-school years, we women teachers/mothers would gladly come back into teaching even if it were on a part-time basis.'

SUMMARY AND DISCUSSION

Many highly qualified women seek to combine work and family life rather than give up one for the sake of the other. Women graduates show an array of patterns of work and family life – from remaining single without the intention of marrying, marrying and not having children, to the other extreme of marrying and following a conventional homemaker role with no intention ever to work. The aim of this chapter has been to describe the nature and dimensions of the various patterns found, and to assess their characteristics – in terms both of potentials for the labour force and of implications for the individuals and their families. Within each of the patterns described, a set of influences exists – positive and negative – which affect women's attitudes, behaviour and intentions. These influences include the nature of home and family life in relation to work life, and in relation to resources in the environment, and the nature of the marital relationship.

First, in sorting out people's values in relation to family life and work, it should be noted that the kind of people studied place great value on family life, particularly that part of it that relates to the children. This does not mean that graduates want large families. They want to have the sort of family life from which they can derive major satisfaction and, at the same time, regard work life as important to them. Career and family are the two most important areas of life from which personal satisfactions are derived. Most of the graduates move, as they marry and have children, in the direction of having a self-owned home, in which the basic family of father, mother and children live as a relatively self-sufficient unit.

Though the graduate population are relatively 'liberal' in their ideas about male and female roles, when they marry and have children, the actual division of labour in the household remains substantially as in traditional homes. Even assuming a level of income that makes it possible to get as much help as they need, *most* of the graduates studied indicate that they would prefer the kind of division of labour which left most domestic activities in the wife's hands – particularly cooking and child care. Help would be used by a substantial majority of the population for cleaning activities, but even such relatively 'drudgery' activities as washing, ironing and mending of clothes would remain by choice of both men and women in the hands of the wife. The only area which tends to be chosen by both men and women as the husband's area has to do with minor repairs. Joint activities, for most, are budgeting, gardening, shopping and arranging social activities. When one compares preferences with actualities, it transpires that even such areas as household cleaning, which ideally are delegated to helpers, are in fact done by the wife herself in most cases. Where there is help, it tends to be at the 'wrong' time from the point of view of making women available for the labour force. Rather than having help after they have children (which might enable them to work), women have less help at this point – presumably because they are earning less and because they are at home and therefore on hand to do the household work themselves. A vicious circle tends to arise out of which it is difficult for most married women with children to break.

A study of the relationships among attitudes expressed about doing all of the household activities shows that while there is a strong general inter-correlation, i.e. people either like to do household things generally or not, child care is associated generally in people's minds (English graduates particularly) with cleaning (rather than with feeding, as in the American study). However, cleaning is not enjoyed as much as child care, and would be more easily delegated by most.

Clearly this is a matter not only of enjoyment, but of responsibility as well. Most of the parents in the sample studied have very stringent requirements about the conditions under which they would leave their children to be looked after even partially by others in order to allow wives to work. The preferred alternative is a relative in one's own home. This, however, is not available for the most part, and will probably be less and less so in the future. It is therefore likely that their preference for a relative in the home will be supplanted by their second choice: *excellent* day-care facilities. While a majority would accept excellent facilities, very few would accept merely 'adequate' facilities. Here is the nub of the problem, for desiring and having children relates very directly to the possibility of one's remaining continuously at work, and the more children one has the less likelihood there is that one will be working.

Having children, however much this is jointly desired by both partners, does not affect both equally. The arrival of the first child signals the interruption of the work career for all but the most committed women, or those who work for reasons other than commitment to vocation. The withdrawal of the majority of women into maternal role activities brings immediate gratifications. However, these gratifications are temporary (many who would not return to work while their first child was under 3 intend to do so when subsequent children are under 3), and there are frustrations and irritations as well as satisfactions in the new role. This is indicated by the increase in 'disagreements' between husband and wife following the arrival of children.

There is, of course, more to disagree about when a child arrives: all the decisions not only on the new division of labour, but of the strategy and tactics of child rearing, in which many men take an active interest while leaving the responsibility to their wives. It is at this stage, however, that the complex of variables which will keep a woman 'domestic' or press her to continue work, or at least return at some point, make themselves felt.

Perhaps the most important complex of variables for the woman herself is that of 'commitment'. By this is meant her orientation to the idea of women having careers. Three definite positions are discernible and in addition two modified positions have special importance of their own. The three 'clear' positions are:

a Non-commitment: where the woman is quite happy to accept the domestic role and to continue in it, returning if at all only when it is convenient all round to do so, ordinarily after her children are in their teens.

b Secondary commitment: where the woman wants to have a career, but accepts that this must be clearly secondary to the requirements of her husband's career and cannot be planned out of that context. The intention is definitely to return, but to do so when the probabilities of conflict are minimized – as between her own and her husband's career (i.e. after he is established), and in relation to ideals, norms and dilemmas relating to child rearing. This is emerging as the new-conventional pattern among highly qualified women.

c Full commitment: where the individual feels that women should pursue careers with involvement equal to that of their husbands, and that where conflicts or dilemmas arise, solutions should be worked out on the basis of joint optimization rather than automatic male priority. This is a minority position, but one that provides the base for women's most serious career effort.

Intermediate between the positions of 'conventional' and the 'secondary' commitment is one that has been termed 'mixed'. Individuals showing this pattern indicate a good deal of ambivalence about whether they think women really should have a career at all, as distinct from just having a job when convenient, or doing voluntary activities. (It is interesting that this is the largest group of married women with children.)

It is accepted that her career should be secondary to her husband's. The other intermediate pattern is between 'secondary' and 'full', where the individual has 'medium' commitment. The general idea of a career is accepted, but the issue remains of how much of a career the wife should have and how much it should be of equal salience in the family to that of the husband.

On the husbands' side, commitment to the idea of women's careers is also important and sets an environment of norms and attitudes which influences the women in their choices about whether or not and how much to continue working. Also important, however, is the position the husband himself holds and expresses behaviourally, as well as in his attitudes, about the relative importance in his own life of career, family and other activities and involvements. The men who mention both career and family as the two primary areas of life from which they derive their major personal satisfactions are termed 'integrated' – those with family first 'family-integrated', those with career first 'career-integrated'. The men who mention career as their first or second area of primary satisfaction but do not mention family as the other top area, are called 'career-non-integrated', and those that do the same for family are designated 'family-non-integrated'.

The husbands' orientations to career and family, and their attitudes to women's careers, affect their wives' attitudes, their wives' patterns of work, and the degree of marital happiness experienced in the family. 'Careerist' (career-non-integrated) husbands have the highest proportions of wives at work, but these wives are not the most committed to the idea of women's careers.

The husbands' commitment to the idea of women's careers affects the proportions of women who work. For the most part the wives of 'high-commitment' husbands work more frequently than do the wives of 'low-commitment' husbands. The only situation in which this is not so is for the wives of family-non-integrated men, where a greater proportion of the low-commitment husbands' wives work – perhaps because these men are low performers in the occupational sphere themselves, at least at this point in their careers.

The proportions of 'very happy' marriages relate to whether the husband is family-orientated (i.e. involved in his family as a major area of life satisfactions); or whether the husband's perceived commitment and the wife's commitment to the idea of womens' careers are concordant and whether the woman is actually working at present.

In considering the whole issue of the relationship between women's working and marital happiness, several points should be made.

a. There is a very high level of reported marital happiness among the graduates studied.
b. Where lower proportions of 'very happy' marriages are reported, factors other than the woman working are involved. The husband's

attitudes and behaviour in relation to the wife's work are of crucial importance. Also, as will be shown in the next chapter, early life experiences underly the sort of character syndromes that make for a career-emphasis in women, and this may produce a lower likelihood of a 'very happy' response to a question on marital satisfaction, regardless of whether the woman works.

c. There is no way to know, from the data presently available, whether working women would be more satisfied or more dissatisfied maritally if they were not working.

d. Aside from early life experiences and current marital attitudes and patterns, some of the stress that may contribute to lower proportions of 'very happy' marriages, noted among working wives, stem from contemporary societal attitudes and pressures which could be alleviated.

In sum, there is no 'working woman' type, and no 'family situation' that is in any simple sense the right type for a working woman. There are different types, different family situations ·and different family effects. On the whole the most favourable conditions are those where the husband is involved in his family and sympathetic to his wife's views on women's careers. However, there are many combinations of husband and wife behaviour and attitude that can result in the wife working on the one hand and marital satisfaction on the other.

Obvious as this seems when written in this way, much of the discussion of this problem, even at very informed levels, is conducted as though this complexity were not appreciated. There are traditional family situations with happy housewives and assertive men effectively fulfilling their 'breadwinner' roles. There are also many situations in which the wife is in the traditional role but does not like it – just as there are some working wives who work out of boredom, necessity or to compensate for an unhappy marital relationship. There are, finally, some wives who work – either continuously or interruptedly either full-time or part-time – who like it and would like to sustain their pattern or increase their involvement.

Certainly the happy housewives should not be disturbed. They have a major contribution to make to society. Most, however, are not in this conventional role but in the 'new-conventional' role, whereby they intend to return to work as soon as feasible. The mixed or ambivalent types of people really would like something different but do not know how to bring it about. For these women something can be done to improve the situation from the point of view both of the labour force and of their personal and marital satisfactions. The most important elements in this seem, from the data available in

297

this study (which in general confirms and refines previously available analyses):

Engendering in women a greater sense of vocational commitment;
Engendering in men a greater acceptance of the idea of women's vocational commitment;
Sanctioning for men the legitimacy and desirability of accepting in themselves the value of participation in family activities;
Providing *excellent* facilities for delegating child care.

Both work and family life have aspects of drudgery and aspects that engender gratifications and potentials for personal development. Many women put up with the drudgery of family life to obtain its gratifications, particularly in the early phases of child care. They are often given more than their share of the drudgery in the occupational sphere (particularly if they work part-time and do not stay around for the 'extras' of camaraderie, etc., that often take place over long lunch hours and later afternoon meetings). Many men put up with the drudgery of their work to obtain its satisfactions. Somehow, by opening the gratifications of the work place more to women and by allowing men to feel it legitimate to enjoy the gratifications of the family, a more favourable balance may be possible for both sexes.

REFERENCES

Bailyn, Lotte, 'Notes on the Role of Choice in the Psychology of Professional Women', *Daedalus*, Vol. 93, 2, pp. 700-10, 1964.
Bailyn, Lotte, Unpublished memo on career patterns of the married couples in the sample.
Bailyn, Lotte, Article to be published in *Human Relations*, 1970.
Bott, Elizabeth, *Family and Social Network*, London: Tavistock Publications, 1957.
Bradburn, S. R., and Orden, N. M., 'Working Wives and Marriage Happiness', *American Journal of Sociology*, Vol. 74, 4, 1969.
Ginzberg, Eli, *et al.*, *Life and Styles of Educated Women*, New York: Columbia University Press, 1966.
Golding, J., 'The Battery Society', *Sunday Times*, September 21, 1969.
Hunt, Audrey, *Survey of Women's Employment*, Government Social Survey, 55, 379, 1968.
McQuitty, L. L., 'Hierarchical Linkage Analysis for the Isolation of types', *Educ. Psychol. Meas.*, 20, 55-67, 1960.
Mill, J. S., *Utilitarianism*, London: Great Books, 1955.
Mulvey, M. C., 'Psychological and Sociological Factors in Prediction of Career Patterns of Women', *Genetic Psychology Monographs*, Vol. 68, pp. 309-86, 1963.

FAMILY PATTERNS AND WORK

Rossi, Alice, 'Barriers to the Career Choice of Engineering, Medicine or Science Among American Women', in *Women in the Scientific Professions*, pp. 79-82 (eds. Mattfield and Allen), M.I.T. Press, 1965.
Sonquist, John A., and Morgan, James N., *The Detection of Integration Effects*, Monograph No. 35 Survey Research Centre, Institute for Social Research, University of Michigan.
Tennyson, Alfred, 'The Princess'.

299

Chapter VIII

Career Pathways:
What Produces the Work-prone Woman?

The discussion in the preceding chapters has highlighted some questions which require further consideration. The current chapter aims to contribute something towards their answers. The key questions are:

(1) Is there a better way of classifying highly qualified women in relation to their career potentials? It has been seen that classifications according to current work situation or aspirations are affected by overriding current situational pressures, notably the bearing and rearing of young children. Other indicators, such as the value placed on the idea of women's careers, and intention to return to work at specified points later in the family cycle, have some utility, but can they be combined to form a still better way of estimating the potential contribution of such married women? The complexities of this question were brought out in the last chapter. The need now is for a more synoptic view which at the same time provides a simpler form of classification.

(2) How much can the career-patterns, synoptically viewed as suggested above, be seen as the result of early life determinants (such as the quality of relationships in the individuals' parental family) and how much as the result of more current antecedent factors (such as the state of the marital relationship)? While there are limitations to the answers that can validly be provided by the survey method in unravelling the relative influences of early and late life experience, it is important to investigate this area as fully as possible because of the policy implications as well as the theoretical interest. Which are the effective factors of experience which produce the work-prone woman? Do they arise in early or late life experience? Or is there some particular combination?

In examining various life experiences to study their effect on the work/career patterns of highly qualified married women, selections have been made. The selections are based on what seems promising from prior research results. In the larger social environment of childhood, for example, it is known that the geographic area, schooling and social class sometimes play an important part in determining the sort of experiences an individual will have. In the family constellation, it is fairly well accepted that the individual's position in the birth order, and the degree of organization/disorganization, warmth/tension in the family atmosphere affect the developing child's character. In addition, the relationship with significant figures like father, mother and siblings are known to have a formative influence.

All of these early factors have an influence which may be life-long in their effects but they may be either reinforced or countered by subsequent experiences and influences. The main point that this chapter will bring out is that the more immediate influences – particularly in the marital relationship – are the most powerful overall factors in determining work/career pattern, but that they have different effects in relation to people with different sorts of early backgrounds.

CAREER AND WORK PATTERNS OF MARRIED WOMEN

In the last chapter it was seen that highly qualified married women could usefully be classified in terms not only of their actual work at present but also of their expected work patterns. The patterns of work expectation are of three major types: non-work-oriented, non-continuous-work-oriented, and continuous-work-oriented (p. 223). The distributions are shown in Table VIII.1.

The non-continuous work pattern is the modal orientation both for married women with and those without children. However, the women with children are more likely than those without children to choose a continuous work pattern. This difference can be explained in different ways, but the interpretation already suggested in Chapter VII, and which seems to fit the diverse elements in the evidence, is that many of the married women without children tend to idealize the state of having children. This is the 'traditional dream', as Bailyn terms it, where women, before having children, anticipate that their presence will be all-fulfilling (Bailyn, 1969). This dream does not always come true with their arrival, or last as long as is necessary to counterbalance the demands of child care. As Rossi points out, the cycling of maternal role enjoyment is quicker in its pay-off and briefer than similar stages of career roles (Rossi, 1968). This makes it initially more attractive but gives rise to discontent after a time, and envy of the career-oriented wife who has been building up more slowly to a pay-off point. It has been noted above that many women, particularly those who have high aspirations (as in the

301

vignettes presented in Chapter VII), modify downward their idea of how many children they wish to have after having one or two. Given the contemporary situation – with prevailing values about marital and domestic sex roles, prevailing lack of facilities for excellent child care, and prevailing difficulties in reconciling work and family roles – the 'easiest' and most 'successful' pattern is the 'non-continuous-work' pattern. In this pattern the woman *does* work but *not* when her children are very young.

The first step in establishing a more satisfactory overall framework for analysis is to see how different types of orientation to work generally relate to the individual's own feelings about work and her own work intentions. The various types of commitment can first of all be grouped into two, the 'non-committed' and the 'committed',

Table VIII.1

Expected Work Patterns

1960 Graduates: Married Women[1] (Percentages)

	Married women no children	Married women with children
Non-work-oriented	35	22
Non-continuous-work-oriented	45	43
Continuous-work-oriented	19	34
Totals Percentages	99	99
N =	(73)	(298)

in order to be able to distinguish between those who are committed to women's careers and those who are not.[2] The commitment variable, as it is here defined, relates only to values about women's careers generally. An additional component to the classification is

[1] Non-work-orientated respondents are those who do not specifically say that they intend to work, even after their children are grown; or if they do work prior to this at any point their intention is to withdraw from work. Non-continuous-work-oriented respondents are those who specifically indicate they intend to return to work, but only after their children are of school age or later. Continuous workers intend to return to work when their youngest child is still under 3. The answers on which the index are based are a mixture of actual descriptions of their current *work patterns and intentions for the future.* Where respondents did not indicate their intentions about working at a particular period they were assumed to be not definitely work-oriented. This does not mean that they will not work later, only that they do not now intend to do so.

[2] 'Non-committed' consists of those who are, in terms of the variable described above, 'non-committed' and 'mixed'; 'committed' are those who are 'secondary', 'medium' or 'full' in their commitment. See Chapter VI, Appendix.

necessary to relate these value orientations to the individual respondent's own norms for herself. An individual is career-committed only if she both holds the idea of women's careers as generally described *and* herself derives major satisfaction from her own work or career. Individuals who indicate major satisfaction from their careers (either first or second choices) were combined into a 'career-satisfied' group, and all others were designated as 'non-career-satisfied'. These two variables were combined to form four types of 'career orientation'. Table VIII.2 shows the distribution of these types in the sample of married women with children.[1]

Table VIII.2

Career Orientations

1960 Graduates: Married Women with Children (Percentages of all Married Women with Children)

	Career-satisfied	Not-career-satisfied	N
	Career-oriented	*Only-ideological*	
Committed	17 (52)	25 (74)	(126)
	Only work-oriented	*Conventional*	
Non-committed	11 (33)	47 (139)	(172)
N =	(85)	(213)	

'*Career-oriented*' people are those who are 'committed' to the idea of women having careers, and who actually obtain major satisfaction from their careers. As this depends partly on being currently employed, the proportions here are smaller than they would be if work 'intention' were to be added.

'*Only work-oriented*' women are those who obtain major satisfactions from work but are not highly committed to the general idea of women having careers (as distinct from 'jobs').

'*Only ideological*' women are those who *are* committed to the ideal of women having careers, but who do not obtain major satisfaction from careers themselves – in this case usually because of the presence of small children entailing interruption of career.

'*Conventional*' women are those who are neither committed to the general idea of women having careers nor do they personally derive major satisfaction from their career.

This typology of four basic types makes sense in terms of a

---

[1] Married women without children show a similar overall distribution, though the fact that more of them are working brings larger proportions of them within the career-satisfied categories.

value position – both generally and in relation to individual respondents – but it becomes still more meaningful if related to expected work patterns. Expected work patterns can be accounted for better by using the 'career-orientation' classification than by using either of the two component variables alone (i.e. commitment to the general value, or one's own personal satisfactions from work or career). Taking only the career-satisfied, 48 of the 85 'career-satisfied' respondents (or 56 per cent) have a 'continuous' work expectation. If only the 'commitment' variable is used, only 60 of the 127 'committed' women have 'continuous' work expectations (47 per cent). Taking the combined category of 'career-orientated', 65 per cent expect to work continuously.

A combination of career-orientations with the expected work patterns, then, provides the best combination of characteristics distinguishing different types of married women workers/careerists, actual and potential. The typology of work/career patterns which results is as follows:

Table VIII.3

Types of Work/Career Patterns

| | | Career orientations | | | |
		Conventional	Only ideological	Only work-orientated	Career-orientated
Expected work patterns	Non-work-oriented	A. Conventional	B. Conflicted non-worker	B. Conflicted non-worker	B. Conflicted non-worker
	Non-continuous-work-oriented	C. New-conventional	D. Transitional	D. Transitional	E. Interrupted career
	Continuous-work-oriented	F. Conflicted worker	F. Conflicted worker	G. Non-career worker	H. Career

It can be seen that the twelve possible types are reducible to eight meaningful types; these are distributed in Table VIII.4 for all married women with children.

The *'Conventional'* pattern is represented by the woman who is not committed to the idea of careers for women, who does not get major satisfaction from a job or career and who does not state an intention to work when her youngest child is under 3 nor subsequently.

The *'Conflicted Non-Worker'* also does not intend to work when her youngest child is under 3, or later; but she is different from the 'conventional' in being committed to the idea of women's careers in general, though she does not herself get major satisfactions from the work area of life.

The *'New-conventional'* is defined as the woman who expects to have an interrupted work pattern, returning to work when her children are older; however, she is not committed to the idea of women's careers nor does she get major satisfactions from a paid job. This is the model category for women graduates but it holds for only a quarter of the population.

The *'Transitional Worker'* also intends to follow an interrupted pattern of work. She is committed in general to the idea of women's careers, but does not herself get major satisfaction from work.

Table VIII.4

Career Patterns

1960 Graduates: Married Women with Children[1]

		Percentage	(N)
Non-work-oriented	A. Conventional	15	(46)
	B. Conflicted non-worker	7	(22)
Non-continuous-work-oriented	C. New-conventional	22	(66)
	D. Transitional	15	(46)
	E. Interrupted career	6	(17)
Continuous-work oriented	F. Conflicted worker	18	(53)
	G. Non-career worker	5	(15)
	H. Career	11	(33)
		99	(298)

The *'Interrupted Career'* women is both committed to the idea of careers for women and herself gets major satisfaction from work. However, she does not intend to work continuously through the period of young children, returning some time after her youngest child is over 3.

The *'Conflicted Worker'* is the woman who intends to work

[1] Married women with children and those without children show nearly identical distributions, except that slightly more of the women without children expect to have an interrupted career, and slightly more of those with children are 'Conflicted Workers'. The former makes sense in terms of the 'traditional dream' interpretation mentioned above, and the latter in terms of the actual stresses associated with the dual-career family, as will be discussed below. For most of the chapter, the focus is on married women with children, as they are crucial in highlighting contemporary barriers to the development of women's careers.

continuously (i.e. even when her youngest child is under 3) and who either is uncommitted to the idea of women's careers and gets no satisfaction from work, or is committed to the idea of women's careers in general, but does not get major satisfaction from this area herself.

The '*Non-Career Worker*', the smallest of the categories, is the one where the woman gets major satisfaction from the work area but is not committed to careers for women. She intends to work continuously nevertheless.

The '*Career*' woman intends to work continuously, is committed to the idea of women's careers and gets major satisfaction from working.

In a sense, the above types may be seen as representing an evolutionary trend from the pure '*Conventional*' to the '*New-Conventional*', where there is an intention to return to work eventually, to the '*Interrupted Career*' pattern where a specifically *career* orientation (in the sense of a long-term work development plan) is added, and finally to the '*Career*' pattern, where there is not only a career orientation but also an intention to continue rather than to interrupt work participation. From the point of view of studying the women whose orientations are most likely to lead them to senior jobs, it is probably worth considering the 'Interrupted Career' and the 'Career' patterns together as likely candidates. They make up 17 per cent of the population of married women with children.

The 'Conflicted' and 'Transitional' types are not seen as 'pure types' in the same sense, but as patterns of behavioural resolution in a difficult situation in which there are inconsistencies which will ultimately probably have to be resolved. The inconsistencies with which these women live often give rise to stress symptoms.[1]

---

[1] A list of 'stress symptoms' was provided ('all kinds of aches and pains', 'not vigorous enough to do what I'd like to', 'short of breath', 'heart beats hard', 'sleeplessness', 'nervousness', 'sweaty hands'). The number of symptoms per person in each category was calculated, and a pattern emerged that seems to lend support for this conception of 'pure types' and 'intermediate or conflicted types'. Three out of the four 'pure types' – Conventional, New-Conventional, Interrupted Career – had a ratio of 1·3 or 1·4 symptoms per person; whereas the Conflicted Non-Workers had a ratio of 1·7, the Transitionals a ratio of 1·7, and the combined Conflicted Workers and Non-Career Workers a ratio of 1·5. The Career pattern people were different from the other types in having a high ratio of 1·7; but this may be attributable not to the logical inconsistencies of their position, but to the stresses of performing in this pattern, as the next chapter brings out. These findings are consistent with the analysis of how personal and marital satisfactions relate under different circumstances of work as brought out in Chapter VII. These findings must be taken as suggestive rather than definitive. Further study of stress and its management for the various patterns is required.

The patterns described above incorporate the most important work-relevant variables mentioned in the last chapter – namely commitment to the idea of women's careers, source of personal satisfactions and work expectations. The typology is therefore, by definition, highly intercorrelated with these variables. Work/career pattern is also influenced by level of aspiration.

Table VIII.5

Level of Aspiration and Work/Career Pattern

1960 Graduates: Married Women with Children[1]

		Percentage High Aspirers* in each pattern		
Non-work-oriented	{ Conventional	12	{ 10	(46)
	{ Conflicted non-worker		{ 17	(22)
Non-continuous-work	{ New-conventional		{ 9	(66)
	{ Transitional	8	{ 8	(46)
	{ Interrupted career		{ 0	(17)
Continuous work	{ Conflicted worker		{ 29	(53)
	{ Non-career worker	30	{ 8	(15)
	{ Career		{ 40	(33)
	High aspirers N =			(41)
	Total N =			(298)

*'Get to top' or 'hold a high position'

This table shows that while the proportion of married women with children who have a high level of aspiration is small (14 per cent overall), the level of aspiration does affect work/career pattern; the high aspirers are more heavily represented among the continuous workers than among the non-continuous or non-work-oriented women. Level of aspiration, as was shown in Chapter VI, also affects commitment to careers, work performance and work intentions – hence it is only to be expected that it relates to the composite index based on elements of all three dimensions of women's careers.

Table VIII.6 shows the relationship between work/career pattern and actual hours of paid employment.

Though the 'Continuous Work' group comprises only 16 per cent of the married women with children, 8 out of the 14 (57 per cent)

---

[1] The married women without children, consistently with the contrasts brought out earlier between their intentions and those of the married women with children, are less concentrated in the 'continuous work-oriented' groups and more in the 'non-continuous'.

who are full-time current workers are continuous-work-oriented. Indeed, as expected, in part-time as well as full-time employment categories, the continuous-work-oriented women are heavily represented.[1]

Table VIII.6

Weekly Employment and Work/Career Pattern
1960 Graduates: Married Women with Children (Percentages)

Number of hours employed per week	Conventional	Conflicted non-worker	New-conventional	Transitional	Interrupted career	Conflicted worker	Non-career worker	Career
0	87	62	87	89	75	32	13	3
10 or less	7	19	11	9	13	55	47	25
11—30	6	5	2	2	6	10	33	51
31+	0	15	0	0	6	4	7	22
Totals Percentages	100	101	100	100	100	101	100	101
N-NA	(45)	(21)	(63)	(45)	(16)	(53)	(15)	(32)
NA = (8)	(8)							
N = (298)	(298)							

ANTECEDENT FACTORS

There are a number of antecedent factors in early life experience that have been mentioned in the literature or are part of generally held conceptions of the origins of different sorts of adult career patterns which it is useful to examine in the data available from the 1960 graduate survey. What early experiences shape later work/career patterns? How do these earlier experiences combine with the current circumstances of the adult married woman – such as her marital relationship and her social circle – in affecting work/career patterns?

Some of the antecedent variables which are hypothetically important can be disposed of relatively briefly, either because the data available are inconclusive in relation to later career patterns, or

---

[1] It should be noted that the apparently higher proportion (15 per cent) of full-time workers among the 'conflicted non-work' group is due to the presence of a small number of women who are working full-time, presumably because of their specific circumstances (though they have a child), and who intend to drop out of work as soon as feasible and not return.

because the patterns revealed are of only fragmentary interest. Others indicate possible influence, but their action is somewhat muted or confusing. Where these are of theoretical interest, they will be examined first in this section, and then again in the following section in interaction with more proximate intervening variables.

The factors which are not very illuminating in the survey data are: type of school attended, geographical area of early residence, and war-time experience of separation from one or both parents. Two aspects of the data on schools were examined, namely, type of school (grammar, direct grant, independent, etc.) and whether the school attended was single-sex or co-educational. Nearly all the respondents went to one of three types of school: grammar, direct grant or independent. There are no appreciable differences in the women's distributions by type of school in the different work/career patterns.[1] The same is true for whether or not the individual attended a single-sex or co-educational school. Among married women without children there is a slight tendency for the 'Conventionals' to have gone to single-sex schools, and correspondingly more of the 'Career' pattern women to co-educational schools. Among the married women with children on the other hand, 'Career' pattern women have a higher proportion of single sex school graduates, as do the 'Non-Work' patterns. However, the differences are too small to be conclusive.

The analysis of locality of early residence as an antecedent factor is also inconclusive. There is a slight tendency for the more 'Career-oriented continuous workers' to come from villages rather than towns or cities. The towns and suburban areas seem to have more of the 'Conventional' and non-work patterns, while women reared in central-city areas are almost never in the non-work patterns. However, once again, the differences are not great enough to be very compelling.

War-time separations, often mentioned by informants as an important experience in moulding character and values, for better or worse, are not related to career patterns of women in the present data. Interestingly, there is a slight relationship between war-time separation from father and performance in career by men. The men who choose the lower-paying types of occupations and therefore tend to show up as lower-income types tend slightly more often to have experienced a war-time separation from father while remaining with mother. This is consistent with some research findings by Whiting and his colleagues on the effects of early sexual identifications. In a study of Harvard students who were young children

[1] Among the high-income men there is a notably higher proportion from direct grant schools, but for the women this difference is not operative.

during the Second World War, it was found that the young men who had experienced the absence of father for any prolonged period tended to choose the humanities and arts emphases more frequently (Kuckenberg, 1970). This type of concentration is likely to lead to occupations that are relatively unremunerative as compared with business or engineering for example. Most of the occupations which form the lower-income groups are occupations more heavily sex-stereotyped as 'feminine' – notably teaching and social work – as was indicated in Chapter VI.

Though war-time separations as such do not contribute meaningful influences to the formation of career patterns for women, there are other indications of identification with one or other parent that are of interest. Respondents were asked to indicate which of their parents they 'take after' in 'personality and temperament', and in 'outlook on life'. They were given the options of replying: 'neither', 'mother only', 'father only', 'both parents but mother more than father', 'both parents but father more than mother', 'both parents equally' and 'don't know'.

Comparing only those who emphasize likeness with father with those who emphasize taking after mother, i.e. those who said 'father only' or 'both but father more than mother' vs. those that said 'mother only' or 'both but mother more than father', the following pattern emerges.

Table VIII.7

Parental Identification and Career Patterns

1960 Graduates: Married Women with Children[1] (Percentages)

| | Personality and temperament | | Outlook on life | |
	Father emphasis	Mother emphasis	Father emphasis	Mother emphasis
Conventional	17	13	15	14
Conflicted non-worker	7	9	5	14
New-conventional	18	32	18	23
Transitional	13	13	15	21
Interrupted career	7	5	11	5
Conflicted worker	15	17	12	12
Non-career worker	8	4	7	7
Career	16	8	16	7
Totals Percentages	101	101	99	103
N =	(128)	(105)	(73)	(77)

[1] The married women without children show a very similar pattern.

310

This table shows a tendency for 'father-emphasizing' women to be slightly more *career* oriented. Mother-oriented women are particularly strong among the 'New-conventionals'.[1]

There are other early antecedent factors which are equivocal in their patterning, and which may best be understood in their interaction with more proximate factors to produce a better explanation of observed career patterns: these include social class, sibling or birth order position, and family warmth.

Social class is indicated by father's occupation, though the interest in classifying fathers' occupations is not a direct concern with what the father did at work, but rather as an index of a general style of life associated with occupational status.

Perhaps more generally considered important as an antecedent factor is whether or not the woman's mother worked and how her mother felt about it. Some girls are more easily able to follow a career if they have mothers who have done so and have provided them with an environment in which this was a normal expectation. Others are pressed to have careers if their mothers did not work but were frustrated at not being able to pursue a career. Women of this type sometimes encourage their daughters to accomplish what they failed to do themselves. On the other hand, some mothers who worked may have done so reluctantly and set up a situation in which the daughter felt that she must avoid this if at all possible. Similarly, some mothers who did not work may have set up the expectation that 'happy' family life depends on the mother being at home with her children (Banducci, R. 1967).

In fact, these countervailing tendencies and influences operate to some extent but not entirely to cancel out the patterns in the data. There is no discernible relationship between whether or not the mother worked when the respondent was a child, and whether or not the respondent is working now; nor does the respondent's recollected childhood attitude about her mother working show any patterned relationship to current work.[2] On the other hand, there is a

---

[1] Collapsing the data on work/career patterns to 'career' and 'all other groupings', differences in emphasis on 'outlook on life' are not statistically significant, but differences in 'personality and temperament' are barely significant at ·05 level (using the chi-square test); the women with father-emphasis are more likely to be in the 'career' pattern.

[2] Respondents' current attitudes towards their mothers' work histories provide strong post-hoc rationalization. Women who are currently working full-time are much more likely to indicate approval of their mothers' having worked than those who are either part-time workers or not working. Conversely, the housewives are very much more likely retrospectively to disapprove of their mothers having worked. And of all the married women with children who express disapproval retrospectively, 80 per cent are now not working at all. This compares

relationship between how the respondent reports what her mother felt about her work and current work/career patterns. Table VIII.8 shows the relationship between mother's work situation and attitude about her work situation in relation to two groupings of the respondents' work/career patterns.

Table VIII.8

Mothers' Work Situation and Attitudes Towards It and Respondents' Work/Career Pattern

1960 Graduates: Married Women with Children (Percentages)

| | Mother didn't work | | Mother did work | |
| | And was happy about it | And was unhappy about it | And was very favourable towards it | But wasn't very favourable towards it |
Respondents have				
Non-work pattern (i.e. 'Conventional' or 'Conflicted' non-worker')	23 ⎫ 10 ⎭ 33	12 ⎫ 7 ⎭ 19	9 ⎫ 9 ⎭ 18	15 ⎫ 10 ⎭ 25
Non-continuous work pattern (i.e. 'New-conventional' 'Transitional' and 'Interrupted career')	20 ⎫ 14 ⎬ 40 6 ⎭	17 ⎫ 20 ⎬ 42 5 ⎭	24 ⎫ 15 ⎬ 46 7 ⎭	22 ⎫ 17 ⎬ 49 10 ⎭
Continuous work pattern (I.e. 'Conflicted worker', 'Non-career worker' or 'Career').	16 ⎫ 2 ⎬ 27 9 ⎭	17 ⎫ 15 ⎬ 39 7 ⎭	15 ⎫ 4 ⎬ 36 17 ⎭	17 ⎫ 0 ⎬ 27 10 ⎭
Totals Percentages	100	100	100	101
N =	(81)	(41)	(54)	(41)

It is clear from this table that when the mother did not work and was happy about it, the 1960 graduate wife is much less likely to be a worker than wives from any other situation. At the other extreme, it is both these daughters of happy housewives and daughters of

with 55 per cent of the married women with children who stop work though they retrospectively favour their mothers having worked. This portion of the group of married women with children contains a high proportion who intend to return to work at the earliest opportunity.

working mothers who were not 'favourable' towards their work who are lowest in their tendency to have careers or continuous work patterns. The highest proportions of continuous workers among graduate wives are drawn from among those whose mothers either worked and were very much in favour of it, or whose mothers did not work, but were unhappy about their situation.

The mother's work experience is of considerable further interest as an antecedent variable, and will be examined again in relation to proximate influences in the next section.

Father's occupation is another antecedent variable of importance because it is an index of social class. Thus it provides a style of life and cultural norms which may have a very general effect on life values as well as providing a specific type of role model for the developing individual. The data from the 1960 graduates' survey shows the following pattern.

Table VIII.9

Father's Occupational and Career Pattern

1960 Graduates: Married Women with Children (Percentages)

	Professional/ Managerial	Other non- Manual	Manual workers
Conventional	19 ⎫ 27	14 ⎫ 21	14 ⎫ 22
Conflicted non-worker	8 ⎭	7 ⎭	8 ⎭
New-conventional	29 ⎫	17 ⎫	10 ⎫
Transitional	9 ⎬ 41	21 ⎬ 49	20 ⎬ 36
Interrupted career	3 ⎭	11 ⎭	6 ⎭
Conflicted worker	11 ⎫	21 ⎫	22 ⎫
Non-career worker	8 ⎬ 32	1 ⎬ 29	2 ⎬ 40
Career	13 ⎭	7 ⎭	16 ⎭
Totals Percentages	100	99	98
N =	(127)	(95)	(49)

This table shows that the daughters of professional or managerial fathers tend a little more than the daughters of men of other occupations to be 'non-work' oriented. Their most frequently indicated work/career pattern is the 'New-Conventional'. Non-manual workers' daughters are most heavily concentrated in the non-continuous work/career patterns. Daughters of manual workers tend to have a more 'continuous work' pattern, their most frequently chosen pattern being 'Conflicted Worker'. Indeed, a breakdown within this group shows that the daughters of unskilled manual workers have the greatest proportion in the 'Continuous' patterns (62 per cent), though they do not concentrate in the 'Career' category particularly. Once women from an unskilled manual background break away and get through university, they tend to be more 'continuous-work-oriented' whether or not they do so as part of a commitment to women's careers. This may represent a perpetuation of the working-class working mother pattern (Jackson, Young and Willmott).

Position in birth order is another variable which may be important but which produces equivocal results in a gross analysis in relation to career patterns. The findings of other studies are to some extent inconsistent and relate to only a limited range of possible situations in the birth order. Most of the work has to do with the effects of being a first-born child. The eldest child, whether male or female, has been found to be more conscientious, more highly motivated, more performance oriented, expressive, serious and methodical (Price, 1969; McArthur, 1956; Sampson, 1965; Warren, 1966; Altus, 1966). The inconsistency of the findings relates to whether these qualities are applied in a conservative direction with the acceptance of traditional patterns, or whether they may be associated with innovative thrust as well. Kammeyer, for example, found that in a sample of American college women, first-born girls were more traditionally-oriented towards the feminine role and tended to hold more traditional views about feminine personality traits (Kammeyer, 1966). Bradley found that first-born children tend more to meet teachers' expectations, show more susceptibility to social pressure, exhibit more information-seeking behaviour, are more sensitive to tension and are more frequently judged serious and low on aggression than others, which tends to strengthen their achievement and enhance their academic performance (Bradley, 1969). This begins to sound more as though the patterns adopted by the first-born will depend on intervening variables, such as the advice or encouragement received, and the general atmosphere. There is some evidence that social norms and pressures aside, first and only children achieve highly not only within the set structural framework, but may be unusually innovative as well when favourable conditions are present.[1]

The evidence from the 1960 graduates' study shows that all categories of men and women except the married women with children are working in too great proportions to see any gross

---

[1] There is a certain amount of discussion supported by research on other birth-order situations. For example, women with only elder brothers may tend to emulate the 'masculine role' and therefore be less oriented to traditional feminine roles (Kammeyer, 1967). However, literature is very scant in these areas and contributions are very much needed (Smelser and Stewart, 1968).

314

effect of birth order on current employment. For married women with children there is a slight tendency for women in three categories mentioned in the literature – only children, eldest daughter with younger sisters, and younger child with an elder brother – to be employed in slightly greater proportions than women from other birth order positions (about 40-50 per cent chance as compared with overall chance of about 35 per cent).

Examining the birth order variable in relation to actual performance at work (as distinct from the mere fact of working at this stage) a slight relationship is found between birth order position and

Figure VIII.1

Birth Order Position as a Determinant of Income

1960 Graduates: All men and Women[1]

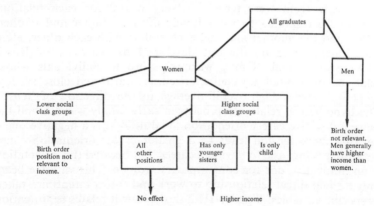

income. Figure VIII.1 indicates the way in which birth order relates to income.

Birth order seems to make a small difference for certain sub-groups of the total graduate population. One of these sub-groups is the women from higher social class backgrounds. Other sub-groups will be defined below when the interaction between this variable and more proximate variables is examined. Eldest children under certain circumstances may function as pioneers, repeating their early familial experience of pioneering the child-role. In addition, where the eldest sister has only younger sisters, she may consciously or unconsciously be the object of her parents' conventional wishes for a male heir and may be invested with many of the aspirations

[1] Based on A.I.D. analysis using Income as the dependent variable for the whole population.

315

that go with this family role. Structurally, she may be in an authoritative position in relation to her siblings more often than daughters in other positions.

An examination of the more differentiated set of career and work patterns in relation to birth order is inconclusive. Viewed in isolation, the birth order variable does not seem to contribute much. 'Only children' show a bi-modal pattern, with a slightly higher proportion in the 'Career' category than for most other groups, but also more in the 'conventional' non-working category. The same holds for those who have 'younger sisters only'.

This variable will be examined again later in the chapter as it combines with intervening variables to produce interactive effects.

Another variable from early experience, suggested by Rossi, is the overall warmth or tension of family relationships. Early family warmth is measured by an index made up of the overall score on a scale from 'very tense' to 'very warm' for each relationship in the respondent's early family life (e.g. father and mother, father and me, mother and me, each sibling with each other, etc.). This index, based on the one developed by Alice Rossi (Rossi, 1968) gives a high 'family warmth' score to individuals whose relationships overall are characterized as 'warm and close'; a low score indicates a high overall average in the direction of 'tense'. The hypothetical relationship between early family warmth and the more innovative career orientation in adulthood is a negative one – i.e. that more tension leads to a greater career orientation – not because it is intrinsic to having a career, but because this orientation is an innovative one for contemporary women. This variable bears only a slight direct relationship to work and career intentions, taken as specific variables. Figure VIII.2 shows how it relates to 'Intention to work when youngest child is under 3', i.e. to have a 'continuous' expected work pattern.

This figure shows that Family Warmth in the individual's background is important as a determinant of work intentions only for those women who at the time of the survey are not working and are happy with the homemaker role *for the time being*. More of those with a 'tense' background expect to return to work eventually than those with a 'warm' background.

The analysis of Family Warmth scores in relation to work/career patterns does not contribute anything to this picture; only insignificant differences in Family Warmth Index scores are found among the different patterns.

This variable, too, will be re-examined as it combines with proximate variables in the women's immediate environment to produce an interactive effect on career orientation.

316

Figure VIII.2

Family Warmth and Women's Intention to Work when Youngest Child Under 3[1]

1960 Graduates: All Married Women

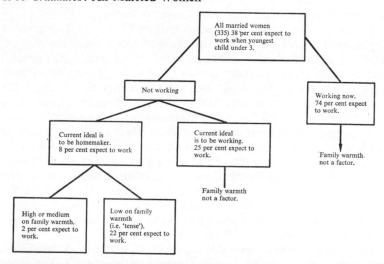

INTERACTION OF ANTECEDENT AND CURRENT INFLUENCES

Because of the conflict-laden situation confronting most married women, particularly those with children, who wish to pursue occupational careers, many are of two minds about whether they want to continue their careers or not. Therefore current influences are unusually likely to override predispositions set up by antecedent influences. The central argument of this section, and indeed the chapter as a whole, is that, although the influence of proximate factors is overriding, at the same time, both for scientific and practical reasons, it is important to recognize that both sets of influences may operate and interact together to create a given result. Scientifically it is potentially important because it may be possible through considering both sets of influences interactively to account for more of the observed patterns than is possible with either set alone. It is also of practical importance because if effective policy is to be formulated in relation to current factors – e.g. child care facilities or educational efforts directed at the marital relationship – expected reactions may be determined by earlier antecedent variables

[1] Based on A.I.D. analysis with 'Intention to work when youngest child is under 3' as dependent variable.

317

which set up dispositions one way or another towards adopting given work/career patterns.

Three of the more proximate influences are examined independently, and then interactively with the antecedent factors. The first of these, marital happiness, was discussed in the last chapter. It is now examined in relation to work/career patterns.

In the previous chapter, marital happiness was looked at as a dependent variable associated with the work situation of the women. Working eight years after graduation and commitment to the general idea of women having careers is associated with a lower level of 'very happy' marital relationships; but what is really the 'cause'? Do women with an early history that predisposes them to tension show lower levels of marital happiness regardless of current employment, or is current employment the crucial factor? Is it profitable to pursue the line that a lower level of marital happiness is the cause for working; or is this true only where there is a predisposing set of factors in the early background experience? The position taken here is that marital happiness is best seen as an intervening variable – on the one hand produced by earlier situations in the individual's personal history and on the other hand as a determinant of current modes of organizing work-family relationships.

By putting together several dimensions of women's occupational patterns – ideals, intentions and actual satisfaction – the more complex set of work/career patterns was derived (p. 304) and in Table VIII.10 the relationship between marital happiness and the different work/career patterns is examined for married women with children.

This table shows that, over the whole career perspective, the proportionately highest levels of 'very happy' marital relationships are found among the 'non-continuous' workers. This is consistent with earlier analyses in that this is the group which makes the most generally acceptable resolution of inner aspirations and supported cultural patterns – it is the 'in-out-in' pattern recommended by most 'accommodative' observers of the current scene. In this grouping are the 'New-Conventionals'.

One of the most interesting findings in this table is that, taking the whole life perspective (rather than current employment only), the level of marital happiness is lower both for the continuous worker and for the non-workers – though it would seem for different reasons. In the latter case, the lack of resolution of the 'captive housewife' dilemma is probably a prominent feature, whereas in the former, the stresses and strains of adopting a non-conventional pattern (e.g. the dual-career family) are probably of paramount importance.

318

A second proximate variable is that of the husband's commitment to the idea of women's careers. In Chapter VII it was shown separately for the graduate men and the graduate women in the sample that both the husbands' commitment and their wives' commitment are important in determining whether or not married women are working currently. The issue now is to determine the relationship between her perception of her husband's commitment (which is only partly accurate, as was shown in the couples' analyses) and her

Table VIII.10

Marital Happiness and Work/Career Patterns

1960 Graduates: Married Women with Children (Percentages)[1]

		'Very happy'	'Not very happy'
Non-work oriented	Conventional	15 ⎫ 21	16 ⎫ 25
	Conflicted non-worker	6 ⎭	9 ⎭
Non-continuous workers	New-conventional	28 ⎫	15 ⎫
	Transitional	16 ⎬ 50	15 ⎬ 35
	Interrupted career	6 ⎭	5 ⎭
Continuous work oriented	Conflicted worker	16 ⎫	20 ⎫
	Non-career worker	4 ⎬ 29	6 ⎬ 40
	Career	9 ⎭	14 ⎭
	Totals Percentages	100	100
	N =	(168)	(130)

own work/career pattern. Whatever the actual strength of the husband's commitment, the operative influence is how that commitment is seen by the wives. Table VIII.11 shows the pattern that emerges.

This table shows that the woman's perception of her spouse's commitment to the idea of women having careers is an important determinant of her own pattern of work/career orientation. A greater percentage of wives who perceive their husbands as committed have a continuous work pattern than is true for the wives whose husbands are not seen as so committed. The effects on the 'non-work' end of the continuum are much more marked, with the wives of non-committed husbands being much more likely to have a 'non-work' pattern than those of the husbands perceived to be

---

[1] 'Very happy' here is the concordant index – i.e. respondent's assessment and her perceived spouse's assessment.

committed. The negative attitude of the husband has, it would seem, a more powerful determining effect than his support – which makes sense in terms of the additional barriers still to be crossed outside the home if a woman is to have a career.

The final variable examined as a proximate influence is the attitude of the married women respondents' social circles towards women and their careers. The reason this variable was thought to be

Table VIII.11

Perceived Commitment of Spouse to the Idea of Women's Careers and Work/Career Pattern

1960 Graduates: Married Women with Children (Percentages)

	Spouse is perceived as	
Respondent's work/career pattern is:	Not committed (i.e. 'None', 'Mixed' or 'Secondary')	Committed (i.e. 'Medium' or 'Full')
Conventional	19 ⎫	3 ⎫
Conflicted	⎬ 26	⎬ 11
non-worker	7 ⎭	8 ⎭
New conventional	27 ⎫	7 ⎫
Transitional	12 ⎬ 42	26 ⎬ 48
Interrupted career	3 ⎭	15 ⎭
Conflicted worker	18 ⎫	17 ⎫
Non-career worker	6 ⎬ 32	1 ⎬ 40
Career	8 ⎭	22 ⎭
Totals Percentages	100	99
N =	(226)	(72)

important was that though to some extent one's social circle is self-selected and may be chosen to reinforce one's own values, in fact a social circle develops according to various criteria among which orientation to women's careers is not prominent. In fact, one's circle or 'network' of friends and associates is an amalgam of people selected on various grounds – neighbourhood, spouse's employment, children's school friends, etc. The type of attitude they hold towards women's careers is usually found as a secondary attribute.

One question the respondents were asked was: 'Looking at your social circle as a whole, how would you describe their attitude towards women working?' The following options were given:

'Most people feel that women ought to have the same opportunity to pursue an important career as men.'
'Most people feel that women ought to be able to work a bit, but not so as to allow it to interfere with home and family obligations.'
'Women ought not to work outside the home.'
'Very mixed feelings (some like the first, some like the second, some like the third option above).'
and 'Not relevant, no social circle.'

As would be expected, most of the respondents answer that their social circles tend to favour the second option, namely, 'women ought to be able to work a bit'.

Not to work at all is a very scarce reply, and is therefore grouped with 'mixed' replies, the latter being a major category of response comparable in frequency to the 'same as men' responses.

Table VIII.12 shows the distribution of responses by work/career patterns.

Table VIII.12

Attitude of Social Circle towards Women's Employment and Type of Work/Career Pattern Adopted

1960 Graduates: Married Women with Children (Percentages)

Respondent's work pattern is	Should not work or very mixed feelings expressed	Women[1] should only work a bit	Women should have same career opportunity as men
Conventional	26 ⎫	15 ⎫	6 ⎫
Conflicted	34	22	11
Non-worker	8 ⎭	7 ⎭	5 ⎭
New-conventional	21 ⎫	24 ⎫	19 ⎫
Transitional	11 ⎬ 34	17 ⎬ 46	16 ⎬ 46
Interrupted career	2 ⎭	5 ⎭	11 ⎭
Conflicted worker	15 ⎫	21 ⎫	16 ⎫
Non-career worker	5 ⎬ 31	5 ⎬ 33	6 ⎬ 44
Career	11 ⎭	7 ⎭	22 ⎭
Totals Percentages	99	101	101
N-NA	(62)	(165)	(64)

NA = 5
N = (291)

[1] Only one married woman in this sample indicated a social circle that felt that women should 'not work'.

The women who experience their social circle as expressing 'very mixed feelings' – i.e., that their social circle is heterogeneous with respect to women working – are the most conservative in the sense that they have the largest proportions in the 'non-work' categories. Where the social circle is perceived as favouring women's careers, the largest proportion of women are in fact 'continuous' and indeed 22 per cent are in the 'career' pattern category as compared with only 7 per cent in this category for the women who report a social circle who feel that women should 'work a bit' and 11 per cent of women who characterize their social circle as expressing very mixed feelings on this topic.

It will now be valuable to examine the effects produced by combining some of the early antecedent influences with some of the more proximate influences. It has already been noted that several antecedent influences – Social Class, Birth Order Position, Family Warmth and Mother's Work Experiences – have a discernible though rather restricted and weak effect on the subsequent career patterns of graduate women. On the other hand, some more proximate influences – notably husband's perceived commitment to the idea of women's careers, marital happiness, and the attitudes of the social circle – are also effective and on the whole more powerful than are the antecedent influences. Does the consideration of early and late influences in combination produce a better explanation of current career patterns than either alone? The examples used here are only illustrative of how the early and late influences may be seen to operate interactively. Of course, deficiencies of data will affect the results, particularly as 'early factors' are subject to problems of retrospective bias. Nevertheless, an examination of the patterns of response combining these variables is instructive if results are taken as suggestive rather than definitive.

Earlier in the chapter, the relation between mothers' work experiences and current career patterns of graduate women was examined. Mothers' work experiences and attitudes towards them were shown to influence current work/career patterns: mothers who did not work and were unhappy with it are associated with daughters who are more likely to work; this is also true for mothers who worked and were in favour of it. Conversely, the happy housewife mothers and the unwilling working mothers tended to produce more traditionally non-working oriented daughters. It was also noted that the happiness of the current marital relationship is a factor in relation to a given pattern of work/career; there are proportionately fewer 'very happy' marriages among the 'continuous' workers than among the 'non-continuous', but there are also proportionately fewer 'very happy' marriages reported among the 'non-work' pattern wives.

What kinds of work/career patterns are associated with the interaction between the antecedent factors of mother's work situation and the more proximate factors of current marital happiness?

Table VIII.13 shows the results for the different work/career pattern groupings produced first by interaction with one of the antecedent factors (mother's work experience), then with a proximate variable (marital happiness), and finally by the combination of the two. The table excerpts those parts of the antecedent variables that hypothetically predispose to a more work-involved pattern. Taking, therefore, only the situations most likely to produce work-prone women – i.e. that the mother worked and was very much in favour of it, and that the current marital relationship is characterized as 'not very happy', the following pattern emerges:

Table VIII.13

Mother's Work Experience, Current Marital Relationship and the Interaction Effect of Both on Work/Career Pattern

1960 Graduates: Married Women with Children (Percentages)

Work/career pattern	Mother worked and was 'very much in favour'	Marital relationship 'not very happy'	Mother worked 'very favourable' *and* marital relationship 'not very happy'
Conventional	9 ⎫ 18	16 ⎫ 25	16 ⎫ 21
Conflicted non-worker	9 ⎭	9 ⎭	5 ⎭
New-conventional	24 ⎫	15 ⎫	21 ⎫
Transitional	15 ⎬ 46	15 ⎬ 35	11 ⎬ 43
Interrupted career	7 ⎭	5 ⎭	11 ⎭
Conflicted worker	15 ⎫	20 ⎫	26 ⎫
Non-career worker	4 ⎬ 36	6 ⎬ 40	0 ⎬ 37
Career	17 ⎭	14 ⎭	11 ⎭
Totals Percentages	100	100	101
N =	(54)	(130)	(19)

This table shows that the combined effect of mother's favourable attitudes and behaviour in relation to work *and* a not very happy current marital situation does not produce a higher proportion of married women with children who expect to work continuously. The specific character of mother working and being favourable to it in combination with marital happiness may not be the most powerful combination, though each separately is relatively influential.

If the second strongest aspect of factors influencing work/career pattern is studied, an interesting line of argument begins to emerge. For example, 'mother didn't work and was unhappy' is the next most productive category in the particular antecedent factor of mother's work experience. When this is studied in combination with current marital happiness, there is actually a small drop as a result of the interaction effect. Thirty-nine per cent of the married women with children whose mothers did not work and were unhappy about it were in the 'continuous' work pattern. Combining this variable with the marital situation of 'not very happy', the percentage in 'continuous work' remains at 36 per cent despite the fact that if the 'not very happy' marital relationship is taken on its own there are 40 per cent who are continuous workers. The further analysis of this data yields an interesting interpretation. Given the fact that there are two components to the mother's work situation, her behaviour (working or not working) and her attitude towards it (favourable or unfavourable, happy or unhappy), a daughter may be primarily responsive to her mother's behaviour regardless of attitudes or her mother's attitudes regardless of her behaviour ('do as I say, not as I do'). The data, as set out in Table VIII.14, show that women with less happy marital relationships tend more to follow their mother's behaviour, and women with more happy marital relationships their mother's attitudes.

Table VIII.14

Mother's Work Experience and Current Work Patterns According to Marital Happiness

1960 Graduates: Married Women with Children (Percentages)

Work/career patterns	'Very happy marriage' Mother worked unfavourable attitude	Mother did not work unhappy	'Not very happy marriage' Mother worked unfavourable attitude	Mother did not work unhappy
Conventional	14 ⎫ 28	11 ⎫ 11	16 ⎫ 21	14 ⎫ 28
Conflicted non-worker	14 ⎭	0 ⎭	5 ⎭	14 ⎭
New-conventional	23 ⎫	21 ⎫	21 ⎫	14 ⎫
Transitional	23 ⎬ 55	21 ⎬ 42	11 ⎬ 43	18 ⎬ 41
Interrupted career	9 ⎭	0 ⎭	11 ⎭	9 ⎭
Conflicted worker	9 ⎫	32 ⎫	26 ⎫	5 ⎫
Non-career worker	0 ⎬ 18	11 ⎬ 48	0 ⎬ 37	18 ⎬ 32
Career	9 ⎭	5 ⎭	11 ⎭	9 ⎭
Totals Percentages	101	101	101	101
N =	(22)	(19)	(19)	(22)

324

This table shows that there is a tendency for women from the less happy marriages to behave more like their mothers, i.e. not to work if their mothers did not work even if they were not happy about not working, and to work if their mothers worked regardless of whether their mothers were in favour of working or not. The women with very happy marriages, in contrast, are more governed by their mothers' attitudes, not working in greater proportions if their mothers were unhappy with working.[1]

The above has shown that there is some interaction effect between antecedent and proximate influences, but that it is not an automatic one. Sometimes they can interact to diminish the overall effect despite the commonsense expectation that the net effect should be additive. In some instances, the net effect is more cumulative and in still others the effect may be reversed.

An example of how the interaction analysis may lead to a different sort of result from naive expectation is seen in relation to early Family Warmth.

Earlier tables have shown that there is a slight tendency under some conditions for women with a more 'tense' background to be more prone to continuous work patterns or to return to work when they adopt a temporary housewife role than are comparable women from a more 'warm' family background. Women from 'warm' family backgrounds, furthermore, tend to have marital relationships that they characterize as 'very happy', as shown in Table VIII.15.

Table VIII.15

Early Family Warmth and Current Marital Happiness

1960 Graduates: Married Women with Children (Percentages)

Marital Happiness (Concordant Index)	Early Family Warmth		
	Low (Tense)	Medium	High (Warm)
'Very Happy'	38	59	65
Not 'Very Happy'	62	41	35
Totals Percentages	100	100	100
N=	(59)	(155)	(83)

Thus family warmth seems to predispose towards marital happiness which in turn promotes conventionality of work/career pattern. An

[1] Conversely, married women with children with 'very happy' marriages whose mothers did not work and were happy about it adopt the non-work patterns more frequently than other groups. Twenty-one out of sixty-three or 33 per cent are in non-work patterns as compared with an overall 24 per cent. See Appendix for full tables.

SEX, CAREER AND FAMILY

analysis of how they combine begins to suggest a more complex formulation.

Table VIII.16 shows the relationship between Work-Career pattern and Family Warmth on its own, Marital Happiness on its own, and the two in combination.

Table VIII.16

Family Warmth, Marital Happiness and the Interaction of Both on Producing Work Orientation

1960 Graduates: Married Women with Children (Percentages)

Careers or work pattern	Family warmth		Marital relationship 'Not very happy'	Marital relationship 'Not very happy' and Family warmth	
	Tense	Warm		Tense	Warm
Conventional	19 ⎫ 27	21 ⎫ 28	16 ⎫ 25	25 ⎫ 36	17 ⎫ 27
Conflicted non-worker	8 ⎭	7 ⎭	9 ⎭	11 ⎭	10 ⎭
New-conventional	19 ⎫	19 ⎫	15 ⎫	11 ⎫	7 ⎫
Transitional	15 ⎬ 39	16 ⎬ 43	15 ⎬ 35	8 ⎬ 24	10 ⎬ 24
Interrupted career	5 ⎭	8 ⎭	5 ⎭	5 ⎭	7 ⎭
Conflicted worker	19 ⎫	14 ⎫	20 ⎫	22 ⎫	24 ⎫
Non-career worker	3 ⎬ 34	5 ⎬ 29	6 ⎬ 40	3 ⎬ 39	10 ⎬ 48
Career	12 ⎭	10 ⎭	14 ⎭	14 ⎭	14 ⎭
Totals Percentages	100	100	100	99	99
N =	(59)	(83)	(130)	(36)	(29)

This table shows that though there is a slight relationship between having a tense family background and a continuous work/career pattern it is the 'warm' background women who are most likely to be continuously career oriented when their marital relationship is 'not very happy'. One reaction of the 'warm' background people to a less than 'very happy' marital relationship is to become continuous workers. This can be understood as an adaptive mechanism. When faced with the strains of a less than 'very happy' marital relationship, the 'tense' background women tend as much to stay at home as to work, seeking other gratifications, e.g. increased involvement with their children; they often withdraw altogether from work as their high proportions in the non-work pattern suggest.[1]

Birth order is another variable whose functioning is mediated by

[1] The people with 'very happy' marriages concentrate particularly heavily in the interrupted work pattern; they are the 'new-conventional' group *par excellence.*

Table VIII.17

Birth Order Position, Perceived Husband's Commitment to the idea of Women's Careers, and Work/Career Pattern

1960 Graduates: Married Women with Children

Work/career pattern	Only child Husband's commitment Low	Only child Husband's commitment High	Eldest daughter with sisters only Husband's commitment Low	Eldest daughter with sisters only Husband's commitment High	All other birth order positions Husband's commitment Low	All other birth order positions Husband's commitment High
Conventional	26 } 32	7 } 21	32	19	15 } 23	4 } 11
Conflicted non-worker	6	14			8	7
New-conventional	26	14 } 35	42	44	32 } 42	5 } 51
Transitional	13 } 41	7			9	32
Interrupted career	2	14			1	14
Conflicted worker	15 } 28	14 } 43	27	37	9 } 34	13 } 38
Non-career worker	4	4			3	0
Career	9	25			22	25
Totals Percentages	101	99	101	100	99	100
N =	(47)	(28)	(34)	(16)	(117)	(56)

intervening variables. This will be shown only illustratively in Table VIII.17, which indicates how two of the birth order variables which have some effect on work/career pattern are sensitive to the husband's perceived attitudes about women's careers. Husband's commitment to the idea of women having careers is examined as an intervening variable in the relationship between birth order position and work career pattern.

This table shows that there is a considerable shift, both for only children and for women who are the eldest sisters of only other

Table VIII.18

Single-Sex or Co-ed Secondary School and Work/Career Pattern by Current Marital Happiness

1960 Graduates: Married Women with Children (Percentages)

Work/career pattern	Single-sex school		Co-ed school	
	'Very happy' marriage	'Not very happy' marriage	'Very happy' marriage	'Not very happy' marriage
Conventional	14 ⎫ 21	17 ⎫ 27	19 ⎫ 19	12 ⎫ 16
Conflicted non-worker	7 ⎭	10 ⎭	0 ⎭	4 ⎭
New-conventional	27 ⎫	15 ⎫	31 ⎫	12 ⎫
Transitional	15 ⎬ 49	15 ⎬ 36	22 ⎬ 56	12 ⎬ 28
Interrupted carrer	7 ⎭	6 ⎭	3 ⎭	4 ⎭
Conflicted worker	15 ⎫	17 ⎫	19 ⎫	32 ⎫
Non-career worker	5 ⎬ 30	5 ⎬ 36	0 ⎬ 25	12 ⎬ 56
Career	10 ⎭	14 ⎭	6 ⎭	12 ⎭
Totals Percentages	100	99	100	100
N =	(136)	(105)	(32)	(25)

sisters, in the direction of increased continuous work patterns when they perceive their husbands' commitment to women having careers as high. The husband's commitment accounts for an increase of about 15 per cent in continuous work orientation of only children, and 10 per cent for eldest daughters with younger sisters, as compared with 4 per cent of people in other positions. It is interesting to note the slight tendency toward bimodality in these 'only' and 'eldest' daughter cases. These two categories have higher proportions in the Conventional work patterns than the others; and this tendency is accentuated when there is the perception of a Conventional attitude on the husband's part. This finding may be interpreted as reflecting the dual aspect of only children's orientations as described above – on the one hand rather conventional in orientation and eager to please in the established ways, and on the other hand potentially creative under the right conditions. For female only children, this would suggest the crucial importance of the attitudes of the principal male in their intimate environment – namely their husband's. Given the character of the data, however, these findings must be considered suggestive rather than conclusive.

Another finding which supports this line of analysis relates to the type of school the respondent attended. Table VIII.18 shows the effect of having attended a single-sex or co-ed secondary school on work and career patterns under different conditions of marital happiness.

This table indicates that for girls who attended single-sex schools an unhappy marital situation produces a polarizing effect – i.e. an increase both in the conventional and in the continuous work orientations; but for the girls who attended co-ed schools, where there is a less than 'very happy' marital situation, the effect is overwhelmingly in the direction of more work. Once again, the small numbers and the nature of the sample require that these data be treated as suggestive only, but their general characteristics are consistent with what has already been indicated in preceding analyses.

SUMMARY AND DISCUSSION

Given the fact that women's occupational performance must be assessed differently from men's at the present stage, an index of work-career patterns was developed that takes into account not only whether the woman is currently employed, but also the nature of her orientation to her work in terms of its salience to her, her commitment to the idea of women having careers and her intentions about working at different stages of the family life cycle. This set of considerations, of special importance in assessing the state of affairs for married women with young children – most of whom have interrupted their major occupation participation – comprises eight patterns. These are further grouped into three major patterns: the non-work, the non-continuous work, and the continuous work patterns.

The issue of what produces the work-prone woman was then examined, though with no claim that this was an exhaustive analysis. Much of the literature relevant to this issue can be divided into a consideration of variables in the early life experience which are thought to have a formative effect (e.g. social class, schooling, relationships with parents and other family members, position in birth order) and a consideration of variables of a more immediate,

SEX, CAREER AND FAMILY

proximate kind which are alive in the current intimate environment
of the woman (e.g. the state of her marital relationship, her husband's
attitudes towards women and their careers, the attitudes of their
social circle towards women's careers).

A preliminary examination of some of the early variables in
comparison with those that are more proximate indicates that the
early ones generally have a much less apparent impact, though they
usually seem to operate in the generally expected direction. There is
a tendency for the more continuous-work oriented women to feel
that they are more like their fathers in personality and temperament;
and to be more inclined to work if their mothers either worked and
were favourable towards it or did not work and were unhappy
about it. Daughters of professional managerial fathers tend to be
somewhat more conventional than those of other social class
backgrounds (though there is a tendency towards bi-modality with
these women), and daughters of manual workers tend to be more
frequently found among the continuous work pattern women.
Birth order position is of only slight importance, with two patterns
having slight prominence – the only children (a group which also
tends towards bi-modality) and the eldest daughters with younger
sisters only. If the early family environment is characterized as
somewhat tense (by a composite index based on the perceived
nature of each of the early family relationships) the woman is likely
to show a greater tendency to intend to return to work if she is
currently a housewife.

Among the proximate factors, marital satisfaction relates to
work/career pattern (with a tendency for those with a lower level
of 'very happy' marriages to be more likely to be continuous workers);
the perception that the husband is committed to the idea of women
having careers bears an important relationship to continuous work;
and if the respondent's social circle considers that women should
have equal career opportunities to men, a continuous-work pattern
is again more likely.

The issue of how early experiences combine with later life situations
to produce given work/career patterns was then examined. As the
early patterns seem on the whole to account by themselves for very
little of the variation in current work/career patterns and as the
proximate situational variables seem to account for a good deal of
variation, the value of analysing their combined results was considered. There is a body of literature which attributes to early
experiences great importance in determining subsequent attitudes
and behaviour. The issue is how the more current factors mediate
the early experiences to produce different effects.

The three interactive combinations that were examined provided

330

interesting insights as to how these mechanisms seem to work, though the results must be taken as suggestive rather than conclusive. Furthermore they are only illustrative of the many combinations that are potentially operative for highly qualified women at this stage in their family life. The work experience of the respondents' mothers was examined as it interacted with current marital happiness. In gross terms, there is no increase in the proportions of continuous workers that are produced by combining the two most predisposing conditions of mothers' employment experience (mother worked and was favourable towards the idea; and, mother didn't work and was unhappy with this) and the most predisposing situation in the current marital relationship (i.e. not 'very happy' marriage). However, further analysis shows that the two predisposing conditions of mothers' employment have different effects in relation to the marital situation. When the marital situation is 'very happy', the women tend to be responsive to their mothers' *attitudes* regardless of what their actual behaviour was (i.e. they are more likely to be continuous-work-orientated if the mothers were either favourable about working or unhappy about not working). Where the marital relationship is 'not very happy', the women tend to be responsive to their mothers' behaviour – i.e. they are work-oriented if their mothers worked and not work-oriented if their mothers did not work regardless of the mothers' attitudes. Contemporary married women do as their mothers said rather than as they did mainly under conditions of a happy marital relationship.

A second interactive pattern was examined in relating early family warmth with current marital happiness to the work/career pattern. Though in some circumstances it is the individual with the 'tense' background who is predisposed to break away from the more conventional pattern, and though in general 'warm' background people have a higher predisposition towards 'very happy' marriages, it was found that it was precisely in the not 'very happy' marital situations that the 'warm' background people are more likely to be continuous-work-oriented. Thus, if a warm background woman does not find herself in the preferred situation of a 'very happy' marital relationship, her response is to divert her energies into work and career. The individual with the more 'tense' background in a not 'very happy' marital situation seeks compensation in domestic involvements more frequently.

Finally, the issue of birth order in relation to the current work situation was examined – using another variable in the current marital situation, namely the wife's perception of her husband's commitment to the idea of women having careers. Though being an 'only child' and being the 'eldest daughter with only younger

331

sisters' are found to predispose women to current employment (though not particularly to the more overall life-pattern of work/career), only the former (being an only child) situation predisposes the women to be particularly sensitive to their husbands' perceived attitudes. Only children are much more likely to become continuous workers if they perceive their husbands as committed than if they perceive them as non-committed. For the other categories of birth order, the effects of husbands' perceived commitment are there and of importance, but less so than for the only children. This seems to be relevant to a good deal of the discussion about only children and their characteristics – under some circumstances they are seen as more conventional in their performance, and in others more innovative. The attitudes of the significant male in their immediate environment are of particularly great importance to women in this birth order position.

In conclusion, it should be noted that while this chapter concentrated on the early family experiences and the current marital relationship. particularly of married women with children, it is suggested that many of the observations have a more general relevance. While the evidence of this study provides support for the notion that behaviour and attitudes of husbands are of crucial importance – his integration of work and family, his commitment, the degree of happiness in the marital relationship, etc. – it is suggested that he is only one among a range of important figures affecting the disposition of women to the more involved work/career patterns. As has been shown, the attitudes of the social circle are also important. Though beyond the scope of this chapter to demonstrate, it is also suggested – and clearly implied in the findings of other parts of the study – that the attitudes of work-mates, bosses and others in the occupational situation are also important. The general point is that highly qualified women, particularly those in the family stage of child rearing, have a particular susceptibility to the attitudes of those in their important social environment. This is not only a matter of support – though overall it is the supportive attitudes that make the most difference. Where there is less support – as with the career-non-integrated husbands, or in the marital relationships that are less than 'very happy – the women are thrown more on to their own resources, and it is primarily those with the warm early familial background who are able to re-adapt with their own occupational careers in the face of a disappointing family situation. The adaptations of the more 'tense' wives who remain in the marital situation that is not 'very happy' tend more frequently to be domestic rather than occupational – though of course many do seek occupational compensation often of a reluctant worker, non-career type.

REFERENCES

Altus, William D., 'Birth Order and Academic Primogeniture', *Journal of Personality and Social Psychology*, 2(6), 872-6, 1965.

Bailyn, Lotte, Unpublished memo, 1969.

Banducci, R., 'The Effect of Mother's Employment on the Achievement, Aspirations and Expectations of the Child', *Personnel and Guidance Journal*, 46(3), 263-7, 1967.

Bradley, Richard W., and Sanborn, Marshall P., 'Ordinal Position of High School Students Identified by Their Teachers as Superior', *Journal of Educational Psychology*, 60(1), 41-5, 1969.

Carlsmith, K. G. Kuckenburg, 'Effect of Early Father Absence in Scholastic Aptitude', *Harvard Educational Review*, 34, pp. 3-21, 1964.

Jackson, Brian, *Working Class Community*, London: Routledge and Kegan Paul, 1968.

Kanmeyer, Kenneth, 'Birth Order and the Feminine Sex Role Among College Women', *American Sociological Review*, 31(4), 504-16, 1966.

Kanmeyer, Kenneth, 'Sibling Position and the Feminine Role', *Journal of Marriage and the Family*, 29(3), 494-9, 1967.

McArthur, Charles, 'Personalities of First and Second Children', *Psychiatry*, 19, 47-54, 1956.

Price, John, 'Personality Differences Within Families: Comparison of Adult Brothers and Sisters', *Journal of Bio-Social Science*, Vol. 1, 177-205, 1969.

Rossi, Alice, 'Social and Psychological Origins of Family Role Expectations', unpublished chapter draft, 1968.

Sampson, E. E., 'The Study of Ordinal Position: Antecedents and Outcomes', in *Progress in Experimental Personality Research*, (ed. B. A. Maher), Academic Press, New York, 1965.

Smelser, William T., and Stewart, Louis H., 'Where are the Siblings? A Re-Evaluation of the Relationship Between Birth Order and College Attendance', *Sociometry*, 31(3), 294-303, 1968.

Warren, Jonathan R., 'Birth Order and Social Behaviour', *Psychological Bulletin*, 65(1), 38-49, 1966.

Young, Michael and Willmott, Peter, *Family and Kinship in East London*: Routledge & Kegan Paul, 1957.

Chapter IX

The Reconciliation of Work and Family Life:
The Dual-Career Family

Given the fact that women are working more in addition to (rather than instead of) getting married and having a family, the issue of reconciling work and family life becomes increasingly acute. Participation by women in responsible jobs in contemporary society requires an organization of effort, and commitment to work that can be characterized as a 'career-orientation', rather than an orientation that allows for working without expectations of development and/or advancement. The probability of a career-orientation as distinct from other orientations to work and to family life is higher for a population of graduate women than for one that is randomly selected, although even here, as already indicated, there is a range of orientations among both women and men. In addition, it is expected that most of the patterns and processes that have been found for graduate women hold as well for a wide range of highly qualified women as they attempt to reconcile work and family life.

Among the different types of families, there is one which is characterized by both the woman and the man having a high degree of commitment and aspiration in the world of work: both seek to exercise their competences as fully as possible in their occupations and to perform highly productive or responsible jobs. Such a family we term the 'dual-career family', in contrast to the conventional pattern where the husband is the breadwinner and the wife is the mother-housewife.

The concept of the dual-career family does not necessarily require that both members work full-time. Depending on their situation and the nature of their occupations, the amount of paid work put in at any given time may vary. The crucial element in distinguishing the dual-career family from other forms of family structure is the high commitment of both husband and wife to work on an egalitarian basis and a life-plan which involves a relatively full participation and advancement in work.

There has been a definite change in the recent history of women's increased participation in work. In the previous traditional situation the model pattern was for the woman to be committed to the housewife role while her husband filled the provider role. The more recent trend is for many women to work before having children and then to drop out and re-enter at a later date, perhaps on a part-time basis, increasing perhaps to more full-time participation after the children are grown.

There is now a bi-modal pattern in which women (even those who are highly qualified) differentiate into those who choose the conventional pattern as a stable one (using their education within the family and for social and community affairs) and those who choose to return to work once they have discharged their family obligations. Indeed, the position of Myrdal and Klein has supported the development of this second mode, arguing that the dilemmas of women's 'two roles' could best be resolved by scheduling – concentrating first on one and then on the other (Myrdal and Klein, 1956). More recently a persuasive study has emerged which argues that highly qualified women prefer less than full-time work on their re-entry (Williams, 1969). This study regards the dropping-out situation as 'axiomatic' for women, though it finds in its unsystematic sample that over a third of the women return after only a brief maternity leave. In keeping with the book's overall emphasis, it stresses the possibility that some of these are 'reluctant' returners: 'Their comments made it clear that in many cases this was imposed by a fear of losing touch rather than choice' (p. 24).

Without discussing the deficiences of the conclusions of this study from a scientific point of view (How many cases? Why is the wish to keep in touch not a choice? Do not men as well as women experience this fear of being away – e.g. on a training programme, etc.?), the general attitude does represent a widely prevalent viewpoint which is accommodating to the contemporary situation.

There are, then, three basic patterns: the conventional homemaker (who may work initially if highly qualified but who intends, once she drops out for marriage or childbirth, to stay out indefinitely); the non-continuous worker (who is 'in, out and in again'; this type of woman expects and usually wants to stay out for a substantial period during the early child-rearing years and then to re-enter part or full-time employment); and the 'continuous-in worker' (where withdrawal is minimal and participation in work is full or part time).

VARIATIONS IN PATTERNING OF WORK-FAMILY RELATIONSHIPS

The pattern which has been traditional in our society since the Industrial Revolution and earlier is neither universal nor inevitable. While, as D'Andrade finds in cross-cultural analysis, men have tended everywhere and always to be concerned with warfare and women with infant nurturance, this is not absolutely inevitable. The legendary Amazons aside, one finds among some of the 'developing' countries such phenomena as women paratroopers and, in the most highly civilized societies, men child welfare officers. In some societies women have held the chief responsibility for finance in the family, as in the markets of some African and South American countries. In some societies it is the women who do the arduous physical labour, for example the farming among the Alorese; indeed, where the couvade is practised, women are found returning to their work in the fields immediately following childbirth while the men take to their hammocks to protect the newborn infant from evil spirits (D'Andrade 1967).

The degree to which the separation of work and family life has been emphasized in our own society owes something to the Protestant Ethic and the capitalist form of organization of industry, though there are deep roots in the whole Judaeo-Christian-Islamic tradition that emphasize the women's place in the shelter of the home. The Industrial Revolution and the rise of capitalism brought about a 'rationalization' of the workplace through the separation of the fiscal affairs of the enterprise from those of the family – allowing entrepreneurs to employ the most competent help independently of familial obligations so as to be better able to compete on the open market (Weber, 1947 and Smelser, 1959). Secondarily, humane tendencies were operating to protect women from the odious conditions of work that sometimes prevailed in the earlier industrial situations. As a consequence of this, a sharp division has resulted between the domestic side of life, which is under the guardianship of women, and the workplace, which is under the control of men who funnel the economic benefits of productive industry into the household. As the household shed its productive functions and became a unit of consumption, the economic dependence of the women on their men became increasingly marked. Women's participation in work at these earlier stages reflected deficiencies in the male role in the family – as with widows, spinsters, divorcees, etc. More recently there are new trends at work associated with increased education and universal education for both sexes.

While the world as a whole has been moving towards a conception of family life which, in most cases, tends to produce something like the Western nuclear family, the situation in the Western countries is one of differentiation (Goode, 1963). As the nature of work changes and as men and women are exposed more equally to educational influences – with their value and skill components – a range of patterns emerges within the basic framework of the nuclear family. Women are beginning to articulate with the world of work as effectively as men – with the differences increasingly being due to differences in individual competence rather than to sex-linked stereo-typed conceptions of work capacity. With women's jobs ranging as variously as men's, an enormous spectrum of possible combinations is coming into being. Husband and wife may work together or separately; they may work at similar or different kinds of jobs; they may be commensurate or incommensurate in their earnings or fame or power; they may be similar or different in relation to the importance of work to them as individuals. Similarly, family considerations and participation may vary greatly for different men and women.

THE PLACE OF THE DUAL-CAREER FAMILY

The dual-career family is a statistically minor variant. A recent survey of all English working women shows that even among the most highly qualified women there is a strong tendency to drop out of work at the time of having the first baby and not to return until many years later (Hunt, 1969). Where the return is successfully negotiated, this becomes the 'in-out-in' pattern referred to above. The length of the 'out' period varies greatly according to the size of the family and the environmental circumstances of the individual woman – as well as her personal level of ambition and her husband's attitudes, etc. The analyses presented above indicate how some of these variables operate in a sample of university graduates. Our reason for concentrating in this chapter on the small minority of 'dual-career' families, in which the woman maintains the involvement fairly continuously, is that it is disproportionately from within this group that the women with senior accomplishments and responsibilities are found. To the extent that this becomes a more important pattern in future, the small group now demonstrating this pattern may be thought of as 'pioneers', or as a 'creative minority'. These are not pioneers in the sense used earlier in describing women and their careers – of breaking new ground in professions previously closed to women. That battle has been nearly successfully concluded – or at least its end is in sight. Today's pioneers are the men and women who work out new patterns of relationships between work and family that

337

will facilitate the wife's pursuit of an effective career if she wants this.

As the analyses in previous chapters have indicated, the life career of a highly qualified woman may be defined in critical path terms with various options available at different points. The life career as a whole, as indicated in Chapter V, is punctuated by critical transitions. Traversing them in a given way constitutes a career pathway. Regarding specifically the work-family aspects of the pathway, the following diagram presents a simplified version of some major options.[1]

Figure IX.1

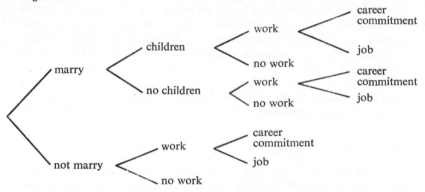

Underlying each choice of option is a motivational syndrome. One marries or does not marry according to one's motivation and circumstances. Our data provide much suggestive material about the single people (both men and women) that indicates the nature of some of these motivational syndromes. The same is true of the decision to have children. The culturally normal and statistically normal situation is to marry and have children, but important variant patterns exist. Similarly, the culturally normative pattern is for the man only to work, particularly in the period of early child-rearing. But here, as in the other variant patterns, important variations are seen and are becoming more prevalent. Indeed, it is one of our basic observations that in periods of social change, it is from among the variant patterns that the most creative innovations may be found. In relation to women's careers, the dual-career family pattern is in this category.

Aside from the motivational syndromes influencing the acceptance of some options and not others, consideration must be given to the consequences of having embarked on a given pathway, in terms of the satisfactions experienced by the person in the pattern. Thus, the

[1] See also Rossi (1968) on 'role-cycling' phenomena.

person who decides to marry, have children and not work may either be a satisfied conventional housewife, or a dissatisfied 'captive housewife' (Gavron, 1966). Similarly, not all the workers are happy in this situation. Two major orientations to work are contrasted – the 'career orientation', where work is highly important to the person and an organized developmental job sequence is sought, and the 'job-orientation' where work is engaged in for other reasons and without an organized sequence. The person who married and has children but who works out of economic necessity (e.g. with an improvident husband) may be a reluctant worker, the one who works out of boredom to fill in time may be a low commitment worker, and so on. This does not mean that the high aspiring and highly committed married women careerist – classic partner in the dual-career family – is necessarily happy and satisfied. However, the tendency where such a pattern exists is for the drive in this direction to be relatively high – given the obstacles and stresses that must be overcome. Consequently, even if the individual concerned is not willing to characterize herself as 'satisfied', it would seem from our qualitative information safe to say that she would be highly dissatisfied if she were not able to carry out her career commitment.

THE DUAL-CAREER FAMILIES IN THE STUDY

Intensive studies were made of the life careers, family backgrounds, marital relationships and patterns of working of 13 fully functioning dual-career families from a range of occupations. In addition, three families were studied in which the women, though highly qualified and formerly on the way to success in their professions, had decided to stop working for an indefinite period. This 'dropping out' is a matter of degree; some 'drop outs' in fact maintain a partial practice of their profession, some intend to return at a later date, others do not. The methods used for data collection include interviews with the couples and, wherever possible, with others who knew them, and the development of a collaborative relationship with the couples in which they contributed directly to the writing up of the research reports.

The women in the dual-career families were in the following occupations:

5 Architects:
    one in partnership with her husband
    one in separate practice (though married to an architect)
    one, also married to an architect, employed by the Civil Service
    two who have temporarily stopped working

2 Entrepreneurs:
   one operating an employment agency
   one operating a clothes designing firm working closely with
   manufacturers
3 Industrial Managers:
   each from a major firm oriented to the market
4 Civil Servants:
   all Administrative Class, comprising: three assistant secretaries
   one, a principal, who had temporarily stopped working
2 Television professionals

The criteria for inclusion in the sample were: being married; living with spouses who were themselves earning at a high level; having at least one child; and being considered by her organization as at, or on their way to high-level jobs.

The reason for including the criterion that husbands should be successful in their own right was to exclude economic necessity as a primary motivation for work on the part of the women. The five architects were all married to architects; the two business enterpreneurs were married to businessmen; the three industrial managers were also married to businessmen, two in other large firms and one in his own small business; of the four Civil Servants, three were married to other Civil Servants of the same or higher rank, and one was married to a non-Civil Service Administrator; of the two television professionals, one was married to a professional person outside television and the other to another television professional.

All the families had at least one child still residing in the family home, but the age range was very wide with two of the families giving birth during the period of the study (one a functioning dual-career family who had a prior child; the other a 'drop-out' having her first child just prior to being interviewed). The other end of the range included adolescents of differing ages.

An overall picture of these couples can be obtained from the following general description of their family backgrounds and current attitudes:

These are families in which both husbands and wives value the possibility of the women continuing in their careers. They feel that various arrangements should be made, or at least the options provided, to facilitate this. The reasons for this kind of view tend to be multiple. Some men profess strong egalitarian values. Others, who are away from home frequently, prefer to know that their wives are feeling happy and fulfilled by working rather than being pent-up and lonely at home. Others like to share the financial burden and the higher level of income that this makes available to the family. Still others like to work with their wives, or at least to interact with them over work issues. They enjoy sharing the elements both of their domestic lives and of their intellectual or professional lives. The motivational syndromes underlying these attitudes are discussed in greater detail below.

The husband-wife relationship in the fully functioning dual-career families tends to be egalitarian, with a good deal of mutual accommodation. While there is wide variation in styles of relating, degree of closeness, volatility, tension and so on, the common factor to all the couples is that neither of the partners considers the relationship in a hierarchical framework – husband as the 'lord and master', and wife as chattel, to caricature the conventional attitude. This is a general trend in contemporary society and the dual-career families are not much distinguished from others in this respect.

The support provided for one another by the dual-career couple should not be idealized. There are many stresses and strains involved, ambivalence and undercutting, conflicts and so on. These are described in the next section. However, it should be stated at the outset that the balance in the families studied was positive; the benefits were perceived as outweighing the costs. Dual-career families that had broken up were not studied. Only families with an intact marriage as well as two careers were selected. No information is available about the relative incidence of broken homes among dual-career families and other kinds of families.

The overwhelming tendency – though not the universal feature – in these families is that both husband and wife value family life and children as well as involvement in careers. On the whole these people are very busy. They have to cut down, for the most part, on their formal leisure and community participation activities. These have to take place at weekends, and tend to be organized around household and children though, to different extents, friends and relatives play a part.

One of the striking features about child-rearing practices in the families studied is the degree to which the children are brought into their parents' lives and participate in many of the interests and concerns of the parents, becoming part of the egalitarian ethos of the families.

ANALYSIS OF IMPORTANT DIMENSIONS IN THE LIVES OF THE DUAL-CAREER FAMILY

In analysing the ways in which the dual-career family 'works', i.e. how the couples have managed to accomplish what is for them a pattern of life consistent with their egalitarian ideals, various approaches could be used. The three approaches taken here reflect the concerns of the couples studied; they are also important in the analysis of trends of social change that are central to this study. The three dimensions discussed are:

a dilemmas confronted by the couples: the strains imposed by these dilemmas and how the couples manage them.

b motivational syndromes: the types of motives that seem to underlie a woman's desire to work and the likelihood of her husband making it possible or allowing it in the context of a continuing marital relationship.

c viability factors: the elements in the situation other than personal motives which make it possible for a woman to have a career and at the same time to reconcile it with family life – such factors as possibilities for organizing time schedules, making job demands flexible, and finding helpers or facilitators to enable the woman to involve herself in her career in spite of her handicaps (seen in terms both of stereotyped prejudices and of competing family demands).

a *Dilemmas confronted by the couples*

There are many dilemmas that might be abstracted from the data. Indeed, it is obvious that in the lives of complex people living in complex metropolitan society, life is continually punctuated with dilemmas. However, five areas of dilemma are selected which seem to represent foci around which many of the important sources of strain cohere. These are not exhaustive but they cover a good deal of the ground, at least as experienced by the couples studied. The five foci are;

I. Dilemmas arising from sheer 'overload'.
II. Dilemmas arising from experiencing in one's important environment strongly conflicting ideas and directions about what is considered right and proper in a given area of behaviour.
III. Dilemmas arising from conflicts within oneself about whether one is being a good person (good human being, good wife and mother, good woman) in leading a certain type of existence.
IV. Dilemmas arising from conflicts in obligations, attachments, desires, and so on relative to one's network of relatives, friends and associates.
V. Dilemmas arising from the conflicts between roles that may be variable in their demands at different times – e.g. the marital role demands in relation to the work demands of each partner at different points in the life cycle.

342

1. Overload dilemmas

'It always seems to me as far as our own situation is concerned, that it is tremendously dependent on good health; this husband and wife team, and the survival of the pair with individual work potential, is almost entirely an energy thing. It may be that a lot of the fall-out (i.e. women dropping out) is actually physical . . . you do run out of steam. We know two couples – one of the children's teachers, both husband and wife teach and the children are about the same age as ours. It's extraordinary the energy pull of that family. I'm always amazed how they survive until the holidays. You can actually see them physically diminishing as the term runs on because it is so physically taxing.'

The old folk expression 'behind every successful man there is a woman' stands not only for a social psychological situation where the wife gives emotional support and advice, but also for a whole culture complex of activities and relationships within which the wife is a helpmeet – attending to the shopping, child rearing, housekeeping and general social tasks necessary to provide a smoothly operating base to which the male can retreat after the rigours of a day's work and from which he can sally forth refreshed and emotionally supported. One of the couples studied began the interview by reversing the expression, stating that 'behind every successful woman there is a man'. What they meant by this, however, was that the man encouraged his wife to face and cope with problems arising in her work, provided consultation on financial matters and co-operated in various ways. They did *not* mean to indicate that the husband gave the same sort of backing – through shopping, mending, cooking, child minding and so on that would be the obverse of the traditional picture. When only the man is following a career, it is usual for his wife to provide the domestic 'back up', but in a dual-career family there is not usually a total reversal of the traditional roles (though role reversals do exist). The most usual situation among the study couples where both husband and wife pursue careers is a rearrangement of the domestic side of their lives. Some of the household tasks are delegated to others and the remainder is reapportioned between husband, wife and children. In effect, each member of the couple both pursues a career and performs some household and child rearing activities. Among the couples studied, the overload experienced seems to have been a function of at least four factors.

a The degree to which having children and a family (as distinct from simply being married) *is salient*. With the exception of one of

343

the couples studied, family life in general and rearing children in particular was highly salient. The couples were very concerned with the possible effects on their children of their both pursuing careers. This implied a limitation in the degree to which the couples were willing to delegate child care, even assuming the availability of satisfactory resources. Aside from the sheer number of things to be done by the conjugal pair who are both working and who, at the same time, value and enjoy interaction with their families, there is an element of psychic strain involved in allowing two major areas of life, so different in their demands and characteristics, to be highly important. The overload involved here, then, is not a simply arithmetical increase in the number of tasks to be accomplished, but is related to the duality of emotional commitment and concern, and is thus far more difficult to assess.

b *The degree to which the couple aspire to a high standard* of domestic living. Most of the couples aspired to a high standard of living, including a pleasant home and garden and high standards of decor, cleanliness, cooking and so on. This made the problem of managing the domestic side of their lives more complex, albeit by choice, than if they had kept to a lower standard. The notion of a lower maternal standard, though, is almost a contradiction in terms of the notion of career success, since a certain standard of life is implied in occupational achievement. The process in fact tends to become circular in that once a taste for high standards has been acquired, the impetus to continue working and career development is increased.

c *The degree to which satisfactory arrangements for the re-apportionment of tasks is possible.* Here we found various combinations of conjugal role reorganizations and delegations of parts of the domestic work to children and helpers of various kinds.

d *The degree to which the sheer physical overload of tasks and their apportionment is adumbrated by a social-psychological overload* which comes from struggling with the conflicts that are described in the issues that follow: normative conflict, sex role identity maintenance, network management and role-cycling. Couples vary enormously in the degree to which these other sources of tensions feed into the family system and the degree to which they can manage them once they are present.

For all the couples the overload issue was salient; they all emphasized the importance of physical health and energy as a prerequisite for making the dual career family a possibility. They regarded it as important for their children to be healthy too. Generally speaking there was little room for illness in the systems that were evolved. For example, Mr Y says:

'I don't think that we're particularly fit or anything, but we're never ill in any serious sense, and I think that we attach more importance to that one fact for our survival capacity than anything else'.

To help them to deal with the overload issues, all of the dual-career families studied spent much thought and effort on arranging a system of domestic help. This problem can be seen as having two sides: the availability of different kinds of domestic helpers on the one hand and the preferences of the couples as to which elements of the domestic roles they wish to delegate.

Our survey indicates that, at a point seen after graduation, domestic role tasks become differentiated into different types. Graduate women become aware that they would like to delegate the activities which are impersonal: washing, cleaning, ironing, etc. – tasks which can absorb a great deal of time, particularly in households with a high standard of living. They tend to wish to retain the more people-oriented activities, particularly in relation to child-care and feeding. Among the couples studied intensively, the delegation of the less desirable aspects of domestic labour was both the expected and the observed tendency. Given the low value placed on domestic work as an occupation in our society, the dual-career couples have all had to devote considerable energy to improvising viable arrangements. A wide range of types of domestic help arrangements are found: short-term and long-term; full-time and part-time; live-in and live-out; nannies, *au pairs*, dailies, students, secretaries-doubling-as-baby-sitters, domestic help couples where husband and wife divide up the domestic part of the employing couples' household affairs, unmarried mothers and their babies taking over part of the premises, and so on. Most of the couples used at least a duplex system; often they would shift from one type of system to another following a major transition like having a child, having the last child enter school, etc. Sometimes the shift was associated with a difficult experience with the previous system; sometimes it was based on the couple's conception of a better arrangement for a particular stage, e.g. the dropping of a nannie and the taking on of an *au pair* instead as the infant reaches school age. Simple as the tasks of household maintenance may be, the difficulties involved in obtaining reliable personnel to whom they may be delegated are so great in contemporary British and American society that all sorts of perquisites are called for. In the couples studied, domestic helpers were not only offered the usual salary and private room arrangements (often with separate TV) but in addition were sometimes given the use of one of the family cars and, in one case, a specially built flat.

Not everyone had the same idea of what was most desirable in a domestic helper but one view was that some helpers made minimal demands and knew 'instinctively' what was wanted in the situation:

Mrs S indicates this about the first helper she had when her first child was born:

'I seemed to be able to surmount that hurdle quite easily. . . . I happened to have a very delightful nurse with me who . . . was so complementary to me that she became a pillar in the household. She was a most wonderful, modest, intelligent and superior being. . . . I had such utter confidence that she knew much more than I did about babies because she was an experienced baby-nurse. . . . When I asked her to watch how I fed the baby, she did it, only twice as good, and so I found myself in good hands . . . it was superb. She was very efficient, intelligent, delightful . . . a great help and a calming influence. . . .'

Mr Y indicates this about one of their previous dailies:

'The woman always knew what to do – she had proper natural housewife's instincts . . . just fantastic, . . . the one or two things we asked her to do were marvellous. We never had to say 'will you do this or that'. She knew the proper cycle of cleaning. It didn't have to be written down.'

The operation of an overlapping or duplex system was often aimed at avoiding crises in domestic help. Mrs O took in an *au pair* as well as a nanny because if nanny was ill, Mrs O had to stay home for the day. The Ys used a combination of secretary (working in their office at home), daily, and live-in student help (though they preferred not to have too much interaction with a living-in person, particularly after work). They regarded the overlaps as important because otherwise there was 'this terrible emotional insecurity'. The students tended not to be blindingly useful, and they have their own students' problems, and the dailies may not be good with the children. To increase reliability, they were considering shifting to a system of 'two household helps because paying a bit extra most of the time might save us when the crunch comes'.

Few of the couples studied used their parents in a major way, though many used them occasionally to look after children while they were away, say for a conference or a long weekend. The Ts had most contact with their respective families and Mr T said:

'We are lucky in having two sets of grandparents living within easy reach – 3 miles up the road one way and 2 miles up the road the other way . . . this sort of family set-up is another of the things that makes our mode of existence possible. . . . About 10 years ago we thought of going out of London to live but ruled it out. Although there were all sorts of things which led to this decision, one thing was the contact with the parents.'

The Ts have six children, and over weekends, one or another child may go off to one or other set of grandparents. During the holidays:

'Although the children are not parked on their grandparents, every other day they go up to Hampstead . . . or my mother comes to take them out or something. This is a variation – an incident in the holidays, as it were, that is largely provided by their grandparents.'

As indicated above, child care presents special problems. While most of our couples valued interaction with their children and felt that their children's welfare and development was of primary importance, they had to delegate at least part of the child-care to pursue their careers.

Most families made deliberate arrangements within their job framework to set aside time to see their children and to participate in activities with them – perhaps more deliberately than in families with a more ordinary work structure. For example, Mrs N tries to arrange her work schedule to allow flexibility at points when children's demands may be high, so that she could meet them where possible:

'Most of one's time one isn't in a meeting, one is pretty free and this is a great advantage. . . . Most meetings I do go to are meetings where I have some important information to get so I can't miss them. If the children have a concert . . . then I can keep this date free. . . . I put school engagements into my diary to keep them free and I take half a day's leave. . . .'

Mr Y indicated how the degree of involvement with their children that they favoured had effected the development of their work careers.

'In a general way our children are very mixed up in our lives to an extent that you'd hardly believe. . . . They are in and out of the office, or in and out of other people's offices. I don't know why, but we are either not good at it or we worry too much about leaving them with strangers, and so on, therefore they tend to be just around. Sometimes it's extremely embarrassing . . . it's conditioned the kind of work we can accept and the sort of organization we have built . . . you have to accept the work and build the organizations in which this behaviour is tolerated.'

Precisely because the children were so important to the couples, the issue of how to arrange child care contributed heavily to the overload picture for these couples. As many of them put it, if the house got dirty it was unfortunate but could be ultimately remedied and anyway was not crucial. However, serious lapses in relation to the children's care simply could not be allowed to occur. Most of the families were aware of and concerned with modern conceptions of child development and the importance of parental involvement in it. As one couple put it: 'We are all victims of our culture in this Spockean age' (i.e., this child-centred age). While compromises could and often were made in the domestic care areas, none of the couples was willing self-consciously to adopt a policy which would have meant possible harm to their children's physical or psychological development. It was not possible within the scope of the study to assess the effects on their children of the child-rearing practices of the dual-career couples. However, from the detailed interviews it was striking how low the level of reported disturbance appeared to be. While the couples were quite aware of potential negative effects they also pointed to some of the positive effects of their pattern of life. Thus, their pattern was seen as possibly fostering independence; getting children to help with household chores was seen as fostering the growth of responsibility; redistributing domestic role allocations resulted in fathers spending more time with their children; providing a student companion for the children was seen as useful in giving them someone to 'talk nonsense' with – something enjoyable to the children when their parents were away or preoccupied with work tasks, and so on. Most of the families interviewed had read or heard about the relevant research work and were concerned with the issue of whether or not a mother working would constitute for the child a potentially harmful situation of 'maternal deprivation'.

Most of the couples tried to take precautions against placing complete reliance on any one helping figure and they tended to monitor very carefully the interaction between children and domestic helpers. One mother describes the degree to which she had to rely on help and how distasteful it was to a strong and independent minded person to have to be made to feel dependent in this way as follows:

'I had no one, so I had to go from hand to mouth. I never knew, in fact, when I could make appointments ahead. It was such a strain that I got not ill but terribly upset, unable to cope, you know, and I put a high value on being able to cope.'

The vulnerability of the woman, in particular, to malfunctioning in the domestic help area is expressed by Mrs Y: she indicated that even when they are working or travelling, there is a 'little corner of my mind somewhere that is thinking and worrying about the management of the children'. Mr Y, in contrast, reserves the comparable 'little corners' in the back of his mind for forward planning of their work and the family's finances. The general tendency among the couples studied was to place high value on having children and developing a close relationship with them. Even in the rare instances where children were sent to boarding school, the reason for doing so (with one possible exception) was not to unload the care of the children on to an institution but rather because of tradition (father and grandfather had gone to that school) or the child's own wishes.

In general most of the couples interviewed were of the opinion that the main consequences of their both working was that there was 'very little slack left in the system'. Several indicated that they were both 'whacked' by the time they got home and that they had very little energy left over for extra activities particularly on week-nights. The following quotations indicate the kinds of expression used: A husband: 'After a hard day in the office she is sometimes very spiky in the evening. . . .'

A wife, speaking of their situation where her husband's job keeps him out during the day as a producer and her job keeps her out during the evening as a performer (talking of shared leisure).

'It's something that strongly has to struggle for existence, really. It's a matter of a night off every now and then and a weekend that we try and organize every few weeks to try and keep something apart from our work. . . . We'd like to have more time off when we can see one another, but what happens is that when I'm off he might be on and it creates tensions. . . .'

While leisure activities tend to disappear first under the impact of overload, the repercussions may spill over into the work lives of one or both of the partners, and couples vary in the degree to which they protect these activities, as a higher priority than other areas like activities with the children. Mr S. illustrates part of this pattern of spill-over into work. In discussing how he concerns himself with his wife's business problems, he says:

'One takes up time during the day thinking over these problems instead of perhaps dining with someone one ought to dine with for one's own business career . . . or, one comes home to have a quiet evening and one can't because the wife is really worn out and exhausted and can't cope with it . . . one has to commiserate and work out a problem. . . .'

349

Thus, the overload issues seem to arise acutely as a stress when both members pursue careers. The strains are felt first in relation to leisure and recreation activities which are often sacrificed very early and second, either in relation to the children and the degree and quality of relationships with them or in relation to one's work. Characteristic patterns of coping with these strains are:

(i) Deliberately to 'work' at leisure – to discipline oneself to take holidays, weekends in the country to 'unwind', frequent trips away, etc. To conserve health and energy deliberately as a human resource. Thus, the Ys, for example, have a country cottage and they:

'Generally go down there every third weekend for a minimum period of three days. . . . In children's holidays we sometimes go for longer. . . . When we're here in town we work pretty solidly . . . if you're here and the work is here, you turn to work; if I go away, I never work except just reading. . . . They the children will miss a day of school but we regard it as therapeutic. They are also very healthy, partly we think that this getting them away from London contributes to keeping them healthy.'

(ii) To delegate as much as possible of the less desired chores. Mrs V describes the delegation of some of the domestic chores, as follows:

'The girl keeps it all running, all the trivia that a housewife would do when she wasn't spring-cleaning, she manages to cope with. She does the shopping – that's how she learns her English. She'll do the cooking, but if I am here I will do that myself at midday. She does all the washing of the children's clothes, and the ironing, bits of mending, taking phone calls when I am not here – general things about the house which it is difficult to catalogue really.'

For most couples the purpose of delegating the routine chores is to leave the mother and father free for providing affectional relationships for their children without having to waste what is left of their energy on domestic chores. In some instances, where the parents recognize that they do not provide the most nurturant atmosphere for the children, they delegate this aspect as well, in the interests of the children's best developmental influences. Mrs Z illustrates this in describing her domestic helper:

'For the past 10 years we have had an Irish housekeeper who manages the household with the help of an *au pair*. The housekeeper is very warm and motherly, and the children get a lot of consistent love and affection from her, though there is no question about who is the mother.'

Strategies to provide the child with the best possible environments at home, school and so on, consume major proportions of the time of the couples studied. Some of this is described in greater detail below under 'dilemmas of personal norms'.

(iii) To modify one's work involvements in such a way as to make them compatible with the other partner's and to diminish the strain of 'over-spill', e.g. from an excessively complicated, demanding or otherwise difficult work situation. Travelling, for example, or getting too deeply involved with complex relationships at work is likely to impinge more on the other's capacity to function at work. Thus, most of the couples made choices that attempted to avoid unnecessary involvements of this kind so as to optimize participation of both partners in work and family spheres. Some of this is described in detail below under conflicts and role-cycling. An example of some of the adaptation required is given for couple T.

Mrs T was prepared to take on a larger share of the housework than usual to enable her husband to take on the presidency of a professional organization:

> 'The work fit at the moment is a bit of a mystery. There are not enough hours in the day to get the right balance, and the balance at the moment is shifted from me away from home, which in turn makes things tougher than they inherently are for my wife. I saw this coming three or four years ago and said, shall I let myself stand for the vice-presidency because it's going to mean a terrible sweat in three years' time, things going the normal way. Knowing myself what it meant and she not knowing what it meant, said yes. . . . I think she thinks it is worthwhile, not just my entertainment as it were, but something on the whole worth doing, and both of us have had to bend things around to make it work a bit.'

Mr T accepts a reasonable limitation on his career, namely the fact that Mrs T prefers to stay in London, because there are more jobs in London and therefore a wider range of jobs available to her. If he moves there must be a job available for her. On another occasion when Mr T had the opportunity to move up to Edinburgh, his wife did not want to go and so they did not move.

II. Dilemmas arising from the discrepancy between personal and social norms

The women in the intensive case study reported here have found ways to continue their careers even after childbirth, stopping work only for a minimal period which did not interfere with their career development. In doing so they have had to deal with dilemmas. Arising from the clash between their personal norms (i.e., what they felt was right and proper behaviour for themselves) and social norms (i.e. the norms they felt that people around them held (Bott, 1957).

These dilemmas arise, as indicated above, because of the fact that most women, even the most highly qualified, tend to drop their careers to fulfil traditional domestic roles even if this is accompanied by personal frustration (Gavron, 1966). It is accepted by the majority of people in our society as the right and proper thing to do, and is supported from childhood by a pervasive set of cultural symbols and manifestations: for example, the importance attributed to 'mothering' (assumed to be always by the biological mother except in abnormal cases), the sanctity of the home and the housewife role, etc. The men and women in our study have deliberately adopted a varient pattern, which reflects their assumption that men and women have similarly valuable potentials and are equally able to realise them in work. For various reasons and under various circumstances they arrive at this pattern and the dilemma for them becomes resolved and dormant.

Some circumstances, however, reactivate the dilemmas, causing the variant norms to collide with the more traditional norms, and thus require a fresh solution. Three examples of such circumstances are:

(a) critical transition points in the family life cycle (particularly birth of the first child);
(b) critical transition points in the career (or occupation) life cycle of *either* partner (role enlargement or contraction); and
(c) critical events in the life space of the children (e.g., illness, school problems, etc.)

One particular critical point in the family life cycle that reactivates these dilemmas is the birth of the first child. For example, when Mrs O's baby was born, she had to overcome the feeling of distress when 'well-meaning' neighbours who had got to know her better while she was at home during the final phase of pregnancy and expected her to remain at home following the birth of the baby made such remarks as: 'Oh well, I suppose you won't mind when your baby doesn't recognise you as its mother'. It took her some time to overcome the heightening of the conflict aroused by such remarks before she resumed her preferred pattern of pursuing both career and family interests.

These remarks are manifestations of a larger set of cultural norms related to child-rearing practices. Most of the couples who were studied experienced pressure from these norms. Mrs O, a Civil Servant, with a good social science degree, sums up how she resolved her dilemma as follows:

'When I first went back to work (after having the baby) there were women who quoted (a noted child-psychiatrist) to me, you know. I got so fed up with this man. I got all his books out before I went back permanently. Really it made me feel a criminal. . . . I really came to the conclusion that he was taking for his children those who had been in institutions on the one hand and comparing them with the kind of children who were in an ordinary mother's care . . . and it seemed to me to be such a long way off from what I was going to do. . . . I think a lot of mothers have gripped on to it to justify what they are doing. I went to see a number of friends of mine who have combined both and whose children are, in the main, older and who have turned out into well-adjusted, independent, happy, thoroughly normal sort of children who seem to have a perfectly normal relationship with their parents, as far as one could judge. I was a bit unconvinced.'

An example of how a critical transition in the occupational situation can reactivate these dilemmas is seen with the S's. Mrs S, a clothing designer, discussed how she had been thrown into conflict (which immediately became a family conflict) when an offer was received from a large fashion group of companies to take over her firm and promote her products in a really 'big way'. Mrs S says that this conflict was exacerbated by its timing, coming at a period of life (age about 40) when she was in any case reviewing her personal norms and values (Jaques, 1965).

Mrs S describes how the pros and cons of her continuing to work weigh up in relation to the effects on her children and their attitudes:

'Well I think I am much more prone to look for things like that (i.e., negative effects on the children) because, you know, we are being bogged with an awful lot of literature, and an awful lot of people and an awful lot of things are said to provide more guilt feelings than are necessary. I have seen women who are at home from morning to night with problem children, where it obviously stems from within the child or from her own attitudes or from her own inhibitions or whatever, but not certainly from the fact that she has another life so to speak. In my case I would say there has been a lot of pride in my little girl – say for instance, "my mummy designed the new school uniform", she said to me the other day: "All the little new girls have come to me to show me their uniforms", and said "Isn't it your mummy who designed it?"

M

and I say "Yes", and I could see that there was a little bit of pride in her which obviously helps her; and it became part of life and I must say the periods where I have had excellent help – I was thinking of a trained nanny who lasted alas too short a time (because she had some romantic problem that made it necessary for her to leave here)–she was excellent for the children and at that time I was able to move mountains and I felt wonderful . . . the children were absolutely happy and I remember at that time – it was last year about this time – we had a show in which I asked my daughter and her friend to participate, you know, to come in and wear the little children's things, and the glowing enthusiasm, it was tremendous to have a mummy who was doing something, you know, it was lovely, and naturally this made up for an awful lot of "Oh mummy, I wish you were home".'

She felt that before she would realize it, the children would have grown up and left home. In attempting to resolve this dilemma, Mr and Mrs S each played the devil's advocate with the other. When Mr S was arguing in favour of maximizing familial values, he would say it was bad enough that the father could not spend more time at home with the children but to have mother away so much in addition was 'terrible'. Mrs S would counter this with how a more senior position would enable her to be more flexible with her work hours, have more assistance and how they would have more and better holidays and be able to remove financial worries about the children's future. Then when she took the position that she could stay home, spend more time with the children, pursue cultural interests and so on, Mr S would argue that it would be doing something to her which they would both regret later as she had so much invested in her career and derived so much satisfaction from it. They indicated that this was a period of 'brinkmanship' in which each pushed the other right up to the brink until they had worked their way through the feelings of both of them about a new resolution to the dilemma. The resolution finally adopted was one in which she agreed to the take-over but with a number of new perquisites allowing for more time with the family and contractual safeguards against her being drawn too deeply into the firm's business involvements.

There are several instances reported of events in the children's life space reactivating the dilemmas. This may occur around a major focused crisis – e.g. the child's disturbance or poor performance at school. More usually it is aroused by small occurrences. Most of the working mothers cite the feelings aroused when they see other mothers wheeling their prams in the park, e.g. while they are at the office, but they tend to put down these feelings relatively easily saying that probably many of these mothers would rather be going to work, or that they would soon be bored with doing only this every day. Occasionally, however, the dilemma is made more acute, e.g. when the child 'uses' the fact that the mother works for 'playing up' the mother's guilt (e.g. by saying that she prefers her granny's house, or the house of a non-working mum of a school friend). In continuing their work, most of these dual-career family mothers emphasized the positive elements of the situation and that their children by and large agreed (e.g. having a happier and more interesting mum, having a mum who is on TV, etc.).

III. Dilemmas of identity

This section concentrates on dilemmas arising within the person about fundamental characteristics of the self – whether one is a 'good' person, a 'good' man or woman and so on. This is at a deeper level and more internally generated than the conflicts arising over specific behavioural patterns, as in the discussion above on normative dilemmas. This set of dilemmas stems from the socio-cultural definitions of work and family as intrinsically masculine and feminine. The quintessence of masculinity is still, in our culture, centred on work and on competing successfully in the 'breadwinning' roles. The quintessence of femininity is still centred on the domestic scene. While there are some occupations which have come to be defined as acceptable for women – even preferable – such as nursing, primary school teaching and social work, these tend to be as temporary, part-time or for unmarried women. Conversely, where men enter these occupations it is probable that they encounter internal dilemmas of identity stemming from the same source of social stereotyping. In analysing the dilemmas observed in this area, it is important to note that these dilemmas are considered to be a product of the contemporary socio-cultural situation. They would be different under different circumstances or at different points in the social process.

With respect to the specifically sexual component of the identity dilemmas, i.e. whether the individual feels himself to be a 'good' or a 'real' man or woman, there seem to be at least three levels at which the issues are discussed in the literature: the physical, the psychological and the socio-cultural. Some observers seem to assume that confusion arising at one level will necessarily be reflected in confusions at other levels. Thus one colleague at the outset of the research indicated that men and women who cross sex lines socio-culturally (as have all of the women in the study to some extent by pursuing careers in preponderantly 'masculine' areas or levels) would be characterized by a psycho-biological confusion of sexual identity as well. The assumption here is that women who want to enter the male world of competition would be highly motivated by competitiveness with men and, as a consequence, would tend to emasculate their husbands. The assumption follows that these couples' sex lives would be characterized by impotence and frigidity. This was assumed to be enhanced by their tendency to choose mates with complementary needs.

While the study did not focus on the sex lives of the couples in detail, the data does seem to indicate that while these stereotyped conceptions may be present in some (doubtless the types of cases most seen in clinical practices), this is by no means the universal picture. The impression is one of a 'normal' range of sexual experience. This makes sense when consideration is given to the actual patterns of motivation that seem to be present among these people and also to their ways of coping with dilemmas and issues that arise in their relationships. Competitiveness with men may be a prominent motive among some of the women but it is only one of many that seem important. Most of these women are involved rather with issues relating to financial security; the need to be creative (in ways that are difficult for them if focused on the household); and the desire to be effective as an individual person. However, while autonomy is a prominent part – financial, psychological and otherwise – it is coupled with, rather than exclusive of, the wish to be interdependent with their husbands. The occupational world is used by all of the women studied as an area in which they develop their separate personal identities. This makes it possible for both husband and wife to relate as two individuals, *each* having a separate identity as a person. To the extent that each has a clear personal sexual identity associated with his physical make-up, the issues of physical relationships may even be enhanced. But it would take a more focused and detailed study to investigate this aspect.[1]

[1] Alice Rossi (1964, p. 648) in discussing the issue says:
'It goes beyond the intended scope of this essay to discuss the effects of a social pattern of equality between men and women upon their sexual relationship. A few words are, however, necessary, since the defenders of traditional sex roles often claim that full equality would so feminize men and masculinize women that satisfactory sexual adjustments would be impossible and homosexuality would probably increase. If the view of the sex act presupposes a dominant male actor and a passive female subject, then it is indeed the case that full sex equality would probably be the death knell of this traditional sexual relationship. Men and women who participate as equals in their parental and occupational and social roles will complement each other sexually in the same way, as essentially equal partners, and not as an ascendant male and a submissive female. This does not mean, however, that equality in non-sexual roles necessarily de-eroticizes the sexual one. The enlarged base of shared

What actually seems to happen in the case of the couples studied is that they are able to go a certain way towards establishing the ideal individual identities that they have formulated for themselves independently of socio-cultural definitions, but in each case indications of discomfort arise under specific circumstances. This is also true for the husbands who form part of the whole pattern. They seem to say in effect: 'This is as far as I can go in experimenting with a new definition of sex-roles without having it "spill over" into my own psychological sense of self-esteem and possibly my physical capacity to carry on in this relationship.' This represents a limit to which an individual's psychological defences are felt to be effective, and in each of the couples studied one or more of these limits seem to have evolved beyond which each knew it was dangerous to push the other. We have called these limits identity 'tension lines'.

Manifestations of identity tension lines are as follows:

In some families the central issue is authority. Mr X, for example, wanted his wife to follow her profession and to achieve the security that she wishes for in it; he even welcomed her earning more than himself and stabilizing the family income so that he could get on with what he valued more highly, namely, creative designing work. However, he did not wish actually to have her in authority over jobs in which he himself was working.

In other families, the matter of income is a crucial point, and

---

experience can, if anything, heighten the salience of sex *qua* sex. In Sweden, where men and women approach equality more than perhaps any other Western society, visitors are struck by the erotic atmosphere of that society. Sexually men and women do after all each lack what the other has and wishes for completion of the self; the salience of sex may be enhanced precisely in the situation of the diminished significance of sex as a differentiating factor in all other areas of life. It has always seemed paradoxical to me that so many psychoanalysts defend the traditional sex roles and warn that drastic warping of the sexual impulses may flow from full sex equality; surely they are underestimating the power and force of the very drive which is so central a position in their theoretical framework. Maslow is one of the few psychologists who has explored the connections between sex experience and the conception of self among women. With a sample of one hundred and thirty college-educated women in their twenties, he found, contrary to traditional notions of femininity and psychoanalytic theories, that the more "dominant" the woman, the greater her enjoyment of sexuality, the greater her ability to give herself freely in love. Women with dominance feelings were free to be completely themselves, and this was crucial for their full expression in sex. They were not feminine in the traditional sense, but enjoyed sexual fulfilment to a much greater degree than the conventionally feminine women he studied. See A. H. Maslow, "Dominance, Personality and Social Behaviour in Women," *Journal of Social Psychology*, 10 (1939), 3-39; and "Self-Esteem (Dominance Feeling) and Sexuality in Women", *Journal of Social Psychology*, 16 (1942), 259-294; or a review of Maslow's studies in Betty Friedan, *The Feminine Mystique*, pp. 316-326.'

tensions may develop if the wife's income is greater than the husband's.

Manifestations of the sexual identity 'tension line' are sometimes found in subtle, often unrecognized, undercutting behaviour by the husband towards the wife. This seems to be an indication of strain and a defensive manifestation rather than the preferred mode, as it occurs in couples where the husbands make such statements as:

Mr X   'My wife has at least as good an education as I have; she earns as much as I do, I don't see any reason why we shouldn't regard ourselves as equal partners, and that is what we do. . . .'

Mr R   'We see our family as a collection of individuals each with different skills and interests and as having evolved the capacity to live together.'

Mr Y   'Our marriage is a form of partnership, and has to be understood in terms of the characteristics of partnerships. . . .'

Clearly these are statements of fundamental ideals on which the dual-career family is based. In actually observed or reported interactions, however, when the tension point was approached the men tended to undercut their wives. Examples of this were seen in the way some husbands cut across their wives in the interview situation, not allowing them to answer fully, as though to say: 'I'm really better at this than you, dear.' One husband did in fact preface his interruptions with statements of that type. Another example was when a husband described his wife's business practices; he tended to make a bit of a joke of them, not expecting her to deal with her management role as 'for real' as he did himself. He expressed surprise when a larger firm thought his wife's business worth a take-over bid but was reassured when they offered a ridiculously low sum. In another instance the husband indicated that he thought that his wife was basically unemployable except for his help. It must be emphasized, however, that these manifestations were subordinated to the more dominant aspect of their relationship, which was that the husband did in fact support, sponsor, encourage and otherwise facilitate his wife's career. It is to be expected that there would be some 'backlash' of other feelings, stemming from the sacrifices and threats that the pattern involved. These processes of 'undercutting' and supporting are also present on the women's side of the symbiotic relationship. Where the dual-career situation persists, as it has in the couples studied, a balance is achieved which constitutes a resolution of the dilemma.

In the families which are also a professional partnership (as with the Ys, an architectural husband-wife partnership) these processes are accentuated. Where the working partnership is conducted at home a method must be developed of softening the modes of relationship found in the cut and thrust of critical competitive work lest it erode the husband-wife relationship. The Ys recognize that criticism is important for the maintenance of work standards and to stimulate creativity. Mr Y, indicating how they resolve this, says: 'It is important if one is to preserve this kind of relationship to learn to criticize *with love*; and to accept criticism in work matters as different from attacks on the person. . . .' The Ys themselves recognized that this is easier said than done, and have learned to accept a good deal more overt conflict in their relationship than, for example, that to which their parents were accustomed.

Some of the wives had developed distinctive ways of handling their dilemmas in relation to the sex-role identity issue. Where their occupational roles called for aggressive behaviour or other patterns of behaviour sharply inconsistent with their conceptions of the wifely role, they more or less consciously segregated the two sets of roles. Examples of the segregation mechanism are:

Mrs P   'When I'm at work I'm very authoritarian. I wear a white coat at work and I try to hang up my working personality with it when I leave the office.'

To this was added her husband's view:

Mr P   'I once visited my wife's company on business and by chance I saw her there. She was so different, I hardly recognized her. She seemed like someone else – some sort of tycoon – certainly not my wife.'

In another case, the switch-over was not so deliberate but nevertheless decisive:

Mrs O   'My friends who know me in both capacities say that I am two different people at home and at work.... I am much more domineering and aggressive in the office than I am at home in that I will fight a point in the office in a way that I would never fight in a domestic situation, or want to.'

Another way in which at least two of the wives dealt with the identity dilemmas that tended to arise if they gave too much emphasis to their career ambitions was to play down their ambitions almost deliberately. They presented their careers as a series of improvisations which allowed them to do something interesting rather than as a series of steps taken towards a career ambition or goal. A given couple may have more than one identity tension line operating and the tension lines may shift through time. When either individual is pushed into a pattern which is too discrepant with his or her sense of personal (and sexual) identity, defensive behaviour begins to develop. The form this takes – attack, withdrawal of support and so on – varies with the couple constellation.

IV. Social network dilemmas

Each couple relates to its social environment through a network of relationships. The social network of each family is variously composed of kin, friends, neighbours, work associates, services relationships and so on. The networks vary in their size, multidimensionality and interconnectedness. Network composition is affected by many elements, e.g. personal preferences, convenience, obligations and pressures of various kinds. Family phase and occupational affiliation are of central importance in determining composition and the quality of relationships. At different stages in the life cycle people may be added or dropped from the 'active' network, while others are carried along from stage to stage in a relatively more 'latent' capacity. For example, when a woman works, some of her work relationships may be important for the family in a way similar to the work relationships of her husband. (In both cases, these will vary according to the general importance of work relationships in the specific occupations and in the national cultures concerned.) When a family has children they may enter into relationships with service personnel connected with the children's care and activities and they may form relationships with families of their children's friends to whom they might otherwise not have related. As well as sheer quantity of relationships, there is the matter of quality of relationships, some being kept rather superficial and others 'deeper', some relating only to a sector of one's interests and others being more general.

The population in focus here has several definite characteristics relating to this area. They are very busy people, committed to occupations which are very demanding. In addition they have their own families which they value highly; as these families are at the stage where there are growing children at home, this creates yet another very demanding situation. Because of the heavy demands in these immediate spheres, the couples tend to enter into a smaller amount of active involvement with kin and friendships than may prevail among other professional middle class families, where there is a greater 'slack' for visiting and sociability outside the round of pressing work and family duties (cf. overload). While some of the couples in the sample interacted heavily with relatives and some kin were drawn on to help with children occasionally, the more general pattern was for difficulties to appear in this area because of the divergence of the dual-career family from expected norms of kin behaviour. This is one of the areas in which network dilemmas tended to arise. The second area in which distinctive dilemmas arose was that of friendship formation. Each of these can be illustrated. They both involve difficulties in reciprocating conventional role expectations and they both give rise to dilemmas since in each case while there is a wish to sustain the relationship, there is also a wish to protect oneself from it in anticipation of the criticism a career wife and mother can usually expect in these relationships.

The kin dilemma is illustrated by Mrs O's experience. Because her husband was very close to his widowed mother who lived with his spinster sister, she wished to be as nice to them as possible. On the other hand, Mr O's in-laws found it difficult to accept that not only was she a working wife but she also had a very demanding schedule. Mrs O described a characteristic incident as follows:

'She (mother-in-law) will call up and ask if she can just drop around for a visit. I've got her pretty well trained now to realize that I cannot just have a chat with her or prepare things for her. . . . Early on, even my husband didn't realize what a problem this was. When she telephoned once, I heard him say: "Yes, she'll be home on Thursday, drop in any time in the afternoon." He didn't realize how precious that afternoon was for me . . . how many things I'd saved and planned to get done on that day, I couldn't spend it chatting with his mother. I've got her trained now to accept every third weekend.'

Mrs S described similar difficulties with her husband's mother. Mr S, as with most of the men in our study, felt that he had a special relationship with his mother. In this case, although Mr S had four brothers, it was he who had always been close to her in her later years and who carried the burden of his mother's difficulties. This was a recurrent source of conflicting loyalties in relation to his wife and family and a high level of tension developed when his mother became seriously ill with a long terminal illness. Mrs S says:

'This was the first time I felt that my marriage might break up. He would return late at night from staying up with her and then be so disturbed about it that we couldn't get any rest. This was the same time as there were heavy demands being made on me to keep my business going. Even when none of the others in the family would lift a finger he felt so guilty about it that it disturbed our own relationship.'

The situation for one of the couples was that as the husband's mother lived in a self-contained flatlet in a wing of their large house, the wife and mother worked out a routine daily contact for a few minutes between the wife's arrival home from work and the beginning of the television programme that the mother watched each evening in her own quarters. Aside from this contact, communication was largely by notes left by the wife in the morning about how to deal with the matters that might arise, e.g. when tradesmen were expected.

The dilemma over friendship is less a matter of the necessity of modifying obligations in the light of the wife's career demands than a matter of deviating from the usual choice patterns for friends. There seems to have been established, particularly among professionals and executives in the business world, a pattern of friendship based on the male's occupational associates (Lazarsfeld and Merton, 1954; Babchuk and Bates, 1965). Typically, however, the male's occupational associates are married to women who do not themselves pursue careers though there is some variation in this. It is far less likely that the associates of a businessman will be married to women who are pursuing careers than might hold for those in the professions. Where either of these categories applied for the couples studied, however, there was a tendency for the women in the sample to report a discomfort with social situations in which the wives of the relevant couples were not at least positively oriented towards women having careers. In other situations there tended to be at best a lack of shared interests and at worst an awkward situation arising out of expressions of criticism.

The circumstances of the dual-career family tended to produce, among the couples studied, a situation in which friendships were formed in different ways from what might be expected in mono-career families. Aside from the general tendency for overload to crowd out many contacts with friends and to make relationships very selective (as with leisure activities generally) there were other tendencies too. Neighbourhood was perhaps less important than in the mono-career family because, as Mr O indicates above, casual visiting patterns are so difficult. In only one family was the neighbourhood a source of friends and in this case the neighbourhood was a suburb with people of the same type as themselves, i.e. a high density of dual-career families or families in which the women had high qualifications and wanted to work at some point.

A striking feature of the dual-career families in the study was the tendency for them to form their friendships on a *couple* basis. While traditional families, particularly in the middle class, assume a minimal degree of acceptance by both partners of any friendships that they form, the tendency is for the wife to accommodate to the husband's choice and for the women and men to relate separately according to traditional lines of division in activities and interests. In the dual-career families, because of the sharp difference in outlook and situation between the career wife and non-career wives, most of the families studied tended to associate primarily with other couples like themselves where the wife was involved in an occupation. This produces a situation in which it is the wife who has a crucial role in selection of friendships though the end product is a couple-based relationship. There is a greater range of acceptable couples purely from the man's point of view than from the woman's point of view, and the selection process is left to centre on the woman's sense of comfort and acceptance. This is further accentuated by the fact, as mentioned above, that overload falls most heavily on the wife, so that it is up to her to indicate whether she can handle friendships which are both gratifying and demanding.

V. Role-cycling dilemmas

There is a considerable amount of literature dealing with the life cycle and with cycles within specific spheres of life, such as the family life cycle. The family, for example, passes through phases which are named in the culture: engagement, honeymoon, marriage, parenthood, and so on. Each culture distinguishes different sub-phases and not all possible phases are named and identified as separate. For example, in ordinary usage in our own culture we do not have a designation to distinguish the phase of the family life cycle before having children and later, the phase in which children leave home. In our culture, we class all these phases as 'parenthood', referring not to the whole family situation but only to the roles of the marital partners. Sociologists have attempted greater precision of terminology, e.g. the 'novice' stage, the 'full house plateau', and so on (Lopata, 1966; Duvall, 1957; Hill, 1966; Rodgers, 1964). In other spheres, e.g. the occupational sphere, there is a plethora of terms depending on the specific occupation – training, apprenticeship (internship, residency), establishment and so on, to retirement. In complex organizations there are hierarchies that contain named stages, e.g. in the Administrative Class of the British Civil Service there are stages of Assistant Principal, Principal, Assistant Secretary, Under-Secretary, Secretary; other organizations have other hierarchies and stages of the career associated with them.

Alice Rossi indicates the utility of thinking in terms of *role-cycles* (Rossi, 1968). When a young man marries he enters the role of husband and he has a cycle of experience in the husband role. When he takes the additional role of father, he has another set of experiences which has its own cycle. The role cycles in different spheres have

363

SEX, CAREER AND FAMILY

different properties and may be in or out of phase with one another. Rossi conceptualizes the role-cycle as having four phases: the *anticipatory* or preparatory phase, the *honeymoon* or early establishment phase (in which efforts are directed towards stabilizing ways of managing the role, usually accompanied by heightened interest and involvement) and a *plateau* or steady-state phase (during which the role is 'fully exercised'). Then, eventually, there comes a phase of *disengagement* from the role which is given up voluntarily or under the force of circumstances. The process of making these transitions from one social role to another has been thought of in social-psychological dynamic terms as status-transitional critical junctures in which the structural potentialities for change are very great and a process of disequilibration occurs followed by reorganization (Rapoport, 1961; Rapoport and Rapoport, 1964, 1965).

The couples studied and reported here were mostly in the stage with regard to familial roles that would be termed the *plateau* in that they were married, had children and were functioning as parents in a family that was established and growing, with children still at home. In three instances there were new first babies, so the plateau stage was barely entered at the time of the study. In all the others it was well established. Our data indicate two basic types of role-cycling conflicts: between the occupational roles of husband and wife and their family roles; and between the occupational role of the husband and the occupational role of the wife. Two potential conflicts will be discussed: the career-family cycling dilemma and the dual-career cycling dilemmas.

In relation to the career-family role-cycling dilemmas, the parental role is one into which women are to some extent pushed by cultural expectations. The woman is, in addition, particularly vulnerable as she may be catapulted into becoming a parent accidentally, even with modern methods of birth control (Rossi, 1968). The parental role is largely irrevocable and one for which parents tend to be relatively poorly prepared. While none of our couples report having been catapulted into parenthood, it is clear that the pressures to become parents were more keenly felt by the women than by the men and several of the couples described the decision to have their first child as one that was pressed by the woman and with which the man tended to acquiesce. The timing of this step in relation to the career role-cycle was something that received considerable attention from our couples and two points of view were expressed.

Some couples stressed the importance, in their continuing to work, of having been occupationally established before having children. This meant that they had a high income, a secure position with flexibility and perquisites of one kind or another; they could

364

therefore afford domestic help and were able to take time off to see that things worked out well. Their commitment to work was by this time so well established that dropping out seemed unthinkable.

Mr K indicated that there is no financial need to have Mrs K to work:

'From our point of view there's no possible financial reason for keeping going really. I mean it would be a decision to work purely for work's sake.'

He drew a contrast with couples where the wife needed to work because of financial considerations:

'I think a lot depends on when people start. People who started having children very young, some of them felt they had almost no alternative financially and once having started had to keep going, the incentive was to keep on.'

Mr K indicated how much his wife's decision was her own and how he had not expected it:

'I suppose what struck me when I responded to this – it was a decision for my wife to take in that she was going to be the one who was primarily affected either way. From my own point of view, looking at it purely selfishly, it is much more convenient from the man's point of view if his wife is at home – particularly if one is in the fortunate position that we are, you know, having resources. My wife having worked for so many years, you know, we're quite well off. So there's no financial stringencies as a result. I think on the other hand I was slightly surprised and won't be at all surprised if she changes her mind.'

One of the 'drop-out' couples argued, in contrast, that as they had both reached the plateau stage of their careers, there was no need for the wife to work any longer as her husband would be earning a high salary and they had accumulated savings through having had a surplus income for so long. The couple felt that for those in the establishment phase, struggling to make the grade, the pressure on women to continue working after becoming a mother was greater. As Mrs K had previously established herself, they felt she could re-enter occupationally whenever she wished; had she become a parent earlier she may not have had sufficient status and contacts to make this possible.

The Ls apparently did not discuss the issue of whether or not Mrs L should continue working after having children. They both took it more or less for granted and described the issue as follows:

Mrs L   'Well we didn't discuss whether I'd go on working after I had the children but you know by the time it came to having the children it seemed a good thing to do.'

Mr L   'If you earn as much money as this there's more to be said for going on with it.'

Mrs L 'Yes, because you can afford the nursery help this is the thing really. So many jobs you can't pay out of your salary for somebody to do the things you would be doing if you were at home and it's interesting work and of course the longer you stay on at it the more sort of involved in it you get.'

The difference between these viewpoints seems to depend to some extent on the specific occupational situation and to some extent on the values and style of life of the specific couple. An example of the latter is the style of life of the Ks (above) who lived at a level set by what one income would allow; other couples lived at levels that required both incomes. An example of the way in which the specific occupational situation affects the likelihood of women staying at work after becoming mothers is seen in the architectural profession. Martin and Smith, in a survey of women architects, show that if they are married to architects they have a higher chance of continuing their careers than if they marry men of other occupations. The early marriers, restricted as their social lives are, to include mainly fellow students, are more likely to marry architects than are later marriers (Martin and Smith, 1968).

None of the couples expressed strong feelings about the degree to which women had to curtail career involvements in favour of family demands as compared with men. This might have been more pronounced had we studied a series of 'captive housewives'. For the most part the women felt fortunate that they had been able to work out a situation where their careers were as full as they had currently managed to achieve. They tended to accept as 'inevitable' for the present that women would have to bear the main brunt of child-care and domestic organization, so that there would 'naturally' tend to be more strain on the wife's career-family cycling problems than on the husband's. The general tendency was to be 'thankful for small mercies', such as having a husband who did not invite guests home for dinner at the last minute or who did not mind running a vacuum cleaner over the carpets. There were only a few who were very outspoken about their wives that 'jointness' and equality in the marital relationship should be equality in the degree to which *each* must curtail the demands of career in favour of their joint familial commitments.

The second type of role-cycling conflict, i.e. between demands of the two careers, was expressed by most of the couples. When Mrs O wished to diminish the demands being made on her by her career so that she could have more time to spend with her growing children, although she wished to continue in a senior professional job of some kind, she considered taking a less demanding post in another part of England. Mr O, however, could find no job in that area comparable to the one he held. So Mrs O had to give up the opportunity. When Mr P was offered a promotion with his industrial firm if he would move to the north of England, he turned it down because there was no chance there for his wife (a research scientist) to obtain a job comparable to the one she held in the London area. Mr S gave up a promising career in politics in order to stabilise a home base and income to underpin the development of his wife's career as a designer.

These compromises that are often necessary for dual-career families can be seen in greater detail in a description of Mr S's career pattern. Mr S had begun to succeed in a career as a television performer but was not sufficiently established by the time of his marriage to provide a solid financial basis for support. He was still in the 'honeymoon' phase of that particular role-cycle and he describes the conflict between the demands of developing that role and the demands of family life as he experienced it at the time:

'I certainly felt that being married immediately curbed my ability to take risks and be very brave and bold about my immediate career . . . and this was complicated by the fact that my mother was becoming ill . . . so there was this feeling that I had bitten off more than I could chew so to speak – I had married, had a child and my mother to look after and my wife anxious to develop a career. . . .'

Before going into the career in which he ultimately succeeded in as a business manager, Mr S had a fling at politics, with similar results:

'I began to look around for some other activities at a higher level of income – as a partner in a business or at least in a top management position . . . but I found myself being asked to stand as a candidate for the Liberal Party . . . and this was something I got on terribly well with, loved every moment of it. This view was not shared by my wife, and I think that there were many aspects of what I was doing that didn't please her – being away and mixing in these circles, the insincerity of the whole thing. . . . The show business world didn't appeal to her – and she didn't have an understanding of the meaning of it to me beyond the wish to please, which is similar to what she gets when she designs things and when people applaud when her things are being shown . . . this she understands . . . so if we were to be happy as a team and to mix with people that we could both like, it seemed to me that I had to withdraw from the political and show business activities – which I did.'

An example of a dilemma arising between the woman's career role and the parental role is seen most crucially at the point of childbirth. As indicated, this is when most women drop out, at least for an extended period. Our data from the 1960 graduates' survey indicates that there is a point following childbirth when the woman's occupational aspirations rise again. In all the couples studied stress was present – both within the individual making the career sacrifice and to some extent between the pair. Therefore two kinds of stresses must be resolved if the woman is to return to work: first, the potential stresses associated with work and family role-cycling and second, the potential stresses associated with the demands of wife's career *vis-a-vis* the demands of the husband's career.

b *Motivational syndromes*

There are several motivational syndromes prominent among married women who follow careers and their husbands.

1. Financial security. It is sometimes said that there is a great difference between women who must work for financial reasons (widows, spinsters, low-income wives or wives with inadequate husbands) and those who do so primarily for other reasons. In fact, it is clear from our data that although economic factors play a part in the motivation of most women who pursue careers, the degree and kind of importance they have in the overall motivational syndrome varies greatly. Financial issues, while not primary, are important in accounting for some of the motivational power underlying the formation and maintenance of the dual-career family. Many women, like many men, see their level of earnings as some kind of measure for personal worth in the world, though when mentioned in this way it is usually stated to be a secondary consideration; this is a tendency among professionals in general.

Some of the women in the study experienced early economic deprivation and are very much aware that this factor has been important in driving them towards a goal of economic security. By the time they became prominent enough to have been included in the study they were successful enough and sophisticated enough to deflect this kind of motivation from the area of personal acquisitiveness. They mentioned the wish to provide for their children so that they would be able to have the best education, the greatest range of options for themselves and so on. The husbands support this and, in fact, often obtain direct gratification from their wives' earning ability.

Another aspect of the financial element is where the father of the woman was felt to be defective in some sense: not a good breadwinner, absent or unstable in some way. This seems to have set up a strong motivation not to rely on a man for one's source of livelihood – and this is translated into the marital situation in a generalized way which may not be specific to the actual marriage partner. The women with this attribute were not in fact married to men whom they saw as unstable or inadequate as providers. They simply felt that it was most comfortable for them in life to be financially independent of anyone else, even their husbands. It was an independence which had its roots rather obviously in a family experience that had unsettled them in this respect in early life.

The third element within the financial area is a much more contemporary issue. When both partners are working prior to having children, a standard of living is created which cannot easily be given up after the birth of the first child when a cut in the overall family income would occur if one partner ceased to work. Though the husband's income may be rising as he passes through the establishment phase of his career and stabilizes at a higher level, the couple may have become attuned to a higher standard of living than even this escalation achieves; in addition a further financial incentive is provided by an accumulated pension investment so that it is important as a future retirement policy for the wife to continue working if at all possible.

All these financial aspects are important although they do not in fact appear to be the primary element in the motivational syndromes for the women in the study. As indicated above, none of the men in the sample was a poor earner; this type of situation was deliberately excluded so as to avoid situations in which financial considerations overpowered all other elements in the motivational picture. It is interesting, nevertheless, that the financial considerations came through strongly despite this research strategy. Other motivational factors to which the financial reasons are secondary will be examined in the next section.

While most of the women in the sample illustrated one or more of the points made above, Mrs S seemed to incorporate many of them, since she grew up in a refugee family which experienced economic deprivation after having been well off.

Mrs S had always wanted financial security and was seeking through making a 'momentous capital gain' in her business to provide for her children's future. She accounted for this element of her motivation in terms of her history:

'The only one thing I have never done is to have had *no* actual earning capacity of my own. I've always had – and I think basically having been a refugee I have much more instability in this respect and need much more bolstering up financially – the need for that little bit of security, you know. I have often tried to reason this one out, and I can't because the opposite ought to be true; having had it proved to me in 1938 that no matter how much you have it could be all taken away and you could be nothing. Yet I feel that this is a little something that tends to push me, you know.'

In another context she says:

'If you are an employee in this country, you honestly never stand a chance if you have a certain level at which you want to live. . . . I've always maintained that you can only eat three meals a day, and I am not the "status symbol seeker" type, neither is my husband. But I think that there is a level of living that most of us enjoy, and as an employee it is jolly difficult to save . . . whereas if I do this (go into the specific business deal which involved the chance for a major capital gain) I'm the one who is able to rise at the end of that period of time and to know that there is going to be X thousand pounds for my little boy and my little girl. This is a lovely thought, and lots of people would think that this is the thing to go for because this is very positive and everything else is a matter of emotions. . . .'

2. Divergence in relation to traditional sex roles. Examining the couples from a qualitative point of view, there do not seem to be any clear-cut lines of classification that make them personally distinguishable from others not in the dual-career family pattern. While the men helped a lot at home, they were not noticeably 'feminine' in their character traits. On the contrary, emphasis was given by some to the need for a man to be especially strong so as to be able to tolerate an actively successful wife. The women were active and successful in non-traditionally women's work roles, but for the most part they were not particularly 'masculine' in their manner or apparent motivation. On the contrary, many operated in a specifically 'feminine' way in their work, sometimes justifying this kind of behaviour – which often went against their egalitarian ideals – in terms of using what advantages they had to compensate to some extent for their disadvantages as women at work.

The commonly used character-types – neurotic, introverted, dominant, tough-minded – do not seem to hold for the couples studied. In some of the couples the women were 'highly strung' and steadied by husbands who could take the strain; in other couples the women were very steady and sometimes balanced their husbands' somewhat erratic performance. The idea of either of the marital partners in the dual-career families being 'dominant' in any simplistic sense was inapplicable. The tendency, rather, was for each member to have primary authority in particular spheres of the family life, but not along conventional lines of women inside the house and men outside.

A relevant categorization would be the concept of 'divergence' developed by Liam Hudson (Hudson, 1966). These were people who diverged *behaviourally* from the traditional patterns prescribed by sex-role norms; they did so in a complementary manner which involved the participation of husband and wife. The motivation underlying this divergence differed and in this sense, Hudson's concept is not strictly applicable as he was concerned with a motivational syndrome underlying behaviour. In this series of couples, the motivational syndromes seemed diverse, but the behavioural consequences were similar. None of the women in the sample gravitated towards their specific type of work role because they thought of it in sex-stereotyped terms. The fact that society defined these work roles as predominantly 'masculine' was not salient for them – either positively or negatively. It was in this sense that they diverged, for the general patterning of thought and action in their social environment tended precisely in the direction of sex-typing jobs as predominantly suitable for men or for women.

Mrs X was described by her former supervisor (an architect) as 'the sort of girl who had to work', who had a serious vocational orientation to her work comparable to that of the most professionally committed male architects.

Mrs M was described by her husband as the sort of woman who 'Naturally worked'. There was never any question about it.

Mrs Y said that, while she expected that she would always do some kind of work, the specific creative partnership that she and her husband had worked out probably happened largely accidentally as they were not able to get a house until after the first five years of marriage, by which time they had evolved a pattern of working together. Their way of life was also reinforced by the fact that they were very successful as a professional partnership, and while working very hard were able to be quite selective about the projects they were willing to take on, organising their work in a way that suited them both. Mrs Y describes her own feeling about the work as follows:

'In a way it's probably quite self-indulgent – you know – doing it this way which is the way we like doing our work – but in another

371

way it's like George Stephenson – knocking himself out to make the railways because he wanted to do that and could only be happy doing so – though it meant working extremely hard.'

The overall impression was that most of the women in the dual-career families studied worked simply 'because it was there'. Where they were doubtful about the costs of pursuing their interests in the face of difficulties in reconciling work and family roles, they some-times tried not working for a while only to have their essential need to work reinforced:

> Mrs V: 'I was very gloomy (when I wasn't working) – not exactly gloomy because I'm not really a gloomy person. But I was subject to restlessness. I got neurotic. I used to start thinking I was ill, and then I would get tearful, and I would get the feeling suddenly that I would want to do mad things – all, you know, from this feeling of restlessness. But when the work came along it definitely satisfied these various things, whatever they were, and now I enjoy it. I'm absolutely perfectly happy (despite the strains and tensions of mixing work and family).'

Examining the motivational syndromes underlying the behaviour patterns both of husbands and wives in the dual-career families studied, some very interesting patterns emerge, though their con-firmation with more rigorous methods of appraisal and with suitable control groups will be necessary. First, patterns concerning the women. Some research has seemed to suggest that women who cross the line – diverge from traditional sex-typed occupations – have a motivational syndrome which involves masculine identification. Roe, for example, found that among female engineers, identification with the father seemed prominent (Roe, 1956). This syndrome of masculine identification may occur in some situations, and it may hold for many professional women – particularly in the earlier pioneering generation. However, among the contemporary younger group of dual-career women – 'younger' meaning in mid-life – the pattern seems somewhat different. It seems that the fathers of many of the women in the study series were in some way disappointing to their mothers. To be very speculative, it might be that far from being the figure with whom the women identified, the women may have tried to make up for the father's deficiencies as perceived by their mothers. For example, Mrs Z's father was seen as something of a disappointment to her mother (though he was 'objectively' quite successful as a senior Civil Servant) because the mother had higher political aspirations for him. Mrs V's father was seen as very domesti-cated, doing things around the household much earlier than the era in which it became fashionable for British men to help; in this sense he was not a disappointment but perhaps the opposite. Mrs V felt particularly close to him and had an awkward relationship with her mother. Mrs S's father had been wealthy and successful in Germany but on fleeing the Nazis and resettling in England had to take menial jobs and was really unable to adjust to the new circumstances very successfully, depending on the rather more effective mother to cope.

In fact this is the secondary pattern found among at least three of the women – of a father towards whom the relationship was particularly close and warm compared with a mother with whom the relationship was awkward. Mrs R illustrates this pattern:

'He was a marvellous father. I adored him. We were very good friends and I got on with him much more than with my mother and this happened right through to adult life, although when I became an adult I understood my mother much more – she was a sharper person altogether and my father was a much gentler sort of person and he used to take me for long walks and tell me stories and that I remember very much as my childhood. But, as a husband I don't think he was a very good provider, he was too vague, and he was never any good at adding the money together.'

For the men in the dual-career families, the pattern is reversed. For nearly every man in the series, there was a particularly close and empathic relationship with the mother – presumably setting up a particular sympathy with women and their concerns. Mr O was a bachelor living at home with mother and sister until late in his 30s when he met and married his wife. Mr R was the one who looked after his aged widowed mother, though his sister and her family lived in the same town and might have easily cared for her from many points of view. Mr S, though only one of five brothers, was the one closest to mother, and it was he who stood by her when the others abdicated their responsibility when she was old and infirm – so much so that it became a source of strain between his wife and himself. Mrs S says:

'I know that it is normal for a son to love his mother and that a good wife should understand, but sometimes this is very difficult to take. For example, I was pregnant at the time and I had problems about establishing my business, and this was the time we had to cope with my mother's residence as well and his mother's residence and there was this terrible medical problem involved. In every family there is someone who takes it upon themselves to do their duty by a parent. My husband was closest to the mother and more sensitive to her needs, and her disease was both physical and 'nervous'. He understood the nervous part and didn't let himself be unduly influenced by the medical opinions on how to deal with it.'

Mr S says that this happened early in their marriage, and that he now feels that it was in a way unfair to his wife, but: 'I used to wake up in the middle of the night in a cold sweat worried about my mother. I engaged nurses and so on.'

In other cases it was the sort of situation, as with Mr Y, where the boy was the only child and there was a special understanding between mother and son because of some kind of similarity of outlook and temperament. In Mr Y's case his mother was a schoolteacher, and he felt that she understood his problems at school and helped particularly effectively. It was Mr Y who expressed concisely how the divergent outlook common to all the couples studied occurred without their experiencing the perspective of being very different or deviant, in contrast with what is often found among more flagrantly divergent kinds of people, such as sexual deviates. Mr Y was asked whether he felt 'different' while at school and he answered 'no', that he felt 'perfectly dead-ordinary'. On reflection, however, he said that he had just recently looked at a picture of his school class, and 'hilariously' he seemed to be the only 'normal one' – the rest looked 'kooky'. Implied in this is the impression that those in the sample studied who diverged did so for the most part without conscious protest against the established norms (only one in the sample was a militant reformist or 'feminist'). At the same time, they were not particularly conformative. They were, rather autonomous and individual, following their interests and personal needs to find the kinds of work and marital partner that seemed right to them.

Considering them as individuals, the most telling finding about them is not that they have been motivated to cross sexual roles as such but that they have not been as much concerned as their more traditional-minded contemporaries about developing patterns that may diverge from the traditional sex-differentiated roles. This shows not only in the fact that they engage in areas stereotypically attributed to members of the opposite sex – the women undertaking careers, the men helping at home – but also in the fact that at an inter-personal level of relating, there does not seem to be such a chasm between men and women as in some traditional couples. The individuals do not feel that the opposite sex world is sharply contrasting and alien to them as individuals. It is unusual to find the intelligent woman asserting that she 'hasn't got a brain in her head' or a 'sense of figures'; or the obviously sensitive and intuitive men avoiding any knowledge of, or interest in, anything domestic. These are, however, fairly familiar patterns among traditionally sex-differentiated couples. In fact, members of these couples enjoy being with the opposite sex, and not only socially or in sexual relations. They are comfortable with members of the opposite sex on the same grounds of discussion and there is a lack of any sense of a 'sex war'.

How did this ease of expression and sympathy with the concerns of both sexes arise? Most of the women were either close to their father and/or felt that they had to take on many functions of the father's role because of the mother's sense of disappointment with the father's way of handling it. Most of the men in the sample were close to their mothers. This did not mean that they were effeminate or 'mother's boys' but that, for a variety of reasons, they were the ones in their families who were especially close to or were left to look after their mothers. Their mothers may have been strong women with strong ideas but as often as not they were simply women who had a close relationship with this particular son among their children. Their wives may or may not have been strong, and the needs of their wives may or may not have been 'imposed' on the men through pressures of dominance or egotism. As often as not the wives were hesitant and full of self doubts, and the sympathy of the husband acted to push them across the hurdles of their hesitancy – helping them to make career decisions, deal with awkward situations with employers or clients as well as with kin and other persons in their social networks.

3. The meaning of work; self-expression. The dual-career families were selected so that the financial motive for working would not necessarily be paramount for the wife as the husband himself was earning at a high level. As indicated above, this does not mean that the financial motive was absent, but only that it tended not to be given as of primary importance. The overriding impression created by the reasons actually given for working among women of this sample can be summarized in the term 'self-expression'. For women of this type not to work made them feel in some sense personally untrue to themselves – wasted, unfulfilled, restless and bored – or, in more extreme cases, not to work was simply considered impossible. Work was essential for these women's self-conception and therefore for their mental health. Mrs N (a manager) says the following:

'I'm not concerned with advancement in terms of position and money. One likes to have money, but after a while it really doesn't matter that much. . . . I enjoyed administering and managing, and this is where I wanted some development. Being able to organize a department and being responsible for policies and the organization and seeing things went smoothly is what attracted me, and there are not many jobs at that level financially for women. . . . I think that this job will continue to grow in satisfaction. In terms of development of me in the job, I've got a long way to go, and this is where the satisfaction is going to come.'

The husbands, on the other hand, have tended to be less vertically ambitious than many men in similar positions. They have sometimes given up their own *status* advancement to accommodate to the situations in which their wives find themselves, and they have made concessions in terms of supports and lessening of demands on their wives in order to help with their wives' careers. The empathy that the men felt for their wives' needs for personal fulfilment may be understood in terms of the motivational syndromes described above. Mr S illustrates this very well when he describes how his wife's wish to develop a business of her own could be understood by him, and he was able to help her almost as a hobby for himself because he too shared her sense of excitement in the business.

'I have always felt that it would be a very, very nice, pleasurable thing to have a business of one's own. I have never had, I have always been working for people, an executive in a company, and oddly enough there seems to be something of a change coming over people in corporations and the business world, whereby people are tending to become more and more employed executives, some of them in a very dynamic way. I am not in a very dynamic way, but in a reasonably comfortable way. However, I have always thought that it would be so pleasant to have a business of one's own; even if it isn't one's only activity it is pleasant; not only is there added income, but there is somehow a sense of greater independence because one is doing something that one has created and is in all senses of the word a master of the destiny of a particular enterprise rather than simply being employed. This may be an illusion, I don't know, but I have always felt that it would be desirable. I think essentially I am a salesman, perhaps in a more refined way, not in the worst sense of the word but in the best sense of the word, so I could sell the idea of the success of the business to other people in order to get finance for my wife. And it always gave me a certain amount of excitement and a great kick to have a hand in some of the decision-making on prices, to say, "yes, we will sell it at that price", you know, "tell him so and so", or "I'll write that letter, we'll do this, or we will change it and do that". There is a great deal of fun attaching to that especially if you make your mistakes and nobody, but nobody can say boo to you.'

So, the women tend to work to find self-expression, and the men tend to support them by sharing their interests and preoccupations. The men's motivational syndromes in using their wives' activities in some sense as extensions of their own has been touched upon. What other factors can be added to a knowledge of the wives' own motivational syndromes? Only part of the picture has been touched on in the preceding section on divergence and sexual identifications.

Most of the women in the dual-career families grew up in the kind of family situation we have described as the 'lonely/only' syndrome. Many were only children or eldest children or in some way children who carried a great responsibility in their early childhood and related closely to adults and adult roles. For them, work from an early age was taken for granted as part of the adult world and the world of being responsible and grown-up, rather than being (as it may have been in the past) associated with masculinity pure and simple.

Mrs Q describes herself as a rather lonely child, despite having a privileged existence from many points of view:

'My greatest regret of my childhood was being shut up in the nursery while there was fun going on downstairs. I remember hanging over the bannister and listening to them opening champagne and that kind of thing. My parents were either giving dinner parties or they were out. We had only three servants and they needed a fourth to play at whist and bridge, so they taught me and I used to go down to the kitchen and play whist. I don't suppose my parents ever knew. I was alone in the daytime. . . . I used to go and talk to the gardener.'

Her relationship with her mother, once again, was difficult, though her relation with her father was easier:

'My mother was a very gay, bright person. She used to say "I don't know anything" and do whatever father said. . . . I got on reasonably well with my father but I got on badly with her. We were unable to talk to each other and were always having rows. I don't know what about, probably nothing.'

Mrs Y indicates loneliness in relation to the environment in which her family lived. She was an only child and her family were culturally isolated in a northern town; they were the only intellectuals on the scene:

'It's a very odd business, this not being able to get on with people, finding yourself culturally different. It was almost like being a black child entering a community of white people. . . .'

Several of the women reported unhappy school experiences. Thus Mrs Y:

'You see, I went to a private school, and I think that I got the worst of all worlds. I think somehow in spite of the terrible dialect one would have been stuck with, maybe a primary or elementary school would have been better. The actual working class are much kinder. When I went to do this year at grammar school, they were much jollier girls than I had ever known, and there was none of the catty back-biting and whispering in corners (that was the way in the private school). . . .'

Mrs Y was continually aware of her marginality in the community and refers to their position in the town as being 'almost like Jews'.

In general, there is some evidence in the research literature to indicate that firstborn children are significantly different from their brothers and sisters, in a number of traits relating to ability and capacity to accept responsibility (Price, 1969). The evidence of our small sample suggests the utility of focusing on the special case of only children. Both only children and first children are, furthermore, subtypes of a larger and less easily definable group that we term 'lonely' children.

c *Viability factors*

   i. *What makes the dual-career family viable?*

At the heart of the factors that make a dual-career family viable lie the motivational syndromes of both husband and wife, which we refer to as dual-salience. Work and family are important spheres of involvement, and for both husband and wife there is a will to find a pattern that will make it possible for each of them to enjoy involvement in these spheres. True, this is a matter of degree; there are families even in the dual-career situation where the husband tolerates rather than assists his wife in her drive towards combining both sets of activities, and there are other families in which a very actively helping, even pushing, husband presses the wife over a line of hesitancy in working out this pattern. These variations, however, fall within a more limited range than prevails in the population as a whole, where the man is expected to maximize his involvement in

378

career and the woman in family – whatever residues of time and interest each may have in the sphere that is primarily salient for the other.

There are also some pre-conditions which must be present to make the pattern work – both in the personal motivational syndromes of the participants and in their external environment. The individuals concerned must have a relatively high energy level because so much of what is involved at the present time is contrary to custom and requires extra energy, and in addition there are too few supportive external institutions to help take up the slack. This means that if the pattern is to work, a great deal depends upon the individuals' sheer drive and persistence.

The issue of flexibility in the work and family situations was one which is much discussed by the study couples and various viewpoints were presented. One thing is clear as a *sine qua non*, and that is that there must be *some flexibility* in both the work and the family situation – ideally in co-ordination with one another. That is, when there are domestic crises, the work situation must be such as to allow the employed person a means of dealing with them. This is true for men as well as women, only more so for women at the present time because the assumption is that domestic crises are largely her responsibility. It is felt to be illusory however to assert that complete flexibility is the answer. Women, for example, who are artists, writers or architects and who work at home may find that their creativity and productiveness are inhibited because they are subject to continuous interruptions and do not have the supports of an external work situation. On the other hand, complete rigidity of the work environment is not conducive to the dual-career family situation – either for the man or the women – because in many of these instances the man covers whatever rigidities there may be in the woman's situation by coping himself with specific domestic crises. Many of the women in the study would like to see both an element of structure and an element of flexibility. When the work situation is structured, for example, one knows that the work is finished at 6 p.m., and that there will not be a great deal of carry over into evenings and weekends. On the other hand some employers recognizing that flexibility is of great assistance to women, have allowed the women to do the job in their own time according to their own hours, making it possible for them, for example, to be with their children in the afternoons. In such situations the danger is that the women will be loaded with impossible expectations because only a limited amount of energy, time, and so on is available for everything. The work may, under such circumstances, go un-completed, and the employer may draw the erroneous conclusion that flexibility is a wrong idea. The point is, of course, that flexibility is not enough. There is an optimum combination of flexibility and structure – different for different occupations and for different family constellations – which makes the pattern viable.

Added to these factors there are a whole series of *coping mechanisms*, which individuals and couples develop apart from their personalities *per se* and their external situations which allow them to deal with the situations in which they find themselves. These are learned patterns of behaviour which make it possible for the couples so to organize their time, energy, finances and other resources that the kind of life they have chosen can be seen as feasible. In this sense the family-work situation may be viewed in a management framework. Some of the couples are better than others at, for instance, managing their resources, delegating housework (and office work), gathering necessary information and making decisions, and delineating issues and drawing boundaries about what is legitimate and possible by way of involvements.

ii. *Factors that will affect the diffusion of the pattern*

In this section the concern is not with the larger societal perspective, which will be presented in the concluding section of the book. The societal perspective will need to deal with such overall issues as how much society wants to foster women's participation, how much it wants to sacrifice traditionally satisfying alternative patterns in order to gain women's participation, and how much the economy can absorb or needs the extra inputs of human resources. Here the emphasis is on the participants viewpoint – the individuals and couples who may form the highly qualified work force if this trend is to continue. Which factors will affect their responsiveness and capacity to make it possible for more women as well as men to have careers? Four areas seem to be central and have top priority.

a *Housing*. It would seem that either better forms of domestic help or patterns of residential architecture (or both) are needed so that each individual family does not have to carry all the current burdens of household maintenance. There are various possible solutions, such as upgrading domestic help and providing communal housing facilities for cleaning, laundry and shopping. All will make it more possible for more people with less exceptional coping patterns to enter into a dual-career family pattern.

b *Child care*. It would seem that this is perhaps the most important single area because in a child-centred culture people are unlikely to want to give up *en masse* their interest in children and their development or easily delegate parts of these tasks. Child-care tasks will be delegated on a more widespread basis only if parents (particularly highly qualified mothers and fathers) feel that their children as well as themselves are benefiting from the arrangement. Play groups, nursery groups and care groups of various kinds must be of a very high standard and must be seen as beneficial for the child if parents are to use them in greater numbers; and they must be well integrated to the home and family, not separated from it. Here again, architectural reforms seem called for as well as the upgrading of the relevant professional groups. Only then will a new ideology of socialization become possible, one that is less fearful of the potentially damaging consequences of any separation between mother and child.

c *Sex-role equalization.* The state of husbands accepting more easily their wives working, having incomes and having opinions of their own, is another pre-condition for increasing women's participation in the dual-career pattern. If any but the most strongly motivated women are to venture over the traditional lines of participation, they must be made to feel that they are not threatening another highly held value, namely their relationship with loved persons of the opposite sex.

d *Work attitudes.* To the extent that women are helped in their work attitudes by being given flexibility and by supportive attitudes towards the idea of women filling relevant work roles, more women are likely to venture into career positions. Such problems as access, short journey to work, positive discrimination, are not dealt with in this report, though they are obviously interlinked issues.

Aside from these four 'core' issues which will affect the trend towards increasing the prevalence of dual career families, there are a number of other aspects to the situation which may be mentioned. One element is the diffuse climate of opinion. If it is generally felt and felt strongly and nearly universally (or at least sufficiently widely to lend itself to the formation of culturally supportive subgroups) that it is good and right that men and women should be able to carry out dual-career family patterns, the situation will be eased for families who wish to pursue this line. The normative dilemmas and self-doubts that were mentioned above tend to lose force. The climate of opinion in any one country is to some extent affected by the opinions of other countries. The fact that the Swedes or Russians, or Israelis, or Americans have made certain kinds of advances in terms of either human rights or human productivity, or both, affects the readiness of another country to consider a given solution, e.g. in housing. Publicization is preferable to propaganda.

and to the extent that this dual-career family pattern is publicized as desirable, socially approved, and rewarding, young people are more likely to at least consider the exemplars as models for their own behaviour. It is not yet known how much the traditional family structure is now functioning as a negative role model, stimulating young people to reject their parents' marital norms rather vigorously, but this is certainly a possibility that should not be overlooked.

Another element in the situation has to do with the general level of affluence in our society and the definitions of work. While in a sense affluence makes it less critical to use *all* available human resources for production – bolstering the forces and tendencies which divert women on the whole from the work force – there are other elements to the affluence situation. No matter how affluent our society is as a whole it must make choices as to the best use of its human resources – male and female. Furthermore, with work changing in character to less physical, less dirty, less traditionally 'masculine' modes, the basis for the sex-based division of labour between work and home is becoming considerably eroded. Competence and aspiration rather than conventional outlooks are becoming increasingly effective as bases for the division of labour in society.

The kind of affluent society ideal where both members of the dual-career family work less than full time was not found among the couples studied, though it may well become a pattern of the future. In fact, the concept of 'full-time' work may itself alter radically.

REFERENCES

Babchuk, N., and Bates, A. P., 'The Primary Relations of Middle Class Couples: A Study of Male Dominance', *American Sociological Review*, 28, 1963.

Bott, Elizabeth, *Family and Social Network*, London: Tavistock, 1967.

D'Andrade, Roy, *see* Maccoby, E.

Dewall, Evelyn M., *Family Development*, Philadelphia: Lipincott, 1957.

Fishbein, M., *Readings in Attitude Theory and Measurements*, New York: J. Wiley, 1968.

Gavron, Helen, *The Captive Wife*, London: Routledge & Kegan Paul, 1966.

Goode, W. J., *World Revolutions and Family Patterns*, New York: Free Press, 1963.

Hadden, J. K. and Borgatta, M. L. (eds), *Marriage and the Family*, Illinois: Peacock Press, 1969.

Hill, Reuben, 'Contemporary Development in Family Theory', *Journal of Marriage and the Family*, 1966.

Hudson, Liam, *Contrary Imaginations*, London: Methuen, 1966.

Hunt, A., *Survey of Women's Employment*, H.M.S.O., 55, 379, 1968.
Lazarsfeld, P. G. and Merton, R. *see* Bergestal, M.
Lopata, Helena, Hadden, J. K. and Borgatta, M. L., 1969.
Maccoby, E., *The Development of Sex Differences*, London: Tavistock, 1967.
Martin, F. and Smith, H., 'Women in Architecture', Mimeo (P.E.P.), 1968.
Myrdal, Alva, and Klein, V., *Women's Two Roles, Home and Work*, London, Routledge & Kegan Paul, 1956.
Price, John, 'Personality Differences Within Families: Comparison of Adult Brothers and Sisters', *Journal of Biological Science*, 1, 177-205, 1969.
Rapoport, Rhona, 'Normal Crises, Family Structure and Mental Health', *Family Process*, 2, 68-80, 1961.
Rapoport, Rhona and Robert, 'New Light on the Honeymoon', *Human Relations*, 17, 33-56, 1964.
Rapoport, Robert, and Rhona, 'Work and Family in Contemporary Society', *American Sociological Review*, 30, 38-394, 1965.
Rodgers, Roy H., 'Towards a Theory of Family Development', *Journal of Marriage and the Family*, August, 1964.
Roe, Anne, *The Psychology of Occupations*, New York: Wiley, 1956.
Rossi, Alice, 'Transition to Parenthood', *Journal of Marriage and the Family*, 30, No. 1, 1968.
Smelser, Neil, *Social Change in the Industrial Revolution*, London: Routledge & Kegan Paul, 1959.
Sussman, Marvin B., 'Some Conceptual Issues in Family-Organizational Linkages', paper presented at the American Sociological Association Meetings, San Francisco, August 1969.
Weber, M., *The Theory of Social and Economic Organization*, London: Hodge, 1947.
Williams, Pat, *Working Wonders*, London: Hodder & Stoughton, 1969.

Part Four

Occupational Prospects

Chapter X

The Occupational Studies

The general review of women's achievements and prospects in high level careers in Part Two, filled out from specifically British studies in Part Three, suggests a situation something as follows. It is not necessary today to ask in a country like Britain, any more than in Eastern Europe, whether women with the high qualifications relevant to a professional or managerial career are likely to use them. In the West as in the East, such women do now normally work not only up to but after their child-bearing years, and on towards retirement. Within this pattern individuals still differ in both the quantity and the quality of their work commitment. A woman who works through most of her life does not necessarily do so out of any strong sense of commitment to a career or of career development. Conversely, a woman with a strong career commitment may nevertheless interrupt her career. Differences like these can extend to whole professional groups. Doctors, for example, tend everywhere to work relatively continuously and to show a particularly strong career commitment. Women also still tend, even in Eastern Europe, to work on the average for a smaller proportion of their total potential career period than men. These differences are important, and need to be borne in mind when considering the career prospects and value to an employer of women as individuals or in particular professions. But the background to the handling of these individual and particular cases is that today it is nearer the truth to assume that a highly qualified woman will remain, like a man, a life-time worker than that she will retire into the role of a permanent housewife.

Nor is it today necessary to argue whether women are able or willing to acquire qualifications at graduate and professional level, although here again there are distinctions to be made. Girls in Britain remain somewhat less likely than boys to persist to the end of a course of full-time higher education, and much less likely to persist to the end of part-time courses. Women are less likely than men to go on to postgraduate qualifications. In Western countries women remain much slower than in Eastern Europe to qualify for professions such as engineering, accountancy, or the law. But these limitations must be considered against the background of a high and rising tide of women qualifying at graduate and professional level, and a demonstrated capacity by women – taking one country with another – to qualify for and do well in all major fields of work.

Nor is there any need to argue further the existence of women with the potential for top jobs, as distinct from those who can do well in the basic grades of a profession but may go no further. The experience of Britain alone would be reasonably convincing in this area. When it is added to that of other countries, both Western and Eastern, there can be no doubt that top potential of both a managerial and a professional kind exists. The question is rather: on what terms and for what sort of top jobs is this potential available, and are the terms on which it can be used worth while from the point of view of the economy and society as well as of individuals? Part Three looked at this question from the standpoint of the individual in relation to her (or his) family. Part Four puts the same question in terms of the relation between the interests of individuals and those of employers and the economy.

For practical purposes the issues in this Part can be combined under three headings:

(i) Granted that differences between masculine and feminine roles, attitudes and abilities exist and are likely to continue to do so, what difference should this make to the proportion of women recruited to highly qualified occupations of different kinds? How do masculine-feminine differences affect women's potential for top leadership – or better, for different kinds of top leadership – within each occupation? Given the experience of the past and the known wide overlap between men's and women's interests and abilities, it can be assumed from the start that some women and some men are likely to have the potential for entry into and success in practically every occupation at professional or managerial level. But can anything be said about a distinctive contribution to be made by men or women to each occupation or each level within it, and about the proportion of men or women likely to be appropriate in each case?

(ii) Granted that women – primarily of course married women – follow and are likely still to follow a different life cycle from men, how would procedures for recruitment, promotion and education or training both up to and beyond graduate level need to be changed to enable highly qualified women's potential as workers to be more fully used, on terms acceptable both to their employers and to the women themselves? What costs, in money or in the trouble needed to adapt to a new situation, would these changes involve for em-

THE OCCUPATIONAL STUDIES

ployers or education authorities? Will they find it worthwhile to incur these costs?

(iii) Do employers, education authorities and others concerned have a clear picture of women's as well as men's work potential and of what is involved in realizing it to the best advantage? Are they in a position to make an objective assessment of the situation and the problems it raises, and, if not, what stands in their way?

A number of British studies bearing on these questions already exist, and several of them were referred to in Chapters I, III and IV. Most of the more specialized studies refer to fields such as school-teaching, social work or medicine – both doctors and nurses – where women have long been well established. Material also exists, however, on fields such as university teaching, the Church of England ministry, politics, business and engineering, where women have found it harder to break in on a substantial scale; or even, in the case of the Church of England ministry, to break in at all.[1] The Fawcett Society keeps an invaluable collection of press cuttings and similar material on women's progress in a wide range of fields back to and before the First World War. For the present enquiry it was decided, as has been said, to add to the material available from these sources five studies of, from women's point of view, relatively non-traditional occupations: architects, managers in two large firms, company directors, the B.B.C., and the Administrative Civil Service. These five were chosen not only because they are non-traditional but because they illustrate between them the main types of environment in which, or by passing through which, it is possible to make a high-level career:

a *As the principal of a free professional practice or as an owner-manager*, with full control of his or her own time and effort. The principals of a private practice in architecture remain as close as the members of any profession in Britain to the traditional model of the free and independent professional man. The owner-manager of a small firm, whether he or she reached the top by inheritance or marriage, by creating the business, or by climbing the ladder of promotion within it, may face much the same problems and have much the same freedom in facing them as the head of a large professional practice.

b *As an entrepreneurial bureaucrat*, the managing director as apart from the manager. A distinction relevant to women's careers emerges,

[1] See e.g. in addition to the sources used in Chapters I, III and IV, R. Messenger, *The Doors of Opportunity*, Femina, 1967 (biography of the engineer Dame Caroline Haslett); Margery Hurst, *No Glass Slipper*, Arlington, 1967 (autobiography of a businesswoman); *Women and Holy Orders*, Report of the Archbishops' Commission, Church Information Office, 1966.

389

both in the five studies and in material on other occupations, between
the employee who is senior, responsible, yet still working within a
framework laid down for him by others, and the manager or professional at the top who has the steering wheel in his, or her, own
hands. Too much precision must not be asked in this distinction;
it is a case of shades and mixtures, not of a sharp separation. But it
is certainly there, and is found at different levels in different occupations. In the Administrative Civil Service the line runs approximately
between Assistant Secretaries, who may be earning £5,000 a year but
nevertheless are usually working within a framework of policy rather
than determining what the policy is to be, and Under-Secretaries and
above who are concerned with policy formation; though, of course,
not even the highest Civil Servant controls policy finally. In the
entertainment and communications industry, as illustrated by the
B.B.C., the division comes somewhat lower. A producer, paid at a
level corresponding to a Civil Service Principal, works within a
policy determined by others. But heads of larger B.B.C. units, who
may be paid no more than Assistant Secretaries, may have to invent
the future, to develop their own vision of what the B.B.C. should be
doing, and to fight for their ideas and the resources to implement
them in a way which an economist will easily recognize as entrepreneurial. Similar distinctions can be found in firms, or between a
local authority's Chief Architect or Chief Planning Officer and professional staff at lower levels.

c *As an employee with managerial or professional responsibility, but
within a predetermined framework;* the project architect or assistant
in a local authority or private office, the middle-level industrial manager, the B.B.C. producer, the Civil Service Principal.

The family case studies reported on in Part Three were chosen, as
has been said, so as to throw further light on the areas of the five
occupational studies. Four of the occupational studies themselves
are published in full in the second volume of this report.[1] Here,
therefore, this material will be used, not to present a history of
women's achievement in each of the five occupations, but analytically
to help in answering the three questions just set out.

[1] *Women and Top Jobs – Four Studies in Achievement.* The Study on architects
is being published separately.

390

Chapter XI

Women's Performance on the Job

THE WORK STYLE AND PERFORMANCE OF WOMEN ALREADY SUCCESSFUL IN THEIR CAREERS

There is no evidence from the five occupational studies, nor from studies outside the P.E.P. series, that women who are at present in top jobs or effectively on their way to them adopt a basically different style of working from men or achieve a very different level or type of performance.

For the Civil Service generally (not only the Administrative Grade) Walker found at the end of the 1950s a 'scarcity of important differences between the attitudes of men and women', and 'no evidence that women were in fact less willing to delegate', or that in other respects women in management positions adopt a markedly different management style from men.[1]

The P.E.P. study of the Administrative Grade confirms this. The Civil Service has no 'women's sphere'. There is some tendency for men and women administrators to go to different departments; men and women are equally likely to be in economic or 'other' ministries, but a relatively high proportion of men are in technical ministries and women in ministries dealing with social services. But this is a question of balance, not (with very few exceptions) of the exclusion of members of either sex from areas open to the other. A woman like a man may find herself administering technology or the docks or the planning of a region; all these are actual recent cases. When the performance of members of the grade who have entered as Assistant Principals since the early 1950s is ranked on a three-factor scale (rank reached, efficiency in present job, and future promise), men's and women's ratings run practically level, with men only a very short head in front. Men who entered just after the Second World War receive ratings higher than either women who entered at that time or men who entered later, but this phenomenon seems to have been once for all. Women tend to provide the 'bread and butter' of the

[1] Walker, N., *Morale in the Civil Service*, Edinburgh, 1961, pp. 251 and 228.

Administrative Grade, neither the best nor the worst. They tend to be promoted rather later than men and to be seen as providing fewer potential Under-Secretaries and above. On the other hand they receive a higher proportion of 'average' and a lower proportion of 'below average' ratings on their performance in their present job.

The German study of women heads of businesses quoted earlier found them to have attitudes and characteristics close to those to be expected among men. When questioned about their management style they had 'astonishingly little' to say about traditionally feminine qualities such as intuition, tact or easy personal contacts. They might use a 'feminine' approach as an extra tool of management, but its usefulness was marginal. The style and quality of leadership which they saw as chiefly important had nothing to do with femininity. They thought that people outside their immediate circle tended on the one hand to accept them as effective business leaders – a judgment objectively justified by the rapidly growing number of women employers in Germany during the 1950s and early 1960s – but on the other to criticize them as unfeminine: coarsened, battleaxes, androgynes, bossy and busy brooms.[1]

The impression gained from the P.E.P.'s study of women directors is similar. Leading factors in the business success of British women directors are education, intelligence and:

'The capacity for making rapid decisions based on further qualities of knowledge and experience, the ability to communicate clearly across the board and down the line, coupled with a talent for persuasion and the ability to win the co-operation, loyalty, and trust of colleagues, employees, and clients . . . the ability to see and to seize an opportunity when it presents itself, to rapidly estimate the consequences of alternative courses, to have the self-confidence to take a calculated risk. . . .'[2]

Other factors include the ability to stand the strain of failure or hostility, to be aggressive when required, to prepare decisions fully and then take them firmly:

'Before a decision do your homework, the rest is a calculated risk· A bad decision is better than no decision at all. In making a decision I would first look at the product to see whether it is marketable, then at capital outlay and cost. I would ask for all the figures to determine its profitability and the space and work needed. Then a long board discussion plus separate thinking. A solution is then hammered out. . . .'[3]

---

[1] Hartmann, H., *Die Unternehmerin*, Westdeutscher Verlag, Köln, 1968.
[2] Allen, J., *Women Directors*, pp. 30-31.   [3] *Ibid.*, p. 34.

An account of factors in men's business success would not be likely to read differently. Compared to factors like these any specifically feminine traits which might have helped or hindered the business careers of these women were secondary.

In British universities the key factor in prestige and academic standing in recent years has been research. Sommerkorn[1] finds that women members of university staffs show a stronger interest than men in teaching rather than research, but nevertheless publish as many books and only marginally fewer articles. That fewer articles are published can be accounted for at least in part by the somewhat higher proportion of the women than of the men who are below age 30. There is a similar finding for the United States. Younger women Ph.Ds working full-time in American universities and colleges publish rather more books than men in science, but rather fewer in social science and the humanities.[2]

In the P.E.P. study of women architects informants repeatedly insist that architecture is a highly personal thing and that the differences between good and bad architects or between the practitioners of this or that style or specialism, whether men or women, tend to outweigh by far the marginal differences between men and women as such. Men as well as women may prefer design work to site supervision or like to leave pre-stressed concrete calculations to others. Whether an architect is or is not strong on the financial side of running his office tends to depend not on sex but on the kind of architect he or she is: research-orientated or production- and profit-orientated as the case may be. A study by the Royal Institute of British Architects on *The Architect and His Office* classifies certain offices as interested in innovation or in a high standard of service to the client, irrespective of what will be covered by the recognized scale of fees. There is no evidence that women architects gravitate to these less economically motivated offices either more or less than they do to others.

When women began to enter architecture in the 1920s and 1930s a number of predictions were made about the types of architectural work in which they were likely to be at either an advantage or a disadvantage. These predictions have not stood the test of time. Women have not proved to have any great or general advantage in detailed work or interior layouts. Nor have they shown any particular lack of ability in the design of massive structures or extensive

[1] Sommerkorn, I., *The Position of Women in the University Teaching Profession in England*, University of London Ph.D thesis, 1966.
[2] Simon, R. J., Clark, S. M., and Galway, K. 'The Woman Ph.D.: A Recent Profile', *Social Problems*, Fall 1967. The study covers women who graduated as Ph.Ds in 1958-1963.

complexes, from Elizabeth Scott's Shakespeare Memorial Theatre in the 1920s to Jane Drew's town developments overseas or Alison and Peter Smithson's *Economist* building. Some common differences between men and women architects can certainly be picked out, sometimes to women's advantage and sometimes to their disadvantage. But these tend to be marginal to the much more important differences, irrespective of sex, between individuals and architectural schools. Findings concerned with the communications industry – for example successful B.B.C. producers – or with medical consultants or top practitioners of market research are similar.

MEN AND WOMEN: MARGINAL DIFFERENCES IN STYLE AND PERFORMANCE AND THEIR EFFECTS

The occupational studies do nevertheless bring out a number of differences between the work styles and interests of men and women and indicate that these differences should not be played down. They may have only marginal significance for women who do in fact achieve successful careers in present conditions. They are always liable to be overridden by differences between individuals, whether men or women. They are a matter of statistical probability, which can never be assumed to hold in any particular case; cases must be considered individually, not only as examples of a category. But when all this has been said, differences between men's and women's work styles and interests turn out to have some significance for the careers even of women currently at the top of their professions, and a good deal more for the type and degree of career success achieved by other women.

There was much truth in the past in the idea that successful career women are, as P.E.P.'s study of women directors puts it, a 'subspecies of women' who succeed because they are willing and able so take on what would normally be masculine roles. The higher levels of most occupations still remain a man's world. If other women, more closely matching typical feminine norms, have found it harder to enter this man's world at the top, it is in a basic sense true that the reason is denial of opportunity. Measures could have been taken, but were not, to make it less of a man's world, or to equip these women better to make their way into it. But to speak without qualification of 'denial of opportunity' is to give too crude and simple an idea of the nature of the barriers which have not been removed. The point, as the occupational studies indicate in line with the rest of the evidence of this report, is neither that the barriers are irremovable nor that they are only of a negative and discriminatory kind. It is that the world of work at the top can be a woman's world as well as

394

a man's, but that to bring this about calls for a process of mutual adaptation, changing on the one hand women's as well as men's norms and on the other employment practices geared, not necessarily or even usually to the discouragement of women, but to encouraging the men who in the past appeared alone or practically alone in so many higher employment fields. The next chapter will deal with adapting employment practices to maternity and women's different life cycle. This chapter considers the effects of differences between the work styles and interests of typical men and women as expressed while actually on their jobs, and the adaptations which might be made in the light of them.

So far as the present chapter is concerned, the differences brought out by the studies run in the directions already indicated in Parts Two and Three. They fall under six heads.

a *Women tend to have wider interests than men, and to be less exclusively motivated to reach top levels of power and wealth. Their ambitions tend to be 'horizontal' rather than 'vertical'.*

On this point there seems to be near unanimous agreement among women and men informants in occupations of all kinds. The occupational studies confirm the findings of the family studies and Rossi's parallel findings from America.[1] Women graduates tend to share with men an interest in originality and creativity, but to be less oriented than men towards the goals of money and power and more oriented towards service to and work with people. Their ambitions tend to be more diffuse, to be 'horizontal' rather than 'vertical'. Women are more likely than men to be concerned with a balanced performance in a number of areas rather than a peak performance in one.

The point is not that money and power – especially money – are treated by British women in the professions and management as unimportant. Equality of pay is an important consideration. In the two companies studied by P.E.P.:

'Women kept a very close eye on their market values, and were very much aware of how they related to men. Even if they agreed

[1] For the family studies see especially Chapter VI. See also Chapter II, p. 84 (on Eastern Europe) and A. Rossi, in *Women and the Scientific Professions*, M.I.T. symposium, 1965, pp. 109-121. An outstanding British document on this point is *Working Wonders*. Note however the analysis of the eight-years-out graduate sample (Chapter VI, Table 3) that this is primarily a contrast between *married* men and women. The aspiration levels of *single* men and women graduates resemble each other more than either resembles the level for married people of their own sex. Single women show more 'vertical' ambition than married women, and single men less than married men.

that they were earning good money, which most of them did, nevertheless they did not feel that they ought to be paid any less than men doing equivalent work.'[1]

So is the contribution of a professional salary to the family income. As a senior company scientist comments:

'In my generation it never happened – but with youngsters today, if they both work, they can easily have a joint income of over £4,000. When they come to have a baby, I've seen girls near tears because of the drastic cut in the family income.'[2]

The higher a woman's earnings, the more likely she is to work continuously.[3] But women in all the occupations covered tend to feel less pressure than men to aim for the maximum attainable earnings, as apart from earnings at a good professional level.

They tend also, quite apart from the money aspect, to be less ready than men to seek – or even to accept when offered – the top administrative and managerial jobs to which top earnings are often attached. Women appear more than men to reject administrative work and to prefer to remain involved in directly producing or making something. This tendency is particularly noticeable in the B.B.C. study, but runs also through the rest. Often it is accompanied by a stronger tendency among women than among men to avoid posts which entail office politics or the building and defence of empires.

In general, the studies show that women tend more than men to settle for a reasonably well-paid job which they like, either because of its content or because it is relatively sheltered from competition and discrimination, and not to press on towards further promotion.[4] They also seem readier than men to reject an area of work because it does not appeal to them, irrespective of the pay and status offered; for example to reject business because of what is thought of as its money-grubbing or anti-intellectual accent, or to refuse the more routine and bureaucratized sorts of work in architecture. They are more likely than men to adopt Junker's 'game-like' attitude to employment.

From the point of view of employers this state of affairs has advantages as well as disadvantages. Firms and public authorities lose the benefit of some women's services in top jobs, but gain in that women who opt out of the topmost levels can fill a role not so

---

[1] Allen, I., *Women in Two Companies*, p. 54.
[2] *Ibid.*, p. 53.
[3] Chapter VI, Table 19; see also Chapter IX, pp. 368-370 for findings from the studies of dual-career families.
[4] See also *Working Wonders* and Brock, *op. cit.*, pp. 84 and 88; and generally, Chapter VI.

suitable for men or women still in the race. These women appear in several of the studies as loyal and impartial advisers with no axe to grind, as having the confidence of senior men who do not have to fear them as competitors, and as free to speak out because they have no promotion to lose. Men can fill this sort of role, like women, but when a woman does so her position is often more apparent and clear-cut. At a low level a role of this sort can be taken by what one study calls the 'office wife': the secretary (rather than the executive) who does the office equivalent of a manager's domestic chores and provides him with personal and emotional support. It also however appears at a much higher level in the person of the senior manager or specialist who is all the more effective as the chief executive's right hand man because she is not seeking, and is known not to be seeking, the top job.

One large distributive firm, with an outstanding reputation both for commercial success and for staff conditions, has developed a complete philosophy of women's employment in ancillary but not controlling roles at all levels: a concept of what might be called the 'womanly woman', responsible for the welfare of a staff largely of women, and acting as the manager's right-hand man, but never as the executive manager herself. A related line of thought is developed by Rogaly, discussing in the *Financial Times* what firms have to gain from offering better opportunities to the many women graduates whom he found to be under-employed in secretarial and similar jobs. After referring sympathetically to measures to open opportunities to women in senior jobs of all kinds, he goes on:

> 'But there is a third (policy) open to business. This is to look to these graduates as a potential source of middle and lower management, as some American companies have so successfully done. This is half a revolution; the top positions held by men are not directly threatened, but the shortage of middle and lower management of quality would be alleviated. This is the line of thought . . . I would like to put forward.'[1]

It seems, then, that the tendency of women, more than men, to limit their 'vertical' ambitions and to prefer directly creative work to administration is frequently seen as a fact, and one from which at least some employers and their advisers are able to draw advantage. But how far has this fact to be treated as permanent or necessary?

For some women, particularly older women who came up against strong career blocks, the adoption of attitudes like these has certainly been a case of making a virtue of necessity. If there was in any case

[1] Rogaly, J., 'This Learned Regiment of Women', *Financial Times*, 29th July 1969.

no chance of getting to the top, especially in administrative and managerial posts, why not settle for a more congenial post lower down? Attitudes which arose in that way might be expected to change as opportunities improve, and this does in fact seem to be happening. Even in the particularly difficult atmosphere of business, the studies note that younger women are much less ready than the generation now in their forties or over to accept that there is a bar to their reaching any particular level or entering a particular field.

Women's tendency to reject certain areas of work may also be due to unfamiliarity. The studies bring out repeatedly the part played by accident in the careers which lead women to jobs as directors or senior managers, the lack of effective career guidance either before finishing school or university or while on the job, and the absence, very often, of effective communication within an organization between senior managers and young women specialists or management trainees.[1] Top-level direction and administration, especially in business, happens to be an area of work of which not many women hitherto have either known or been helped to learn much. If more younger women could be helped to see the interest and value of work in some of the areas which they now avoid, as experienced by women who have actually done this work, there is every reason to think that more of them would turn that way.

There may be some marginally greater tendency among women actually occupying posts as directors or as senior managers or administrators than among men at the same level to feel that administration is a wearisome chore, and that the politics of managing a big organization are a discreditable nuisance. But the studies show that plenty of the women as well as the men actually in these positions, in business as well as in the Civil Service, find their work stimulating and rewarding. It offers not only money and power but scope for idealism, personal contacts and intellectual skill; not forgetting, in some types of business, the excitement of a gamble. No doubt many professionally qualified women, like many professionally qualified men, will always prefer to stay with the drawing board or the television cameras, or in direct contact with the client, rather than move to an administrative job. But it seems very likely that better knowledge would narrow if not remove the gap between the proportions of women and of men who make this choice.

---

[1] One of the authors has a particularly vivid memory of a morning spent with the women management trainees of one large firm, followed by a lunch with the directors of the same firm to discuss women's abilities and prospects. The firm is one with a well-deserved reputation for training and personnel management as well as for commercial efficiency, but the contrast of expectations and the block in communications was near enough complete.

398

This does not mean that the case for entering a career leading to a top managerial job should necessarily be put to women in the same way as to men. If girls acquire from their early upbringing and education a different set of interests from boys, different (though equally valid) aspects of various fields of work may need to be emphasized to them to catch their attention. Rossi, for example, notes that the most characteristic value patterns of men and women graduates partly match and partly diverge from the patterns characteristic of entrants into business management. So far as this goes, either men or women might be suited to management careers. But there is a difference between the respects in which men's and women's patterns correspond to typical business management patterns and can be made the basis for an appeal to enter business careers. For men it might be advisable to stress money and power, for women working with and service to people. For both it might be advisable to lay more stress on the originality and creativity of business management than appears to have been used in the past.

There remains however the third and most basic reason why women tend, as compared to men, to limit their 'vertical' ambitions and to spread their life aims over a wider area, namely their family commitments. As seen through the eyes of informants in the occupational studies these take effect in a number of ways.

The most obvious is simply the pressure of overload through doing two jobs. On this point, the occupational material in P.E.P.'s and other reports confirms the findings of the family studies and presents a consistent picture of 'particularly conscious and conscientious middle-class mothers'.[1] The conscientiousness operates in both directions. On the one hand women tend to give their family responsibilities at least equal priority with their work, even at the highest work levels. On the other the evidence is that married women at these levels tend to be particularly careful not to get into a situation where their job commitments would exceed the time and effort they can spare from their families, and they would therefore have to fall short on what they or others currently understand as their obligations to their job. A number of single women informants, even more than men, suspect that married women do often get into this position and 'let the side down'. But the evidence does not bear out that this actually happens. Married women at senior professional and managerial levels seem, where their responsibility to their employers is concerned, to be a particularly conscientious group. If their double load seems likely to be inconsistent with seeking and holding a top job, they are likely to let the job go. Men and women respondents

---

[1] Sommerkorn, *op. cit.*, p. 201.

in the family studies agree that 'substantial success' in an occupation can be achieved with a 'medium' expenditure of time and energy, but that to get to the top requires 'maximum' energy. When asked further what degree of time and energy will be required to reach the position where each respondent him- or herself wants to be, 31 per cent of single women and 35-40 per cent of men reply 'maximum', but for married women with children this proportion drops to 17 per cent and for those without children to 9 per cent. In much greater proportions than men or single women, married women accept a 'medium' but disclaim a 'maximum' work commitment.[1]

Another way in which family commitments have their effect follows from the tradition that the husband is the family's main bread-winner. Informants note how men at senior levels tend to feel themselves obliged as family supporters to seek promotion whether or not the higher job is attractive in itself. Quite apart from their own or their families' feelings, their superiors tend to expect this behaviour from them and to press them to conform to it. Women tend not to be put under the same pressure either by their families or by their firms. It is easier for them, therefore, to adopt the gamelike attitude once expected of the man of means: the man who, because his livelihood is assured, can take the role of the gifted amateur, with its advantages as well as its disadvantages, its independence on the one hand and lack of full professional commitment on the other.

Thirdly, informants note a tendency in women to avoid a situation in which a wife is clearly superior in rank, pay, or professional skill to her husband. In husband and wife partnerships, for example in architecture, it is common to find the husband acting as the front-line operator even when the wife is quite clearly playing an equal if not a superior role in the partnership and is well able to fill the front role herself.

Family commitments do not, of course, exist in a vacuum. Their significance for women's as for men's careers depends on the obligations imposed by work at senior levels. These obligations could well change, or be made to change, in ways favourable to women's opportunity of reaching the top. The possibility that work patterns could be re-designed, without loss of efficiency, to provide for women's different life cycle will be considered in Chapter XII. For men as well as for women, the commitment of time and effort required for the production of material goods and services is likely to diminish as affluence grows. That is likely to make it easier for women to reconcile family commitments with what will be accepted in more affluent conditions as a 'maximum' contribution to work; some aspects of

[1] Ch. VI. p. 207.

this will be considered in Chapters XII and XIII. Attitudes and the sharing of responsibilities within the family, the material equipment of families, and the personal and social services available to them, could all change further – on top of the extensive changes which have already taken place – in directions facilitating women's promotion. All these threads, and the possibilities to which they lead for the future, will be drawn together in Chapter XIII. But as things now stand, family commitments, from one angle or another, continue to constitute for many women a strong bar to entry into posts whose attainment calls for 'maximum' effort.

b *Women tend to be less forceful and competitive than men in their work and in pursuing their careers*

Whatever the level or field of work at which women ultimately aim, the occupational studies agree that more women than men fall short in drive, decisiveness and the ability to impose their authority or to devise and sell their own policies, for the purpose either of the job they are doing or of promoting their own career.

A young man in senior management in one company summed up the views of many others thus:

'A manager in a line management position must be an entrepreneur, and I don't know any woman in this organization who has these entrepreneurial qualities. You find them in little shops sometimes, but the girls who come in here are all too nice. I find that a lot of them lack personality – all a bit faceless. I look for individuals. . . . I reckon business is authoritarian. If you give people responsibility, they must get the job done. A lot of people talk about team spirit and co-operation, and women often get things done by coaxing. I don't think this is the way. I think it's very difficult to take a woman seriously. A man goes into a meeting determined to get something out of it. If I go into a meeting, something has got to happen at the end. Women can give nice little presentations, but they don't turn the knife – they don't leave the impression that they're going to make no concessions and that what they want must be done. I think women lack persistence and a competitive feeling. There are some men I'm scared of, but no women. . . . I wouldn't promote a woman above a certain level, even if she were better than a man, because (*a*) I wouldn't trust her to stay and (*b*) I don't think she could set the standards.'[1]

The Civil Service, the B.B.C. and industry have their share of forceful women. But comments from all these fields agree that, when women

[1] I. Allen, *Women in Two Companies*, pp. 13-15.

who enter or apply to enter through the entry gates most likely to lead to top jobs are compared to men entering by the same gates, rather fewer of the women prove to have the force and initiative which mark them out as possible top managers or members of the Civil Service's policy grades.[1] Comments even by women informants tend also to agree that women are more likely than men to prove 'not very good at being in positions of authority', and may try to avoid such positions altogether; a further reason for the tendency just noted for women to draw back from promotion into positions of line management. More women than men architects, for example, seem to avoid work involving large-scale line management responsibility even when there is no obviously compelling reason for them to do so.

'Authority' here refers to two things. The first is style of management. Walker's study of a Civil Service office handling the routine administration of national insurance – a straightforward executive situation, with a minimum of innovation – showed that in this type of situation a relatively firm, aloof type of leadership based strongly on technical expertize gives better results, in terms of efficiency, than a style based on sympathy for staff and good personal contacts. Women supervisors, it also showed, tend to adopt the more permissive and men the more authoritarian style. As a result, the productivity and efficiency of the women's sections studies tended to rank relatively low. The women showed more dislike than the men for the supervisory part of their job and preferred posts where they could work as individuals, preferably meeting members of the public face to face.[2]

This finding can be generalized from the P.E.P. studies. Women are more likely than men, situation for situation, to adopt a persuasive, non-authoritarian approach: power with rather than power over, in Mary Parker Follett's phrase. There will be plenty of exceptions, since this, like the other tendencies discussed in this part of this chapter, is a matter of statistical probability and of marginal differences; a matter of there being a rather lower percentage of authoritarians among women than among men, not of women generally being non-authoritarians. The qualification 'situation for situation' is important. A role like that of a mental hospital matron, for example, may be defined by custom and the hospital's medical staff in either an authoritarian or a non-authoritarian way, and the man or woman who holds it is likely, irrespective of sex, to tend either to

---

[1] Under-Secretary and upwards. Assistant Secretaries and below tend to be more concerned with administering existing policy. The distinction is, however, only rough.

[2] Walker, *op. cit.*, pp. 100 and 102.

conform to, or to be selected because, he or she fits the style chosen. A woman who pioneers as the first entrant to a traditionally masculine profession may find it necessary to be either exceptionally conciliatory or exceptionally hard-driving. With all these reservations, however, the generalization stands, at least for women qualified at the level with which the P.E.P. studies have been concerned; in the existing conditions of British culture, women appear, other things being equal, to be more likely than men to use a non-authoritarian style of supervision and management.

In situations of change and development a less authoritarian style will often be appropriate, whereas in situations of simple execution it is often out of place. In that sense women could be better equipped than men for the situations typically met with in top jobs, but men would be likely to do better in more routine managerial or supervisory roles. This, however, is not the end of the story. For, secondly, the suggestion that fewer women than men are likely to be able to carry authority well refers not simply to their choice of management styles but, more generally, to the ability of both women and men to get decisions made in any management style at all. A woman with long experience of recruiting and promoting women graduates in a large company said that, if she had to name two things which she had found lacking in girls' education, one would be mathematics and the other decision-making: the idea that decisions are needed and must be made, plus the skill and personal force to get them made. This theme recurs repeatedly in the P.E.P. studies. Women are said to be more liable than men to nag, to whine, to 'flap like wet hens' when something goes wrong, to be unaware of how to handle colleagues, or to react to extremes: dragons in an older generation, ineffectual nice mice in the present one; in any case ineffective as managers in whatever style.

Further, it is said by a number of employers covered in the studies that women in professional and managerial work have proved to be less self-propelled than men as regards their own careers. Case-histories show, as has been said, a high degree of accident – though there are also the committed few – in the way young women drift into careers outside traditional women's fields; there is probably a higher degree of accident than among men, though luck and accident count heavily for men as well. Having drifted into a particular field, able women are reported by employers as more likely than able men to enter at too low a level – perhaps as a secretary or a B.B.C. Programme Operations Assistant – so giving their competitors several years' start. They are less likely than men – though men as well often fall short here – to develop a long-range career strategy and the arts of office politics needed, in Hegarty's regrettable but revealing phrase,[1] to 'curry favour with the power'. In general they fail to realize that it is up to them to sell themselves to the organization and to go out and do so. A man in a company famous for its marketing success commented that:

> 'Women don't get any further than they do (in this company) because they're not thinking right. They're not thinking in terms of a career. They're not thinking of the job after next. I'm a politician . . . not of the back-stabbing sort. I consciously foster things which will do me some good in my career. I really feel that women ought to learn to market themselves a bit better. First of all they ought to get the product right. This means they shouldn't wear mini-skirts or look too much like pretty dollies, because nobody will take them seriously. On the other hand, they mustn't look masculine. Then, once they've got the product right, they've got to learn to advertise it. They've got to project what they've got. I'm very conscious of my image. When I started, I was appalling. I was very much of a grafter, not a chatter. Now I'm a chatter – very good in meetings. I used to be very diffident. You've got to grab yourself by the bootlaces and pull yourself up. And then there's the public relations aspect. You have to develop relations – you've got to be seen in the right places. If you're capable, it's a good idea to get into the right situation, and then be seen to be talking good sense. I just don't think women go about all these things in the right way.'[2]

Women tend to show too much diffidence, employers insist, and to wait for the employer to develop them instead of going out to seek development for themselves.

A similar situation as regards both career development and job performance is found in architecture. Informants insist on the need, at point after point in an architectural career, for a high degree of tough-mindedness and self-confidence. A student needs this to organize him- or herself through the chaos of architectural education. A qualified architect needs it to survive criticism and correction in the early stages of practical training and acquire a matter of fact attitude to such things as the rejection of a design; to cope with builders and contractors and carry major professional responsibility; to go out and build a network of contacts and bring work into the office; and to sell himself into the principal or chief officer level of work and develop and apply the relevant skills in office politics. A married woman architect needs an additional degree of the same qualities to

---

[1] Hegarty, E. J., *How to Succeed in Company Politics*, McGraw-Hill, 1964, Ch. IV.
[2] Allen, I., *Women in Two Companies*, pp. 43-44.

organize her family alongside her professional life and, if necessary, to re-start a broken career at a relatively junior level and build up quickly to the professional standing which others have reached by continuing work. At all these points, informants suggest, women architects tend to meet a confidence barrier and to fall at least marginally short of men in determination and drive.

The point in all this is not that women necessarily lack the drive and political skill to reach or do well in top jobs, nor that lack of a self-propelled quality or the ability to carry authority well is confined to women. It is that there appears to be a higher proportion of women than of men who have the underlying ability for these purposes, but need special grooming and encouragement to bring it out. The exact extent to which this is so is difficult to measure, since it is hard to disentangle the effects of women's own tendency to be less forceful and competitive from those of the obstacles put in women's way. The qualities needed to overcome or survive among the obstacles – for example a very conciliatory or a 'battleaxe' approach – are not necessarily those most likely to put women in line for promotion to the top. As a delegate to the 1969 U.N. seminar on the Status of Women put it, a champion steeplechaser is not the same as a champion on the flat. But certainly a need exists to promote the development among highly qualified women of forcefulness and competitiveness. The example has already been quoted of how women who are 'catapulted' into the role of head of a business or a professional practice by some accident of inheritance, marriage, or widowhood often fill it successfully, but might have had neither the skill and drive nor the motivation to seek and achieve this role for themselves.

Younger women, several of the P.E.P. reports note, are tending to succeed much better than those now middle-aged or nearing retirement in combining femininity with forcefulness both on the job and in promoting their own careers. Informants remember an older 'battleaxe' generation of women who were the first to break through into the senior levels of a number of occupations, and whose ferocity caused the stoutest male heart to quail. Women informants repeatedly disclaim any intention of adopting what they perceive as that generation's too aggressive style. That generation was followed by another, quiet, much more reluctant to be identified with feminism or any kind of agitation; it is to this generation that what was said above about the non-aggressiveness of women in high-level careers particularly applies. The suggestion of the reports is that a third generation, of women who have entered careers in the last ten years, has learnt from the experience of its two predecessors and is now beginning to find a workable middle way between them: more forceful and competitive than the generation immediately before it, but without the loss of femininity of the 'battleaxe' age.[1]

The reports do not, however, suggest that the problem of women's tendence to excessive diffidence in work situations is fully solved, even in the younger generation, nor that it will necessarily solve itself automatically. Approaches to a further solution could be along either of two lines.

One is to accept that women tend to be relatively diffident but to change their working environment so as to minimize the loss of high-quality working capacity which their diffidence causes to employers and the loss of career opportunity which it causes to women themselves. Some relatively 'gentlemanly' environments, like that of the Administrative Civil Service or of the 'old' B.B.C. in the time of Lord Reith, have proved particularly favourable to women's promotion. These are environments which are co-operative rather than competitive and preferably are equipped, like the Civil Service, with promotion procedures for drawing people forward instead of waiting for them to push forward. A conscious effort by senior members of staff to sponsor the promotion of promising young women can also help. Sponsors ('office uncles') play an important part in the careers of many men, and the studies show that they do and could play a still greater part in the careers of women.

But an approach based only on employers' or sponsors' initiative or on changing the work environment, useful as it is, would be likely on its own to prove neither reliable enough nor wide enough in scope. Sponsorship can be an unreliable resource. In the long run it will not necessarily help a young man's career to be known as the boss's blue-eyed boy. A sponsorship relation between a senior man and a junior woman may be even more suspect. If a sponsor's career fails, so may that of the man or woman he sponsors. In any case the availability of a sponsor cannot be guaranteed. A gentlemanly, uncompetitive environment is neither practicable nor desirable in many changing and developing fields where forceful entrepreneurship is required. Even in the Civil Service, though quieter qualities can win promotion up to and including Assistant Secretary, posts above that level tend to demand an extra element of drive and initiative of the kind in which, the experience of the service suggests, women are more likely than men to fall short.

Gentlemanliness, in any case, can bury women's problems as well as solve them. If women's problems in a particular occupation or

[1] See also the findings of the family studies on the absence of masculine identification among younger and middle-aged dual-career women (Chapter IX, pp. 372-375) and on some informants' ability to be 'two different people at home and at work', and much more authoritative at work (Chapter IX, p. 359).

industry have not been solved, a 'gentlemanly' tradition such as that of 'Company B' or the Civil Service may make it harder to bring them into the open and solve them than in environments where a more aggressive approach is acceptable. The studies suggest that women may actually have a better chance of growing through the cracks of a chaotic and informal promotion system than of being promoted in an organization where formal career planning has been introduced. Under formal plans for talent-spotting and career design, they may, and in some of the cases studied do, get less attention and grooming than men, and their last state under such plans may be worse than their first.

The second and more generally promising approach is to help women themselves to develop the qualities needed to progress in a competitive environment, in so far of course as this is an objective which they want to pursue.[1] Traditionally the difficulty in the way of doing this, whether in Britain or in other countries,[2] has been, as Sommerkorn says of women teachers in British universities:

'The fact that no unequivocal role pattern has yet been evolved for professional women. There is a strain caused by the conflicting demands made by the role requirements of the new feminism on the one hand, and the demands inherent in the academic career on the other. How can one keep up in one's intellectual field, if at the same time it is advisable not to appear to be too engrossed in it, in other words if the role expectations of one role are disfunctional to the performance of the other? In short the crucial problem of modern academic women seems to be how to deal successfully with the anomaly of a woman performing an instrumental role.'[3]

This point recurs in the P.E.P. studies. Women executives in business or the B.B.C. are liable to be overlooked if they fail to act forcibly and aggressively, but criticized as unfeminine if they do act in these ways. Women graduates, one of the studies suggests, have been the victims in their university years of an anti-intellectual tradition which prevents them from appearing as men's intellectual equals or superiors.

But the occupational studies also show that it should be more practicable today than at any time in the past to resolve the dilemma whether professional women should or can afford to play an aggressive role. The increased experience which has accumulated since the

---

[1] Above, p. 396.
[2] See e.g. the discussion by Hartmann, *op. cit.*, of how German women business heads have had in effect to write their own role prescription, or by M. Cussler in *The Woman Executive*, Harcourt Brace, 1958.
[3] Sommerkorn, *op. cit.*, p. 185.

'battleaxe generation' is one key factor. Another is what might be called the professionalization of decision-making. A feature of management studies in the last decades has been the analysis of styles and techniques of management and the development of standards to show to which decisions or stages of decision each style or technique is appropriate. Whether to use a directive or a participative approach, a management hierarchy or a network, a formal or an informal procedure, or whether to be forcible or persuasive are matters not of personal predilection or of sex-typing, but, as with scientific techniques, of what best suits the task in hand. An understanding of these distinctions is becoming common currency among younger trained managers in all fields. Women who learn and apply them may well find themselves accepted in the same way as women scientists, not as exponents of a feminine or a masculine approach but simply as doing what is necessary for the job. One of the reasons why women progress relatively easily in the Civil Service is that the Administrative Grade already has, to a greater extent than any of the other occupations studied, a distinctive management style which can be adopted by administrators of both sexes without raising any question of whether this means that they are behaving in a masculine or feminine way. A condition of women gaining from the professionalization of management is, of course, that they must themselves become actively involved in management studies. There have been a number of outstanding women research workers in this field, but at the student level, for a variety of reasons – not only firms' reluctance to back women for management courses, but also some reluctance from the side of women themselves and a shortage of women in the posts from which staff are usually seconded for top-level courses – the proportion of women in major courses has hitherto been very small.[1]

---

[1] Some figures for the proportion of women at particular schools are:
London Business School, two-year courses: 1967-68, one woman; 1968-69, two women (out of 41 students); 1969-70, none. The age group for these courses is 20-30.
　　Manchester Business School, 1968-69: One-year graduate course: 3 women out of 39 students: age typically 21-28. Number of women in each of last four years: 1, 1, 3, 3.
　　Twelve-week middle management course (2 courses): 1 woman out of 100 students. Age typically 45-55.
　　Senior executive course (2 courses). One course had one woman out of 26 students, the other no women. Age typically 30-40.
　　Ashridge Management College, 1967-9: 44 women (including one on a course designed for senior management) out of 4,948 students.
　　Sundridge Park, 1968-69: one woman out of 900 students (age range 35-45).
　　British Institute of Management: estimated 10 per cent of women on general management courses.

408

Another helpful factor – as in the case of women's different motivation and aspirations – is the improvement that is now beginning, compared to the past, in understanding the unreality of the conceptions held by men and women of the behaviour expected of them by the other sex. Women have tended to believe to a much greater extent than is actually the case, as the Steinmann studies show, that educated men prefer a soft, conventionally feminine woman to one who adds intellect and force to traditional feminine qualities, and have tended to damp their own drive and intellectual expression to match this pattern. Men, similarly, have tended to believe that educated women wish to influence them to behave in a more 'feminine' way than men themselves would wish to do, and have resisted forceful action by women accordingly. Though conflicts based on misconceptions like these remain common, they are at least becoming better understood and to that extent easier to resolve.

The argument is not that differences between men and women in management style, and especially in forceful and aggressive behaviour, are to be ruled out altogether. Sex-typed as well as personal differences may remain. But it should be possible to set them in a framework which makes clear to all that the differences which remain are the reflection, not of some feminine or masculine bias irrelevant to the job in hand, but of the 'law of the situation' – again Mary Parker Follett's phrase – as determined on the one hand by the job to be done and on the other by the personalities of those engaged in doing it.

The primary responsibility for developing and securing the adoption of objectively correct styles of management rests on employers and on the organizations engaged in management research and teaching. But informants stress that for girls in particular training needs to begin much earlier, and that schools and universities need to pay more attention to this side of girls' education than, in the view of managers concerned with recruitment, they have done hitherto. The occupational studies do not show that Sommerkorn's problem of evolving an 'unequivocal role pattern' for professional women in the matter of drive, aggression and carrying authority has been solved. What they present rather is a challenge to employers, educators, and women themselves to tackle their problems in conditions where, for the first time since women began to move into senior professional and managerial work in Western countries, a solution could be in sight.

c *Women tend more than men to adopt an informal, personal, expressive ('emotional, talkative') style of working.*

d *Women are more likely than men to be tense, self-conscious, conscientious over details, disinclined to delegate, and better at routine than at initiation.*

German university professors, as reported in Anger's study, hold determinedly that 'women cannot think', are too emotional for the life of a university teacher, 'cannot do research', and are industrious but uncreative. They are 'God's poorest creatures', intellectual life is for men, and the best professors marry non-academics.[1] Recent British studies throw up nothing so ferocious as this.[2] The views they report on points (3) and (4), like the rest of those reported in this chapter, refer to what informants see as marginal, not basic, differences between typical or modal men and women. These differences may run, from women's point of view, in either a favourable or an unfavourable direction; they may be overlaid in particular cases by the wider differences between individual men and women, and in any case do not stand out as either permanent or fundamental. As P.E.P.'s Civil Service report puts it:

'The theme of the women's discussions of differences between men and women administrators was that the differences were not those of fundamental approach or capacity but sprang from the kinds of adjustment that women made to their minority situation.'[3]

With this reservation, the P.E.P. reports agree that women do tend rather more than men, so far as the opportunity is open to them, towards flexible fields of work where they are not bound too much by formal procedures, and where there is plenty of opportunity for personal contacts. They are more likely than men to rely strongly on feel, intuition, talking through a situation, and generally on an informal approach, and less likely to structure a situation formally or to proceed by abstract thinking.

Academic women are more likely than men to prefer teaching to research. They tend to criticize formal administrative procedures as ways of becoming bogged down in forethought instead of getting on with the job, and to see them as a peculiarly masculine defect:

[1] Anger, H., *Probleme der Deutschen Universität*, Mohr, Tübingen, 1960, pp. 468-484. We cannot resist quoting the view of John Knox on this and on the previous point of women in authority: 'Such be al women, compared unto men in bearing of authority. For their sight in civil regiment, is but blindnes: their strength, weakness: their counsel, foolishnes: and judgement, phrenesie, if it be rightly considered.'

[2] The nearest is V. A. Demant's dismissal of the case ordaining women as Anglican priests in the Report of the Archbishops' Commission on *Women and Holy Orders*, Church Information Office, London, 1966, pp. 96-114.

[3] Walters, P., *Women in the Administrative Civil Service*, p. 38.

410

'Men seem to love it; they spend half their time on committees, they adore sitting there. That would bore me to tears anyway. Men are more committee-minded than women. They sit on committees for hours and talk about nothing and get nowhere.'[1]

B.B.C. women are more likely than men to avoid posts with formal administrative authority and to prefer work like that of the 'anchor man' of a production team, whose network of contacts is wide but informal.

Women business heads tend to gravitate towards situations where:

'As we have discovered from their career histories, their position allows or obliges them to exercise considerable flexibility in dealing with administrative matters, staff relations and customers. Within this specialized framework, either of the small business or in a more advisory capacity, whether owner, entrepreneur, aide-de-camp, or trouble-shooter, they learn, if they are to prosper, not only how to operate to maximum advantage but to live with their limitations.'[2]

Like academic women, they tend to criticize men as:

'More given to posturing, to pompous displays, to express themselves in stilted phrases, not to be themselves, to be unwilling to face the facts.'[3]

and generally, the male tradition of 'brave fronts and stiff upper lips' and the rites and ceremonies of the City of London.

Women architects, similarly, are said by some informants to score through not being over-professionalized. They may bring to problems a freshness of outlook which allows them to spot an unconventional solution while their men colleagues continue to batter their heads against a brick wall of standard practice. They may also have at least a marginal advantage on what might be called the more personal side of architecture. Though men as well as women can be successful interior designers, a number of informants insist that women have been particularly successful in taking the client's-eye view of such things as colours, shapes, and the design and location of interior equipment, not only in homes but in shops, offices, and schools. It seems that women architects tend to show at least a marginally greater interest in the service and human relations aspects of their work – in personal service to the customer, in ensuring that

[1] Sommerkorn, *op. cit.*, p. 121.   [2] Allen, J., *op. cit.*, p. 35.
[3] Allen, J., *op. cit.*, p. 42.

under-privileged groups are taken into account and that the architect produces 'a total sculpture where people belong' (Jane Drew), or in helping other members of the profession rather than in going straight out for their own careers.

The tendency of many women to adopt a personal, loosely structured style of working has both positive and negative aspects. As a technique of problem-solving and as a ground for either favouring or disfavouring women in particular posts it may be more or less useful according to the problems to be solved. An informal, flexible, approach is likely, as was said above,[1] to be more effective in situations of change and development than in routine administration, especially where this is on a large scale. It is likely to be more useful in small units, what one architectural report calls 'the vehicle of the master craftsman', than in big organizations which depend more on formal structures and procedures. As regards the prospects for women's careers these considerations might tell either way. On the one hand managerial and professional work has tended to become increasingly professionalized and organized into large-scale units. On the other, the pace of change is increasing, greater stress is being laid on creativity as apart from routine management, and there is a general revolt against bureaucracy and demand for a more personal style of work and management in all fields.

Men informants tend to stress the risks of the informal, personal approach. They emphasize the danger of using this approach where it is out of place, of being over-emotional and over-talkative, of letting personal considerations count too heavily in deciding cases, of mixing personal with business life, and of despising, failing to understand, and therefore mismanaging large-scale organizations. Women informants point out that men too may have these problems, and in addition may tend too much towards formality and abstract, impersonal thinking. Flair, personal relationships and informal networks are fundamental to efficient working for men in senior positions as well as for women. A major problem for women in many occupations, as the P.E.P. studies underline, is not so much that they are over-involved in informal networks as that they are not accepted into the informal male networks through which much of the effective business is done.

The question, as before, is not whether the informal, personal, approach which is thought to be marginally commoner among women is better or worse than the more formal and abstract approach commoner among men, but whether women (or men) can learn to recognize and use the approach that fits each particular situation.

[1] See also the account of the Y.M.C.A./Y.W.C.A. case in Chapter IV.

Situations are not rigidly divided. The same problem can often be handled in different ways, leaving room for personal style and an element of sex-typing. The question is whether sex-typing can be limited to these cases, and not allowed to influence methods of handling problems which call for an informal or formal approach as the case may be.

On this the P.E.P. studies are encouraging. They suggest that women in an older generation might have been inclined either to use a 'feminine' style of working uncritically – for example to commit themselves emotionally to a particular cause or field of work, to the extent that they no longer worked effectively as members of a larger team – or else to suppress their feelings unduly and to develop by way of reaction the style of a dragon or martinet. Younger and even not so young women, however, seem readier to choose the style that fits the case. Women Civil Servants, as the quotation on page 410 shows, tend to see a 'feminine' approach as a controlled reaction useful in particular cases, notably as compensation for the fact that 'some of the traditional male techniques for softening up the work situation . . . talking it over, over a drink or a meal, could not easily be initiated by a woman'.[1] Men, one woman Civil Servant comments, are perfectly well aware that this game is being played and accept it as a legitimate gambit. A woman director notes that women, or men, whose current role is unfamiliar and insecure may tend to be emotional, but that this proves to be a passing phase once they have come fully and securely to grips with the job. Another says:

'If women are engaged in non-emotional work they are no more emotional than men, but otherwise – for example matrons in schools – they get emotionally involved.'[2]

When logic rather than intuition is needed, the study of women directors finds that logic can be and tends to be acquired. A woman manager in P.E.P.'s study of two companies comments that she is a completely different person at home and at work. Her work requires a very different style of behaviour, but she finds no particular difficulty in switching roles. In general what was said above about the professionalization of management styles and the ways in which they might make it easier for women to choose, and be seen to have chosen, an appropriate style applies in this area as well.

It remains, however, to consider the question raised by point (4) of whether women can be expected to unwind enough and be free enough from tension to let them choose and exercise appropriate

[1] Walters, P., *op. cit.*, p. 38.
[2] Allen, J., *op. cit.*, p. 49.

working styles with the flexibility required. A double thread runs through the reports. On the one hand women are seen by both men and women informants as tending to be more conscientious than men, and better at handling details; or, as women rather than men tend to put it, that men are too much inclined, as compared with women, to get the main lines of a decision right and hope that the details will work themselves out. On the other, women are seen as tending to be less creative and less able to see the wood for the trees. On both counts the indication seems to be, on the lines of Rogaly's suggestion quoted on page 397, that women are likely to provide a better flow of candidates for middle and junior management and for relatively routine jobs at the top than for genuine policy-making jobs. When Civil Servants or applicants for the B.B.C.'s General Trainee scheme are rated, women do in fact tend to supply a relatively high proportion of the good, competent, applicants or administrators, but relatively few who rate a grading as A+.

Behind this situation there lie factors in the work situation as well as others which reach further back. Women in the junior and middle and to some extent even at the most senior levels of the occupations studied tend to feel themselves under closer scrutiny by superiors, colleagues, subordinates, and clients than would be normal in the case of a man. They are less accepted, more on probation, and consequently tend to be more tense and to feel less able to risk mistakes or to be casual over matters like time-keeping. If customers or contacts in another department start with a suspicion that a woman is likely to be incompetent, she may feel that an effective way to establish her position is to master her job with a detailed thoroughness unnecessary for a man. If colleagues think that a married woman with children is unlikely to be fully available for her job – the strongest suspicion seems to come from single women, not from men – an effective answer is to be meticulous in observing office hours, to miss no meetings, and to take on, voluntarily, extra tasks.

Though this answer is effective in one direction, it may be at the price of greater loss in another. A married woman who has in any case a heavy load of work at home may find, as a Civil Service comment notes, that even without being over-meticulous at the office she may be overloading herself and that her work, though done competently, loses the cutting edge of its creativity. The Administrative Civil Service has developed during the last generation a tradition of overload and overtime which is not on the face of it helpful to efficiency. If overload and overtime can damage the efficiency of men or of single women, they are likely to be still more damaging, as the P.E.P. report underlines, in the case of married women and especially of those married women who feel themselves to be under pressure to be unusually conscientious and meticulous in their work.

Another factor in many women's work situation which makes for over-concern with detail is that they may be forced into over-specialization because the paths which they are allowed to follow are more limited than those open to men. The business and B.B.C. reports note that, because posts in certain fields – especially general and production management – have not usually been available to women, there may be a tendency to recruit women as specialists or, if they are recruited for general management training, to give them in practice a less wide job rotation than is usual for men. Since men are called on to cover a wider field, they are not expected to be too familiar with the detail of any part of it, but on the other hand are more likely to be expected to develop a wide view and a capacity for seeing the wood rather than the trees.

An important factor making for tenseness and lack of confidence among married women is the high degree of upset to which their careers are liable as compared to those of single women or men. At a time when men or single women are settled, secure and confident in their careers, married women are liable to need to contract out into an unusual career pattern or to drop out of work altogether, and have then to re-establish themselves. Like men who have a similar career upset – but far more married women meet this problem than men – they tend at this point not only to lose the benefit of the confidence which their previous career had won for them from others, but, and experience shows this to be even more important, to lose confidence in themselves.

The effects of factors like these on women's work behaviour should not be over-stressed. As Walker's Civil Service study points out, it is one thing to suspect women of being over-conscientious and unwilling to delegate and another to find solid evidence that this actually is so. In fact he found none. All factors of this kind arising out of the work situation tend, in any case, to become less important once women reach really senior levels. At this point, as a number of the company women who have broken the seniority barrier point out, a woman who has proved herself is likely to be accepted and even favoured. There may still be doubt as to whether she should be promoted further, but not as to her competence in her present job. She is likely to be visible and well-known in the circle with which she deals; indeed more so than a man, since she is so rare. When a Civil Servant reaches Assistant Secretary or Under-Secretary grade, not only is her own competence likely to be beyond suspicion, but she is also likely to be in a better position than a Principal to control her own time and to delegate work. The same applies to the principal of an architectural practice as compared to an assistant.

The work factors which make for tenseness and over-conscientiousness would, for the most part, disappear if qualified women could rely on career patterns adapted to women's life cycle, on the lines to be discussed in the next chapter; if women at senior levels became more numerous and accepted; and if women were helped, on the lines suggested above, to improve their capacity for promoting their own careers and for handling decisions. Behind the work factors, however, lies, as has been shown,[1] a further range of factors reaching back into education and the family. Press comments on radio and television performers have repeatedly noted that women from a wide range of backgrounds share a tendency, especially in comment and discussion programmes, to be more tense and self-conscious than men, as well as more diffident and informal or, by reaction, too brightly self-assured. Exceptions, the comments suggest, include some older women intellectuals, some of the younger women television professionals, and those involved in the relatively relaxed atmosphere of Woman's Hour.[2] The general tendency towards tenseness, over-meticulousness, and lack of creativity of which employers complain shows itself already at the point where graduates enter employment and in girls' earlier educational record.

e *Women are not acceptable in certain fields as colleagues, superiors or business partners*

Women can be rejected as members of a work team on the ground of actual or alleged features of their work performance, such as those just discussed, or because of a vaguer resentment at 'having women around'. The two, obviously, are difficult to disentangle. So far as they can be disentangled, it is the vaguer feeling of preferring women's room to their company that is referred to here.

The P.E.P. reports show very clearly that this feeling still exists in many quarters in Britain. Very often it is a case, not of what an employer's own staff might think themselves, but of what they fear that others might think. An engineering firm in a traditionally male-dominated industrial area reports keeping quiet the appointment of a woman to its board, even though her competence can be shown by all the usual criteria of business success. A number of firms are reluctant to accept women into their sales force on the ground not

---

[1] Above, Ch. III, p. 128, and Ch. IV, p. 149.

[2] E.g. *Telegraph*, September 7, 1957; *Observer*, February 5, 1961; *The Times*, April 27, 1963; *Telegraph*, July 13, 1963; *Sunday Times Magazine*, July 18. 1965; *Evening Standard*, February 23, 1966; *Radio Times*, May 4, 1967.

only that they might not adapt to conditions on the road but that the customer might not like it. Civil Servants and architects report that quite often the customer in fact does not like it. A number of businessmen, particularly though not exclusively in the north, show reluctance to do business with a woman Civil Servant or to treat a woman architect or husband-and-wife partnership as being on a full business basis. The same problem may arise in dealing with trade unions or with foreign businessmen.

Often unacceptability is also found within an organization's own ranks. A number of factory management messes and executive dining rooms are reported to remain closed to women. Women at a sales or management conference may be left out not only of informal drinking circles but even of a formal dinner. Women executives or Civil Servants may have to find alternative routes of doing business to replace informal eating, drinking and entertaining relationships used by men, but from which women are shut out. The company studies report that among able men there is little problem of resentment by men against women, but that considerably more is found among routine middle managers and generally among men of lower ability. Opinion polls show a general tendency for both men and women to be more likely to prefer a man rather than a woman as a superior. In some fields the degree of preference is marginal, but it is repeatedly said that male manual workers are likely to resent taking orders from a woman whether in a factory or on a building site.

At first sight this is a phenomenon of historical interest only: a survival which may take time and effort to sweep away, but has no lasting roots. The frontier of resentment is continually moving. The resistances met today among stockbrokers or north-country businessmen were once met among senior Civil Servants, but the generation of Civil Servants who resented the presence of women is now retiring or retired. Once women have moved in significant numbers into any field or level of work (one or two may not be enough) resentment of 'having women around' tends to fall sharply. Women have by now overlapped into enough traditionally male fields to show that resistance to them can be overcome in the remaining areas of resentment as well. Probably the strongest remaining resistance is that shown by male manual workers. But many women architects do in fact succeed in establishing their authority among building workers on the site, and a number of B.B.C. women note that they are well able to achieve co-operative and friendly relations with camera crews and other male technical staff. Walker, having noted that Civil Servants show a somewhat stronger preference for men as superiors than for women, adds that it is difficult to find any objective basis for this, and asks whether it may not be a matter of status rather than of the attitude of subordinates to women themselves. If women commonly hold low-status positions, units headed by them may be seen as of low status as well.[1] When the instances in all occupations in which resentment of women is reported are grouped together, a law seems to emerge: the higher the educational and intelligence level of those in a given occupation, the younger the age group, the more developed the culture, and the less tradition-bound the occupation, the less is likely to be the resentment of women as women (as apart from the question of their practical competence) in a managerial, professional or business partner role.

In other ways, however, the position is not so simple. Sex – the personal relations between men and women – does introduce a new element into the communication patterns of an organization used to operating with members of one sex alone. The new element can be positive, but can also in certain circumstances cause 'noise in the system', complicating the patterns of communication and perhaps cutting across the patterns most effective from the organization's point of view.

Whether it will do so depends in the first place on accurate understanding by men and women about each other's motives and interests.[2] Secondly, it is necessary to find the right pattern of accommodation between men's and women's roles, given not only their work capacities but the rest of their personal make-up. As the P.E.P. reports show, particularly those concerned with business, architecture, and the Civil Service, resentment of women in senior jobs tends to be lowest among men with first-class capacity; and the point is not simply the one just made that the first-class men may be less traditional and more open to new ideas. It may also be that they, like first-class women, are more likely than people with less ability to be able to cope with the problems of living in a world where men's and women's roles are more varied and flexible than in the past. Certainly such men are likely to be better able to cope with the extra strains of a full dual-career pattern if that is what seems indicated for their own family. The sources quoted in Chapters III and IV show that traditional conceptions of masculine and feminine roles tend to remain more deeply rooted among families at working- and lower middle-class levels than at the graduate level. While historical survival certainly plays its part in this, there may also be a genuine need to adapt the division of sex roles to each group's level of ability. People of lower ability may need to be presented with a more clear-

[1] Walker, *op. cit.*, pp. 241-2. On the general point of resentment by men of women, see the finding from the survey of graduates in Ch. VI, Table 7.
[2] See Ch. IV, p. 155, and above, p. 409.

cut, less complicated division of roles, tending to work out on somewhat traditional lines, than is appropriate at higher levels. This is
at present no more than a hypothesis needing further research, but
it is one which at least deserves consideration. If it should prove to
be correct, the resistance from manual workers and others of less
than top ability to women in senior jobs could be much more than a
historical survival.

Thirdly, labour market factors may be relevant. Irrespective of
their personal qualities, women constitute a distinct and identifiable
category of competitors whose presence in an area where opportunities are scarce may not be welcome. This applies at the top as well
as the bottom. Resentment of women at the top drops sharply, as
several of the studies report, once it is clear that they have put themselves out of the running for the topmost and scarcest jobs of all.

The fact that women's entry into certain fields is resisted, whether
it is due to a generalized resistance by men to women as such or to
an estimate of women's working capacity, means not only that
women lose the opportunity of entering these particular fields – and
their employers the chance of employing them there – but that
women may find the normal road towards promotion into other
more senior jobs blocked. Men in business or the B.B.C. commonly
follow a zig-zag pattern to the top, taking in a variety of experiences
in areas such as sales, reporting and comment on current affairs,
production management, or general management, to which women
are commonly not admitted. Women have to follow more specialized
paths and, at the time when they might have become eligible for the
most senior jobs, may be thought to lack sufficiently wide experience.
Architecture has in the past been an interesting case to the contrary,
inasmuch as in relatively small architectural offices, with limited
specialization, there cannot be so many reserved or protected spheres,
and architects, whether men or women, employed at any but the
most junior level have had to undertake a full range of work. But
this may change as the scale of architectural offices and the specialization within them increases. For women the results of increasing scale
and specialization could be superficially helpful, inasmuch as a
woman who prefers (for example) to avoid working directly with
male labour on building sites will find it easier to do so. But at a
more basic level it could be damaging, in that women could too
easily be cut off from areas of experience needed to qualify for a
principal's or chief officer's job.

If resistance to women's entry into particular fields is merely a
historical fact, the right answer is clearly to work, as fast as is practicable, towards a situation in which they enter these areas on
exactly the same footing as men. But in so far as more permanent

factors are at work, it may be necessary to think in terms of alternative strategies by which women can, if not by-pass, at any rate limit their participation in certain work areas and still find their way to the top.

f Women are said to be a bad risk

One of the commonest reasons for saying that women are a bad risk, at least in jobs which demand continuity and long experience in the same organization, is the suspicion that they will not stay: that family obligations will make them leave. This will be taken up again in the next chapter. Apart from this, however, the idea that women are a bad risk sums up all the doubts already explored in this chapter about their performance on the job, especially on jobs with a wide-ranging responsibility for staff and capital. On the face of it the idea that, because women have not done a job, they should therefore not be risked in it, is like the rule of Cornford's *Microcosmographia* that nothing should ever be done for the first time. For an employer, however, with a major job to fill and a choice between an untried category of staff and a category whose qualities (for better or worse) are well known, the question is real enough. One can sympathize with the view expressed when women's admission to the Administrative Civil Service was being considered, and echoed in several of the present P.E.P. reports, that it would be a good thing if some other employer tried the experiment first.

Individual women, like individual men, can of course be failures at their jobs. The P.E.P. studies have thrown up female examples of practically all the forms of moral and mental incompetence practised by males, from bank fraud to a catastrophic radio commentary on the Grand National. But as regards the argument that the risk of failure by women in top jobs is too high for it to be reasonable to ask employers to face it, several things can be said:

First, no evidence has appeared in the P.E.P. studies that women are so lacking – or at any rate need be so lacking – in the ability to exercise any of the main types of professional and managerial responsibility usually entrusted to men that they are not worth considering as candidates for these responsibilities along with men. Men's and women's capacities tend at present to differ somewhat, and some of these differences could be permanent. But they can, as has been shown, be to women's advantage as well as disadvantage, and where they are to women's disadvantage they can to a significant though not always very clear extent be removed. A particularly interesting piece of evidence on this comes from 'Company A', where the opportunities offered to women differ widely between the company's different departments. In some areas of work (for example market research) they are given opportunities equal to those of men. In others they are treated 'as a pair of hands'. What is striking is the way that women – nothing different, of course, would be expected in the case of men – live up or down to the expectations held of them in these differing environments. In the favourable environment they not only do well on the job but stay with it; their turnover rate and average length of service is similar to that of men. In the environment of low expectations they live down to what is thought of them and (like men in similar cases) quickly leave.

Some environments seem basically more suited to women in top jobs than others. The Civil Service report, for example, points out that the Administrative Grade's strong tradition of service, of un-aggressive and conciliatory rather than entrepreneurial behaviour towards colleagues and outsiders, and of stress on qualities such as honesty, openness, impartiality, and pragmatism, fits very well with the typical slant of women's qualities, the range of qualities in which they tend at present to differ at least marginally from men. In more entrepreneurial environments women prove to have more to learn and further to go. But for none of the occupations studied can it be said, on the evidence collected, that women are or at least need be in any fundamental way disqualified.

Secondly, in so far as employers or others have had rational grounds for not hurrying to encourage women's movement into the higher levels of the occupations studied, it is clear that the problem has often been one not of long-run or permanent obstacles but of thresholds deterring advance in the short run. Situations of this kind arise in many areas of economic and social life. A typical example might be the choice between a familiar and an unfamiliar location for a firm's new plant. Left to itself, the firm may have plausible, perhaps convincing reasons for not spending the time, effort and money needed to verify that the unfamiliar location might be as profitable or more profitable than the other in the long run. If however it is pressed into giving the unfamiliar location serious considera-tion, or if a far-sighted management chooses to risk the extra effort to do so, it may find that location to be an excellent bargain. Investi-gators of British policy on the location of industry have documented cases of this kind often enough to justify treating them almost as the rule rather than the exception.

The same situation seems regularly to have arisen in the course of women's movement into senior levels in the occupations studied in the present report. Repeatedly, employers have found short-term reasons by reference either to women's ability (as in this chapter) or to their availability (as in the next) for not risking them in higher

SEX, CAREER AND FAMILY

jobs. But repeatedly, also, some accidental event has come along –
war, or a shortage of staff in some field, or the sheer persistence of
some exceptional, pioneering woman – and the experiment has been
made after all, and has succeeded; once over the threshold, women's
performance has justified their promotion. In the Civil Service the
push over the threshold came largely from political and trade union
pressure, though in the two wars and in recent years staff shortages
have helped as well. Around the time of the First World War, when
the question of allowing women to enter the Administrative Civil
Service first arose, doubts were expressed about admitting them, not
necessarily because they could not do the work, but on the typical
'threshold' ground that the decisive consideration should be the
interests of the Service, not of women, and that there were plenty
of competent men candidates available. Outside pressure, however,
provided the push to take the Civil Service over the top. Gradually
the level of Civil Service work which it was suspected that women
were not qualified to undertake moved upwards, one step ahead of
the level which competent women administrators had reached at any
time. Where once it had been doubted whether they were suited for
administrative work at all, the doubt presently came to be about
whether they were suited for the top posts of the service; until at last
women did in fact become successful Under-Secretaries, Deputy
Secretaries, and Permanent Secretaries, and the last doubts about
women as a category (as apart from the question of individuals'
capacities) were laid to rest.

Another analogy can be taken from marketing, for in principle
there is no difference between promoting women's entry into higher
jobs and the marketing of any other service. The piecemeal, often
accidental, process by which women have made their way into higher-
level work closely resembles the description by Andrews[1] and others
of how firms edge into new markets in the absence of a major marketing effort. Most markets have to be made to work, at any rate if
they are to work well, and the market for highly qualified women's
services is no exception. An entrepreneurial, marketing approach is
likely to be called for not only from individual women[2] but from
public and private agencies interested in seeing that women's services
are fully used. The analogy of the location of industry raises the
question whether the marketing approach may not need to be supplemented with more forceful measures to compel, not merely persuade, employers' attention. These and other questions about the

[1] Andrews, P. W. S., *Manufacturing Business*, Macmillan, 1949; see also the
summary in M. P. Fogarty, *Personality and Group Relations in Industry*, Longmans, 1956.
[2] Above, p. 404.

strategy or mixture of strategies required will be taken up in Chapter XIII.

First, however, it is necessary to consider what in practice will probably remain the most serious obstacle to women's promotion into top jobs. This is not their performance in top jobs or on the way to them, but their availability for them: the question of how far women, and especially married women, can be expected to make enough of their time available at the right times to earn promotion or to enable them to fill senior posts. As was said in Chapter III, if women's access to higher posts depended only on their interests and abilities as they now exist – let alone any more favourable patterns that might be developed in future – women might be rather differently distributed from men in the higher ranks of each industry and profession, but would be represented there more or less in proportion to the number of qualified women coming in through the entry-gates at the bottom of each field. A higher percentage of women than of men might be specialists rather than managers; or middle managers rather than top leaders with the extra drive and aggression which reaching, and sometimes filling, top leadership posts requires; or in jobs with personal contacts rather than those demanding abstract and lonely thought. But, overall, women would have much the same share of middle and senior jobs – or a share at most only marginally different – as men of the same ability and qualifications.

In fact, as the figures in Chapter III show, this is far from being the case. Women's share falls far short of men's. Outright discrimination accounts for part of the difference, but only for a diminishing part. It certainly cannot account for the fact that women's share of senior posts has tended to level off[1] at a time when discrimination has been decreasing. The major factor, and the greatest single obstacle for the future, is the question of women's availability for work, or rather of women's different life cycle compared to men's. This will be the subject for the next chapter.

SUMMARY AND CONCLUSION

Not surprisingly, the views of men and women informants on a number of issues raised in this chapter often show widely differing angles of approach. Whereas men may say simply that women tend to have such-and-such qualities, and leave it at that, women are more likely to say that they adapt to their social circumstances in ways which could well be different if the circumstances changed. Differences of approach also show themselves among different categories

[1] See also Chapter I, Tables I.1 and I.2.

of women. In the occupational as in the family studies, single women tend to take a conservative line on their married colleagues' potential.

Nevertheless, out of the variety of viewpoints certain reasonably clear conclusions emerge. First, there do appear to be certain common or typical differences between men's and women's performance on a job. Women are more likely than men to balance their work commitment with other commitments, and less likely to be 'vertically' ambitious and seek to reach the peaks of their profession. They are more likely than men to want to stay with 'real' rather than administrative work. They are less likely to be aggressive and competitive, and more inclined to use an informal, personal, 'expressive' style of working. They are often tenser, more self-conscious, tending to be meticulous and strong on details, and less inclined to delegate. In a very general way, the presence of both sexes on a job is a factor not to be ignored, whether its effect is positive or, on the contrary, to create 'noise in the system' or a situation of mutual unacceptability.

These observed existing differences are in some ways favourable to women's work prospects and in others unfavourable. A catalogue of the traits more common among highly qualified working women than among similarly qualified men reads from one point of view like a specification for the ideal middle manager, second-in-command, non-managerial specialist, or staff assistant. From another it describes the sensitive, unbureaucratic, maintainer of communications – the general facilitator – needed to operate a network or 'organic'[1] system of management such as is specially appropriate to conditions of development and change. These traits do seem, however, to be less favourable for entrepreneurial leadership or the direction of large-scale, formalized bureaucracies. Distinctions of this kind correspond broadly, as was shown in Chapter III, to the types of post in which women tend in fact to be more or less commonly found; though it is also clear that women have nowhere near the share of the posts for which their observed traits give them an advantage which might be expected from this consideration alone.

The observed differences between the working behaviour of highly qualified women and men are, however, as has been said, marginal – not necessarily great in extent – and a matter of statistical probability, not a universal rule. There are many exceptions; many women are more like most men than they are like most women, and *vice versa*. In particular, no substantial (as apart from marginal) or even general differences are observable between the working styles of women who have actually reached the top and those of men at the same level.

---

[1] Burns' and Stalker's phrase in their *Management of Innovation*, Tavistock, 1961.

Further, the evidence shows that the work traits common or typical among highly qualified women can to an important extent be changed. In some ways they are changing already as a result of the greater familiarity of women in and with the working world, of the accumulated experience of successive generations of working women since women began to move into high-level employment before and around the First World War, and of continuing high levels of employment. In other respects changes could be made if wished. More could be done to familiarize women, in terms likely to attract them, with the interest of high-level managerial work, and to develop promotion and coaching procedures which will draw women on in spite of their tendency to greater diffidence. In families and schools more could be done to develop girls' capacity for forceful and decisive action and for taking a broad rather than a meticulous view, and to forestall the growth of mutually obstructive misconceptions, like those highlighted by Steinmann, of what each sex expects of the other. The professionalization of management should help women's prospects, provided that women are recruited on a large enough scale into the business schools, where at present they are poorly represented. Simply to treat women on equal terms, assume that they have the same range of ability as men, and offer them equal opportunity, can, as in the experience of certain departments of 'Company A' or of the Administrative Civil Service, call up qualities which women might otherwise not be thought to possess. Commonly the problem of what looks like women's unsuitability for a particular post turns out to be no more than a threshold difficulty which can be overcome by a good push. Too often in the past this push has been left to come, not from a considered policy, but from some emergency or accident.

It would also be possible to make further changes in patterns of work organization and behaviour and in roles within the family so as to open the road more easily to women's high-level careers, and this is the area to be covered in the next chapter. The present chapter has dealt with women's ability in high-level work; the next deals with their availability.

425

Chapter XII

Adapting Employment Practices to Women's Life Cycle

Whatever may happen in the longer run, it is clear from the evidence brought together in Part Three that in the immediate future only a small proportion of well-qualified married women are likely to work full-time during the years when they have small children. Most intend to take a more or less long break while they have children under nursery school age, or at least to cut their work commitments drastically. Many intend to work for less than a standard working week when their children are over this age but still growing up. Many, like those whose evidence is collected in *Working Wonders*, never intend to return to full standard working hours at all, or at any rate (whatever the total number of hours they work) to let themselves be bound by standard starting, finishing, or holiday times. Those who do intend to work full hours according to standard timetables may still be reluctant to accept undefined commitments to overtime or to coping with out-of-hours emergencies.

The fact that many women limit their time commitments in these ways does not imply that they are less committed than men to a lifetime career. Employers in the past assumed, rightly, that in most parts of Britain – the textile districts were the chief exception – and at all levels of work only those women could be relied on as lifetime workers who were single, widowed, or separated and were beyond the normal age for marriage or re-marriage. This is no longer true of women at any level of qualification, and least of all, as has been shown, of women with high qualifications. Among highly qualified women in Britain today it is those who do not intend to work in middle age and towards retirement who are the exceptions; and this is as true of the normal woman who married and has children and a stable family life as of the exceptional woman who does not.

But though the services of highly qualified women with a normal family life are today likely to be available to employers over the full span of a working life, they are likely to be available on a timetable different from that of a man. A successful young male executive will probably move in a regular and even sequence of steps along a smooth age-salary-capacity curve at the level appropriate to his ability.[1] In industry and commerce he may change his employer 'every two to three years to provide greater responsibility, wider experience, and new challenges'.[2] In any field of employment he is likely to rotate, or be rotated, into new types and levels of work. But in terms of the level of work which he achieves by a given age and of the salary associated with it his progress is likely to be fairly smooth and steady. To have made constant progress and acquired experience in a range of work as wide as his number of years in employment permits will be a main consideration in promoting him further. Conversely, if his progress drops below the curve normal for a man of his ability, he is likely to be seen as a problem or as having missed his chance. He will have lost his place in his age-group, and fallen out of the race for promotion.

None of this applies to the equally able and, so far as her life-time career is concerned, equally committed young woman in the same type of career, unless she is one of the few who are willing to work through full-time. She can start out along the same curve as the man, provided that she is allowed to do so and is not blocked from key steps in experience and promotion. But she is likely to drop below what would be a man's normal curve of progress, and perhaps even below her own previously achieved level, during the years when she has small children. Later she will have either to accelerate back on to this curve or to settle for a slower pace of advance to a lower final level. She is all the more likely to make, or be forced to make, the latter choice since her working time may remain limited even in later years, and the years during which she is likely to have to slow down her commitment to work include those commonly decisive in a man's career. It is around the age of thirty, as has been pointed out, that a man with top potential tends to be regarded as having completed his training and to be considered for the appointments which lead most directly to the top. The woman who is out of the race at that time, unlike the man who has had his full time available but has not had the ability or determination to make the grade, cannot be said to have failed or fallen short; her case is more like that of the man whose career has been interrupted by war service.

[1] On the model of the 'Earning progression data sheets' developed by E. Jaques, *Equitable Payment*, Heinemann, 1961.

[2] D. C. Duncan, *Managerial Success – A Pilot Study*, paper to XV International Congress of Applied Psychology, 1964, p. 5. Graduate Appointments Register, *Salary Survey*, October, 1966, shows that half of all men graduates can be expected to have left their first firm in just over four years; half of all women go within around two years.

But so far as the practical effects on her further career are concerned she may and often does find herself treated in the same way as the man who has had his chance and failed to take it.

To these difficulties in the way of the married woman has to be added that of relative geographical immobility. Many careers today, particularly at graduate level, require movement from one district or country to another either on changing employers (as in local government) or within a single organization. Women, and especially married women, remain on recent evidence far more reluctant than men to make moves of this kind.[1]

The present chapter considers this situation from the point of view of employers and the economy. How serious is the obstacle of immobility, and how far is it economic to adapt recruitment and promotion practices to women's different timetable? Adaptations to consider include:

(1) Maintaining the continuity of women's work experience during the time when they have small children, for example by part-time work or by guaranteeing their right to return to a job after maternity without loss of rank, fringe benefits or social security rights.

(2) Re-launching women who for a time have dropped out of work altogether.

(3) Opening the way for women of high ability to accelerate back to the curve of career progress which they started to follow, but have not been able to follow continuously.

(4) Organizing top jobs themselves so that they can be filled by women – or if the case applies, men – whose time commitment has to be limited or whose timetable has to be flexible.

Judgments on measures like these may well differ – as do, for example, judgments on industrial training – from the point of view of an individual employer, of an industry or profession as a whole, and of the whole economy. The individual employer, especially the medium or small employer, may be satisfied if he can fill his senior posts satisfactorily from the men who are already competing for them. Rightly or wrongly, he may see little point in spending effort and money to make it easier for another category of applicants to enter the race, especially since the full pay-off on training a woman is likely to be postponed further into the future, because of the small-child break, than is usual in the case of a man. He may be more impressed with the short-run difficulties of the break than with

Harris, A. I. and R. Clausen, *Labour Mobility in Great Britain*, Government Social Survey, ss333, H.M.S.O. 1966, pp. 23-26.

the long-run gains from enlarging the field for recruitment to top jobs and improving its quality.

For an industry or profession as a whole, or for a large and established firm, long-run considerations may count much more. As in the case of industrial training, short-term costs and immediate productivity may seem less urgent at this level than they do to smaller employers, and the pay-off on a long-range investment may count much more. The same applies to the economy as a whole, with the addition that for the economy, by contrast even with a whole industry, let alone an individual firm, labour is an overhead cost. A firm can take or leave a particular recruit. A profession can limit its numbers to match demand. But for the managers of the whole economy, willing and able workers, whether highly qualified or otherwise, are an asset already on the books. From the economic point of view there is a question of obtaining the best return on this asset. The best return may be zero, if it costs less to keep the asset idle than to use it. But, if so, it must be proved; if the asset is on the books, it is necessary at least to consider what use can be made of it. From the social point of view, full employment of willing and able workers is one of the accepted responsibilities of a modern economy. It cannot always be made consistent with other objectives, but has at least to be considered along with them.

Judgments on measures to adapt employment practices to women's life cycle may also differ according to the level of work considered. After the experience of recent years it no longer needs to be argued that in a fully employed economy it can be economic to employ women part-time on routine office and factory work, especially if they are available on no other terms.[1] Whether it is also economic to extend part-time employment into senior managerial and professional work is another question, which must be argued separately.

Questions about what degree of adaptation to women's different life cycle is economic lead on to others about what is perceived to be economic and what is actually done to ensure optimum results. These form part of a wider question which relates also to the last chapter. How rational are employers in judging the potential of highly qualified women, and also the cost and benefit of the adaptations needed to realize their potential in full? On the evidence of the occupational studies, have employers developed a considered view of this? Are they ahead of events and in control of them, or are they reacting *ad hoc* on the basis of the circumstances of the moment rather than of a considered long-range policy?

[1] See A. P. Jephcott, B. M. Seear and J. H. Smith, *Woman, Wife and Worker*, H.M.S.O., 1962.

CONTINUITY OF EXPERIENCE: BRIDGING THE
SMALL CHILD GAP

A woman who drops out of highly qualified work for a substantial
length of time, say for a year or more, loses professional qualification
in several respects. The least important is what might be called the
routine tricks of the trade. A woman architect, for example, may
find that she is less handy than she was with a pencil on a drawing
board. But that type of skill can be very quickly recovered. Informants
in architecture comment that a married woman who has been out of
architectural work even for several years, and who returns at a
routine assistant level, is likely to be a far better proposition from
her principal's point of view than a new graduate straight from
architectural school.

What is much more important, especially for a woman who is
looking for promotion, is that if she leaves her occupation for any
considerable time she drops out of both its personal and its technical
information networks. The scientist, the B.B.C. producer, the Civil
Servant, or the industrial manager who has been out for some time
no longer knows who is who, what is going on, which developments
are significant or insignificant, or where to lay hands on the information or the personal contacts needed to handle a problem quickly.

This loss can be remedied fairly quickly so far as concerns the
capacity to solve limited, specialist problems, in a narrow field even
if at a high level. But the characteristic difference between the brilliant
young performer and the man or woman qualified for senior posts
with a strong management element is that the former may have the
knowledge and contacts to break through on a limited front – for
example to make an outstanding scientific discovery – but the latter
has the wider network of information and contacts, including historical memory, needed for administrative and socio-technical problems in which many considerations interlock. Jaques has argued per-
suasively that the essential difference between highly responsible and
less responsible jobs lies in the size of their holders' information
networks and their capacity for processing the information which the
network throws up.[1] He has coined the phrase 'sculpted creativity'
to distinguish the creativity in depth characteristic of the older administrator from what might be called the 'point' creativity of the
brilliant young inventor.[2] The woman, or for that matter the man,
who drops out of the information network for long may be losing

---

[1] As a development of his work in *Equitable Payment*.

[2] Jaques, E., 'Death and the Mid-Life Crisis', *International Journal of Psycho-
analysis*, 1965, p. 513. On the 'point' creativity of young inventors see H. C.
Lehman, *Age and Achievement*, Princeton, 1953.

in terms not merely of her capacity to handle problems immediately on her return but of the investment in information and in the means of getting and using it which would pay dividends in the longer run in terms of qualification for promotion to top levels.

The woman, or the man, who drops out of an occupational field for long is also likely to drop out of what might be called its expectations network. The ranks close behind her. She no longer has a recognized place among those in line for promotion. The superiors who knew her move to other jobs, and she is no longer visible to their successors. Equals and subordinates move into the place she has left, and when she eventually returns there is liable to be resentment if she takes her old place in the queue. Commenting on men, not women, informants from the B.B.C. and from Companies A and B note that it is risky to second any but the best men for service overseas because it is so hard to fit the returners back into the organization's structure. Not only is the returner likely to have dropped out of the home information network; there is also likely to be frustration among home staff members who see the man from overseas slipping back into the line ahead of them.

Last, but very important, the woman who is absent for long is likely herself to feel a double loss of confidence when she comes back. On the one hand she is liable to lose confidence in her ability to handle a new job if she gets it. On the other she faces an unfamiliar situation in actually obtaining her new job and starting in it. She is not a beginner (a situation which she has met already) but a relatively mature worker who may have nevertheless to drop to a more junior level or start a new apprenticeship. This problem of the double confidence barrier, like that of the information and expectations networks, is not confined to women. The central problem in re-launching Forces officers or business executives who have had to switch to a new employer in mid-career has proved to be that of giving them the confidence to start; this will be taken up again below. But if loss of confidence is a problem for men, it is likely to be still more of a problem for women. The occupational studies show that this is the case. Women are less likely than men to have the aggressive self-confidence to make their way successfully in an environment with which they are no longer familiar. They are more likely than men to have had a complete break away from work, and perhaps more likely to wish to change their professional field. The problem of re-starting is likely to be particularly great in the case of women who have once committed themselves, even temporarily, to the role of a full-time housewife. On the evidence of the family studies, women who have once made this commitment are less likely than women with similar career interests and aspirations, but who have stayed in employment, to re-start their careers quickly after a birth, and so are likely not only to lose seniority and experience but to incur greater re-starting difficulties.[1]

For all these reasons it is important that a woman who hopes to reach the top should maintain the greatest practicable continuity of contact with her job. Since it is often neither desirable nor practicable to do this by working through with only the minimum physiologically necessary break at the time of a birth, two other sorts of measure have to be considered.

a *Institutionalizing maternity leave*

A woman who is working and is paying full national insurance contributions is entitled to 18 weeks of flat-rate maternity benefit, which, however, is at a rate too low – £4 10s a week in 1969 – to be more than a marginal replacement for a professional woman's or manager's salary. Public services such as the Civil Service or the B.B.C. have their own regular and more generous provision for maternity leave. A woman Civil Servant can take two months' maternity leave, to be counted against her allowance of up to six months' sick leave in any twelve months. She can and commonly does take additional time as annual leave, unpaid leave or (with a medical certificate) sick leave.

Industry and commerce, on the other hand, are astonishingly lacking in their own provision for maternity, nor is there any general legislation to compel them to make provision. The United Kingdom shares with the United States the doubtful distinction of having 'no general regulations with regard to the employment of expectant mothers'.[2] A 1965 survey of provisions for leave of absence in companies of various sizes in a wide variety of industries noted well organized arrangements for contingencies such as court cases and jury service, army reserve training, local government or other political work, marriage, illness in the family, or medical and dental appointments, but as regards maternity leave recorded that:

> 'The majority of participating companies have no policy of leave of absence for maternity. Employment is usually terminated, leaving employees to re-apply for work when they wish.'

Just over one in five of the companies covered allowed maternity leave, not necessarily paid or as of right. Of those not allowing it, some replied bluntly and to the point:

[1] Chapter VI, pp. 42-46.
[2] Klein, V., *Women Workers—Working Hours and Service, O.E.C.D.*, 1965, p. 57. Pp. 57-58 give a brief summary of provisions in other *O.E.C.D.* countries.

'Employment is terminated 11 weeks prior to confinement.'

'Employment is terminated at the point of entitlement to National Health Insurance benefit.'

The two large companies studied in P.E.P.'s enquiry employ many married women part-time in routine factory and office work and have made a wide variety of arrangements to enable them to continue working. But neither appears to have thought seriously about how to handle maternity breaks in the case of women at managerial and professional level. Younger women in Company A felt that they were expected to work through full-time, with only a minimum maternity break, or – perhaps even preferably – to leave the company:

'They felt resentful that the choice was apparently made so clear-cut to them – work or nothing. . . . Only one of the young women interviewed had ever spoken to a superior about the possible dilemma. The others all thought that the moment they mentioned the possibility of their having a baby their superiors would immediately assume that they were about to do so, and that that would put paid to their chances of promotion.'[1]

Superiors' attitudes in this company are in fact less ruthless than the younger women interviewed supposed: 'There was clearly an enormous breakdown in communications.'[2] Nevertheless there is substance in the younger women's fears. Over the last generation the common attitude of industrial and commercial employers to maternity has passed through two stages. At the start the common assumption was that in peacetime, outside a few districts and occupations, maternity meant the end of a woman's career. Over the years this has been replaced with the idea of married women as three-phase workers who will drop out and eventually at some indefinite date 're-apply for work when they wish', possibly sooner, possibly later, but quite probably after a long gap and not in the same job. What seems not yet to have become established is the idea that an increasing number of women, especially professional women, may wish to find a middle way between rushing through maternity with only the physiologically necessary minimum break and giving up the prospect of a continuous and developing career. Judging by the amount of maternity leave which women Civil Servants actually take, women who move in this direction are likely to want a substantial break at the time of a birth. But it will be a break in a continuous career, not a transition from work to prolonged concentration on the role of a housewife.

---

[1] Allen, I., *Women in Two Companies*, p. 57.   [2] *Ibid.*

The obvious suggestion to consider is that Britain, or individual British employers, might protect working mothers who wish to follow this pattern by adopting rules on the lines of those already operating in Western countries such as Denmark, Austria or Israel as well as Eastern Europe. In Denmark non-manual workers are entitled to three to five months' maternity leave on half pay.[1] In Israel a mother has a right to three months' paid leave, and then to a further nine months' unpaid leave without losing her right to return to her job. In Austria, similarly, a mother's right to return to her own or a similar job is protected for up to a year from her child's birth; during this time she receives a social security allowance. A possible scheme for Britain might include:

(i) A ban, on the lines of Soviet legislation, on dismissing, refusing to employ, or refusing to promote a woman on the grounds of actual or possible pregnancy.

(ii) A right for any woman worker to take, say, three months' maternity leave, and to return to her previous job at the end of it; the leave to be paid if the woman has been in the same or other employment for at least a minimum time beforehand. As the Soviet experience quoted by Souter and Winslade[2] shows, even this basic period of maternity leave does not need to be a complete break from work, especially for women at professional and managerial levels. A woman specialist or manager can keep in touch with her office during her maternity leave by telephone, by occasional visits, and on special occasions by having work sent home.

(iii) A right to take further paid maternity leave if medically required, and in any case to take unpaid leave or leave at reduced pay up to a further, say, nine months over and above the basic three months' paid leave. At the end of this time a woman would be entitled to return, not necessarily to her old job, which cannot be kept open indefinitely, but to a new posting at the same level in the same employment. Israel legislation has a safeguard that the right to additional unpaid leave does not apply if a woman has births in two successive years.

(iv) All these periods of leave, whether paid or unpaid, to be treated as working time for the purpose of superannuation, social security, and other rights related to seniority and length of service.

The details of a scheme like this are a matter for discussion. The periods of leave suggested follow the rather cautious examples of Austria and Israel. Some East European schemes, as has been

[1] Klein, op. cit.   [2] Chapter II, p. 92.

434

shown, go much further; especially Hungarian legislation, which guarantees a mother's right to return up to three years after a birth. But the cases of Israel and Austria are more relevant since these countries have economies of Western type, with many small independent employment units. If provisions of this sort are workable there, it is reasonable to assume that they are equally workable elsewhere in the West.

Judging from the occupational studies, a clear set of rules of this kind to protect the position of working mothers is likely to have considerable advantages for employers. The absence of such rules has led in some of the cases studied to under-employment of highly qualified women even before they reach the stage of maternity, and to the extra cost of replacing proved and experienced employees with newcomers. When a woman with five or six years' service leaves a firm, her immediate replacement will no doubt be as competent and well-trained, or nearly so, as herself. But back along the line, as one employee after another moves up into the chain of vacancies created by her going, it becomes necessary to fill the ultimate gap with a raw recruit, who in professional and managerial work may take up to two years to train to the point where he earns his money. The prospect that trained women will leave also encourages managers to use them in relatively routine jobs where they can be easily replaced, instead of in jobs which fully stretch their ability, and so reduces the return on the employer's investment in training them. Under-employment and the prospect of being forced out, as the occupational studies show, frustrate well-qualified women and damage their morale to the disadvantage of their employers as well as themselves. If a clear set of rules on maternity can bring about a situation in which it is common and expected for well-qualified women to return to work with the same employer after a reasonable break, employers as well as women themselves are likely to gain.

It does not follow that the whole cost or responsibility of setting up and operating rules of this kind need or should fall on employers. The community too stands to gain, over and above the gain to individual employers, through the conservation and development of women's working capacity. The actual employer for whom a woman is working at the time of maternity will not necessarily get the full benefit from this, since she may not work for him throughout her career; but the gain to her profession and the economy as a whole will be clear. Maternity is a social contingency, not arising out of the operations of any particular industry. It applies to all women, whoever their employer may be, and, once rules for the protection of mothers' right to maternity leave and their jobs are established, no group of women is likely to be willing to be left out.

Although, therefore, individual employers might experiment with schemes on these lines, there would seem in this case to be strong grounds for laying down a general set of rules by law and for carrying the cash cost of maternity leave – an earnings-related maternity benefit – through some form of social insurance. This could be direct State insurance or one or another form of statutorily supported occupational scheme or family benefit fund. Which is to be chosen depends on controversies about the financing of the social services into which it would be out of place to enter here. The White Paper on *Proposals for Earnings-related Social Security*,[1] which proposes that the process of transferring British social security from flat-rate to earnings-related benefits be completed, does not commit itself to a definite plan for maternity benefit but does note the need for 'consequential changes' in this area following on the general move towards earnings-relation.

b *Part-time work and flexible hours*

'Part-time' is an unfortunate phrase. It conveys an impression of half-heartedness and of sharply limited time commitment which is very far from the reality shown by the material collected in the present enquiry. Part-timers – doctors, for example – may be fully as career-committed and job-centred as full-timers. Often the point of 'part-time' is not so much shorter hours as more flexible hours. Where hours are shorter than standard they may be only marginally shorter; or it may be a question of working, not shorter hours each day, but full hours or overtime on a limited number of days a week, or of working full hours and weeks but with extra leave for school holidays and other family contingencies. These points apply with particular force to women in managerial and professional work. The Government Social Survey's 1965 *Survey of Women's Employment* found women in these categories to be much more likely than others to return themselves as working variable hours or numbers of days in the week, and as working from their own homes.[2] 'Part-time' is used here to cover any or all of these arrangements for enabling mothers to continue their careers during the period when their responsibility for small children makes it hard for them to fit into standard time-tables.

The issue here is concerned specifically with the years in which mothers have very young children, and so are likely themselves to be young – usually under 30, or a little over it – and either in rela-

[1] Cmnd. 3383, 1969; see especially paragraph 93.
[2] Government Social Survey, Survey of Women's Employment, ss379, 1968, vol. ii, Tables B4(d), B5(3), B8(d), B14(c).

tively junior posts or willing to accept a postponement of promotion to more senior levels till the children are older. The question of part-time work at older ages and more senior levels is taken up below. Here the issue is: how far is it economic for employers to meet the demand of many married women for part-time professional or managerial work at relatively young ages and junior levels?

The answer from the occupational studies is unequivocal, and falls into two parts. On the one hand, in every occupation studied, it is possible to point to a range of jobs at this level which can be and are being done part-time on a basis which pays the employer and makes it possible for a woman to keep up her professional contacts and skill, and in a number of cases, to develop towards higher responsibility. The outstanding profession for part-time work is teaching. Potentially, however, an even more interesting case is the plan now being developed in the medical profession to enable women hospital doctors not merely to get part-time work but to follow a sequence of part-time jobs qualifying them for promotion to the top.[1] The Royal Commission on Medical Education recommended in 1968 that:

'Women doctors with family responsibilities should be given every opportunity to undertake part-time training over a longer period, with provision made for creches at the hospital and for maternity leave as required. We have been impressed by the scheme introduced in the Oxford region for the return of married women doctors to employment in hospitals in part-time posts in which training and experience are given. We should like to see schemes on similar lines introduced in all regions so that women might more easily obtain, particularly in highly competitive specialities, part-time posts which have been approved for general professional training.'[2]

The Department of Health issued in 1969 a memorandum recommending this approach to Hospital Boards and backing it with finance:

'The Secretary of State is prepared to consider sympathetically proposals for increases in medical establishments at all levels for part-time posts specifically for women doctors.'[3]

[1] Final Joint Report on Negotiations between the Health and National Health Service Hospital Doctors and Dentists, Ministry of Health and Scottish Home and Health Departments, 1968, pars. 64-69; Report of the Royal Commission on Medical Education, Cmnd. 3569, 1968 par 82; Department of Health and Social Security, memorandum H.M.(69) 6, on Re-Employment of Women Doctors, February 1969.

[2] Cmnd. 3569, *ibid*.   [3] H.M. (69) 6, *ibid*.

Part-time work is specially easy in fields like market research or systems analysis where many projects can be packaged and taken away to be worked on at home. One informant called systems analysis and related work 'practically a cottage industry'. In radio and television there are a variety of opportunities for free-lance and part-time work. Architectural informants agree that part-time work is economic in a wide range of offices for specialist work or for sections of a job. This refers particularly to the routine work of an architectural assistant. But a number of the women architects interviewed for the P.E.P. study have been able to arrange themselves part-time jobs which are not only convenient in terms of family ties but are also at a respectable level of responsibility, and these jobs are spread through all major sections of the profession: private offices, large and small units of local government, commerce and the Civil Service. Among the occupations covered in P.E.P.'s studies the least favourable for part-time work are industrial management and the Administrative Civil Service, in each case for the reason that managerial work is thought to be particularly difficult to sub-divide. But even in these occupations there proves to be a range of work – research, information, and relatively self-contained projects – at junior and middle levels which can be handled part-time.

But there is only a handful of professions, headed by teaching, in which the problems and possibilities of part-time work have been seriously thought through. The chief impression from nearly every occupation studied is of improvization by employers and self-help by women rather than of a considered and developed plan. B.B.C. women criticize particularly:

'The relative lack of opportunities for free-lance or part-time work. . . . They felt that an organization like the B.B.C. could provide far more opportunities for free-lance and part-time work and mentioned the fact that much of this work was given out on what they called the 'network' basis rather than in an official or organized way. Most of the women interviewed stressed the necessity of keeping up good contacts with colleagues if they wanted this kind of . . . work.'[1]

Women architects who have found themselves part-time work above the routine level turn out to owe more to their own drive and planning, usually helped out with a good dose of luck, than to any organized policy on the part of the profession or of individual offices. In Company A some departments take trouble over part-time work and get good results from it, while others do not bother. As with so

[1] Allen, I., *Women in the B.B.C.*, p. 41.

many other issues connected with women's work, results which are seen after the event to be economic and satisfying to all concerned tend to have been brought about *ad hoc*, by the accident of local pressures and particular women's drive, rather than by systematic policy.

One reason for this has simply been employers' unfamiliarity with part-time work at professional and managerial levels and with the fact that it is often an economic proposition on a current basis alone, even disregarding its value for maintaining and developing the capacity of fully qualified staff for work in the future. Part-time work for men in senior positions is not unknown to British employers. A figure of 2,660 part-time male 'managers, large establishments' was returned for England and Wales at the Census of 1961 and 4,000 part-time male graduate professional employees. But these made up no more than 0·5 per cent and 1 per cent respectively of all men economically active in these grades, and most of the men concerned were elderly or retired. Part-time is familiar enough in the case of lower-skilled women workers; of employed women aged 35-59 in 1961, two-fifths were working part-time. But for graduate women professional employees this proportion dropped to one-fifth, of whom the overwhelming majority[1] would be in teaching (including university teaching) and the medical professions. Among women 'managers, large establishments' it dropped to one in twenty.

A second factor has been confusion in the minds not only of employers but of women themselves between the case for part-time as a phase in a career at a relatively young age and junior level and for what might be called permanent part-time for older and more senior staff. Whereas the former is increasingly acceptable, the latter raises different and more difficult problems for employers and meets resistance from many women and women's organizations themselves.[2]

A third factor has been the slowness of employers, as in the case of institutionalizing maternity leave, to appreciate the strength and continuity of work commitment on the part of highly qualified women today, and the amount that employers collectively as well as individually have to gain from assisting it, if they provide opportunities for part-time at the appropriate stage of a married woman's career.

[1] Aregger, *op. cit.*, Table XI.

[2] See e.g. Sommerkorn, *op. cit.*, pp. 222-223 on the resistance of many women university teachers in Britain to the Robbins Committee's recommendation in favour of part-time work; and the cautious attitude, moving from rejection to conditional acceptance, in the International Federation of University Women's Report to the I.L.O. on *Pratique du Travail à Temps Partiel par les Femmes Diplomées des Universités*, 1962.

By contrast with the question of maternity leave, there does not seem to be any case for the state to provide a permanent subsidy for encouraging part-time work, whether at professional and managerial or at other levels. It is part-time at junior and middle, not top, levels, which is under discussion here. Since well-planned part-time work at this level can be fully economic from the employer's point of view, there is no need to raise the issue of subsidizing an activity which is profitable from the community's point of view but not from that of the employer's. The salary of a part-time worker is, like any other wage or salary, a cost arising directly out of the process of producing goods and services and which it is reasonable to charge to it in full.

Legislation and administrative action have, however, a part to play in creating a framework and atmosphere encouraging to well-planned part-time work. There has recently been discussion in France of a measure to entitle both men and women, at least in the public services, to claim to change to part-time work for limited periods for specific purposes. The reasons could include not only family problems but also, for example, a man's wish to take time to study for a degree or professional qualification. Generally, legislation and administrative practice need to be checked to ensure that they do not discourage part-time work; for example that social security contributions or selective employment tax are no more than proportionate to actual earnings and time worked. There may in addition be a case for temporary financial inducements to prime the pump in both the public and private sector. The example of the medical scheme in allowing a larger establishment and more finance to divisions of a public service which develop an approved policy for part-time working might well be followed both in other public services and in large private organizations.

Beyond this, the problem is to force the pace of employers' education in the short- and long-term economics of part-time work at junior and middle professional and managerial levels, and to press for the adoption by more and more employers of considered policies for part-time on the lines of those now being developed in medicine. This is largely a matter for education through professional organizations and the bodies concerned with training in management and manpower planning, supplemented by pressure from women's organizations and from trade unions or professional associations.

RE-LAUNCHING

Even if provisions for maternity leave and part-time work are improved, there are likely, on the evidence of Part Three, still to be

440

many highly qualified women who take several years away from work while they have young children. Their first need when they are ready to return is for an open door: for the right at least to be considered for posts at a level corresponding to their qualifications and allowing them to resume their career. The occupational studies bring out that in many fields their chances of doing so have been till recently, and often still are, very poor.

The reasons for this have been concerned partly with women themselves and partly with the attitude of managers and personnel specialists to career planning and patterns for men as well as women. The family studies show that women are less likely than men to have fixed career aims from the time when they graduate, and are more likely to wish to change their field, so that they present themselves to employers, not as trained though rusty, but as new beginners at a relatively advanced age. On the side of employers, as career structures and a professional attitude to career planning have developed, the chances for late entrants have diminished. Organizations have tended to stress promotion from within on grounds of both efficiency and morale, and – recognizing that other organizations do likewise – to suspect the quality of men who change employers in middle age. Established career expectations have been set up, and there has been reluctance to disturb them by bringing men in from outside to relatively senior positions; or even, as has been said, by bringing men back into a promotion line after a long period of secondment to other organizations or to subsidiaries overseas. There has also in recent years been an accent on youth as a qualification for senior posts, on the ground both that younger people with recent training are more likely to be up to date in their knowledge and that creativity, adaptability, and drive tend to fall off in middle age. If younger people are to be promoted to senior posts, they must have an appropriate amount of relevant recent experience. The delay imposed by women's different life and career cycles is such that it may be difficult for them to obtain this experience in time.

The bureaucratization of career patterns can help women as late entrants or re-entrants, as well as in other respects, once the custom of giving consideration to women who apply for re-entry has been established. The rules of the bureaucracy can then ensure that this consideration is given regularly and on a reasonable basis. But in the actual conditions of the last generation bureaucratization has in fact often worked in the opposite direction. The relatively informal and personal patterns of recruitment and promotion in the B.B.C. in the early years allowed many women their chance. But 'in the 1930s professionalism set in and kept women out'.[1] Many of the

[1] Adams, Mary, letter to *The Times*, March 22, 1962.

women covered in P.E.P.'s study of women directors got their chance by climbing through the cracks of the business system, but would not have had the right formal qualifications at the right age to achieve a similar level in a regular business bureaucracy, or perhaps even to be employed there at all.

For a number of reasons the conditions experienced in the last generation now seem to be changing. Staff shortages have forced professions such as teaching, medicine, and the Administrative Civil Service to consider late entrants and the re-recruitment of women, and the Companies study suggests that a similar development may be on the way in at least some areas of industrial research and management. The conception of a continuous, life-time career for a man with one organization is being eaten away from both ends. At one end there has been increasing acceptance both by new graduates and by their employers that the years of working life up to 30 or 35 are a 'trial progression region' in which job-changing can be the rule rather than the exception. This is reflected in the figures quoted earlier for turnover in first jobs.[1] At the other end there is greater mobility in middle age, as more men are forced by industrial change into a new career; less suspicion by employers of those who do move, and more acceptance of Drucker's thesis[2] about the advantages of switching older men at least into a new job, if not into a new professional field. The Fulton Committee makes a strong case for increasing mobility into and out even of a field like that of the Civil Service where the need for a high degree of stability is obvious, and says that 'late entry should be considerably expanded'.[3] Recent research, of which more will be said below, has undermined the idea that the dynamism, adaptability, and learning capacity of highly qualified men and women need fall off sharply in middle age.

These changes in opinion create new possibilities both for the late promotion of women who return after a career break and for their late recruitment or re-recruitment. But in several of the occupations studied the new conditions have made only a limited impact as yet, especially as regards formal and regular procedures. Late promotion will be considered in the next section of this chapter. As regards recruitment or re-recruitment the Administrative Civil Service has liberalized its rules for the re-admission of these former women Civil Servants who choose to apply, but:

> 'As a useful expedient in a time of labour shortage rather than something which they ought to encourage . . . . Certainly little con-

[1] Jaques' term in Equitable Payment, *loc. cit.*, and see Duncan, *op. cit.*
[2] Ch. III, p. 124.
[3] Report of the Committee on the Civil Service, Cmnd. 3638, 1968, par. 124.

sidered thought had been given to married women ex-administrators who might form a possible recruiting pool. Equally, whilst women at present in the service are becoming more aware of the possibility of leaving and returning, little is done to make women administrators consider the possibility. There is certainly nothing like a register of women leavers who are circularized when the labour situation is acute. . . . The feeling was that women would not be able to count on the assurance of re-employment . . . rather they must be prepared to chance their luck if and when they sought to return.'[1]

In the B.B.C. a woman 'would have to apply in the usual way and take her chance in the normal competitive channels',[2] and might then, if her past record was good, get sympathetic but not preferential treatment. Like the Civil Service, the B.B.C. has developed no regular recall procedures. Companies A and B have little experience of women returning at anything more than routine levels.

A woman who wishes to return to work in environments like these will need to push hard for it. How is she to be equipped to do so? The crucial problem, as has been said, is not technical training – though that may be needed too – but the double confidence barrier which arises from lacking or having partly lost the skills and contacts needed in a new job, and from unfamiliarity with the action which a mature re-starter, as apart from a beginner, needs to take in order actually to obtain a job and to work her way successfully into it.

The Architectural Association's major drive in 1964 to attract housewives back into the profession illustrates both the importance of the confidence barrier and – going back to the previous point about employers' attitudes – what can be and may need to be done to make prospective employers aware of what returners have to offer. The Association organized a course with strong stress on re-acquiring professional skills and on bringing the women attending up to date on the most recent developments in the profession. But in fact the course made its main impact through restoring married women's confidence and increasing principals' awareness of married women as a source of useful recruits, who still had their professional skill or were quickly able to recover it. Women attending the course, and many others reached through propaganda about it disseminated along professional channels and through broadcasting and the press, were reminded that the profession needed them and was willing to

[1] Walters, *op. cit.*, pp. 51-52.
[2] Allen, I., *Women in the B.B.C.*, p. 41.

443

offer a helping hand, and that the skills which many of them had thought were rusty or obsolete were still relevant and usable. After the event, it could be seen that the chief justification for the course was that it established in the minds both of employers and of married women architects themselves that returning married women have a valued place in the profession.

In so far as technical training or re-training is needed, P.E.P.'s architecture report points out that the right place to give it, especially for women, will often be on the job rather than in a course beforehand. The woman who switches entirely to a new field may need a basic course of training. But women are less likely than men to be able to be away from home for long periods, and specialized courses to fill out the training of a handful of women re-entering a higher occupation cannot often be economically provided within commuting reach of their homes. Older men and women in any case tend to learn best by doing. The most effective approach will normally be that developed by the Department of Health for women doctors re-entering the National Health Service. Under the Department's circulars of 1966 and 1969 arrangements can be made for a re-entering doctor to serve in effect a new short apprenticeship on the job. She can 'sit at the feet' of a general practitioner or be appointed to a hospital in a training grade. This will not of course exclude her from also participating in formal courses whether during or after her re-apprenticeship, so far as is necessary and practicable. But these will be courses forming part of the normal training and re-training process for doctors, not a special provision for re-training women.

The easiest way to overcome the confidence barrier – leaving aside such straightforward cases as that of the woman architect married to the principal of an architectural practice – is for employers themselves to take the initiative in calling prospective re-entrants back to work. This is what is being attempted for women doctors on a national scale by the Department of Health. Case histories from occupational fields of all kinds show again and again that re-entry has occurred because, and often only because, an employer or some other sponsor took the initiative, or at least some personal link existed. So for example in the case of women teachers in universities:

'Comments of the few married women in this sample pointed to psychological problems connected with re-entry. Although they had toyed with the idea for some time, they did not have the courage to implement it. Had it not been for outside initiative, generally in the way of the offer of a post in their old university where they were known, or through some personal contact, they might not have returned to the profession. But even with these helpful circumstances the respondents considered their initial period of coming back very difficult.'[1]

But as this quotation suggests, even the returner who is called back by her employer may need to show force and initiative. This is even more true for the woman who has to find her own way into a new and at least neutral if not hostile environment. To build the confidence and skills needed for this is the central task of any re-launching programme. The most successful programme for this purpose in Britain has been one predominantly for men, namely that for former Forces officers, for whom the career break and transition to an unfamiliar environment on leaving the Forces is often particularly sharp. In *Women and Top Jobs* the authors drew attention to certain features of the Forces scheme which could be incorporated into more general schemes for re-launching either women alone or women along with men – civilian or Forces – who make a career break. Among these are:

(i) Early fixing of a target date for returning to work or moving to work of a new kind. In the Forces or for men in civilian jobs this date will often be decided by the ending of the old job. For returning housewives it is a matter of voluntary decision. There is a case for a regular procedure to remind highly qualified women who are not currently in paid work of the need to make this sort of decision in good time. The procedure might take the form of periodic circulars from former employers or, on a more general basis, from the Department of Employment and Productivity; from these women's own professional organizations; or from the centres providing the appreciation courses suggested below. Once the basic decision has been made the period before actually taking up employment can be used to obtain long-range guidance from employment and occupational guidance agencies, and such technical training or re-training as is necessary and convenient; and encouragement for this can be built into the procedure.

(ii) Near the time of moving into new work, attendance at an appreciation course designed not so much to convey technical knowledge as to help candidates to understand the possibilities open to them, the sort of work which each involves, and how best to go after it. This is the key area in the Forces procedure; the point at which it is brought home to candidates, as it was for women architects in the Architectural Association's course, that there are real and worthwhile prospects ahead of them and what these prospects are. It is

[1] Sommerkorn, *op. cit.*, p. 223.

here that, as one informant put it, 'we get the colonels' tails up'. An important part of a course of this kind is to give candidates a realistic understanding of the action and the skills, including letter-writing, interview techniques and how to act on starting in a job, which they need in order to get and keep the right job in practice. An appreciation course of this kind does not train a candidate to do a job. It does train him or her, to his prospective employer's advantage as well as his own, to play a more positive and effective part in the process by which jobs and candidates are matched.

(iii) Hard selling by the candidate him- or herself over a period beginning two to four months before a job is actually wanted. One study of Forces officers' experience showed that it can take a candidate up to 120 letters to employers, with an average of 25, to obtain an average of two job offers.

(iv) Direct support by employment agencies acting for the candidate, and indirect support by general measures to create a favourable climate of public opinion. In the case of ex-Forces officers, government statements, press articles, advertising, and direct contact with business leaders, trade unionists, and service representatives, have been used to build up the idea that officers' resettlement is both a national duty and the employer's opportunity.[1]

Whether what is envisaged is technical training or training to beat the confidence barrier and get the best out of the job market, the family studies underline the importance attached by married women to part-time training, payment, and facilities for child care during the training period. For the woman who is available only for part-time work it is essential that training opportunities too should also be part-time, in the sense either of occupying part of a day or week or at least of being broken up into manageable short blocks of time. Payment for training is important not only as an inducement but for covering extra domestic or travelling expenses and as a way of lifting the returning housewife out of an amateur into a professional atmosphere. Married women respondents to the survey of graduates put it high in their priorities.

It would be wrong to lay exclusive stress on formalized as apart from informal procedures whether for recall, technical training, or training in the art of getting the best out of the job market, and whether on the analogy of the Forces procedure or on the lines developed for the recall of married women doctors or teachers. A vast amount of satisfactory matching of employers with housewives

---

[1] *Women and Top Jobs*, pp. 43-45. See also articles and correspondence in the *Daily Telegraph*, May 8 and 26, 1969, and *Sunday Telegraph*, March 30 and April 6, 1969.

446

who are returning to work takes place, as *Working Wonders* points out, by an informal process in which personal contacts, the initiative of former employers and of women themselves, and sheer accident all play their part without much planning or formal decision. What must however be doubted, in the light of P.E.P.'s as well as of previous enquiries, is whether these informal processes cover enough potential returners, or ensure them a good enough chance of matching their abilities with prospective jobs, to be satisfactory whether from the point of view of the economy and employers or from that of women themselves. Even when they are satisfactory from the point of view of the woman who wants a job of some kind with interest and responsibility, but not necessarily with further prospects, they are not necessarily so for the 'vertically ambitious' woman who is interested in prospects as well as in the immediate job. There is a strong case for supplementing these processes with more formal procedures for recall, re-motivation, and re-apprenticeship, so long as this does not involve costs out of proportion to the gains in working capacity and morale which result.

In so far as the problem is to re-launch married women in their former professions it does not seem that any disproportionate cost need be incurred. The married woman doctor who returns to work in a hospital or as a trainee general practitioner or the architect who returns as an assistant is likely very quickly to be earning her money. There would obviously be difficulty if she were put straight into the level of work which she might have reached if she had had a continuous career. If, however, she re-starts at a level appropriate to her actual current capacity, she is very likely, as with the part-timer, to be a more economic proposition to her employer than the raw recruit who would have to be brought in, somewhere back along the line, if the returner were not available. In *Women and Top Jobs* the authors quoted a 1967 estimate of the cost of a very thorough type of appreciation course, such as might be developed for both men and women with high qualifications who make career breaks in middle age. The cost per case, including capital costs and help with making employer contacts, came to under £200. The cost per head of recall procedures, of the services provided by employment agencies, and of measures of general propaganda will normally be much lower. Since for married women all these costs arise directly out of maternity, it seems reasonable that they should be carried, at least in married women's case, by the community rather than by employers or by the women themselves. This might well be treated as one of the training services to be financed out of levies under the Industrial Training Act. Employers with well-developed recall and re-training procedures of their own could, under the normal procedure of that Act, be allowed

447

to deduct part or all of the cost incurred by them from the levy which they would otherwise have to pay.

The cost of training – not re-training – the returning housewife who decides to change her profession may of course be a very different matter. It is also a separate issue, since from the point of view of her new profession she is not a returner but a new entrant. The economics of training and recruiting her have to be considered in the context not of returning housewives but of the need of each profession for new recruits generally and for inter-professional transfers.

The specific details of regular provision for the re-launching and re-apprenticeship of highly qualified women need further consideration along with the measures now increasingly needed to provide for mobility and re-training among highly qualified middle-aged men. But so far as the principle of this provision is concerned it seems that the case for regular procedures is strong: that these procedures seem likely, in the case of the housewife returning to her old profession, to entail no more than an economic cost; and that the charge for them should fall primarily on the community as a whole.

ACCELERATING BACK TO THE TOP

Granted that both part-time work at relatively modest levels of responsibility and re-launching can be economic, what are the chances that a woman who has slowed down or broken her career and dropped behind her men contemporaries can accelerate back up to the level which she might have reached by a continuous career? This question can be answered at both the theoretical and the practical level.

From the theoretical side the question might be put as follows. A number of qualities important for top leadership, such as energy, initiative and creativity, are often said to fall off towards and sometimes well before retiring age. Suppose then that a woman who has slowed down her career acquires the experience needed for promotion to the highest jobs only at, say, age 45 or even 50, whereas a man of equal ability competing for the same promotion might have acquired it by 35 or 40. Is the difference between the energy and creativity of the candidate of 35 to 40 and the candidate of 45 likely to be so great, or alternatively is the gap between the time when a candidate of 45 is at the peak of his or her powers and the time when his or her powers begin to decline sharply so short, that, if it is known that a candidate is likely to become available for top responsibility only at 45 or over, it will not seem worthwhile to groom that candidate for a top position in the first place?[1] There certainly is evidence that:

'With increasing age there is less energy available to the ego for responding to or maintaining formal levels of involvement in the outside world. The implication is that the older person tends to respond to inner rather than to outer stimuli, to withdraw emotional investment, to give up self-assertiveness, and to avoid rather than to embrace challenge.'[2]

The drop in drive at some point after age 50 can be traced, for example, in the earnings curves of practitioners in professions paid by fees, such as the Bar or general medical practice.[3] There is evidence that ability to solve new problems rapidly – not necessarily to solve them when given time – does fall off with advancing age. The capacity to make a sharp breakthrough on a narrow front, as with a scientific discovery, does in many fields seem to reach a peak in the thirties or even earlier, and then to decline.[4]

But these findings are subject to strong reservations of a kind very relevant to the case discussed here. A number of recent studies suggest that:

'The reason why so many people come to a dead end in middle age is not that their powers have declined but that they lack any adequate stimulus.'[5]

Levelling off in middle age may in fact be culturally conditioned and could therefore be culturally altered;[6] given a suitable challenge, middle-aged people can show the ability to rise to it. They need not lose the capacities they acquired earlier, and these capacities can include not only routine skills, such as the clerk's ability to write fast, but the capacity to learn, especially in fields of which the learner already has much experience.[7] There is evidence that it is less

[1] In addition to other sources specifically cited, the section following relies on a bibliographical memorandum on *Some Aspects of Middle Age* by Sister M. Cabrini.

[2] Neugarten, B. L., *et al.*, *Personality in Middle and Late Life*, New York: Atherton, 1964, p. 99.

[3] See data in M. P. Fogarty, 'Portrait of a Pay Structure' in Meij (ed.), *Internal Pay Structures*, North Holland; and *The Just Wage*, Geoffrey Chapman 1961, 105-107.

[4] E.g. Lehman, *op. cit.*: A. T. Welford, *Ageing and Human Skill*, Oxford, 1958, Ch. 11: and R. H. Williams (ed.), *Processes of Ageing*, New York: Atherton, 1963, Vol. 1, p. 75.

[5] Tizard, L. J. and Guntrip, H. J. S., *Middle Age*, Allen and Unwin, 1959, p. 58.

[6] Cf. the comment in K. Soddy and M. C. Kidson, *Men in Middle Life*, Tavistock, 1967, p. 43.

[7] E.g. Sorenson, H., 'Adult Ages as a Factor in Learning', *Journal of Educational Psychology*, 1930.

P

inevitable than earlier studies had suggested that creativity in the sense of breaking through to new scientific findings must decline after age 40.[1] An American study reports that:

'Contrary to the folk-lore, and the initial expectations of the investigators, the sixty-year-old subjects were on the average no more or less flexible, mentally or emotionally, than the fifty- or forty-year-olds.'[2]

Nor was there any consistent change with age in factors such as 'ego transcendence', the capacity to engage in a direct, active, and emotionally satisfying way with the people and events of daily life and to show concern for others' well-being; nor in 'ego differentiation', the capacity to pursue and enjoy a variety of activities and to use and value oneself for a wide range of personal attributes. Among gifted and highly educated people there does not seem to be the same fall in general intellectual ability with age as among people of lower ability. Nor is there the same fall in vocabulary.[3]

The same data which show that earnings in the free professions tend to drop sharply after age 50 shows that this drop is much less marked among the most able than among those of lower ability. A British enquiry for 1955-56[4] showed for a range of professions, both fee-paid and salaried, that whereas the incomes of earners at the lower quartile of nearly every profession were a smaller percentage of the median for their age-group and profession at ages 55-64 than at 40-44, earners at the upper quartile or upper decile were likely to be proportionately even further above the median at 55-64 than they had been in their forties. In a number of professions the top earners continued to raise their absolute as well as their relative income on towards retiring age. In particular, capacity for managerial and administrative work of a kind representing statesmanship – Jaques' 'sculpted creativity' – rather than sharp breakthrough on a narrow front, and resting on a wide network of contacts and extensive information, appears to rise towards retiring age.[5]

In a general way, 'Chronological age is at best only a convenient means of ordering developmental data'.[6] It is 'a very poor guide to

[1] References in J. E. Birren (ed.), *Handbook of Ageing and the Individual*, Chicago, 1959, pp. 729-730 and 785-786.

[2] Neugarten, *op. cit.*, Ch. 2.

[3] E.g. Ghiselli, E. E., 'The Relationship between Intelligence and Age among Superior Adults', *Journal of Genetic Psychology*, 1957, and Raven's study of vocabulary quoted in Birren, *op. cit.*

[4] Report of the Royal Commission on Doctors' and Dentists' Remuneration, Cmnd. 939, 1960, pp. 37 and 35, and cf. Jaques' studies.

[5] E.g. Lehman, *op. cit.*; and see R. H. Williams, *op. cit.*, p. 23.

[6] Birren, *op. cit.*, pp. 892-893.

the state of a man's physical well-being or mental alertness', for the changes it brings may be great or insignificant, and differences between individuals tend to increase with age.[1] In so far as chronological age does provide a reliable guide to functional ability, this may be simply a case of self-justifying prophecy. People are led to believe that their powers will decline at a certain age, therefore they act accordingly.[2]

To these findings, which refer to both men and women – though particularly to men – can be added others which suggest that comparisons between the working capacity of men and women, and especially of those who are highly qualified and in responsible jobs, are likely to change to women's advantage at higher ages. If 'masculine' qualities such as force and initiative are thought to be desirable, it is significant that women seem to maintain their share of these qualities into their fifties and sixties better than men.[3] It is not that they become more masculine than they were; there is a tendency for men to over-estimate the extent to which this happens.[4] But whereas in the case of men 'masculine' qualities fall off rather sharply towards retiring age, this does not seem to happen in the case of women. The gap between men and women in emotional stability, after widening in the forties, tends to narrow again very sharply in the fifties.[5] The same is true of women's sickness absence. By age 55-59 working women in Great Britain average fewer spells of sickness each year than working men. Their average days lost through sickness – the number of spells multiplied by the average number of days in each spell – is still at this age 60 per cent higher than the average for men, but at age 40-44 the excess of the women's average over the men's was not 60 per cent but 150 per cent.[6] Various studies suggest that older women tend to gain relative to men in reasoning and short-term memory,[7] and perhaps slightly in general intelligence,[8] that middle-class women gain relatively to men in their fifties and sixties in interest in the future, capacity for personal relations, and sense of their own identity, and tend to experience more tension and be less settled and self-satisfied;[9] and that women in their fifties

[1] Heron, A., and Chown, S., Age and Function, Churchill, 1967, p. 137.
[2] Cf. Neugarten, op. cit., pp. 147-148.
[3] Terman, L. C., and Miles, C. C., Sex and Personality, McGraw-Hill, Ch. 7.
[4] Ibid., pp. 457-458: and see Neugarten, op. cit., Ch. 3, esp. Table 3.5.
[5] Heron and Chown, op. cit., p. 113.
[6] Smith, G. T., and Israel, S., 'Sickness Absence – Defining the Problem', in Sickness Absence Control, Industrial Society Information Report, Chs. 6 and 7, 1968. The figures are for Great Britain in 1960-1.
[7] Ibid.
[8] Studies summarized by Cabrini, loc. cit., p. 17.
[9] Neugarten, op. cit.; Ch. I and Table I.3; see also p. 85.

compare to their advantage with men on qualities such as absence of dogmatism, logical rather than anecdotal reporting, concern for others' views and for learning, interest in and optimism about the future, and self-improvement rather than self-indulgence.[1] On the debit side there is evidence of more paranoid disorders among women over 60 than among men.[2] But another study notes that though tendencies towards 'magical mastery' – towards reinterpreting reality on the principle that wishing will make it so – develop in many women in their fifties and sixties, they also develop in many men.[3]

'The age of any given population group', one investigator suggests, 'is its life expectancy in reverse'.[4] The excess of women's life expectancy over men's has widened in England and Wales since 1920 from under three years to six years,[5] and by the test of life expectancy women in their fifties or early sixties are substantially younger than men. An American study finds that married women are more likely than married men to be active in public and social organizations in their fifties, and that the women's advantage reaches its peak at ages 54-58.[6] Another finds that older women are less likely than men to accept 'the remorseless logic of social and biological loss' and to 'withdraw from the world and prepare for death', but attributes this not so much to their functional as apart from chronological age as to their lesser readiness to let themselves be bound by the logic of 'objective definitions of their capacities and their prospects'.[7]

Carried away by enthusiasm for the career prospects of middle-aged women, one French writer exclaims:

'The mature woman acquires a sense of well-being, a degree of aggressiveness and objectivity and above all of stability in emotion and action, which – when added to the specific qualities of her sex – explain the impressive development which occurs at this age, that of the most brilliant feminine careers known.'[8]

Neither the general findings quoted nor those specifically referring to women will completely justify this claim. But they do so to a substantial degree. They justify advising employers that, particularly in the case of jobs of top responsibility which require people of top

[1] *Ibid.*, Ch. VII, especially Table VII.1.   [2] Birren, *op. cit.*, p. 385.
[3] Neugarten, *op. cit.*; Ch. VI and Tables VI.1 and VI.2.
[4] Williams, *op. cit.*, p. 571.
[5] Registrar-General's *Statistical Review of England and Wales*, 1966 Part II.
[6] Kuhlen in Birren, *op. cit.*, p. 862.
[7] Neugarten, *op. cit.*, pp. 147-148, and see Ch. 9 for the general tendency of which this is a case in point.
[8] Denard-Toulet, A., quoted from *Esprit* in International Federation of University Women, *The Occupational Outlook for the Mature Woman*, 1964, p. 32.

ability and educational level, there is no *a priori* reason why a delay of a few years beyond the normal age for promotion to top jobs need cause a woman's – or indeed a man's – prospective length of service at the top to be too short to make her, or him, worth consider-ing. In some occupations, for example research, efficiency may be more at risk at high ages than in others. Obviously also it is necessary to look carefully at the individual cases of women as well as of men, since at this age the development of individuals' capacities can diverge even more than at younger ages. Also it is clear that for men as well as women the methods currently used by employers to train, promote, and get the best service from their older highly-qualified staff are often deficient. But these points are marginal to the main conclusion. Whereas in jobs demanding less ability, and in physical as apart from mental work, there is evidence of a general and sometimes sharp fall in capacity towards retirement age, beginning in some occupations as early as the thirties, no such general rule can be made for people qualified for top jobs;[1] and women seem, if anything, to compare better with men in working capacity in their fifties and sixties than they did at earlier ages. Employers need to beware of judging the potential of older highly qualified staff, both women and men, on the basis of experience with staff at a quite different level, or by their performance under conditions which are not in fact likely to get the best service from them.

There remains however the practical question whether, given that there is no *a priori* reason why a woman whose career has been broken or delayed should not accelerate back to the point which she would have reached with a continuous career, she will in fact be given the opportunity to do so. P.E.P.'s studies have turned up a number of cases where this happened, but these have tended to be in the free professions or in independent business rather than in either a public or a private bureaucracy.

The type of case where this sort of adjustment is particularly easy would be that of a woman architect who, after qualifying and acquir-ing some years' experience, marries and goes into professional partnership with another architect and presently drops out of work to raise a family. When, in due course, she wishes to re-start she may begin by working at an elementary level, quite possibly below that at which she previously ceased work, till she has reacquired her pro-fessional skill and contacts. Then, rather quickly, she accelerates back through the normal stages of professional responsibility, taking inde-pendent charge of projects and an increasing share in the general work of the office, until, after a few years, she is carrying the full

[1] Cf. Fogarty in Meij, *op. cit.*, and F. LeGros Clark and A. C. Dunne, *Ageing in Industry*, Nuffield Foundation, 1955.

weight of a principal of an important partnership; at an age, possibly, not very different from that at which a man might have reached the same position.

This case, which is taken from life, has three main features. The married woman architect:

(1) Is free to come back and develop at her own pace. She can start at as elementary a level as she likes without losing prestige or prejudicing her prospects. She can adjust her volume and level of work upwards as and when she is ready for it.

(2) Is provided with easy access to information and material relevant to all levels of her office's work, and has the chance to familiarize herself with it before taking full responsibility for action on it. She has coaching available as required.

(3) Is visible to the current head or heads of the office, who determine how work shall be distributed and who shall have promotion. She is in a position to insist that her interests and abilities shall be considered.

In theory these conditions are no more than a man or woman with good potential for promotion might expect to find in any well-run organization. In practice, as P.E.P.'s enquiries make clear, they are often not available in large bureaucracies even to men who depart from standard career patterns, let alone to women. Whereas in a small architect's office information about all aspects of the business can be easily and informally available, and senior members of the staff are directly available for coaching, in a big bureaucracy coaching and rotation to gain wide experience are likely to require an organized effort. This will often be made only for those who have become visible as candidates for the top. The candidate's problem in that case is to become visible, and late entrants or re-starters may easily fail to achieve this.

Informants on experience with civilian careers for ex-Forces officers note than an Army officer who hopes to go far in a big firm will need either to move into civilian life early enough – certainly before age 35 – to fit into the normal development plans under which trainees and promising young managers are groomed for the top, or to start at a level high enough, probably not below £2,000-£2,500 a year, to be directly visible to senior managers. If he does not fit into one of these categories he is liable to be blocked for many years behind a layer of routine middle managers who have neither the vision nor the interest to push a flyer forward. So also women interviewed in Company A note that the key step for a woman is to get beyond the middle management barrier and become visible to managers of higher quality at the top; or alternatively to move out into a smaller company where 'a woman has more chance to shine and to be judged specifically on her individual contribution rather than be regarded as a junior member of a team'.[1] A number of women in Companies A and B and the B.B.C. feel, rightly or wrongly, that even women who come in as regular management trainees in their twenties – let alone late entrants or re-entrants – are given less grooming and are watched less carefully for promotion than men of similar ability entering through the same gate.

Some occupations may already have their promotion procedures well enough organized to pick up high flyers who enter late or re-enter, and to provide them with a well-rounded job experience and quick promotion if they earn it. This could well be true of the Civil Service, especially if the Fulton proposals for late entry and greater mobility into and out of the service are adopted; including notably the committee's proposal for a regular two-year probation for late entrants,[2] which might also be applied to re-entrants after a long break. It could become true of the medical profession if the Department of Health's re-entry scheme operates as planned. Organizations such as Companies A and B and the B.B.C. are still a step behind. It is not a step that raises any severe problem of cost or administration. There is no special difficulty about giving good late entrants or re-starters, whether Forces officers or women returners, accelerated promotion in a bureaucracy once they are classified into a category which lets their merits be noticed, and the rules of the bureaucracy have been re-written so as to legitimate their claims to consideration. Legitimation may be required in the eyes of colleagues and subordinates even more than of superiors, bearing in mind what was said above about unfavourable reactions often met by those who try to re-enter or catch up in promotion lines. A senior manager responsible for selection and recruitment in Company A says of the whole group of problems arising out of women's career patterns:

> 'I think we could help to establish a climate of opinion towards the recruitment of girls and in particular the re-recruitment of highly qualified women. We could let men managers know that part of the assessment of them as complete managers is how they solve this problem.'[3]

PERMANENT PART-TIME

It is clear that many highly qualified women wish for flexible hours or a less than full-time commitment to work, not simply as a

[1] Allen, I., *Women in Two Companies*, p. 55.
[2] Cmnd. 3638, *op. cit.*, par. 143.
[3] Allen, I., *Women in Two Companies*, p. 49.

temporary arrangement while they have small children but from then on throughout their working life. This demand can be met economically at the junior levels of many occupations. How far is it practicable and economic to do so at the top?

Whereas, as has been shown, part-time work in the wide sense defined earlier is economic and acceptable as a transitional arrangement in posts at relatively junior levels, informants on the employer's side of nearly all the occupations studied resist strongly the suggestion of part-time in senior or even middle-level posts, especially if it is intended as a permanent arrangement and not as a temporary aid during the time when a married woman has small children. In this view they are often joined by highly qualified women themselves. The 1962 report by the International Federation of University Women on part-time work, although withdrawing the opposition to organized part-time work which had been expressed in a report of 1954, insisted that:

'Certain types of work can be done only full-time; posts of supervision and direction, high-level and important research projects and, generally, posts of major responsibility.'[1]

The case against a reduced or flexible work commitment at senior levels reduce to four arguments:

(1) The holders of genuine top jobs, or those who aspire to hold them, need as the basis for the day-to-day decisions a very high level and quantity of up to date information. For this they need to build and maintain an information network, personal and documentary, on a scale and by methods which are more likely to require overtime than to permit part-time. One of the reasons why so much time and effort is required is that at this level much information-gathering is and must be non-logical. It cannot be programmed or delegated and depends on feel, hunch and the immersion of the person who is seeking information directly and personally in the information flow. Top performance in science as well as in management requires a heavy investment in personal contacts,[2] and the research worker or teacher who cannot take the time for this risks being tarred with the brush of amateurism or 'becoming a mere technician'.[3] A part-timer might keep up by giving all of her time to gathering information, but in that case would be left with no time

[1] International Federation of University Women, report to the I.L.O. on *Part-time Women Graduates*, 1962, p. 17.
[2] Cf. Hobsbawm, E. J., 'Global Villages', *New Society*, June 19, 1969.
[3] E.g. Sommerkorn, *op. cit.*, p. 224 (British women university teachers). The quotation is from International Federation of University Women, *op. cit.*, p. 12 (from the IFUW's Belgian affiliate).

456

actually to do her work. Even at what might be called routine professional levels, a part-timer, or her employer, often finds it much harder than a full-timer both to do the immediate job in hand and to find time for the meetings, training courses, and informal contacts around the office needed for full efficiency in the long run.[1] She is less likely than a full-timer to be in touch with all sides of the work of her office, may find it necessary to specialize more narrowly, and so is likely to be a less generally useful member of the staff, and less able to stand in for others in emergencies.

(2) Successful day-to-day operation in many professions depends on all members of a particular network being available simultaneously at regular working hours for a quick response to unforeseeable needs. There is for example a crisis in the child-care office or on the building site, or a parliamentary question comes in to a Civil Service department; if a key member of the network needed to handle the problem is absent, the network cannot function with the speed and efficiency required.

'The usual reaction of (Civil Service) administrators to the subject of part-time working was:

> "It would so gum up the works if Mrs X didn't work conventional hours. A full-time administrator can drop what he is doing to go to a meeting, deal with a parliamentary question or letter to a Minister. Part-timers cannot be called from home, and no one else, despite the extensive filing system, can stand in for Mrs X." '

One administrator quoted his permanent secretary as saying:

> 'Administrators are paid for being here rather than doing anything.'[2]

A limited number of breaks in the network can be tolerated, for example those due to annual holidays. But extensive use of part-timers would 'gum up the works', not only by increasing the number of occasions when someone must stand in for Mrs X but because, for the reason mentioned in the last paragraph, it is likely also to be harder for Mrs X than for a full-timer to stand in for others.

(3) Emergencies also arise outside normal working hours, or spells of regular overtime may be required. Part-timers whose work commitments are strictly limited cannot cope with these.

(4) The difficulties raised in the last two paragraphs might in

---

[1] See notably the discussion of part-timers in social work in H. Curtis and C. Howell's *Part-time Social work*, National Council of Social Service, 1965.
[2] Walters, *op. cit.*, p. 52.

theory be met by filling one full-time post with two part-timers, providing full-time coverage between them. This, however, doubles the number of persons to and from whom information about each case or about the office generally has to be transmitted. The complexity, difficulty of operating, and risk of error and delay in an information network increases not arithmetically but geometrically as the number of persons in the network rises.

These are powerful arguments, but are subject to certain reservations. Difficulties over the time required to obtain personal information or over emergencies outside working hours do not apply with equal force to all part-timers. The woman who needs to work unusual hours or to be free in school holidays may be able to work as long hours as an official full-timer, especially if she can work partly from home, and may cope as easily with out-of-doors emergencies. Out-of-doors emergencies, regular overtime, and difficulty in finding time for both action and information-gathering or in obtaining information without direct personal enquiry may in any case be symptoms of poor work organization which need to be done away with and not to be catered for. The Civil Service report notes among administrators a 'cult of *not* clock-watching'[1] and a tendency to acquire merit by overtime. Persistent overtime at less eminent levels has recently, since D. J. Robertson's devastating study of a Glasgow shipyard[2] and Esso's pioneering productivity bargain at Fawley, been more and more regarded in Britain not as a useful activity but as a sign of bad management. The author of P.E.P.'s study of the Civil Service raises tentatively the question whether this might not be the right view for the Civil Service as well. In social work:

> 'The novelty of the part-time situation has undoubtedly created new problems for the employers and employees alike, but it also high-lighted difficulties which have long been familiar in social work. Amongst these the most prominent are ill-defined areas of responsibility, little spare time for professional contacts, inadequate clerical help, and, above all, work pressure.'[3]

If these general obstacles to efficiency in social work were removed, there would be much less difficulty in getting efficient service from part-timers.

Company B's scientists note the difficulty of reconciling scientific experiments, for example the growth of a culture, with a domestic

---

[1] Walters, *op. cit.*, p. 46.
[2] Robertson, D. J., *Factory Wage Structure and National Agreements*, Cambridge University Press, 1960.
[3] Curtis and Howell, *op. cit.*, p. 105.

timetable. But a university scientist in Sommerkorn's sample comments that:

'If you want to do your research from the late afternoon to midnight you can, and you can be with your children during the day. . . . The argument . . . that one cannot fit research into the odd hours, I do not think is quite true. People always think they cannot but, if you have got to, it is surprising how you can. On the surface it may seem very difficult to catch the same train every evening to go home, as I have to do, but if you have more or less got to because the children are pleased if you turn up, you design your experiments in such a way that they fit. You manage somehow with a bit of ingenuity. Whereas if you have got all day and it doesn't matter when you go home, you tend not to move on and not design the thing carefully.'[1]

In technically advanced industries several tendencies seem likely to increase the possibility of part-time at senior levels. Among these are the separation of operating from other functions, the increase in the number of senior specialists not having general management responsibility, and the changing nature of information flows and of middle to senior management decisions. It is increasingly possible to deliver to a manager at any level direct from the computer much of the information which he needs for his decisions, and for him in turn to feed information direct into the computer for others' use without passing through personal channels. In advanced process industries decisions are increasingly determined by objective technical facts visible to those on the spot and needing no reference to other functions or to higher authority. The job of the senior manager then becomes not so much to arbitrate between his juniors, but more and more to take decisions in fields other than theirs; and even the decisions which he takes himself may be largely programmed, and leave little margin for choice.

In these conditions the fact that a plant is controlled by two people working part-time instead of by one working full-time need not mean confusion or contradiction. Each will receive the same information from instruments or from the computer. Technical conditions, understood similarly by any technically competent person, will determine most of the decisions to be made.[2] Plants and services on shift work or stores which remain open six days a week while the staff work five are in any case well accustomed, whether or not they

[1] Sommerkorn, *op. cit.*, p. 218.
[2] Cf. Woodward, J., *Industrial Organization*, Oxford 1965, and articles in *Harvard Business Review*, September-October 1965, by J. Diebold and H. I. Ansoff.

employ advanced technology, to the idea that responsibility for a single area of work can be shared among several managers.

Directorial as apart from managerial posts in business are already commonly held part-time, and so are a wide range of posts in the free professions. At the time of the Royal Commission on Doctors' and Dentists' Remuneration less than half of all medical consultants worked full-time for the National Health Service, and one fifth worked four days a week or less.[1] Earnings records show that many older barristers, solicitors, accountants, and architects must be working substantially less than full-time.[2] P.E.P.'s study of architects found husband and wife partnerships where both partners operate at a highly responsible level and control between them major construction projects, but do between them less than two full-time jobs.

There is thus a good case for exploring further the possibilities of part-time at higher levels, especially since it is clear both from P.E.P.'s samples and from *Working Wonders* that it is only as part-timers that many well-qualified older women will be available at all. But there remains substance in the argument that, when all unnecessary obstacles have been cleared away, full-timers will still be more economic than part-timers for a wide range of senior jobs.

Eventually, much of the conflict between full- and part-time is likely to be resolved by a cut in working hours which brings regular full-time hours, whether measured by the week or by the year, down to the level now acceptable to many part-timers: say from a present office week of 34-38 hours, excluding the lunch break, to 25-30 hours worked in either four or five days. A six-hour day might well be worked without a lunch break at all. As Myrdal and Klein suggest,[3] one reasonable use for the profit to the economy from married women's employment might well be to reduce the hours of men as well as women to a level which releases men for their families as well as helping married women themselves. There would then no longer be any question about the need to accept arrangements for double manning posts, and otherwise coping with the problem of short hours for senior staff, which seem uneconomic so long as staff prepared to work longer hours can be found.

Even if this were to occur, however, and even supposing that there were a vast improvement in information services, in programmed decision-making, and in supporting services for senior staff, it seems likely that the first of the four arguments against shortened hours at senior levels would still hold for many professional people and

---

[1] Cmnd. 1064, supplement to Cmnd. 939, *op. cit.*
[2] *Ibid.*   [3] Ch. III, p. 105.

managers who are at or proceeding to the top. The top is the point where very many channels of information and decision come together. It could also be defined, picking up a hint from Woodward, as the area where in even the most advanced technical conditions programmed information and decision-making ceases to be enough, and has to be supplemented with methods of a more time-consuming kind. People at this level may and commonly do fill several roles at once. Each of these roles taken separately may be part-time, and not all need be performed in an office or in standard office hours. But, taken together, they seem likely in the foreseeable future as in the past to continue to add up to what would now be regarded as full-time or more.

In the next years, in any case, there will be an interval during which many employers will continue to find part-time work at senior levels unacceptable – often with good reason – and the gap between part- and full-time work will not yet have been closed by reducing full-time hours. During this interval the most effective way to reconcile efficiency with the wishes of holders of senior posts who want more time for their families seems likely to be, not to press for part-time, but to build flexibility into full-time work by longer and more flexible leave entitlements. Complete flexibility of hours, as the dual-career studies bring out,[1] is not usually desirable; it is liable to leave a woman – or a man – confused and disoriented. It is a combination of a well-structured working day with a good margin of flexibility for family and other emergencies which seems likely to give the best results.

The suggestion is not that there should be some extra holiday or family leave entitlement for women with families. Provisions of this kind might well be rejected by women themselves, and would certainly be rejected by many women's organizations. There runs through the P.E.P. reports a widespread reluctance on the part of married women to let themselves be singled out among workers as a category apart and, commonly, treated as a result as second-class. A special leave allowance for wives but not for husbands would also weight the scales unnecessarily in favour of a segregated role pattern within the family. The point is rather that Britain in recent years has lagged behind most other European countries in holiday provision for both men and women, and for professional and executive as well as routine office and manual grades. An advance is due on this front in the interests of men as well as women, and could be particularly helpful from married women's point of view.

The teaching professions, including the universities and technical colleges, are of course outstanding as regards convenience of holidays

[1] Ch. IX, pp. 379-380.

as well as of daily hours, and several of the P.E.P. reports note the pull which they can therefore exert on able married women from other professions. But the experience of a number of other professions and organizations, including certain firms and the Civil Service, which already have generous and flexible leave allowances underlines how greatly this can reduce the strain for married women and facilitate their promotion to senior levels. With, say, four working weeks' holiday – senior Civil Servants have six – it becomes possible to take three weeks in the summer and nearly a fortnight at Christmas, including the normal public holiday and a weekend. If a husband as well as a wife has holidays on this scale and an overlap can be arranged, a substantial part of the problem of school holidays is solved. Alternatively, a number of days can be kept in reserve for family emergencies and special occasions without cutting into the time needed for a reasonable family holiday. Hours tend in any case to be less rigid and casual days' leave easier to arrange at senior than at routine levels. The next step is to see that this flexibility is general and operates in the framework of adequate overall allowances of leave.

THE PROBLEM OF GEOGRAPHICAL MOBILITY

Most of the problems of adapting employment practices to women's different cycle so far mentioned are capable of being solved, and without unreasonable cost. There remains the less tractable issue of mobility.

Mobility, in the day-to-day sense of being free and willing to travel in connection with the job, does not stand out from either the occupational or the family studies as causing notable difficulty to women at the level of work and income studied. Women in professional and managerial work tend generally to be better equipped for day-to-day mobility than women in more junior jobs, not least because they are more likely not only to have cars but to use them for their work.[1] For women in the dual-career studies day-to-day travel is simply one among the various duties which make it necessary for them to be away from home. If they can cope with the other reasons for absence, they can cope with this as well. Business women, Civil Servants, and radio or television workers appear in the family case studies and occupational studies not only to be managing successfully any complications which day-to-day travel may bring to their family life but to be finding travel a particularly interesting and stimulating part of their job. In certain of the occupations studied,

[1] Hunt, A., *A Survey of Women's Employment*, Government Social Survey, SS 379, H.M.S.O., 1968, p. 45.

if women are not at present given the chance of posts involving travel—for example of gaining experience as salesmen in Companies A or B or in outside broadcasting in the B.B.C.—the reason seems often to be not that a woman herself will not travel but that men assume that she will not, or think that the customer or the team with whom she would travel would not like it. Practice in occupations like these often shows inconsistencies suggesting lack of consideration or simply discrimination:

> 'It is often said by men that women cannot stand the discomfort of the outside broadcast life – up early, working under cold and draughty conditions, long hours, and so on – but the production secretary on these expeditions is always a woman.'[1]

On the other hand, mobility in the sense of readiness to move to a job in another area remains one of the most intractable problems of married women's employment. But the findings of the occupational studies and the survey of graduates together suggest that this problem, at least in the social group studied, may both be less acute and be becoming less exclusively a women's problem than it once seemed. As with day-to-day mobility, it seems that the reason why at least some women do not move is not that they will not but that they are not asked. A woman in Company B comments that:

> 'It is always assumed that women won't move, so they never ask us. This means that we're never given opportunities to move out or up.'[2]

The family studies bring out that among today's younger graduates, men as well as women accept that a man should be prepared to move to a new district and look for a new job if this will let his wife seize a major chance for her own career. Men graduates still show a majority for the proposition that it is more important for a wife to help her husband's career than to have one herself. But around 40 per cent of married men graduates of 1960 reject this proposition, and among married women graduates with children the proportion rejecting it reaches 50 per cent. The married women graduates still accept that it is difficult for them to make long-range plans for their own careers because they must adapt to their husbands', but are calling for, and seem likely to get, a good deal of adaptation the other way. Instances turned up in the family case studies where a husband did in fact turn down a good opportunity for his own career or drop out of a satisfactory job because his wife's career required this.

The career decisions of managers and professional men have

[1] Allen, I., *Women in the B.B.C.*, p. 24.
[2] Allen, I., *Women in Two Companies*, p. 19.

always of course been influenced by their wives.[1] The difference now is that the wives' influence seems likely to be concerned not only with factors such as housing and schools but more and more with the wife's own career. There is no reason yet to think that men in management and the professions have ceased to be readier than women to move to a new district to work. But among highly qualified people, where women tend to have a relatively high career commitment and degree of continuity in their working life, the point seems likely increasingly to be not that men are mobile and women are not, but that the mobility of men as well as women will be determined by the career situation of both spouses together and not of one alone. This will not necessarily make it easier to persuade a married woman to move to a new district when her employer or her own career requires this. But in the eyes of an employer it should reduce the *relative* disadvantage of employing her as compared to employing a man, for one of the most important brakes to her mobility, consideration for her spouse's career, will now apply to many married men as well.

The implications of this not only for personnel policy but for town planning and plant location could be far-reaching. In the family studies married women graduates showed a modest but noticeable interest – interest from the men's side was markedly smaller – in the idea of 'more extensive hiring of professional husbands and wives by the same employer'.[2] Where this is not desirable or practicable, there is likely to be growing interest in the idea of seeking jobs within reach of an industrial and office complex large enough to offer openings at a responsible professional or managerial level to husband and wife alike.

CONCLUSION: DO EMPLOYERS IN ANY CASE NEED WOMEN WITH 'AVERAGE' OR 'TYPICAL' LIFE CYCLES?

A recurring theme in this as in the previous chapter has been that employers in Britain, and indeed in most Western countries, appear to have given little thought to the practical problems of employing at even moderately senior, let alone top, levels women who marry and have children, unless and until the need to do so is forced on them (as has happened in teaching or medicine) by a shortage of men and single women. As a recent study of the prospects for women business executives in Britain notes:

[1] See e.g. Pahl, R. E. and J. M., *The Manager: His Wife, His Family and His Career*, Graduate Appointments Register, April 1968 and Holstrom, Lynda L., *Career Patterns of Married Couples*, Paper to Seventh World Congress of Sociology, Varna, 1970.

[2] Among 1960 graduates 30 per cent of married women with children took a favourable view of this proposition, and just under 2 per cent of married men with children.

'There was generally a lack of imagination about how women can be used; and interviews showed that most employers tended to consider women suitable only for 'back room' jobs. Many showed surprise when confronted with the question of a career in their firms and very few had even considered the idea of promotion in connection with female executives.'[1]

In the light of the evidence of the occupational studies, it seems once again that this is for the most part a matter of 'threshold' costs holding up progress rather than of any fundamental obstacle. The chief exception is over geographical mobility, and even in that case women's relative disadvantage may be, or be becoming, smaller than it used to appear.

To institutionalize maternity leave, to provide openings for part-time work during married women's small-child period, or to re-launch qualified women who return to work in their former profession can, it seems, be done economically in the sense both that the cost to employers is unlikely to be great – especially if the community bears its share of the costs of maternity, including re-launching – and that it is likely to be outweighed by the gain from improving the supply of well qualified and experienced staff and from avoiding the cost of training raw recruits. It appears that older women *can* accelerate back and regain the professional ground which they lost in their small-child period, and that for women as for men a delay of a few years beyond what are at present the common ages for top promotion need not make their promotion uneconomic. The procedures needed to identify mature women with top potential and to accelerate their promotion are no different from those which a well run organization uses in any case to identify and promote its future leaders. The point is simply that mature women, too, need to be brought within the selectors' range of vision. It has been seen that there is a case for going further into the practicability of reduced or flexible hours even in senior jobs, for in a number of cases part-time even at this level may be more economic than it has seemed hitherto. Longer holidays and (more remotely) shorter weekly hours will probably come in any case, through pressures not arising specifically or specially from the problems of married women. One economic gain towards offsetting their cost could be an increase in the number of well-qualified married women who are willing to accept full-time jobs if generous, and flexible, leave arrangements can be built into them.

Nevertheless, though re-designing jobs and career patterns to suit

[1] Gordon Yates Bureau, *Is There a Future for Female Executives?* 1969, p. 14.

the typical life-cycles of women as apart from men seems on all these counts a practicable and economic proposition, progress in their direction is not being made, or is made only piecemeal and half-heartedly. The view of a manager in Company B remains widespread; 'Let the other chap be the first to start re-designing jobs for married women'.[1] The reasons for this, like those quoted in the last chapter for neglecting or under-estimating women's potential work performance, run parallel to those found in studies of employers' policies on industrial training or on plant and office location.

Employers do have a great deal to gain in the long run from re-designing senior jobs and the career patterns which may lead married women to them. First and foremost there is the question of the quality of top appointments. Widening the field from which candidates can be drawn helps to ensure that the best possible quality of candidates are effectively in the running for top jobs.

Secondly, there is the question of the repercussions of policy on top jobs on performance lower down. The report on Company A, in particular, raises the question whether, with the attitudes and expectations now developing among women graduates, employers can expect good service and low turnover from highly qualified women employed even at junior levels if these women have reason to feel that they are treated as second-class citizens, expected to abandon their careers on having children, and denied the consideration for promotion given to men of the same ability. The contrast mentioned in Chapter XI between women's performance in the departments of Company A which do and do not give these women the chance to reach senior posts is particularly revealing.

Thirdly, a number of organizations report problems of quantity: a shortage of well-qualified staff, not perhaps at the very top, but for senior posts somewhat lower down. Company B reports a potential shortage of scientists. The Administrative Civil Service would have been willing to take more recruits in recent years if men or women of the right standard had been available. Unilever's quarterly, *Progress*, stated in 1964 that:

'The limits to Unilever's expansion will largely be set by its managerial resources. Sometimes we have had to postpone a proposal for a new venture because the necessary management to put the plan into effect could not be deployed. In spite of hopes that management would become less scarce as time went on and the fruits of postwar management planning became ripe for picking, we are still having to search for the right man in the right place. . . .

[1] Allen, I., *Women in Two Companies*, p. 48.

The scarcity of management talent has introduced a further responsibility, which is that no talent is overlooked by the organization wherever and at whatever level it is to be found.'

Women and Top Jobs noted a number of general factors which may tend to increase the demand for very highly qualified and experienced staff over the next generation.[1] One factor could be a tendency to adopt 'organic' rather than 'mechanistic' patterns of management:

'Not so much a pyramid as a network of communication and authority linking autonomous decision centres of which first one and then another becomes a 'hot centre' and gives the current lead. Authority becomes decentralized and is spread in a fluid and fluctuating way between different ranks and functions. The leadership in a particular project is allowed to come from whatever point is most appropriate in that particular case.'[2]

This type of management is likely to become more widespread because it is particularly suited to rapidly changing conditions; and it can use a much higher proportion than can pyramid patterns of highly qualified staff with the capacity for independent decisions. Another possibility is that organizations and sectors of the economy which at present use few highly qualified staff may employ more. Another is that, as tends in any case to happen in advanced countries, levels of qualification will continue to rise throughout the job structure as the number of qualified people increases, without the structure necessarily changing its shape; that technicians will replace craftsmen, technologists technicians, and so on up the line.

But *Women and Top Jobs* also noted that though the demand for highly qualified managerial and professional staff may be strengthened by these long-run tendencies, this could be offset by an increase on the supply side as the flood of graduates accelerates.[3] Meantime, in the shorter run, inquiries from a wide range of organizations for the present study show that few of them feel that they face a serious shortage of staff for really senior jobs. There may be shortages lower down, but as pyramids narrow towards the top the competition becomes fiercer and, if selectors find themselves short of candidates, it is more likely to be because they have failed to take normal steps to plan for the succession to top jobs than because potential candidates are not to be found. Organizations which in the short run can fill their top jobs adequately are liable to see as marginal the long-range advantages of being able to select from a still wider field if

---

[1] *Women and Top Jobs*, pp. 22-29.   [2] *Ibid.*, p. 26.
[3] See above, Ch. III, p. 122.

the doors are opened more to women, of having candidates of still better quality, or of minimizing discontent in the lower ranks.

In these circumstances employers may not and commonly do not think that the effort needed to re-design career paths and employment practices in order to take more married women into senior levels is worthwhile; especially if it involves pioneering, not merely applying procedures developed by others. Yet, because there is after all a long run gain to be achieved, these same employers might well be grateful if others – women themselves, unions or professional associations, or public opinion or the government – took the initiative in pushing them over this particular threshold. To use once again the analogy of the location of industry, the case of these employers is exactly parallel to that of the firm which does not think it worthwhile on its own to explore widely for sites for a new plant or office, but may and often does have reason to be grateful if agencies with a wider and longer view do in fact force on its attention opportunities which it would otherwise have overlooked.

It is here that the difference pointed out at the beginning of this chapter between the individual employer's point of view and that of community agencies, including each profession or occupation as a whole, becomes particularly relevant, for these wider groupings do have a much clearer incentive than most individual employers to make the effort to re-design career patterns so that more women may climb to the top. Individual employers' view of reform in recruitment and employment practices is necessarily focused primarily on the near future and on the needs of their own particular form of production or service, though it need not and should not stop there.[1] The community, in the wide sense of agencies – professional, governmental, or other – above the level of the individual employer, can and must take a wider view.

The efficiency of particular enterprises is of interest, not only to individual employers, but to the community as a whole. But the community also has a wider economic interest in the full use of willing and available labour; particularly in Britain, where the prospective demographic increase in the working population to 1980 is no more than $4\frac{1}{2}$ per cent: the third lowest rate in Europe.[2] It has a social interest both in the full use of ability and in working out to

---

[1] The P.E.P. series of publications bearing on employers' wider obligations include broadsheets by B. Shenfield on *Company Giving*, M. Fogarty on *Wider Business Objectives, Beyond Jenkins* and *A Companies Act 1970*; and books by C. de Hoghton (ed.), on *The Company: Law, Structure and Reform in Eleven Countries*, 1970, and by B. Shenfield on the social responsibilities of British company boards (forthcoming).

[2] Economic Commission for Europe. *The European Economy in 1968*, Ch. III, Table 25.

the best advantage the changes in social and especially family life, for men as well as women, which married women's new career commitments imply. The community's incentive to act on the problems raised by married women's careers at senior – or other – levels is clear even when the individual employer's is not. It is therefore reasonable that a major part of the initiative towards solving these problems should come from the community, and that the community should relieve employers of certain of the costs which arise from this initiative, especially the direct costs of maternity. The next chapter considers among other things what this community initiative is in practice to mean, and which agencies in the community should be involved.

Part Five

Conclusions

Chapter XIII

The Enquiry's Findings and the Future

Most of the findings of this report are neither new nor special to Britain. They confirm that the same problems and tendencies exist in Britain as in other industrialized and urbanized countries in Eastern and Western Europe, and from Israel to North America. What the report sets out to do is to knit together a number of strands of thought and factual research so as to increase understanding of the social and psychological processes underlying these tendencies, and in this way to lay a more solid foundation of fact for future policies. As was said in the Foreword and Chapter I, there has been a double shift of accent as the enquiry has proceeded. Originally the subject was women's access to and prospects in jobs that are 'top' in the sense of being at the peak of a managerial or professional hierarchy. Increasingly, it has come to be their prospects in the much greater number of jobs at senior but not necessarily 'top' levels. At first the question of access to senior or top jobs was taken up as a problem of and for women. But here too the accent has shifted from women alone to men and women together and the whole complex of problems around the relationship between family and work. What modifications are needed in this complex in recognition of the fact of highly-qualified women's interest in careers, and how can these modifications best be achieved through the efforts of men and women together and in the interests of both?

HIGH-LEVEL CAREERS FOR WOMEN (NOTABLY FOR MARRIED WOMEN) CAN BE PRACTICABLE AND DESIRABLE FROM BOTH THE FAMILY AND THE ECONOMIC POINT OF VIEW

A first general finding is that workable patterns can be found for giving access to senior and top jobs not only to single women but to married women with children and a normal family life. There is nothing to be gained from pressuring able women who are mothers of families into pursuing in addition a career aimed at high levels

473

if they themselves do not judge it right to do so. It is for them to choose the course which fits best with their personal and family circumstances, work opportunities and social responsibilities. But the findings show that there is also no convincing general case, from the angle either of the family or of economic efficiency, for discouraging those mothers who do wish to pursue high-level careers from doing so.

a *Need women's high-level careers damage the family?*

The survey of graduates shows that, at least in the group of women studied here, the extreme forms of 'feminine mystique'[1] have vanished practically without trace. Highly qualified women today are decisively committed to being lifetime workers. Four out of five of those British women graduates of 1960 who are married with children have a firm intention of being in employment, most of them full-time, after their children have grown up, and only 1 per cent have a firm intention *not* to be so. Four out of five also intend to be in employment when their children are between 6 and 12, but in this case most of the employment would be part-time.[2]

But this does not imply that these wives propose to neglect their family responsibilities. They are the same women who figure in previous chapters as 'particularly conscious and conscientious mothers'. When asked to express a preference between a range of possible attainments, 'to be a good parent' and 'to help my children develop as I think they should' come overwhelmingly at the top of their list. Most of them refuse to work at all while their youngest child is under 3, and only one in twenty works or intends to work full-time at that stage.[3] By a heavy majority they express their intention to leave work, or to drop down to part-time work, if one of their young children shows signs of severe disturbance. The proportion who think a wife should stop work altogether in this case is, however, matched by the proportion who think that the answer is for husband and wife jointly to reorganize their working life so as to spend more time at home. This latter solution is supported even more commonly by husbands than by wives. The great majority of wives would also drop to part-time work if they thought that full-time working was damaging their relationship to their husband.[4]

---

[1] Betty Friedan's phrase, in her book of the same title (Penguin, 1965), for exclusive devotion to the housewife role.
[2] Ch. VI, Table 14.
[3] Ch. VI, Table 14; and Ch. VII, Table 5.
[4] Ch. VII, pp. 281-285.

Of the wives in the sample very few want fewer than two children, and not far short of half of those who specify any particular number mention three or more. It tends, however, to be the more continuous workers who prefer to have two children or fewer.[1] These wives prefer to do much of their own housekeeping, especially cooking, and are reluctant to delegate child care.[2] If they do delegate it, only the best will do: 'adequacy' is not enough.[3] For children under 3 care outside the home tends to be rejected altogether.[4] If a specially favourable opportunity for a wife's career opens up, men as well as women in the sample expect the husband to adapt to this even at some inconvenience to himself. Wives themselves divide about equally on the principle of whether they ought to give some preference to their husbands' careers. But they tend to accept that it is, in practice, hard for a wife to make long-range plans for her own career, since these must depend on her husband's career.[5]

General evidence was quoted earlier[6] that 'mother working' is not a particularly useful category for predicting good or bad effects on children. It depends on the circumstances surrounding each case and on the skill and other resources available to handle it. The mothers considered here are not only 'conscious and conscientious' but are also particularly well equipped with resources of ability, knowledge and cash. A similar conclusion emerges from the evidence of the family studies on the effect of the employment of highly qualified women on their relations with their husbands. Among husbands for whom the family has top priority, it makes very little difference to happiness in marriage whether or not their wives work; these husbands tend anyway to rate the happiness of their marriages high. Husbands who are chiefly career-centred, but for whom the family nevertheless means a great deal, tend to feel that their marriages are happier if their wives are working. Those who are career-centred and give the family low priority tend to feel that their marriages are happier if their wives do not work. Taking all families together, it cannot be said that in the social group investigated 'wife working' has any clear-cut effect, whether positive or negative, on husbands' estimate of the happiness of the marriage.[7]

As regards the relationship between a wife's work and her own estimate of the happiness of her marriage, much depends on the attitudes of her husband and of her social circle and on whether she knows her own mind. Dithering wives, who do not know their own mind for or against women's careers, tend to feel their marital

[1] Ch. VII, Tables 4 and 6.
[2] *Ibid.*, pp. 242-243.
[3] *Ibid.*, Table 5.
[4] *Ibid.*, p. 250.
[5] *Ibid.*, pp. 262, 264, 282.
[6] Ch. IV, pp. 141-144.
[7] Ch. VII, Table 18.

happiness to be under more strain when they work than when they do not; but once a woman does make up her mind – in whichever direction – this no longer holds.[1] A wife whose husband agrees with her in his attitude to women's careers is likely to see her marriage as much happier than if he does not, whether or not she is currently working. Wives' attitudes to women's careers do as a matter of fact tend to agree with their husbands'; many men in the sample, as well as many women, have at least a 'secondary', if not a 'medium' or 'full', commitment to women's careers. There remain, however, many clashes of attitude to diminish wives' estimate of happiness.[2] 'Wife's job' is not a noticeably direct factor in disputes in the families investigated, but Table VII.10 illustrates the possibility of its giving rise to disputes indirectly; where the wife is working, disagreements over the division of labour in the home tend to be commoner.

Wives with differing degrees of career commitment tend to find their way into social circles where there is a good deal of support for their own position. But, overall, attitudes about women's work in the social circles in which these wives move tend to be mixed or weighted towards the idea that 'women ought to be able to work a bit'. Only in a small minority of cases is there clear support for equality of careers. It is, accordingly, not surprising to find in Table VII.17, that, whereas wives who fit the socially approved pattern and are uncommitted to women's careers, or committed only to 'working a bit', show much the same level of satisfaction in their marriage whether they are working or not, those with a stronger career commitment, diverging from the standard pattern, show a less high level of marital satisfaction and more strain when they go out to work. Their level of satisfaction can be expected to rise as and when the 'break-even' point suggested in Chapter III is passed and the balance of social support swings over on to the side of women with careers.[3]

The impact of a highly qualified wife's work on her family as a whole can be tested particularly thoroughly from the evidence of Chapter IX on dual-career families. These families represent the boundary case, which departs furthest from formerly conventional patterns and raises the most problems for married couples themselves. The remarkable thing about the findings of Chapter IX is, in a sense, that they are so unremarkable. These are families which are undoubtedly exceptional, in which both husband and wife are pursuing full-scale, high-level – often very high-level – and strenuous

[1] Ch. VIII, Table 17.
[2] Ch. VII, Tables 15 and 19.
[3] Ch. VIII, Table 12, and see Ch. VII, Tables 17 and 19, and Ch. VIII, Table 10.

careers. Yet when these families are examined closely it appears that there is no very general or obvious difference between the quality of life which they experience and which is found in families following other patterns. The dual career families examined certainly have their problems, some special, for example difficulty in finding time for contacts with relatives and neighbours,[1] others common to them and to families of other patterns. But they cope with their problems just as effectively as other families, if sometimes in different ways.

Wives and husbands who follow dual careers at high level have necessarily to delegate many aspects of housekeeping and child care. But the impression which emerges from the dual-career case studies is not of professionalized and bureaucratized family life from which the humanity has departed: of children kept at arms' length, nor of the situation so encouragingly suggested to one dual-career mother by the neighbour who said, 'I suppose you won't mind when your baby doesn't recognize you as its mother'.[2] There is time for children in these families; even perhaps more time, as the kibbutz parallel quoted earlier suggests,[3] than in many families which are under less pressure to organize their day carefully. There are friends and close links with relatives, though, once again, on a less casual basis than in many other families. Interest in community activities does not seem a high priority for the dual-career families studied, but neither is it for young British men and women graduates generally.

Certainly in dual-career families time-schedules are tight and family management becomes a skilled art. But the point of skilled management and working to a tight schedule in a family of this kind is to leave room for the necessary warmth of family life and 'time for free time'. The evidence of the case studies is that this can be and often is successfully achieved, on the condition that a deliberate effort is made by all concerned. And, bearing in mind what was said above about the relation between marital unhappiness and a wife's uncertainty over her own attitude to work, it is an advantage for the quality of life in these families that the wife as well as the husband at least starts by knowing what her attitude to work is.

There is no evidence from the experience of the dual-career families studied, nor indeed from the rest of the family or occupational studies – as was pointed out in the Foreword – that a dual-career pattern leads to the masculinization of women or the feminization of men. The direct evidence of the dual-career studies is that the men and women who adopt this pattern are more likely than others to be

1 Ch. IX, p. 360.   2 *Ibid.*, p. 352.
3 Ch. IV, p. 144.

familiar with and sympathetic to the interests of the other sex, and less likely to be worried at taking up activities (such as careers for wives) which cross older conventional sex-role lines; but not that they themselves cross sex lines, nor that they are confused over their sex identity.[1] The occupational studies indicate that this is particularly likely to be true of younger women who are placed at the end of the cycle of action and reaction which began with the 'battleaxe' generation. Many of the pioneering women of that generation adopted a strongly masculine style. This was followed by a sharp reaction in the generation now middle-aged. Today's younger generation appears to be finding a balanced position between its two predecessors.[2] The graduate sample studies suggest that one reason for the emergence of the wrong belief that women with high-level careers become masculinized is simply that so many of the women with high-level careers in the last two generations were single. For among those women, and men, who remain single a relatively high proportion do diverge from the norms of their own sex towards those of the other.[3]

It does not follow that every married couple in which the wife is highly qualified either should or will adopt the particularly demanding dual-career family pattern. Reasons against that thesis will be presented below. What can be said is that the evidence of the dual-career studies shows that dual careers can with good management be reconciled with a satisfactory family life, and that marital satisfaction does in fact tend to be high where the wife is a highly-committed continuous worker, though somewhat less high[4] than in families where the wife's commitment is to 'work a bit'. The marginal difference in favour of 'working a bit' is likely to be in part temporary, due to the lack in present conditions of social support for continuous working patterns. It may well also be at least in part an optical illusion, for dual-career couples aim at a difficult and sophisticated target, and seem likely to be more critical than more easy-going couples of their own performance and less ready to describe it in glowing terms. John Stuart Mill's analogy of Socrates dissatisfied, already quoted, could be relevant here.

If even in present conditions a dual-career pattern can be reconciled with a flourishing family life—provided that it is thought out and managed with skill—this is likely also to be true *a fortiori* of other patterns which are less demanding from the family's point of view; in particular the common[5] three-phase pattern with a strong commitment to employment, but a clear and substantial break during the

[1] Ch. IX, pp. 355-360. [2] Ch. XI, pp. 405-6.
[3] Ch. VI, especially pp. 200-213. [4] Table VIII, 10.
[5] Ch. VI, Table 8; and Ch. VIII, Table 5.

time when children are small. As a general judgment it seems that any of a range of patterns—dual careers, or a more traditional pattern with the housewife at home, or an intermediate pattern—can be consistent with the happiness of a marriage provided that at least one partner, or preferably both, gives high priority to maintaining and developing the family relationship, whether alongside or in substitution for that partner's own career; and provided that attention is given to the specific problems of the pattern chosen. In a dual career pattern it is important to have the resources and organisation to lighten what could otherwise become the intolerable burden of overload. In a traditional pattern, with the housewife at home, it may be more important to work at developing common spheres of activity between husband and wife and ensuring that their life activities do not drift completely apart.[1]

It is true, as was stressed in Chapter I, that careers raise different and more difficult problems for highly qualified women and their husbands from those experienced at lower levels. But the evidence is that they can solve these problems successfully, even in existing conditions, thanks to their high level of resources, and could of course solve them still better if the social climate gave more support and unnecessary material difficulties were removed.

The differences between lower and higher level careers appear most clearly in the case of women who aim to reach not simply *some* post of high qualification and responsibility but the actual top of their profession. A woman (like a man) who hopes to reach the top by climbing a career ladder – women who are pressed or catapulted into top jobs, by inheritance or otherwise, are of course another matter – needs, as an informant from Company A inelegantly but revealingly put it, to decide what package she is selling to employers and colleagues. She must design her package with care, and go about selling it in an orderly way. Unlike the woman who will be content with some combination of a more or less satisfying job and family life, she cannot afford to be casual. On the side of the family, she may find several patterns of living to be consistent with high-level careers: for example to have children quickly after graduating or qualifying, and then make in effect a new clear start to a career; or to take a break for children or a period of part-time after becoming well established in a career; or to work through on a dual-career pattern. Though the evidence of Chapters VII and XII is that she will be well advised to maintain a large degree of continuity in her career, it is not impossible that she might reach the

[1] L. Bailyn, 'Marital Satisfaction in Relation to Career and Family Orientations of Husbands and Wives', *Human Relations*, 1970.

top after a considerable break. So far as the work situation itself is concerned, she may be able to reach the top by choosing a single career path early and pursuing it to the end, or by seizing opportunity as it comes. But whatever strategy she chooses on either the work or the family side, she needs to pursue it persistently and actively. A degree of drift, in terms of decisions affecting either work or such matters as family size and spacing, may be consistent with *some* combination of satisfying work with family life. But it is unlikely to be consistent with the sort of combination which leads to the top; above all in the case of married women, given the extra difficulty which they in any case experience in planning their lives and careers.

Even in those careers where a woman is not reaching for the ultimate peaks of her profession, the tension between work and family life is liable in a number of ways to be greater for her if she is in highly qualified work. Highly qualified women tend, as has been said, to have a particularly high degree of career commitment, and one which rests more than among lower qualified women on interest in the job itself and less on features such as income or the social relations surrounding the job. Their careers require a relatively high degree of continuity. It is not so easy for them simply to take work or leave it as their family commitments may require. The domestic problems which are caused by their work, especially the problems over bringing up children, may not be more difficult to solve than those of women with lower qualifications. But they may well be felt more keenly and give rise to more feelings of guilt among these 'particularly conscious and conscientious parents', whose standards of child care are exceptionally high; whose standard of living is in any case high enough to make the wife's work a matter of choice rather than necessity; yet who cannot be as free as women in routine work to drop their work casually when the family seems to need them.

The problem for most women in highly qualified careers and for their husbands is not, obviously, that they must struggle to make ends meet; although a number of very low-earning husbands appear in the samples, and there is a noticeable connection between husband's low earnings and full-time working by the wife.[1] For most of these women the question is how to design for themselves and their families the 'multi-faceted' pattern of living to which *Working Wonders* refers, and to be organized enough and quick enough on their feet (to borrow *Working Wonders*' phrase again) to make this pattern work. But the lesson of these studies is that they can as a matter of

[1] Ch. VII, p. 266.

fact often succeed in doing so, given that their greater difficulties are matched by their greater personal and financial resources.

This, is seems, is the point which employers, relatives, and neighbours are liable to miss. If they notice at all the typical differences between highly qualified women and women of lower ability working at lower levels, they are liable to do so in a one-sided way. They see the family and work problems to which a high-level career commitment by a wife as well as a husband can give rise, but not the extra resources for coping with these problems which highly qualified women and their husbands are likely to possess. Neighbours and relatives may judge by the experience of families with smaller personal and financial resources, and think that parents in a dual-career family are taking undue risks over child care when in fact they are well able to manage their child care successfully. Employers often judge highly qualified women in terms of experience with women of similar age and family commitments but smaller resources, and so underestimate the level and continuity of performance which they can expect from them.

b *The gain to employers and the economy*

On the side of work, some of the problems over women's promotion to senior posts are proving less difficult to solve than they once seemed. Given that highly qualified women can today be expected to be lifetime workers and to return to their careers even if they make a break, the traditional argument that training and promotion for able young women is wasted because their careers will cease on marriage or on the birth of their children has clearly lost its force. It was never wholly sound; women doctors, for example, have always tended to work during most of their lives.[1] Today it has ceased to be true of highly qualified women generally. Young graduates, whether men or women, are now likely to change employers possibly several times in their first career years. In the case of men, employers have learned to look on this mobility as a necessary and in some ways profitable nuisance. One employer's loss is another's gain, and mobility helps to widen young managers' or professional men's experience. In the case of women, employers tended in the past to see departure from a job, especially on marriage or after a birth, as a final loss. This view is no longer justified. The young highly qualified woman who leaves a job, like the highly qualified young man, is not lost to the world of work. In her case as in the man's one employer's loss will eventually – even if after a longer interval, if she leaves for family reasons – be another's gain.

[1] Table III.3 (iii) (e).

Difficulties over geographical mobility will continue to tell against opportunities for married women. But in some respects these difficulties are less acute than they are often thought to be. Problems over day-to-day travel do not seem particularly salient for women at the high occupational level studied here, and often exist more in the imagination of employers and fellow-employees than in the view of the women themselves. Difficulties over moving to a job in a new area are likely to remain real and in particular cases serious. But, as was argued in Chapter XII, married women's *relative* as apart from absolute disadvantage in this respect by comparison with men may well diminish. As the number of wives with strong career commitment increases, husbands too are becoming more tied than they used to be in their geographical choice of a job by consideration for the careers of their wives.

The difference between men's and women's life cycles remains a substantial obstacle to the promotion of highly qualified women. Even women committed to a dual-career pattern are likely at least to slow down their progress during their child-bearing years, if not to drop out altogether. For others the norm is to drop out of work while they have young children. Women are not available, or as freely available, for promotion at the time when high-flying men reach the point of take-off. Compared with men, the high-flyers among the women are likely to have to drop behind and to catch up later. Is it then likely to be economic for employers to adapt their recruitment, appointment, and promotion practices to fit the life cycles of able women and give them a more equal chance of reaching the top? This has been a central question for the enquiry. The answer, from the findings summarized in Chapter XII, is clearly positive. Certainly it is reasonable for employers to ask the community to meet some of the costs arising out of this adaptation, notably the cost of pay during maternity leave and of certain re-launching programmes. But whether costs are carried directly by employers or by the community at large, it seems that it is practicable and economic to provide the necessary programmes for maternity leave, part-time work during the small-child period, re-launching, and promotion for older women. These programmes *can* be operated at costs adequately offset by expected returns.

Is there, however, enough of the right sort of ability among women to make them worth considering for higher posts, especially in the categories where widespread doubts about women's capacity are still found: posts with a high content of management and entrepreneurship, and some technical posts? Once again the answer is clearly positive. The material from both Eastern Europe and the West summarized in Part Two, together with the findings of Chapter

XI, make it clear that though the work interests and abilities of women tend to differ from those of men in certain respects, every level and type of ability can be found, or developed, among women as among men. *A priori* arguments that women are incapable of handling this or that type or level of work have again and again collapsed under the test of experience. No convincing reason can be found for assuming that women are likely to perform so poorly in particular types of managerial or professional work that they are not worth considering for them. The family studies add the point that, over and above the fact that women graduates today are lifetime workers, many of them have a strong and positive commitment to a career; though still, usually, with less 'vertical' aspiration than is found among men.[1]

Nor can the exclusion of women from competition for top jobs be justified by the argument that the supply of candidates for these jobs is already sufficient, both in quality and numbers, to make further competition unnecessary and perhaps undesirable. This argument is still commonly used, implicitly if not explicitly. There has been a tendency in Britain as in other Western countries to call on women's services chiefly in times of labour shortage. To some extent, as was shown in Chapter II, this is true of Eastern Europe as well. At routine levels of office and factory work the pressure of demand in the labour markets of advanced countries such as Britain is now strong enough to ensure a consistently high level of demand for women workers. But there tends still to be strong competition for top jobs, since, as the pyramid of jobs narrows towards the top, the ratio of qualified candidates to available posts rises. Interviews show that the question whether, in that case, it is worth taking the trouble of grooming yet another category of applicants for top jobs is very much in employers' minds.

Nevertheless, it is clear that there are good economic grounds – apart from any question of personal interest and satisfaction or of civil rights – for enlarging the field so as to give women too their chance of selection for the top. Top jobs need the best available talent. In so far as women's work abilities and interests cover the same range as men's, it is in employers' and the economy's interest that women with great ability should have the chance to replace men of less ability. In so far as women's interests and abilities differ from men's, it is important that the distinctive contribution which able women can make should be put to use. Masculine-feminine differences – which in any case must not be exaggerated – are a matter not of superiority and inferiority but of qualities which are complementary in high-level and managerial work as well as lower down,

[1] See, e.g., Ch. VII, Table 11.

especially in the changing conditions of an advanced economy and under advanced methods of management. Refusal of access to top jobs can also have damaging repercussions at lower levels. In organizations where women are refused consideration for career ladders leading to the top this tends, as was shown in Chapter XI, to cause under-employment, low morale, and excessive turnover among able women even in lower ranks. In certain occupations, in any case, staff shortages which could be relieved by women are found even at senior levels.

NO SINGLE PATTERN OF WORK AND FAMILY LIFE PROVIDES THE ANSWER: A RANGE OF OPTIONS IS NEEDED TO SUIT DIFFERENT CASES AND TIMES

In Chapter I, when the values held by the research group were described, it was noted that the research began with the expectation that no single pattern of work and family living would prove ideal. What was likely to be required was a range of options fitting the circumstances of different individuals and families according to case, time, and place. The choice of one or another option should be equally open, and should be free from criticism on general social grounds, as apart from criticism of the suitability of each couple's choice to that couple's own circumstances. Society should support and facilitate couples in working out the solution most suited to their own case in the circumstances of their own time, and make it clear that, so long as the solution discovered fits a couple's objective circumstances, it will have social support.

The findings of the enquiry have given the group no reason to withdraw from this position. It is clear that the choices of highly qualified as of other men and women are likely to spread over the whole range of patterns from the traditional or neo-traditional, where the husband concentrates on the world of work and the wife on her home, by way of complementary-job or three-phase patterns, up to full-scale dual careers. Each of these patterns has had its defenders in recent writing. Leach has put the case against 'the curious assumption that men and women (are) socially interchangeable':

'Instead of training our women to be imitation second-class males we should recognize the basic facts of existence and make a clear distinction between male and female roles, concentrating our attention on raising the social status of the female role.'[1]

Working Wonders puts the case for the job as complementary, Myrdal and Klein for the three-phase pattern, and Alice Rossi, with

[1] E. Leach, address to the British Humanist Association. *The Times*, July 26, 1969.

her 'melting-pot model',[1] or the authors of the Swedish report on *The Status of Women*, for dual-career or other continuous-career patterns and the modification of conventional sex roles which needs to underlie them.

The actual distribution of choices among British women graduates of 1960 who are now married shows that 34 per cent expect to be continuous workers, whether or not they are personally committed to the idea of women's careers or obtain much satisfaction from their work; 43 per cent expect to have interrupted careers, but to return to a substantial level of work once their children are grown; and 22 per cent expect to work less when their children are grown than when they are at age 6 to 12, including a very few who expect not to work at all.[2] These are *expected*, not necessarily *preferred*, categories. The preferred pattern would be different, but it cannot be said precisely how much. Uncertainty centres particularly on the large group of women who are ambivalent in their attitude to work and likely, when they do work, to describe their marriages as something less than 'very happy'; but who cannot make up their minds clearly whether they want to go forward to a fuller career commitment or back towards a traditional housewife role.[3]

The career and, generally, the sex-role patterns which are commonly held to be appropriate have already changed, and are likely to change further in future. Fifty or sixty years ago, when the 'battleaxe' generation were moving into careers, many women felt the need to choose between a traditional housewife role and the outright renunciation of family life, for only the woman whose hands were free could hope to make the extra commitment of time, effort and resistance to social pressure needed for a full-scale career. This view was appropriate to the circumstances of that time, and there are still occupations which could use a 'battleaxe' generation. But the need for so stark a choice has already been modified over the years. If, now, employment structures are changed to fit the needs of married women, and if more and more social and occupational groups pass the break-even point at which the weight of social approval falls onto the side of the working wife, the patterns of work and family life judged appropriate are likely to change still further. More and more 'average' or 'typical' women are likely, in that case to choose work and family patterns which can lead to the top. It will in any case be reasonable to encourage change where present work and family patterns are unsatisfactory: in cases where women cannot make up their minds about their attitude to work, or where there are discrepancies between the attitudes to women's

---

[1] Ch. IV, p. 148.   [2] Ch. VIII, p. 302.
[3] Ch. VII, Tables 2 and 17.

careers of husbands and wives, or between 'careerist' husbands' nominal commitment to their wives' careers and their actual failure to support them. In many of these cases the appropriate change will be towards a stronger career commitment by women; for example in the case of those women who have not made up their own minds about work, but whose husbands are already fully committed to the principle of women's careers.[1]

The upshot could well be that a greater proportion of families will come to prefer a dual-career pattern to the three-phase patterns common in recent years. But this neither need nor should mean imposing a new dual-career stereotype in place of the traditional stereotype of segregated roles, as official policy has tried to do in Eastern Europe. The point should be no more than that there will be a greater statistical probability that a dual-career pattern will fit any particular family's circumstances. The strains of a full dual-career pattern, as recorded in Chapter IX, are very real and the choices favoured by wives and couples may still with reason go in other directions.

One of the striking features of Chapter VII is the high degree of satisfaction shown by those married women who have committed themselves definitively and in principle to the role of a full-time housewife, whether or not they happened to be in this role at the time of the enquiry. That chapter also brings out the relatively uniform and high marital satisfaction among married women with 'secondary commitment' – three-phase or complementary-job workers – whether they are in or out of work.[2] In terms of married couples' own satisfaction, there seems no reason to disturb wives who freely and for valid reasons choose any of these patterns, including the full-time housewife role.

In terms of demography and of general advantage to families and society, the evidence of Eastern Europe as well as of the West suggests that in many families there is still a great deal to be said for a relatively traditional division of labour, with the wife either interrupting her career for long periods or becoming a housewife for life. This case rests not only on the care of small children – especially in the families of three or more children which play a key part in maintaining the population – but on differences in husbands' and wives' own personality, career needs and attitudes to their careers, and on families' responsibilities for elderly or disabled relatives, for relationships within the extended family, and for voluntary social and political action. Some of these responsibilities can be and will be taken over by professionals, but it is neither desirable nor practicable

---

[1] *Ibid.*, Tables 13-18.   [2] Ch. VII, Tables 11 and 18.

for professionals to take over this area completely. The woman (or man) who becomes the focus for an extended family has a valuable social function which no professional can replace. Political activities can be carried on by paid agents and full-time politicians, but it is highly undesirable that there should be no voluntary participation in this field. Many functions in mental health or the care of the aged need to be put back into the community rather than taken out of it by separate institutions. A wide range of movements is developing for participation at local level, for example by tenants in running housing estates or by parents in running nursery schools and play-groups. Parent-teacher associations are showing belated signs of growth in Britain. Participation and community responsibility of a time-consuming kind could well become a main theme of British political and social development through the next generation. Traditional inequalities within the family have gone, but, in the light of all these possible circumstances of the family and demands made on it, a traditional type of division of labour may for many families continue to be justified.

Tendencies for the balance of society's interest, and of married couples' own satisfaction, to shift in a way encouraging to dual careers may well show themselves most strongly among women who are highly qualified. It is these women, especially if they are married to similarly qualified men, who have both the strongest incentive to move in this direction and the best resources to cope with any difficulties to which the move gives rise. Grounds are likely to remain, however, for as far ahead as can usefully be foreseen, for many even of highly qualified couples to choose not dual careers but a three-phase or complementary-job pattern, or even the once conventional pattern of segregated roles.

THE PROBLEM IS ONE OF MEN AND WOMEN, NOT OF WOMEN ALONE

In an investigation such as the present one, which is directed mainly towards long-term problems, a number of obvious current issues about women's employment are less prominent than would be expected in a study with more immediate objectives. Taxation, for instance, has not been a particularly salient issue even in the family case studies, and equal pay, though it figures in a number of the underlying reports, is much less salient than it has been in the general discussion of women's problems in the last few years. Discrimination, though an important short-term issue, seems unlikely to be the basic issue in the long run. P.E.P.'s enquiry has been more concerned, as was said in Chapter IV, with the issues which will remain when discrimination has gone.

These longer-term issues, it is clear from the findings, are not primarily or particularly about women – though problems currently experienced by women may be the original reason for raising them – but about men and women together. As was said in Chapter IV, the leading edge of discussion about women's movement into professional and managerial work is shifting. Once, the point was to remove obstacles to entry into what would still be essentially a man's world. Now it is increasingly to change the structures of work and the family so as to take account of the presence in the world of work, not merely of a few unusual women, but of 'average' or 'typical' women with husband, children, and a distinctively feminine life cycle and outlook. This change in structure involves adaptation by both sexes and co-operation by both in working out what the adaptations are to be and how they are to be brought about.

In some cases the point is simply that problems experienced by women are equally of interest to men. Women who reach the top are often able to overcome the obstacles and handicaps in their way only with the help of a sponsor or 'facilitator', but find that this relationship gives rise to a number of difficulties. For men too, however, coaching and sponsorship are important. Coaching is a recognized responsibility of all supervisors and managers, and men as well as women have an interest in seeing that it is properly carried out. The relationship of a 'crown prince' or 'blue-eyed boy' can also create difficulties for men, though the special complication of sex is not present in the same way. Men, like women, have an interest in promotion procedures which seek out and develop all the talent available in an organization, not merely certain favoured categories; in acceptance by employers that older members of staff may be suitable for promotion; or in a move towards shorter hours, longer and more flexible holidays, and, generally, more free time for their responsibilities and interests as fathers and husbands. To have a mother in responsible, highly qualified, respected, and well paid work can have a very positive value for children, especially older children, and this is something which fathers as well as mothers can appreciate. For a woman to pursue a high-level career it is important that she have the support of her husband. But a man, equally, needs the support of his wife, and the condition of this support is likely increasingly to be that, in the matter of careers, he makes his wife's interests his own, on a basis of mutual obligation such as that set out in East German family law. A man may wish to pursue his career ruthlessly in disregard of his family, but, if so, will do well to be warned by the findings of Chapter VII. For most men as for most women the family is a central source of satisfaction which can be disregarded only at high cost. Most men need to give the family high priority in their lives. But in families where this happens, wives tend to have or develop a relatively high degree of career commitment; and marital satisfaction, particularly as estimated by wives, is linked strongly to agreement between husband and wife in their attitudes to women's careers.[1]

In other cases the point is that if women are to be treated fairly they must be judged by the same standards as men. Men do not have the same pattern of emotional problems as women, nor do they have maternity absences or drop out of work when their child is born. But they do have other emotional problems, and types of absence to which women are less liable, for example for political work or for Forces reserve training. In certain respects they tend to be less stable in their jobs than women. As the occupational studies bring out, an employer has a good chance in present conditions of finding that an able man drives harder than a woman for his next move or promotion and is less content to settle to the job in hand. There has been a tendency in the past for employers to treat the problems arising from men's employment at senior levels as a fact of life with which an employer must live, but those arising from women's employment as a nuisance with which he ought not to be asked to put up. This might have been reasonable when women were not career workers and were a dispensable part of the work force, at least at the levels discussed here. It has ceased to be reasonable now that these conditions have changed.

The findings of the Steinmann studies[2] about the capacity of the two sexes for mutual misinterpretation are fully borne out by those of the P.E.P. studies. P.E.P. has been concerned largely with misunderstanding by men about women, but for the men on the research team it has also been a revealing experience to meet the image of people like themselves in the minds of highly intelligent and responsible women who have commented during the studies on the managers and professional men with whom they work. Men as they appear in a number of these comments are egotistic and more concerned with their own advancement than with the job in hand. They are abstract thinkers, remote from the commonsense realities of work and family life, and lacking in intuition for people and situations. They are over-formal, given to ceremonial dinners and to long, smoke-filled committees with endless reading of minutes, but are also more heavily involved than women in back-stairs office intrigue. They conduct the real business of the office in public

[1] Ch. VII, especially Table 16 and Table 19.
[2] Ch. IV, p. 155; and Ch. XI, p. 410.

houses, where the level of conversation is not (though some informants seem in two minds over this) such as women wish to take part in. When eventually they do return to the office, they start, as one informant put it, 'pawing the unmarried office girls'.

Misunderstandings of this splendidly general kind are not confined to the relations between men and women. They are generally characteristic of relations between groups or between classes in a hierarchy. What the foreman thinks of the shop steward is not at all the same, research shows, as what the shop steward thinks that the foreman thinks. The same is true of what the shop steward thinks of the foreman or manager, or of what the white man thinks of the black and the black man of the white. The relations between men and women are one of a number of areas where this sort of misunderstanding is both widespread and damaging.

Behind the question of judging men and women by the same standards, and of men's and women's common interests, there lies a general and fundamental issue, that of (borrowing again Marcuse's terminology) one-dimensional versus multi-dimensional man. Are the standards by which men's aspirations and performance have been judged in the past the right ones, or could men have something to learn from the tendency of women to follow broader aims; to be 'horizontally' rather than 'vertically' ambitious? The tradition in Western society is that men in or on their way to top jobs throw themselves increasingly into their work and become deeply involved and identified with it. This tradition is very clearly seen in the occupational studies. Men are likely to be under pressure from superiors and, generally, from their environment to drive for the highest-paid and top-status jobs in circumstances where a woman would be left free to decide whether to press on or to stay with an interesting job which she already holds.[1] For women both the traditional and the actual state of affairs are different. The findings show that most women at the levels of ability and qualification considered in these studies refuse to let their interests be over-concentrated on the role of a housewife. But to many women for whom work is very important, it is important in different ways from men, and attitudes on the part of their employers and of their environment tend to support them in this. These are women who look at work from the point of view, not of using their skills and abilities to get to the top, but of enriching their personal life and social relationships and of serving others. Their ambition is often 'horizontal' in the sense that their aim is not to drive towards power and wealth, but to create a certain environment and condition of life, and a certain human quality in work.

[1] Ch. XI, p. 400.

490

Bearing in mind the high level of satisfaction shown by strongly family-centred men,[1] whether or not their careers also provide them with major satisfactions, it seems likely that many men too would find work situations more satisfactory and their alienation diminished if they had more freedom to switch from the 'vertical' to the 'horizontal' approach. Many men – as indeed many women – enjoy the pressure and excitement of competition for top jobs and would not wish to give it up. But excitement and pressure have their price in terms of time, particularly the time taken from family life; of immediate strain; and of a higher incidence of stress diseases, crime, and death on those for whom the pressure proves too much. Why not, it might be asked, work less, or rather work differently, with a better balance of time and effort between interests on and off the job?

From society's point of view this line of argument raises difficult issues. The ideal of 'multi-dimensional man' is attractive. It was once the aim of the 'universal man' of the Renaissance. Marx foresaw the general adoption of 'universal' or 'multi-dimensional' living as one of the achievements of the final stage of communism. There is certainly a case for saying that advanced industrial societies no longer need the total, specialized commitment to work, in the sense of providing society's material needs, which used to be vital in earlier stages of development. High-quality work can in any case be done with only a limited commitment of time and effort. The present studies have shown a number of instances where men and women are doing work highly valued by society, yet do not apparently need to commit themselves beyond the equivalent of an ordinary or even a reduced working day.

But the question remains whether the highest levels of creativity, or top leadership of the quality needed to be effective in the complex and swiftly changing conditions of advanced societies, can be promoted on this basis. The 'universal man' of the Renaissance was not only learned in many spheres but an expert practitioner in several of them, aiming not merely for the competence of an amateur but for the highest professional achievement and fame. He knew well how to combine work and leisure, family life, public life, and employment into a many-sided work of art for 'the harmonious development of (his) spiritual and mental existence'.[2] At the modest level of the ordinary practitioner of professional work or management, many-sidedness like this is practicable enough. It can be an attainable aim for an increasing number of men as it already is for many women. When it comes to performance at top levels, however,

[1] Ch. VII, Table 17.
[2] Burckhardt, J., *The Civilization of the Renaissance in Italy*, Phaedon, 1950, Pt. II, esp. pp. 84-87.

491

how many men or women even with top ability can match the towering performance of the outstanding men of the Renaissance in more than one field? There were not so many of these towering performers even in the age of the Renaissance itself, when the body of knowledge needed for expert performance in many fields was far smaller, and often also less changeable, than it is now. How far is it actually possible to go today in re-directing men's or women's ambitions towards 'horizontal' goals, without losing the sharp edge of creativity and leadership? The answer, as was said in Chapter XI, must for the moment be left open. There is plenty of scope for experiment in this area, but not yet for final decision.

It is natural to think of women's advancement into high-level careers and top posts as a question of special interest to women and likely to be solved largely by women's own action in pioneering their way into new lines of work and putting pressure on men to remove barriers. This certainly is one aspect of the problem. What might be called the 'women's trade union' approach can be justified by reference both to women's special interest in the results to be attained and to strategy and tactics. The strategy of Lysistrata, with or without her particular tactics, remains evergreen. But the research team wish to underline their conviction, which began as a working hypothesis and has been strengthened by the whole trend of the enquiry's findings, that the 'women's trade union' approach should not be the primary one for the long run. Having regard both to goals and to methods, the main line of approach should be by way of a joint enterprise of men and women, a process of 'joint optimization' rather than of pressure by and in the interests of one sex alone.

Men, as the class in control of top jobs, have obviously to give up something if women are to move in. The number of top jobs is limited, and if more able women get them, men who are less able will not. The way of life at the top has in most professions been a masculine way, geared to men's ways of thinking and patterns of working. Both in work and in family life men will need to adapt substantially, in ways not always welcome to them, if great numbers of women are to reach the top. It is all the more important, therefore, to underline the fact that men's own self-interest in conditions of employment, satisfaction with family life, or the move towards 'multi-dimensional man' will often encourage them to co-operate in adapting the structures of work and family life in the ways which have been indicated. Altruism will also tend to draw men that way; but there is no need to rely on altruism alone. Men have a great deal to gain from these reforms, and this needs to be stressed.

Even if there were more ground for conflict between men and

women over reforms like these than there in fact is, there will be more chance, as in collective bargaining, of any solutions that are reached being feasible if they are worked out jointly than if they are imposed by one side alone. This is true at every level of decision at which changes in sex roles have to be worked out, and in particular is true of change at the level of individual married couples or families. Wide, sweeping measures to bring about changes on a national scale or in large social groups need not be ruled out. Some are necessary and (as, for example, better protection for mothers' job rights) have been suggested earlier. But such broad and general measures cannot by themselves be enough. Account must be taken of individual differences between husbands, wives, and children; of class differences such as those between the career commitment of women with higher and lower qualifications; and of differences in factors such as married couples' access to grandparents and other relatives, the social facilities which it is practicable to make available in each district, or the availability in different labour markets of various types of job. When allowance is made for all these differences and the many ways in which they can be combined, it is clear not only that there must be many options for the division of roles within a family, but that no one but the individual family itself is likely to see families' particular circumstances clearly enough to choose the right option for each. The role of each husband and wife within marriage, in work as well as inside the family, must be worked out case by case by the husband and wife themselves in the light of their own personal and social circumstances. Society can offer facilities, suggest a variety of options, and perhaps weight the scales in favour of some of them, but it cannot replace the responsibility of each married couple for working out its own formula. And couples are likely to be fully successful in working out their own formula only if their method of doing so is a joint enterprise, aimed at what might be called 'joint optimization'.

POSITIVE ACTION IS LIKELY TO BE REQUIRED, NOT MERELY THE REMOVAL OF BARRIERS

It is of central importance for future policy that many of the problems to be solved over highly qualified women's careers and the general re-thinking of sex roles cannot be expected to sort themselves out automatically through individual initiative or the unguided processes of society and the labour market. It is not enough to free the market from restrictions and leave individuals or individual married couples to find their own way. Collective, organized action will be needed as well.

493

There is no single key to the problem of providing access for more women to higher careers and top jobs. A summary list of lines of action suggested by the findings of the previous chapters might run something as follows:

a *At the stage of schooling and upbringing*
   (i) To widen the range of girls' qualifications.
   (ii) To develop in them numeracy, capacity for decision-making and the 'self-propelled' quality and capacity to market their own abilities which many employers at present consider them to lack.
   (iii) To forestall or remove boys' and girls' misunderstanding of each others' role, and misunderstanding by each sex of how members of the other sex perceive the first sex's role; and to encourage individual rather than sex-typed perceptions of members of each sex, whether by members of the other sex or of their own.
   (iv) To bring home to both boys and girls – particularly, informal enquiries in the present study suggest, to boys – the new choice of life-patterns opening up as a result of women's changing role in the family and work.
   (v) To bring home especially to girls the need for a clear commitment, one way or the other, in the matter of careers, and the unhappiness which can follow from ambivalence: from being one of 'the in-between women, the half-emancipated generation, who . . . find the most difficulty in fulfilling their roles'.[1]
   (vi) To bring home especially to boys the importance for the marital satisfaction of husbands as well as wives of a positive and supporting attitude by the husband to his wife's career; and, generally, of 'family-integration' and family-centredness on the part of the husband.

b *As regards marriage and family life*
   (i) Guidance to help married couples towards a more considered choice of the division of roles and the timetable of family development which best suits their particular circumstances.[2]
   (ii) More experiment with patterns of communal living which suit urban conditions, as for example the pattern of an Israeli kibbutz, in Israel's own experience, does not: patterns which are consistent with autonomy and privacy for individual families, but which make it easier to share child care and to find catering and other facilities

---

[1] Allen, J., *op. cit.*, p. 75.
[2] See T. A. Ratcliffe's pamphlet for the National Marriage Guidance Council on *The Development of Personality*, which notes (e.g. p. 31) the wide variety of role patterns which can be open to married couples today and the need both for a considered choice between them and for society to accept the choice made.

at hand. On an international comparison, the one area of this kind in which Britain has so far been noticeably innovative is the provision of private but officially supervised day-care centres. There is room for experiment in private as well as public housing, and in developments based on the neighbourhood principle as well as in apartment blocks on the lines of Swedish 'service houses'.

(iii) More rapid development of existing facilities of proved value such as nursery schools and home cleaning and home help services, whether commercial or public.

c *In the world of work*

(i) An attack on the remaining formal barriers to women's entry into particular fields or levels of work, backed with a campaign to catch influential employers' positive interest in opening to women opportunities to show what they can do in work from which they have so far been barred.

(ii) Encouragement of job enlargement schemes, at all levels of work, to ensure that the greatest practicable opportunity is provided for the use of high-grade ability on the part of both men and women.

(iii) A review of recruitment propaganda to ensure, especially in fields not traditional for women such as technology or management, that it is designed to appeal as effectively to women as to men.

(iv) Education to ensure that managers understand accurately both the positive and the negative ways in which women's work interests and abilities tend to differ from those of men, and how to take the most positive account of these differences; for example to bring home to managers that a woman may be as competent as a man in doing a senior job once she is promoted into it, but less aggressive in seeking it, and may need more than a man to be pulled up into it.

(v) More generally, education to remove in work situations, as well as in the schools or through marriage guidance, misunderstandings by men and women about the interpretation put by each sex on its own and the other sex's role, and to encourage individual rather than sex-stereotyped perception of members of both sexes.

(vi) Action to gear personnel practices to women's life cycle, for example to open the door for them to enter or re-enter potentially top-level careers at an age unusual for men, or to be considered for promotion in spite of the delay caused by a career break. Are there opportunities at appropriate points in a woman's career for a spell of part-time work of a kind likely to help her career, or for attending a re-launching course; and are there satisfactory schemes of maternity leave and reasonably long and flexible holidays? In one way and another, are highly qualified women given enough chance to maintain continuity in their careers? Is rapid enough progress being made towards shortening working hours and the working week on a scale which would let much of the present distinction between part- and full-time work die a natural death; for example towards a six-hour day or a four-day week? Given that women, and especially married women, have been the marginal work force in the economy, and that their contribution has provided the marginal increment of the country's affluence, has reasonable account been taken of women's own needs in deciding whether this increment shall be used to permit shorter and more convenient hours of work or for other purposes?

d *As regards the law and other formal systems of rules*
These rules, for example pay structures, embody society's formal definition and proclamation of sex roles in both work and the family, and need to be brought into line with the new patterns for work and the family which are now emerging. Women's autonomy and equality need to become more clearly defined in matters such as taxation, pay, job security, access to jobs, the mutual responsibility of husband and wife, the ownership of property acquired during marriage, and social security and other pension rights. This list includes items, such as taxation, which, as has been said, have not been particularly salient in the present enquiry, but also others, such as job security for mothers, which have stood out strongly. Measures of all these kinds are in any case important not only for their direct and material respects but for symbolising equality in status, opportunity, and obligations.

These lines of action are not novel or revolutionary. They look and are familiar, and in every case it is possible to point to practical experience, in Britain or elsewhere, on which action can be based. The point made in this report is a different one. It is that the measures required form a web of such complexity that individual women, or married couples, or heads of schools, or employers cannot reasonably be left to do on their own all that needs to be done. If they are left to act separately it will be only too easy for them to become bewildered and frustrated, to choose paths which are not the best for their particular circumstances, or simply to give up and seek the easiest way out, often by falling back on some traditional pattern. The difficulty does not simply arise from ignorance or misunderstanding, though these are of course present as well. It has to do with the structure of the situation. The responsibility and incentive to act in the areas listed is spread widely over individuals, employers and community agencies, and one line of action often interlocks

496

with the next, so that progress on one may be blocked till an advance is made along others.

Certainly it is true that many changes in work and the family likely to help women's access to high-level careers have taken place, and may be expected still to take place, through the pioneering of individual women or married couples, the enlightened self-interest of individual employers, and the automatic outcome of labour market processes or of general changes in the national income or in social custom and practice. The tide of innovation seeps in almost imperceptibly, with no general plan, as one married couple after another picks up a new way of living; or new occupations open up and women, following the line of least resistance, move into the cracks between existing sex-typed fields; or a woman makes a successful career in a particular type of employment and opens the road for others behind her. This sort of local, individual pioneering is indispensable, first because it is effective, and secondly because the final aim is, not to impose some particular pattern of family life or manpower distribution, but a situation where people have been helped to and do make the most appropriate choices for themselves. In interviews for this project the research team has found repeatedly a tendency for people and organizations who could well take action at their own level to pass the buck. Schools claim that the lead must come from parents or employers, employers that it should come from the schools. Women blame the discrimination and negligence of men, and men the inertia and lack of drive of women. In actual fact there is always scope for individuals and individual organizations to act, and much of the most useful progress over women's careers and sex roles comes and must continue to come in this way.

But scattered and individual pioneering, valuable as it can be, is not enough. Patterns of family living are part of the social structure and, if individuals wish to make innovations in them, difficulties arise over finding what needs to be done in a many-sided and tangled situation, as well as from the sanctions by which the existing situation is defended, and from the threshold costs which face an individual innovator where they might not face an agency organizing collective action. Individual married couples can break away from socially approved patterns only at the cost of effort and tension which not many can stand or can reasonably be asked to accept. A woman starting in a new field of employment can make the best of the employment practices which she finds there, but cannot be expected on her own, or in a short time, to change a profession's or even an individual employer's rules for promotion or maternity leave or part-time work. What she herself is able and willing to attempt is in any case limited not only by factors which she ought to be able to

497

influence, such as her husband's attitude to women's careers, but by antecedent factors beyond her control, such as the warmth of her parental background or her own mother's attitude to and experience of work.[1]

If in his turn the employer asks why he as an individual should take the lead in changing practices of this kind, he may well have a case. Though he may have something to gain by taking the initiative, if he acts alone he will not necessarily gain enough to compensate for the trouble which this will involve in the short run. Let others, he may and often does argue, work out new patterns first. Let the community take its own responsibilities for women's initial training and for the costs of maternity leave or re-launching courses. Then he can follow without the trouble and expense of pioneering. Employers in a number of fields, for example in teaching or personnel management, report that the supply of women qualified for and interested in top jobs is at present too small to allow the filling even of all those jobs for which a woman would specifically be preferred. Why then, an individual employer may reasonably ask, should I develop new patterns to facilitate women's access to top jobs when it is not even certain that qualified women will be available as candidates for these jobs? Can the individual employer be expected to act until the schools and universities increase the supply of women with appropriate qualifications and motivation, and society changes its work and family patterns in such a way that the pool of women with the right level of experience and interest becomes large enough to offer him a worth-while choice? It is the whole fabric of society that needs to be re-woven to allow for the fact of women's careers, not some single section of it, easy to isolate and to review on its own.

In some cases the point, in economic terms, may be that social costs and benefits differ from the private costs and benefits of the people immediately responsible for a decision. As was argued in Chapter XII, the community can often expect a clearer gain – economic and psychological – than the individual employer from ensuring the full use of assets, such as highly qualified women, who are currently on the community's books but not on those of the employer. But often the point seems to be rather that made by Keynes that, in a situation of bewildering variety where individuals are in control of only a few factors in their immediate environment, it is natural for individuals to act as best they can in the light of such circumstances as they can understand and control, even though if account were taken of all the circumstances their actions would be seen to harm not only the community but also themselves. This is the lesson of Keynes's trade cycle theory and of the experience

[1] Ch. VIII.

already several times quoted of re-shaping the location of industry. In cases of either of these kinds, right decisions are likely to be reached only if an agency with an overall view enters the picture to supplement – not necessarily or normally to replace – the decisions of individuals.

From another point of view, there is here a classic problem of marketing. Marketing is understood today not simply as selling but as a way of looking at and co-ordinating the whole process of developing and producing goods or services, and delivering them to customers who have been made aware both of their need for them and of how to make the best use of them. Its purpose is not to replace the competition of producers or the decisions which individual consumers make in the light of their own circumstances. It is to make the individual and autonomous decisions of producers and customers effective by bridging information gaps and ensuring that a well-balanced sequence of facilities exists, so that no one's decisions need be held back by ignorance of the market or of the supply situation or by fears of a breakdown in the chain of production and demand.

Marketing in this sense may involve anything from organizing a supply of raw materials or trained labour, through quality control in the production process, to advertising, salesmanship, and guiding the final user in how to make the best use of the goods and services supplied, or financing him to do so. In terms of the present study, it may involve reaching back into the schools, or into marriage guidance or children's clinics, to influence boys' and girls' early upbringing and choice of qualifications; or examining the recruitment process by which initial career choices are or are not made effective, or the processes by which young married couples work out their respective roles during the first years of married life; or reaching forward into employers' organizations to show them how to adapt to use highly qualified women to the best advantage. In any case it involves developing a strategy; selecting the most favourable points on which to concentrate a promotion effort; and choosing targets attainable in the short and the long run. Marketing in this wide sense is the central function of entrepreneurship; and it is entrepreneurship, in this sense, that is currently needed to facilitate women's access to top jobs.

WHAT SORT OF AGENCIES ARE NEEDED?

Entrepreneurship and marketing on the lines just suggested can be undertaken by agencies of an almost infinite variety of types. In *Women and Top Jobs* the research team suggested a fourfold classification of agencies.

At the centre are individual men and women themselves. Next are the people and agencies most directly involved in decisions at key points in individuals' careers: parents, teachers, husbands or wives, employers. Next again is the circle of advisers and intermediaries, the agencies which advise and influence both individuals and the agents involved at the previous stage. The Marriage Guidance Councils and a variety of family and parents' groups and child welfare agencies influence parents. Training colleges, university departments of education, teachers' organizations, or the Schools Council for Curriculum Development influence teachers and schools. New entrants to the labour market are advised by schools careers advisers, the Youth Employment Service, university appointments boards, university science and social science departments, and professional associations such as the Institute of Personnel Management or the R.I.B.A.; along with some agencies, such as the Women's Employment Federation or the Women's Engineering Society, which are specially concerned with women's employment. Selection consultants and other employment brokers influence the recruitment of staff who have already begun their careers. Employers are advised on their recruitment and promotion policies not only by consultants but by professional associations and bodies such as the Industrial Society or the British Institute of Management. Polytechnics and technical colleges are increasingly involved in 'recycling' men and women who change careers in mid-life; some of them also play an active part as employment brokers. Finally, a fourth circle includes the general body of political and public opinion-forming agencies: the press, television, the political parties, the churches, the T.U.C., the national women's organisations.

All these agencies have or can have a part to play in the major re-shaping of social customs and practices, both in the family and at work, in the perspective of the 'post-industrial society', which has been suggested here. To the complexity of the problems analysed in this report there corresponds, of necessity, a complex pattern of solutions and of agencies promoting them. There is no single, simple solution, and no one Ariadne's thread for finding a way through the labyrinth of problems and considerations involved. Successful solutions will necessarily involve initiatives and decision at many points. For the purpose of solving the problems of family and work, agencies like those listed constitute, together with those on which special stress is laid below, a network in which the activities of each agency reinforce – or often fail to reinforce – those of every other. Initiative can in principle start from anywhere within the network and radiate outwards from where it starts.

There is however a need, as has just been suggested, to lay on one

500

or more centres a special responsibility for animating activity and rousing initiative throughout the area covered by this report. The responsibility and potential for action is divided among many agencies, delay or obstruction at one point can have repercussions at many others, and mistakes can easily arise out of the limited information and views of particular agencies. It is important that some agency or agencies should take a general overview and be responsible for eliminating bottlenecks, filling gaps and promoting initiatives wherever in the network this is needed. For this function of reviewing and animating the whole field three candidates suggest themselves, not as alternatives but as each having a part to play.

a *Organization by or for women themselves*
Although, as has been said, the main accent for the long run should be on the idea of a joint enterprise of men and women rather than on the 'women's trade union' approach, the latter is certainly not to be ruled out; especially in the immediate future, when action to break barriers and remove discrimination is likely to play a bigger part than should be needed later on. P.E.P.'s studies show reluctance on the part of most of the women interviewed to see themselves as a class apart or to accept that anything in the nature of feminist agitation or of organization by and for women is needed today. In her study of British women university teachers, Sommerkorn[1] notes as a general rule – not only for the universities – that people who experience discrimination may find it shaming to admit it, and be slow to face the need to fight their own case and to prove to others' satisfaction that they themselves are being valued below their true ability. Whatever its cause, this tendency to regard organization and collective action by women on women's problems as unnecessary or even objectionable does not correspond to the actual state of professional and managerial women's problems today. Promotional activity, sometimes including pressure, is needed to get these problems solved, and often this activity will be forthcoming only if women themselves take organized action to ensure it.

Organized action by women or directly on women's behalf can take many forms. It can be very informal. In several countries the authors have found what might be called a women's *maquis*: a network of women, strategically placed to influence public opinion or important action agencies, keeping close informal touch with one another, and exerting an influence out of proportion to their apparent strength.

[1] Pinder, *op. cit.*, pp. 639-640.

Equally, however, there can be room for agencies of a very formal and official kind. In the United States the Women's Bureau of the Department of Labour has a semi-political responsibility for informing and influencing government departments, public authorities, and public opinion generally on all issues affecting women's progress in the field of work. Canada also has a Women's Bureau, which however works more as a Civil Service department, and does not have as independent a role in influencing public and political discussion. The West German Ministry of the Interior has a Women's Branch to co-ordinate policy on women's constitutional rights, and there are more specialized Women's Branches in a number of other ministries.

In between the fully official and the informal levels of action come the national women's organizations. They are a particularly obvious candidate for the marketing and entrepreneurial role, for they can bring massive political and social weight to bear behind their policies. In her P.E.P. study of *Women at Work* Mrs Pinder shows how in Britain they have been slow to be effective even on so obvious and immediate an issue as equal pay. There are similar findings from other countries, chiefly Sweden. But she suggests that more effective action might be possible on the basis of an alliance more representative of all women than any existing organization or group of organizations: an alliance which would bring together, as has tended not to happen in the past, women from the trade unions with the general and middle-class women's associations.[1]

An alliance of that kind would be a matter of large-scale, massive organization. It could well be supplemented with a stronger development than has yet occurred in Britain of small radical action groups, often nearer to the 'women's maquis' than to mass organization, such as have grown fast recently in North America: N.O.W., W.I.T.C.H., W.R.A.P., and generally the Women's Liberation Movement.[2] The positions taken by groups like these tend to be more explosive and one-sided than is likely to be acceptable to the majority of women, and their effectiveness is limited in the long run. Extremist militants, in this as in other fields, tend to attack as the enemy the very groups – in this case men – with which they must ultimately work if they are to achieve a satisfactory result. Ultimately, tactics like these are counter-productive. Violence and discord too easily escalate, and sooner or later a deliberate effort has to be

---

[1] Sommerkorn, *op. cit.*, pp. 169-171.
[2] National Organization of Women, Women's International Terrorist Conspiracy from Hell, Women's Radical Action Project.

made to reach a stage of 'joint optimization'. But though new structures have ultimately to be built not with dynamite but with cement, dynamite has its place for breaking a situation open and clearing the way to build. As in industrial relations, though bargaining and consultation are ultimately the way to solve conflicts between groups, in the face of rigid resistance force may be needed to open the way to the bargaining table.

Mrs Pinder's criticism does not in any case apply with the same force, if at all, to action by specialized associations of women in their own professional fields, as apart from action by the larger national women's organizations on issues of general interest. Groups such as the Medical Women's Federation or the Women's Engineering Society have played a part in advancing women's interests in their particular professions which can best be appreciated by considering the state of affairs in professions where organizations of this kind do not exist. P.E.P.'s report on the Administrative Civil Service notes the disadvantages which have followed from the premature decision of the former organizations of women Civil Servants to dissolve themselves. The attainment in the Civil Service of equal pay and of formal equality of opportunity was taken, incorrectly, to bring to an end the need for separate and distinctive representation of women's interests, as apart from the representation of women along with men through unions or associations covering both sexes. Women's problems still exist in the Civil Service, but the organizations which could once be relied on to identify and examine them and present a well-prepared case specifically from women's point of view have gone. If the Civil Service has seemed slow to think through women's more recent problems and develop something more than *ad hoc* policies on them, this has certainly been a contributory cause. So also in the two companies studied, in the B.B.C., and in architecture, it is hard to believe that policy on women's issues could have remained as unconsidered as it has done if there had been in and around each of these organizations or professions a well-organized group of women to speak for their colleagues, identify their problems, develop policies, and press women's cause home.

In the research team's view all five of the lines of approach just mentioned deserve to be pushed further in Britain than they have yet been: special interest groups in each organization or profession where these do not already exist, Mrs Pinder's suggestion for a new grouping in the national women's organizations, the 'women's *maquis*' approach, radical action groups, and the idea of a women's department or bureau. As an immediate line of action at the official level, there is a strong case for pressing for the establishment

SEX, CAREER AND FAMILY

within the Department of Employment and Productivity of a Women's Department with a head at Under-Secretary level. Its responsibility would be to promote (not necessarily in all or even most cases to undertake) the whole range of measures, from vocational guidance to the re-design of promotion patterns and the specifications of top jobs, already listed as needed to ensure full opportunity for women and use of their abilities in employment. Other official agencies concerned jointly with men's and women's problems will be suggested below; the Women's Department would be concerned with women specifically. Its terms of reference would need to extend to all women's employment, but should in particular include the promotion of women's prospects in higher careers and top jobs. The right model for it is probably not the US Women's Bureau, which has a semi-political head and is close to being a sub-ministry on its own, but the Women's Bureau in Canada, whose practice fits better into that of the British Civil Service.

An immediate task for the Women's Department could be to promote, in collaboration with the Civil Service Department, the re-design of the Government's own jobs and recruitment and promotion patterns to fit women's life cycle. Private enterprise is often as well placed as the Government, or better, to pioneer some new employment practice. But when it comes to a decision or principle and its general implementation, the Government with its centralised control, or at least influence, over a very large work force, and its freedom from the pressure of competition, has the advantage. In 1955–61 the Government preceded private enterprise in the widespread application of equal pay; private enterprise is only now being brought into line through a further Government measure, the Equal Pay Act of 1970. The Government could well be pressed to take a similar lead over the re-design of jobs.

b *Anti-discrimination agencies*
A modest further amount of help could be expected from the agencies dealing with discrimination generally. In the United States the Equal Employment Opportunity Commission, set up under the Civil Rights Act of 1964, deals with discrimination on grounds of sex as well as race. It has been cautious in its approach to any but the most obvious cases of sex discrimination, for, whereas discrimination *prima facie* exists wherever two men or two women are treated differently on the ground of their skin colour, it is by no means so clear that it exists when men and women are treated differently on grounds of sex. In Britain it has not hitherto been thought wise to complicate the task of the chief official agencies for eliminating discrimination, the Race Relations Board and the Community

504

Relations Commission, by expecting them to deal with sex discrimination as well.

Nevertheless there is a case for extending their responsibility, and especially that of the Commission, to sex discrimination as soon as they have made enough progress with their primary responsibility, colour discrimination, to be able to give substantial attention to discrimination on grounds of sex. It is, as has been said, fairly straightforward to identify and attack formal discrimination, as where a job is advertised for men only, or a woman is offered less pay for the same job, or where women executives are excluded from dining rooms or other facilities appropriate to their rank. Less formal discriminations can be hard to identify, as recent debates on equal pay have underlined, especially in individual cases. But they may still be identified, though less sharply, when they amount to a persistent course of conduct: for example if the percentage of women in certain grades or occupations in an organization falls consistently short of what would be expected on the experience of other organizations or from the number of women candidates available, or if factors in a job evaluation scheme are seen to be weighted against jobs commonly held by women.

If measures against sex discrimination were confined to cases which could be clearly and sharply identified, or to the negative task of removing barriers, they would cover only a fraction of the ground on which this report shows action to be required. Even in removing barriers the cases likely to arise will often be in grey areas where information and education are appropriate, rather than the hard enforcement of a judgment in black and white. What is important for the long run is, as has been said, not simply the removal of barriers to women's entry into a world of work which would otherwise remain unchanged, but the positive promotion of new attitudes and practices on the part of both men and women, at work and in the family, to take account of the new fact of women's high-level careers. In fact, however, a large part of the work being done on race relations is already concerned with grey areas and does have this positive slant. It consists not simply of beating down resistance and bursting through barriers but of positive action to promote new and better patterns of community relations. Action on race discrimination is building up a growing volume of practical experience of positive as well as preventive procedures which it will be well worth while to bring to bear on the problems of women's work.

c *Men and women together: agencies for action on family and work*
There remains however the major point that many of the issues in this report, including the most basic issues about sex roles,

involve promoting the interests not simply of women but of men and women together, and call for action by both sexes jointly. To make women's organizations or anti-discrimination agencies the main focus for action in the areas covered by the report would be to miss one of its central points.

What sort of joint agencies are required? The Swedish Government's report on *The Status of Women*, having made clear its view that sex roles in general rather than women's interests in particular should be the focus of policy and action, goes on to reject the idea for their purpose of 'special sections within a department, a central unit of Government, a national commission on the status of women, a joint committee of liaison officers'. The issues of employment, social welfare, taxation, family matters, and education with which special *ad hoc* agencies like these might deal can be handled, the report suggests, with less delay and in a wider perspective by the departments, committees, or other agencies generally and normally responsible for each of these fields.

The research group would largely agree with this comment. It is for example for the Department of Education and Science, rather than some *ad hoc* body, to take the lead in reconsidering school curricula and texts, co-education and separate education, the work of careers advisory services in schools, colleges, and universities and the development of related branches of research, in the light of new thinking about family, work and sex roles. This reconsideration is, as the Swedish report insists, something to be worked into the whole texture of a department's activities rather than to be segregated in some section apart. The same might be said of the responsibility of the departments dealing with health, social security, employment, taxation, and housing and community design, of social research in universities and independent institutes, or of professional associations, trade unions, and the parties in collective bargaining.

But the Swedish report itself indicates that the principle it lays down should not be taken too absolutely. Countries less well advanced in the sex role debate, it points out, may need an *ad hoc* agency or agencies 'to point out deficiencies and problems . . . and thus provide a stimulus to further reform'. The debate on sex roles in Sweden reaches back over several decades and rose to a peak in the sixties. 'There are probably few countries in which the roles of men and women in the family have been so thoroughly analysed and discussed as in Sweden during the 1960s.'[1] Public and official opinion in Sweden have already been penetrated with a new set of ideas. A non-departmental post of Minister for Family Affairs has been created. If Sweden can afford to do so without further special

[1] *The Status of Women*, p. 23.

agencies, it does not follow that a country like Britain which is at an earlier stage of the debate on sex roles can do the same.

It has just been argued that to ensure the proper representation of women's interests as apart from the joint re-consideration of men's and women's roles, a number of special agencies continue to be needed in Britain; some already exist and others would have to be created. As regards the wider question of family and work, and generally of re-thinking sex roles, the research group makes four suggestions. The first two refer to action needed on this complex of questions generally, not only in the case where women have high-level careers. The other two refer to the more specific problems raised by that case.

(i) *A Minister for the Family.* There is at present no focus within Britain's machinery of government for debate and action on sex roles, whether in the family or elsewhere. For the reasons indicated by the Swedish Government, it would be inadvisable to create anything in the nature of a Family Department or Department of Family and Work; the many departments involved must continue to carry their own responsibilities. But it would be valuable to have, preferably within a department concerned generally with the status of the citizen rather than one biased towards particular aspects of family and work, a small but strong secretariat, preferably headed by a Minister, to promote the reconsideration of policies on family and work both outside and within the Government's machinery. Israel has a small secretariat within the Prime Minister's office to perform this function, in effect though not formally. Sweden has its non-departmental Minister for Family Affairs. Drawing on both analogies, the research group suggests that a Minister of State for the Family be appointed to the Home Office, with terms of reference which makes it clear that he – or she – is concerned with the whole range of problems of family and work. He should have a small but high-level secretariat around which inter-departmental collaboration on issues connected with family and work could be expected to focus.

(ii) *An institute for family, work, and environment.* A number of research and action institutions deal with aspects of the relationship between family, work, and community participation, as they affect one another and affect and are affected by prevailing conceptions of sex roles. But none deals with it in its full breadth. There has been a tendency for institutions to concern themselves either with family and community problems or with work problems alone. What is

507

needed is an institute which will deal with all these in relation to each other and work outwards from this into feeding informed discussion and stirring up initiatives in the whole network of agencies outlined earlier. There are many analogies in other fields: among others the Institute for Community Studies, the Institute for Race Relations, the Overseas Development Institute or the Institute for Strategic Studies. The normal way to establish such an Institute will be for interested individuals to take the initiative and seek finance from sources such as the Social Science Research Council – or, seeing that the Institute would have an important action as well as research element, a direct government grant – or from industry or charitable foundations.

(iii) *A national working group, or groups, to promote national measures on the special problems arising for families and employers when a wife has a high-level career.* The two previous proposals provide the general setting for a third, concerned specifically with issues arising from highly qualified women's careers. The successful handling of these issues depends, certainly, among other things on obtaining the right general climate of opinion and on wide sweeping measures affecting women and men at all levels, such as those needed to protect the employment and social security rights of mothers or to re-design school curricula in the light of new thinking about sex roles. But the problems of families and employers in the case where wives follow a highly qualified career are, as has been said, special, and need special and specific attention. Though the right general setting is important, they can and must be solved to some extent on their own, and action on them need not wait on more general measures.

Highly qualified women and their husbands are a small group, easily visible to administrators and educators. The best way to deal with their specific problems will usually be quietly, by direct approach to key employers, career advisers or educators, rather than by mass propaganda. The word '*maquis*' was used earlier. It might be taken to imply something too underground and sinister to be acceptable, but its other implication of informality is very much to the point. The research group would like to see the establishment of one or two working groups, including both men and women, to spread both among employers and among young graduates as family members and employees an understanding of the possibilities which this report has opened up for re-shaping employment practices and family life. The working group or groups should operate with little publicity, by identifying and working with the gatekeepers through whom influence in each field can be brought to bear: for example through direct contact with large or innovative employers, university and college appointment agencies, marriage guidance agencies and heads of schools. It will need to develop both short-term and long-term strategies. There is an immediate possibility, on the lines suggested by Rogaly in the article quoted earlier,[1] of increasing rapidly the intake of women into middle management and specialist roles in which they already have a strong foothold, and of formalizing the arrangements about maternity breaks, part-time work, or re-launching which have tended to grow up informally. Longer-range action will be needed for the full scale reshaping of family roles, or on the side of employment for arriving at the six-hour day and to achieve full equality for women in admission to top management jobs.

A working group of this kind need not have massive finance. It must however have enough to pay a small highly qualified, full-time staff, and it will be an advantage if it can itself be the gatekeeper for funds which can be used to prime pumps: to promote experiments in re-launching, or the development (as in the Department of Health's plan for married women doctors) of new ladders of part-time work, or new developments in marriage guidance, child guidance, nursery education, or the re-orientation of older boys and girls with a traditional upbringing, or to encourage further research. An established working group of this kind could well have a case for a state grant. In its experimental phase its funds could come best from foundations or from industry, which in this case would have a very material interest in the work to be done.

(iv) *Professional and local action groups.* The need to maintain in each profession or occupation special groups to promote women's interests was stressed above. These groups, however, will not achieve all they might if they stop at a 'women's trade union' approach. The national working group of men and women just proposed will also not achieve all it might unless it is briefed and supplemented through action at local and professional level. Putting these two ideas together, it will be useful to develop a network of local and occupational action groups, more or less formal as the circumstances of each environment may require, in any case including both men and women, to concentrate more precisely on the problems of particular occupations, districts, or social groupings than a national agency can hope to do.

[1] Ch. XI, p. 397.

POSTSCRIPT

This study began with limited and somewhat technical terms of reference: a review of how best to make use of the country's main reserve of high working ability, namely highly qualified women. It has widened out by the nature of its material into a prospect of a new society. The people with whom the report deals are already living beyond the fiercer pressures of economic need. In Britain as in most other advanced countries the pressure in recent years for economic growth has led to the question: growth for growth's sake, or growth for what? This report deals with people whose own circumstances already make this question very real.

As regards the answer to that question, the material collected verifies the vision of Marx, Marcuse, and many others of 'multi-dimensional man', from the point of view both of its attractiveness and, for many people and married couples in the group investigated, its practicability.

Looking at employment, the research team has found itself interviewing women as well as men who are not alienated from their work but deeply and increasingly committed to it. It has found it to be practicable and economic for employers to adapt their recruitment and career patterns so as to match women's (especially married women's) different life cycle, and to allow them as well as men or single women access to satisfying and high-level careers.

Looking at family life, the team has found not only that it is possible to reconcile a wife's high-level career with a satisfactory family life – though, especially under present social conditions, it takes considerable skill and effort to make this pattern succeed – but that in a number of ways one can be the condition of the other. The family-centred husbands whose wives are most likely to feel free to commit themselves to a career are also those whose own happiness in their family life tends to be greatest. Nor need this family-centredness stand in the way of the husband's own career. In this group of people the most prevalent pattern is for men to be 'integrated', with a strong interest in both their career and their family, and to be happy in this combination. No reason has shown itself why a well-managed dual-career pattern need operate to children's disadvantage.

The team has raised the question whether complete 'multi-dimensionality' will be as practicable for those who aim at the peaks of creativity or managerial leadership – except for the few 'Renaissance men' who can perform at top level in several fields at once – as for those whose careers stop a step lower down. This question has been left open. It is clear, however, that 'multi-dimensionality' or some approach to it could be made far easier to achieve than it is now. A full, well managed dual-career pattern has been achieved so far only by a small minority of higher qualified men and women, who have been able to withstand the social pressure in favour of patterns involving a smaller work commitment for the wife, and to overcome by their initiative the shortage in present British society of supporting institutions from kindergartens to promotion patterns adapted to women's life cycle. Obstacles like these can be removed. As Myrdal and Klein rightly point out, the extra working power provided by women could well be used more to shorten hours and lengthen holidays and less exclusively to increase production. In that case many of the present difficulties of combining careers with family and leisure life could, in the foreseeable future, be made largely or wholly to disappear. The new balance of working and non-working life which could then be created could be highly attractive not only to women but also to men.

This study has looked beyond the present stage of often petty discrimination against women, needing to be countered with one-sided action by women themselves or on their behalf: with what has been called here the 'women's trade union' approach. For the moment there is still a battle to be fought against crude discrimination left over from the past, both at work and at home. But the accent will need, as has been shown, to shift more and more from defence and pressure by women towards the idea of a joint enterprise on the part of men and women to revise work and family roles to the advantage of both.

The difficulties in the way of the advances proposed have not, it is hoped, been understated. In particular, it is right to stress again the danger of thinking that any one formula will provide all the answers; perhaps dual careers instead of traditionally segregated sex roles. That is the trap into which many East European countries have fallen, in spite of their excellent progress in other areas covered by this report. With increased education and attractiveness of work in high-level jobs, it is to be expected that wives will choose increasingly to participate in the world of work. But the choice must remain a free one. There must continue to be room for work and family patterns of all types. The aim should be, as it has been in this report, to clarify the options so that each married couple may select the pattern best suited to its own circumstances, and the difficulties and complexities of bringing this about are great. The research team would like to end its report by laying the accent, not on the difficulties to be met, but on the vision of new ways of living which will make the overcoming of these difficulties worth while.

511

Statistical
Appendices

APPENDIX TO CHAPTER III

Table III.1

Participation by women in the Work Force in Western Countries

(i) All women: percentage in each age group working or expected to be working

	Year	20–24	25–29	30–34	35–39	40–44	45–49	50–54	55–59
Austria	1951	65½			45			40	
	1961	71			45			44	
	1961	75	59	55	55	53	51	47	40
	1980	75	59	55	55	53	51	47	37
Belgium	1947	40½	29½	26	25	24	22	20	17
	1961	52	36½	31	30	30	28	25	20
	1961	52	36½	31	30	30	28	25	20
	1980	65	50½	42	42	44	38½	34	24
Denmark	1950	64	42		43		43		36½
	1960		36½		37		38		
	1960	59	39	34	36	38	38	37	34
	1980	62	54	53	59	52	51	43	34

Country	Years	(1)	(2)	(3)	(4)	(5)	(6)	(7)	(8)
Finland	1950, 1960	64	{57 / 56				{60 / 58		53
France	1960, 1980	61 / 59	57 / 61½	56 / 60		{59½ / 64	{60 / 58	57 / 59	51 / 48
France	1954, 1962	57 / 61½	{40½ / 42	40½ / 45	{42 / 40		57 / 62	{46½ / 45	}39 / 38
France	1962, 1980	61			{41 / 47			{47	}35
Germany (West)	1950, 1961	70 / 72	50½ / 51	40½ / 45		36 / 45	37 / 46	35 / 38	30 / 33
Germany (West)	1961, 1980	72 / 66½	51 / 50½	45 / 42	46 / 44½	45 / 47	42 / 45	38 / 39	33 / 34
Ireland	1951, 1961	65 / 67	41½ / 39	27 / 24	{25 / 31	21 / 19	{21 / 21	20 / 19	}22 / 22½
Ireland	1961, 1981	70					23		17
Netherlands	1947, 1960, 1980	51 / 53 / 54	26 / 22½ / 27	23 / 16 / 20	22 / 15 / 20	21 / 16 / 20	20 / 17 / 18	19 / 16 / 17	17 / 14 / 12½

Table III.1(i)—(continued)

	Year	20–24	25–29	30–34	35–39	40–44	45–49	50–54	55–59
Norway	1950	51	31	20		23		25	
	1960			19		21		26	
	1960	48	26	19	19	20	22½	25	27
	1980	59	43	34	36	29	35	37	36
Sweden	1950	57	37	27	26	28½	31	30	26
	1960	57	42	36	35	36½	37	37	32
	1965	56	44	41	46	49	49	46	39½
	1980	55	49	42	49	57	57½	58	54
United Kingdom	1951	66	37		34		34		28
	1961	62½	38		42		43		37
	1965	63	39	39	48	52	54	51	45
	1975	54	39	39½	52	52	58½	57	51
U.S.A.	1965	50	38		46		50½		47
	1970	50	39		47½		55		51½

United Nations, Economic Commission for Europe, *The European Economy in 1968*, Ch. III, Appendix IV, and OECD, *Demographic Trends 1965–1980 in Western Europe and North America*, 1966, p. 61.

Table III.1—(continued)

(ii) Percentage of women of each marital status in each age group who are working

a. England and Wales, Ireland, U.S.A., West Germany

	Year	20–24	25–29	30–34	35–39	40–44	45–54	55–59	60–64
Single									
England and Wales	1961	90	90	88	{85}		82	75	39
Ireland	1961	84	79	70	64	62	56½	{46}	
U.S.A.	1964	74	88	86	{83}		86¹ 83²	75	67
West Germany	1964	87	90½	90	90	89	75	75	48
Widows and divorced									
England and Wales	1961	62½	69	69	{72}		67	52	28
Ireland	1961	39	40	46½	49	50	46	{37}	
U.S.A. (including 'husband absent')	1964	50	67	54	{64}		70	{53}	
West Germany	1964	81	77	75	74	66	53¹ 45²	37	21
Married, husband present									
England and Wales	1961	43	30	30	{37}		36	27	13
Ireland	1961	8	6	4	4	5	6	{6}	
U.S.A.	1964	37	29	32	{39}		45	{31}	
West Germany	1964	52	40	36	38	40	38¹ 33²	28	19

¹ 45–49 ² 50–54

Table III.1 (ii)—(continued)

b. France, Norway, Sweden

	Year	20–24	25–29	30–39	40–49	50–59	60–64
					Age		
Single							
France	1962	74	80	78	76	71	57
Norway	1960	76½	80	76	73½	71	59
Sweden	1960	74	82	79	74	66	46
Widows and divorced							
France	1962	74	68	70	71	60	40½
Norway	1960	58½	63	65	68	58	38
Sweden	1960	72	75	77	74	58	30
Married							
France	1962	45	36	33	36	37	27
Norway	1960	18	13	10	10	10	5
Sweden	1960	34	30	28	29	23	10

M. Dubrulle, *L'Emploi Féminin en Europe*, paper C.48 of the European Population Conference, Council of Europe, 1966; US Department of Labor, *Handbook of Women Workers*, 1965; *Bericht der Bundesregierung über die Situation der Frauen in Beruf, Familie, und Gesellschaft*, Deutscher Bundestag, Drucksache V/909, 1966, pp. 357–358.

Table III.1—(continued)

(iii) Percentage of men and women in or expected to be in the work force, United Kingdom, 1967-1981

Age	Men	Single women	Married women			
	Percentages assumed for all years		1967	1972	1977	1981
25-29	96½	92	30	30	30	30
30-34	97	87	35	36½	38	39
35-39	97	87	45	47½	50	52
40-44	97	80	50½	54½	57½	59½
45-49	97	76	52½	56½	59½	61½
50-54	97	69	50	54	57	59
55-59	96½	61	40½	45½	50½	54½
60-64	91	29	24	25	25½	26
65-69	37½	44½	8	8	8	8
70 and over	13½	4½	8	8	8	8

Employment and Productivity Gazette, March 1969, p. 215.

(iv) Percentage of women aged 20-54 who are working in certain countries of Eastern and Western Europe

	All Women	Urban Women only
U.S.S.R. (1959)	77	
Romania (1966)	77	60
E. Germany (1964)	69[1]	
Poland (1960)	66	53
Czechoslovakia (1961)	63	
Hungary (1960)	50	61
Yugoslavia (1961)	48	
Finland (1960)	58	61
Austria (1961)	56	
W. Germany (1961)	49	
France (1962)	45	45
U.K. (1961)	44	
Denmark (1960)	40	45
Sweden (1960)	40	47
Switzerland (1960)	38½	
Belgium (1961)	33	
Italy (1961)	32	
Iceland (1961)	30	
Norway (1960)	25	37
Netherlands (1960)	23	

[1] 21-54.

United Nations, Economic Commission for Europe, *The European Economy in 1968*, Table 28.

Table III.2

Employees in Each Region as Per Cent of the Population Resident in the Region and Aged 15 or Over, 1968

	South East England[1]	South East	East Anglia	South Western	West Midlands	East Midlands	Yorks & Humberside	North Western	Northern	Wales	Scotland	Great Britain[2]
Employees aged:												
15–24 Men	76	78	61	65	79	77	79½	78	72	67½	74	75½
Women	68	69	57	54	63½	63	62	65	63	53	65	64
25–44 Men	88	90	73	75	89	83	84	86	77½	77	88	85
Women	47	48	38	35	44	41	43	48	37	35	44	44
45–64 Men	88	89	81	75	87	86	84	87	85	77	84	85
45–59 Women	53	54	42	43	54	50	48	55½	39	35	49½	50
65 & over Men	20	20	14	12	21	16	18	17	11	10	16	17
60 & over Women	11½	12	5	8	11½	10	10	10	8	6	10	10
Total aged:												
15 & over Men	77	78	65	63½	78	74	75	76	70	66	74½	74
Women	42½	43	33	32	43	39	39	42	35	30	40	40

[1] The South East of England is a grouping of the South East and East Anglia standard regions.
[2] Includes some Civil Servants overseas not allocated to regions.

Employment and Productivity Gazette, July 1969, pp. 652-653.

Table III.3

Persistence of Women in Higher Careers – Britain

(i) *Percentage of women with certain qualifications who were in paid employment, 1965*

a *By age at date of completing full-time education*

	Percentage in paid employment	
Age on completing education	Married	Single, widowed, divorced
15 or under	43	73
16-18	42	89
19 and over	51	89

b *By school examinations passed*

	Percentage of women not now in full-time education who are:		
	Working		Not
	Full-time	Part-time	working
No examinations passed	30	22	48
G.C.E. 'O' level or equivalent	47	$13\frac{1}{2}$	$39\frac{1}{2}$
'A' level or equivalent	55	13	33

c *By type of further education institution attended*

Type of institution attended	Percentage of women not now in full-time education who are working
None	52
'Other'	51
Evening Institute	57
Secretarial college etc.	58
Technical college	57
Teachers' training college	67
University, College of Advanced Technology	66

Government Social Survey, *A Survey of Women's Employment*, SS 379, 1968, Vol. I, pp. 27, 138, 143.

Table III.3—(continued)

(ii) *Factors which may make a job pleasant for a woman: all women in paid employment in Britain, 1965*

Percentage of respondents who rank each factor among the top three

Age of respondent on completing full-time education

	15	16–18	19 and over
Easy travelling distance from home	54	50	51
Management shows understanding attitude to domestic difficulties	28	28	24
Pleasant working companions	74	68	56
Good working conditions	61	54	52
High wage or salary	39	35	25
Opportunity to use skills and qualifications	16	32	61
Opportunity for training	11	10	4
Opportunity for promotion	$16\frac{1}{2}$	$20\frac{1}{2}$	18

ibid. Vol. II p. 287.

(iii) *Career persistence of particular groups of qualified women in Britain*

a *Cambridge women graduates of 1937-8 and 1952-3*

Percentage of graduates of each year who were working in 1961

	Married		All	
	1937–38	1952–53	1937–38	1952–53
Full-time	17	14	42	36
Part-time	27	21	19	15
Total	44	35	61	51

C. Craig, *The Employment of Cambridge Graduates*, Cambridge 1963, pp. 69-70.

Table III.3 (iii)—(continued)

b *All women graduates, 1965*

	Percentage who were working		
	Full-time	Part-time	Total
Single, widowed, divorced	84	3	87
Married: all	35	25	60
Mothers with:			
All children below school age	10	29	39
One or more children under 18:			
at least one at home	24	32	56
none at home	47	8	55
All children aged 18 or over	38	20	58

C. Aregger (ed.), *Graduate Women at Work*, Oriel 1966, pp. 16 and 22.

c *Women social administration students Manchester University, 1940-60*

	Percentage of married ex-students working in December, 1960		
Year of completing course	Full-time	Part-time	Total
1940-45	11	11	22
1946-50	19	10	29
1951-55	12	15	27
1956-60	54	10	64
All married ex-students	21	12	33

B. M. Rodgers, *A Follow-Up Study of Social Administration Students at Manchester University*, 1940-60, Manchester 1963, p. 23.

d *Women professional engineers, 1967*

	Percentage who are in each age group and work status				
Working	25 and under	26–35	36–45	46 and over	Total
Full-time	13	19	17	16	65
Part-time	1	1	3	5	10
Total	14	20	20	21	75
Retired or un-employed	1	6	3	14	24
	15	26	23	35	99

Proceedings of the Second International Conference of Women Engineers and Scientists, Cambridge 1967.

Table III.3 (iii)—(continued)

e *Women doctors*

(i) *Graduates of St Mary's Hospital Medical School, 1916-24: percentage working in 1934*

	Single	Married	
		No children	With children
Full-time	93	59	35
Part-time	1	14	30
Total	94	73	65

M. H. Kettle, 'The Fate of a Population of Medical Students', *The Lancet*, 13 June, 1936.

(ii) *All women doctors: percentage working in 1962*

	All	Years since qualification				
		Under 5	5–9	10–14	15–19	20 and over
Single						
Full-time	82	96	91	88	83	68
Part-time	13	1	6	10	15	22
Total	95	97	97	98	98	90
Married (not widowed or divorced)						
No children						
Full-time	54	58$\frac{1}{2}$	55	60	55	46
Part-time	29	21	34	28	34	33
Total	83	79$\frac{1}{2}$	89	88	89	79
With children						
Full-time	24	17	15	20	24	33
Part-time	48	38	50$\frac{1}{2}$	49	51	48
Total	72	55	65$\frac{1}{2}$	69	75	81

J. E. Lawrie, M. C. Newhouse, P. M. Elliott, 'Working Capacity of Women Doctors', *British Medical Journal*, 12 February, 1966. See also A. G. W. Whitfield, 'Women Medical Graduates of the University of Birmingham 1959-1963', *British Medical Journal*, 5 July, 1969.

Table III.3 (iii) e—(continued)

(iii) *Graduates of the Oxford Medical School. Percentage of potential working time since graduation actually worked up to 1960*

Year of graduation	Single	Widowed or divorced	Married Husband a doctor	Other
1922–30	89	90	52	57
1931–40	100	73	65	50
1941–50	93	72	54	46

A. H. Robb-Smith, 'The Fate of Oxford Medical Women', *The Lancet*, December 1, 1962.

Table III.4

Persistence of American and French Women in Higher Careers: Percentage of Women of Each Age, Educational Level and Marital Status Who Work

(i) *America, 1964*

Education	All women aged					Single	Married	
	20–24	25–34	35–44	45–54	55–64		Husband present	Husband absent¹
Elementary:								
less than 8 years	34	31½	39½	43	30	—	—	—
8 years	44	39	44	43½	37	55	29	30
High school:								
1–3 years	34½	36	45	50	41	55	34	47
4 years	54	36	45	55	46	76	37	58
College:								
1–3 years	49	35	44	55	47	55	36	52½
4 years	77	48	50	61	59	83	45	58
5 years or more	71	65	66	85½	85	84	63	84

¹ Widowed, divorced, separated, or husband otherwise absent.

(ii) *France, 1962*

Education	All women aged							
	20–24	25–29	30–34	35–39	40–44	45–49	50–54	55–64
No diploma	57	37	32	34	36	42	43	37
Baccalauréat	88	75	61	60	65	69	67	37
Higher education diploma	86	80	69	66	67	70	69	60

Sample Survey Census of 1962

526

Table III.5

Women's Participation in High School and Higher Education: Women's
Qualifications and Occupations

a *Britain*

(i) England and Wales: Boys and girls in school at age 17 (actual and
forecast)

	Numbers		As per cent of all boys or girls of that age	
	Boys	Girls	Boys	Girls
	000s			
1954	24	20	9	7
1961	42	32	13	10
1966	62	48	16	13
1971	66	49	20	15
1976	84½	62	23	18
1981	112	81	26	20
1986	127	91	29	22
1990	149	107	32	24

Statistics of Education—Schools, 1966, Vol. I, H.M.S.O. 1967,
Table 44.

(ii) England and Wales: Subjects studied by sixth form pupils in first
year 'A' level courses

	Percentages of boys and girls studying subjects in each group	
	Boys	Girls
Mathematical and science subjects only:		
1963	53	21
1966	47	17
Other subjects only:		
1963	39	66
1966	40	68½
Subjects in both groups:		
1963	9	13
1966	13	15
Totals		
1963	100	100
1966	100	100

ibid. Table 10.

Table III.5a—(continued)

(iii) England and Wales: Percentages of boys and girls leaving school at age 17-19 who obtain a given level of G.C.E. result (actual and forecast)

	Actual 1965-66	Forecast
1 or more A level passes		
leaving age		
17 boys	32	32 rising to 41 in 1986-87
girls	25	27 rising to 39 in 1986-87
18 boys	85	86
girls	80	80
19 boys	87	86
girls	79	78
2 or more 'A' level passes		
leaving age		
17 boys	26	26 rising to 36 in 1986-87
girls	18	21 rising to 33 in 1986-87
18 boys	70½	70
girls	62	61
19 boys	69½	73
girls	58	62

Statistics of Education, 1966, Vol. 2: H.M.S.O. 1968: p. xxiii.

(iv) a. Entrants of each sex into higher education as percentage of their age group, 1954-67 Great Britain

		Full-time			Part-time				
	University	Teacher training	Further education	All Full-time	Day	Evening	All part-time	Private study	Total
Men									
1954	4·5	0·9	0·8	6·2					
1959	6·1	1·5	2·0	9·6	4·3	2·7	7·0		
1961	5·7	1·4	2·5	9·5	5·4	3·7	9·1	2·1	20·7
1961[1]	6·5	1·5	1·8	9·8					
1967[1]	8·8	2·6	4·6	16·0					
Women									
1954	1·8	3·2	0·5	5·5					
1959	2·2	4·1	0·7	7·0	0·2	0·1	0·3		
1961	2·5	3·7	0·9	7·0	0·3	0·1	0·4	—	7·4
1961[1]	2·5	3·7	0·6	6·8					
1967[1]	3·8	7·1	1·7	12·6					

[1] England and Wales: Colleges of Advanced Technology are included in Universities and excluded from Further Education.

Report of the Committee on Higher Education, Cmnd. 2154, 1963, Appendix I, pp. 150-152, and information from the Higher Education Unit of the London School of Economics.

Table III.5a—(continued)

b. Number of students in full-time higher education 1961 and 1967 (numbers have been rounded to nearest ten)

		Universities (including former Colleges of Advanced Technology)	Colleges of Education	Further Education	All full-time Higher Education
England and Wales					
1961	Men	78,590	11,950	19,400	109,940
	Women	24,010	24,550	4,400	52,960
	Total	102,600	36,500	23,800	162,900
1967	Men	122,920	27,930	51,550	202,390
	Women	44,660	68,500	14,410	127,570
	Total	167,580	96,430	65,960	329,960
Scotland					
1961	Men		970		
	Women		4,680		
	Total	20,830	5,650	3,100	29,580
1967	Men	22,040	2,010	2,700	26,450
	Women	10,060	8,810	2,200	21,070
	Total	32,100	10,820	4,900	47,520
Great Britain					
1961	Men		12,920		
	Women		29,240		
	Total	123,430	42,160	26,900	192,480
1967	Men	144,960	29,940	54,250	229,140
	Women	54,710	77,310	16,610	148,630
	Total	199,670	107,250	70,860	377,770

Information from the Higher Education Unit of the London School of Economics.

Table III.5a—(continued)

(v) England and Wales: initial entrants to full-time higher education having two or more 'A' levels (students from Britain only) as a percentage of the output of those with the same qualification in the same year

		Entering			Total
	University	Teacher training	Further education	No full time higher education	
Men					
1955	78	3	5	14	100
1958	79	6	9	6	100
1961	63	7	11	19	100
1961[1]	71	7	6	16	100
1967[1]	67	7	10	16	100
Women					
1955	57	20	3	20	100
1958	49	31	3	17	100
1961	47	26	4	23	100
1961[1]	49	$26\frac{1}{2}$	3	$21\frac{1}{2}$	100
1967[1]	44	29	$5\frac{1}{2}$	21	100

[1] Revised estimates: former Colleges of Advanced Technology included with Universities and excluded from Further Education. Cmnd. 2154, Appendix I, p. 273, and information from the Higher Education Unit of the London School of Economics.

Table III.5a—(continued)

(vi) Great Britain: subjects studied by full-time students at universities

Percentage of students of each sex studying
each group of subjects

	Men		Women	
	1953-54	1964-65	1953-54	1964-65
Arts	} 36·3 {	23·9	} 63·7 {	53·1
Social studies		13·0		11·9
Science:				
pure	22·2	27·9	17·6	22·9
applied	16·3	19·7	0·7	1·3
Medical:				
medicine	17·0	10·1	14·7	8·2
dentistry	3·7	2·5	1·5	1·5
Agricultural:				
agriculture	2·9	1·8	1·4	0·7
veterinary science	1·6	1·1	0·4	0·4
	100	100	100	100

University Grants Committee, *Returns from Universities and University Colleges*, Cmnd. 3106, 1966, p. 3.

(vii) Great Britain: examination results of men and women university students, first degree examination, 1966

	Level of degree (percentage of all graduating)		
	1st Class	2nd Class	Other
Arts			
Men	5.9	66·7	27·4
Women	4·4	67·5	28·1
Social studies			
Men	3·1	59·0	37·9
Women	2·1	62·6	35·3
Pure science			
Men	11·5	52·9	35·6
Women	6·3	53·6	40·1

University Grants Committee, *First Employment of University Graduates 1965-6*, H.M.S.O., 1967.

Table III.5a—(continued)

(viii) Great Britain: destination of first degree graduates, 1965-66 (excluding medicine, dentistry, and veterinary science)

	Numbers		Total (Percentage)		By faculties (percentage)							
					Arts		Social Studies		Pure Science		Applied Science	
	Men	Women	Men	Women	Men	Women	Men	Women	Men	Women	Men	Women
Research or further academic study	5,336	1,039	23	12	19½	10	15½	12	35	16	16	17
Teaching: Teacher training	2,331	2,473	10 }14	29 }41	24 }31	37 }48	6 }11	15 }27	10½ }14½	24 }38	1 }2	9 }18
Employment in education in UK	956	1,033	4	12	7	11	5	12	4	14	1	9
Other training	1,324	914	6	11	5	13	1½	16	5	4	5	2
Employment in UK: Public service (except teaching)	1,162	735	5	8	5	5½	15	7	3½	10	6	13
Industry and commerce (including accountancy, insurance, banking)	7,315	749	31	9	12	3	21¼	4½	29	19	54½	31
Other	677	224	3	3	5¹	2½¹	7¹	4½¹	1	2	1	2
Employment overseas (UK graduates)	4,461	1,437	19	17	6	7	3	5	3	4	5	8
Overseas students returning home					2	1	7	1	1	½	6	1
Still seeking employment					4	2	3	3	2	1½	6	1
Not seeking employment					4	5	6	5	2½	3	3	4
Unknown					6	4	6	6	4	2	5	3
Total	23,562	8,604	100	100	100	100	100	100	100	100	100	100

University Grants Committee, *First Employment of University Graduates, 1965-6*, HMSO 1967, pp. 4 and 11.

¹ Including:

	Arts		Social Studies	
	Men	Women	Men	Women
Solicitors (private practice)	0·1	0·1	4·9	2·1
Publishers, cultural organizations, entertainment	2·8	2·0	1·2	1·0
Other	2·2	0·5	1·1	1·4
	5·1	2·6	7·2	4·5

Table III.5(a)—(continued)

(ix) Great Britain: distribution of higher degree graduates between main fields of study, 1965-66[1]

All	Numbers		Percentage	
	Men	Women	Men	Women
	5,307	514	91	9
Arts	797	177	15⎫	34⎫
Social studies	567	87	11⎪	17⎪
Science:			⎬100	⎬100
pure	2,501	225	47⎪	44⎪
applied	1,442	25	27⎭	5⎭
Of which:				
Doctorates	3,011	217	57	42
Other	2,296	297	43	58

[1] Excluding medicine, dentistry, veterinary science.

ibid. p. 29.

(x) Great Britain: occupations of women graduates who are in employment

	Full-time	Part-time	All	All earning over £2,000 p.a.
Teaching (school)	55½	51	55	27
Teaching (university or technical college: research)	16	7	14	22
Medicine, dentistry	14½	24	16	39
Social work	4	2	4	1½
Other	10	16	11	11
	100	100	100	100

Aregger, *op. cit.* (1966), Table XI.

Table III.5a—(continued)

(xi) Great Britain: highest qualifications held by men and women, 1963

	Per cent having each qualification			
	In employment during last ten years		All, including full-time housewives and retired	
	Men	Women	Men	Women
Degree	2·0	1·0	1·9	0·9
Diploma: membership of professional body	2·8	0·9	2·6	0·7
Minor professional (nurses, teachers, H.N.C., H.N.D., etc.)	0·8	5·3	0·7	4·1
'A' level or equivalent	1·1	0·7	1·3	0·6
'O' level or equivalent	7·1	6·7	7·6	5·8
Minor technical (O.N.C., O.N.D., City and Guilds, etc.)	4·3	1·0	4·0	0·7
Commercial and R.S.A.	7·1	6·8	6·7	5·6
Served or serving recognized apprenticeship	17·8	5·5	17·2	5·8
Skilled but not apprenticed[1]	24·5	21·4	23·7	17·7
No qualification	32·5	50·7	34·3	58·1
	100·0	100·0	100·0	100·0

[1] Claiming to be skilled by virtue of experience.

A. I. Harris and R. Clausen, *Labour Mobility in Britain*, Government Social Survey, SS 333, H.M.S.O. 1966, pp. 104, 106.

Table III.5a—(continued)

(xii) a. Great Britain: professional associations classified by their proportion of women (See also Table I.2, Census of 1966)

Women's occupations (women 80 per cent or over of membership)

Almoner	Occupational therapist
Church of England Council for Social Work	Orthoptician
	Physiotherapist
Dietician	Psychiatric social worker
Moral Welfare Worker	Radiographer
Nurse	

Intermediate (Majority of women)	*Unclassified, substantial number of women*
Chiropodist	Child care officer
Librarian	Institutional manager
Medical laboratory technician	Psychologist

Intermediate (majority of men)

Doctor	Optician
Hotel and catering manager	Personnel manager
Housing manager	Pharmacist[1]
Landscape architect	Probation officer
Market research	Public relations
	Welfare officer

Men's occupations (under 10 per cent of women)

Accountant (including Municipal)	Insurance
	Patent agent
Advertising	Photographer
Architect	Physicist
Auctioneer, estate agent	Plastics technologist
Chartered or corporate secretary	Remedial gymnast
	Solicitor
Chemist	Statistician
Engineer	Surveyor
Industrial artist	Veterinary surgeon

[1] See however the subdivision of the 1969 membership survey by the Pharmaceutical Society of Great Britain. Women are a large majority among hospital pharmacists, but a minority in other fields.

Based on V. Klein, 'The Demand for Professional Womanpower', *British Journal of Sociology*, June 1966, Table 1.

Table III.5—(continued)

b *France*

(i) Percentage of each age group attending school or college (actual or forecast)

Age	1955 Men	1955 Women	1970 Men	1970 Women
17	25	26	41	47
21	7	4	10	9

(ii) Women as per cent of all qualifying for the baccalauréat

1905	0·4
1910	2
1920	13
1930	24
1940	33½
1950	42½
1960	49
1962	50
1963	48

(iii) Women as per cent of all university students (actual and forecast)

1900	2
1910	6
1920	10
1930	26
1939	32
1950	36
1961	43
1970	44½

These figures do not include teachers' training colleges. In 1961-62 women made up 55 per cent of the students at these colleges.

Table III.5b—(continued)

(iv) Faculty distribution of women university students

	Numbers		Women as per cent of all students in each faculty	
	1930	1960	1930	1960
Letters	7,800	31,025	47	57½
Science	2,800	20,305	18	32[1]
Law	2,500	8,675	12½	29½
Medicine	2,800	7,655	17	27
Pharmacy	1,500	4,670	30	60
Total	17,400	72,330	23½	40

[1] The number of women in the main engineering schools remains 'very restricted'.

F. Guelaud-Léridon, *La Situation de la Femme dans la Société*, cyclostyled report to the Commissariat Général du Plan, 1965, and *Le Travail des Femmes en France*, Presses Universitaires de France, 1964, p. 57.

c *West Germany*

(i) Schools

a. Social origins of boys and girls in the final year of Gymnasium, 1965

Parents	Per cent of students from each social background	
	All	Girls
Graduates	30	34
Other	67	63
Without occupation or unknown	3	3
	100	100

b. Percentage of boys and girls in the final year of Gymnasium, 1964, who are in schools with various specialisms:

	Boys	Girls
Humanities	25	5
Modern languages	41	82
Science	34	13
	100	100

Table III.5c (i)—(continued)

c. Percentage of the relevant age group who:

	were in a high school in their 18th year		obtained the *Abitur* (higher leaving certificate) as students of a Gymnasium[1]	
	Men	Women	Men	Women
1950	—	—	5·5	3·0
1953	—	—	4·5	2·1
1957	7·8	4·2	6·1	3·2
1960	10·5	6·3	6·8	4·0
1963	11·1	7·0	8·7	5·6
1965	—	—	8·7	5·3

[1] Excluding external students. The median age for obtaining the *Abitur* is 20 for women and 20-21 for men.

d. Percentage of leavers with full high school education who proceeded to universities and colleges:

(*A*) Percentage of men and women who obtained the *Abitur* in 1957-59 and proceeded to study at:

	Men	Women
Universities	90	55
Teacher training colleges	7	31
	97	86
Neither	3	14
	100	100

(*B*) Percentage of leavers from the final year of the Gymnasium, 1965, who proceeded to:

	Men	Women
Universities and colleges	87	87
Employment	8	11
Military service	3½	—
Other	1½	2
	100	100

Table III.5c—(continued)

(ii) Universities

a. Women in German universities and other colleges (including technical high schools) of university rank

	Number of students		Women as per cent of all
	All	Women	
1950-51	116,000	19,000	16½
1965	258,000	61,600	24

For universities alone the proportion of women in 1965 was 29 per cent.

b. Women as per cent of students in various faculties of German universities, 1959-60 and 1964-65

	1959-60	1964-65
Humanities, theology:		
German	43	44
English and French	53	52
Classics	25	26
Evangelical theology	14	12
Catholic theology	2	0·3
Law, economics:		
Law	11	11
National economy	19	16
Enterprise economy	9	8
Science:		
Mathematics	16	17
Chemistry	9	10
Physics	4	7
Medicine, pharmacy:		
Medicine	37	32
Pharmacy	61	56½
Architecture	12	14
Agriculture, forestry:		
Agriculture	18	13
Forestry	1	2

Table III.5 c (ii)—(continued)

c. Field of qualification of all women with university degrees (irrespective of year of graduation), 1961

	Percentage of women graduates whose qualification is in each field	Women as a percentage of all graduates in each field
Humanities, education, theology	68	44
Art	5	28
Law, economics, administration	5½	9
Science	4	17
Medicine, pharmacy, etc.	16	25
Technology	0·3	1
Agriculture, forestry	1	10
	100	27

d. Field of employment of employed men and women graduates, 1961:

	Per cent of all employed men and women graduates who were working in each field	
	Men	Women
Teaching:		
School	24 ⎫ 27	62½ ⎫ 63½
University	3 ⎭	1 ⎭
Medicine and pharmacy:		
Doctors	11 ⎫	9 ⎫
Dentists	3 ⎬ 16	2 ⎬ 15
Pharmacists	2 ⎭	4 ⎭
Business	8	2
Public administration	5	1
Legal professions	6	1
Technologists (including architecture)	13	1
Clergy, nuns, etc.	5	0·2
Other	20	16
	100	100

Information from the section *Bildung* of *Bericht der Bundesregierung über die Situation der Frau in Beruf, Familie, und Gesellschaft, Deutscher Bundestag, Drucksache* V/909, 1966; and from unpublished data supplied by I. Sommerkorn: summarized in her article *Studien und Berufsaussichten der Abiturientinnen*, Neue Sammlung, January/February, 1969.

Table III.5—(continued)

d *U.S.A.*

(i) Students graduating from high school or college, 1900-65

	High school			College Numbers	
	Numbers		Both sexes students as per cent of their age		
	Boys	Girls		Men	Women
	000s		group	000s	
1900	38	57	6	22	5
1920	124	188	17	32	17
1940	579	643	51	$109\frac{1}{2}$	77
1950	571	629	59	329	103
1960	898	966	65	254	138
1964	1,121	1,169	76	298	201
1965	1,303	1,337	72	318	217

Statistical Handbook of the U.S.A., 1966 and 1967.

(ii) Percentage of the population of each sex of each age who were in school or college:

| Age | 1950 | | 1964 | |
	M	F	M	F
14-17	84	82	94	92
18-19	35	24	51	34
20-24	14	5	24	11
25-29	6	0·4	8	3
30-34	$1\frac{1}{2}$	0·4	4	2

U.S. Department of Labor, *Handbook on Women Workers*, 1965, Ch. 4.

(iii) Students of each sex enrolling in colleges for the first time in each year as a percentage of the high school graduates of their sex in that year

	Men	Women
1950	56	31
1964	62	45

ibid.

(iv) College graduation: Percentage of all degrees earned by women in:

	1900	1930	1960	1964
Bachelor's or first professional	19	40	35	40
Master's	19	40	32	32
Doctor's	6	15	$10\frac{1}{2}$	11

ibid.

Table III.5d—(continued)

(v) Distribution of women graduates' qualifications by subject. Bachelor's and first professional degrees conferred on women as per cent of:

	All such degrees conferred on women		All such degrees conferred on men or women in each field	
	1956	1964	1956	1964
Education	45	42½	72	76
Humanities, arts	18	22	44	54
Social Science	21	20½	—	—
including:				
Economics	1	1	10	10
Business, commerce	4	2	10	8
Home economics	4	2	99	98
Politics	1	1	20	22
Sociology	3	3	57	60
Social Work and Administration	1	1	66	62
Psychology	2	3	45	41
History	3	4	30	35
Librarianship	1	1	77	78
Science (pure and applied) including:	13	13	17	21
Biological Sciences	3	3	23½	28
Health professions	7	5½	34	43½
Mathematics	1	3	33	32
Physical sciences	1	1	13	14
Other	0·4	0·5	1½	2
Other	1	1	8½	7
	100	100	36	40

Ibid.

Table III.5d—(continued)

(vi) Women as per cent of all workers in selected professional occupations, 1900-60

Occupation	1960	1950	1940	1930	1920	1910	1900
College Professors, Presidents Instructors	19	23	27	32	30	19	
Doctors	7	6	5	4	5	6	
Lawyers[1]	3½	3½	2	2	1	1	
Engineers	1	1	0·3				
Dentists	2	3	1½	2	3	3	
Scientists	10	11					
Biologists	28	27					
Chemists	9	10					
Mathematicians	26	38					
Physicists	4	6½					
Nurses	97	98	98	98	96	93	94
Social Workers	57	66	67	68	62	52	
Librarians	85	89	89	91	88	79	
Clergy	6	8½	2	4	3	1	4

C. Epstein, *Women's Place, The Salience of Sex Status*, Paper 2, Annual Meeting of the American Sociological Association, August 1967, Table (1).

[1] Hankin and Mrabake, *The American Lawyer*: 1964 Statistical Report 29 (1965): give adjusted figures:

1963	1960	1957	1954	1951	1948
2·7	2·6	2·7	2·3	2·5	1·8

Table III.5—(continued)

e *Sweden*
Percentage of first degrees or professional qualifications and
of higher degrees in each subject obtained by women, 1958
and 1965

	First		Masters		Doctorate	
	1958	1965	1958	1965	1958	1965
Arts	47[1]	59[1]	17	31	3	4
Law	14	22				
Economics	6	12				
Theology	11	14				
Science	24[1]	32[1]	11	17	3	7
Engineering	1	5				
Medicine	18	25			5	0

Sweden Today, p. 41.

[1] Including degrees both with and without a teaching qualification.

f *Various Western countries:* percentage of women in selected
professions, 1960-66

	Doctors	Dentists	Lawyers	Engineers
U.S.A.	6½	2	3½	1
U.K.	16	7	4	negligible
Germany (West)	20	n.a.	5½	3
Sweden	15	24	6	1
Denmark	16	70	n.a.	n.a.
Italy	5	n.a.	3	1

Epstein, *op. cit.*

Table III.6

Women's occupational achievement

(i) *Industrial and general*

    a. England and Wales, 1961: women managers, large establishments (see also Table I.1, Census of 1966)

			Women as per cent of all managers in each group
Total		76,430	12·9
of whom:			
education	20,190	selected public service groups: 34,700	44·0
medical	8,170		53·8
national government	3,260		11·7
local government	3,080		8·2
retail distribution	13,960	selected distributive and service groups: 23,560	24·9
wholesale distribution	1,550		7·1
catering, hotels	3,280		39·0
laundries, dry cleaning	1,890		41·2
miscellaneous services	2,880		20·4
food, drink, tobacco	1,540	selected industries: 8,980	7·3
engineering, electrical goods	2,550		4·9
textiles	1,390		7·8
clothing, footwear	2,010		15·2
paper, printing, publishing	1,490		7·8
all other[1]		9,190	3·8

[1] Including extractive industries: bricks, pottery, glass, cement; chemicals; metals, shipbuilding, vehicles (including repairing) etc; leather; timber, furniture; miscellaneous manufacturing; construction; gas, water, electricity; transport; communications; dealing in coal, grain, industrial raw materials, machinery; insurance, banking; finance; religion; professional and scientific services (including law and accountancy) not otherwise mentioned.

Table III.6 (i)—(continued)

b. Great Britain: women as per cent of total in certain occupations, 1968

Members of the Institute of Directors	2½
Employees in manufacturing industry:	
Managers and superintendents	4
Scientists, technologists	3
Draughtsmen	1
Other technicians	7
Clerks, office staff	62
Other administrative, technical, and commercial	17
Foremen and chargehands	13
Apprenticed craftsmen:	
maintenance	1
production	5
Other production workers (skilled or other)[1]	45
Warehouse, packing, and despatch workers	28
Road transport drivers	1
Canteen staff	91
Labourers	6
Other	38
Total	29

Information from the Institute of Directors and Department of Employment and Productivity, *Statistics on Incomes, Prices, Employment and Production*, March 1969.

[1] For some but not all industries this category is broken down into more and less skilled and experienced. Women's share of more skilled jobs compares much better with men in this category than in the apprenticed crafts. In footwear and pottery women have a larger share of skilled and experienced than of less skilled jobs. In textiles, leather, clothing, and woodworking their share in skilled jobs comes close to their share in less skilled. For an overall view on this point see Table III.5a (xi).

Table III.6 (i)—(continued)

c *France*

(i) Whole population: women as per cent of total in certain categories, 1954 and 1962

	1954	1962
Employers and members of their families working with them:		
farming	41	39
industry and commerce	37	36
Free professions and higher managerial and professional employees:		
free professions	14	
engineers	2	
college teachers, scientists, literary professions	40	
other higher professional/managerial	8½	
	—13	17
Middle professional and managerial:		
teachers: medical and social workers	68½	
technicians	9	
other	25	
	—37	39
Office and sales workers	53	58
Plant etc. workers	23	22
Service workers	81	80
Farm workers	15	12
Other[1]	26	22
Total	35	34

F. Guélaud – Léridon: (1) *Le Travail des Femmes en France*, Presses universitaires de France, 1964, pp. 29-30: (2) *Le Travail des Femmes en France*, Notes et Etudes Documentaires, November 12, 1966.

[1] Including for example, army, artists, clergy.

Table III.6 (i) c—(continued)

(ii) Certain occupations: women as per cent of total in each grade or branch

	1954	1962
Managers and administrators:		
higher	12	13
other	38	42
Civil Servants:		
Category A (Highest)		26
B		58
C		37
D		62
Health:		
Doctors	10	15
Dentists	24	28
Pharmacists	38	48
Nurses	83	86
Teaching:		
higher	14	21
secondary	46	51
primary	65	64

Notes et Etudes, loc. cit.

d. Sweden, 1966: women as percentage of all in certain categories of employees in mining and manufacturing

	Technical	Office	Works supervisory
Managers (excluding top executives)	0·3	1	
Other personnel in responsible positions including:	2	11	
General foremen			1
Foremen			3
Technical and clerical (general)	3	37	
Technical and clerical (assistants)	28	68	

The Status of Women in Sweden, p. 98.

Table III.6—(continued)

Public service

a. Britain: women as percentage of Civil Servants of certain categories, 1968

Administrative including:		8
Permanent Secretary	nil	
Deputy Secretary	2½	
Under-Secretary	3	
Assistant Secretary	6	
Principal	10	
Assistant Principal	17	
Executive including:		15
Senior Executive Officer	11½	
Chief Executive Officer	5	
Higher Executive Officer	16	
Executive Officer	26	
Clerical including:		49
Higher Clerical Officers	41	
Clerical Officers	49	
Other Clerical	45	
Clerical Assistants	64	

b. Sweden: women as percentage of Civil Servants in certain salary brackets, 1966

Monthly salary (kr.)	Number Men	Women	Women as per cent of total in each category
5,800-10,000			
grades 4-8 (highest)	273	1	—
2-3	607	6	1
1	2,138	42	2
4,200-5,700			
grades 6-7	315	6	2
5	2,467	94	4
2-4	108	12	11
1,000-4,000	141,855	84,628	37

The Status of Women in Sweden, p. 92.

Table III.6—(continued)

c. U.S.A.: women as percentage of Federal Civil Servants in white-collar grades, 1961

Grade

15-18 (highest)	1·4
12-14	4
9-11	12
7-8	32
1-6	67

President's Commission on the Status of Women: Report of the Committee on Federal Employment, 1963, Appendix D.

d. Germany: women established members of the senior Civil Service in Federal ministries, 1965

Rank	Women as per cent of all civil servants of each rank	Number of women			
			Of whom, holding posts as		
		Total	Assist-ants	Principal Officers	Division heads and deputies
State Secretary, Ministerial-direktor or – dirigent	—	—			
Ministerialrat	1	7	—	7	—
Regierungsdirektor	2	7	1	6	—
Oberregierungsrat	3	27	21	6	—
Assessor up to (inclu-sive) Regierungsrat	5	38	37	1	—
	3	79	59	20	—

Bericht der Bundesregierung über die Situation der Frauen in Beruf, Familie, und Gesellschaft: Deutscher Bundestag, Drucksache V/909: pp. 416-41.

Table III.6—(continued)

(iii) *Universities*

a. Great Britain: women university staff as per cent of total in each grade, 1961-62 and 1965-66

	1961-62	1965-66
Professor	2	2
Reader	7 ⎫	
Senior Lecturer	8 ⎬	7
Lecturer	10	9
Assistant Lecturer	16	18
Other (e.g. research)	18	—

Committee on Higher Education, *op. cit.*, Appendix III, Annex G: and University Grants Committee returns.

b. Germany, 1960: women as per cent of certain staff in universities and colleges of university rank

Full Professors	0·6
Other fully qualified (*habilitierte*) staff	3
Other teaching staff	8
Assistants	9

Frauen im Bildungswesen, Wirtschaft und Statistik, 1965-66, p. 388.

c. U.S.A. 1963-64: women as per cent of certain grades of teaching staff in colleges and universities

Professors	9
Associate professors	16
Assistant professors	20
Instructors	31

Handbook of Women Workers p. 153.

Table III.6—(continued)

(iv) *Medical*

England and Wales: women as per cent of all hospital doctors of each grade, 1968

Consultants	7
Medical Assistants and Senior Hospital Medical Officers	25
Senior Registrars	10
Registrars	14
Senior House Officers	18
House Officers:	
post-registration	25
pre-registration	$25\frac{1}{2}$

Information from the Department of Health.

(v) *School Teachers: England and Wales, 1967*

a. Women as per cent of staff in each grade

	Primary	Secondary
Heads	47	
modern		20
grammar		33
comprehensive		16
other		28
Deputy heads, second masters and mistresses	60	46
Other heads of departments	54	29
Holders of graded posts:		
Scale 3 (highest)	$53\frac{1}{2}$	32
2	52	34
1	62	39
Other assistants	85	55
All	74	41

b. Number of men and women in each grade (primary and secondary)

	Men	Women
Heads	16,779	12,214
Intermediate posts	71,499	48,841
'Other assistants'	36,994	102,415
Total	125,272	163,470

Statistics of Education 1967, Vol. 4.

APPENDIX TO CHAPTER V

There are three sample surveys mentioned *passim* in Chapters V-IX. As the VIth form survey analysis was not completed in time for this publication, it will not be described here. A subsequent publication will give details. Of the other two surveys – the 1967 Graduates and the 1960 Graduates eight years out – it is the latter that is more heavily drawn on in the present volume. The field-work for both of these surveys was executed for us by Research Services Ltd., under the supervision of Gerald Hoinville. The research instruments used had as their core adaptions of the N.O.R.C. Survey instruments used by Davis, Rossi and Spaeth. Only a few comparisons are drawn in the present volume, but ultimately it should be possible to make more detailed comparisons.

The 1967 Graduates:

The sample target was 1,000 full-time students of both sexes who were in the final year of their first degree courses at Universities and Colleges of University status in England and Wales. A basic control matrix for all of the academic bodies of this type was available from official statistics.

A sample stratified by type of university and by faculty was drawn, and the following distribution of responses achieved:

Sample of Universities

1967 Graduate: Survey

	Number	Per cent of Sample
(i) London (4 Colleges)	128	12
(ii) Oxford and Cambridge (10 Colleges 5 each)	88	9
(iii) 'Redbrick' (9 Universities)	667	65
(iv) 'New' (2 Universities)	46	4
(v) 'Technological' (3 Universities)	104	10
Total	1033	100

The Universities were chosen to provide a spread across the United Kingdom as well as among the different types, and within this array samples were drawn to represent in proportionate numbers students finishing their first degree in (*a*) Arts and Social Sciences, (*b*) Pure and Applied Sciences and (*c*) Medicine, Dentistry and Veterinary Science. Women were over-represented in the respondent sample, particularly those in Pure and Applied Science faculties. This was done to ensure adequate numbers for analysis.

S

Students were contacted individually on the basis of lists of names provided by the Universities and asked for their co-operation. The initial response rate was reasonably high (varying from 80 per cent at Oxbridge to 55 per cent at the Technological Universities). The difference between the target and achieved samples was made up by substituting respondents of appropriate sex, university and faculty.

The 32-page questionnaires were, for the most part, completed under supervision in accommodation provided by the Universities. In some instances, where students indicated a willingness to co-operate but were not able to turn up at the appointed times and places and in the three instances where no accommodation could be provided for invigilating the surveys, questionnaire forms were left to be completed and returned by post.

The 1960 Graduates:

A National Survey of 1960 Graduates directed by Professor R. K. Kelsall with Mrs Anne Poole and Mrs Annette Moore served as the sampling frame for the current sample. This study, sponsored by the Department of Education and Science from March 1965 to March 1970, after an initial suggestion by the University Appointments Boards' Statistics Committee, had traced almost 80 per cent of these graduates who, by the time our own questionnaire reached them, had been out of University for 8 years. Graduates who had co-operated in the National Survey had been assured of anonymity and before we were provided with any addresses 1,000 of the original 4,702 men and 1,000 of the original 3,582 women were asked by letter if they would agree to receive another questionnaire on the topic of the study. Of the original 2,000 asked, some had moved and could not be traced, others were overseas and were discarded from our sample; but 1,071 remained of those who had agreed to co-operate, and they are distributed as follows:

Categories of Respondents

1960 Graduate: Survey

Respondent Category	Number	Per cent of Sample
Single men	84	8
Married men, no children	81	7
Married men, with children	320	30
Single women	137	13
Married women, no children	82	8
Married women, with children	367	34
Total	1071	100

In addition, spouses of Married Women in the Sample were asked to fill up questionnaire forms, making a potential further response number of 449.

Of the total of 1,520 who were issued questionnaires, the response rates were as follows:

Response Rates

1960 Graduate: Survey

Respondent Category	Number	Per cent	Response Rate	Per cent in National Survey
Men: Single	58	7	69	20
Married no children	79	9	97 ⎫	
Married with children	245	29	77 ⎬	52
Women: Single	112	13	82	7
Married no children	73	9	90 ⎫	
Married with children	298	34	81 ⎬	20
	865	101		99
Spouse Sub-Sample:				
no children	32	15	45	
with children	177	85	50	
		100		

An analysis of returns by Kelsall *et al.* compared with our own shows that our sample compares very closely (i.e. within 5 per cent) for type of school attended and subject of concentration at University, as indicated above, our sample differs from Kelsall's in that it is designed to have a greater than representative proportion of women than his, which, reflecting the actual distribution of graduates, is disproportionately male. Within the male and female groupings, however, our sample is biased toward a greater proportion having higher class degrees (e.g. about 30 per cent of his men and 23 per cent of his women have first or upper second class degrees, as compared with 42 per cent of our men and 34 per cent of our women).

The method was that of the postal questionnaire. The question-naire was very lengthy and detailed (50 printed pages), and the

555

achieved sample is considered very high for this kind of an instrument. The date of survey was June 1968, making the population one that had graduated from University exactly eight years previously.

The analysis of the information was partly by simple computation of marginals, and cross-tabulations and partly by the formation of indexes as described in the text, and by the use of the A.I.D. method of multivariate analysis, as described by Morgan and Sonquist, 1963.

Further information on the samples and the questionnaires used is available from the authors.

APPENDIX TO CHAPTER VI

Table VI.A1

Commitment to the Idea of Women's Careers[1] and Work Intentions (Full Table)

1960 Graduates: All Married Women with Children (Percentages)

	No commit-ment	Mixed commit-ment	Secondary commit-ment	Medium commit-ment	Full commit-ment	Totals percentage	N =
Not intending to work (or decreasing work intent)	33	21	8	14	10	21	(61)
Non-continuous part-time	27	21	3	10	10	17	(51)
Non-continuous full-time	18	27	47	28	21	27	(81)
Continuous part-time	12	7	14	4	11	9	(26)
Continuous full-time	8	20	28	43	47	26	(76)
Totals percentages	98	96	100	99	99	100	
N-NA	(72)	(96)	(36)	(72)	(19)		(295)
NA	(1)	(2)					(3)
N	(73)	(98)	(36)	(72)	(19)		(298)

[1] The derivations of Work Intention and of Not Committed and Fully Committed categories are described above. Mixed Commitment is derived by mild agreement or disagreement with Q.74, and mixed, neutral or against the proposition in Q.51. All those who did not answer Q.51 were put into the 'mixed' category, but those who did not answer Q.74 were put into 'mixed' only if they answered other than 'in favour' for Q.51. If they did answer 'in favour', they were put into Medium Commitment category. Medium Commitment was ascribed to those who were in favour of the proposition in Q.51, and who mildly agreed with the Q.74 proposition. The Secondary Commitment category was for those strongly agreed with the proposition that a woman cannot make long-range plans for her own career, but at the same time answered in favour of the idea of a woman having a career – placing her career squarely in a secondary position – though, as the patterning of response in relation to intentions confirms, still on the side of the positive commitment groupings of full and medium commitment.

Table VI.A2

Area of Life Giving the Greatest Satisfaction (Percentages)

	Single men	Married men no children	Married men with children	Single women	Married women no children	Married women with children
Career or occupation	53	42	29	42	19	4
Family relationships	11	42	59	14	58	82
Leisure/recreation	18	10	4	21	10	3
Religious beliefs/activities	8	0	4	14	6	1
Participation as a citizen in community affairs	2	1	0	0	0	1
National or international betterment activities	0	0	1	0	0	1
Running a home	2	3	2	0	4	7
Other	3	1	0	7	4	1
NA	3	0	2	1	0	1
Totals percentages	100	99	101	99	101	101
N =	(58)	(79)	(245)	(112)	(73)	(298)

APPENDIX TO CHAPTER VII

Table VII.A1

Correlational matrices of housekeeping activity preferences (women)

1967 Graduates	1	2	3	4	5	6	7	8
1 Daily cooking	100	81	79	87	55	86	85	81
2 Special cooking		100	38	63	47	31	54	57
3 Child care			100	70	44	50	59	57
4 Weekly clean				100	92	92	60	80
5 Seasonal clean					100	77	63	61
6 Clothes care						100	87	77
7 Mending							100	80
8 Gardening								100

Table VII.A1a

Housekeeping activity preferences (women)

1960 Graduates	1	2	3	4	5	6	7	8	9	10
1 Daily cooking	100	83	15	22	67	78	65	62	57	45
2 Special cooking		100	34	26	34	38	16	18	29	33
3 Child care			100	54	11	30	16	16	−02	28
4 Weekly clean				100	85	86	54	37	40	26
5 Seasonal clean					100	70	56	54	58	51
6 Clothes care						100	75	51	49	54
7 Mending							100	63	68	67
8 Decorating								100	81	71
9 Household repairs									100	61
10 Gardening										100

Table VII.A2

Housekeeping activity enjoyment (women)

Eight year out Graduate (1960)

		1	2	3	4	5	6	7	8	9	10	11	12
1	Budgeting	100	40	−27	12	57	38	08	35	09	15	02	−04
2	Daily cooking		100	74	32	16	10	16	56	08	29	24	34
3	Special cooking			100	09	−77	−59	22	29	19	16	21	51
4	Child care				100	41	50	32	06	−08	19	14	22
5	Cleaning					100	89	63	41	−01	61	79	−32
6	Washing clothes						100	19	46	18	00	93	−38
7	Gardening							100	02	−07	16	42	13
8	Food shopping								100	46	59	84	03
9	Clothes shopping									100	88	−09	38
10	Furniture shopping										100	23	50
11	Minor household repairs[1]											100	44
12	Family social activity												100

[1] The correlations of these items are not meaningful because the numbers who stated enjoyment of them is too small.

Table VII.A2a

Anticipated activity salience (women)

1967 Graduates		1	2	3	4	5	6	7	8	9
1	Home activities	100	34	03	−26	75	45	82	−51	91
2	Hobbies		100	12	09	02	12	15	05	−10
3	Community work			100	−04	16	08	09	51	−03
4	Career				100	−35	04	−26	18	−35
5	Child care					100	51	62	−08	61
6	Contact parents						100	92	−12	04
7	Contact in-laws							100	−06	51
8	Political work								100	−40
9	Home management									100

Table VII.A3

Resolution patterns of marriage disagreements

1960 Graduates: (Percentages)

	Married men without children	Married men with children	Married women without children	Married women with children
By a row	21 (17)	20 (51)	23 (17)	22 (67)
Rational discussion	31 (25)	28 (71)	36 (27)	37 (110)
Giving in in turns	26 (21)	24 (60)	13 (10)	13 (40)
Keep it to self – give in	3 (2)	1 (2)	8 (6)	3 (9)
Get own way	6 (5)	10 (25)	1 (1)	3 (10)
They aren't resolved	14 (11)	17 (43)	19 (14)	22 (65)
(N)	(81)	(252)	(75)	(301)

Table IX.A1

Work Intentions by Family Stage:

Women 1960 Graduates: (Percentages)

	After Marriage but before children			Children under 3			Children 6-12			Children working or married		
	Single	Married without children	Married with children	Single	Married without children	Married with children	Single	Married without children	Married with children	Single	Married without children	Married with children
Full-time	62	84	82	5	8	5	8	12	20	47	41	55
Part-time	20	11	12	7	20	33	51	59	61	23	36	26
Not at all	8	2	5	75	54	61	25	15	4	7	3	1
Don't know	10	3	0	13	18	2	16	15	16	23	20	18
N-NA:	61	62	295	61	61	290	61	61	287	60	61	288
Total sample N	112	73	298	112	73	298	112	73	298	112	73	298
Modal pattern	Full	Full	Full	None	None	None	Part	Part	Part	Full	Full	Full/Part

Subject Index

Absence, level of, 151, 451
Acceleration of career progress, 428, 448-55
Accountancy, as career, 21, 126, 219, 388, 460
Achievement, 189
    motive, 196
    by women in top jobs, 77, 120, 137, 545-52
Adaptations to take account of women's life cycle, 138, 158, 428-69, 488
    acceleration of career progress, 428, 448-55
    continuity of work experience, 428, 430-40
    relaunching, 428, 440-8, 509
Administrative Civil Service,
    as career, 19, 20, 23, 24, 25, 30, 43, 132, 137, 138, 219, 363, 430, 438, 442, 443, 458, 466, 503
    dual-career families, 340
    salary levels, 28
    as study of work environment, 182, 389, 390, 398, 401, 406, 408, 410, 414, 417
Agencies for marketing women's potential, 499-510
    anti-discrimination, 504-5
    educational bodies, 500
    government departments, 502, 504
    individuals, 500
    Institute for family, work, and environment, 507-8
    local action groups, 509-10
    Minister for Family Affairs, 507
    national working groups, 508-9
    professional associations, 500, 503

welfare agencies, 500
women's organisations, 501-4
Ambition,
    and birth order, 169
    eminence type, 195, 196
    and family relationships, 169
    material type, 195, 196
    in school children, 35
    in women, 150, 197
    see also Career aspiration
'Ambivalent commitment',
    see Commitment typology
America, 43, 99, 128, 140, 153, 155, 381, 393, 473, 502, 504
    ambition, 395
    attitudes to women's careers, 190-2
    career commitment, 26
    child-care, 101, 246-7
    domestic help, 345
    equal pay, 135
    feminine identity, 94
    feminist movements, 502
    household activities, 246-7
    legislation, 138
    occupational choice, 126, 543, 544
    women in senior positions, 130, 526, 550, 551
    women in work force, 112, 115, 516, 517
    women's participation in higher education, 122, 123, 124, 541-2
Antecedent factors, as determinants of career patterns, 300, 308-17, 498
    father's occupation, 311, 313
    geographical area, 301, 309
    interaction with current influences, 317-29
    mother's work experience, 311-13, 322

563

Name Index

577

579

GEORGE ALLEN & UNWIN LTD

Head Office:
40 Museum Street, London, W.C.1
Telephone: 01-405 8577

Sales, Distribution and Accounts Departments
Park Lane, Hemel Hempstead, Herts.
Telephone: 0442 3244

Athens: 7 Stadiou Street, Athens 125
Auckland: P.O. Box 36013, Auckland 9
Barbados: Rockley New Road, St. Lawrence 4
Bombay: 103/5 Fort Street, Bombay 1
Calcutta: 285J Bepin Behari Ganguli Street, Calcutta 12
Dacca: Alico Building, 18 Montijheel, Dacca 2
Hornsby, N.S.W.: Cnr. Bridge Road and Jersey Street, 2077
Ibadan: P.O. Box 62
Johannesburg: P.O. Box 23134, Joubert Park
Karachi: Karachi Chambers, McLeod Road, Karachi 2
Lahore: 22 Falettis' Hotel, Egerton Road
Madras: 2/18 Mount Road, Madras 2
Manila: P.O. Box 157, Quezon City, D-502
Mexico: Serapio Rendon 125, Mexico 4, D.F.
Nairobi: P.O. Box 30583
New Delhi: 4/21-22B Asaf Ali Road, New Delhi 1
Ontario: 2330 Midland Avenue, Agincourt
Rio de Janeiro: Caixa Postal 2537-Zc-00
Singapore: 248C-6 Orchard Road, Singapore 9
Tokyo: C.P.O. Box 1728, Tokyo 100-91